A Complete History of Connecti

HISTORY

OF

CONNECTICUT.

A Complete History of Connecticut, Civil and Ecclesiastical

A Complete History of Connecticut, Civil and Ecclesiastical

BENJAMIN TRUMBULL, D.D.

A
COMPLETE
HISTORY
OF
CONNECTICUT,
Civil and Ecclesiastical,

FROM THE EMIGRATION OF ITS FIRST PLANTERS,

FROM ENGLAND, IN THE YEAR 1630,

TO THE YEAR 1764;

AND TO THE CLOSE OF THE INDIAN WARS.

IN TWO VOLUMES.

BY BENJAMIN TRUMBULL, D. D.

Vol. I.
WITH AN APPENDIX,

Containing the original Patent of New-England, never before published in America.

NEW-HAVEN:
PUBLISHED BY MALTBY, GOLDSMITH AND CO.
AND SAMUEL WADSWORTH.

1818.

District of Connecticut, ss.

BE it remembered, that on the twenty-second day of June, in the 42d year of the Independence of the United States of America, Maltby, Goldsmith & Co. and Samuel Wadsworth, of the said district, have deposited in this office the title of a book, the right whereof they claim as proprietors, in the words following, to wit: "A complete History of Connecticut, civil and ecclesiastical, from the emigration of its first planters, from England, in the year 1630, to the year 1764; and to the close of the Indian wars. In two volumes. By Benjamin Trumbull, D. D. With an Appendix, containing the original Patent of New-England, never before published in America"—In conformity to the act of the Congress of the United States, entitled, "An act for the encouragement of learning, by securing the copies of maps, charts, and books, to the authors and proprietors of such copies, during the times therein mentioned."

R. I. INGERSOLL,
Clerk of the District of Connecticut.

T. G. Woodward, Printer,
State-St. New-Haven.

PREFACE.

AUTHENTIC history is of great utility; especially, to the countries and people whose affairs it relates. It teaches human nature, politics and morals; forms the head and heart for usefulness, and is an important part of the instruction and literature of states and nations. While it instructs, it affords an exalted pleasure. No man of genius and curiosity can read accounts of the origin of nations, the discovery, settlement, and progress of new countries, without a high degree of entertainment. But in the settlement of his own country, in the lives of his ancestors, in their adventures, morals, jurisprudence and heroism, he feels himself particularly interested. He at once becomes a party in their affairs, and travels and converses with them, with a kind of filial delight. While he beholds them braving the horrors of the desert, the terrors of the savage, the distresses of famine and war, he admires their courage, and is pleased with all their escapes from danger, and all their progress in settlement, population, opulence, literature and happiness. While he contemplates their self-denial and perseverance in surmounting all dangers and enduring all hardships, to form new churches, and lay the foundations of new colonies and empires, and the immensely happy consequences of their conduct in turning the wilderness into gardens and fruitful fields, and in transmitting liberty and religion to posterity, he is struck with a pleasing astonishment. The pious man views a divine hand conducting the whole, gives thanks, adores and loves. No history is better calculated to produce these happy effects, than that of New-England and Connecticut.

Connecticut, originally consisting of two colonies, replete with Indians, and connected as it was with the neighboring colonies, affords much interesting matter for history. An authentic and impartial account of the affairs of the colony had long been an object of the wishes of the legislature, and of many gentlemen of principal character both in church and commonwealth.

In these views the writer, many years since, determined to attempt the compilation of the history which is presented to the public in the following sheets. He wished for the improvement which such a work might afford him, and for the pleasure of contributing his mite to the service of the community in which he received his birth and education, and has enjoyed such distinguished liberty and immunities.

In pursuance of his design, he collected all books and manuscripts from which he could expect assistance. He read the records of Connecticut, New-Haven and the United Colonies; and extracted whatever he judged important. He made a journey to Boston, examined the collection of the Rev. Mr. Prince, and minuted every thing which he could find relative to Connecticut. To him, at the time he was about writing the Chronological History of New-England, the ancient ministers, and other principal gentlemen in Connecticut, had transmitted accounts of the settlement of the towns and churches to which they respectively be-

PREFACE.

longed. In this collection, important information was found, which could have been obtained from no other source. The author visited most of the principal towns, and places of burial, and obtained from records, monuments, and men of intelligence, whatever they could communicate on the subject. The ministers and clerks of the respective towns, and other gentlemen of character, assisted him in his researches. The honorable legislature, having been made acquainted with his design, passed a generous resolve, which gave him access to their records and papers on file.

His excellency governor Trumbull, than whom no man had a more thorough acquaintance with the history of the colony, employed his influence and friendship for his assistance, and furnished him with many important papers. In a letter to him on the subject, he expresses himself in this manner—"I wish you success, and to afford you all the assistance in my power. I imagine the earliest times of the colony will be attended with the most difficulty, to collect the facts with sufficient certainty— wherein the great excellency of a history consists. Such an one I have long desired to see. It must be a work of time and indefatigable labour and industry, since it has been so long neglected, and the materials, many of them, almost lost, and others scattered, and all need so much care in collecting, time in comparing, and judgment in compiling." The truth of these observations, the author hath fully experienced; how far he hath acted upon them must be determined by the public opinion.

The honorable George Wyllys, Esq. late secretary of the state, was second to none in the assistance and encouragement which he afforded. From these various sources, the author, in 1774, found himself possessed of an ample and important collection; and determined to write the first volume of the history, as soon as might be, with convenience. But before he had entered upon the work, the war commenced between Great-Britain and her colonies, and the universal attention was turned to a very different object. It was conceived to be dangerous for any of the public papers to be kept so near the sea coast as the place of his residence. A great number of papers, therefore, which he had received from governor Trumbull, and others which had been taken out of the office at Hartford, were returned to their respective offices.

For a number of years after the war, the state of the country was altogether unfavorable for publications of this kind. It was nevertheless still hoped that an opportunity would present for the publication of such a work to advantage, and the design of writing was not wholly given up.

However, before the writer had entered upon the work, he was invited, by a vote of the General Association of the state, to compile a different history. Many objections presented themselves to his mind against engaging in the work proposed by that venerable body. But after these had been fully communicated, the solicitation was renewed. In consequence of which, and the opinion and advice of some principal gentlemen of the legislature, he was induced to undertake the writing of a general history of the United States of America, from the first discovery of this northern continent until the year 1792, including three complete centuries. In making collections for this, and in the compilation of it, all the leisure hours which he could possibly redeem, by early rising and an indefatigable attention to business, from the stated labours of his office, have been, for nearly ten years, employed.

In the progress of this work it became necessary to have frequent recourse to his former collections, which, by this time, had been in a manner forgotten. By this means the ideas of the ample materials which had been prepared, for the history of Connecticut, were revived in his mind. When he contemplated the pains and expense at which they had

PREFACE.

been collected, the countenance which he had received from the legislature, and the general expectations which had been entertained with respect to a history of Connecticut, it appeared to him not very consistent with that respectful and generous treatment which he owed more particularly to his own state, to publish a large history of the United States, while he neglected theirs. It also appeared to be a duty, which he owed to himself and family, as well as the public, not to suffer all his former pains and expense, in his collections for the history of Connecticut, to be lost. Upon a mature view of the case, and the advice of a number of his brethren in the ministry, he determined to suspend the writing of the history of the United States, until he should publish one volume, at least, of the history of Connecticut. If this should meet the public approbation, it might assist him in introducing a larger work, and render it more extensively useful. If the history of Connecticut should be unpopular, it would give him a profitable admonition, and prevent a greater misfortune, by a larger and more expensive publication.

About the middle of December, 1796, he began to look over and arrange his papers and to compile the following history. Since that time he hath examined the papers on file in the secretary's office, and taken out such as were necessary, composed and copied off with his own hands the history now published, besides preaching twice on every Lord's day, lectures on proper occasions, and attending the other duties of his office.

The death of that truly worthy gentleman, the honorable George Wyllys, the former secretary, considerably retarded the work, as more time has been employed in examining the files than otherwise would have been necessary.

In compiling the history, great pains have been taken to exhibit the state of the country when the first settlements commenced, to present every important transaction in a candid and clear view, and to make such an arrangement of the whole, as that every preceding chapter might prepare the way for the next, and add perspicuity to the story.

As this is the first history of the colony, and as time effaces ancient records and papers, and eradicates from the mind of man the remembrance of former transactions, the compiler judged it expedient to make it more full and particular, than otherwise might have been necessary or proper. He imagined, that no person would, probably, hereafter have the same advantages which he has had, nor take the same pains which he has taken, to examine the ancient records, histories and manuscripts of the country. He wished to assist future historians, and that nothing useful and important, respecting church or state, might be lost. As he has aimed at information and usefulness, he has avoided all circumlocutions, reasonings and opinions of his own, and attempted to fill every page with history. The florid and pompous style has been avoided, as unnatural and improper in historic writings, and the easy and familiar has been attempted. The compiler has judged his time too precious, and the field of usefulness before him too extensive, to busy himself in rounding periods, and guarding against every little matter which might afford business for the critic. He has, however, aimed at authenticity, propriety and perspicuity. He has wished to avoid the dull and dry manner, and to write with a becoming deference to the public.

The account which has been given of the sources whence the compiler has obtained his information, the quotations in the body of the work, the references made in the marginal notes to authors, records, and manuscripts, with the appendix, it is imagined, will be abundantly sufficient to authenticate what has been written. Indeed, very little has been taken upon tradition.

Had the history been written more leisurely and with fewer avocations

PREFACE.

it might have been more perfect; but as it was desired to make as short a pause as possible in writing the history of the United States, it was judged inexpedient to employ more time upon it.

The author is under great disadvantages for historic writing. He can command no time for himself. The work of the ministry, which is his chosen and beloved employment, after all his application, so engrosses his time, that sometimes for weeks and months, after all his application, he cannot find a single day for the compilation of history. When he has attempted it, he has been able scarcely to write a page without interruption. Often he has been so fatigued with other studies, as to be in circumstances not the most favorable for composition.

It may, possibly, be thought a great neglect, or matter of partiality, that no account is given of witchcraft in Connecticut. The only reason is, that after the most careful researches, no indictment of any person for that crime, nor any process relative to that affair, can be found. The minute in Goff's journal, published by governor Hutchinson, relative to the execution of Ann Coles, and an obscure tradition that one or two persons were executed at Stratford, is all the information to be found relative to that unhappy affair.

The countenance and assistance which the honorable legislature have given the writer, by allowing him a free access to the public records and papers, is most respectfully acknowledged.

The attention and complaisance with which he has been treated by the secretaries of the state, and their respective families, while he has had occasion to examine the public records and papers, challenge the warmest expressions of his gratitude.

To his brethren in the ministry, the gentlemen of the bar, and the towns who have so generously encouraged and supported the subscription, he returns his grateful acknowledgments.

The labor of collecting the materials for the history and compilement, has been almost incredible. The expense of publication will be great. However, should it meet a favorable reception, assist the legislator or divine, the gentlemen of the bench or of the bar; should it afford instruction and pleasure to the sons and daughters of the state, and in any degree advance its morals or literature, it will be an ample compensation.

CONTENTS.

CHAPTER I.

INTRODUCTION. The discovery of North-America and New-England. Captain Smith's discovery. The country is named New-England. New-Plymouth settled. The great patent of New-England, and patent of Massachusetts. The settlement of Salem, Charlestown, Boston, and other towns in Massachusetts. Mr. Warham, Mr. Phillips and Mr. Hooker, with others of the first planters of Connecticut, arrive and make settlements at Dorchester, Watertown, and Newtown. Their churches are formed and they are ordained.

CHAPTER II.

THE patent of Connecticut. The situation, extent, boundaries and area of the settled part of the colony. The discovery of Connecticut river; a description of it, and the signification of its name. The colony derives its name from the river. Description of other rivers. Plymouth and Dutch houses. Prospects of trade upon the river.

CHAPTER III.

THE state of the country of Connecticut when the settlement of the colony began. Its trees and fruits. Its animals. Number, situation, genius, manners, arms, utensils and wars of the Indians.

CHAPTER IV.

THE people at Dorchester, Watertown, and Newtown, finding themselves straightened in the Massachusetts, determine to remove to Connecticut. Debates in Massachusetts relative to their removal. The general court at first prohibited it, but afterwards gave its consent. The people removed and settled the towns of Windsor, Hartford and Weathersfield. Hardships and losses of the first winters.

Vol. 1.   B

CONTENTS.

CHAPTER V.

The war with the Pequots. The origin of it. The murder of Captain Stone and Norton, of Mr. Oldham and others. Mr. Endicot's expedition against them. The Pequots kill a number of the garrison at the mouth of the river, and besiege the fort. Captain Mason is sent down from Connecticut with a reinforcement. The enemy make a descent on Weathersfield, torture and mock the English. The court at Connecticut declares war against them. Captain Mason takes Mistic fort. Sassacus destroys his royal fortress and flees to the westward. A second expedition is undertaken against the Pequots conjointly, by Massachusetts and Connecticut. The great swamp fight. The Pequots subdued. Sassacus flying to the Mohawks was beheaded. The captivated and surviving Pequots, after the war, were given to the Moheagans and Narragansets, and their name extinguished.

CHAPTER VI.

Effects of the war. Great scarcity in Connecticut, and means taken to relieve the necessities of the people. Settlement of New-Haven. Plantation covenant. Means for the defence of the colony. Captain Mason made major general. Civil constitution of Connecticut, formed by voluntary compact. First general election at Connecticut. Governors and magistrates. General rights of the people, and principal laws of the colony. Constitution and laws of New-Haven. Purchase and settlement of several towns in Connecticut and New-Haven.

CHAPTER VII.

The progress of purchase, settlement, and law in the colonies of Connecticut and New-Haven. The effect of the conquest of the Pequots on the natives, and the manner in which they were treated. Purchases of them. Towns settled. Divisions at Weathersfield occasion the settlement of Stamford. Troubles with the Dutch and Indians. Capital laws of Connecticut. The confederation of the united colonies. Further troubles with the Indians. Victory of Uncas over the Narragansets, and capture of their sachem. The advice of the commissioners respecting Miantoninoh. His execution. Precautions of the colonies to prevent war. The Dutch, harassed by an Indian war, apply to New-Haven for assistance.

CHAPTER VIII.

Public fasts appointed. Indians continue hostile, and commit murder. Acts of the commissioners respecting them. Branford settled. Towns in Connecticut. Message of the commissioners to the Narragansets. Their agreement respecting Uncas. Long-Island Indians taken under the protection of the United colonies. Massachusetts claim part of the Pequot country and Waranoke. Determination of the commissioners respecting said claim. Agreement with Mr. Fenwick relative to Saybrook fort and the adjacent country. Fortifications advanced. Extraordinary meeting of the commissioners to suppress the outrages of the Narragansets. War proclaimed and troops sent against them. They treat and prevent war. Fairfield object to a jury of six. Centroversy with the Dutch. The Indians plot against the life of governor Hopkins and other principal gentlemen at Hartford. Damages at Windsor. Battle between the Dutch and Indians. Losses of New-Haven. Dispute with Massachusetts relative to the impost at Saybrook. Mr. Winthrop's claim of the Nehantick country. Settlement of accounts between the colonies.

CHAPTER IX.

SETTLEMENT of New-London. Salaries first granted to civil officers. Troubles with the Narraganset Indians. Rhode-Island petitions to be united with the colonies in confederation. The Massachusetts resume the affair of the impost. Mr. Westerhouse complains of the seizure of his vessel by the Dutch, in the harbour of New-Haven. Murders committed by the Indians;—resolutions respecting the murderers. Body of laws compiled. Debates relative to the settlement of Delaware. The Pequots revolt from Uncas, and petition the English. Resolution respecting them. Mr. Westerhouse petitions to make reprisals from the Dutch. Letter to the Dutch governor. Further altercation respecting the impost. Final issue of that affair. The conduct of the Massachusetts upon its decision, and the declaration of the commissioners respecting it. Their treatment of Connecticut respecting the line between the colonies. The court at Connecticut determine to avenge the death of John Whitmore, and detach men to take the murderer.

CHAPTER X.

COURT of election at Hartford. Grants to captain Mason. The commissioners meet and dispatch captain Atherton to the Narragansets. Their message to Ninigrate. The Dutch Governor arrives at Hartford, and refers the differences between him and the colonies to arbitrators. Their determination, and the line is fixed between the English and Dutch plantations. Agreements with Mr. Fenwick occasion general uneasiness. Committees are appointed to explain and ascertain them. Towns are invited to attend the committees, by their deputies, at Saybrook. An act for the encouragement of Mr. Winthrop in seeking and improving mines. Norwalk and Mattabeseck settled and made towns. The colony of New-Haven make another attempt to settle at Delaware. The Dutch Governor seizes the company and frustrates the design. He pursues his former line of conduct towards the colonies. The resolutions of the commissioners relative to his conduct, to the settlement of Delaware, and the tribute to be paid by the Pequots. French commissioners from Canada. Their proposals. Reply to them. The Dutch governor and Indians concert a plan to extirpate the colonies. The commissioners meet, and dispatch agents to the Dutch governor. They determine upon war, unless he should manifest his innocence, and redress the grievances of the colonies. They determine on the number of men to be raised, and draw a declaration of the reasons of the war. The agents return unsuccessful. The commissioners meet again, and determine to make war upon the Dutch and Narraganset Indians. The general court of Massachusetts refuses to raise men, and prevents the war. Altercations between that general court and the commissioners, and between that and the general courts of Connecticut and New-Haven. The alarm and distress of the plantations in these colonies. Their general courts protest

CONTENTS.

against the court of Massachusetts, as violaters of the articles of confederation; and write to Cromwell and the parliament for assistance. The tumultuous state of the inhabitants in several of the towns.

CHAPTER XI.

The death and character of Governor Haynes. The freemen of Connecticut meet and appoint a moderator. Mr. Ludlow removes to Virginia. The spirited conduct of the people at Milford, in recovering Manning's vessel. The freemen add to the fundamental articles. Fleet arrives at Boston for the reduction of the Dutch. The colonies agree to raise men to assist the armament from England. Peace prevents the expedition. The general court at New-Haven, charge the Massachusetts with a breach of the confederation. They refuse to join in a war against Ninigrate, and oblige Connecticut and New-Haven to provide for the defence of themselves and their allies. Ninigrate continuing his hostile measures, the commissioners send messengers to him. His answer to them. They declare war, and send an army against him. The art of Massachusetts and the deceit of Major Willard, defeat the designed expedition. The number of rateable polls, and the amount of the list of Connecticut. The Pequots are taken under their protection. Ninigrate persisting in his hostilities against the Indians upon Long-Island, the general court adopt measures for the defence of the Indians and the English inhabitants there. New-Haven perfect and print their laws. The answer of New-Haven to the protector's invitation, that they would remove to Jamaica. Reply of the commissioners to the Dutch governor. Uncas embroils the country. Deaths and characters of Governors Eaton and Hopkins. Settlement of Stonington. Mr. Winthrop chosen governor. The third fundamental article is altered by the freemen. Mr. Fitch and his church and people remove to Norwich. Final settlement of accounts with the heirs of Mr. Fenwick. Deputy governor Mason resigns the Moheagan lands to the colony.

CHAPTER XII.

The general court of Connecticut declare their loyalty and submission to the king; determine to address his majesty, and apply for charter privileges. A petition to his majesty is prepared, and a letter addressed to lord Say and Seal. Governor Winthrop is appointed the colony's agent, to present their petition, and solicit a patent. Regicides condemned. Whalley and Goffe arrive at Boston; escape to New-Haven, and are kindly entertained, and kept from their pursuers. New-Haven falls into great trouble and danger on that account. New-Haven excuse themselves; decline sending an agent; but join with Massachusetts in supporting one. The king proclaimed. Governor Winthrop obtains the charter of Connecticut. First governor and council under the charter. Representation of the constitution it ordains, and the privileges it conveys. Difficulties of the colony of New-Haven. Governor Leet's address. Charter of Connecticut arrives. Proceedings of Connecticut in consequence of the charter. They extend their jurisdiction to all places within the limits of their patent, and challenge New-Haven colony, as under their jurisdiction. Controversy between the two colonies. Settlement of Killingworth. Patent of the duke of York. Colonel Nichols and commissioners arrive; reduce all the Dutch settlements. Their extraordinary powers. Important crisis of Connecticut. The general court make a present to the commissioners. Answer to the propositions from his majesty, and reply to the duke of Hamilton's claim and petition. Boundaries between Connecticut and New-York. Union of Connecticut and New-Haven.

CHAPTER XIII.

A VIEW of the churches of Connecticut and New-Haven, from their first settlement, until their union, in 1665. Their ministers. The character of the ministers and first planters. Their religious and political sentiments. Gathering of the churches of New-Haven and Milford. Installation of Mr. Davenport and Mr. Prudden. Church formed at Guilford. Number of ministers in Connecticut and New-Haven before the union. Proportion of ministers to the people, before, and at the union. Harmony between the civil rulers and the clergy. Influence of the clergy, and the reasons of it. Their opposition to Antinomianism. Assisted in the compilation of Cambridge Platform. Ecclesiastical laws. Care to diffuse general knowledge: its happy influence. Attempts to found a college at New-Haven. No sectaries in Connecticut nor New-Haven, until after the union; and for twenty years the churches generally enjoyed great peace. Deaths and characters of several of the first ministers. Great dissensions in the church at Hartford soon after Mr. Hooker's death. Dissensions and controversies in the colony and churches in general, relative to baptism, church-membership, and the rights of the brethren. A new generation arises, who had not all imbibed the spirit of their fathers. Grievances presented to the general court of Connecticut, on the account of the strictness of the churches, and that sober people were denied communion with them, and baptism for their children. The court of Connecticut send to the other general courts for advice. Laws against the Quakers. Massachusetts and Connecticut agree in appointing a synod at Boston. General court at New-Haven oppose the meeting of a synod, and decline sending their elders. Questions proposed for discussion. The synod meet and answer them; but it had no good effect on the churches: they would not comply with their decisions. Dissensions continued at Hartford. Acts of the general court respecting them. Councils from Massachusetts. Difficulties in some measure composed. Divisions and animosities at Weathersfield. Act of the general court respecting the church there. Mr. Russell and others remove from Weathersfield and Hartford and settle Hadley. Mr. Stow dismissed from the ministry at Middletown, by a committee of the general court. Synod at Boston. Its determination relative to baptism, and the consociation of churches. Division in the synod and in the churches relative to those points. The court at Connecticut send no elders to the council, nor take any part in the controversy, until some time afterwards.

CHAPTER XIV.

CONDUCT of the king's commissioners. Counties and County Courts regulated. Governor Winthrop's estate freed from taxation. Towns settled. Controversy with Rhode-Island. The grounds of it. Courts appointed in the Narraganset country. Laws revised and printed. War with the Dutch. Claims and conduct of major Edmund Andross, governor of New-York. Protest against him. Conduct of capt. Thomas Bull. Proclamation respecting the insult received from major Andross. Philip's war. Captains Hutchinson and Lothrop surprised

CONTENTS.

and slain. Treachery of the Springfield Indians. Hadley attacked by the enemy. The assembly make provision for the defence of Connecticut. Expedition against the Narraganset Indians. The reasons of it. The great swamp fight. Loss of men. Courage exhibited and hardships endured. Captain Pierce and his party cut off. Nanunttenoo taken. Success of captains Denison and Avery. Captain Wadsworth and his party slain. Death and character of governor Winthrop. Success of Major Talcott. Attack upon Hadley. The enemy beaten and begin to scatter. They are pursued to Housatonick. Sachem of Quabaug and Philip killed. Number of the enemy before the war. Their destruction. Loss of the colonies. Connecticut preserves its own towns and assists its neighbours.

CHAPTER XV.

Measures adopted to discharge the public debt, and settle the country in peace. The reasons of the colony's claim to Narraganset. The former settlers and owners of land there apply to Connecticut for protection. Major Treat goes to the upper towns upon Connecticut river, to treat with the Indians. Fasts appointed through New-England. Act concerning the conquered lands in Narraganset. Navigation act grievous to the colonies. Governor Leet takes the oath respecting trade and navigation. Answers to queries from the lords of trade and plantations. Protest against Sir Edmund Andross's claim to Fisher's Island. Character of governor Leet. Commissioners appointed by his majesty, to examine and make report concerning all claims to the Narraganset country, or king's province. They report in favour of Connecticut. Answers to the renewed claim of the duke of Hamilton, and opinions on the case. Connecticut congratulate the arrival of colonel Dungan, governor of New-York, and agree with him respecting the boundary line between that colony and Connecticut. Petition to king James II. Settlement of Waterbury. Quo-warrantos against the colony. The assembly petition his majesty to continue their charter privileges. Sir Edmund Andross made governor of New-England. Arrives at Hartford: takes the government by order of his majesty. The oppression and cruelty of his administration. Distressed and sorrowful state of the people.

CHAPTER XVI.

Revolution in New-England. Connecticut resume their government. Address to king William. Troops raised for the defence of the eastern settlements in New-Hampshire and the province of Maine. French and Indian war. Schenectady destroyed. Connecticut dispatch a reinforcement to Albany. Expedition against Canada. The land army retreats, and the enterprise proves unsuccessful. Leisler's abuse of major-general Winthrop. The assembly of Connecticut approve the general's conduct. Thanks are returned to Mr. Mather, agent Whiting, and Mr. Porter. Opinions respecting the charter, and the legality of Connecticut's assuming their government. Windham settled. The Mohawk castles are surprised, and the country alarmed. Connecticut send troops to Albany. Colonel Fletcher, governor of New-York, demands the command of the militia of Connecticut. The colony petition king William on the subject. Colonel Fletcher comes to Hartford, and, in person, demands that the legislature submit the militia to his command: but they refuse. Captain Wadsworth prevents the

CONTENTS.

reading of his commission; and the colonel judges it expedient to leave the colony. The case of Connecticut relative to the militia stated. His majesty determines in favour of the colony. Committees are appointed to settle the boundary line between Connecticut and Massachusetts. General Winthrop returns, and receives public thanks. Congratulation of the Earl of Bellemont, appointed governor of New-York and Massachusetts. Dispute with Rhode-Island continues. Committee to settle the boundaries. Expenses of the war. Vexatious conduct of governor Fletcher. Peace, joy, and thanksgiving.

CHAPTER XVII.

GENERAL Winthrop is elected governor. The assembly divide and form into two houses. Purchase and settlement of several towns. The boundary line between Connecticut and New-York surveyed and fixed. Attempts for running and establishing the line between Massachusetts and Connecticut. Owaneco and the Moheagans claim Colchester and other tracts in the colony. Attempts to compose all differences with them. Grant to the volunteers. The assembly enacts, that the session in October, shall, for the future, be in New-Haven. An Act enlarging the boundaries of New-London; and acts relative to towns and patents. Measures adopted for the defence of the colony. Appointment of king's attorneys. Attempt to despoil Connecticut of its charter. Bill for re-uniting the charter governments to the crown. Sir Henry Ashurst petitions against, and prevents the passing of the bill. Governor Dudley, Lord Cornbury, and other enemies conspire against the colony. They exhibit grievous complaints against it. Sir Henry Ashurst defends the colony, and defeats their attempts. Quakers petition. Moheagan case. Survey and bounds of the pretended Moheagan country. Dudley's court at Stonington. The colony protest against it. Dudley's treatment of the colony. Judgment against it. Petition to her majesty on the subject. New commissions are granted. Act in favor of the clergy. State of the colony.

CHAPTER XVIII.

THE country is alarmed. Means of defence. The assembly decline the affording of any assistance in the expedition against Port Royal. Grant assistance to the frontier towns. New townships granted and settled. The Rev. Gurdon Saltonstall chosen governor. Act empowering the freemen to choose the governor from among themselves at large. Acts relative to the settlement of the boundary line with Massachusetts. Garrisons erected in the towns on the frontiers. Expedition against Canada. First emission of paper money. Address to her majesty. Loss of the colony at Wood Creek. Expedition against Port Royal. Expedition against Canada, under the command of Admiral Walker and general Nicholson. Fleet cast away, and the enterprise defeated. The colony petition her majesty, and send the only pilot from Connecticut, to England, to represent to her majesty the loss of the fleet truly as it was. Acts respecting the superior court. Settlement of the boundary line between Massachusetts and Connecticut. Reasons why the colony consented to such a settlement. Return of peace. The colony happy in the preservation of their frontiers. Towns settled under Massachusetts. State of the colony. Observations.

CHAPTER XIX.

A VIEW of the churches of Connecticut, from 1665 to 1714, continued from chapter XIII. The general assembly appoint a synod to determine points of religious controversy. The ministers decline meeting under the name of a synod. The assembly alter the name, and require them to meet as a general assembly of the ministers and churches of Connecticut. Seventeen questions were proposed to the assembly, to be discussed and answered. The assembly of ministers meet and discuss the questions. The legislature declare, that they had not been decided, and give intimations that they did not desire, that the ministers and churches of Connecticut should report their opinion upon them. They express their desires of a larger council from Massachusetts, and New-Plymouth. The Rev. Mr. Davenport removes to Boston. Dissension at Windsor. Mr. Bulkley and Mr. Fitch are appointed by the assembly to devise some way in which the churches might walk together, notwithstanding their different opinions relative to the subjects of baptism, church communion, and the mode of church discipline. The church at Hartford divides, and Mr. Whiting and his adherents are allowed to practice upon congregational principles. The church at Stratford allowed to divide and hold distinct meetings. Mr. Walker and his hearers, upon advice, remove and settle the town of Woodbury. Deaths and characters of the Rev. Messrs. John Davenport and John Warham. General attempts for a reformation of manners. Religious state of the colony in 1680. Attempts for the instruction and christianising of the Indians in Connecticut. Act of the legislature respecting Windsor. The people there required peaceably to settle and support Mr. Mather. Owning or subscribing the covenant introduced at Hartford. College founded, and trustees incorporated. Worship according to the mode of the church of England, performed in this colony, first at Stratford. Episcopal church gathered there. Act of assembly requiring the ministers and churches of Connecticut to meet and form a religious constitution. They meet and compile the Saybrook Platform. Articles of discipline. Act of the legislature adopting the Platform. Associations. Consociations. General Association. Its recommendations relative to the examination of candidates for the ministry, and of pastors elect previous to their ordination. Ministers, churches, and ecclesiastical societies in Connecticut, in 1715. Degree of instruction. The whole number of ministers in the colony from its first settlement, to that period.

APPENDIX.

CONTAINING various documents referred to in this volume, with the great original PATENT OF NEW-ENGLAND, never before published.

THE HISTORY OF CONNECTICUT.

CHAPTER I.

Introduction. The discovery of North-America and New-England. Captain Smith's discovery. The country is named New-England. New-Plymouth settled. The great patent of New-England, and patent of Massachusetts. The settlement of Salem, Charlestown, Boston, and other towns in Massachusetts. Mr. Warham, Mr. Phillips and Mr. Hooker, with others of the first planters of Connecticut, arrive and make settlements at Dorchester, Watertown and Newtown. Their churches are formed and they are ordained.

THE settlement of New-England, purely for the purposes of Religion, and the propagation of civil and religious liberty, is an event which has no parallel in the history of modern ages. The piety, self-denial, sufferings, patience, perseverance and magnanimity of the first settlers of the country are without a rival. The happy and extensive consequences of the settlements which they made, and of the sentiments which they were careful to propagate, to their posterity, to the church and to the world, admit of no description. They are still increasing, spreading wider and wider, and appear more and more important.

The planters of Connecticut were among the illustrious characters, who first settled New-England, and twice made settlements, first in Massachusetts, and then in Connecticut on bare creation. In an age when the light of freedom was but just dawning, they, by voluntary compact, formed one of the most free and happy constitutions of govern-

Book I. ment which mankind have ever adopted. Connecticut has ever been distinguished by the free spirit of its government, the mildness of its laws, and the general diffusion of knowledge, among all classes of its inhabitants. They have been no less distinguished by their industry, economy, purity of manners, population and spirit of enterprise. For more than a century and half, they have had no rival, as to the steadiness of their government, their internal peace and harmony, their love and high enjoyment of domestic, civil and religious order and happiness. They have ever stood among the most illuminated, first and boldest defenders of the civil and religious rights of mankind.

The history of such a people must be curious, entertaining and important. It will exhibit the fairest models of civil government, of religious order, purity and human happiness. It is the design of the present work to lay this history before the public.

As the planters of Connecticut were among the first settlers of New-England, and interested in the first patents and settlements, sketches of the discovery of the country, of the patents by which it was conveyed and divided to the different colonies, and of the first settlements, will be necessary to illustrate the history of Connecticut and be a natural preliminary to this work.

Oct. 12, 1492. CHRISTOPHER COLUMBUS, a Genoese, discovered the western isles, and first communicated to Europe the intelligence of a new world: but the Cabots had the honor of discovering the great continent of North-America.

1494. JOHN CABOT, a Venetian, born in England, in 1494 discovered Newfoundland and the island of St. Johns. In consequence of this discovery, king Henry the seventh of England, in whose service he was employed, conferred on him the honor of knighthood; and gave him and his sons a commission to make further discoveries in the new world. John Cabot died soon after he received this commission. His son Sebastian, in 1497, sailed with the fleet, which had been preparing for his father, and directing his course by his journals, proceeded to the 67th degree of north latitude, and, returning to the southward, fell in with the continent in the 56th degree of north latitude; and thence explored the coast as far south as the Floridas. From these discoveries originated the claims of England to these parts of the northern continent.

1602. In 1602, Bartholomew Gosnold discovered some part of New-England. He first touched on its eastern coast, in about 43 degrees of north latitude; and, sailing to the southward, landed on the Elizabeth Islands. He made some

CHAP. I.   CONNECTICUT.   19

discoveries of the adjacent parts, and gave the name to Cape Cod and Marthas Vineyard.

Captain Henry Hudson, commissioned by king James I. in 1608, sailed, in the employment of several London merchants, to North-America. He came upon the coast in about 40 degrees of north latitude, and made a discovery of Long-Island and Hudson's river. He proceeded up the river as far as the latitude of 43, and called it by his own name.

About two years after he made a second voyage to the river, in the service of a number of Dutch merchants; and, some time after, made sale of his right to the Dutch. The right to the country, however, was antecedently in king James, by virtue of the discovery which Hudson had made under his commission. The English protested against the sale; but the Dutch, in 1614, under the Amsterdam West-India company, built a fort nearly on the same ground where the city of Albany now is, which they called fort Aurania. Sir Thomas Dale, governor of Virginia, directly after dispatched captain Argall to dispossess the Dutch, and they submitted to the king of England, and under him to the governor of Virginia.*

The same year captain John Smith, who some years before had been governor of Virginia, made a voyage to this part of the continent. He ranged the coast from Penobscot to Cape Cod; made a discovery of the river Pascataqua, and the Massachusetts islands. On his return to England, he published a description of the country, with a map of the sea coast, and gave it the name of New-England.

In 1620, a number of pious people, part of Mr. John Robinson's church and congregation, who, by the violence of persecution, had been driven from their pleasant seats and enjoyments in England, arrived on the coast; and, after braving every danger, and enduring almost every hardship and distress of which human nature is capable, effected a permanent settlement in this part of North-America. They gave it the name of New-Plymouth. By voluntary compact they formed themselves into a small commonwealth, and had a succession of governors. They settled all that part of Massachusetts included in the county of Plymouth. By making permanent settlements, to which others might resort, on their first arrival in New-England, or afterwards in times of distress; by making treaties with the Indians, by which the peace of the country was preserved; by their knowledge of it, and the experience

*Smith's history of New-York, p. 2.

Book I.

1608.

1610.

1614.

New-Plymouth, settled, 1620.

which they had gained, they were of peculiar advantage to those who came over and made settlements after them. They were a pious, industrious people, and exhibited towards each other the most striking examples of fraternal affection. They continued a distinct colony for about seventy years, until their incorporation, by the charter of William and Mary, in 1691, with the colony of Massachusetts and the province of Maine.

Patent of New-England, Nov. 3, 1620. November 3d, 1620, just before the arrival of Mr. Robinson's people in New-England, king James the first, by letters patent, under the great seal of England, incorporated the duke of Lenox, the marquises of Buckingham and Hamilton, the earls of Arundel and Warwick, and others, to the number of forty noblemen, knights and gentlemen, by the name "of the council established at Plymouth in the county of Devon, for the planting, ruling and governing of New-England in America"—"and granted unto them, and their successors and assigns, all that part of America, lying and being in breadth from forty degrees of north latitude, from the equinoctial line, to the forty eighth degree of said northerly latitude inclusively, and in length of, and within all the breadth aforesaid, throughout the main lands from sea to sea." The patent ordained that this tract of country should be called New-England in America, and by that name have continuance for ever.

This grant is the broad basis on which stand all the other grants made to the colonies in New-England. This prepared the way for future grants and the immediate settlement of New-England.

Patent of Massachusetts, March 19, 1628. On the 19th of March, 1628, the Plymouth company granted unto Sir Henry Roswell, Sir John Young, knights, Thomas Southcoat, John Humphry, John Endicott and Simon Whitcomb, their heirs and assigns forever, all that part of New-England in America, which lies and extends between Merrimack river and Charles river, in the bottom of Massachusetts bay, and three miles to the north and south of every part of Charles river, and three miles south of the southernmost part of said bay, and three miles to the northward of every part of Merrimack river, and "all lands and hereditaments whatsoever lying within the limits aforesaid north and south, in latitude and breadth; and in length and longitude, of and within all the breadth aforesaid throughout the main lands there, from the Atlantic sea and ocean on the east part, to the south sea on the west part."

Confirmed March 4, 1629. On the 4th of March, 1629, king Charles the first confirmed this patent under the great seal of England. This

CHAP. I.   CONNECTICUT.

was the patent of Massachusetts bay, under which the settlement of that colony immediately commenced.

At this time, liberty of conscience could not be enjoyed in the parent country. No indulgence was granted even to the most pious, loyal, and conscientious people, who would not strictly conform to the habits, ceremonies, and worship of the church of England. All non-conformists were exposed to fines, imprisonments, the ruin of their families, fortunes, and every thing which ought to be dear to men. The most learned, pious, orthodox, and inoffensive people, who did not conform to the church of England, were treated, by the king and his bishops, with far greater severity, than drunkards, sabbath breakers, or even the most notorious debauchees. They were condemned, in the spiritual courts, without juries; without having the witnesses against them brought into court, to depose face to face; and, sometimes, without knowing the crime alledged against them, or who were the witnesses by whom it was to be proved. Many of the pious people in England, were so harassed and persecuted for their non-conformity, that they determined, if possible, rather to make settlements in a dreary wilderness, at the distance of three thousand miles from their native couuntry, than endure the persecution and sufferings, to which they were constantly exposed from the hands of those who ought to have cherished and defended them. This cruel treatment of our venerable ancestors, was the cause of the settlement of the New-England colonies and churches. It will ever be the distinguishing glory of these colonies, that they were not originally formed for the advantages of trade and worldly emolument, but for the noble purposes of religion, the enjoyment of liberty of conscience in the worship and ordinances of God. The pious fathers of these colonies wished to enjoy the uncorrupted gospel, administered in all its ordinances in purity and power, and to transmit the invaluable blessings of civil and religious liberty to their remotest posterity. With these views they left their native country, their pleasant seats and enjoyments in Europe, and made settlements in the wilds of America.

The same year in which the patent of Massachusetts received the royal confirmation, Mr. John Endicott was sent over, with about three hundred people, by the patentees, to prepare the way for the settlement of a permanent colony in that part of New-England. They arrived at Naumkeak in June, and began a settlement, which they named Salem. This was the first town in Massachusetts, and the second in New-England.

Book I.

No liberty of conscience in England.

1629.

New-England settled for the purposes of religion.

Salem settled, June 24th.

Book I. About a hundred of the planters who came over with Mr. Endicott, removed very soon to Mishawam, and began a plantation at that place. Here they erected a very spacious house, and made other preparations for the accommodation of those who were expected from England the next year. They called their settlement Charlestown.

Charlestown settled.

At a meeting of the company for the planting of the Massachusetts, in England, August 29th, it was voted, that the patent and government of the plantation be transferred to New-England.*

The next year, therefore, seventeen ships were prepared, with all necessaries for the settlement of a colony. Eleven or twelve of these ships made a safe arrival in New-England by the middle of July, and they all arrived before the close of the year.† In these came over governor Winthrop, and the magistrates of the colony, who had been previously chosen in England. With them also came a number of ministers, to illuminate the infant churches, and preach in the wilderness the glad tidings of salvation.

1630.

On the 10th or 12th of July, governor Winthrop arrived at Charlestown, with about fifteen hundred people. They encamped in cottages, booths, and tents, upon Charlestown hill. Their place of public worship was under a large spreading tree. Here Messrs. Wilson and Phillips preached their first sermons to these pious pilgrims.‡ In the ships which arrived this year, there came over about seventeen hundred people. In this and the last year, there came into New-England two thousand planters. These settled about nine or ten towns or villages. A considerable number settled at Boston and Charlestown. Many of the principal characters fixed their abode in these towns. Governor Winthrop lived in the great house, which had been erected the preceding year at Charlestown. Mr. Isaac Johnston, who married the lady Arabella, sister of the earl of Lincoln, and who had the best estate of any of the company, fixed his residence at Boston. He was the great promoter of the settlement of the capital of the Massachusetts.§ Sir Richard Saltonstall, who was another of the magistrates, with his company, settled at Watertown. They made choice of Mr. Phillips for their pastor. Mr. Pyncheon, and another company, began a settlement at Roxbury, and the famous Mr. John Elliot and Mr. Weld, who came into New-England the next year, were elected their ministers. Other companies settled Medford and Weymouth. Boston and Charlestown, the first year, con-

Gov. Winthrop arrives at Charlestown, July 10th.

Towns settled in Massachusetts, 1630.

* Prince's Chron. p. 192. † Ibid. part ii. p. 10. ‡ Ibid. p. 240
§ Ibid. part ii. sect. 2, p. 2.

sidered themselves as one company, and chose Mr. Wilson for their pastor.

In one of the first ships which arrived this year, came over the Rev. Mr. John Warham, Mr. John Maverick, Mr. Rossiter, Mr. Ludlow, Mr. Henry Wolcott, and others of Mr. Warham's church and congregation, who first settled the town of Windsor, in Connecticut. Mr. Rossiter and Mr. Ludlow were magistrates. Mr. Wolcott had a fine estate, and was a man of superior abilities. This was an honourable company. Mr. Warham had been a famous minister in Exeter, the capital of the county of Devonshire. The people who came with him, were from the three counties of Devonshire, Dorsetshire, and Somersetshire.

Some time before the 20th of March, just as they were about to embark for New-England, upon a day of solemn fasting and prayer, they were formed into a congregational church, in the new hospital at Plymouth, in England. They then made choice of Mr. Warham and Mr. Maverick to be their pastor and teacher, and they were ordained, or re-installed to the care of this particular church. The famous Mr. White, of Dorchester, preached and assisted on this occasion.†

They sailed from Plymouth, in England, on the 20th of March, in the ship Mary and John, of 400 tons, and arrived at Nantasket on the Lord's day, May 30th. The next day, captain Squeb, master of the ship, put them and their goods on shore, at Nantasket point, and, in this situation, left them to shift for themselves.‡ But, by the assistance of some of the old planters, they obtained a boat, and proceeded up Charles river, to the place since called Watertown. Here they landed their goods, and erected a shelter to cover them; but as they had many cattle, and found a neck of land at Mattapan, affording good accommodations for them, they soon removed and began a settlement there. They named their town Dorchester.

Sir Richard Saltonstall's people, who settled at Watertown, were the first settlers of Weathersfield, in Connecticut. Mr. Phillips, who was elected their pastor, at Watertown, had been minister at Boxford, in the county of Essex. Most of them were, probably, the people of his former charge, and from the same county.

The emigrants who came into New-England with Mr. Endicott and governor Winthrop, soon after their arrival,

Book 1.
1630.

Mr. Warham arrives, May 30th, with the first settlers of Windsor.

1630.
Planters of Weathersfield.

Mortality and losses of the first years.

† Prince's Chron. p. 200.
‡ Ibid. p. 207. Captain Squeb was, afterwards, obliged to pay damages for this conduct.

Book I. were visited with uncommon sickness and mortality. Of the company who came with Mr. Endicott the last year, eighty were in their graves before governor Winthrop arrived. He found the colony in very miserable circumstances. Many of those who were yet living, were in a weak and sickly condition. The people had scarcely a sufficiency of provisions for their subsistence fourteen days. Besides, they had sustained a capital loss in their servants. They brought over with them a hundred and eighty. These cost them more than three thousand pounds sterling. But they were so straightened for provisions, that they were necessitated to give all those who survived the sickness, their liberty, that they might shift for themselves.*

Many of the ships which arrived this year, had a long passage of seventeen or eighteen weeks; in consequence of which, numbers had the scurvy, and came on shore in a sickly condition. By reason of wet lodgings, in cottages and miserable huts, for the want of fresh food and other conveniences, this sickness increased. Other diseases also, soon attacked them with violence; so that, in a fortnight or three weeks, the sickness became general. In a short time, so many fell sick, that the well were not sufficient properly to attend them, and bury the dead. Great numbers died, and were buried on Charlestown hill.† The sickness and mortality greatly retarded the necessary labours and affairs of the colony; so that many of the people were obliged to lie in tents, or miserable huts, during the winter. By the next spring, a hundred and twenty, or more, were among the dead. Of this number were Mr. Johnson and Mr. Rossiter. The charming lady Arabella, celebrated for her many virtues, died before her husband. She was sister to the earl of Lincoln; and, for the sake of religion, came from a paradise of ease, plenty, and delight, in the house of a renowned earl, into a wilderness of toil, disaster, and misery.

1630.

About a hundred of the people were discouraged, and returned to England; two hundred were dead, and some went to Piscataqua. About seventeen hundred remained; a little more than a hundred and eighty persons, or thirty families, on an average, to each town. The greatest numbers fixed themselves at Boston and Watertown. In these towns, there were, probably, nearly sixty families: in Charlestown and Dorchester, about forty; and in the other towns, not more than fifteen or twenty families.‡

Famine, 1631.

In addition to all the other calamities, with which these

* Prince's Chron. p. 209, 210. † Ibid. p. 242.
‡ Ibid. part ii. p. 1 and 31.

plantations had been visited, they, this year, experienced the distress of famine. By the beginning of February, bread failed in every house, except the governor's, and even in this the family were reduced to the last loaves. Such were the necessities of the people, that they fed on clams, muscles, ground-nuts, and acorns. Indeed, in the winter season, it was with great difficulty that the people procured these poor articles of subsistence. The governors foreseeing, in the fall, that they should want provisions, dispatched a ship to Ireland to procure them a supply. Her happy arrival on the 5th of February, prevented their perishing with famine. The return of health in the spring, the arrival of other vessels, with provisions, afterwards, and a plenteous harvest, gave the affairs of the colony a more prosperous appearance.

While affairs were thus transacting in the colony, the violent persecution of the puritans in England made great numbers look towards America as the only safe retreat from the impending storm. This, annually, occasioned a large accession of new planters to the settlements in New-England.

In 1630, the Rev. Mr. Thomas Hooker, a gentleman of great abilities, and a famous preacher, at Chelmsford, in the county of Essex, was silenced for non-conformity. To escape fines and imprisonment, he fled into Holland. He was held in such high and universal esteem among his acquaintance, that forty-seven ministers, in his vicinity, petitioned the bishop of London in his favour. These were all conformists, and witnessed for Mr. Hooker, that they esteemed him, and knew him " to be, for doctrine orthodox, for life and conversation honest, for disposition peaceable, and no wise turbulent or factious." However, as he was a non-conformist, no personal or acquired excellencies, no testimonials of his good conduct, nor prayers of his friends, could save him from prosecutions and deposition.

He was so esteemed as a preacher, that not only his own people, but others, from all parts of the county of Essex, flocked to hear him. The noble earl of Warwick, though he resided at a great distance from Chelmsford, was so delighted with his public performances, that he frequently attended them. Great numbers not only attended his ministry, but experienced its salutary effects, and found themselves willing to emigrate into any part of the world, to enjoy the happiness of such a pastor. No sooner, therefore, was he driven from them, than they turned their eyes towards New-England. They hoped that, if comfortable settlements could be made in this part of America, they

D

Book I. might obtain him for their pastor. Therefore, in 1632, a large body of them came over and settled at Newtown, since called Cambridge, in Massachusetts. Numbers of them, it seems, came over at an earlier period, and began to settle at Weymouth, but, this year, they all removed to Newtown. They had expressed their earnest desires to Mr. Hooker, that he would come over into New-England, and take the pastoral charge of them.

1632.

Mr. Hooker arrives, Sept. 4th, 1633.

At their desire he left Holland, and having obtained Mr. Samuel Stone, a lecturer at Torcester, in Northamptonshire, for an assistant in the ministry, took his passage for America in the Griffin, a ship of 300 tons, and arrived at Boston, Sept. 4th, 1633. With him came over the famous Mr. John Cotton, Mr. John Haynes, afterwards governor of Connecticut, Mr. Goff, and two hundred other passengers, of importance to the colony.

1633.

Mr. Hooker, soon after his arrival at Boston, proceeded to Newtown, where, finding himself in the midst of a joyful and affectionate people, he was filled with joy himself. He embraced them with open arms, saying, in the language of the apostle, "Now I live, if ye stand fast in the Lord."* These were the pious people who afterwards settled the town of Hartford.

Messrs. Hooker and Stone ordained, Oct. 11th, 1633.

Mr. Phillips ordained at Watertown, Aug. 27th, 1630.

Soon after Mr. Hooker's arrival, he was chosen pastor, and Mr. Stone teacher of the people at Newtown. On the 11th of October the church was gathered, and, after solemn fasting and prayer, the pastor and teacher were ordained to their respective offices. The church at Watertown, had been gathered before, on the 27th of August, 1630, and Mr. Phillips ordained pastor. Thus, the three churches of Windsor, Hartford, and Weathersfield, were gathered antecedently to their settlement in Connecticut, and it does not appear that they were ever re-gathered afterwards.

* Magnalia B. III. The Life of Hooker.

CHAPTER II.

The patent of Connecticut. The situation, extent, boundaries, and area of the settled part of the colony. The discovery of Connecticut river; a description of it, and the signification of its name. The colony derives its name from the river. Description of other rivers. Plymouth and Dutch houses. Prospects of trade upon the river.

THE great Plymouth company wished to make grants of their lands as fast as they could find purchasers; and conformity was so pressed, and the times grew so difficult in England, that men of quality, as well as others, were anxious to provide, for themselves and their friends, a retreat in America. Another patent, therefore, containing a large tract of country in New-England, soon succeeded that of Massachusetts.

On the 19th of March, 1631, Robert, earl of Warwick, president of the council of Plymouth, under his hand and seal, did grant and confirm unto the honourable William Viscount Say and Seal, Robert Lord Brooks, Robert Lord Rich, Charles Fiennes, Esq. Sir Nathaniel Rich, Sir Richard Saltonstall, and others, to the number of eleven, and to their heirs, assigns, and associates, for ever, "All that part of New-England, in America, which lies and extends itself from a river there, called Narraganset river, the space of forty leagues upon a strait line near the sea shore, towards the south-west, west and by south, or west as the coast lieth towards Virginia, accounting three English miles to the league, and all and singular the lands and hereditaments whatsoever, lying and being within the bounds aforesaid, north and south in latitude and breadth, and in length and longitude of, and within all the breadth aforesaid, throughout all the main lands there, from the western ocean to the south seas; and all lands, grounds, soil, wood and wood lands, ground, havens, ports, creeks and rivers, waters, fishings and hereditaments whatsoever, lying within the said space, and every part and parcel thereof; and also, all islands lying in America aforesaid, in the said seas, or either of them, on the western or eastern coasts, or parts of the said tracts of land, by these presents to be given or granted."* The council of Plymouth, the preceding year, 1630, granted this whole tract to the earl of Warwick, and it had been confirmed to him by a patent from king Charles the first.

Old patent of Connecticut, 1631.

* See this patent in the Appendix, No. 1.

BOOK I. This is the original patent of Connecticut. The settlers of the two colonies of Connecticut and New-Haven were the patentees of Viscount Say and Seal, lord Brook, and their associates, to whom the patent was originally given.

Extent of the Connecticut patent.

President Clap describes the extent of the tract, conveyed by this patent, in the words following: "All that part of New-England which lies west from Narraganset river, a hundred and twenty miles on the sea coast; and from thence, in latitude and breadth aforesaid, to the south sea. This grant extends from Point Judith, to New-York; and from thence, in a west line to the south sea: and if we take Narraganset river in its whole length, this tract will extend as far north as Worcester: it comprehends the whole of the colony of Connecticut, and much more."* Neal, Douglass, Hutchinson,† and all ancient historians and writers, have represented all the New-England grants as extending west from the Atlantic ocean to the south sea. Indeed the words of the patent are most express, declaring its extent to be south west or west, towards Virginia, to be in length and longitude throughout all the main lands to the south sea.

1631.

The colony of the Massachusetts, and the commissioners of the united colonies of New-England, understood the patents in this light, and hence extended their claims to the westward of the Dutch settlements. The Massachusetts, in the year 1659, made a grant of lands, opposite to fort Aurania, upon Hudson's river, to a number of principal merchants, in the colony, who were planning to make settlements in those parts.‡ The same year, the commissioners of the united colonies asserted their claim of all the western lands to the south sea. In a letter to the Dutch governor, September 1st, 1659, they write, "We presume you have heard from your people of the fort of Aurania, that some of our people, the English, have been lately in those parts, upon discovery of some meet places for plantations, within the bounds of the patent of the Massachusetts colony; which from the latitude of 42 degrees and a half, or 42 degrees and 33 and a half minutes, and so northerly, extends itself from east to west, in longitude through the main land of America, from the Atlantic ocean to the south or west sea."

The patents to Virginia, the Carolinas, and Georgia, have ever been understood to have the same westerly ex-

* Manuscripts of president Clap.
† Neal's history N. E. vol. i. p. 148. Douglass, vol. ii. p. 90 and 160; and Hutchinson vol. i. p. 64 and vol. ii. p. 203.
‡ Hutchinson vol. i. p. 159.

tension. In the same light have they always been viewed, by the British kings, and have been pleaded and acted upon, in treaties, between the court of Great-Britain, and the French and Spanish monarchs. By virtue of this construction of patents and charters of the American colonies, it was, that all the western territories, as far as Mississippi, were, in the late peace with Great-Britain, ceded to the states of America. From the same construction of the patents, congress have taken a formal surrender of the unappropriated western lands from particular states, and from Connecticut no less than from others.

The situation of the settled part of Connecticut is chiefly from 41 to 42 degrees of north latitude, and from 72 to 73 degrees and 45 minutes west longitude. It is bounded south by the sea shore about 90 miles, from Byram river, in the latitude of 40 degrees and 58 minutes, and longitude 72 degrees and 25 minutes, to Pawcatuck river, in latitude 41 degrees and 17 minutes, and in longitude 72 degrees and 25 minutes; east on the colony of Rhode-Island 45 miles; north on Massachusetts 72 miles, the line running nearly in the latitude of 42 degrees; and west on New-York about 73 miles. It contains 4,730 square miles, and 3,020,000 acres. One twentieth part of the colony is water and highways.* Exclusive of these there are 2,869,000 acres. Of this about 2,640,000 are estimated improvable. The land is excellently watered, and liberal to the husbandman. Though, in some places, it is mountainous and broken, yet the greatest part of this is profitable either for wood or grazing. There are some thin lands, but these are profitable with proper manuring and cultivation.

Situation, and area of Connecticut.

The present population is more than fifty souls to every square mile, including land and water. It is about one person to every ten or twelve acres of land.

Degree of population.

The first discoveries made of this part of New-England were of its principal river and the fine meadows lying upon its bank. Whether the Dutch at New-Netherlands, or the people of New-Plymouth, were the first discoverers of the river is not certain. Both the English and Dutch claimed to be the first discoverers, and both purchased and made a settlement of the lands upon it nearly at the same time.

In 1631, Wahquimacut, a sachem upon the river Connecticut, made a journey to Plymouth and Boston, earnestly soliciting the governors of each of the colonies to send

Invitation to settle on the river.

---

* To find the quantity of water and highways, an accurate computation was made of the proportion of water and highways in a particular town, which was supposed to contain an average with the towns in general.

Book I. men to make settlements upon the river. He represented the exceeding fruitfulness of the country, and promised that he would supply the English, if they would make a settlement there, with corn annually, and give them eighty beaver skins. He urged that two men might be sent to view the country. Had this invitation been accepted it might have prevented the Dutch claim to any part of the lands upon the river, and opened an extensive trade, in hemp, furs, and deer skins, with all the Indians upon it, and far into Canada.

1631. The governor of Massachusetts treated the sachem and his company with generosity, but paid no further attention to his proposal. Mr. Winslow, the governor of Plymouth, judged it worthy of more attention. It seems, that soon after he went to Connecticut, and discovered the river and the adjacent parts. The commissioners of the united colonies, in their declaration against the Dutch, in 1653, say, "Mr. Winslow, one of the commissioners for Plymouth, discovered the fresh river when the Dutch had neither trading house nor any pretence to a foot of land there."*

It very soon appeared that the earnestness, with which the Indian sachem solicited the English to make settlements on the river, originated in the distressed state of the river Indians. Pekoath, at that time, the great sachem of the Pequims, or Pequots, was conquering them, and driving their sachems from that part of the country. The Indian king imagined that, if he could persuade the English to make settlements there, they would defend him from his too powerful enemies.†

1632. The next year, the people of New-Plymouth made more particular discoveries, upon the river, and found a place near the mouth of the little river, in Windsor, at which they judged a trading house might be erected, which would be advantageous to the colony.

The Indians represented that the river Connecticut extended so far north, and so near the great lake, that they passed their canoes from the lake into it; and that from the great swamps about the lake came most of the beaver in which they traded.

One of the branches of Onion river, in Vermont, is within ten miles of Connecticut river. This was anciently called the French river. The French and Indians from Canada came by this river, and from this into Connecticut, when they made their attacks on the northern frontiers of New-England and Connecticut.

* Records of the United Colonies.
† Winthrop's Journal, p. 25.

Chap. II.   CONNECTICUT.   31

Connecticut river has its source in that grand ridge of mountains which divides the waters of New-England and Canada, and extends north-easterly to the gulph of St. Lawrence. The source of its highest branch is in about 45 degrees and a half, or 46 degrees of north latitude. Where it enters New-England, in 45 degrees of north latitude, it is ten rods in breadth, and in running sixty miles further, it becomes twenty-four rods wide. It forms the boundary line between New-Hampshire and Vermont about two hundred miles. Thence running through the states of Massachusetts and Connecticut, it disembogues its waters into Long-Island sound, between Saybrook and Lyme. It runs with a gentle flow, as its course is, between three and four hundred miles. Its breadth through Connecticut, as a medium, is between a hundred rods and half a mile. In the high spring floods it overflows its banks, and in some places is nearly two miles in breadth. As its banks are generally low, it forms and fertilizes a vast tract of the finest meadow; feasible, fertile, and in which a stone is scarcely to be found. The general course of this beautiful river, above, and between the states of New-Hampshire and Vermont, is nearly south west; thence it turns and runs but a few degrees west of south to its mouth. At a small distance from its mouth is a bar of sand, apparently formed by the conflux of the river and tide. Upon this there is but ten feet of water at full tide. The bar is at such a distance from the mouth of the river, that the greatest floods do not increase the depth of the water. This is some obstruction to navigation, but any vessel, which can pass the bar, may proceed without obstruction as far as Middletown, thirty miles from the sound; and vessels of eighty, and a hundred tons, go up to Hartford, fifty miles from the river's mouth. By means of locks and cuts, at the falls, it is now navigable, for boats, more than three hundred miles.

In Connecticut, there is one exception to the lowness of the river's banks. About three miles below Middletown the river makes its way through two mountains, by which its breadth is contracted to about forty rods. This occasions the waters, sometimes, in the spring floods, to rise, even at Hartford, twenty feet above the common surface of the river. This, for the length of its course, its gentle flow, its excellent waters, the rich and extensive meadows which it forms, and the immense quantities of fish, with which it abounds, is one of the finest rivers in New-England.

None of the ancient adventurers, who discovered the

Book I. great continent of North-America, or New-England, made any discovery of this river. It does not appear that it was known to any civilized nation, until some years after the settlement of the English and Dutch, at Plymouth and New-Netherlands.

Connecticut named from its principal river. From this fine river, which the Indians called Quonehtacut, or Connecticut, (in English, the long river,) the colony, originally took its name. Indeed this is one principal source of its wealth and convenience.

Description of rivers. The Housatonick and the little or Farmington river, westward of it, and Pequot river, now called the Thames, on the east, are also considerable sources of its opulence and prosperity. The Housatonick, now commonly called Stratford river, has two principal branches. One rises in Lanesborough, and the other in Windsor, in the county of Berkshire, in Massachusetts. Where it enters Connecticut, between Salisbury and Canaan, it is about fifty rods wide, and running through the whole length of the colony, it empties into the sound between Milford and Stratford. It is navigable twelve miles to Derby. Between Milford and Stratford it is about eighty rods wide, and there is about four fathoms of water. Were it not obstructed, by a bar of shells, at the mouth, it would admit large ships. Between Salisbury and Canaan is a cataract where the water of the whole river falls perpendicularly sixty feet. The fall produces a perfectly white sheet of water, and a mist in which various floating rainbows are exhibited, forming a scene exquisitely grand and beautiful.

Of Naugatuck The Naugatuck, or Waterbury river, is another considerable branch of the Housatonick. Its source is in Torrington, and running through Harwinton, Plymouth and Waterbury, it empties itself into said river at Derby.

Of the little river. The little, or Farmington river, rises in Becket, in Massachusetts, crosses the boundary line between the colonies at Hartland, and passing through Barkhempsted and New-Hartford, runs south considerably below the centre of Farmington first society; then, making a remarkable turn, it runs back nearly a north course, twelve or fourteen miles into Simsbury; where it turns easterly, and running into Windsor, discharges its waters into Connecticut river nearly in the centre of the town. This formerly was replenished with all kinds of fish in as great a profusion as Connecticut. The numerous dams, which more lately have been erected upon it, have very greatly obstructed their passage.

Of Pequot. Pequot river, or the Thames, empties into the sound at New-London. It is navigable fourteen miles, to Norwich

CHAP. II.   CONNECTICUT.

landing. Here it loses its name, and branches into Shetucket on the east, and Norwich or little river on the west.

About a mile from the mouth of the little river, is a remarkable romantic cataract. A perpendicular rock, about twelve feet high, extends itself across the whole channel: over this the river pitches, in one entire sheet, on to a bed of rocks; here it is compressed by a very narrow and crooked passage, between two craggy cliffs, and for fifteen or twenty rods, forces its way over numerous pointed rocks, with the most violent agitation; thence it flows into a large bason, which spreads itself for its reception. The long and constant falling of the waters, have excavated the rocks, even to admiration. In some, cavities are made, of a circular form, not less than five or six feet deep. The smooth and gentle flow of the river above the fall, the regularity and beauty of its descent, the roughness and foam of the waters below, and the rugged, towering cliff impending the whole, presents the spectator with a scene majestic and pleasing beyond description.

The Shetucket, which name it bears as far only as the southern boundary of Windham, is formed by the Willamantick and Quenibaug rivers. The Willamantick has its source in Massachusetts, enters Connecticut at Stafford, and is the boundary line between Tolland and Willington, Coventry and Mansfield, and passing by Windham, loses itself in the Shetucket. Quenibaug rises in Brimfield, in Massachusetts, and passing through Sturbridge and Dudley, crosses the line between that state and Connecticut, at Thompson; and dividing Pomfret from Killingly, Canterbury from Plainfield, and Lisbon from Preston, flows into the Shetucket.

The colony is watered and fertilized by numerous other rivers, of less extent and utility.

As the people at Plymouth had explored Connecticut river, and fixed upon a place convenient for building and commerce, and found the original proprietors of the soil desirous of their making settlements among them, they judged it an affair worthy of public, and immediate attention.

In July, 1633, Mr. Winslow and Mr. Bradford therefore made a journey to Boston, to confer with governor Winthrop and his council, on the subject. Governor Winslow and Mr. Bradford proposed it to them, to join with Plymouth, in a trade to Connecticut, for hemp and beaver, and to erect a house for the purposes of commerce. It was represented as necessary, to prevent the Dutch from taking possession of that fine country, who, it was reported

E

Margin notes: Book I. Description of the cataract at Norwich. Of Shetucket, Willamantic, and Quenibaug.

Book I.
~~~
1633.

September

ed, were about to build upon the river: but governor Winthrop declined the motion: he objected that it was not proper to make a plantation there, because there were three or four thousand warlike Indians upon the river; and because the bar at the mouth of it was such, that small pinnaces only could enter it at high water; and because that, seven months in the year, no vessels could go into it, by reason of the ice, and the violence of the stream.

The Plymouth people therefore determined to undertake the enterprise at their own risk. Preparations were made for erecting a trading house, and establishing a small company upon the river. In the mean time, the master of a vessel from Massachusetts, who was trading at New-Netherlands, shewed to Walter Van Twiller, the Dutch governor, the commission which the English had to trade and settle in New-England; and that his majesty the king of England, had granted all these parts to his own subjects. He therefore desired that the Dutch would not build at Connecticut. This appears to have been done at the direction of governor Winthrop; for, in consequence of it, the Dutch governor wrote a very complaisant letter to him, in which he represented, that the lords, the States General, had granted the same country to the West-India company. He requested therefore, that the English would make no settlements at Connecticut, until the affair should be determined between the court of England, and the States General.* This appears to have been a piece of policy in the Dutch governor, to keep the English still, until the Dutch had got a firm footing upon the river.

Several vessels, this year, went into Connecticut river to trade. John Oldham, from Dorchester, and three men with him, also travelled through the wilderness to Connecticut, to view the country, and trade with the Indians. The sachem upon the river made him most welcome, and gave him a present in beaver. He found that the Indian hemp grew spontaneously in the meadows, in great abundance: he purchased a quantity of it; and, upon trial, it appeared much to exceed the hemp which grew in England.

William Holmes, of Plymouth, with his company, having prepared the frame of a house, with boards and materials for covering it immediately, put them on board a vessel, and sailed for Connecticut. Holmes had a commission from the governor of Plymouth, and a chosen company to accomplish his design. When he came into the river, he found that the Dutch had got in before him, made a light fort, and planted two pieces of cannon: this was erected

* Winthrop's Journal, p. 55.

CHAP. II.   CONNECTICUT.

at the place since called Hartford. The Dutch forbid Holmes' going up the river, stood by their cannon, ordered him to strike his colours, or they would fire upon him: but he was a man of spirit, assured them that he had a commission from the governor of Plymouth to go up the river, and that he must obey his orders: they poured out their threats, but he proceeded, and landing on the west side of the river, erected his house a little below the mouth of the little river, in Windsor.* The house was covered with the utmost dispatch, and fortified with palisadoes. The sachems, who were the original owners of the soil, had been driven from this part of the country, by the Pequots; and were now carried home on board Holmes' vessel. Of them the Plymouth people purchased the land, on which they erected their house.† This, governor Wolcott says, was the first house erected in Connecticut.‡ The Dutch, about the same time, erected a trading house at Hartford, which they called the Hirse of good hope.§

Book 1. Plymouth house erected at Windsor, Oct. 1633.

Dutch house at Hartford.

It was with great difficulty that Holmes and his company erected and fortified their house, and kept it afterwards. The Indians were offended at their bringing home the original proprietors, and lords of the country, and the Dutch that they had settled there, and were about to rival them in trade, and in the possession of those excellent lands upon the river: they were obliged therefore to combat both, and to keep a constant watch upon them.

Troubles from the Dutch and Indians.

The Dutch, before the Plymouth people took possession of the river, had invited them, in an amicable manner, to trade at Connecticut; but when they were apprised that they were making preparations for a settlement there, they repented of the invitation, and spared no exertions to prevent them.

On the 8th of June, the Dutch had sent Jacob Van Curter, to purchase lands upon the Connecticut. He made a purchase of about twenty acres at Hartford, of Nepuquash, a Pequot captain. Of this the Dutch took possession in October, and on the 25th of the month, Curter protested against William Holmes, the builder of the Plymouth house. Some time afterwards, the Dutch governor, Walter Van Twiller, of fort Amsterdam, dispatched a reinforcement to Connecticut, designing to drive Holmes and his company from the river. A band of seventy men, under arms, with banners displayed, assaulted the Plymouth

Oct. 25.

Dec. 1634.

---

* Manuscripts of governor Wolcott.
† Prince's Chron. part ii. sec. 2, p. 94, 95, 96.
‡ In his manuscripts.
§ Smith represents this house as built ten years before it was. Hist. of New-York, p. 2.

house, but they found it so well fortified, and the men who kept it so vigilant and determined, that it could not be taken without bloodshed: they therefore came to a parley, and finally returned in peace.

The Dutch were always mere intruders. They had no right to any part of this country. The English ever denied their right, and when the Dutch placed a governor at New-Netherlands, and the court of England made complaint of it to the States General, they disowned the affair, and said it was only a private undertaking of an Amsterdam West-India company. King James the first commissioned Edward Langdon to be governor, at New-Netherlands, and named the country New-Albion. The Dutch submitted to the English government, until the troubles in England, under the administrations of king Charles the first and the long parliament.* Taking the advantage of the distraction of those times, they again usurped and established their government, until they were reduced by king Charles the second, in 1664. They gave great trouble to both the colonies of Connecticut and New-Haven.

Trade in fur.

The people of New-Plymouth had carried on a trade upon Connecticut river for nearly two years before they erected a trading house. They found the country to be excellent and the trade profitable; but that, were there a house and company to receive the commodities which were brought down from the inland country, the profits would be much greater. The country abounded with beaver. The Dutch purchased not less than ten thousand skins annually. Plymouth and Massachusetts people sometimes sent, in a single ship, for England, a thousand pounds sterling worth of otter and beaver skins. The extent of Connecticut river, the numerous Indians upon it, and the easy communication which they had with the lakes, and natives of Canada, gave an extensive opening for a trade in furs, skins, corn, hemp and all kinds of commodities which the country afforded.

1633.

This was a year of great sickness at Plymouth. They lost twenty of their people. Some of them were their principal and most useful inhabitants.

Mortality among the Indians in Nov. and Dec.

It was a dreadful year to the Indians in the Massachusetts. Two sachems with a great part of their Indians died. The small pox, which spread among them, was the occasion of the mortality. The people of Massachusetts shewed them great kindness in their distress. Several towns received their children to prevent their taking the infection, and to nurse and save them if they had taken it;

* Doug. vol. ii. p. 222.

but the most of them died, notwithstanding all the care and pains which could be exercised towards them. When their own people forsook them, the English, who lived near them, went to their wigwams and ministered to them. Some families spent almost their whole time with them. One Englishman buried thirty of their dead in one day.*

CHAPTER III.

The state of the country of Connecticut when the settlement of the colony commenced. Its trees and fruits. Its animals. Number, situation, genius, manners, arms, utensils and wars of the Indians.

WHEN the English became first acquainted with that tract comprised within the settled part of Connecticut, it was a vast wilderness. There were no pleasant fields, nor gardens, no public roads, nor cleared plats. Except in places where the timber had been destroyed, and its growth prevented by frequent fires, the groves were thick and lofty. The Indians so often burned the country, to take deer and other wild game, that in many of the plain, dry parts of it, there was but little small timber. Where lands were thus burned there grew bent grass, or as some called it, thatch, two, three and four feet high, according to the strength of the land. This, with other combustible matter, which the fields and groves produced, when dry, in the spring and fall, burned with violence and killed all the small trees. The large ones escaped, and generally grew to a notable height and magnitude. In this manner the natives so thinned the groves, that they were able to plant their corn and obtain a crop.

The constant fall of foliage, with the numerous kinds of weeds and wild grass, which annually died and putrified on the lands, yielded a constant manure, and exceedingly enriched them. Vegetation was rapid, and all the natural productions of the country luxuriant.

It abounded with the finest oaks of all kinds, with chesnut, walnut and wild cherry trees, with all kinds of maple, beech, birch, ash and elm. The butternut tree, buttonwood, basswood, poplar and sassafras trees, were to be found

Trees.

1633.

* Winthrop's Journal, p. 59.

HISTORY OF — Chap. III.

Book I. generally upon all tracts in Connecticut. White, yellow and pitch pine, white and red cedar, hemlock and spruce, grew plenteously in many places. In the north and northwestern part of the colony were excellent groves of pine, with spruce and fir trees. The white wood tree also, notable for its height and magnitude, making excellent boards and clapboards, was the natural growth of the country. In some towns white wood trees have grown in great abundance. All other kinds of small trees, of less utility, common to New-England, flourish in Connecticut.

Natural fruits. The country abounded with a great variety of wild fruit. In the groves were walnuts, chesnuts, butternuts, hazlenuts and acorns in great abundance. Wild cherries, currants and plumbs, were natural productions. In the low lands, on the banks of the rivers, by the brooks and gutters, there was a variety and plenty of grapes. The country also abounded with an almost endless variety of esculent and medicinal berries, herbs and roots. Among the principal and most delicious of these were strawberries, blackberries of various kinds, raspberries, dewberries, whortleberries, bilberries, blucberries and mulberries. Cranberries also grew plenteously in the meadows, which when well prepared furnish a rich and excellent sauce. Juniperberries, barberries and bayberries, which are of the medicinal kind, grow spontaneously in Connecticut. The latter is an excellent and useful berry, producing a most valuable tallow. It is of a beautiful green, and has a fine perfume. Beside these, there was a profusion of various other kinds of berries of less consideration. Some even of these, however, are very useful in various kinds of dyes and in certain medicinal applications.

The earth spontaneously produced ground nuts, artichokes, wild leeks, onions, garlicks, turnips, wild pease, plantain, radish, and other esculent roots and herbs.

Medicinal vegetables. Among the principal medicinal vegetables of Connecticut are the blood root, seneca snakeroot, liquorice root, dragon root, pleurisy root,* spikenard, elecampane, solomon's seal, sarsaparilla, senna, bittersweet, ginseng, angelica, masterwort, motherwort, lungwort, consumption root,† great and small canker weed, high and low centaury, sweet and blue flag, elder, maidenhair, pennyroyal, celan-

---

* Esclepias decumbens.

† This is the Geum Urbanum of Linnæus. It is known in Britain by the name of *Herb Bennet*, or common *Avens*. Dr. Buchhave, from long experience, recommends it as much superior to the Peruvian bark, in the cure of periodical and other diseases. Medical commentaries by a society of Physicians in Edinburgh, vol. vii. p. 279 to 288. He represents three ounces of this root, as equal to a pound of the cortex.

dine, mallow, marsh mallow, slippery elm, adder's tongue and rattlesnake weed. Indeed a great proportion of the the roots and plants of the country, with the bark, buds and roots of many of the trees, are used medicinally. There is a great variety of plants and flowers, the names and virtues of which are not known.§

[margin: Book I. 1633.]

The country was no less productive of animals, than of natural fruit. In the groves there were plenty of deer, moose, fat bears, turkies, herons, partridges, quails, pigeons, and other wild game, which were excellent for food. There were such incredible numbers of pigeons in New-England, when the English became first acquainted with it, as filled them with a kind of astonishment. Such numerous and extensive flocks would be seen flying for some hours, in the morning, that they would obscure the light. An American historian writes, "It passeth credit, if but the truth were written."

[margin: Animals.]

Connecticut abounded in furs. Here were otters, beaver, the black, gray, and red fox, the racoon, mink, muskrat, and various other animals, of the fur kind. The wolf, wild cat, and other animals, common in New-England, were equally so in Connecticut. Wolves were numerous in all parts of New-England, when the settlements commenced, and did great damage to the planters, killing their sheep, calves, and young cattle.

The country afforded an almost incredible plenty of water fowl. In the bays, creeks, rivers, and ponds, were wild geese, and ducks of all kinds, wigeons, sheldrapes, broadbills, teal of various sorts, and other fowl, which were both wholesome and palatable. In the waters, on the shores, and in the sands, were lobsters, oysters, clams, and all kinds of shell fish in abundance. Most of these are reckoned among the dainties of the table.

[margin: Fowl.]

In the seas, bays, rivers, and ponds, there was a variety, and an innumerable multitude of fish. Connecticut river, in particular, was distinguished for that plenty and variety which it afforded in the proper season: especially for those excellent salmon, with which its waters were replenished.

[margin: Fish.]

As Connecticut abounded in wild animals, so it did also with wild and savage men. In no part of New-England were the Indians so numerous, in proportion to the extent of territory, as in Connecticut. The sea coast, harbors, bays, numerous ponds and streams, with which the country abounded, the almost incredible plenty of fish and fowl

[margin: Indians numerous in Connecticut.]

§ The roots and flowers of America, would be the most valuable addition to the works of the celebrated Linnæus, which could be made.

BOOK I.
1633.

which it afforded, were exceedingly adapted to their convenience and mode of living. The exceeding fertility of the meadows, upon several of its rivers, and in some other parts of it, the excellence of its waters, and the salubrity of the air, were all circumstances, which naturally collected them in great numbers to this tract. Neither wars, nor sickness, had so depopulated this, as they had some other parts of New-England.

Their numbers.

From the accounts given of the Connecticut Indians, they cannot be estimated at less than twelve or sixteen thousand. They might possibly amount to twenty. They could muster, at least, three or four thousand warriors.* It was supposed, in 1633, that the river Indians only could bring this number into the field.† These were principally included within the ancient limits of Windsor, Hartford, Weathersfield, and Middletown. Within the town of Windsor only, there were ten distinct tribes, or sovereignties. About the year 1670, their bowmen were reckoned at two thousand. At that time, it was the general opinion,

Situation.

that there were nineteen Indians, in that town, to one Englishman. There was a great body of them in the centre of the town. They had a large fort a little north of the plat on which the first meeting-house was erected. On the east side of the river, on the upper branches of the Podunk, they were very numerous. There were also a great number in Hartford. Besides those on the west side of the river, there was a distinct tribe in East-Hartford. These were principally situated upon the Podunk, from the northern boundary of Hartford, to its mouth, where it empties into Connecticut river. Totanimo, their first sachem with whom the English had any acquaintance, commanded two hundred bowmen. These were called the Podunk Indians.

Forts.

At Mattabesick, now Middletown, was the great sachem Sowheag. His fort, or castle, was on the high ground, facing the river, and the adjacent country, on both sides of the river, was his sachemdom. This was extensive, comprehending the ancient boundaries of Weathersfield, then called Pyquaug, as well as Middletown. Sequin was sagamore at Pyquaug, under Sowheag, when the English began their settlements. On the east side of the river, in the tract since called Chatham, was a considerable clan, called the Wongung Indians. At Machemoodus, now called East-Haddam, was a numerous tribe, famous for their pawaws, and worshipping of evil spirits.‡ South of these,

* Winthrop's Journal, p. 51. † Manuscripts from Windsor.
‡ Manuscripts of the Rev. Mr. Hosmer.

in the easternmost part of Lyme, were the western Nehanticks. These were confederate with the Pequots. South and east of them, from Connecticut river to the eastern boundary line of the colony, and north-east or north, to its northern boundary line, lay the Pequot and Mohegan country. This tract was nearly thirty miles square, including the counties of New-London, Windham, and the principal part of the county of Tolland.§

Historians have treated of the Pequots and Mohegans, as two distinct tribes, and have described the Pequot country, as lying principally within the three towns of New-London, Groton, and Stonington. All the tract above this, as far north and east as has been described, they have represented as the Mohegan country. Most of the towns in this tract, if not all of them, hold their lands by virtue of deeds from Uncas, or his successors, the Mohegan sachems. It is, however, much to be doubted, whether the Mohegans were a distinct nation from the Pequots. They appear to have been a part of the same nation, named from the place of their situation. Uncas was evidently of the royal line of the Pequots, both by his father and mother; and his wife was daughter of Tatobam, one of the Pequot sachems.* He appears to have been a captain, or petty sachem, under Sassacus, the great prince of the nation. When the English first came to Connecticut, he was in a state of rebellion against him, in consequence of some misunderstanding between them; and of little power or consequence among the Indians.

The Pequots were, by far, the most warlike nation in Connecticut, or even in New-England. The tradition is, that they were, originally, an inland tribe; but, by their prowess, came down and settled themselves, in that fine country along the sea coast, from Nehantick to Narraganset bay. When the English began their settlements at Connecticut, Sassacus had twenty-six sachems, or principal war captains, under him. The next to himself, in dignity, was Mononottoh. The chief seat of these Indians, was at New-London and Groton. New-London was their principal harbor, and called Pequot harbor. They had another small harbor at the mouth of Mystic river. Their principal fort was on a commanding and most beautiful eminence, in the town of Groton, a few miles south-easterly from fort Griswold. It commanded one of the finest prospects of the sound and the adjacent country, which is to

§ President Clap's manuscripts, and Chandler's map of the Mohegan country.

* Preface to Capt. Mason's history, and genealogy of Uncas, upon the records of Connecticut.

Book I.
1633.

be found upon the coast. This was the royal fortress, where the chief sachem had his residence. He had another fort near Mystic river, a few miles to the eastward of this, called Mystic fort. This was also erected upon a beautiful hill, or eminence, gradually descending towards the south and south-east. The Pequots, Moheagans, and Nehanticks, could, doubtless, muster a thousand bowmen. The Pequots only were estimated at seven hundred warriors. Upon the lowest computation we therefore find at least three thousand warriors on the river Connecticut, and in the eastern part of the colony. If we reckon every third person a bowman, as some have imagined, then the whole number of Indians, in the town and tract mentioned, would be nine thousand; but if there were but one to four or five, as is most probable, then there were twelve or fifteen thousand.

West of Connecticut river and the towns upon it, there were not only scattering families in almost every part, but, in several places, great bodies of Indians. At Simsbury and New-Hartford, they were numerous; and upon those fine meadows, formed by the meanders of the little river, at Tunxis, now Farmington, and the lands adjacent, was another very large clan. There was a small tribe at Guilford, under the sachem squaw, or queen, of Menunkatuck. At Branford and East-Haven there was another. They had a famous burying ground at East-Haven, which they visited and kept up, with much ceremony, for many years after the settlement of New-Haven.

At Milford, Derby, Stratford, Norwalk, Stamford, and Greenwich, their numbers were formidable.

Milford Indians.

At Milford, the Indian name of which was Wopowage, there were great numbers; not only in the centre of the town, but south of it, at Milford point. In the fields there, the shells brought on by the original inhabitants are said to be so deep, that they never have been ploughed, or dug through, even to this day. On the west part of the town was another party. They had a strong fortress, with flankers at the four corners, about half a mile north of Stratford ferry. This was built as a defence against the Mohawks. At Turkey hill, in the north-west part of Milford, there was another large settlement.

Paugusset and Stratford Indians.

In Derby, there were two large clans. There was one at Paugusset. This clan erected a strong fort against the Mohawks, situated on the bank of the river, nearly a mile above Derby ferry. At the falls of Naugatuck river, four or five miles above, was another tribe.

At Stratford, the Indians were equally, if not more numerous. In that part of the town only, which is comprised within the limits of Huntington, their warriors, after the English had knowledge of them, were estimated at three hundred; and, before this time, they had been much wasted by the Mohawks.

The Indians at Stamford and Greenwich, and in that vicinity, probably, were not inferior in numbers to those at Stratford. There were two or three tribes of Indians in Stamford, when the English began the settlement of the town. In Norwalk were two petty sachemdoms; so that within these towns, there was a large and dangerous body of savages. These, with the natives between them and Hudson's river, gave extreme trouble to the Dutch. The Norwalk and Stamford Indians gave great alarm, and occasioned much expense to the English, after they made settlements in that part of the colony.

In the town of Woodbury, there were also great numbers of Indians. The most numerous body of them was in that part of the town, since named South-Britain.

It would doubtless be a moderate computation, to reckon all these different clans at a thousand warriors, or four or five thousand people. There must therefore have been sixteen, and it may be, twenty thousand Indians in Connecticut, when the settlement of it commenced.

East of Connecticut were the Narraganset Indians: these were a numerous and powerful body. When the English settled Plymouth, their fighting men were reckoned at three or four thousand.* Fifty years after this time, they were estimated at two thousand. The Pequots and Narragansets maintained perpetual war, and kept up an implacable animosity between them. The Narragansets were the only Indians in the vicinity of the Pequots, which they had not conquered. To these their very name was dreadful. They said Sassacus was "all one God; no man could kill him."†

On the northeasterly and northern part of the colony, were the Nipmuck Indians. Their principal seat was about the great ponds in Oxford, in Massachusetts, but their territory extended southward into Connecticut, more than twenty miles. This was called the Wabbequasset and Whetstone country; and sometimes, the Moheagan conquered country, as Uncas had conquered and added it to his sachemdom.‡

* Prince's Chron. p. 116.
† Major Mason's history of the Pequot war.
‡ President Clap's manuscripts, and Chandler's map of the Moheagan country.

BOOK I. The Connecticut, and indeed all the New-England Indians, were large, strait, well proportioned men. Their bodies were firm and active, capable of enduring the greatest fatigues and hardships. Their passive courage was almost incredible. When tortured in the most cruel manner; though flayed alive, though burnt with fire, cut or torn limb from limb, they would not groan, nor show any signs of distress. Nay, in some instances they would glory over their tormentors, saying that their hearts would never be soft until they were cold, and representing their torments as sweet as Englishmen's sugar.* When travelling in summer, or winter, they regarded neither heat nor cold. They were exceedingly light of foot, and would travel or run a very great distance in a day. Mr. Williams says, "I have known them run between eighty and a hundred miles in a summer's day and back again within two days." As they were accustomed to the woods, they ran in them nearly as well as on plain ground. They were exceedingly quick sighted, to discover their enemy, or their game, and equally artful to conceal themselves. Their features were tolerably regular. Their faces are generally full as broad as those of the English, but flatter; they have a small, dark coloured good eye, coarse black hair, and a fine white set of teeth. The Indian children, when born, are nearly as white as the English children; but as they grow up their skin grows darker and becomes nearly of a copper colour. The shapes both of the men and women, especially the latter, are excellent. A crooked Indian is rarely if ever to be seen.

The Indians in general were quick of apprehension, ingenious, and when pleased, nothing could exceed their courtesy and friendship. Gravity and eloquence distinguished them in council, address and bravery in war. They were not more easily provoked than the English; but when once they had received an injury, it was never forgotten. In anger they were not, like the English, talkative and boisterous, but sullen and revengeful. Indeed, when they were exasperated, nothing could exceed their revenge and cruelty. When they have fallen into the power of an enemy, they have not been known to beg for life, nor even to accept it when offered them. They have seemed rather to court death.† They were exceedingly improvident. If they had a supply for the present, they gave themselves no trouble for the future. The men declined all labor, and spent their time in hunting, fishing,

* Hubbard's Narrative, p. 130 and 172.
† Jefferson's notes, p. 102, 103, and Hubbard's narrative, p. 130, 172.

shooting, and warlike exercises. They were excellent marksmen, and rarely missed their game, whether running or flying.

"They imposed all the drudgery upon their women. They gathered and brought home their wood, planted, dressed and gathered in their corn. They carried home the venison, fish and fowl, which the men took in hunting. When they travelled, the women carried the children, packs and provisions. The Indian women submitted patiently to such treatment, considering it as the hard lot of the woman. This ungenerous usage of their haughty lords, they repaid with smiles and good humour."

It has been common among all heathen nations, to treat their women as slaves, and their children, in infancy, with little tenderness. The Indian men cared little for their children when young, and were supposed at certain times, to sacrifice them to the devil. Christianity only provides for that tender and honorable treatment of the woman, which is due to the sex formed of man. This alone provides for the tender care, nursing and education of her offspring, and is most favorable to domestic happiness, to the life and dignity of man.

"The Indian women were strong and masculine; and as they were more inured to exercise and hardship than the men, were even more firm and capable of fatigue and suffering than they." They endured the pains of child-bearing without a groan. It was not uncommon for them, soon after labor, to take their children upon their backs and travel as they had done before.*

The clothing of the Indians in New-England, was the skins of wild beasts. The men threw a light mantle of skins over them, and wore a small flap which was called Indian breeches. They were not very careful, however, to conceal their nakedness. The women were much more modest. They wore a coat of skins, girt about their loins, which reached down to their hams.—They never put this off in company. If the husband chose to sell his wife's beaver petticoat, she could not be persuaded to part with it, until he had provided another of some sort.

In the winter, their blanket of skins, which hung loose in the summer, was tied or wrapped more closely about them. The old men in the severe seasons also wore a sort of trowsers made of skins and fastened to their girdles. They wore shoes without heels, which they called mockasins. These were made generally of moose hide, but

* Wood's prospect of New-England, Neal and Hutchinson, Neal's Hist. N. E. vol. i. p. 45. Hutchinson, vol. i. p. 462 to 467.

Book I.
1633.
Ornaments.

sometimes of buck skin. They were shaped entirely to the foot, gathered at the toes and round the ankles, and made fast with strings.

Their ornaments were pendants in their ears and nose, carved of bone, shells and stone. These were in the form of birds, beasts and fishes. They also wore belts of wampompeag upon their arms, over their shoulders and about their loins. They cut their hair into various antic forms and stuck them with feathers. They also, by incisions into which they conveyed a black or blue, unchangeable ink, made on their cheeks, arms, and other parts of their bodies, the figures of moose, deer, bears, wolves, hawks, eagles and all such living creatures as were most agreeable to their fancies. These pictures were indelible, and lasted during life. The sachems, on great days, when they designed to show themselves in the full splendor of majesty, not only covered themselves with mantles of moose, or deer skins, with various embroideries of white beads, and with paintings of different kinds; but they wore the skin of a bear, wild cat or some terrible creature upon their shoulders and arms. They had also necklaces of fish bones, and painting themselves in a frightful manner, made a most ferocious and horrible appearance. The warriors who, on public occasions, dressed themselves in the most wild and terrific forms, were considered as the best men.

Habitations.

The Indian houses or wigwams, were, at best, but poor smoky cells. They were constructed generally like arbours, of small young trees, bent and twisted together, and so curiously covered with mats or bark, that they were tolerably dry and warm. The Indians made their fire in the centre of the house, and there was an opening at the top, which emitted the smoke. For the convenience of wood and water, these huts were commonly erected in groves, near some river, brook or living spring. When the wood failed, the family removed to another place.

Food.

They lived in a poor low manner: their food was coarse and simple, without any kind of seasoning: they had neither spice, salt, nor bread: they had neither butter, cheese, nor milk: they drank nothing better than the water which ran in the brook, or spouted from the spring: they fed on the flesh and entrails of moose, deer, bears, and all kinds of wild beasts and fowls; on fish, eels, and creeping things: they had good stomachs, and nothing came amiss. In the hunting and fishing seasons, they had venison, moose, fat bears, racoons, geese, turkies, ducks, and fish of all kinds. In the summer, they had green corn, beans, squashes, and the various fruits which the country naturally produced. In the winter they subsisted on corn, beans, fish, nuts, groundnuts, acorns, and the very gleanings of the grove.

They had no set meals, but like other wild creatures, ate when they were hungry, and could find any thing to satisfy the cravings of nature. Some times they had little or nothing for several days; but when they had provisions, they feasted. If they fasted for some time, they were sure at the next meal to make up for all they had lost before. They had but little food from the earth, except what it spontaneously produced. Indian corn, beans and squashes, were the only eatables for which the natives in New-England labored. The earth was both their seat and their table. With trenchers, knives, and napkins, they had no acquaintance.

Their household furniture was of small value. Their best bed was a mat or skin: they had neither chair nor stool. They ever sat upon the ground, commonly with their elbows upon their knees: this is the manner in which their great warriors and councillors now sit, even in the most public treaties with the English. A few wooden and stone vessels and instruments, serve all the purposes of domestic life. They had no steel nor iron instrument. Their knife was a sharp stone, shell, or kind of reed, which they sharpened in such a manner, as to cut their hair, make their bows and arrows, and served for all the purposes of a knife. They made them axes of stone: these they shaped somewhat similar to our axes; but with this difference, that they were made with a neck instead of an eye, and fastened with a withe, like a blacksmith's chissel. They had mortars, and stone pestles, and chissels: great numbers of these have been found in the country, and kept by the people, as curiosities. They dressed their corn with a clamshell, or with a stick, made flat and sharp at one end. These were all the utensils which they had, either for domestic use, or for husbandry.

Their arts and manufactures were confined to a very narrow compass. Their only weapons were bows and arrows, the tomahawk and the wooden sword or spear. Their bows were of the common construction: their bowstrings were made of the sinews of deer, or of the Indian hemp. Their arrows were constructed of young elder sticks, or of other strait sticks and reeds: these were headed with a sharp flinty stone, or with bones. The arrow was cleft at one end, and the stone or bone was put in and fastened with a small cord. The tomahawk was a stick of two or three feet in length, with a knob at one end. Some times

Book I. it was a stone hatchet, or a stick, with a piece of deers horn at one end, in the form of a pick axe. Their spear was a strait piece of wood, sharpened at one end, and hardened in the fire, or headed with bone or stone.

1633.

With respect to navigation, they had made no improvements beyond the construction and management of the hollow trough or canoe. They made their canoes of the chesnut, whitewood, and pine trees. As these grew strait to a great length, and were exceedingly large as well as tall, they constructed some, which would carry sixty or eighty men:* these were first rates; but commonly they were not more than twenty feet in length, and two in breadth. The Pequots had many of these, in which they passed over to the Islands, and warred against, and plundered the Islanders. The Indians upon Long-Island had a great number of canoes, of the largest kind.

Indian canoes constructed.

The construction of these, with such miserable tools as the Indians possessed, was a great curiosity. The manner was this: when they had found a tree to their purpose, to fell it they made a fire at the root, and kept burning it and cutting it with their stone axe, until it fell: then they kindled a fire at such a distance from the butt as they chose, and burned it off again. By burning and working with their axe, and scraping with sharp stones and shells, they made it hollow and smooth. In the same manner they shaped the ends, and finished it to their wishes.

Nets and hooks.

They constructed nets, twenty and thirty feet in length, for fishing; especially for the purpose of catching sturgeon: these were wrought with cords of Indian hemp, twisted by the hands of the women. They had also hooks, made of flexible bones, which they used for fishing.

Religion and morals

With respect to religion and morals, the Indians in New-England were in the most deplorable condition. They believed that there was a great SPIRIT, or GOD, whom they called KITCHTAN. They imagined that he dwelt far away in the southwest, and that he was a good GOD. But they worshipped a great variety of gods. They paid homage to the fire and water, thunder and lightning, and to whatever they imagined to be superior to themselves, or capable of doing them an injury.† They paid their principal homage to Hobbamocko. They imagined that he was an evil spirit and did them mischief; and so, from fear, they worshipped him, to keep him in good humour. They appeared to have no idea of a sabbath, and not to regard any particular day more than another. But in times of uncommon

* Winthrop's Journal, p. 54.
* Magnalia, b. iii, p. 192.

distress, by reason of pestilence, war, or famine, and upon occasion of great victories and triumph, and after the ingathering of the fruits, they assembled in great numbers, for the celebration of their superstitious rites.* The whole country, men, women and children, came together upon these solemnities. The manner of their devotion was, to kindle large fires in their wigwams, or more commonly in the open fields, and to sing and dance round them in a wild and violent manner. Sometimes they would all shout aloud, with the most antic and hideous notes. They made rattles of shells, which they shook, in a wild and violent manner, to fill up the confused noise. After the English settled in Connecticut, and they could purchase kettles of brass, they used to strain skins over them, and beat upon them, to augment their wretched music. They often continued these wild and tumultuous exercises incessantly, for four or five hours, until they were worn down and spent with fatigue. Their priests, or powaws, led in these exercises. They were dressed in the most odd and surprising manner, with skins of odious and frightful creatures about their heads, faces, arms, and bodies. They painted themselves in the most ugly forms which could be devised. They sometimes sang, and then broke forth into strong invocations, with starts, and strange motions and passions. When these paused, the other Indians groaned, making wild and doleful sounds. At these times, they sacrificed their skins, Indian money, and the best of their treasures. These were taken by the powaws, and all cast into the fires and consumed together. After the English came into the country, and they had hatchets and kettles, they sacrificed these in the same manner. The English were also persuaded, that they, sometimes, sacrificed their children, as well as their most valuable commodities. No Indians in Connecticut were more noted for these superstitions than those of Wopowage and Machemoodus. Milford people observing an Indian child, nearly at one of these times of their devotion, dressed in an extraordinary manner, with all kinds of Indian finery, had the curiosity to inquire what could be the reason. The Indians answered, that it was to be sacrificed, and the people supposed that it was given to the devil. The evil spirit, which the New-England Indians called Hobbamocko, the Virginia Indians called Okee. So deluded were these unhappy people, that they believed these barbarous sacrifices to be absolutely necessary. They imagined that, unless they appeased and conciliated their gods in this manner, they would neither suffer them to have

* Magnalia, B. III. p. 192.

Book I. peace, nor harvests, fish, venison, fat bears, nor turkeys;
but would visit them with a general destruction.

1633.
Morals.
With respect to morals, they were indeed miserably depraved. Mr. Williams and Mr. Callender, who, at an early period, were acquainted with the Indians in Rhode-Island, Mr. Hooker, and others, have represented them as sunk into the lowest state of moral turpitude, and as the very dregs of human nature.* Though the character which they gave them was, in some respects, exaggerated and absurd, yet it cannot be denied, that they were worshippers of evil spirits, liars, thieves, and murderers. They certainly were insidious and revengeful, almost without a parallel; and they wallowed in all the filth of wantonness. Great pains were taken with the Narraganset and Connecticut Indians, to civilize them, and teach them christianity; but the sachems rejected the gospel with indignation and contempt. They would not suffer it to be preached to their subjects. Indeed, both made it a public interest to oppose its propagation among them. Their policy, religion, and manners, were directly opposed to its pure doctrines and morals.

Courtship and marriage.
The manner of their courtship and marriages manifested their impurity. When a young Indian wished for marriage, he presented the girl with whom he was enamoured, with bracelets, belts, and chains of wampum. If she received his presents, they cohabited together for a time, upon trial. If they pleased each other, they were joined in marriage; but if, after a few weeks, they were not suited, the man, leaving his presents, quitted the girl, and sought another mistress, and she another lover.† In this manner they courted, until two met who were agreeable to each other. Before marriage the consent of the sachem was obtained, and he always joined the hands of the young pair in wedlock.

Plurality of wives.
The Indians in general kept many concubines, and never thought they had too many women.‡ This especially was the case with their sachems. They chose their concubines agreeably to their fancy, and put them away at pleasure. When a sachem grew weary of any of his women, he bestowed them upon some of his favourites, or chief men. The Indians, however, had one wife, who was the governess of the family, and whom they generally kept during life. In cases of adultery, the husband either put away the guilty wife, or satisfied himself by the infliction

---

* Williams' manuscripts, and Mr. Callender's sermon.
† Hutchinson, vol. i. p. 461, 462.
‡ Neal's Hist. N. E. p. 58, 59.

of some severe punishment. Husbands and wives, parents and children, lived together in the same wigwams, without any different apartment, and made no great privacy of such actions as the chaster animals keep from open view.

BOOK I.
1633.

The Indian government, generally, was absolute monarchy. The will of the sachem was his law. The lives and interests of his subjects were at his disposal. But in all-important affairs, he consulted his counsellors. When they had given their opinions, they deferred the decision of every matter to him. Whatever his determinations were, they applauded his wisdom, and without hesitation obeyed his commands. In council, the deportment of the sachems was grave and majestic to admiration. They appeared to be men of great discernment and policy. Their speeches were cautious and politic. The conduct of their counsellors and servants was profoundly respectful and submissive.

Indian government.

The counsellors of the Indian kings in New-England, were termed the paniese. These were not only the wisest, but largest and bravest men to be found among their subjects. They were the immediate guard of their respective sachems, who made neither war nor peace, nor attempted any weighty affair, without their advice. In war, and all great enterprises, dangers, and sufferings, these discovered a boldness and firmness of mind exceeding all the other warriors.

The paniese.

To preserve this order among the Indians, great pains were taken. The stoutest and most promising boys were chosen, and trained up with peculiar care, in the observation of certain Indian rites and customs. They were kept from all delicious meats, trained to coarse fare, and made to drink the juice of bitter herbs, until it occasioned violent vomitings. They were beaten over their legs and shins with sticks, and made to run through brambles and thickets, to make them hardy, and, as the Indians said, to render them more acceptable to Hobbamocko.

These paniese, or ministers of state, were in league with the priests, or powaws. To keep the people in awe, they pretended, as well as the priests, to have converse with the invisible world, and that Hobbamocko often appeared to them.

Among the Connecticut Indians, and among all the Indians in New-England, the crown was hereditary, always descending to the eldest son. When there was no male issue, the crown descended to the female. The blood royal was held in such veneration, that no one was considered as heir to the crown, but such as were royally descended on

The crown hereditary.

Book I.
1633.

both sides. When a female acceded to the crown, she was called the sunk squaw, or queen squaw. There were many petty sachems, tributary to other princes, on whom they were dependant for protection, and without whose consent they made neither peace, war, nor alliances with other nations.

Revenues of the prince.

The revenues of the crown consisted in the contributions of the people. They carried corn, and the first fruits of their harvest of all kinds, beans, squashes, roots, berries, and nuts, and presented them to their sachem. They made him presents of flesh, fish, fowl, moose, bear, deer, beaver and other skins. One of the paniese was commonly appointed to receive the tribute. When the Indians brought it, he gave notice to his sachem, who went out to them, and by good words and some small gifts, expressed his gratitude. By these contributions, his table was supplied; so that he kept open house for all strangers and travellers. Besides, the prince claimed an absolute sovereignty over the seas within his dominion. Whatever was stranded on the coast, all wrecks and whales floating on the sea, and taken, were his.* In war, the spoils of the enemy, and all the women and royalties of the prince conquered, belonged to him who made the conquest.

Sachems judges and executioners.

The sachem was not only examiner, judge, and executioner, in all criminal cases, but in all matters of justice between one man and another. In cases of dishonesty, the Indians proportioned the punishment to the number of times in which the delinquent had been found guilty. For the first offence, he was reproached for his villainy in the most disgraceful manner; for the second, he was beaten with a cudgel upon his naked back. If he still persisted in his dishonest practices, and was found guilty a third time, he was sure, besides a sound drubbing, to have his nose slit, that all men might know and avoid him. Murder was, in all cases, punished with death. The sachem whipped the delinquent, and slit his nose, in cases which required these punishments; and he killed the murderer, unless he were at a great distance. In this case, in which execution could not be done with his own hands, he sent his knife, by which it was effected. The Indians would not receive any punishment which was not capital, from the hands of any except their sachems. They would neither be beaten, whipped, nor slit by an officer: but their prince might inflict these punishments to the greatest extremity, and they would neither run, cry, nor flinch. Indeed, neither the crimes nor the punishments are esteemed so infamous,

* Magnalia, B. VI. p. 51.

among the Indians, as to groan or shrink under suffering. The sachems were so absolute in their government, that they contemned the limited authority of the English governors.

"The Indians had no kind of coin; but they had a sort of money, which they called wampum, or wampumpeag. It consisted of small beads, most curiously wrought out of shells, and perforated in the centre, so that they might be strung on belts, in chains and bracelets. These were of several sorts. The Indians in Connecticut, and in New-England in general, made black, blue and white wampum. Six of the white beads passed for a penny, and three of the black or blue ones for the same. The five nations made another sort, which were of a purple colour. The white beads were wrought out of the inside of the great conchs, and the purple out of the inside of the muscle shell. They were made perfectly smooth, and the perforation was done in the neatest manner. Indeed, considering that the Indians had neither knife, drill, nor any steel or iron instrument, the workmanship was admirable." After the English settled in Connecticut, the Indians strung these beads on belts of cloth, in a very curious manner. The squaws made caps of cloth, rising to a peak over the top of the head, and the fore part was beautified with wampum, curiously wrought upon them. The six nations now weave and string them in broad belts, which they give in their treaties, as a confirmation of their speeches and the seals of their friendship.*

The Indians of Connecticut and New-England, although consisting of a great number of different nations and clans, appear all to have spoken radically the same language. From Piscataqua to Connecticut, it was so nearly the same, that the different tribes could converse tolerably together.† The Moheagan or Pequot language was essentially that of all the Indians in New-England, and of a great part of the Indians in the United States.‡ The word Moheagans, is a corruption of Muhhekaneew, in the singular, or of Muhhekaneok in the plural number. Not only the natives of New-England, but the Penobscots, bordering on Nova-Scotia, the Indians of St. Francis, in Canada, the Delawares, in Pennsylvania, the Shawanese, on the Ohio, and the Chippewaus, at the westward of lake Huron, all spoke the same radical language. The same appears evident

---
* Colden's history, vol. i. p. 3, 4, 71, 72.
† Hutchinson, vol. i. p. 479.
‡ Dr. Edwards' observations on the language of the Muhhekaneew Indians.

Book I.
1633.

also with respect to the Ottowaus, Nanticooks, Munsees, Menomonees, Missifaugas, Saukies, Ottagaumies, Killistinoes, Nipegons, Algonkins, Winnebagoes and other Indians. The various tribes, who evidently spoke the same original language, had different dialects; yet, perhaps, they differed little more from each other, than the style of a Londoner now does from that of his great grandfather. The want of letters and of a sufficient correspondence between the several nations may well account for all the variations to be found among the natives in New-England, and between them and the other tribes which have been mentioned. All the New-England Indians expressed the pronouns both substantive and adjective by prefixes and suffixes, or by letters or syllables added at the beginnings or ends of their nouns.§ In this respect there is a remarkable coincidence between this and the Hebrew language, in an instance in which the Hebrew entirely differs from all the ancient and modern languages of Europe.

Affinity of the Indian and Hebrew languages.

From this affinity of the Indian language, with the Hebrew, from their anointing their heads with oil, their dancing in their devotions, their excessive howlings and mourning for their dead, their computing time by nights and moons, their giving dowries to their wives, and causing their women at certain seasons to dwell by themselves, and some other circumstances, the famous Mr. John Eliot, the Indian apostle, was led to imagine that the American Indians were the posterity of the dispersed Israelites.* They used many figures and parables in their discourses, and some have reported that, at certain seasons, they used no knives, and never brake the bones of the creatures which they eat. It has also been reported, that in some of their songs the word Hallelujah might be distinguished.†

The Indian language abounds with gutterals and strong aspirations, and their words are generally of a great length,‡ which render it peculiarly bold and sonorous. The Indian speeches, like those of the eastern nations, generally were adorned with the most bold and striking figures, and have not been inferior to any which either the English or French have been able to make to them. The Indians in general, throughout the continent, were much given to speech making. As eloquence and war were, with them,

§ Dr. Edwards' observations on the Indian language.
* Magnalia b. iii. p. 192, 193.   † Hutchinson vol. i. p. 473.
‡ Nummatchekodtantamoonganunnonash was a single word, which in English, signifies, Our lusts. Noowomantammoonkanuunnonash was another, signifying, Our loves. Kummogkodonattoottummooctiteaonganunnonash was another, expressing no more than, Our question. Magnalia b. iii. p. 193.

the foundations of all consequence, the whole force of their genius was directed to these acquisitions. In council, their opinions were always given in set speeches; and to persons whom they highly respected, it was not unusual, on meeting and parting, or on matters of more than common importance, to address their compliments and opinions in formal harangues. The Indians commonly spake with an unusual animation and vehemence.

The Indians in New-England, rarely if ever admitted the letters L and R into their dialect; but the Mohawks, whose language was entirely different, used them both. Some of the western Indians, who speak the same language radically, with the Mohengans, use the L. The Mohegan language abounds with labials, but the Mohawk differs entirely from this, and perhaps from every other, in this respect, that it is wholly destitute of labials. The Mohawks esteemed it a laughable matter indeed, for men to shut their mouths that they might speak.*

The Indians in Connecticut, and in all parts of New-England, made great lamentations at the burial of their dead. Their manner of burial was to dig holes in the ground with stakes, which were made broad and sharpened at one end. Sticks were laid across the bottom, and the corpse, which was previously wrapped in skins and mats, was let down upon them. The arms, treasures, utensils, paint and ornaments of the dead, were buried with them, and a mound of earth was raised upon the whole. In some instances the Indians appear to have used a kind of embalming, by wrapping the corpse in large quantities of a strong scented red powder.† In some parts of New-England, the dead were buried in a sitting posture with their faces towards the east. The women on these occasions painted their faces with oil and charcoal, and while the burial was performing, they, with the relatives of the dead, made the most hideous shrieks, howlings and lamentations. Their mourning continued, by turns, at night and in the morning, for several days. During this term all the relatives united in bewailing the dead.

When the English began the settlement of Connecticut, all the Indians both east and west of Connecticut river, were tributaries, except the Pequots, and some few tribes which were in alliance with them. The Pequots had spread their conquests over all that part of the state east of the river. They had also subjugated the Indians on the sea coast, as far eastward as Guilford. Uncas therefore,

* Golden's history vol. i. p. 16.
† Neal's history N. E. vol. i. p. 20.

Book I. after the Pequots were conquered, extended his claims as far as Hammonasset, in the eastern part of that township.*
1633. The Indians in these parts were therefore tributaries to the Pequots.

The Mohawks had not only carried their conquests as far southward as Virginia, but eastward, as far as Connecticut river. The Indians therefore, in the western parts of Connecticut, were their tributaries. Two old Mohawks, every year or two, might be seen issuing their orders and collecting their tribute, with as much authority and haughtiness as a Roman dictator.

It is indeed difficult to describe the fear of this terrible nation, which had fallen on all the Indians in the western parts of Connecticut. If they neglected to pay their tribute, the Mohawks would come down against them, plunder, destroy, and carry them captive at pleasure. When they made their appearance in the country, the Connecticut Indians would instantly raise a cry from hill to hill, a Mohawk! a Mohawk! and fly like sheep before wolves, without attempting the least resistance.† The Mohawks would cry out, in the most terrible manner, in their language, importing "We are come, we are come, to suck your blood."‡ When the Connecticut Indians could not escape to their forts, they would immediately flee to the English houses for shelter, and sometimes the Mohawks would pursue them so closely as to enter with them, and kill them in the presence of the family. If there was time to shut the doors they never entered by force, nor did they, upon any occasion, do the least injury to the English.

When they came into this part of the country for war, they used their utmost art to keep themselves undiscovered. They would conceal themselves in swamps and thickets, watching their opportunity, and all on a sudden, rise upon their enemy and kill or captivate them, before they had time to make any resistance.

Mohawks surprise Paugusset. About the time when the settlement of New-Haven commenced, or not many years after, they came into Connecticut, and surprised the Indian fort at Paugusset. To prevent the Connecticut Indians from discovering them, and that not so much as a track of them might be seen, they marched in the most secret manner, and when they came near the fort travelled wholly in the river. Secreting themselves near the fort, they watched their opportunity, and suddenly attacking it, with their dreadful yellings and violence, they soon took it by force, and killed and capti-

* Manuscripts of Mr. Ruggles.
† Colden's history vol. 1. p. 3.   ‡ Wood's prospect of N. England.

CHAP. III. CONNECTICUT.

vated whom they pleased. Having plundered and destroyed, at their pleasure, they returned to their castles, west of Albany.

As the Indians in Connecticut were slaughtered and oppressed, either by the Pequots or Mohawks, they were generally friendly to the settlement of the English among them. They expected, by their means, to be defended against their terrible and cruel oppressors. They also found themselves benefited by trading with them. They furnished themselves with knives, hatchets, axes, hoes, kettles and various instruments and utensils which highly contributed to their convenience. They could, with these, perform more labor in one hour or day, than they could in many days without them. Besides, they found that they could exchange an old beaver coat, or blanket, for two or three new ones of English manufacture. They found a much better market for their furs, corn, peltry, and all their vendible commodities.

The English were also careful to treat them with justice and humanity, and to make such presents to their sachems and great captains, as should please and keep them in good humor.

By these means, the English lived in tolerable peace with all the Indians in Connecticut, and New-England, except the Pequots, for about forty years.

The Indians, at their first settlement, performed many acts of kindness towards them. They instructed them in the manner of planting and dressing the Indian corn. They carried them upon their backs, through rivers and waters; and, as occasion required, served them instead of boats and bridges. They gave them much useful information respecting the country, and when the English or their children were lost in the woods, and were in danger of perishing with hunger or cold, they conducted them to their wigwams, fed them, and restored them to their families and parents. By selling them corn, when pinched with famine, they relieved their distresses and prevented their perishing in a strange land and uncultivated wilderness.

Book I.

1633.

Motives inducing the Indians to permit the English settlements.

Indian kindness.

H

CHAPTER IV.

The people at Dorchester, Watertown and Newtown, finding themselves straitened in the Massachusetts, determine to remove to Connecticut. Debates in Massachusetts relative to their removal. The general court at first prohibited it, but afterwards gave its consent. The people removed and settled the towns of Windsor, Hartford and Weathersfield. Hardships and losses of the first winters.

1634.

SUCH numbers were constantly emigrating to New-England, in consequence of the persecution of the puritans, that the people at Dorchester, Watertown and Newtown, began to be much straitened, by the accession of new planters. By those who had been at Connecticut, they had received intelligence of the excellent meadows upon the river: they therefore determined to remove, and once more brave the dangers and hardships of making settlements in a dreary wilderness.

May.

Upon application to the general court for the enlargement of their boundaries, or for liberty to remove, they, at first, obtained consent for the latter. However, when it was afterwards discovered, that their determination was to plant a new colony at Connecticut, there arose a strong opposition; so that when the court convened in September.

September, there was a warm debate on the subject, and a great division between the houses. Indeed, the whole colony was affected with the dispute.

Arguments for removing to Connecticut.

Mr. Hooker, who was more engaged in the enterprise than the other ministers, took up the affair and pleaded for the people. He urged, that they were so straitened for accommodations for their cattle, that they could not support the ministry, neither receive, nor assist any more of their friends, who might come over to them. He insisted that the planting of towns so near together was a fundamental error in their policy. He pleaded the fertility and happy accommodations of Connecticut: That settlements upon the river were necessary to prevent the Dutch and others from possessing themselves of so fruitful and important a part of the country; and that the minds of the people were strongly inclined to plant themselves there, in preference to every other place, which had come to their knowledge.

Arguments against it.

On the other side it was insisted, That in point of conscience they ought not to depart, as they were united to

| CHAP. IV. | CONNECTICUT. |

the Massachusetts as one body, and bound by oath to seek the good of that commonwealth: and that on principles of policy it could not, by any means, be granted. It was pleaded, that as the settlements in the Massachusetts were new and weak, they were in danger of an assault from their enemies: That the departure of Mr. Hooker and the people of those towns, would not only draw off many from the Massachusetts, but prevent others from settling in the colony. Besides, it was said, that the removing of a candlestick was a great judgment: That by suffering it they should expose their brethren to great danger, both from the Dutch and Indians. Indeed, it was affirmed that they might be accommodated by the enlargements offered them by the other towns.

BOOK I.
1634.

After a long and warm debate, the governor, two assistants, and a majority of the representatives, were for granting liberty for Mr. Hooker and the people to transplant themselves to Connecticut. The deputy-governor however and six of the assistants were in the negative, and so no vote could be obtained.*

The court divided.

This made a considerable ferment, not only in the general court, but in the colony, so that Mr. Cotton was desired to preach on the subject to quiet the court and the people of the colony. This also retarded the commencement of the settlements upon the river. Individuals, however, were determined to prosecute the business, and made preparations effectually to carry it into execution.

It appears, that some of the Watertown people came this year to Connecticut, and erected a few huts at Pyquag, now Weathersfield, in which a small number of men made a shift to winter.†

While the colonists were thus prosecuting the business of settlement, in New-England, the right honourable James, Marquis of Hamilton, obtained a grant from the council of Plymouth, April 20th, 1635, of all that tract of country which lies between Connecticut river and Narraganset river and harbour, and from the mouths of each of said rivers northward sixty miles into the country. However, by reason of its interference with the grant to the lord Say and Seal, lord Brook, &c. or for some other reason, the deed was never executed. The Marquis made no settlement upon the land and the claim became obsolete.

May 2, 1635.

The next May, the Newtown people, determining to settle at Connecticut, renewed their application to the gene-

---
* Winthrop's Journal, p. 70.
† This is the tradition, and the Rev. Mr. Meeks of Weathersfield in his manuscripts says, Weathersfield is the oldest town on the river.

Book I. ral court, and obtained liberty to remove to any place which they should choose, with this proviso, that they should continue under the jurisdiction of the Massachusetts.‡

1635.

A number of Mr. Warham's people came this summer into Connecticut, and made preparations to bring their families, and make a permanent settlement on the river. The Watertown people gradually removed, and prosecuted their settlement at Weathersfield. At the same time, the planters at Newtown began to make preparations for removing to Hartford the next spring.

Meanwhile, twenty men arrived in Massachusetts, sent over by Sir Richard Saltonstall, to take possession of a great quantity of land in Connecticut, and to make settlements under the patent of lord Say and Seal, with whom he was a principal associate. The vessel in which they came over, on her return to England, in the fall, was cast away on the isle Sable.†

August.

As the Dorchester men had now set down at Connecticut, near the Plymouth trading house, governor Bradford wrote to them, complaining of their conduct, as injurious to the people of Plymouth, who had made a fair purchase of the Indians, and taken a prior possession.*

The Dutch also, alarmed by the settlements making in Connecticut, wrote to Holland for instructions and aid, to drive the English from their settlements upon the river.†

Oct. 15th, the planters on the river remove their families to Connecticut.

The people at Connecticut having made such preparations as were judged necessary to effect a permanent settlement, began to remove their families and property. On the fifteenth of October, about sixty men, women, and children, with their horses, cattle, and swine, commenced their journey from the Massachusetts, through the wilderness, to Connecticut river. After a tedious and difficult journey, through swamps and rivers, over mountains and rough ground, which were passed with great difficulty and fatigue, they arrived safely at the places of their respective destination. They were so long on their journey, and so much time and pains were spent in passing the river, and in getting over their cattle, that, after all their exertions, winter came upon them before they were prepared. This was an occasion of great distress and damage to the plantations.

Oct. 5th, Mr. Winthrop arrives at Boston.

Nearly at the same time, Mr. John Winthrop, son of governor Winthrop, of Massachusetts, arrived at Boston, with a commission from lord Say and Seal, lord Brook,

‡ Winthrop's Journal, p. 82. † Winthrop's Journal, p. 83 and 89.
* Winthrop's Journal, p. 86.   † The same, p. 86.

and other noblemen and gentlemen interested in the Connecticut patent, to erect a fort at the mouth of Connecticut river. Their lordships sent over men, ordnance, ammunition, and 2000 pounds sterling, for the accomplishment of their design.‡

His commission.

1635.

Mr. Winthrop was directed, by his commission, immediately on his arrival, to repair to Connecticut, with fifty able men, and to erect the fortifications, and to build houses for the garrison, and for gentlemen who might come over into Connecticut. They were first to build houses for their then present accommodation, and after that, such as should be suitable for the reception of men of quality. The latter were to be erected within the fort. It was required that the planters, at the beginning, should settle themselves near the mouth of the river, and set down in bodies, that they might be in a situation for entrenching and defending themselves. The commission made provision for the reservation of a thousand or fifteen hundred acres of good land, for the maintenance of the fort, as nearly adjoining to it as might be with convenience.*

Mr. Winthrop, having intelligence that the Dutch were preparing to take possession of the mouth of the river, as soon as he could engage twenty men, and furnish them with provisions, dispatched them in a small vessel, of about thirty tons, to prevent their getting the command of the river, and to accomplish the service to which he had been appointed.

Nov. 9th, Mr. Winthrop dispatched a vessel to Connecticut.

But a few days after the party, sent by Mr. Winthrop, arrived at the mouth of the river, a Dutch vessel appeared off the harbor, from New-Netherlands, sent on purpose to take possession of the entrance of the river, and to erect fortifications. The English had, by this time, mounted two pieces of cannon, and prevented their landing.† Thus, providentially, was this fine tract of country preserved for our venerable ancestors, and their posterity.

Dutch not suffered to land.

Mr. Winthrop was appointed governor of the river Connecticut, and the parts adjacent, for the term of one year. He erected a fort, built houses, and made a settlement, according to his instructions. One David Gardiner, an expert engineer, assisted in the work, planned the fortifications, and was appointed lieutenant of the fort.

Mr. Davenport and others, who afterwards settled New-Haven, were active in this affair, and hired Gardiner, in behalf of their lordships, to come into New-England, and assist in this business.‡

‡ Winthrop's Journal, p. 88.   * Appendix, No. II.
† Winthrop's Journal, p. 90, 91.   ‡ Manuscripts of Gardiner.

HISTORY OF CHAP. IV.

BOOK I.
1635.
Agreement respecting the planters in Connecticut.

As the settlement of the three towns on Connecticut river was begun before the arrival of Mr. Winthrop, and the design of their lordships to make plantations upon it was known, it was agreed, that the settlers on the river should either remove, upon full satisfaction made, by their lordships, or else sufficient room should be found for them and their companies at some other place.†

The winter set in this year much sooner than usual, and the weather was stormy and severe. By the 15th of November, Connecticut river was frozen over, and the snow was so deep, and the season so tempestuous, that a considerable number of the cattle, which had been driven on from the Massachusetts, could not be brought across the river. The people had so little time to prepare their huts and houses, and to erect sheds and shelters for their cattle, that the sufferings of man and beast were extreme. Indeed, the hardships and distresses of the first planters of Connecticut scarcely admit of a description. To carry much provision or furniture through a pathless wilderness, was impracticable. Their principal provisions and household furniture were, therefore, put on board several small vessels, which, by reason of delays and the tempestuousness of the season, were either cast away or did not arrive. Several vessels were wrecked on the coasts of New-England, by the violence of the storms. Two shallops laden with goods, from Boston to Connecticut, in October, were cast away on Brown's island, near the Gurnet's nose; and the men, with every thing on board, were lost.‡ A vessel, with six of the Connecticut people on board, which sailed from the river for Boston, early in November, was, about the middle of the month, cast away in Manamet bay. The men got on shore, and, after wandering ten days in deep snow and a severe season, without meeting with any human being, arrived, nearly spent with cold and fatigue, at New-Plymouth.

November.

Famine in Connecticut, the 16th.
Arrived in Massachusetts, the 26th.

By the last of November, or beginning of December, provisions generally failed in the settlements on the river, and famine and death looked the inhabitants sternly in the face. Some of them, driven by hunger, attempted their way, in this severe season, through the wilderness, from Connecticut to Massachusetts. Of thirteen, in one company, who made this attempt, one, in passing the rivers, fell through the ice, and was drowned. The other twelve were ten days on their journey, and would all have perished, had it not been for the assistance of the Indians.

Indeed, such was the distress in general that, by the 3d

† Winthrop's Journal, p. 89. ‡ The same, p. 97.

and 4th of December, a considerable part of the new settlers were obliged to abandon their habitations. Seventy persons, men, women, and children, were necessitated, in the extremity of winter, to go down to the mouth of the river, to meet their provisions, as the only expedient to preserve their lives. Not meeting with the vessels which they expected, they all went on board the Rebecca, a vessel of about 60 tons. This, two days before, was frozen in twenty miles up the river; but by the falling of a small rain and the influence of the tide, the ice became so broken and was so far removed, that she made a shift to get out. She ran, however, upon the bar, and the people were forced to unlade her, to get her off. She was reladen, and, in five days, reached Boston. Had it not been for these providential circumstances, the people must have perished with famine.

Book I.
1635.
December 3d or 4th.
Dec. 10th.

The people who kept their stations on the river suffered in an extreme degree. After all the help they were able to obtain, by hunting, and from the Indians, they were obliged to subsist on acorns, malt and grains.*

The settlers ate acorns and grains.

Numbers of the cattle, which could not be got over the river before winter, lived through without any thing but what they found in the woods and meadows. They wintered as well, or better, than those which were brought over, and for which all the provision was made, and pains taken, of which the owners were capable. However, a great number of cattle perished. The Dorchester, or Windsor people lost, in this single article, about two hundred pounds sterling. Their other losses were very considerable.

Loss in cattle.

It is difficult to describe, or even to conceive, the apprehensions and distresses of a people, in the circumstances of our venerable ancestors, during this doleful winter. All the horrors of a dreary wilderness spread themselves around them. They were encompassed with numerous, fierce and cruel tribes of wild and savage men, who could have swallowed up parents and children, at pleasure, in their feeble and distressed condition. They had neither bread for themselves, nor children; neither habitations nor clothing convenient for them. Whatever emergency might happen, they were cut off, both by land and water, from any succour or retreat. What self-denial, firmness, and magnanimity are necessary for such enterprises! How distressful, in the beginning, was the condition of those now fair and opulent towns on Connecticut river!

For a few years after the settlements on the river com-

* Winthrop's Journal, p. 90, 91, to 98.

BOOK I. menced, they bore the same name with the towns in the Massachusetts, whence the first settlers came.

1636. The Connecticut planters, at first settled under the general government of the Massachusetts, but they held courts of their own, which consisted of two principal men from each town; and, on great and extraordinary occasions, these were joined with committees, as they were called, consisting of three men from each town. These courts had power to transact all the common affairs of the colony, and with their committees, had the power of making war and peace, and treaties of alliance and friendship with the natives within the colony.

First court in Connecticut, April 26. The first court in Connecticut, was holden at Newtown, April 26th, 1636. It consisted of Roger Ludlow, Esq. Mr. John Steel, Mr. William Swain, Mr. William Phelps, Mr. William Westwood, and Mr. Andrew Ward. Mr. Ludlow had been one of the magistrates of Massachusetts in 1630, and in 1631 had been chosen lieutenant-governor of that colony. At this court it was ordered, that the inhabitants should not sell arms nor ammunition to the Indians. Various other affairs were also transacted relative to the good order, settlement, and defence of these infant towns.*

People return to their settlements. Several of the principal gentlemen interested in the settlement of Connecticut, Mr. John Haynes, who at this time was governor of Massachusetts, Mr. Henry Wolcott, Mr. Wells, the ministers of the churches, and others had not yet removed into the colony. As soon as the spring advanced, and the travelling would admit, the hardy men began to return from the Massachusetts, to their habitations on the river. No sooner were buds, leaves and grass so grown, that cattle could live in the woods, and obstructions removed from the river, so that vessels could go up with provisions and furniture, than the people began to return in large companies, to Connecticut. Many, who had not removed the last year, prepared, with all convenient dispatch, for a journey to the new settlements upon the river.

Mr. Hooker removes to Connecticut in June. About the beginning of June, Mr. Hooker, Mr. Stone, and about a hundred men, women and children, took their departure from Cambridge, and travelled more than a hundred miles, through a hideous and trackless wilderness, to Hartford. They had no guide but their compass; made their way over mountains, through swamps, thickets, and rivers, which were not passable but with great difficulty. They had no cover but the heavens, nor any lodgings but

* Records of Connecticut.

those which simple nature afforded them. They drove with them a hundred and sixty head of cattle, and by the way, subsisted on the milk of their cows. Mrs. Hooker was borne through the wilderness upon a litter. The people generally carried their packs, arms, and some utensils. They were nearly a fortnight on their journey.

Book I.
1636.

This adventure was the more remarkable, as many of this company were persons of figure, who had lived, in England, in honor, affluence and delicacy, and were entire strangers to fatigue and danger.

The famous Mr. Thomas Shepard, who, with his people, came into New-England the last summer, succeeded Mr. Hooker at Cambridge. The people of his congregation purchased the lands which Mr. Hooker and his company had previously possessed.

The removal of Dorchester people to Windsor is said to have been disagreeable to their ministers, but, as their whole church and congregation removed, it was necessary that they should go with them. However, Mr. Maverick died in March, before preparations were made for his removal. He expired in the 60th year of his age. He was characterized as a man of great meekness, and as laborious and faithful in promoting the welfare both of the church and commonwealth.

Mr. Maverick died March 3d.

Mr. Warham removed to Windsor in September, but he did not judge it expedient to bring his family until better accommodations could be made for their reception. Soon after the removal of Mr. Warham from Dorchester, a new church was gathered in that town, and Mr. Mather was ordained their pastor.

Mr. Phillips, pastor of the church at Watertown, did not remove to Weathersfield. Whether it was against his inclination, or whether the people did not invite him, does not appear. They chose Mr. Henry Smith for their minister, who came from England in office.

The colony of New-Plymouth professed themselves to be greatly aggrieved at the conduct of the Dorchester people, in settling on the lands, where they had made a purchase, and where they had defended themselves and that part of the country against the Dutch. They represented that it had been a hard matter that the Dutch and Indians had given them so much trouble as they had done, but that it was still more grievous to be supplanted by their professed friends. Mr. Winslow of Plymouth, made a journey to Boston, in the spring, before governor Haynes and some other principal characters removed to Connecticut, with a view to obtain compensation for the injury done to the

Plymouth people aggrieved.

Book I.
1636.

Plymouth men, who had built the trading house upon the river. The Plymouth people demanded a sixteenth part of the lands and 100 pounds as a compensation; but the Dorchester people would not comply with their demands.* There however appeared to be so much justice, in making them some compensation, for the purchase they had made, and the good services which they had done, that some time after, the freeholders of Windsor gave them fifty pounds, forty acres of meadow, and a large tract of upland for their satisfaction.†

Court, June 7th.

At a court holden at Dorchester, it was ordered, that every town should keep a watch, and be well supplied with ammunition. The constables were directed to warn the watches in their turns, and to make it their care that they should be kept according to the direction of the court. They also were required to take care, that the inhabitants were well furnished with arms and ammunition, and kept in a constant state of defence. As these infant settlements were filled and surrounded with numerous savages, the people conceived themselves in danger when they lay down and when they rose up, when they went out and when they came in. Their circumstances were such, that it was judged necessary for every man to be a soldier.

September 1st.

At a third court, therefore, holden at Watertown, an order was given, that the inhabitants of the several towns should train once a month, and the officers were authorized to train those who appeared very unskilful more frequently, as circumstances should require. The courts were holden at each town by rotation, according to its turn.

Springfield settled.

A settlement was made, this year, at Springfield, by Mr. Pyncheon and his company from Roxbury. This for about two years was united in government with the towns in Connecticut. In November, Mr. Pyncheon for the first time appears among the members of the court.

Government at first.

All the powers of government, for nearly three years, seem to have been in the magistrates, of whom two were appointed in each town. These gave all orders, and directed all the affairs of the plantation. The freemen appear to have had no voice in making the laws, or in any part of the government, except in some instances of general and uncommon concern. In these instances, committees were sent from the several towns. Juries were employed in jury cases, from the first settlement of the colony.

This was a summer and year of great and various la-

---

* Winthrop's Journal, p. 96.
† Governor Wolcott's manuscripts compared with governor Winthrop's journal.

Chap. IV. CONNECTICUT.

bors, demanding the utmost exertion and diligence. Many of the planters had to remove themselves and effects from a distant colony. At the same time, it was absolutely necessary, that they should turn the wilderness into gardens and fields, that they should plant and cultivate the earth, and obtain some tolerable harvest, unless they would again experience the distresses and losses of the preceding year. These were too great, and too fresh in their memories, not to rouse all their exertion and forethought. It was necessary to erect and fortify their houses, and to make better preparations for the feeding and covering of their cattle. It was of equal importance to the planters, not only to make roads for their particular convenience, but from town to town; that, on any emergency, they might fly immediately to each other's relief. It was with great difficulty that these purposes could be at first accomplished. The planters had not been accustomed to felling the groves, to clearing and cultivating new lands. They were strangers in the country, and knew not what kinds of grain would be most congenial with the soil, and produce the greatest profits, nor had they any experience how the ground must be cultivated, that it might yield a plentiful crop. They had few oxen, or instruments for husbandry. Every thing was to be prepared, or brought from a great distance, and procured at a dear rate. Besides all these labors and difficulties, much time was taken up in constant watchings, trainings, and preparations for the defence of themselves and children. The Pequots had, already, murdered a number of the English; some of the Indians, in Connecticut, were their allies; and they had maintained a great influence over them all. They were a treacherous and designing people; so that there could be no safety, but in a constant preparation for any emergency.

Some of the principal characters, who undertook this great work of settling Connecticut, and were the civil and religious fathers of the colony, were Mr. Haynes, Mr. Ludlow, Mr. Hooker, Mr. Warham, Mr. Hopkins, Mr. Wells, Mr. Willis, Mr. Whiting, Mr. Wolcott, Mr. Phelps, Mr. Webster, and captain Mason. These, were of the first class of settlers, and all, except the ministers, were chosen magistrates or governors of the colony. Mr. Swain, Mr. Talcott, Mr. Steel, Mr. Mitchell, and others, were capital men. Mr. John Haynes, Mr. Hooker, Mr. Hopkins, Mr. Stone, Mr. George Wyllys, Mr. Wells, Mr. Whiting, Mr. Thomas Webster, and Mr. John Talcott, were all of Hartford. Mr. Ludlow, Mr. Henry Wolcott, Mr. Warham, Mr. William Phelps, and captain John Mason, were some

Book I.
1636.
Labors of this year.

Fathers of Connecticut.

Book I.
1636.

of the principal planters of Windsor. Mr. William Swain, Mr. Thurston Rayner, Mr. Henry Smith, Mr. Andrew Ward, Mr. Mitchell, and Mr. John Deming, were some of the chief men, who settled the town of Weathersfield. These were the civil and religious fathers of the colony. They formed its free and happy constitution, were its legislators, and some of the chief pillars of the church and commonwealth. They, with many others of the same excellent character, employed their abilities and their estates for the prosperity of the colony.

While the three plantations on the river were making the utmost exertions for a permanent settlement, Mr. Winthrop was no less active, in erecting fortifications and convenient buildings at its entrance. Though he had, the last year, sent on one company after another, yet the season was so far advanced, and the winter set in so early, and with such severity, that little more could be done than just to keep the station. When the spring advanced, the works were, therefore, pressed on with engagedness. Mr. Winthrop and his people were induced, not only in faithfulness to their trust, but from fears of a visit from the Dutch, and from the state of that warlike people, the Pequots in the vicinity, to hasten and complete them, with the utmost dispatch. A good fort was erected, and a number of houses were built. Some cattle were brought from the Massachusetts, for the use of the garrison. Small parcels of ground were improved, and preparations made for a comfortable subsistence, and good defence.

There were, at the close of this year, about two hundred and fifty men in the three towns on the river, and there were twenty men in the garrison, at the entrance of it, under the command of lieutenant Gardiner. The whole consisted, probably, of about eight hundred persons, or of a hundred and sixty or seventy families.

CHAPTER V.

The war with the Pequots. The origin of it. The murder of captains Stone and Norton; of Mr. Oldham and others. Mr. Endicot's expedition against them. The Pequots kill a number of the garrison at the mouth of the river, and besiege the fort. Captain Mason is sent down from Connecticut with a reinforcement. The enemy make a descent on Weathersfield; torture and mock the English. The court at Connecticut declares war against them. Captain Mason takes Mistic fort. Sassacus destroys his royal fortress, and flees to the westward. A second expedition is undertaken against the Pequots conjointly, by Massachusetts and Connecticut. The great swamp fight. The Pequots subdued. Sassacus, flying to the Mohawks, was beheaded. The captivated and surviving Pequots, after the war, were given to the Moheagans, and Narragansets, and their name extinguished.

THE Indians in general, were ever jealous of the English, from the first settlement of New-England, and wished to drive them from the country. Various circumstances however, combined to frustrate their designs. The English, on their first settlement at New-Plymouth, entered into such friendly treaties with some of the principal tribes, and conducted themselves with such justice, prudence and magnanimity towards them and the Indians in general, as had the most happy influence to preserve the peace of the country. The animosities of the Indians among themselves, and their implacable hatred of each other, with their various separate interests, contributed to the same purpose. Some of them wished for the friendship and neighbourhood of the English, to guard them from one enemy, and others of them to protect them from another. All wished for the benefit of their trade; and it is probable, that they had no apprehensions, at first, that a handful of people would ever overrun, and fill the country. It was therefore nearly sixteen years before they commenced open hostilities upon their English neighbours. But no sooner had they begun to trade and make settlements at Connecticut, than that great, spirited, and warlike nation, the Pequots, began to murder and plunder them, and to wound and kill their cattle.

In 1634, a number of Indians, who were not native Pequots, but in confederacy with them, murdered captain

Murder of captains Stone and Norton, 1634.

Stone and captain Norton, with their whole crew, consisting of eight men: they then plundered and sunk the vessel. Captain Stone was from St. Christopher's, in the West-Indies, and came into Connecticut river, with a view of trading at the Dutch house. After he had entered the river, he engaged a number of Indians to pilot two of his men up the river, to the Dutch: but night coming on, they went to sleep, and were both murdered by their Indian guides. The vessel, at night, was laid up to the shore. Twelve of those Indians, who had several times before been trading with the captain, apparently in an amicable manner, were on board. Watching their opportunity, when he was asleep, and several of the crew on shore, they murdered him secretly in his cabin, and cast a covering over him, to conceal it from his men: they then fell upon them, and soon killed the whole company, except captain Norton. He had taken the cook room, and for a long time made a most brave and resolute defence. That he might load and fire with the greatest expedition, he had placed powder in an open vessel, just at hand, which, in the hurry of the action, took fire, and so burned and blinded him, that he could make no further resistance. Thus, after all his gallantry, he fell with his hapless companions. Part of the plunder was received by the Pequots, and another part by the eastern Nehanticks. Sassacus and Ninigret, the sachems of those Indians, were both privy to the affair, and shared in the goods and articles taken from the vessel. It was supposed that the Indians had pre-concerted this massacre.*

The Pequots desire peace. The November following, the Pequots sent a messenger to Boston, to desire peace with the English. He made an offer of a great quantity of beaver skins and wampumpeag, to persuade the governor to enter into a league with them. The governor answered the messenger, that the Pequots must send men of greater quality than he was; and that he would then treat with them. The Pequots then sent two messengers to the governor, carrying a present, and earnestly soliciting peace. The governor assured them, that the English were willing to be at peace with them; but insisted, that, as they had murdered captain Stone and his men, they must deliver up the murderers, and make full compensation. The messengers pretended, that captain Stone had used the Indians ill, and provoked them to kill him: that their sachem, who was concerned in the affair, had been killed by the Dutch, and that the Indians who perpetrated the murder, were all dead but two; and that,

* Mason's history, and Hubbard's narrative.

CHAP. V. CONNECTICUT.

if they were guilty, they would desire their sachem to deliver them up to justice. They offered to concede all their right at Connecticut river, if the English should desire to settle there; and engaged to assist them as far as was in their power, in making their settlements. They also promised that they would give the English four hundred fathoms of wampum, forty beaver, and thirty otter skins. After long and mature deliberation, the governor and his council entered into a treaty with them, on the conditions which they had proposed. The English were to send a vessel with cloths, to trade with them fairly, as with friends and allies.*

Book I.

1635.

Treaty with the Pequots.

The reasons of their so earnestly soliciting peace, at this time, were, that the Narragansets were making war furiously upon them; and the Dutch, to revenge the injuries done them, had killed one of their sachems, with several of their men, and captivated a number more. They wished not, at this critical time, to increase the number of their enemies. They artfully suggested to their new allies, the governor and council of Massachusetts, their desire, that they would be mediators between them and the Narragansets. They also intimated their willingness, that part of the present which they were to send, might be given to them, for the purpose of obtaining a reconciliation. Such was the pride and stoutness of their spirits, and so much did they stand upon a point of honour, that though they wished for peace with their enemy, yet they would not directly offer any thing for that purpose. This treaty was signed by the parties, but hostages were not taken to secure the performance of the articles, and the Pequots never performed one of them. Whatever their designs were at that time, they afterwards became more and more mischievous, hostile and bloody.

The next year, John Oldham, who had been fairly trading at Connecticut, was murdered near Block Island. He had with him only two boys and two Narraganset Indians. These were taken and carried off. One John Gallup, as he was going from Connecticut to Boston, discovered Mr. Oldham's vessel full of Indians, and he saw a canoe, having Indians on board, go from her, laden with goods. Suspecting that they had murdered Mr. Oldham, he hailed them, but received no answer. Gallup was a bold man, and though he had with him but one man and two boys, he immediately bore down upon them, and fired duck shot so thick among them, that he soon cleared the deck. The

* Winthrop's Journal, p. 75, compared with Hubbard's narrative, p. 15, 16, 17.

BOOK I.
1636.

Indians all got under the hatches. He then stood off, and running down upon her quarter with a brisk gale, nearly overset her; and so frightened the Indians, that six of them leaped into the sea, and were drowned. He then steered off again, and running down upon her a second time, bored her with his anchor, and raked her fore and aft with his shot. But the Indians kept themselves so close, that he got loose from her; and running down a third time upon the vessel, he gave her such a shock, that five more leaped overboard, and perished, as the former had done. He then boarded the vessel, and took two of the Indians, and bound them. Two or three others, armed with swords, in a little room below, could not be driven from their retreat. Mr. Oldham's corpse was found on board; the head split, and the body mangled in a barbarous manner. He was a Dorchester man, one of Mr. Warham's congregation. In these circumstances, Gallup, fearing that the Indians whom he had taken might get loose, especially if they were kept together, and having no place where he could keep them apart, threw one of them overboard. Gallup and his company then, as decently as circumstances would permit, put the corpse into the sea. They stripped the vessel, and took her rigging, and the goods which had not been carried off, on board their own. She was then taken in tow, with a view to carry her in; but the night coming on, and the wind rising, Gallup was obliged to let her go adrift, and she was lost. The Indians who perpetrated the murder were principally the Block-Islanders, with a number of the Narragansets, to whom these Indians, at this time, were subject. Several of the Narraganset sachems were in the plot, and it was supposed that the Indians whom Oldham had with him, were in the conspiracy. Several of the murderers fled to the Pequots, and were protected by them. They were, therefore, considered as abettors of the murder.

Mr. Endicott's expedition.

The governor and council of Massachusetts, therefore, the next year, dispatched captain Endicott, with ninety volunteers, to avenge these murders, unless the Indians should deliver up the murderers, and make reparation for the injuries which they had done. The Narraganset sachems sent home Mr. Oldham's two boys, and made such satisfaction, and gave such assurances of their good conduct, for the future, as the English accepted; but the other Indians made no compensation. Captain Endicott was, therefore, instructed to proceed to Block-Island, put the men to the sword, and take possession of the island. The women and children were to be spared. Thence he was to sail to the Pequot country, and demand of the Pequots the murderers of captains Stone and Norton, and of the other Englishmen who were of their company. He was also to demand a thousand fathoms of wampum for damages, and a number of their children for hostages, until the murderers should be delivered, and satisfaction made. If they refused to comply with these terms, he was directed to take it by force of arms. He had under him captains John Underhill and Nathaniel Turner. They sailed from Boston on the 25th of August. When he arrived at Block- Island, forty or fifty Indians appeared on the shore, and opposed his landing; but his men soon landed, and, after a little skirmishing, the Indians fled to the woods. The Indians secreted themselves in swamps, thickets, and fastnesses, where they could not be found. There were two plantations on the island, containing about sixty wigwams, some of which were very large and fair. The Indians had, also, about two hundred acres of corn. After the English had spent two days on the island, burning the wigwams, destroying their corn, and staving their canoes, they sailed for the Pequot country. When they had arrived in Pequot harbour, captain Endicott acquainted the Pequots with the design of his coming, demanded satisfaction for the murders which they had committed against the English, and compensation for the damages which they had done them. In a few hours, nearly three hundred of the Pequots collected upon the shore; but soon after they were fully informed of his business, they began to withdraw into the woods, and, instead of treating, answered him with their arrows, from the adjacent rocks and fastnesses. He landed his men on both sides of the harbour, burnt their wigwams, and destroyed their canoes, but made no spirited attack upon them, nor pursuit after them. As their corn was standing, no pains were taken for its destruction. They killed an Indian or two, and then returned to Boston. They all arrived on the 14th of September, unharmed either by sickness or the sword.* Enough, indeed, had been done to exasperate, but nothing to subdue a haughty and warlike enemy.

Sassacus and his captains were men of great and independent spirits; they had conquered and governed the nations around them without controul. They viewed the English as strangers and mere intruders, who had no right to the country, nor to controul its original proprietors, independent princes and sovereigns. They had made settlements in Connecticut without their consent, and brought

Winthrop's Journal, p. 105, 106, 107.

BOOK I.
1636.

home the Indian kings whom they had conquered, and restored to them their authority and lands. They had built a fort, and were making a settlement, without their approbation, in their very neighbourhood. Indeed, they had now proceeded to attack and ravage their country. They were now, therefore, all kindled into resentment and rage: they determined upon, and breathed nothing but war and revenge. They determined to extirpate, or drive all the English from New-England.

Policy of the Pequots.

For this purpose, they conceived the plan of uniting the Indians generally against them. They spared no art nor pains to make peace with the Narragansets, and to engage them in the war against the English. They represented, that the English, who were merely foreigners, were overspreading the country, and depriving the original inhabitants of their ancient rights and possessions: that, unless effectual measures were immediately taken to prevent it, they would soon entirely dispossess the original proprietors, and become the lords of the continent. They insisted, that, by a general combination, they could either destroy, or drive them from the country. With great advantage did they represent the facility with which it might be effected. They said there would be no necessity of coming to open battles: that, by killing their cattle, firing their houses, laying ambushes on the roads, in the fields, and wherever they could surprise and destroy them, they might accomplish their wishes. They represented, that, if the English should effect the destruction of the Pequots,

Savage revenge prevents union.

they would also soon destroy the Narragansets. So just and politic were these representations, that nothing but that thirst for revenge which inflames the savage heart, could have resisted their influence. Indeed, it is said, that, for a time, the Narragansets hesitated.

The governor of Massachusetts, to prevent an union between these savage nations, and to strengthen the peace between the Narraganset Indians and the colony, sent for Miantonimoh, their chief sachem, inviting him to come to Boston. Upon this, Miantonimoh, with another of the Narraganset sachems, two of the sons of Canonicus, with a number of their men, went to Boston, and entered into the following treaty.

Treaty with the Narragansets.

That there should be a firm peace between them and the English, and their posterity: That neither party should make peace with the Pequots, without the consent of the other: That they should not harbor the Pequots, and that they should return all fugitive servants, and deliver over to the English, or put to death, all murderers. The En-

CHAP. V.   CONNECTICUT.

glish were to give them notice, when they went out against the Pequots, and they were to furnish them with guides. It was also stipulated, that a free trade should be maintained between the parties.

Book 1.
1636.

Captain Underhill and twenty men, appointed to reinforce the garrison at Saybrook, lying wind bound off Pequot harbor, after Mr. Endicott's departure, a party of them went on shore to plunder the Pequots, and bring off their corn. After they had plundered a short time, and brought off some quantity of corn, the Pequots attacked them, and they fought a considerable part of the afternoon. At length, the enemy retired, and they returned to their boats. They had one man wounded, and imagined they killed and wounded several of the Indians.

Pequots fight in their own defence.

About the beginning of October, the enemy, concealing themselves in the high grass, in the meadows, surprised five of the garrison at Saybrook, as they were carrying home their hay. One Butterfield was taken and tortured to death. The rest made their escape; but one of them had five arrows shot into him. From this disaster, the place received the name of Butterfield's meadow.

Surprise the English. Oct.

Eight or ten days after, Joseph Tilly, a master of a small vessel, was captivated by the enemy, as he was going down Connecticut river. He came to anchor two or three miles above the fort, and taking a canoe, and one man with him, went a fowling. No sooner had he discharged his piece, than a large number of Pequots, arising from their concealment, took him, and killed his companion. Tilly was a man of great spirit and understanding, and determined to show himself a man. The Indians used him in the most barbarous manner, first cutting off his hands, and then his feet, and so gradually torturing him to death. But as all their cruelties could not effect a groan, they pronounced him a stout man.

Oct. J. Tilly taken and tortured.

The enemy now kept up a constant watch upon the river, and upon the people at Saybrook. A house had been erected, about two miles from the fort, and six of the garrison were sent to keep it. As three of them were fowling, at a small distance from the house, they were suddenly attacked, by nearly a hundred Pequots. Two of them were taken. The other cut his way through them, sword in hand, and made his escape; but he was wounded with two arrows.*

Before winter, the garrison were so pressed by the enemy, that they were obliged to keep almost wholly within

The fort is compassed with Indians.

* Hubbard's Narrative, Winthrop's Journal, and Mason's History of the Pequot war.

Book I. the reach of their guns. The Pequots razed all the out-
houses, burnt the stacks of hay, and destroyed almost eve-
1636. ry thing, which was not within the command of the fort.
The cattle which belonged to the garrison, were killed and
wounded. Some of them came home, with the arrows of
the enemy sticking in them. Indeed, the fort was but little better than in a state of siege, a great part of the winter. The enemy so encompassed it about, and watched
all the motions of the garrison, that it was dangerous, at
any time, to go out of the reach of the cannon.

When the spring came on, they became still more mischievous and troublesome. They kept such a constant
watch upon the river, that men could not pass up and
down, with any safety, without a strong guard. They
waylaid the roads and fields, and kept Connecticut in a
state of constant fear and alarm.

In March, lieutenant Gardiner, who commanded the fort
March at Saybrook, going out with ten or twelve men, to burn the
1637. Men marshes, was waylaid by a narrow neck of land, and as
killed at
Saybrook. soon as he had passed the narrow part of the neck, the enemy rose upon him, and killed three of his men. The
rest made their escape to the fort; but one of them was
mortally wounded, so that he died the next day. The
lieutenant did not escape without a slight wound. The
enemy pursued them in great numbers, to the very fort,
and compassed it on all sides. They challenged the English to come out and fight, and mocked them, in the
groans, pious invocations, and dying language of their
friends, whom they had captivated, when they were torturing them to death. They boasted, That they could
kill English men "all one flies." The cannon loaded
with grape shot were fired upon them, and they retired.

Killed go- Some time after, the enemy, in a number of canoes, being down set a shallop, which was going down the river, with three
the river. men on board. The men fought bravely, but were overpowered with numbers. The enemy shot one through the
head with an arrow, and he fell overboard; the other two
were taken. The Indians ripped them up, from the bottom of their bellies to their throats, and cleft them down
their backs: they then hung them up by their necks upon
trees, by the side of the river, that as the English passed
by, they might see those miserable objects of their vengeance.

The Pequots tortured the captives to death in the most
cruel manner. In some, they cut large gashes in their
flesh, and then poured embers and live coals into the
wounds. When, in their distress, they groaned, and in a

pious manner committed their departing spirits to their Redeemer, these barbarians would mock and insult them in their dying agonies and prayers.

On the 21st of February, the court met at Newtown, and letters were written to the governor of Massachusetts, representing the dissatisfaction of the court with Mr. Endicott's expedition, the consequences of which had been so distressful to Connecticut. The court expressed their desires that the colony of Massachusetts would more effectually prosecute the war with the Pequots.* It was also represented to be the design of Connecticut to send a force against them.

At this court it was decreed, that the plantation called Newtown, should be named Hartford; and that Watertown should be called Weathersfield. It was soon after decreed, that Dorchester should be called Windsor. Hartford was named in honor to Mr. Stone, who was born at Hartford, in England.

Captain Mason was soon after dispatched with twenty men, to reinforce the garrison at Saybrook, and to keep the enemy at a greater distance. After his arrival at the fort, the enemy made no further attacks upon it, but appeared very much to withdraw from that quarter.

A party of them took a different route, and, in April, waylaid the people at Weathersfield, as they were going into their fields to labour, and killed six men and three women. Two maids were taken captive: besides, they killed twenty cows, and did other damages to the inhabitants.

Soon after this, captain Underhill, who had been appointed, in the fall preceding, to keep garrison at Saybrook, was sent from the Massachusetts, with twenty men, to reinforce the garrison. Upon their arrival at Saybrook, captain Mason and his men immediately returned to Hartford.

The affairs of Connecticut, at this time wore a most gloomy aspect. They had sustained great losses in cattle and goods in the preceding years, and even this year they were unfortunate with respect to their cattle. They had no hay but what they cut from the spontaneous productions of an uncultivated country. To make good English meadow, was a work of time. The wild, coarse grass, which the people cut, was often mowed too late, and but poorly made. They did not always cut a sufficient quantity, even of this poor hay. They had no corn, or provender, with which they could feed them: and, amidst the

* Winthrop's journal, p. 122.

Book I. multiplicity of affairs, which, at their first settlement, demanded their attention, they could not provide such shelters for them, as were necessary during the long and severe winters of this northern climate. From an union of these circumstances, some of their cattle were lost, and those which lived through winter, were commonly poor, and many of the cows lost their young. Notwithstanding all the exertions the people had made the preceding summer, they had not been able, in the multiplicity of their affairs, and under their inconveniences, to raise a sufficiency of provisions. Their provisions were not only very coarse, but very dear, and scanty. The people were not only inexperienced in the husbandry of the country, but they had but few oxen or ploughs.* They performed almost the whole culture of the earth with their hoes. This rendered it both exceedingly slow and laborious.

1637.

Every article bore a high price. Valuable as money was, at that day, a good cow could not be purchased under thirty pounds; a pair of bulls or oxen not under forty pounds. A mare from England or Flanders, sold at thirty pounds; and Indian corn at about five shillings a bushel: labour, and other articles bore a proportionable price.

In addition to all these difficulties, a most insidious and dreadful enemy were now destroying the lives and property of the colonists, attempting to raise the numerous Indian tribes of the country against them, and threatened the utter ruin of the whole colony. The inhabitants were in a feeble state, and few in number. They wanted all their men at home, to prosecute the necessary business of the plantations. They had not a sufficiency of provisions for themselves: there would therefore be the greatest difficulty in furnishing a small army with provisions abroad. They could neither hunt, fish, nor cultivate their fields, nor travel at home, or abroad, but at the peril of their lives. They were obliged to keep a constant watch by night and day; to go armed to their daily labours, and to the public worship. They were obliged to keep a constant watch and guard at their houses of worship, on the Lord's day, and at other seasons, whenever they convened for the public worship. They lay down and rose up in fear and danger. If they should raise a party of men and send them to fight the enemy on their own ground, it would render the settlements proportionably weak at home, in case of an assault from the enemy. Every thing indeed appeared dark and

---

* It seems, that at this period there were but thirty ploughs in the whole colony of Massachusetts. Winthrop's journal, p. 114. It is not probable that there were ten, perhaps not five, in Connecticut.

CHAP. V.   CONNECTICUT.

threatening. But nothing could discourage men, who had an unshaken confidence in the divine government, and were determined to sacrifice every other consideration, for the enjoyment of the uncorrupted gospel, and the propagation of religion and liberty in America.

In this important crisis, a court was summoned, at Hartford, on Monday the 1st of May. As they were to deliberate on matters in which the lives of the subjects and the very existence of the colony were concerned, the towns for the first time, sent committees. The spirited measures adopted by this court, render the names of the members worthy of perpetuation. The magistrates were Roger Ludlow, Esq. Mr. Welles, Mr. Swain, Mr. Steel, Mr. Phelps and Mr. Ward. The committees were Mr. Whiting, Mr. Webster, Mr. Williams, Mr. Hull, Mr. Chaplin, Mr. Talcott, Mr. Geffords, Mr. Mitchel and Mr. Sherman.

The court, on mature deliberation, considering that the Pequots had killed nearly thirty of the English; that they had tortured and insulted their captives, in the most horrible manner; that they were attempting to engage all the Indians to unite for the purpose of extirpating the English; and the danger the whole colony was in, unless some capital blow could be immediately given their enemies, determined, that an offensive war should be carried on against them, by the three towns of Windsor, Hartford and Weathersfield. They voted, that 90 men should be raised forthwith; 42 from Hartford, 30 from Windsor, and 18 from Weathersfield. Notwithstanding the necessities and poverty of the people, all necessary supplies were voted for this little army.* No sooner was this resolution adopted, than the people prosecuted the most vigorous measures, to carry it into immediate and effectual execution.

The report of the slaughter and horrid cruelties practised by the Pequots, against the people of Connecticut, roused the other colonies to harmonious and spirited exertions against the common enemy. Massachusetts determined to send 200, and Plymouth 40 men, to assist Connecticut in prosecuting the war. Captain Patrick with 40 men was sent forward, before the other troops, from Massachusetts and Plymouth, could be ready to march, with a view, that he might seasonably form a junction with the party from Connecticut.

On Wednesday, the 10th of May, the troops from Connecticut fell down the river, for the fort at Saybrook. They consisted of 90 Englishmen and about 70 Moheagan and river Indians. They embarked on board a pink, a pin-

Records of Connecticut.

Book I.

1637.

Court May 1st.

Determine on a war against the Pequots.

Massachusetts and Plymouth agree to assist Connecticut.

May 10th, the troops fell down the river.

Book I
1637.
May 15.

Success of Uncas.

His barbarous treatment of his prisoner.

Captain Mason and his council divided in opinion.

Debates in the council of war.

nace and a shallop. The Indians were commanded by Uncas, sachem of the Moheagans. The whole was commanded by captain John Mason, who had been bred a soldier in the old countries. The Rev. Mr. Stone of Hartford went their chaplain. On Monday the 15th, the troops arrived at Saybrook fort. As the water was low, this little fleet several times ran aground. The Indians, impatient of delays, desired to be set on shore, promising to join the English at Saybrook. The captain therefore granted their request. On their march, they fell in with about forty of the enemy, near the fort, killed seven and took one prisoner.

The prisoner had been a perfidious villain. He had lived in the fort, some time before, and could speak English well. But after the Pequots commenced hostilities against the English, he became a constant spy upon the garrison, and acquainted Sassacus with every thing he could discover. He had been present at the slaughter of all the English who had been killed at Saybrook. Uncas and his men insisted upon executing him according to the manner of their ancestors; and the English, in the circumstances in which they then were, did not judge it prudent to interpose. The Indians, kindling a large fire, violently tore him limb from limb. Barbarously cutting his flesh in pieces, they handed it round from one to another, eating it, singing and dancing round the fire, in their violent and tumultuous manner. The bones and such parts of their captive, as were not consumed in this dreadful repast, were committed to the flames and burnt to ashes.

This success was matter of joy, not only as it was a check upon the enemy, but as it was an evidence of the fidelity of Uncas and his Indians, of which the English had been before in doubt. There were other circumstances, however, which more than counterbalanced this joy. The army lay wind bound until Friday, and captain Mason and his officers were entirely divided in opinion, with respect to the manner of prosecuting their enterprise. The court, by the commission and instructions which it had given, enjoined the landing of the men at Pequot harbour, and that from thence they should advance upon the enemy. The captain was for passing by them, and sailing to the Narraganset country. He was fixed in this opinion, because he found that, expecting the army at Pequot harbour, they kept watch upon the river night and day. Their number of men greatly exceeded his: He was informed, at Saybrook, that they had sixteen fire arms, with powder and shot. The harbour was compassed with rocks and thickets, affording the enemy every advantage. They were upon the land, and exceedingly light of foot. He was therefore of the opinion, that they would render it very difficult and dangerous to land, and that he might sustain such loss, as would discourage his men and frustrate the design of the expedition. If they should make good their landing, he was sure that, while they directed their march through the country, to the enemy's forts, they would waylay and attack them, with their whole force, at every difficult pass. Beside, if they should find, on trial, that they were not able to defeat the English, they would run off to swamps and fastnesses, where they could not be found; and they should not be able to effect any thing capital against them. He was not without hopes that, by going to Narraganset, he might surprise them. There was also some prospect, that the Narragansets would join him in the expedition, and that he might fall in with some part of the troops from Massachusetts.

His officers and men in general were for attending their instructions, and going at all hazards directly to the forts. The necessity of their affairs at home, the danger of the Indians attacking their families and settlements, in their absence, made them wish, at once to dispatch the business, on which they had been sent. They did not relish a long march through the wilderness. They also imagined that they might be discovered, even should they determine to march from Narraganset to the attack of the enemy. In this division of opinion, Mr. Stone was desired by the officers most importunately to pray for them, That their way might be directed, and that, notwithstanding the present embarrassment, the enterprise might be crowned with success.

Mr. Stone spent most of Thursday night in prayer, and the next morning visiting captain Mason, assured him, that he had done as he was desired; adding, that he was entirely satisfied with his plan. The council was again called, and, upon a full view of all the reasons, unanimously agreed to proceed to Narraganset. It was also determined, that twenty men should be sent back to Connecticut, to strengthen the infant settlements, while the rest of the troops were employed in service against the enemy; and, that captain Underhill, with nineteen men from the garrison at Saybrook fort, should supply their places.

On Friday, May 19th, the captain sailed for Narraganset bay, and arrived on Saturday at the desired port. On Monday, captain Mason and captain Underhill marched with a guard to the plantation of Canonicus, and ac-

Book I.
1637.

Mr. Stone prays.

May 19th, expedition against the Pequots.

quainted him with the design of their coming. A messenger was immediately dispatched to Miantonimoh, the chief sachem of the Narragansets, to acquaint him also with the expedition. The next day Miantonimoh met them, with his chief counsellors and warriors, consisting of about 200 men. Captain Mason certified him, that the occasion of his coming with armed men, into his country, was to avenge the intolerable injuries which the Pequots, his as well as their enemies, had done the English: and, that he desired a free passage to the Pequot forts. After a solemn consultation in the Indian manner, Miantonimoh answered, That he highly approved of the expedition, and that he would send men. He observed, however, that the English were not sufficient in number to fight with the enemy. He said the Pequots were great captains, skilled in war, and rather slighted the English. Captain Mason landed his men, and marched just at night to the plantation of Canonicus, which was appointed to be the place of general rendezvous. That night there arrived an Indian runner in the camp, with a letter from captain Patrick, who had arrived with his party at Mr. Williams' plantation in Providence. Captain Patrick signified his desire, that captain Mason would wait until he could join him. Upon deliberation it was determined not to wait, though a junction was greatly desired. The men had already been detained much longer than was agreeable to their wishes. When they had absolutely resolved the preceding day to march the next morning, the Indians insisted that they were but in jest; that Englishmen talked much, but would not fight. It was therefore feared, that any delay would have a bad effect upon them. It was also suspected that, if they did not proceed immediately, they should be discovered, as there were a number of squaws who maintained an intercourse between the Pequot and Narraganset Indians. The army therefore, consisting of 77 Englishmen, 60 Moheagan and river Indians, and about 200 Narragansets, marched on Wednesday morning, and that day reached the eastern Nihantick, about eighteen or twenty miles from the place of rendezvous the night before. This was a frontier to the Pequots, and was the seat of one of the Narraganset sachems. Here the army halted, at the close of the day. But the sachem and his Indians conducted themselves in a haughty manner toward the English, and would not suffer them to enter within their fort. Captain Mason therefore placed a strong guard round the fort; and as the Indians would not suffer him to enter it, he determined that none of them should come out. Knowing the perfidy of the Indians, and that it was customary among them to suffer the nearest relatives of their greatest enemies to reside with them, he judged it necessary, to prevent their discovering him to the enemy.

In the morning, a considerable number of Miantonimoh's men came on and joined the English. This encouraged many of the Nihanticks also to join them. They soon formed a circle, and made protestations, how gallantly they would fight, and what numbers they would kill. When the army marched, the next morning, the captain had with him nearly 500 Indians. He marched twelve miles, to the ford in Pawcatuck river. The day was very hot, and the men, through the great heat, and a scarcity of provision, began to faint. The army, therefore, made a considerable halt, and refreshed themselves. Here the Narraganset Indians began to manifest their dread of the Pequots, and to enquire of captain Mason, with great anxiety, what were his real designs. He assured them, that it was his design to attack the Pequots in their forts. At this, they appeared to be panic-struck, and filled with amazement. Many of them drew off, and returned to Narraganset. The army marched on about three miles, and came to Indian corn fields; and the captain, imagining that he drew near the enemy, made a halt; he called his guides and council, and demanded of the Indians how far it was to the forts. They represented, that it was twelve miles to Sassacus's fort, and that both forts were in a manner impregnable. Wequosh, a Pequot captain or petty sachem, who had revolted from Sassacus to the Narragansets, was the principal guide, and he proved faithful. He gave such information, respecting the distance of the forts from each other, and the distance which they were then at, from the chief sachem's, as determined him and his officers to alter the resolution which they had before adopted, of attacking them both at once; and to make a united attack upon that at Mistic. He found his men so fatigued, in marching through a pathless wilderness, with their provisions, arms, and ammunition, and so affected with the heat, that this resolution appeared to be absolutely necessary. One of captain Underhill's men became lame, at the same time, and began to fail. The army, therefore, proceeded directly to Mistic, and continuing their march, came to a small swamp between two hills, just at the disappearing of the day light. The officers, supposing that they were now near the fort, pitched their little camp, between or near two large rocks, in Groton, since called Porter's rocks. The men were faint and weary; and though the rocks were their pillows,

Book I.
1637.
Thursday 25th.

84 HISTORY OF CHAP. V.

BOOK I. their rest was sweet. The guards and sentinels were considerably advanced, in the front of the army, and heard the enemy singing, at the fort, who continued their rejoicings even until midnight. They had seen the vessels pass the harbor, some days before, and had concluded, that the English were afraid, and had not courage to attack them. They were, therefore, rejoicing, singing, dancing, insulting them, and wearying themselves, on this account.

1637.

The night was serene, and, towards morning, the moon shone clear. The important crisis was now come, when the very existence of Connecticut, under providence, was to be determined by the sword, in a single action; and to be decided by the good conduct of less than eighty brave men. The Indians who remained, were now sorely dismayed, and though, at first, they had led the van, and boasted of great feats, yet were now all fallen back in the rear.

Attack on Mistic fort, May 26th.

About two hours before day, the men were roused with all expedition, and briefly commending themselves and their cause to God, advanced immediately towards the fort. After a march of about two miles, they came to the foot of a large hill, where a fine country opened before them. The captain, supposing that the fort could not be far distant, sent for the Indians in the rear, to come up. Uncas and Wequosh, at length, appeared. He demanded of them where the fort was. They answered, on the top of the hill. He demanded of them where were the other Indians. They answered, that they were much afraid. The captain sent to them not to fly, but to surround the fort, at any distance they pleased, and see whether Englishmen would fight. The day was nearly dawning, and no time was now to be lost. The men pressed on, in two divisions, captain Mason to the north-eastern, and captain Underhill to the western entrance. As the object which they had been so long seeking, came into view, and while they reflected they were to fight not only for themselves, but their parents, wives, children, and the whole colony, the martial spirit kindled in their bosoms, and they were wonderfully animated and assisted. As captain Mason advanced within a rod or two of the fort, a dog barked, and an Indian roared out, Owanux! Owanux! That is, Englishmen! Englishmen! The troops pressed on, and as the Indians were rallying, poured in upon them, through the pallisadoes, a general discharge of their muskets, and then wheeling off to the principal entrance, entered the fort sword in hand. Notwithstanding the suddenness of the attack, the blaze and thunder of their arms, the enemy made a manly and desperate resistance. Captain Mason

CHAP. V. CONNECTICUT.

and his party, drove the Indians in the main street towards the west part of the fort, where some bold men, who had forced their way, met them, and made such slaughter among them, that the street was soon clear of the enemy. They secreted themselves in and behind their wigwams, and taking advantage of every covert, maintained an obstinate defence. The captain and his men entered the wigwams, where they were beset with many Indians, who took every advantage to shoot them, and lay hands upon them, so that it was with great difficulty that they could defend themselves with their swords. After a severe conflict, in which many of the Indians were slain, some of the English killed, and others sorely wounded, the victory still hung in suspense. The captain finding himself much exhausted, and out of breath, as well as his men, by the extraordinary exertions which they had made; in this critical state of the action, had recourse to a successful expedient. He cries out to his men, WE MUST BURN THEM. He, immediately entering a wigwam, took fire, and put it into the mats, with which the wigwams were covered. The fire instantly kindling, spread with such violence that all the Indian houses were soon wrapped in one general flame. As the fire increased, the English retired without the fort, and compassed it on every side. Uncas and his Indians, with such of the Narragansets as yet remained, took courage, from the example of the English, and formed another circle in the rear of them. The enemy were now seized with astonishment, and forced, by the flames, from their lurking places, into open light, became a fair mark for the English soldiers. Some climbed the pallisadoes, and were instantly brought down by the fire of the English muskets. Others, desperately sallying forth from their burning cells, were shot, or cut in pieces with the sword. Such terror fell upon them, that they would run back from the English, into the very flames. Great numbers perished in the conflagration.

The greatness and violence of the fire, the reflection of the light, the flashing and roar of the arms, the shrieks and yellings of the men, women and children, in the fort, and the shoutings of the Indians without, just at the dawning of the morning, exhibited a grand and awful scene. In a little more than an hour this whole work of destruction was finished. Seventy wigwams were burnt, and five or six hundred Indians perished, either by the sword, or in the flames.* A hundred and fifty warriors had been sent

Book I.
1637.

Fort burnt.

Six hundred Indians destroyed.

---

* Captain Mason, in his history, says six or seven hundred. From the number of Wigwams, and the reinforcement, the probability is, that about six hundred were destroyed.

Book I.
1637.

on, the evening before, who, that very morning, were to have gone forth against the English. Of these, and all who belonged to the fort, seven only escaped, and seven were made prisoners. It had been previously concluded not to burn the fort, but to destroy the enemy, and take the plunder; but the captain afterwards found it the only expedient to obtain the victory, and save his men. Thus parents and children, the sannup and squaw, the old man and the babe, perished in promiscuous ruin.

Danger and distress of the army.

Though the victory was complete, yet the army were in great danger and distress. The men had been exceedingly fatigued, by the heat, and long marches through rough and difficult places; and by that constant watch and guard which they had been obliged to keep. They had now been greatly exhausted, by the sharpness of the action, and the exertions which they had been necessitated to make. Their loss was very considerable. Two men were killed, and nearly twenty wounded. This was more than one quarter of the English. Numbers fainted by reason of fatigue, the heat, and want of necessaries. The surgeon, their provisions, and the articles necessary for the wounded, were on board the vessels, which had been ordered to sail from the Narraganset bay, the night before, for Pequot harbour; but there was no appearance of them in the sound. They were sensible that, by the burning of the fort, and the noise of war, they had alarmed the country; and therefore were in constant expectation of an attack, by a fresh and numerous enemy from the other fortress, and from every quarter whence the Pequots might be collected.

A number of the friendly Indians had been wounded, and they were so distracted with fear, that it was difficult even to speak with their guide and interpreter, or to know any thing what they designed. The English were in an enemies country, and entire strangers to the way in which they must return. The enemy were far more numerous than themselves, and enraged to the highest degree. Another circumstance rendered their situation still more dangerous, their provisions and ammunition were nearly expended. Four or five men were so wounded that it was necessary to carry them, and they were also obliged to bear about twenty fire arms, so that not more than forty men could be spared for action.

After an interval of about an hour, while the officers were in consultation what course they should take, their vessels, as though guided by the hand of providence, to serve the necessities of these brave men, came full in view; and, under a fair gale, were steering directly into the harbour. This, in the situation of the army at that time, was a most joyful sight.

Immediately, upon the discovery of the vessels, about three hundred Indians came on from the other fort. Captain Mason, perceiving their approach, led out a chosen party to engage them, and try their temper. He gave them such a warm reception, as soon checked and put them to a stand. This gave him great encouragement, and he ordered the army to march for Pequot harbour. The enemy, upon this, immediately advanced to the hill, where the fort stood; and viewing the destruction which had been made, stamped and tore their hair from their heads. After a short pause, and blowing themselves up to the highest transport of passion, they leaped down the hill after the army, in the most violent manner, as though they were about to run over the English. Captain Underhill, who, with a number of the best men, was ordered to defend the rear, soon checked the eagerness of their pursuit, and taught them to keep at a more respectful distance. The friendly Indians who had not deserted, now kept close to the English, and it was believed that, after the enemy came on, they were afraid to leave them. The enemy pursued the army nearly six miles, sometimes shooting at a distance, from behind rocks and trees, and at other times, pressing on more violently, and desperately hazarding themselves in the open field.

That the English might all be enabled to fight, captain Mason soon hired the Indians to carry the wounded men and their arms. The English killed several of the enemy while they pursued them, but sustained no loss themselves. When they killed a Pequot, the other Indians would shout, run and fetch his head. At length, the enemy finding that they could make no impression upon the army, and that wounds and death attended their attempts, gave over the pursuit.

The army then marched to the harbor, with their colors flying, and were received on board the vessels, with great mutual joy and congratulation.

In about three weeks from the time the men embarked at Hartford, they returned again to their respective habitations. They were received with the greatest exultation. As the people had been deeply affected with their danger, and full of anxiety for their friends, while nearly half the effective men in the colony were in service, upon so hazardous an enterprise, so sudden a change, in the great victory obtained, and in the safe return of so many of their children and neighbors, filled them with exceeding joy and

BOOK I.
1637.
Remarkable circumstances.

thankfulness. Every family, and every worshipping assembly, spake the language of praise and thanksgiving.

Several circumstances attending this enterprise, were much noticed by the soldiers themselves, and especially by all the pious people. It was considered as very providential, that the army should march nearly forty miles, and a considerable part of it in the enemies country, and not be discovered until the moment they were ready to commence the attack. It was judged remarkable, that the vessels should come into the harbour at the very hour in which they were most needed. The life of captain Mason was very signally preserved. As he entered a wigwam for fire to burn the fort, an Indian was drawing an arrow to the very head, and would have killed him instantly; but Davis, one of his sergeants, cut the bow string with his cutlass, and prevented the fatal shot.* Lieutenant Bull received an arrow into a hard piece of cheese, which he had in his clothes, and by it was saved harmless. Two soldiers, John Dyer and Thomas Stiles, both servants of one man, were shot in the knots of their neckcloths, and by them preserved from instant death.†

Gallantry and good conduct.

Few enterprises have ever been achieved with more personal bravery or good conduct. In few have so great a proportion of the effective men of a whole colony, state, or nation been put to so great and immediate danger. In few, have a people been so deeply and immediately interested, as the whole colony of Connecticut was in this, in that uncommon crisis. In these respects, even the great armaments and battles of Europe are, comparatively, of little importance. In this, under the divine conduct, by seventy-seven brave men, Connecticut was saved, and the most warlike and terrible Indian nation in New-England, defeated and ruined.

Pequots destroy their fort and flee.

The body of the Pequots, returning from the pursuit of captain Mason, repaired to Sassacus, at the royal fortress, and related the doleful story of their misfortunes. They charged them all to his haughtiness and misconduct, and threatened him, and his, with immediate destruction. His friends and chief counsellors interceded for him; and, at their intreaty, his men spared his life. Then, upon consultation, they concluded, that they could not, with safety, remain any longer in the country. They were, indeed, so panic struck, that, burning their wigwams and destroying their fort, they fled and scattered into various parts of the country. Sassacus, Mononotto, and seventy or eighty of their chief counsellors and warriors, took their route towards Hudson's river.

* Hubbard's Narrative. † Mason's History.

CHAP. V. CONNECTICUT.

Just before captain Mason went out upon the expedition against the Pequots, the Dutch performed a very neighbourly office for Connecticut. The two maids, who had been captivated at Weathersfield, had, through the humanity and mediation of Mononotto's squaw, been spared from death, and kindly treated. The Dutch governor, receiving intelligence of their circumstances, determined to redeem them at any rate, and dispatched a sloop to Pequot harbour for that purpose. Upon its arrival, the Dutch made large offers for their redemption, but the Pequots would not accept them. Finally, as the Dutch had a number of Pequots on board, whom they had taken, and finding that they could do no better, they offered the Pequots six of their own men for the two maids.* These they accepted, and the Dutch delivered the young women at Saybrook, just before captain Mason and his party arrived. Of them he received particular information respecting the enemy.

An Indian runner, dispatched by Mr. Williams, at Providence, soon carried the news of the success of Connecticut against the Pequots, to the governor of Massachusetts. The governor and his council, judging that the Pequots had received a capital blow, sent forward but a hundred and twenty men. These were commanded by Mr. Stoughton, and the Rev. Mr. Wilson, of Boston, was sent his chaplain.

This party arrived at Pequot harbour the latter part of June. By the assistance of the Narraganset Indians, the party under captain Stoughton surrounded a large body of Pequots in a swamp. They took eighty captives. Thirty were men; the rest were women and children. The men, except two sachems, were killed, but the women and children were saved.† The sachems promised to conduct the English to Sassacus, and for that purpose were spared for the present.

The court at Connecticut ordered that forty men should be raised forthwith for the further prosecution of the war against the Pequots, to be commanded by captain Mason.

The troops from Connecticut made a junction with the party under the command of captain Stoughton, at Pequot. Mr. Ludlow, with other principal gentlemen from Connecticut, went also with the army, to advise with respect to the measures to be adopted in the further prosecution of the war. Upon general consultation, it was concluded to pursue the Pequots, who had fled to the westward. The

Book I.
1637.
Captivated maids redeemed.

June.
Pequots taken.

June 26.

* Winthrop's Journal, p. 128.
† Hubbard's Narrative, p. 34, and Winthrop's Journal, p. 130, 132.

M

Book I.
1637.

Origin of sachem's head.

Great swamp fight, July 13th.

army marched immediately, and soon discovered the places, where the enemy had rendezvoused, at their several removes. As these were not far distant from each other, it appeared that they moved slowly, having their women and children with them. They also were without provisions, and were obliged to dig for clams, and to range the groves for such articles as they afforded. The English found some scattering Pequots, as they scoured the country, whom they captivated, and from whom they obtained intelligence relative to the Pequots whom they were pursuing. But finding, that the sachems, whom they had spared, would give them no information, they beheaded them, on their march, at a place called Menunkatuck, since Guilford; from which circumstance, the spot on which the execution was done, bears the name of sachem's head to the present time. In three days they arrived at New-Haven harbour. The vessels sailed along the shore while the troops marched by land. At New-Haven, then called Quinnipiack, a great smoke, at a small distance, was discovered in the woods. The officers supposing, that they had now discovered the enemy, ordered the army immediately to advance upon them; but were soon informed that they were not in that vicinity. The Connecticut Indians had kindled the fires whence the smoke arose. The troops soon embarked on board the vessels. After staying several days at New-Haven, the officers received intelligence from a Pequot, whom they had previously sent to make discovery, that the enemy were at a considerable distance, in a great swamp, to the westward. Upon this information, the army marched with all possible dispatch to a great swamp, in Fairfield, where were eighty or a hundred Pequot warriors, and nearly two hundred other Indians. The swamp was such a thicket, so deep and boggy, that it was difficult to enter it, or make any movement without sinking in the mire. Lieutenant Davenport and others, rushing eagerly into it, were sorely wounded, and several were soon so deep in the mud, that they could not get out without assistance. The enemy pressed them so hard, that they were just ready to seize them by the hair of their head. A number of brave men were obliged to rescue them sword in hand. Some of the Indians were slain, and the men were drawn out of the mire. The swamp was surrounded, and after a considerable skirmish the Indians desired a parley. As the officers were not willing to make a promiscuous destruction of men, women and children, and as the sachem and Indians of the vicinity had fled into the swamp, though they had done the colonies no injury, a parley was granted. Thomas Stanton, a man well acquainted with the manners and language of the Indians, was sent to treat with them. He was authorized to offer life to all the Indians who had shed no English blood. Upon this offer, the sachem of the place came out to the English, and one company of old men, women and children after another, to the number of about two hundred. The sachem of the place declared for himself and his Indians, that they had neither shed the blood of the English nor done them any harm. But the Pequot warriors had too great a spirit to accept of the offer of life, declaring, that they would fight it out. They shot their arrows at Stanton, and pressed so hard upon him, that the soldiers were obliged to fly to his rescue.* The fight was then renewed, the soldiers firing upon them whenever an opportunity presented. But by reason of an unhappy division among the officers, a great part of the enemy escaped. Some were for forcing the swamp immediately, but this was opposed, as too dangerous. Others were for cutting it down, as they had taken many hatchets, with which they were of the opinion it might be effected. Some others were for making a pallisado and hedge round it, but neither of these measures could be adopted.† As night came on, the English cut through a narrow part of it, by which the circumference was greatly lessened; so that the soldiers, at twelve feet distance from each other, were able completely to compass the enemy. In this manner they enclosed and watched them until it was nearly morning. A thick fog arose just before day, and it became exceedingly dark. At this juncture, the Indians took the opportunity to break through the English. They made their first attempt upon captain Patrick's quarters, yelling in their hideous manner and pressing on with violence, but they were several times driven back. As the noise and tumult of war increased, captain Mason sent a party to assist captain Patrick. Captain Trask also marched to reinforce him. As the battle greatly increased, the siege broke up. Captain Mason marched to give assistance in the action. Advancing to the turn of the swamp, he found that the enemy were pressing out upon him; but he gave them so warm a reception, that they were soon glad to retire. While he was expecting that they would make another attempt upon him, they faced about, and falling violently on captain Patrick, broke through his quarters and fled. These were their bravest warriors, sixty or seventy of whom made their escape. About twenty were killed, and one hundred

* Hubbard's Narrative, p. 38.   † Mason's history.

Book I. and eighty were taken prisoners. The English also took hatchets, wampum, kettles, trays and other Indian utensils.

1637. Captives divided.

The Pequot women and children, who had been captivated, were divided among the troops. Some were carried to Connecticut, and others to the Massachusetts. The people of Massachusetts sent a number of the women and boys to the West-Indies, and sold them for slaves. It was supposed that about seven hundred Pequots were destroyed. The women who were captivated, reported, that thirteen sachems had been slain, and that thirteen yet survived. Among the latter were Sassacus and Mononotto, the two chief sachems. These with about twenty of their best men fled to the Mohawks. They carried off with them wampum to the amount of 500 pounds.* The Mohawks surprised and slew them all, except Mononotto. They wounded him, but he made his escape. The scalp of Sassacus was sent to Connecticut in the fall, and Mr. Ludlow and several other gentlemen, going into Massachusetts, in September, carried a lock of it to Boston, as a rare sight, and a sure demonstration of the death of their mortal enemy.†

Sachem's wife and children.

Among the Pequot captives were the wife and children of Mononotto. She was particularly noticed, by the English, for her great modesty, humanity and good sense. She made it as her only request, that she might not be injured either as to her offspring or personal honor. As a requital of her kindness to the captivated maids, her life and the lives of her children were not only spared, but they were particularly recommended to the care of governor Winthrop. He gave charge for their protection and kind treatment.

After the swamp fight, the Pequots became so weak and scattered, that the Narragansets and Moheagans constantly killed them, and brought in their heads to Windsor and Hartford. Those who survived were so hunted and harassed, that a number of their chief men repaired to the English, at Hartford, for relief. They offered, if their lives might be spared, that they would become the servants of the English and be disposed of at their pleasure. This was granted, and the court interposed for their protection.

Covenant at Hartford, Sept. 21st, 1638,

Uncas and Miantonimoh, with the Pequots, by the direction of the magistrates of Connecticut, met at Hartford; and it was demanded by them, how many of the Pequots were yet living? they answered, about two hundred, be-

* Winthrop's Journal, p. 136.
† Winthrop's Journal, p. 134, 135, 136.

sides women and children. The magistrates then entered into a firm covenant with them, to the following effect: that there should be perpetual peace between Miantonimoh and Uncas, and their respective Indians; and that all past injuries should be remitted, and for ever buried: that if any injuries should be done, in future, by one party to the other, that they should not immediately revenge it, but appeal to the English to do them justice. It was stipulated, that they should submit to their determination, and that if either party should be obstinate, that then they might enforce submission to their decisions. It was further agreed, that neither the Moheagans, nor Narragansets should conceal, or entertain any of their enemies; but deliver up or destroy all such Indians as had murdered any Englishman or woman. The English then gave the Pequot Indians to the Narragansets and Moheagans; eighty to Miantonimoh, twenty to Ninnigret, and the other hundred to Uncas; to be received and treated as their men. It was also covenanted, that the Pequots should never more inhabit their native country, nor be called Pequots, but Narragansets and Moheagans. It was also further stipulated, That neither the Narragansets nor Moheagans should possess any part of the Pequot country without the consent of the English. The Pequots were to pay a tribute, at Connecticut annually, of a fathom of wampumpeag for every Sannop, of half a fathom for every young man, and of a hand for every male papoose. On these conditions the magistrates, in behalf of the colony, stipulated a firm peace with all the Indians.*

The conquest of the Pequots struck all the Indians in New-England with terror, and they were possessed with such fear of the displeasure and arms of the English, that they had no open war with them for nearly forty years.

This happy event gave great joy to the colonies. A day of public thanksgiving was appointed; and, in all the churches of New-England, devout and animated praises were addressed to Him, who giveth his people the victory, and causeth them to dwell safely.

* Records of Connecticut.

CHAPTER VI.

Effects of the war. Great scarcity in Connecticut, and means taken to relieve the necessities of the people. Settlement of New-Haven. Plantation covenant. Means for the defence of the colony. Captain Mason made major-general. Civil constitution of Connecticut, formed by voluntary compact. First general election at Connecticut. Governors and magistrates. General rights of the people, and principal laws of the colony. Constitution and laws of New-Haven. Purchase and settlement of several towns in Connecticut and New-Haven.

THOUGH the war with the Pequots was now happily terminated, yet the effects of it were severely felt by the inhabitants. The consequences were, scarcity and a debt, which, in the low state of the colony, it was exceedingly difficult to pay. Almost every article of food or clothing was purchased at the dearest rate: and the planters had not yet reaped any considerable advantage from their farms. Such a proportion of their labourers had been employed in the war, and the country was so uncultivated, that all the provision which had been raised, or imported, was in no measure proportionate to the wants of the people. The winter was uncommonly severe, which increased the distress of the colony.* The court at Connecticut foreseeing that the people would be in great want of bread, contracted with Mr. Pyncheon for five hundred bushels of Indian corn, which he was to purchase of the Indians, and a greater quantity, if it could be obtained. The inhabitants were prohibited to bargain for it privately, and limited to certain prices, lest it should raise the price, while he was making the purchase. A committee was also appointed by the court, to send a vessel to Narraganset, to buy of the natives in that quarter.† But notwithstanding every precaution which was taken, the scarcity became such, that corn rose to the extraordinary price of twelve shillings by the bushel.‡ In this distressful situation a committee was sent to an Indian settlement called Pocomtock, since Deer-

Scarcity in Connecticut.

---

* The snow lay from the 4th of November until the 23d of March. It was, at some times, three and four feet deep. Once in the winter it snowed for two hours together, flakes as big as English shillings. Winthrop's Journal, p. 154.
† Records of Connecticut.
‡ Mason's history. Twelve shillings sterling at that time, was doubtless equal to eighteen or twenty shillings lawful money.

CHAP. VI. CONNECTICUT.

field, where they purchased such quantities, that the Indians came down to Windsor and Hartford, with fifty canoes at one time, laden with Indian corn.§ The good people considered this as a great deliverance. Those, who, in England, had fed on the finest of the wheat, in the beginning of affairs in Connecticut, were thankful for such coarse fare as Indian bread, for themselves and children.

In this low state of the colony, the court found it necessary to order the towns immediately to furnish themselves with magazines of powder, lead and shot, and every man to be completely armed, and furnished with ammunition. The court were also obliged to impose a tax of 550 pounds, to be collected immediately, to defray the expenses of the war. This appears to have been the first public tax in Connecticut. Agawam, since named Springfield, though it sent no men to the war, yet bore its proportion of the expense.* The first secretary and treasurer appears to have been Mr. Clement Chaplin. He was authorised to issue his warrants for gathering the tax which had been imposed.

Captain John Mason was appointed major-general of the militia of Connecticut. The reverend Mr. Hooker was desired to deliver him the military staff. This he doubtless performed with that propriety and dignity which was peculiar to himself, and best adapted to the occasion. The general was directed to call out the militia of each town, ten times in a year, to instruct them in military discipline. He received out of the public treasury 40 pounds annually, for his services.

As it was of the highest importance to the colony to cultivate peace, and a good understanding with the Indians, laws were enacted to prevent all persons from offering them the least private insult or abuse.

While the planters of Connecticut were thus exerting themselves in prosecuting and regulating the affairs of that colony, another was projected and settled at Quinnipiack,† afterwards called New-Haven. On the 26th of July, 1637, Mr. John Davenport, Mr. Samuel Eaton, Theophilus Eaton and Edward Hopkins, Esquires, Mr. Thomas Gregson, and many others of good characters and fortunes, arrived at Boston. Mr. Davenport had been a famous minister in the city of London, and was a distinguished character for piety, learning, and good conduct. Many of his congre-

Book I.
1638.
Relieved.

February 9th.

March 8th.

Mr. Davenport arrives at Boston.

§ Mason's History.
* The tax was laid on the towns in the proportions following: Agawam, 86 pounds : 16 : 0. Windsor, 158 pounds : 2 : 0. Hartford, 251 pounds 2 : 0. And Weathersfield, 124 pounds : 0 : 0.
† This is sometimes spelt Quillipiack, and Quinepioke.

gation, on account of the esteem which they had for his person and ministry, followed him into New-England. Mr. Eaton and Mr. Hopkins had been merchants in London, possessed great estates, and were men of eminence for their abilities and integrity. The fame of Mr. Davenport, the reputation and good estates of the principal gentlemen of this company, made the people of the Massachusetts exceedingly desirous of their settlement in that commonwealth. Great pains were taken, not only by particular persons and towns, but by the general court, to fix them in the colony. Charlestown made them large offers; and Newbury proposed to give up the whole town to them. The general court offered them any place which they should choose.* But they were determined to plant a distinct colony. By the pursuit of the Pequots to the westward, the English became acquainted with that fine tract along the shore, from Saybrook to Fairfield, and with its several harbours. It was represented as fruitful, and happily situated for navigation and commerce. The company therefore projected a settlement in that part of the country.

[margin: Offers to retain him in Massachusetts.]

In the fall of 1637, Mr. Eaton, and others, who were of the company, made a journey to Connecticut, to explore the lands and harbours on the sea coast. They pitched upon Quinnipiack for the place of their settlement. They erected a poor hut, in which a few men subsisted through the winter.

On the 30th of March, 1638, Mr. Davenport, Mr. Prudden, Mr. Samuel Eaton, and Theophilus Eaton, Esquire, with the people of their company, sailed from Boston for Quinnipiack. In about a fortnight they arrived at their desired port. On the 18th of April, they kept their first sabbath in the place. The people assembled under a large spreading oak, and Mr. Davenport preached to them from Matthew vi. 1. He insisted on the temptations of the wilderness, made such observations, and gave such directions and exhortations as were pertinent to the then present state of his hearers. He left this remark, That he enjoyed a good day.

[margin: April 18th, the first sabbath kept at New-Haven.]

One of the principal reasons which these colonists assigned for their removing from Massachusetts, was, that they should be more out of the way and trouble of a general governor of New-England, who, at this time, was an object of great fear in all the plantations. What foundation there was for the hope of exemption from the controul of a general governor, by this removal, had one been sent, does not appear. It is probable, that the motive which had the

[margin: Reasons for removing.]

* Winthrop's Journal, p. 151.

greatest influence with the principal men, was the desire of being at the head of a new government, modelled, both in civil and religious matters, agreeably to their own apprehensions. It had been an observation of Mr. Davenport's, That whenever a reformation had been effected in the church, in any part of the world, it had rested where it had been left by the reformers. It could not be advanced another step. He was now embarked in a design of forming a civil and religious constitution, as near as possible to scripture precept and example. The principal gentlemen, who had followed him into America, had the same views. In laying the foundations of a new colony, there was a fair probability, that they might accommodate all matters of church and commonwealth to their own feelings and sentiments. But in the Massachusetts, the principal men were fixed in the chief seats of government, which they were likely to keep, and their civil and religious polity was already formed. Besides, the antinomian controversy and sentiments, which had taken such root at Boston, were exceedingly disagreeable to Mr. Davenport, and the principal gentlemen of his company. He had taken a decided, though prudent part, against them. He, with his leading men, might judge, that the people who came with them would be much more out of danger of the corruption, and that they should be more entirely free from the trouble of those sentiments, in a new plantation, than in the Massachusetts. These might all unite their influence with Mr. Davenport and others, to determine them to remove and begin a new colony.

Soon after they arrived at Quinnipiack, in the close of a day of fasting and prayer, they entered into what they termed a plantation covenant. In this they solemnly bound themselves, "That, as in matters that concern the gathering and ordering of a church, so also in all public offices, which concern civil order, as choice of magistrates and officers, making and repealing laws, dividing allotments of inheritance, and all things of like nature, they would, all of them, be ordered by the rules which the scripture held forth to them." This was adopted as a general agreement, until there should be time for the people to become more intimately acquainted with each other's religious views, sentiments, and moral conduct; which was supposed to be necessary to prepare the way for their covenanting together, as christians, in church state.

The aspects of Providence on the country, about this time, were very gloomy, and especially unfavourable to new plantations. The spring, after a long and severe win-

Book I. 1638.

Plantation covenant at Quinnipiack.

Book I.
1638.

ter, was unusually backward. Scarcely any thing grew, for several weeks. The planting season was so cold that the corn rotted in the ground, and the people were obliged to replant two or three times.* This distressed man and beast, and retarded all the affairs of the plantations. It rendered the gloom and horrors of the wilderness still more horrible. The colonists had terrible apprehensions of scarcity and famine. But at length the warm season came on, and vegetation exceeded all their expectations.

Great earthquake, June 1st.

On the 1st of June, between the hours of three and four in the afternoon, there was a great and memorable earthquake throughout New-England. It came with a report like continued thunder, or the rattling of numerous coaches upon a paved street. The shock was so great that, in many places, the tops of the chimnies were thrown down, and the pewter fell from the shelves. It shook the waters and ships in the harbours, and all the adjacent islands. The duration of the sound and tremor was about four minutes. The earth, at turns, was unquiet for nearly twenty days. The weather was clear, the wind westerly, and the course of the earthquake from west to east.

The planters at Quinnipiack determined to make an extensive settlement; and, if possible, to maintain perpetual peace and friendship with the Indians. They, therefore, paid an early attention to the making of such purchases and amicable treaties, as might most effectually answer their designs.

The first purchase at New-Haven, Nov. 24th, 1638.

On the 24th of November, 1638, Theophilus Eaton, Esq. Mr. Davenport, and other English planters, entered into an agreement with Momauguin, sachem of that part of the country, and his counsellors, respecting the lands. The articles of agreement are to this effect:

That Momauguin is the sole sachem of Quinnipiack, and had an absolute power to aliene and dispose of the same: That, in consequence of the protection which he had tasted, by the English, from the Pequots and Mohawks,† he yielded up all his right, title, and interest to all the land, rivers, ponds, and trees, with all the liberties and appurtenances belonging to the same, unto Theophilus Eaton, John Davenport, and others, their heirs and assigns, for ever. He covenanted, that neither he, nor his Indians, would terrify, nor disturb the English, nor injure

* Winthrop's Journal, p. 155. Ibid. See also Morton and Hutchinson.
† The Indians of Quinnipiack, in this treaty, declared, that they still remembered the heavy taxes of the Pequots and Mohawks; and that, by reason of their fear of them, they could not stay in their own country, but had been obliged to flee. By these powerful enemies, they had been reduced to about forty men.

CHAP. VI.   CONNECTICUT.   99

them in any of their interests; but that, in every respect, they would keep true faith with them.

The English covenanted to protect Momauguin and his Indians, when unreasonably assaulted and terrified by other Indians; and that they should always have a sufficient quantity of land to plant on, upon the east side of the harbour,* between that and Saybrook fort. They also covenanted, that by way of free and thankful retribution, they gave unto the said sachem, and his council and company, twelve coats of English cloth, twelve alchymy spoons, twelve hatchets, twelve hoes, two dozen of knives, twelve porringers, and four cases of French knives and scissors.†

This agreement was signed and legally executed, by Momauguin and his council on the one part, and Theophilus Eaton and John Davenport on the other. Thomas Stanton, who was the interpreter, declared in the presence of God, that he had faithfully acquainted the Indians with the said articles, and returned their answers.

In December following, they made another purchase of a large tract, which lay principally north of the former. This was of Montowese, son of the great sachem at Mattabeseck. This tract was ten miles in length, north and south, and thirteen miles in breadth. It extended eight miles east of the river Quinnipiack, and five miles west of it towards Hudson's river. It included all the lands within the ancient limits of the old towns of New-Haven, Branford, and Wallingford, and almost the whole contained in the present limits of those towns, and of the towns of East-Haven, Woodbridge, Cheshire, Hamden, and North-Haven.‡ These have since been made out of the three old towns.

The New-Haven adventurers were the most opulent company which came into New-England, and they designed to plant a capital colony. They laid out their town plat in squares, designing it for a great and elegant city. In the centre was a large, beautiful square. This was encompassed with others, making nine in the whole.

The first principal settlers were Theophilus Eaton, Esq. Mr. Davenport, Mr. Samuel Eaton, Mr. Thomas Gregson, Mr. Robert Newman, Mr. Matthew Gilbert, Mr. Nathaniel Turner, Mr. Thomas Fugill, Mr. Francis Newman, Mr. Stephen Goodyear, and Mr. Joshua Atwater.

Mr. Eaton had been deputy-governor of the East India

Book I.

1638.

Second purchase, Dec. 11th, 1638.

Tract purchased.

* This was in the present town of East-Haven.
† Records of New-Haven.
‡ For the last tract of ten miles north and south, and thirteen east and west, the English gave thirteen coats, and allowed the Indians ground to plant, and liberty to hunt within the lands. Records of New-Haven.

BOOK I. company, and was three years himself in the East Indies. He served the company so well, that he received from them presents of great value. He had been on an embassy from the court of England to the king of Denmark. He was a London merchant, who had, for many years, traded to the East Indies, had obtained a great estate, and brought over a large sum of money into New-England.† Others were merchants of fair estates, and they designed to have been a great trading city.

1638.

There appears no act of civil, military, or ecclesiastical authority, during the first year; nor is there any appearance, that this colony was ever straitened for bread, as the other colonies had been.

Mr. Prudden, and his company, who came with Mr. Davenport, continued the first summer at Quinnipiack, and were making preparations for the settlement of another township.

When Mr. Davenport removed to Quinnipiack, Mr. Hopkins came to Hartford, and soon after incorporated with the settlers of Connecticut.

The inhabitants of the three towns upon Connecticut river, finding themselves without the limits of the Massachusetts patent, conceived the plan of forming themselves, by voluntary compact, into a distinct commonwealth.

The original constitution of Connecticut, Jan. 14th 1639.

On the 14th of January, 1639,‡ all the free planters convened at Hartford, and, on mature deliberation, adopted a constitution of government. They introduce their constitution, with a declaration to this effect, That for the establishment of order and government, they associated, and conjoined themselves to be one public state or commonwealth; and did, for themselves and successors, and such as should be, at any time, joined to them, confederate together, to maintain the liberty and purity of the gospel, which they professed, and the discipline of the churches, according to its institution; and in all civil affairs, to be governed according to such laws, as should be made agreeably to the constitution, which they were then about to adopt.

Two general assemblies annually.

The constitution, which then follows, ordains, That there shall be, annually, two general courts, or assemblies;

† The tradition is, that he brought to New-Haven a very great estate, in plate and money. The East India company made his wife a present of a bason and ewer, double gilt, and curiously wrought with gold, weighing more than sixty pounds.

‡ This stands on the records of the colony, January 14th, 1638, which is owing to the manner of dating at that time. The first settlers of the colony, began their year on the 25th of March; and until this time, they dated 1638; but it was most evidently 1639, as the December preceding, was 1638, and the April following, 1639.

CHAP. VI.   CONNECTICUT.

one on the second Thursday in April, and the other on the second Thursday in September: That the first, shall be the court of election, in which shall be annually chosen, at least, six magistrates, and all other public officers. It ordains, that a governor should be chosen, distinct from the six magistrates, for one year, and until another should be chosen and sworn: and that the governor and magistrates should be sworn to a faithful execution of the laws of the colony, and in cases in which there was no express law established, to be governed by the divine word. Agreeably to the constitution, the choice of these officers was to be made by the whole body of the freemen, convened in general election. It provided, that all persons, who had been received as members of the several towns, by a majority of the inhabitants, and had taken the oath of fidelity to the commonwealth, should be admitted freemen of the colony. It required, that the governor and magistrates should be elected by ballot; the governor by the greatest number of votes, and the magistrates by a majority. However, it provided, that if it should so happen, at any time, that six should not have a majority, that in such case, those who had the greatest number of suffrages, should stand as duly elected for that year. No person might be governor, unless he were a member of some regular church, and had previously been a magistrate in the colony. Nor could any man be elected to the office, more than once in two years. No one could be chosen into the magistracy who was not a freeman of the colony, and had been nominated, either by the freemen, or the general court. The assembly were authorised to nominate, in cases in which they judged it expedient. Neither the governor, nor magistrates, might execute any part of their office until they had been publicly sworn, in the face of the General Assembly.

The constitution also ordained, that the several towns should send their respective deputies to the election: and that when it was finished, they should proceed to do any public service, as at any other courts: and, that the assembly, in September, should be for the enacting of laws, and other public services. It authorised the governor, either by himself or his secretary, to issue his warrants for calling the assemblies, one month at least, before the time of their appointed meetings. Upon particular emergencies, he might convene them in seventeen days, or even upon shorter notice, stating the reasons in his warrant. Upon the reception of the governor's warrants, in April and September, the constables of the respective towns were obliged to warn all the freemen to elect and send their deputies.

Book I.
1638.
How composed.

Officers how chosen.

Governor and magistrates to be sworn.

Assemblies how convoked.

BOOK I.
1639.
Number of deputies to be sent.

Powers of the house of representatives.

Constables to convoke a general assembly.

The constitution ordained, that the three towns of Windsor, Hartford and Weathersfield, should each of them send four deputies to every general court; and, that the other towns, which should be added to the colony in future, should send such a number as the court should determine, proportionate to the body of their freemen. The constitution declared the deputies to be vested with the whole power of the respective towns which they represented. It authorised them to meet separately, and determine their own elections, to fine any person who should obtrude himself upon them, when he had not been duly chosen, and to fine any of their members for disorderly conduct, when they were assembled.

Further, the constitution provided, that in case the governor and the major part of the magistrates should, upon any urgent occasion, neglect or refuse to call an assembly, the freemen should petition them to summon one; and, if, upon the petition of a major part of the freemen in the colony, they still refused or neglected, then the constables of the several towns should, upon the petition of the major part of the freemen, convoke an assembly. It also ordained, that when this assembly was convened, it should have power of choosing a moderator; and when it was thus formed, should exercise all the powers of any other general assembly. Particularly it was authorised to call any court, magistrate, or any other person before it, and to displace, or inflict penalties according to the nature of the offence.

All general assemblies, called by the governor, were to consist of the governor, four magistrates, and the major part of the deputies. When there was an equal vote, the governor had a casting voice. The constitution also provided, that no general court should be adjourned or dissolved, without the consent of a major part of the members: and that, whenever a tax was laid upon the inhabitants, the sum to be paid by each town should be determined by a committee, consisting of an equal number from each of the respective towns.

The form of oaths to be administered to the governor and magistrates was also adopted in the general convention of the free planters. This, for substance, was the original constitution of Connecticut.*

With such wisdom did our venerable ancestors provide for the freedom and liberties of themselves and their posterity. Thus happily did they guard against every encroachment on the rights of the subject. This, probably,

* Appendix, No. III.

CHAP. VI.   CONNECTICUT.   103

is one of the most free and happy constitutions of civil Book 1.
government which has ever been formed. The formation
of it, at so early a period, when the light of liberty was   1639.
wholly darkened in most parts of the earth, and the rights
of men were so little understood in others, does great hon-
or to their ability, integrity, and love to mankind. To
posterity indeed, it exhibited a most benevolent regard.
It has continued, with little alteration, to the present time.
The happy consequences of it, which, for more than a century and half, the people of Connecticut have experienced,
are without description.

Agreeably to the constitution, the freemen convened at General
Hartford, on the second Thursday in April, and elected Election at
their officers for the year ensuing.   Hartford
                                                              the second
John Haynes, Esq. was chosen governor, and Roger Thursday
Ludlow, George Wyllys, Edward Hopkins, Thomas in April.
Wells, John Webster and William Phelps, Esquires, were
chosen magistrates. Mr. Ludlow, the first of the six magistrates, was deputy governor. Mr. Hopkins was chosen
secretary, and Mr. Wells treasurer.

The deputies sent to this first general assembly, in Con-
necticut, were Mr. John Steele, Mr. Spencer, Mr. John
Pratt, Mr. Edward Stebbins, Mr. Gaylord, Mr. Henry
Wolcott, Mr. Stoughton, Mr. Ford, Mr. Thurston Rayner,
Mr. James Boosy, Mr. George Hubbard, and Mr. Rich-
ard Crab.

The general assembly proceeded as they had leisure, First law,
and as occasion required, to enact a system of laws. The or bill of
laws at first were few, and time was taken to consider and rights.
digest them. The first statute in the Connecticut code is
a kind of declaration, or bill of rights. It ordains, that no
man's life shall be taken away; no man's honor or good
name be stained, no man's person shall be arrested, restrained, banished, dismembered, nor any wise punished:
That no man shall be deprived of his wife or children; no
man's goods or estate shall be taken away from him, nor
any wise endamaged, under colour of law, or countenance
of authority, unless it should be by the virtue of some
express law of the colony warranting the same, established by the general court, and sufficiently published; or in
case of the defect of such law, in any particular case, by
some clear and plain rule of the word of God, in which the
whole court shall concur.† It was also ordained that all
persons in the colony, whether inhabitants or not, should
enjoy the same law and justice without partiality or delay.
These general precepts bore the same aspect, and breath-

† Old code of Connecticut.

Book I.
1639.

ed the same spirit of liberty and safety, with respect to the subjects universally, which is exhibited in the constitution.

The planters of Quinnipiack continued more than a year without any civil or religious constitution, or compact, further than had been expressed in their plantation covenant.

Meanwhile, Mr. Henry Whitfield, William Leet, Esq. Samuel Desborough, Robert Kitchel, William Chittenden and others, who were part of Mr. Davenport's and Mr. Eaton's company, arrived to assist them in their new settlement. These were principally from Kent and Surry, in the vicinity of London. Mr. Whitfield's people, like Mr. Davenport's, followed him into New-England. There were now three ministers, with many of the members of their former churches and congregations, collected in this infant colony, and combined in the same general agreement.

June 4th, 1639, the planters at Quinnipiack, assemble to form a constitution.

On the 4th of June, all the free planters at Quinnipiack convened in a large barn of Mr. Newman's, and, in a very formal and solemn manner, proceeded to lay the foundations of their civil and religious polity.

Mr. Davenport introduced the business, by a sermon from the words of the royal preacher, " Wisdom hath builded her house, she hath hewn out her seven pillars." His design was to show, that the church, the house of God, should be formed of seven pillars, or principal brethren, to whom all the other members of the church should be added. After a solemn invocation of the Divine Majesty, he proceeded to represent to the planters, that they were met to consult respecting the settlement of civil government according to the will of God, and for the nomination of persons, who, by universal consent, were, in all respects the best qualified for the foundation work of a church. He enlarged on the great importance of the transactions before them, and desired, that no man would give his voice, in any matter, until he fully understood it; and, that all would act, without respect to any man, but give their vote in the fear of God. He then proposed a number of questions in consequence of which the following resolutions were passed.

Its fundamental articles.

I. That the scriptures hold forth a perfect rule for the direction and government of all men in all duties which they are to perform to God and men, as well in families and commonwealth, as in matters of the church.

II. That as in matters which concerned the gathering and ordering of a church, so likewise in all public offices

CHAP. VI.   CONNECTICUT.

which concern civil order, as the choice of magistrates and officers, making and repealing laws, dividing allotments of inheritance, and all things of like nature, they would all be governed by those rules, which the scripture held forth to them.

III. "That all those who had desired to be received as free planters, had settled in the plantation, with a purpose, resolution and desire, that they might be admitted into church fellowship according to Christ."

IV. "That all the free planters held themselves bound to establish such civil order as might best conduce to the securing of the purity and peace of the ordinance to themselves and their posterity according to God."

When these resolutions had been passed and the people had bound themselves to settle civil government according to the divine word, Mr. Davenport proceeded to represent unto them what men they must choose for civil rulers according to the divine word, and that they might most effectually secure to them and their posterity a just, free and peaceable government. Time was then given to discuss and deliberate upon what he had proposed. After full discussion and deliberation it was determined—

V. "That church members only should be free burgesses; and that they only should choose magistrates among themselves, to have power of transacting all the public civil affairs of the plantation: Of making and repealing laws, dividing inheritances, deciding of differences that may arise, and doing all things and businesses of like nature."

That civil officers might be chosen and government proceed according to these resolutions, it was necessary that a church should be formed. Without this there could be neither freemen nor magistrates. Mr. Davenport therefore proceeded to make proposals relative to the formation of it, in such a manner, that no blemish might be left on the "beginnings of church work." It was then resolved to this effect,

VI. "That twelve men should be chosen, that their fitness for the foundation work might be tried, and that it should be in the power of those twelve men, to choose seven to begin the church."

It was agreed that if seven men could not be found among the twelve qualified for the foundation work, that such other persons should be taken into the number, upon trial,* as should be judged most suitable.† The form of a solemn

* Appendix No. IV.
† The twelve persons chosen for trial, out of whom the seven pillars of the house were chosen, were Theophilus Eaton, John Davenport, Robert

O

106   HISTORY OF   Chap. VI.

Book I. 1639.

charge, or oath, was drawn up and agreed upon at this meeting to be given to all the freemen.

Further, it was ordered, that all persons, who should be received as free planters of that corporation, should submit to the fundamental agreement above related, and in testimony of their submission should subscribe their names among the freemen.* After a proper term of trial, Theophilus Eaton, Esq. Mr. John Davenport, Robert Newman, Matthew Gilbert, Thomas Fugill, John Punderson and Jeremiah Dixon, were chosen for the seven pillars of the church.

August 22.

General election at Quinnipiack, Oct. 25th, 1639.

October 25th, 1639, the court, as it is termed, consisting of these seven persons only, convened, and after a solemn address to the Supreme Majesty, they proceeded to form the body of freemen and to elect their civil officers. The manner was indeed singular and curious.

Mode of proceeding.

In the first place, all former trust, for managing the public affairs of the plantation, was declared to cease, and be utterly abrogated. Then all those who had been admitted to the church after the gathering of it, in the choice of the seven pillars, and all the members of other approved churches, who desired it, and offered themselves, were admitted members of the court. A solemn charge was then publicly given them, to the same effect as the freemen's charge, or oath, which they had previously adopted. The purport of this was nearly the same with the oath of fidelity, and with the freemen's administered at the present time. Mr. Davenport expounded several scriptures to them, describing the character of civil magistrates given in the sacred oracles. To this succeeded the election of officers. Theophilus Eaton, Esq. was chosen governor, Mr. Robert Newman, Mr. Matthew Gilbert, Mr. Nathaniel Turner, and Mr. Thomas Fugill, were chosen magistrates. Mr. Fugill was also chosen secretary, and Robert Seely, marshal.

Charge to Gov. Eaton.

Mr. Davenport gave governor Eaton a charge in open court, from Deut. i. 16, 17. "And I charged your judges at that time, saying, Hear the causes between your brethren, and judge righteously between every man and his brother, and the stranger that is with him. Ye shall not respect persons in judgment, but ye shall hear the small as well as the great; ye shall not be afraid of the face of man; for the judgment is God's: and the cause that is too hard for you, bring it unto me, and I will hear it."

Newman, Matthew Gilbert, Richard Malbon, Nathaniel Turner, Ezekiel Cheevers, Thomas Fugill, John Punderson, William Andrews and Jeremiah Dixon.

* Sixty-three subscribed on the 4th day of June, and there were added soon after about fifty other names.

It was decreed, by the freemen, that there should be a general court annually, in the plantation, on the last week in October. This was ordained a court of election in 1639, which all the officers of the colony were to be chosen. This court determined, that the word of God should be the only rule for ordering the affairs of government in that commonwealth.

This was the original, fundamental constitution of the government of New-Haven. All government was originally in the church, and the members of the church elected the governor, magistrates, and all other officers. The magistrates, at first, were no more than assistants of the governor, they might not act in any sentence or determination of the court.* No deputy governor was chosen, nor were any laws enacted except the general resolutions which have been noticed ; but as the plantation enlarged, and new towns were settled, new orders were given; the general court received a new form, laws were enacted, and the civil polity of this jurisdiction gradually advanced, in its essential parts, to a near resemblance of the government of Connecticut.

While these affairs were transacted at Quinnipiack, plantations commenced at Wopowage and Menunkatuck. Wopowage was purchased February 12th, 1639,† and Menunkatuck the September following. Both were settled this year. The churches of Mr. Prudden and Mr. Whitfield were both formed upon the plan of Mr. Davenport's; each consisting of seven principal men, or pillars. They appear to have been gathered at the same time. The planters were in the original agreement made in Mr. Newman's barn, on the 4th of June. The principal men, or pillars in the town of Wopowage, were Mr. Peter Prudden, William Fowler, Edmund Tapp, Zechariah Whitman, Thomas Buckingham, Thomas Welch, and John Astwood. The principal planters of Menunkatuck, were Henry Whitfield, Robert Kitchel, William Leet, Samuel Desborough, William Chittenden, John Bishop, and John Caffinge. The lands in Milford and Guilford, as well as in New-Haven, were purchased by these principal men, in trust, for all the inhabitants of the respective towns. Every planter, after paying his proportionable part of the expenses, arising from laying out and settling the plantation, drew a lot or lots of land, in proportion to the money or estate which he had expended in the general purchase, and to the number

Margin notes: Book 1. 1639. Milford and Guilford purchased and settled. Aug. 22d.

---

* Records of the colony of New-Haven.

† On the records it was 1638, but according to the present mode of dating 1639.

Book I. of heads in his family. These principal men were judges in the respective towns, composing a court, to judge between man and man, divide inheritances and punish offences according to the written word, until a body of laws should be established.

1639.

Most of the principal settlers of Milford were from Weathersfield.* They first purchased of the Indians all that tract which lies between New-Haven and Stratford river, and between the sound on the south, and a stream called two mile brook on the north, which is the boundary line between Milford and Derby. This tract comprised all the lands within the old town of Milford, and a small part of the town of Woodbridge. The planters made other purchases which included a large tract on the west side of Stratford river, principally in the town of Huntington. In the first town meeting in Milford, the number of free planters, or of church members, was forty four.

The Indians were so numerous in this plantation, that the English judged it necessary for their own safety, to compass the whole town plat, including nearly a mile square, with a fortification. It was so closely inclosed with strong pallisadoes, as entirely to exclude the Indians, from that part of the town.

The purchasers of Guilford agreed with the Indians, that they should move off from the lands, which they had purchased. According to agreement they soon all removed from the plantation.

The number of the first free planters appears to have been about forty. They were all husbandmen. There was not a merchant, nor scarcely a mechanic among them. It was at great expense and trouble that they obtained even a blacksmith to settle in the plantation. As they were from Surry and Kent, they took much pains to find a tract of land resembling that from which they had removed. They therefore finally pitched upon Guilford, which, toward the sea, where they made the principal settlement, was low, moist, rich land, liberal indeed to the husbandman. Especially the great plain south of the town. This had been already cleared and enriched by the natives. The vast quantities of shells and manure, which, in a course of ages, they had brought upon it from the sea, had contributed much to the natural richness of the soil. There were also nearly adjoining to this, several necks, or points of land, near the sea, clear, rich and fertile, prepared for immediate improvement. These, with the in-

* Mr. Prudden it seems preached at Weathersfield, the summer before the people removed to Milford.

CHAP. VI.   CONNECTICUT.

dustry of the inhabitants, soon afforded them a comfortable subsistence.*

At the same time when these settlements commenced, two new ones were made under the jurisdiction of Connecticut.

Mr. Ludlow, who went with the troops in pursuit of the Pequots, to Sasco,† the great swamp in Fairfield, was so pleased with that fine tract of country, that he soon projected the scheme of a settlement in that part of the colony. This year, he, with a number of others, began a plantation at Unquowa, which was the Indian name of the town. At first there were but about eight or ten families. These, probably, removed from Windsor, with Mr. Ludlow, who was the principal planter. Very soon after, another company came from Watertown and united with Mr. Ludlow and the people from Windsor. A third company removed into the plantation from Concord; so that the inhabitants soon became numerous, and formed themselves into a distinct township, under the jurisdiction of Connecticut. The first adventurers purchased a large tract of land of the natives, and soon after Connecticut obtained charter privileges, the general assembly gave them a patent. The township comprises the four parishes of Fairfield, Green's farms, Greenfield and Reading; and part of the parish of Stratfield. The lands in this tract are excellent, and at an early period the town became wealthy and respectable.

Settlements commenced the same year at Cupheag and Pughquonnuck, since named Stratford. That part which contains the town plat, and lies upon the river, was called Cupheag, and the western part, bordering on Fairfield, Pughquonnuck. It appears that settlements were made in both these places at the same time. Mr. Fairchild, who was a principal planter, and the first gentleman in the town vested with civil authority, came directly from England. Mr. John and Mr. William Curtiss and Mr. Samuel Hawley were from Roxbury, and Mr. Joseph Judson and Mr. Timothy Wilcoxson from Concord, in Massachusetts. These were the first principal gentlemen in the town and church of Stratford. A few years after the settlement commenced, Mr. John Birdseye removed from Milford, and became a man of eminence both in the town and church. There were also several of the chief planters from Boston, and Mr. Samuel Wells, with his three sons, John, Thomas

BOOK I.

1639.

Mr. Ludlow and others settle the Fairfield.

Settlement of Stratford, or Cupheag.

---
* Manuscripts of Mr. Ruggles.
† It has also been called Pequot swamp, on the account of the memorable battle fought in this place with the Pequots.

Book I. and Samuel, from Weathersfield. Mr. Adam Blackman, who had been episcopally ordained in England, and a preacher of some note, first at Leicester, and afterwards in Derbyshire, was their minister, and one of the first planters. It is said, that he was followed by a number of the faithful into this country, to whom he was so dear, that they said to him, in the language of Ruth, "Intreat us not to leave thee, for whither thou goest we will go; thy people shall be our people, and thy God our God." These, doubtless, collected about him in this infant settlement.

1639.

The whole township was purchased of the natives; but, at first, Cupheag and Pughquonnuck only, where the settlements began. The purchase was not completed until 1672. There was a reservation of good lands at Pughquounuck, Golden hill, and another place, called Coram, for the improvement of the Indians.

The town is bounded upon the east by the Housatonick, or Stratford river; on the south by the Sound; by Fairfield on the west; and Newtown on the north. It comprises these four parishes, Stratford, Ripton, North-Stratford and New-Stratford, and a considerable part of Stratfield. The lands in this town, like those in Fairfield, are good, and its situation is exceedingly beautiful and agreeable.

While these plantations were forming in the south-western part of Connecticut, another commenced on the west side of the mouth of Connecticut river. A fort had been built here in 1635 and 1636, and preparations had been made for the reception of gentlemen of quality; but the war with the Pequots, the uncultivated state of the country, and the low condition of the colony, prevented the coming of any principal character from England, to take possession of a township, and make settlements in this tract. Until this time, there had been only a garrison of about twenty men in the place. They had made some small improvement of the lands, and erected a few buildings in the vicinity of the fort; but there had been no settlement of a plantation with civil priviliges. But about midsummer, Mr. George Fenwick, with his lady and family, arrived in a ship of 250 tons. Another ship came in company with him. They were both for Quinnipiack. Mr. Fenwick and others, came over with a view to take possession of a large tract upon the river, in behalf of their lordships, the original patentees, and to plant a town at the mouth of the river. A settlement was soon made, and named Saybrook, in honour to their lordships, Say and Seal and Brook. Mr. Fenwick, Mr. Thomas Peters, who was the first minister

CHAP. VI.   CONNECTICUT.   111

in the plantation, captain Gardiner, Thomas Leffingwell, Thomas Tracy, and captain John Mason, were some of the principal planters. Indeed, the Huntingtons, Baldwins, Reynolds's, Backus's, Bliss's, Watermans, Hydes, Posts, Smiths, and almost all the names afterwards to be found at Norwich, were among the first inhabitants of Saybrook. The government of the town was entirely independent of Connecticut, for nearly ten years, until after the purchase made of Mr. Fenwick, in 1644. It was first taxed by the colony in the October session, 1645; and it appears by the tax imposed, that the proportion of the towns of Hartford, Windsor, and Weathersfield, were to this, as six to one. The plantation did not increase to any considerable degree until about the year 1646, when Mr. James Fitch, a famous young gentleman, was ordained to the pastoral care of the church and congregation; and a considerable number of families from Hartford and Windsor removed and made settlements in the town. Its original boundaries extended eastward five miles beyond the river, and from its mouth northward six miles; including a considerable part of the town of Lyme. Westward they extended to Hammonasset, the Indian name of the tract comprised in the limits of Killingworth, and north eight miles from the sea. Mr. Fenwick and captain* Mason were magistrates, and had the principal government of the town.

Great difficulties had arisen the last year, between the English at Pyquaug, now Weathersfield, and Sowheag and his Indians. It was discovered, that some of the Indians at Pyquaug, under Sowheag, had been aiding the Pequots in the destruction which they had made there the preceding year, and were instrumental of bringing them against the town. Sowheag entertained the murderers, and treated the people of Weathersfield with haughtiness and insult. The court at Connecticut, on hearing the differences, determined, that, as the English at Weathersfield, had been the aggressors, and gave the first provocation, the injuries which Sowheag had done should be forgiven, and that he should, on his good conduct for the future, be restored to their friendship. Mr. Stone and Mr. Goodwin were appointed a committee to compromise all differences with him. However, as Sowheag could not, by any arguments, or fair means, be persuaded to give up the murderers, but continued his outrages against the English, the court, this

Book I. 1637.

Troubles at Weathersfield with the Indians.

Court at Connecticut, Aug. 2d, determines to despatch

* Though captain Mason was appointed major-general of the militia of 100 men to the colony, yet he was always called captain, or major, upon the records; Mattabesek. in conformity to which I have uniformly given him those titles.

BOOK I.
1639.

year, determined, that a hundred men should be sent down to Mattabeseck, to take the delinquents by force of arms. The court ordered, that their friends at Quinnipiack should be certified of this resolution, that they might adopt the measures necessary for the defence of the plantations. It was, also, determined to have their advice and consent in an affair of such general concernment.

New-Haven objects, and dissuades from the design.

Governor Eaton and his council fully approved of the design of bringing the delinquents to condign punishment; but they disapproved of the manner proposed by Connecticut. They feared that it would be introductive to a new Indian war. This they represented would greatly endanger the new settlements, and be many ways injurious and distressing. They wanted peace, all their men and money, to prosecute the design of planting the country. They represented that a new war would not only injure the plantations in these respects, but would prevent the coming over of new planters, whom they expected from England. They were, therefore, determinately against seeking redress by an armed force. Connecticut, through their influence, receded from the resolution which they had formed with respect to Sowheag and Mattabeseck.

Expedition against the Pequots, September.

Nevertheless, as the Pequots had violated their covenant, and planted at Pawcatuck, in the Pequot country, the court dispatched major Mason, with forty men, to drive them off, burn their wigwams, and bring away their corn.* Uncas, with a hundred men and twenty canoes, assisted in the enterprise. When they arrived at Pawcatuck bay, major Mason met with three of the Pequot Indians, and sent them to inform the others of the design of his coming, and what he should do, unless they would peaceably desert the place. They promised to give him an immediate answer, but never returned.

The major sailed up a small river, landed, and beset the wigwams so suddenly, that the Indians were unable to carry off either their corn or treasures. Some of the old men had not time to make their escape. As it was now Indian harvest, he found a great plenty of corn.

Indian fighting.

While Uncas's Indians were plundering the wigwams, about sixty others came rushing down a hill towards them. The Moheagans stood perfectly still, and spake not a word, until they came within about thirty yards of them; then, shouting and yelling, in their terrible manner, they ran to meet them, and fell upon them, striking with bows, and cutting with knives and hatchets, in their mode of fighting. Indeed, it scarcely deserved the name of fighting. It, how-

* Records of Connecticut.

Chap. VI. CONNECTICUT.

ever, afforded something new and amusing to the English, as they were now spectators of an Indian battle. The major made a movement to cut off their retreat, which they perceived, and instantly fled. As it was not desired to kill, or irritate the Indians more than was absolutely necessary, the English made no fire upon them. Seven Indians were taken. They behaved so outrageously, that it was designed to take off their heads; but one Otash, a Narraganset sachem, brother to Miantonimoh, pleaded that they might be spared, because they were his brother's men, who was a friend to the English. He offered to deliver the heads of so many murderers in lieu of them. The English, considering that no blood had been shed, and that the proposal tended both to mercy and peace, granted the request. The Indians were committed to the care of Uncas, until the conditions should be performed.

The light of the next morning no sooner appeared, than the English discovered three hundred Indians in arms, on the opposite side of the creek in which they lay.

Upon this, the soldiers immediately stood to their arms. The Indians were alarmed at the appearance of the English; some fled, and others secreted themselves behind rocks and trees, so that a man of them could not be seen. The English called to them, representing their desire of speaking with them. Numbers of them rose up, and major Mason acquainted them with the Pequots' breach of covenant with the English, as they were not to settle or plant in any part of their country. The Indians replied, that the Pequots were good men, and that they would fight for them, and protect them. Major Mason told them it was not far to the head of the creek; that he would meet them there, and they might try what they could do at fighting. The Indians replied, they would not fight with Englishmen, for they were spirits; but they would fight with Uncas. The major assured them, that he should spend the day in burning wigwams, and carrying off the corn, and they might fight when they had an opportunity. The English beat up their drum, and fired their wigwams, but they dared not to engage them. The English loaded their bark with Indian corn, and the Indians the twenty canoes in which they passed to Pawcatuck, and thirty more, which they took from the Indians there, with kettles, trays, mats, and other Indian luggage, and returned in safety.*

During these transactions in Connecticut, the Dutch, at New-Netherlands, were increasing in numbers and strength. A new governor, William Kieft, a man of ability and en-

Book 1.

1639.

Apprehensions from the Dutch.

* Mason's History.

P

Book I. terprise, had arrived at their seat of government. Kieft had prohibited the English trade at the fort of Good Hope, in Hartford, and protested against the settlement at Quinnipiack.* These circumstances gave some alarm to the English in Connecticut. The court at Hartford appointed a committee to go down to the mouth of the river, to consult with Mr. Fenwick, relative to a general confederation of the colonies, for mutual offence and defence. The deputy-governor, Mr. Ludlow, Mr. Thomas Wells, and Mr. Hooker, went upon this business. They were, also, instructed to confer with Mr. Fenwick, relative to the patent. The court approved of the conduct of the committee, and, with respect to the article of confederation, declared its willingness to enter into a mutual agreement of offence and defence, and of all offices of love between the colonies. Mr. Fenwick was in favour of an union of the New-England colonies. With respect to the patent of the river, it was agreed, that the affair should rest, until the minds of the noblemen and gentlemen particularly interested, could be more fully known.

1639.

Aug. 15th.

Attempts for a general union.

Governor Haynes and Mr. Wells were appointed to repair to Pughquonnuck, and administer the oath of fidelity to the inhabitants; to admit such of them as were qualified to the privileges of freemen; and to appoint officers for the town, both civil and military. They were, also, authorised to invite the freemen to send their deputies to the general courts at Hartford.†

Oct. 10th, towns incorporated.

At an adjourned General Assembly, the court incorporated the several towns in the colonies, vesting them with full powers to transact their own affairs. It was enacted, that they should have power to choose, from among themselves, three, five, or seven of their principal men, to be a court for each town. One of the three, five, or seven, was to be chosen moderator. The major part of them, always including him, constituted a quorum. A casting voice was allowed him, in cases in which there was an equal division. He, or any two of the court, were authorised to summon the parties to appear at the time and place appointed, and might grant execution against the party offending. They were authorised to determine all matters of trespass or debt, not exceeding forty shillings. An appeal might be made from this court, at any time before execution was given out. This court was appointed to sit once in two months.

Town courts instituted.

* Smith's Hist. N. York, p. 2.
† It was not unusual for the General Assembly to fine its members. Mr. Ludlow, the deputy-governor, was fined for absence, and for his conduct at Pughquonnuck. It was, probably, on the account of the displeasure of the court towards him, that this committee were appointed.

CHAP. VI.   CONNECTICUT.   115

It was ordained, that every town should keep a public ledger, in which every man's house and lands, with the boundaries and quantity, according to the nearest estimation, should be recorded. All lands also granted and measured to any man afterwards, and all bargains and mortgages of lands were to be put on record. Until this was done, they were to be of no validity. The towns were, also, empowered to dispose of their own lands. This was the origin of the privileges of particular towns in Connecticut.

Besides the court in each town, there was the court of magistrates, termed the particular court. This held a session once in three months. To this lay all appeals from the other courts. In this were tried all criminal causes and actions of debt, exceeding forty shillings, and all titles of land. Indeed, this court possessed all the authority, and did all the business now possessed and done by the county and superior courts. For a considerable time, they were vested with such discretionary powers, as none of the courts at this day would venture to exercise.

Nepaupuck, a famous Pequot captain, who had frequently stained his hands in English blood, was condemned by the General Court at Quinnipiack, for murder. It appeared, that in the year 1637, he killed John Finch, of Weathersfield, and captivated one of Mr. Swain's daughters. He had also assisted in killing the three men, who were going down Connecticut river in a shallop. His head was cut off, and set upon a pole in the market place.

It will, doubtless, hardly be granted, in this enlightened age, that the subjects of princes, killing men by their orders, in war, ought to be treated as murderers. Though the first planters of New-England and Connecticut were men of eminent piety and strict morals, yet, like other good men, they were subject to misconception and the influence of passion. Their beheading sachems, whom they took in war, killing the male captives, and enslaving the women and children of the Pequots, after it was finished, was treating them with a severity, which, on the benevolent principles of christianity, it will be difficult ever to justify. The executing of all those as murderers, who were active in killing any of the English people, and obliging all the Indian nations to bring in such persons, or their heads, was an act of severity unpractised, at this day, by civilized and christian nations. The decapitation of their enemies, and the setting of their heads upon poles, was a kind of barbarous triumph, too nearly symbolizing with the examples of uncivilized and pagan nations. The further we are remo-

Book I.

1639.

Oct. 30th.

Book I.
1640.

ved from every resemblance of these, and the more deeply we imbibe those divine precepts, "Love your enemies: Whatsoever ye would that men should do unto you, do ye even so to them,"—the greater will be our dignity and happiness.

CHAPTER VII.

The progress of purchase, settlement, and law, in the colonies of Connecticut and New-Haven. The effect of the conquest of the Pequots on the natives, and the manner in which they were treated. Purchases of them. Towns settled. Divisions at Weatherfield occasion the settlement of Stamford. Troubles with the Dutch and Indians. Capital laws of Connecticut. The confederation of the United Colonies. Further troubles with the Indians. Victory of Uncas over the Narragansets, and capture of their sachem. The advice of the commissioners respecting Miantonimoh. His execution. Precautions of the colonies to prevent war. The Dutch, harassed by an Indian war, apply to New-Haven for assistance.

ALTHOUGH the conquest of the Pequots extended the claim of Connecticut to a great proportion of the lands in the settled part of the colony, yet, to remove all grounds of complaint or uneasiness, the English planters made fair purchases of almost the whole tract of country within the settled part of Connecticut.

Claims of the Indians, and the manner in which the English treated them.

After the conquest of the Pequots, in consequence of the covenant made with Uncas, in 1638, and the gift of a hundred Pequots to him, he became important. A considerable number of Indians collected to him, so that he became one of the principal sachems in Connecticut, and even in New-England. At some times he was able to raise four or five hundred warriors. As the Pequots were now conquered, and as he assisted in the conquest, and was a Pequot himself, he laid claim to all that extensive tract called the Mohengan or Pequot country. Indeed, it seems he claimed, and was allowed to sell some part of that tract which was the principal seat of the Pequots. The sachems in other parts of Connecticut, who had been conquered by the Pequots, and made their allies, or tributaries, considered themselves, by the conquest of this haughty nation, as restored to their former rights. They claimed to be independent sovereigns, and to have a title to all the lands which they had at any time before possessed. The planters therefore, to show their justice to the heathen, and to maintain the peace of the country, from time to time, purchased of the respective sachems and their Indians, all the lands which they settled, excepting the towns of New-London, Groton and Stonington, which were considered as the peculiar seat of the Pequot nation. The inhabitants of Windsor, Hartford, and Weathersfield, either at the time of their settlement, or soon after, bought all those extensive tracts, which they settled, of the native, original proprietors of the country. Indeed, Connecticut planters generally made repeated purchases of their lands. The colony not only bought the Moheagan country of Uncas, but afterwards all the particular towns were purchased again, either of him or his successors, when the settlements in them commenced. Besides, the colony was often obliged to renew its leagues with Uncas and his successors, the Moheagan sachems; and to make new presents and take new deeds, to keep friendship with the Indians and preserve the peace of the country. The colony was obliged to defend Uncas from his enemies, which was an occasion of no small trouble and expense. The laws obliged the inhabitants of the several towns to reserve unto the natives a sufficient quantity of planting ground. They were allowed to hunt and fish upon all the lands no less than the English.

The colonies made laws for their protection from insult, fraud and violence.* The inhabitants suffered them to erect wigwams, and to live on the very lands which they had purchased of them; and to cut their fire wood on their uninclosed lands, for more than a whole century, after the settlements began. The lands, therefore, though really worth nothing at that time, cost the planters very considerable sums, besides the purchase of their patents and the right of pre-emption.

In purchasing the lands and making settlements, in a wilderness, the first planters of Connecticut expended great estates. It has been the opinion of the best judges, who have had the most perfect acquaintance with the ancient affairs of the colony, that many of the adventurers expended more, in making settlements in Connecticut, than all the lands and buildings were worth, after all the improvements which they had made upon them.†

---

* These facts are fully ascertained by the records of the colonies, and of the respective towns.
† This was the general opinion among men of extensive knowledge, in

Book I.
1640.
Election at Hartford.

At the general election in Connecticut, this year, Mr. Hopkins was chosen governor, and Mr. Haynes deputy governor. Mr. Ludlow was chosen magistrate in the place of Mr. Hopkins. The other magistrates were the same who were elected the last year. The same governor, deputy governor and magistrates, who were in office, at New-Haven, the last year, were re-elected for this.

As the colonists, both in Connecticut and New-Haven, were the patentees of Lord Say and Seal, Lord Brook and the other gentlemen interested in the old Connecticut patent, and as that patent covered a large tract of country, both colonies were desirous of securing the native title to the lands, with all convenient dispatch. Several large purchases were made this year both by Connecticut and New-Haven.

Connecticut made presents to Uncas, the Moheagan sachem, to his satisfaction, and on the 1st of September 1640, obtained of him a clear and ample deed of all his lands in Connecticut, except the lands which were then planted. These he reserved for himself and the Moheagans.

The same year, governor Haynes, in behalf of Hartford, made a purchase of Tunxis, including the towns of Farmington and Southington, and extending westward as far as the Mohawk country.

The people of Connecticut, about the same time, purchased Waranoke and soon began a plantation there, since called Westfield. Governor Hopkins erected a trading house and had a considerable interest in the plantation.

Mr. Ludlow made a purchase of the eastern part of Norwalk, between Saugatuck and Norwalk rivers. Captain Patrick bought the middle part of the town. A few families seem to have planted themselves in the town about the time of these purchases, but it was not properly settled until about the year 1651. The planters then made a purchase of the western part of the town.*

About the same time Robert Feaks and Daniel Patrick bought Greenwich. The purchase was made in behalf of New-Haven, but through the intrigue of the Dutch governor, and the treachery of the purchasers, the first inhabitants revolted to the Dutch. They were incorporated and vested with town privileges by Peter Stuyvesant, gov-

Massachusetts, as well as in Connecticut. Governor Hutchinson, in a manuscript which he wrote against the stamp act, observed, that land in New-England, at the time of its settlement, was of no value.
* The first purchases were of the sachem, Mamechimoh. Mr. Ludlow's deed bears date Feb. 26th, 1640, and Capt. Patrick's April 20th, 1640. The western purchase was of a sachem called Buckingkeage. It hence appears that there were two sachems in this town.

CHAP. VII. CONNECTICUT.

ernor of New-Netherlands. The inhabitants were driven off by the Indians, in their war with the Dutch; and made no great progress in the settlement until after Connecticut obtained the charter, and they were taken under the jurisdiction of this colony.

Captain Howe and other Englishmen, in behalf of Connecticut, purchased a large tract of the Indians, the original proprietors, on Long-Island. This tract extended from the eastern part of Oyster bay to the western part of Howe's or Holmes's bay to the middle of the great plain. It lay on the northern part of the island and extended southward about half its breadth. Settlements were immediately begun upon the lands; and by the year 1642, had made considerable advancement.

New-Haven made a purchase of all the lands at Rippowams. This purchase was made of Ponus and Toquamske, the two sachems of that tract, which contained the whole town of Stamford. A reservation of planting ground was made for the Indians.†

Another large purchase, sufficient for a number of plantations, was made by captain Turner, agent for New-Haven, on both sides of Delaware bay or river. This purchase was made with a view to trade, and for the settlement of churches in gospel order and purity. The colony of New-Haven erected trading houses upon the lands, and sent nearly fifty families to make settlements upon them. The settlements were made under the jurisdiction of New-Haven, and in close combination with that colony in all their fundamental articles.

It also appears, that New-Haven, or their confederates, purchased and settled Yennycock, Southhold, on Long-Island. Mr. John Youngs, who had been a minister at Hingham in England, came over, with a considerable part of his church, and here fixed his residence. He gathered his church anew, on the 21st of October, and the planters united themselves with New-Haven. However, they soon departed from the rule of appointing none to office, or of admitting none to be freemen, but members of the church. New-Haven insisted on this as a fundamental article of their constitution. They were, therefore, for a number of years, obliged to conform to this law of the jurisdiction. Some of the principal men were the Reverend Mr. Youngs, Mr. William Wells, Mr. Barnabas Horton, Thomas Mapes, John Tuthill and Matthias Corwin.

Laws were enacted, both by Connecticut and New-Ha-

Book I.
1640.

Purchases of New-Haven.

† The purchase was made by captain Nathaniel Turner, agent for New-Haven. It cost about thirty pounds sterling.

BOOK I. ven, prohibiting all purchases of the Indians, by private persons, or companies, without the consent of their res-
1640. pective general courts. These were to authorize and direct the manner of every purchase.

Sept. 5th. The general court, at New-Haven, this year, made a grant of Totoket to Mr. Samuel Eaton, brother of governor Eaton, upon condition of his procuring a number of his friends, from England, to make a settlement in that tract of country.

At this court it was decreed, that the plantation at Quinnipiack should be called New-Haven.

General election at Hartford, April 6, 1641. At the general election, this year, at Hartford, John Haynes, Esq. was chosen governor, and George Wyllys, Esq. deputy governor. Mr. Hopkins was chosen magistrate, and the other principal officers were re-elected.

Divisions at Weathersfield. The brethren of the church at Weathersfield removed without their pastor, the Rev. Mr. Phillips; and, having no settled minister at first, fell into unhappy contentions and animosities. These continued for a number of years, and divided the inhabitants of the town, as well as the brethren of the church. They were the means of scattering the inhabitants, and of the formation of new settlements and churches in other places. Great pains were taken, by the ministers on the river, to compose the differences and unite the church and town; but they were unable to effect an union. Mr. Davenport and some of the brethren of the church at New-Haven were sent for, to advise and attempt a reconciliation. Mr. Davenport and his brethren gave advice somewhat different from that which had been given by the ministers and churches on the river; and, it seems, suggested the expediency of one of the parties removing and making a new settlement, if they could not by any means be united among themselves. Some were pleased with the advice, others disliked it, and the parties could not agree which of them should remove. The church, which consisted of seven members only, was divided three against four. The three claimed to be the church, and therefore pleaded, that they ought not to remove. The four, as they were the majority, insisted that it was their right to stay.

The church at Watertown, as they had not dismissed their brethren, at Weathersfield, from their watch, judged it their duty to make them a visit, and to attempt to heal the divisions which had sprung up among them. For this benevolent purpose, several of the brethren made a journey to Connecticut; but they succeeded no better in their endeavours, than those who had been before them. It now appeared to be the opinion, that it was expedient for one of the parties to remove, but it could not be agreed which of them should be obliged again to make a new settlement. At length a number of principal men, who were the most pleased with the advice of Mr. Davenport and the New-Haven brethren, and to whom the government of that colony was most agreeable, determined to remove, and settle in combination with New-Haven.

Therefore, on the 30th of October, 1640, Mr. Andrew Ward and Mr. Robert Coe of Weathersfield, in behalf of themselves and about twenty other planters, purchased Rippowams of New-Haven. The whole number obliged themselves to remove, with their families, the next year, before the last of November. This spring the settlement commenced. The principal planters were the Rev. Mr. Richard Denton, Mr. Matthew Mitchel, Mr. Thurston Rayner, Mr. Andrew Ward, Mr. Robert Coe, and Mr. Richard Gildersleve. Mr. Denton was among the first planters of the town, and continued their minister about three or four years. After that time he removed with part of his church and congregation to Hempsted. They settled that town about the year 1643 or 1644.

At the general election, this year, in New-Haven, Theophilus Eaton, Esq. was chosen governor, and Mr. Stephen Goodyear, deputy governor. The magistrates were Mr. Gregson, Mr. Robert Newman, Mr. Matthew Gilbert and Mr. Wakeman. Thomas Fugill was appointed secretary, and Mr. Gregson treasurer.

Upon the general election, this year, at Hartford, there was a considerable change, with respect to civil officers. George Wyllys, Esq. was elected governor, and Roger Ludlow, Esq. deputy governor. Eight magistrates were chosen for Connecticut. This is the first instance of more than six. The magistrates were John Haynes, Esq. Mr. Phelps, Mr. Webster, captain Mason, Mr. Wells, Mr. Whiting, Edward Hopkins, Esq. and Mr. William Hopkins.

The Indians were exceedingly troublesome this year. It was suspected, that they were forming a combination for a general war. All trading with them, in arms or any instruments of iron, was expressly prohibited, both by Connecticut and New-Haven. Each colony concerted all measures of defence. A constant watch was kept in all the plantations. Upon the sabbath a strong guard was set at the places of public worship.

At this court, the magistrates were desired to write to the Dutch, and, as far as possible, to prevent their vending

Book I.
1641.

Election at New-Haven, Oct. 27, 1641.

1642. Election at Hartford.

The Indians are troublesome.

Damages by the Dutch.

ing arms and ammunition to the natives, and to settle all disputes between them and the colony with respect to claims. But notwithstanding all their endeavours, the Dutch behaved with great insolence, and did much damage to both the English colonies.

The Dutch, at Hartford, gave entertainment to fugitives from the English; helped them when confined to file off their irons; and persuaded servants to run from their masters and then gave them entertainment. They purchased goods which had been stolen from the English, and would not return them. They also assisted criminals in breaking gaol.

Besides these misdemeanors, at Hartford, the Dutch governor, William Kieft, caused the English settlements on Long-Island, which had now advanced, on the lands purchased by captain Howe, as far as Oyster bay, to be broken up. Some of the English planters were forcibly seized and imprisoned, and others driven from their settlements. These were injuries done to Connecticut.

To the colony of New-Haven the Dutch were still more hostile and injurious. Notwithstanding the fair purchases which that colony had made, by their agents at Delaware, governor Kieft, without any legal protest or warning, dispatched an armed force, and with great hostility, burned the English trading houses, violently seized and for a time detained their goods, and would not give them time to take an inventory of them. The Dutch also took the company's boat, and a number of the English planters, and kept them as prisoners. The damages done the English at Delaware, were estimated at a thousand pounds sterling.*

The same year the Swedish governor and Dutch agent uniting in a crafty design against Mr. Lamberton, a principal gentleman of New-Haven, made an injurious attempt upon his life. They accused him of having joined in a plot with the Indians to cut off the Swedes and Dutch. They attempted, by giving his men strong drink, and by threatenings and allurements, to influence them to bear testimony against him. They proceeded so far as to imprison and try him for treason. When, notwithstanding these unfair means, and that they were both his accusers and judges, they could not find any evidence against him, they arbitrarily imposed a fine upon him, for trading at Delaware, though within the limits of the purchase and jurisdiction of New-Haven.

At another time, when Mr. Lamberton was occasional-

* Records of the united colonies, and Smith's history of New-York, p. 4.

CHAP. VII.   CONNECTICUT.

ly at Manhatoes, in the capacity of an agent for New-Haven, the Dutch governor, Kieft, by force and threatenings, compelled him to give an account of all his beaver, within the limits of New-Haven, at Delaware, and to pay an impost upon the whole. The Dutch did other damages, and insulted the English in various other instances. Both Connecticut and New-Haven, from year to year, complained and remonstrated against them, but could obtain no redress.

Book I.

1642.

While the colonies were increasing in numbers and settlements, progress in law and jurisprudence, in the regular establishment of courts and the times of their sessions, was also necessary, for the advancement, order and happiness of the respective jurisdictions.

This, so far as the numerous affairs of the colonies would permit, was an object of special attention. The capital laws of Connecticut were, this year, nearly completed, and put upon record. The several passages of scripture on which they were founded were particularly noticed in the statute. They were twelve in number, and to the following effect.

If any man or woman shall have or worship any God, but the true God, he shall be put to death. Deut. xiii. 6. xvii. 21. Exodus xxii. 2.

Capital laws of Connecticut, April 2, 1642.

If any person in this colony shall blaspheme the name of God the Father, Son or Holy Ghost, with direct, express, presumptuous or high-handed blasphemy, or shall curse in like manner, he shall be put to death. Levit. xxiv. 15, 16.

If any man or woman be a witch, that is, hath or consulteth with a familiar spirit, they shall be put to death. Exodus xxii. 18. Levit. xx. 22. Deut. xviii. 10, 11.

If any person shall commit wilful murder, upon malice, hatred or cruelty, not in a man's own defence, nor by casualty against his will, he shall be put to death. Exodus xxi. 12, 13, 14. Numb. xxxv. 30, 31.

If any person shall slay another through guile, either by poisoning, or other such devilish practices, he shall be put to death. Exodus xxi. 14.

If any man or woman shall lie with any beast or brute creature, by carnal copulation, they shall surely be put to death, and the beast shall be slain and buried. Leviticus xx. 15, 16.

If any man lieth with mankind, as he lieth with a woman, both of them have committed abomination; they both shall surely be put to death, except it appear that one of the parties was forced, or under fifteen years of age. Levit. xx. 13.

Book I. If any man lie with his mother, or father's wife, or wife's mother, his daughter, or daughter in law, having carnal copulation with them, both of them have committed abomination; they shall be put to death, except it appear, that the woman was forced, or under fourteen years of age. Levit. xx. 11, 12, 14, and xviii. 7, 8.

1642.

If any man shall forcibly ravish any maid, or woman, by carnal copulation, against her consent, he shall be put to death, provided prosecution and complaint be made forthwith upon the rape. Deut. xxii. 25.

If any man steal a man, or mankind, and selleth him, or he be found in his hand, he shall be put to death. Exodus xxi. 16.

If any person rise up by false witness, wittingly, and of purpose, to take away man's life, he or she shall be put to death. Deut. xix. 16, 18, 19.

It was also enacted, that if any person should conspire against the commonwealth, attempt an insurrection, invasion, or rebellion against it, he should be put to death.

Wilful arson, the cursing and smiting of father or mother, and notorious stubbornness in children, after a certain age, were, soon after, made capital offences, by the laws of the colony, and added to the list of the capital laws.*

Before this time, unchastity between single persons, and wanton behaviour, had been punished with whipping at the tail of the cart, by fining, or obliging the delinquents to marry, at the discretion of the particular courts.

The general court approved of what the particular courts had done, in these cases, and authorised them, in future, to punish such delinquents by fines, by committing them to the house of correction, or by corporal punishment, at the discretion of the court.

As some loose persons deserted the English settlements, and lived in a profane, heathenish manner, a law was enacted, that all persons who should be convicted of this crime, should be punished with three years imprisonment, at least, in the house of correction, with fine, or corporal punishment, as the particular court should direct.†

General court at New-Haven, April 5, 1643.

At a general court in New-Haven, April 5, 1643, considerable progress was made in the laws and government of that colony. Deputies were admitted to the court, and an addition was made to the number of magistrates. Stamford, for the first time, sent captain John Underhill, and Mr. Richard Gildersleve, to represent the town. Mr.

---

* Records of Connecticut, and the old Connecticut code.
† Records of Connecticut. When the Connecticut laws were printed, in 1672, this law was altered, and the term reduced from three, to one year's imprisonment.

Mitchel and Mr. Rayner were nominated for magistrates in Stamford. Mr. Rayner was appointed by the court. Captain Underhill, Mr. Mitchel, Mr. Andrew Ward, and Mr. Robert Coe were appointed assistant judges to Mr. Rayner. This court was vested with the same powers as the court at New-Haven, and was the first instituted in Stamford. Mr. William Leet and Mr. Desborough were admitted magistrates for Menunkatuck, and that plantation was named Guilford. *(Book I. 1643.)*

This year John Haynes, Esq. was elected governor, and Mr. Hopkins deputy governor. Mr. Wolcott and Mr. Swain were chosen magistrates; and Mr. Phelps and Mr. William Hopkins were not elected.* Mr. Whiting was chosen treasurer and Mr. Wells secretary. It appears to have been customary, for a number of years, to choose the secretary and treasurer among the magistrates. *(General election at Hartford, April 13, 1643.)*

Juries appear to have attended the particular courts, in Connecticut, from their first institution. They seem to have been regularly enrolled about the year 1641, or 1642. But the particular courts found great difficulties with respect to their proceedings. There were no printed laws for the inhabitants to study, and many of the common people had attended very little to law and evidence. The jury therefore, very often, would be so divided, that they could not agree upon any verdict; and when they were agreed, it did not always appear to the court that they brought in a just one. A pretty extraordinary law therefore passed this court, regulating the juries. The court decreed, that the jury should attend diligently to the case, and to the evidence, and if they could not all agree in a verdict, they should offer their reasons upon the case to the court, and the court should answer them, and send out the jury again. If, after deliberating upon the case, they could not bring in a joint verdict, it was decreed, that it should be determined by a major vote; and that this should, to all intents and purposes, be deemed a full and sufficient verdict; upon which judgment should be entered, and execution, and all other proceedings should be as though there had been a joint verdict of the jury. It was also provided, that if the jury should be equally divided, six and six, they should represent the case to the court, with their reasons, and a special verdict should be drawn, and a major vote of the court, or magistrates, should determine the cause, and *(An act respecting juries.)*

* Mr. Phelps, I suppose, was now dead, as he appears no more upon the records. He was one of the principal planters of Windsor, and chosen into the magistracy from the first settlement of Connecticut. He appears to have been the ancestor of the Phelpses in this state.

all matters respecting it should be as though there had been a joint verdict of the jury.*

1643. Grand jury to attend the courts.

At this court, it was ordained, that a grand jury of twelve men should attend the particular courts, annually, in May and September, and as often as the governor and court should judge expedient. It was also enacted, that the grand jury should be warned to give their attendance. This is the first notice of a grand jury, at any court.

Proposals for a general union of the N. England colonies.

A general confederation of the New-England colonies, had been proposed, and in agitation for several years. In 1638, articles of union, for amity, offence and defence, mutual advice and assistance, upon all necessary occasions, were drawn, and for further consideration, referred to 1639. Connecticut and Mr. Fenwick agreed to confederate for these purposes. From this time, Connecticut had annually appointed some of her principal men, to go into the Massachusetts, to complete the designed confederacy. Governor Haynes and Mr. Hooker, in 1639, were nearly a month in Massachusetts, laboring to carry it into effect. New-Haven paid equal attention to an affair so important to the colonies. The circumstances of the English nation, and the state of the colonies in New-England, at this time, made it a matter of urgent necessity. For the accommodation of particular companies, the colonies had extended their settlements upon the rivers and sea coasts much farther, and had made them in a more scattering manner, than was at first designed. No aid could be expected from the parent country, let emergencies be ever so pressing. The Dutch had so extended their claims, and were so powerful and hostile, as to afford a just ground of general alarm. All the plantations were compassed with numerous tribes of savage men. The Narragansets appeared hostile, and there were the appearances of a general combination, among the Indians, in New-England, to extirpate the English colonies. There were, notwithstanding, impediments in the way of effecting even so necessary and important an union. The Massachusetts was much more numerous and powerful, than the other colonies. It was in various respects more respectable and important. It was, therefore, a matter of difficulty, to form an union upon equal terms. The other colonies were not willing to unite upon such as were unequal. There were also disputes between Connecticut and Massachusetts. The colony of Massachusetts claimed part of the Pequot country, on the account of the assistance which they afforded in the Pequot war. There was also a difference with respect to

Reasons for the union.

* Records of Connecticut.

the boundary line between Massachusetts and Connecticut. Both colonies claimed the towns of Springfield and Westfield. These difficulties retarded the union.

However, Connecticut, New-Haven, and Plymouth, all dispatched commissioners to Boston, in May, at the time of the session of the General Court. The commissioners from Connecticut were, Governor Haynes and Mr. Hopkins; Mr. Fenwick, from Saybrook; Governor Eaton and Mr. Gregson, from New-Haven; Mr. Winslow and Mr. Collier, from Plymouth. The general court of Massachusetts appointed Governor Winthrop, Mr. Dudley, and Mr. Bradstreet, of the magistrates, and of the deputies, Mr. Hawthorne, Mr. Gibbons, and Mr. Tyng. There appeared, at this time, a spirit of harmony and mutual condescension among the commissioners, and on the 19th of May, 1643, the articles were completed and signed. The commissioners were unanimous in adopting them; but those from Plymouth did not sign them, as they had not been authorised by the court. At the meeting of the commissioners in September, they came vested with plenary powers, and signed them.

The commissioners, in the introductory part, declare, with respect to the four colonies of Massachusetts, Plymouth, Connecticut, and New-Haven, and the plantations under their respective jurisdictions, that, as they all came into these parts of America with one and the same end and aim, to advance the kingdom of our Lord Jesus Christ, and enjoy the liberties of the gospel in purity and peace, they conceived it their bounden duty to enter into a present confederation among themselves, for mutual help and strength in all future concernments; that, as in nation and religion, so in other respects they be and continue one, and henceforth be called by the name of THE UNITED COLONIES OF NEW-ENGLAND.

They declare, that the said united colonies, for themselves and their posterity, did, jointly and severally, enter into a firm and perpetual league of friendship and amity, of offence and defence, mutual aid and succour, upon all just occasions, both for preserving and propagating the truth and liberty of the gospel, and for their own mutual safety and welfare.

The articles reserved to each colony an entire and distinct jurisdiction. By them, no two colonies might be united in one, nor any other colony be received into the confederacy, without the consent of the whole.

Each colony was authorised to send two commissioners annually, always to be church members, to meet on the

Book I.
1643.

first Monday in September, first at Boston, then at Hartford, New-Haven, and Plymouth. This was to be the annual order, except that two meetings successively were always to be at Boston.

The commissioners, when met, were authorised to choose a president from among themselves, for the preservation of order. They were vested with plenary powers for making war and peace, laws and rules of a civil nature and of general concern. Especially, to regulate the conduct of the inhabitants towards the Indians, towards fugitives, for the general defence of the country, and for the encouragement and support of religion.

The expense of all wars, offensive or defensive, was to be borne in proportion to the number of the male inhabitants in each colony, between sixteen and sixty years of age.

Upon notice from three magistrates of any of the colonies of an invasion, the colonies were immediately to send assistance, the Massachusetts a hundred, and each of the other colonies forty-five men. If a greater number was necessary, the commissioners were to meet and determine the number.

All determinations of the commissioners, in which six were agreed, were binding upon the whole. If there were a majority, yet under six, the affair was to be referred to the general court of each colony, and could not be obligatory, unless the courts unanimously concurred.

No colony might engage in a war, without the consent of the whole union, unless upon some urgent and sudden occasion. Even in such case, it was to be avoided as far as possible, consistent with the general safety.

If a meeting were summoned, upon any extraordinary occasion, and the whole number of commissioners did not attend, any four who were met, might, in cases which admitted of no delay, determine upon a war, and send to each colony for its proportion of men. A number, however, less than six could not determine the justice of a war, nor have power to settle a bill of charges, nor make levies.

If either of the confederates should break any article of the confederation, or injure one of the other colonies, the affair was to be determined by the commissioners of the three other confederates.

The articles also made provision, that all servants running from their masters, and criminals flying from justice, from one colony to another, should, upon demand, and proper evidence of their character, as fugitives, be returned to their masters, and to the colonies whence they had made

CHAP. VII.   CONNECTICUT.

their escape; that, in all cases, law and justice might have their course.

This was an union of the highest consequence to the New-England colonies. It made them formidable to the Dutch and Indians, and respectable among their French neighbours. It was happily adapted to maintain a general harmony among themselves, and to secure the peace and rights of the country. It was one of the principal means of the preservation of the colonies, during the civil wars and unsettled state of affairs in England. It was the grand source of mutual defence in Philip's war, and of the most eminent service in civilizing the Indians, and propagating the gospel among them. The union subsisted more than forty years, until the abrogation of the charters of the New-England colonies, by king James the second.

This union was very seasonable. The Indians were so tumultuous and hostile, that its whole influence was necessary to prevent a general war. The troubles originated in the ambitious and perfidious conduct of Miantonimoh, chief sachem of the Narragansets. After the Pequot war, he attempted to set himself up as universal sachem over all the Indians in New-England. The old grudge and hatred which had subsisted between him and the Pequots, he now suffered to embitter and inflame his rancorous heart against Uncas and the Moheagans. Without any regard to the league made between him, the English, and the Moheagans, at Hartford, in 1638, when the Pequots were divided between him and Uncas, he practised murder and war against him. At the same time, he used all the arts of which he was master, by presents and intrigue, to inflame the Indians, and excite a general insurrection against the English plantations. The Indians, through his influence, had been collecting arms and ammunition. There appeared among them a general preparation for war. The colonists were obliged to keep guards and watch every night, from the setting to the rising of the sun, and to guard their inhabitants from town to town, and from one place to another.

Connecticut was for making war immediately, and sent pressing letters to the court at Boston, urging that a hundred men might be sent to Saybrook fort, to assist against the enemy, as circumstances might require. But the court of Massachusetts pretended to doubt of the facts alledged, and would not consent.

In the mean time Miantonimoh, in prosecution of his bloody designs, hired a Pequot, one of Uncas's men, to kill him. He made an attempt, in the spring, and shot Uncas

Book I.

1643.

The vexatious conduct of Miantonimoh.

Book I.
1643.

through his arm. He then ran off to the Narragansets, reporting, through the Indian towns, that he had killed Uncas. But when it was known that Uncas was not dead, though wounded, Miantonimoh and the Pequot contrived together, and reported that Uncas had cut through his arm with a flint, and then charged the Pequot with shooting him. However, Miantonimoh soon after going to Boston, in company with the Pequot who had wounded Uncas, the governor and magistrates, upon examination, found clear evidence, that the Pequot was guilty of the crime, with which he had been charged. They had designs of apprehending him and sending him to Uncas, that he might be punished; but Miantonimoh pleaded, that he might be suffered to return with him, and promised that he would send him to Uncas. Indeed, he so exculpated himself, and made such fair promises, that they gave up their designs, and permitted them to depart in peace. About two days after, Miantonimoh murdered the Pequot, on his return, that he might make no further discovery of his treacherous conduct.

About the same time much trouble arose from Sequassen, a sachem upon Connecticut river. Several of his men killed a principal Indian belonging to Uncas. He, or some of his warriors, had also waylaid Uncas himself, as he was going down the said river, and shot several arrows at him. Uncas made complaint to the governor and court at Connecticut, of these outrages. Governor Haynes and the court took great pains to make peace between Uncas and Sequassen. Upon hearing their several stories it appeared, that Uncas required, that six of Sequassen's men should be delivered to him, for the murder of his man, because he was a great man. Governor Haynes and the court laboured to dissuade Uncas from his demand of six men for one; and urged him to be satisfied upon Sequassen's delivering up the murderer. At length, with much persuasion and difficulty, Uncas consented to accept of the murderer only. But Sequassen would not agree to deliver him. He was nearly allied to Miantonimoh, and one of his peculiar favorites. Sequassen chose rather to fight, than to make Uncas any compensation, expressing, at the same time, his dependance on Miantonimoh for assistance. It is not improbable, that it was through the influence of Miantonimoh, that he came to this resolution. Uncas and Sequassen fought. Sequassen was overcome. Uncas killed a number of his men and burned his wigwams.

Miantonimoh, without consulting the English, according to agreement, without proclaiming war, or giving Uncas the least information, raised an army of nine hundred, or a thousand men, and marched against him. Uncas's spies discovered the army at some distance and gave him intelligence. He was unprepared, but rallying between four and five hundred of his bravest men, he told them they must by no means suffer Miantonimoh to come into their town; but must go and fight him on his way. Having marched three or four miles, the armies met upon a large plain. When they had advanced within fair bow shot of each other, Uncas had recourse to a stratagem, with which he had previously acquainted his warriors. He desired a parly, and both armies halted in the face of each other. Uncas, gallantly advancing in the front of his men, addressed Miantonimoh to this effect, "You have a number of stout men with you, and so have I with me. It is a great pity that such brave warriors should be killed in a private quarrel between us only. Come like a man, as you profess to be, and let us fight it out. If you kill me, my men shall be yours; but if I kill you, your men shall be mine." Miantonimoh replied, "My men came to fight, and they shall fight." Uncas falling instantly upon the ground, his men discharged a shower of arrows upon the Narragansets; and, without a moment's interval, rushing upon them, in the most furious manner, with their hideous Indian yell, put them immediately to flight. The Moheagans pursued the enemy with the same fury and eagerness with which they commenced the action. The Narragansets were driven down rocks and precipices, and chased like a doe by the huntsman. Among others, Miantonimoh was exceedingly pressed. Some of Uncas's bravest men, who were most light of foot, coming up with him, twitched him back, impeding his flight, and passed him, that Uncas might take him. Uncas was a stout man, and rushing forward, like a lion greedy of his prey, seized him by his shoulder. He knew Uncas, and saw that he was now in the power of the man whom he had hated, and by all means attempted to destroy; but he sat down sullen and spake not a word. Uncas gave the Indian whoop and called up his men, who were behind, to his assistance. The victory was complete. About thirty of the Narragansets were slain, and a much greater number wounded. Among the latter was a brother of Miantonimoh and two sons of Canonicus, a chief sachem of the Narraganset Indians. The brother of Miantonimoh was not only wounded, but armed with a coat of mail, both which retarded his flight. Two of Miantonimoh's captains, who formerly were Uncas's men, but had treacherously deserted him, discovering his

BOOK I.
1643.

situation, took him and carried him to Uncas, expecting in this way to reconcile themselves to their sachem. But Uncas and his men slew them. Miantonimoh made no request, either for himself or his men; but continued in the same sullen, speechless mood. Uncas, therefore, demanded of him why he would not speak. Said he, "Had you taken me, I should have besought you for my life." Uncas, for the present, spared his life, though he would not ask it, and returned with great triumph to Moheagan, carrying the Narraganset sachem, as an illustrious trophy of his victory.*

The famous Samuel Gorton and his company had purchased lands of Miantonimoh, under the jurisdiction of Massachusetts and Plymouth; and expected to be vindicated in their claims, by him, against those colonies, and against the Massachusetts and Plymouth sachems, who were the original proprietors. Therefore, when the news of Uncas' victory, and of the capture of Miantonimoh, arrived at Providence, they sent to Uncas to deliver Miantonimoh, threatening him that the power of the English should be employed against him, if he refused a compliance.

Uncas carries him to Hartford, and advises with the governor.

Uncas, therefore, carried his prisoner to Hartford, to advise with the governor and magistrates, with respect to his conduct in such a situation.

The governor and magistrates were of the opinion that, as there was no open war between them and the Narragansets, it was not prudent for them to intermeddle with the quarrel; but advised, that the whole affair should be referred to the commissioners of the united colonies at their meeting in September.

Miantonimoh is kept at Hartford.

How long Miantonimoh continued speechless, does not appear; but it is certain, that when he came to Hartford, his mouth was opened. He most earnestly pleaded to be left in the custody of the English. He probably expected more safety and better treatment with them, than with Uncas. Uncas consented to leave him at Hartford, but insisted that he should be kept as his prisoner. He was, therefore, kept under guard at Hartford, until the meeting of the commissioners.

On the 7th of September, the commissioners met at Boston. Governor Winthrop and Thomas Dudley, Esquires,

* This account is taken from a manuscript of Mr. Hyde, of Norwich, from governor Winthrop's Journal, and from the records of the united colonies, in one or other of which, all the facts are ascertained. The manuscript represents Miantonimoh as having 900, and Uncas 600 men. The records of the united colonies represent, that Miantonimoh had 900, or 1000 men, and that Uncas had not half so many. Governor Winthrop's account is essentially the same.

were commissioners for Massachusetts; George Fenwick and Edward Hopkins, Esquires, for Connecticut; and Theophilus Eaton and Thomas Gregson, Esquires, for New-Haven.* Governor Winthrop was chosen President. The whole affair of Uncas and Miantonimoh was laid before the commissioners, and the facts already related were, in their opinion, fully proved; not only his attempts upon the life of Uncas, but that he had been the principal author of inflaming and stirring up the Indians to a general confederacy against all the English plantations. It also appeared that, instead of delivering the Pequot, who had shot Uncas, as he promised in open court, he had murdered him on the road from Boston to Narraganset. It was also affirmed to the commissioners, that the Narragansets had sent for the Mohawks, and that they were come within a day's journey of the English settlements, and were kept back only by the capture of Miantonimoh: That they were waiting for his release, and then would prosecute their designs against the English, or Uncas, or against both, as the Indians should determine. The commissioners, having fully considered the premises, laid the affair before five or six of the principal ministers in Massachusetts, and took their advice relative to the lawfulness and justice of putting him to death. They gave it as their opinion, that he ought to be put to death. The commissioners finally resolved, "That as it was evident that Uncas could not be safe, while Miantonimoh lived; but that, either by secret treachery or open force, his life would be continually in danger, he might justly put such a false and blood-thirsty enemy to death." They determined Uncas should not do it in any of the English plantations, but in his own jurisdiction. At the same time, they advised, that no torture or cruelty, but all mercy and moderation be exercised in the manner of his execution.

Determination of the commissioners concerning Miantonimoh.

The commissioners also determined, that if the Narragansets, or any other Indians, should unjustly assault Uncas, on the account of the execution of Miantonimoh, the English should, upon his desire, assist him against such violence.†

Governor Winthrop writes, "It was clearly discovered to us, that there was a general conspiracy among the Indians, to cut off all the English; and that Miantonimoh was the head and contriver of it: That he was of a turbulent and proud spirit, and would never be at rest: and that he had killed the Pequot contrary to his promise.‡

* The commissioners for Plymouth are not upon record this year. It is probable that they did not arrive until after the commissioners had formed.
† Records of the united colonies. ‡ Winthrop's Journal, p. 305, 306.

BOOK I.
1643.

The commissioners had received intimations, that the Narragansets had it in contemplation to capture one or more of them, with a view to the redemption of Miantonimoh. Their determination respecting his execution, was therefore kept as a profound secret, until after the return of the commissioners of Connecticut and New-Haven, lest it should inflame and engage them, in earnest, to make the attempt.

July 20th, the Dutch wrote to governor Winthrop.

Previously to the meeting of the commissioners, the Dutch governor had written a letter to governor Winthrop, containing high congratulations on the union of the colonies, and at the same time making grievous complaints of Connecticut and New-Haven, as having committed unsufferable injuries against the Dutch, and as having given misinformation respecting them to their agent in Europe. He desired a categorical answer from governor Winthrop, whether he would aid or desert them, that he might know who were his friends, and who were his enemies.

Governor Winthrop's reply.

The governor, after consulting with some few of his council, who were at hand, wrote an answer, in part, to the Dutch governor, reserving to himself one more full, at the session of the general court. He represented his sorrow for the differences which had arisen between the Dutch and his brethren at Hartford, suggesting that they might be settled by arbitrators, either in England, Holland, or America. He observed, that by the articles of confederation, each colony was obliged to seek the safety and welfare of the other colonies, no less than its own. He hoped however, that this would not interrupt the friendship which had subsisted between them and the Dutch. The governor observed, that the controversy at Hartford was for a small piece of land only, which, in so vast a continent as this, was of too little value to make a breach between protestants so related in profession and religion, as the Dutch and English were. He therefore earnestly desired, that each party would carefully avoid all injuries, until the differences between them should be amicably accommodated, by an impartial hearing and adjudication, either in Europe or America.*

The injurious conduct of the Dutch is laid before the commissioners.

The affair was now brought before the commissioners. Governor Eaton and Mr. Gregson complained of the outrages which the Dutch had committed against the persons and property of the English, within the limits of New-Haven, at Delaware, and in other places, and made proof of the injuries of which they complained. The conduct of the Dutch towards Connecticut was also laid before the commissioners, by governor Hopkins and Mr. Fenwick,

* Winthrop's Journal, p. 303, 304, 305.

Upon which the president was directed to write a letter, in the name of the commissioners, to the Dutch governor, stating the particular injuries which the Dutch had done the English colonies, and to demand satisfaction. It was also directed, that, as governor Winthrop had, in part answered the Dutch governor's letter respecting Connecticut, he would now, in further answer to it, particularize the injuries done, both to Connecticut and New-Haven, and demand an answer. He was also authorised to assure the Dutch, that as they would not wrong others, so neither would they desert their confederates in a just cause.†

Book I.
1643.
They demand satisfaction.

The Indians, at this period were beginning to acquire the use of fire arms. The French, Dutch and others, for the sake of gain, were vending them arms and ammunition. The Indians were in such a tumultuous and hostile state, as had the appearance of a general war. The commissioners therefore gave orders, that the militia, in the several colonies, should be frequently trained, and completely furnished with arms and ammunition. All the companies were to be mustered and reviewed four times in a year. It was ordered, that all the towns should prepare magazines, in proportion to the number of their militia.

The commissioners, having given the necessary directions for the execution of Miantonimoh, and for the general safety of the country, dispersed and returned to their respective colonies.

Immediately, upon the return of the commissioners of Connecticut and New-Haven, Uncas, with a competent number of his most trusty men, was ordered to repair forthwith to Hartford. He was made acquainted with the determination of the commissioners, and, receiving his prisoner, marched with him to the spot where he had been taken. At the instant they arrived on the ground, one of Uncas's men, who marched behind Miantonimoh, split his head with a hatchet, killing him at a single stroke. He was probably unacquainted with his fate, and knew not by what means he fell. Uncas cut out a large piece of his shoulder, and ate it in savage triumph. He said, "it was the sweetest meat he ever ate, it made his heart strong."

Execution of Miantonimoh.

The Moheagans, by the order of Uncas, buried him at the place of his execution, and erected a great heap, or pillar, upon his grave. This memorable event gave the place the name of Sachem's Plain.* Two Englishmen were sent with Uncas, to witness that the execution was

† Records of the united colonies.
* Manuscript of Mr. Hyde. This plain is in the eastern part of the town of Norwich.

BOOK I.
1643.

done, and to prevent all torture and cruelty in the manner of its performance. Connecticut and New-Haven, agreeably to the direction of the commissioners, sent a party of soldiers to Moheagan, to defend Uncas against any assault which might be made upon him by the Narragansets, in consequence of the execution of their sachem.

Message to the Narragansets.

Governor Winthrop, at the same time, according to the orders which he had received from the commissioners, dispatched messengers to Canonicus, the Narraganset sachem, and the Narraganset Indians, to certify them, that the English had noticed their perfidy, in violating the league between them and the English, from time to time, notwithstanding the English had treated them with love and integrity. They assured them, that they had discovered their mischievous plots, in joining with Miantonimoh, in purchasing aid of the Indians, and, by gifts, threats, and allurements, exciting them to a confederacy to root out the whole body of the English. They represented to them their treachery in waging war with Uncas, contrary to their express covenant with him, and with the English. They justified the execution of Miantonimoh, by Uncas, as he was his lawful captive, and as he had practised treachery and murder against him and his subjects. They insisted, that it was both just and agreeable to the practice of the Indians in similar cases. It was declared to be necessary for the safety of Uncas, the peace of the country, and even of the Narragansets themselves. While they firmly and fully represented these facts to them, they, in the name of the united colonies, tendered them peace and safety. They assured them, that they would defend Uncas and all their allies, whether English or Indians, in their just rights: that if they desired peace, they would exercise equal care and friendship towards them.†

The commissioners gave orders, that Connecticut should provide for the defence of Uncas against any assault or fury of the Narragansets, or any other Indians.

Election at New-Haven, Oct. 30th.

Upon the general election at New-Haven in October, governor Eaton and Mr. Stephen Goodyear, were re-elected governor and deputy-governor. Mr. William Fowler and Mr. Edward Tapp were elected magistrates for Milford, and Thurston Rayner for Stamford. This year, for the first time, the general court at New-Haven, are distinctly recorded and distinguished by the names of governor, deputy-governor, magistrates, and deputies.

It appears that the plantation at Yennycock, had not fully attended to the fundamental article of admitting none

† Records of the United Colonies.

CHAP. VII.   CONNECTICUT.   137

to be free burgesses, but members of the church. It was, therefore, at this general court, decreed, "That none should be admitted free burgesses in any of the plantations, but such as were members of some approved church in New-England: that such only should have any vote in elections; and that no power for ordering any civil affairs, should be put into the hands of any but such."

Book I. 1643. Progress of law and liberty at New-Haven.

It was enacted, that each town in the jurisdiction should choose their own judges, in ordinary cases. They were authorised to judge in civil cases, not exceeding twenty shillings, and in criminal cases, in which the punishment did not exceed setting the delinquent in the stocks, whipping him, or fining not exceeding five pounds. If there were a magistrate, or magistrates, in the towns in which these town courts were holden, then the magistrate, or magistrates, were to sit in the court, and judgment was to be given with a due respect to their advice. From these courts, there was liberty of appeal to the court of magistrates.

Plantation courts.

It was granted, that all the free burgesses in the plantations, should vote in the choice of governors, magistrates, secretary, and treasurer. It was also granted, that each town should have a magistrate, if they desired it, chosen from among their own free burgesses.

Privileges of freemen.

At this general court, a court of magistrates was appointed, consisting of all the magistrates in the jurisdiction. They were to meet twice, annually, at New-Haven, on the Mondays preceding the general courts in April and October. This court was authorised to receive appeals from the plantation courts, and to try all important causes, civil and criminal. Every magistrate was obliged, on penalty of a fine, to give his attendance. Four magistrates constituted a quorum. All judgments of the court were to be determined by a major vote. All trials were decided by the bench. It does not appear that juries were ever used in the colony of New-Haven.

Court of magistrates instituted.

The court enacted, that there should be two general courts for this colony, to meet at New-Haven, on the first Wednesday in April, and the last in October, annually. It was decreed, that the general court should consist of a deputy-governor, magistrates, and two deputies from each town. In the last of these general courts, a governor, deputy-governor, magistrates, secretary, treasurer, and marshal, or high sheriff, were to be annually chosen. The governor, or, in his absence, the deputy-governor, had power to call a general court, upon pressing emergencies, and whenever it might be necessary. All the members

Act respecting the general courts.

S

BOOK I.
1643.
General court to provide for the purity of religion.

were obliged to attend, upon penalty of twenty shillings fine, in case of default. It was ordained, that in this court should subsist the supreme power of the commonwealth.

It was particularly ordained, that the general court should, with all care and diligence, endeavour to maintain the purity of religion, and to suppress all irreligion, according to the best light they could obtain from the divine oracles, and by the advice of the elders and churches in the jurisdiction, so far as it might concern the civil power.*

The Dutch apply to New-Haven for help against the Indians.

The Dutch were this year exceedingly harassed and distressed by the Indians, and made application to governor Eaton and the general court, soliciting that a hundred men might be raised in the plantations, for their assistance against such barbarous enemies.

Occasion of the war between the Dutch and Indians.

The war between the Dutch and Indians began in this manner. A drunken Indian, in his intoxication, killed a Dutchman. The Dutch demanded the murderer, but he was not to be found. They then made application to their governor to avenge the murder. He, judging it would be unjust or unsafe, considering the numbers of the Indians, and the weak and scattered state of the Dutch settlements, neglected to comply with their repeated solicitations. In the mean time the Mohawks, as the report was, excited by the Dutch, fell suddenly on the Indians, in the vicinity of the Dutch settlements, and killed nearly thirty of them. Others fled to the Dutch for protection. One Marine, a Dutch captain, getting intelligence of their state, made application to the Dutch governor, and obtained a commission to kill as many of them as it should be in his power. Collecting a company of armed men, he fell suddenly upon the Indians, while they were unapprehensive of danger, and made a promiscuous slaughter of men, women and children, to the number of seventy or eighty. This instantly roused the Indians, in that part of the country, to a furious, obstinate and bloody war. In the spring, and beginning of the summer, they burnt the Dutch out-houses; and driving their cattle into their barns, they burned the barns and cattle together. They killed twenty or more of the Dutch people, and pressed so hard upon them that they were obliged to take refuge in their fort, and to seek help of the English. The Indians upon Long-Island united in the war with those on the main, and burned the Dutch houses and barns. The Dutch governor in this situation, invited captain Underhill from Stamford to assist him in the war. Marine, the Dutch captain, was so exasperated

* Records of New-Haven, fol. vol. i. p. 73, 74, 75.

with this proceeding that he presented his pistol at the governor, and would have shot him, but was prevented by one who stood by him. Upon this one of Marine's tenants discharged his musket at the governor, and the ball but just missed him. The governor's sentinel shot the tenant and killed him on the spot. The Dutch, who at first were so forward for a war with the Indians, were now, when they experienced the loss and dangers of it, so irritated at the governor, for the orders which he had given, that he could not trust himself among them. He was obliged to keep a constant guard of fifty Englishmen about his person. In the summer and fall the Indians killed fifteen more of the Dutch people, and drove in all the inhabitants of the English and Dutch settlements, west of Stamford.

In prosecution of their works of destruction, they made a visit to the neighbourhood where Mrs. Hutchinson, who had been so famous, at Boston, for her Antinomian and familistical tenets, had made a settlement. The Indians, at first, appeared with the same friendship with which they used to frequent her house; but they murdered her and all her family, Mr. Collins, her son in law, and several other persons, belonging to other families in the neighbourhood. Eighteen persons were killed in the whole. The Indians, with an implacable fury, prosecuted the destruction of the Dutch, and of their property, in all that part of the country. They killed and burned their cattle, horses and barns without resistance. Having destroyed the settlements in the country, they passed over to the Dutch plantations on Long-Island, doing all the mischief of which they were capable. The Dutch, who escaped, were confined to their fort, and were obliged to kill and eat their cattle, for their subsistence. Their case was truly distressing.* It demanded succour as far as it could have been consistently given.

Governor Eaton and the general court, having maturely considered the purport of the Dutch governor's letter, rejected the proposal for raising men and assisting in the war against the Indians. Their principal reasons were, that joining separately in war, was prohibited by the articles of confederation; and that they were not satisfied that the Dutch war with the Indians was just.

Nevertheless it was determined, that if the Dutch needed corn and provisions for men or cattle, by reason of the destruction which the Indians had made, the court would give them all the assistance in its power.†

* Winthrop's Journal, p. 272, 273 and 308.
† Records of New-Haven.

Book I. The war continued several years, and was bloody and destructive both to the Dutch and Indians. Captain Underhill had the principal management of it, and was of great service to the Dutch. He collected a flying army of a hundred and twenty, and sometimes of a hundred and fifty men, English and Dutch, by which he preserved the Dutch settlements from total destruction. It was supposed, that, upon Long-Island and on the main, he killed between four and five hundred Indians.†

1643.

The Indians at Stamford too much caught the spirit of the western Indians in their vicinity, who were at war with the Dutch. They appeared so tumultuous and hostile, that the people at Stamford were in great fear, that they should soon share the fate of the settlements at the westward of them. They wrote to the general court at New-Haven, that in their apprehensions there were just grounds of a war with those Indians, and that if their houses should be burned, because the other plantations would not consent to war, they ought to bear the damage.

The Narraganset Indians were enraged at the death of their sachem. The English were universally armed. The strictest watch and guard was kept in all the plantations. In Connecticut, every family, in which there was a man capable of bearing arms, was obliged to send one complete in arms, every Lord's day, to defend the places of public worship. Indeed all places wore the aspect of a general war.

† Dr. Belknap's Hist. vol. i. p. 50.

CHAPTER VIII.

Public fasts appointed. Indians continue hostile, and commit murder. Acts of the commissioners respecting them. Branford settled. Towns in Connecticut. Message of the commissioners to the Narragansets. Their agreement respecting Uncas. Long-Island Indians taken under the protection of the United Colonies. Massachusetts claim part of the Pequot country and Waranoke. Determination of the commissioners respecting said claim. Agreement with Mr. Fenwick relative to Saybrook fort and the adjacent country. Fortifications advanced. Extraordinary meeting of the commissioners to suppress the outrages of the Narragansets. War proclaimed and troops sent against them. They treat and prevent war. Fairfield object to a jury of six. Controversy with the Dutch. The Indians plot against the life of governor Hopkins and other principal gentlemen at Hartford. Damages at Windsor. Battle between the Dutch and Indians. Losses of New-Haven. Dispute with Massachusetts relative to the impost at Saybrook. Mr. Winthrop's claim of the Nehantick country. Settlement of accounts between the colonies.

THE affairs both of Old and New-England, wore so gloomy an aspect, at this time, that the pious people, in the colonies, judged extraordinary fasting and prayer to be their indispensable duty. The flames of civil discord were kindled in England, and the tumultuous and hostile state of the natives in the united colonies, threatened them with a bloody and merciless Indian war. The general court of Connecticut therefore ordained a monthly fast, through the colony, to begin on Wednesday, the 6th of January. New-Haven had before appointed a fast, at the same time, in all the plantations in that jurisdiction. Indeed, this was practised, throughout the united colonies, during the civil wars in England. The colonists sympathized with their brethren, in their native country, and conformed to them in their days of humiliation and prayer. *Public fasting appointed.*

The freemen of Connecticut and New-Haven, exhibited a remarkable example of steadiness in the election of civil officers. Nearly the same persons were chosen annually into places of principal trust as long as they lived. This year Edward Hopkins, Esq. was chosen governor, and *Freemen steady.*

Book I.
1644.

John Haynes, Esquire, deputy-governor. The other magistrates were the same as they had been the last year, except Mr. William Swain, who was chosen into the magistracy. Mr. Haynes and Mr. Hopkins were generally elected, alternately governor and deputy-governor, during their respective lives. The reason of this annual change of them, from governor to deputy-governor, was because the constitution prohibited the choice of any man governor, more than once in two years.

At New-Haven, governor Eaton was annually elected to the office of governor, during his life; and Mr. Stephen Goodyear was generally chosen deputy-governor.

The Indians were no more peaceable this year, than they were the last. Those in the western part of Connecticut, still conducted themselves in a hostile manner. In the spring, they murdered a man belonging to Massachusetts, between Fairfield and Stamford. About six or eight weeks after the murder was discovered, the Indians promised to deliver the murderer, at Uncoway, if Mr. Ludlow would appoint men to receive him. Mr. Ludlow sent ten men for that purpose; but as soon as the Indians came within sight of the town, they, by general consent, unbound the prisoner and suffered him to escape. The English were so exasperated at this insult, that they immediately seized on eight or ten of the Indians, and committed them to prison. There was among them not less than one or two sachems. Upon this, the Indians arose in great numbers about the town, and exceedingly alarmed the people, both at Fairfield and Stamford. Mr. Ludlow wrote to New-Haven for advice. The court desired him to keep the Indians in durance, and assured him of immediate assistance, should it be necessary and desired. A party of twenty men were draughted forthwith, and prepared to march to Stamford upon the shortest notice. The Indians were held in custody, until four sachems, in those parts, appeared and interceded for them, promising, that if the English would release them, they would, within a month, deliver the murderer to justice.

The Indians commit murder.

May 1st.

Woman wounded at Stamford in June.

Not more than a month after their release, an Indian went boldly into the town of Stamford, and made a murderous assault upon a woman, in her house. Finding no man at home, he took up a lathing hammer, and approached her as though he were about to put it into her hand; but, as she was stooping down to take her child from the cradle, he struck her upon the head. She fell instantly with the blow; he then struck her twice, with the sharp part of the hammer, which penetrated her skull. Supposing her to be dead, he plundered the house, and made his escape. Soon after, the woman so far recovered, as to describe the Indian, and his manner of dress. Her wounds, which at first appeared to be mortal, were finally healed; but her brain was so affected, that she lost her reason.

At the same time, the Indians rose in those parts, with the most tumultuous and hostile appearances. They refused to come to the English, or to have any treaty with them. They appeared, in a very alarming manner, about several of the plantations, firing their pieces, and exceedingly terrifying the inhabitants. They deserted their wigwams, and neglected to weed their corn. The English had intelligence that the Indians designed to cut them off. Most of the English judged it unsafe to travel by land, and some of the plantations were obliged to keep a strong guard and watch, night and day. And as they had not numbers sufficient to defend themselves, they made application to Hartford and New-Haven for assistance. They both sent aid to the weaker parts of their respective colonies. New-Haven sent help to Fairfield and Stamford, as they were much nearer to them, than to Connecticut.

After a great deal of alarm and trouble, the Indian, who had attempted the murder of the woman, was delivered up, and condemned to death. He was executed at New-Haven. The executioner cut off his head with a falchion: but it was cruelly done. He gave the Indian eight blows, before he effected the execution. The Indian sat erect and motionless, until his head was severed from his body.*

Both the colonies of Connecticut and New-Haven, were put to great expense, this year, in defending themselves, and they were obliged to bear the whole charge, as the measures adopted for their defence, were taken by the order of their respective legislatures, and not by the direction of the commissioners.

The unhappy divisions which continued at Weathersfield, occasioned another settlement under the jurisdiction of New-Haven. As Mr. Eaton, to whom Totoket had been granted, in 1640, had not performed the conditions of the grant, New-Haven, for the accommodation of a number of people at Weathersfield, made a sale of it to Mr. William Swain, and others of that town. They sold it at the price which it cost them, stipulating with Mr. Swain and his company, that they should unite with that colony, in all the fundamental articles of government. The settlement of the town immediately commenced. At the same time, Mr. Abraham Pierson, with a part of his church and congrega-

* Records of the colonies, and Winthrop's Journal, p. 252.

Book I.
1644.

tion, from Southampton, on Long-Island, removed and united with the people of Weathersfield, in the settlement of the town. A regular church was soon formed, and Mr. Pierson was chosen pastor. The town was named Branford. Mr. Swain was the principal planter, and, a few years after, was chosen one of the magistrates of the colony of New-Haven, as he had previously been of the colony of Connecticut.

Sept. 5th. The meeting of the commissioners, this year, was at Hartford. Mr. Simon Bradstreet and Mr. William Hawthorne were commissioners from the Massachusetts; Mr. Edward Winslow and Mr. William Brown, from Plymouth; Governor Hopkins and Mr. George Fenwick, for Connecticut; and Governor Eaton and Mr. Thomas Gregson, from New-Haven.

Commissioners of Massachusetts claim precedence.

No sooner was the meeting opened, than a proposal was made by the commissioners from Massachusetts, directed by their general court, that the commissioners from that colony should always have preference to the commissioners of the other colonies, and be allowed to subscribe first, in the same order in which the articles of confederation had been signed.

Upon consideration of the proposal, the commissioners were unanimously of the opinion, that no such thing had either been proposed, granted, or practised, by the commissioners of the other jurisdictions, in any of their former meetings, though the articles had been subscribed in the presence of the general court of the Massachusetts. They resolved, that the commission was free, and might not receive any thing, but what was expressed by the articles of confederation, as imposed by any general court. Nevertheless, they determined, that, on account of their respect to the Massachusetts, they willingly granted, that their commissioners in that, and in all future meetings, should subscribe first, after the president, and the commissioners of the other colonies in such order as they were named in the articles; viz. Plymouth, Connecticut, and New-Haven.

The Indians were, this year, almost every where troublesome, and, in some places, in a high state of hostility. In Virginia they generally rose, and made a most horrible massacre of the English,* and it was imagined, that there was a general combination among the southern and New-England Indians, to destroy all the colonies. The Narraganset Indians, regardless of all their covenants with the

* In two days they massacred about 300 Virginians. Many of them were killed so suddenly and unexpectedly, that they knew neither the hand nor weapon by which they fell.

CHAP. VIII. CONNECTICUT.

English and with Uncas, continued in acts of constant hostility against the latter, and so oppressed the sachems and Indians under the protection of the Massachusetts, that they were obliged to dispatch a party of men for their defence and assistance, in fortifying against these oppressors.

Book I.
1644.

The commissioners immediately sent Thomas Stanton, their interpreter, and Nathaniel Willet, into the Narraganset and Moheagan countries, with particular instructions to their respective sachems. They were instructed to acquaint the sachems, that the commissioners were then met at Hartford; and that, if they would appear and lay their respective grievances before them, they would judge impartially between them: that the commissioners had heard the report which they had spread abroad concerning Uncas, that he had taken a ransom, in part, for Miantonimoh, and afterwards had put him to death; and that he refused to return the ransom. They were directed to assure them, that Uncas utterly denied the charge: that nevertheless, if they would go themselves, or send some of their principal men to Hartford, the commissioners would impartially hear this, and all other differences subsisting between them and the Moheagans, and assist them in the settlement of an amicable correspondence between the two nations; and that the parties should have a safe passage to and from Hartford, without any injury from the English. According to their instructions, they demanded of both parties, that they should commit no acts of hostility against each other in their travels to Hartford, nor on their return to their respective countries; and that all hostilities against each other's plantations should cease, during the hearing and treaty proposed. If either of the parties should refuse to go or send to Hartford, the treaty made in 1638 was to be urged against them, and their engagements not to go to war with each other, until they had acquainted the English with their grievances, and taken their advice. Directions were given, that it should be demanded of the party refusing, what their designs were? Whether they were for peace or war? Whether they designed to perform their treaties made with the English of Massachusetts and Connecticut? Or whether they considered them as all broken and void? The interpreter was charged fully to state all these articles to the Indians, and, having taken their answers in writing, to read them to the sachems, that they might understand and acknowledge them to be the very answers which they had given.

Message from the commissioners to the Indians.

In consequence of this message, the Narraganset Indians sent one of their sachems, with other chief men, to prove

T

BOOK I.
1644.
The Indians appear before the commissioners.

their charge against Uncas, and to treat with the English. They, also, bound themselves to confirm what their deputies should do in their name. Uncas, also, made his appearance, and the commissioners went into a full hearing of all differences between the parties. Upon hearing the case, the commissioners found, that there never had been any agreement between the Narragansets and Uncas, for the redemption of Miantonimoh, nor any thing paid, in whole or in part, for his ransom. Notwithstanding, they declared, that if the Narragansets should hereafter be able to prove what they had alledged against Uncas, that they would order him to make full satisfaction. They also resolved, that neither the Narragansets nor Nehanticks should make any war or assault upon Uncas, or any of his men, until they should make proof of the pretended ransom, and that Uncas had refused to make them satisfaction.

Agreement of the Narragansets.

The Narraganset sachem and his counsellors, upon consultation together, stipulated, in behalf of the Narraganset and Nehantick Indians, that no hostility should be committed against Uncas, or any of his Indians, until after the next year's time of planting corn. They also covenanted, that, before they began war, they would give thirty days notice, either to the governor of Massachusetts or Connecticut. Thus, for the present, by the vigorous and prudent exertions of the colonies and their commissioners, an Indian war was prevented.

The Long-Island Indians taken under protection of the colonies.

Yoncho, Wiantanse, Moughmatow, and Weenaganinim, sachems of Monhauset and its vicinity, on Long-Island, with their companies, appeared before the commissioners, and represented, that they, and the Long-Island Indians, had been tributaries to the English ever since the Pequot war, and that they had never injured the English nor the Dutch, but had been friendly to both. They, therefore, desired a certificate of their relation to the English, and to be taken under the protection of the united colonies. Upon this representation, the commissioners gave them a certificate, and declared, that it was their desire, while they continued peaceable, and did not intermeddle with the quarrels of other Indians, they and their companies might enjoy ample peace, without any disturbance from the English, or any in connection or friendship with them.

Massachusetts claims the Pequot country.

In this meeting, the commissioners of Massachusetts laid claim to part of the Pequot country, on the footing of joint conquest. They desired, that a division of the country might be made, or some way prescribed, by which the affair might be compromised.

Mr. Fenwick, in behalf of himself, and the noblemen and

CHAP. VIII. CONNECTICUT.

gentlemen in England, particularly interested in the lands in question, pleaded, that nothing in their absence might be determined against their title. He insisted, that Pequot harbour, and the lands in the adjacent country, were of great consequence to the gentlemen interested in the Connecticut patent. He said they had a special respect to them, in their consultations, relative to a plantation in these parts.

Book I.

1644.

The commissioners judged, that a convenient time ought to be given to those noble personages to plead their right, and that all patents, of equal authority, ought to have the same construction, both with reference to propriety and jurisdiction.

Determination of the commissioners.

The commissioners of Massachusetts also made claim to Waranoke, now Westfield, as lying within the limits of their patent. Mr. Fenwick, at the same time, claimed it as covered by the patent of Connecticut. However, as it appeared to the commissioners, that Mr. Fenwick had promised, before this meeting, either to clear his title to Waranoke, or submit to the government of Massachusetts, they determined, that Waranoke, with Mr. Hopkins's trading house, and the other houses and lands in that plantation, should be under the jurisdiction of Massachusetts, until it should be made evident to which colony they belonged; but that the propriety of the land should belong to the purchasers, provided it should not exceed two thousand acres.

Claim of Massachusetts to Waranoke.

The reverend Mr. Shepard wrote to the commissioners, representing the necessity of further assistance for the support of scholars at Cambridge, whose parents were needy, and desired them to encourage a general contribution through the colonies. The commissioners approved the motion; and, for the encouragement of literature, recommended it to the general courts in the respective colonies, to take it into their consideration, and to give it general encouragement. The general courts adopted the recommendation, and contributions of grain and provisions were annually made, through the united colonies, for the charitable end proposed.

Contribution for scholars at Cambridge.

At this meeting a plan was concerted by the commissioners, for a general trade with the Indians, by a joint stock. It was proposed to begin the trade with a stock of five or six thousand pounds, and to increase it to twenty thousand or more. It was designed, that each general court should approve and establish the trade, with peculiar privileges, for the term of twenty years: but it was never adopted. It seems it did not comport with the views

Book I.
1644.

of the general court of Massachusetts; and this, notwithstanding the confederation, rendered all the determinations of the commissioners void, which were not agreeable to their views and interests.

As the Indians were numerous, and began to learn the use of fire arms, all trading with them, in any of the united colonies, in guns, ammunition, swords, or any warlike instruments, directly or indirectly, was prohibited, upon the penalty of a fine of twenty times the value of the articles thus unlawfully sold. It was also recommended to the several courts, to prohibit all vending of arms and ammunition to the French or Dutch, because they immediately disposed of them to the Indians. Every smith was forbidden to mend a gun or any warlike instrument for an Indian, upon a severe penalty.*

South-Hampton, on Long-Island, was, by the advice of the commissioners, taken under the jurisdiction of Connecticut. This town was settled in 1640. The inhabitants of Lynn, in Massachusetts, became so straitened at home, that, about the year 1639, they contracted with the agent of Lord Sterling, for a tract of land on the west end of Long-Island. They also made a treaty with the Indians, and began a settlement, but the Dutch gave them so much trouble, that they were obliged to desert it, and remove further eastward. They collected nearly a hundred families and made a permanent settlement at South-Hampton. By the advice of the general court of Massachusetts, they entered into a combination among themselves, to maintain civil government. A number of them regularly formed themselves into church state, before they removed to the Island, and called Mr. Abraham Pierson to be their pastor. He had been a minister in Yorkshire, in England. Upon his arrival in New-England, he became a member of the church at Boston, whence he was called to the work of the ministry at South-Hampton.† This year he removed with part of his church to Branford. It seems that they were not pleased that the town had put itself under the jurisdiction of Connecticut.

General court in April.

This year a committee, consisting of the governor, deputy-governor, and several other gentlemen, were appointed by the general court of Connecticut, to treat with George Fenwick, Esquire, relative to the purchase of Saybrook fort, and of all guns, buildings and lands in the colony, which he, and the lords and gentlemen interested in the patent of Connecticut, might claim. The next December

* Records of the united colonies.
† Magnalia, b. iii. p. 95.

CHAP. VIII. CONNECTICUT. 149

they came to an agreement with Mr. Fenwick, to the following effect:

"Articles of agreement made and concluded betwixt George Fenwick, Esquire, of Saybrook fort, on the one part, and Edward Hopkins, John Haynes, John Mason, John Steele, and James Boosy, for, and on the behalf of the jurisdiction of Connecticut river, on the other part, the 5th of December, 1644.

"The said George Fenwick, Esq. doth make over to the use and behoof of the jurisdiction of Connecticut river, to be enjoyed by them forever, the fort at Saybrook, with the appurtenances; all the land upon the river Connecticut; and such lands as are yet undisposed of, shall be ordered and given out by a committee of five, whereof George Fenwick, Esq. is always to be one. The said George Fenwick doth also promise, that all the lands from Narraganset river, to the fort of Saybrook, mentioned in a patent granted by the earl of Warwick, to certain nobles, and gentlemen, shall fall in under the jurisdiction of Connecticut, if it come into his power."*

Book I.
1644.
Agreement with George Fenwick, Dec. 5, 1644.

* About this time died George Wyllys, Esq. the venerable ancestor of the Wyllyses in Connecticut. He was possessed of a fair estate, at Knapton, in the county of Warwick, worth £500 a year. In 1636, he sent over William Gibbons, the steward of his house, with twenty men, to prepare him a seat at Hartford. They purchased, and took possession of a fine tract of land, erected buildings, and planted a garden upon that pleasant plat, which has ever since been the principal seat of the family. In 1638 he came over with his household; and, at the election in 1639, was chosen into the magistracy, in which he continued about five years, until his death. In 1641, he was chosen deputy-governor, and in 1642, governor of the colony. It appears from the manuscripts of the family, that both he and Mrs. Wyllys were eminently pious, living with all the exactness of the Puritans of that day. From love to undefiled religion, and purity in divine ordinances and worship, they exchanged their pleasant seat and easy circumstances in England, for the dangers and hardships of a wilderness in America. He left one son, Samuel, about twelve years of age. He was educated at Cambridge, where he was graduated 1653; and the next year was chosen one of the magistrates for Connecticut, at about twenty-two years of age. It appears by his manuscripts, that he became deeply impressed with the truths and importance of religion, at college, under the ministry of Mr. Shepard; and the spirit of his pious parents descended upon him. He married a daughter of governor Haynes, who appeared equally to have imbibed the spirit of her Saviour. In his manuscripts, he describes the excellent examples which their parents had exhibited, and the pious pains they employed in their education; teaching them, from childhood, to pray always in secret, private and public; to venerate the sabbath, and the divine word; and to attend all christian institutions and duties.

After bearing testimony to the great advantages of such an education, and to the comfort which they had experienced in the duties, in which they had been educated, he warmly recommends them to his children, and their posterity.

The family is ancient, and may be traced back to the reign of Edward the IV. more than three centuries. It has well supported its dignity to the present time. Some of the family have been magistrates or secretaries of

BOOK I. On the part of Connecticut it was stipulated, "That the said George Fenwick, Esq. should enjoy all the housing* belonging to the fort for the space of ten years. And that a certain duty on corn, biscuit, beaver and cattle, which should be exported from the river's mouth, should be paid to him during the said term."

The general court confirm the agreement with Mr. Fenwick, Feb. 4, 1645.

Upon the 4th of February, 1645, the general court of Connecticut confirmed this agreement with Mr. Fenwick, and passed an act imposing a duty of two pence per bushel upon all grain, six pence upon every hundred weight of biscuit, and a small duty upon all beaver exported from the mouth of the river, during the term of ten years, from the first day of March ensuing. It was also enacted, that an entry should be made of all grain laden on board any vessel, of the number of bushels, and of the weight of biscuit, and that a note of the same be delivered to Mr. Fenwick, upon the penalty of forfeiting the one half of all such grain and biscuit as should be put on board and not thus certified. The colony, on the whole, paid Mr. Fenwick 1,600 pounds sterling, merely for the jurisdiction right, or for the old patent of Connecticut. The general court, the

July 19th. next July, ordered that a tax of two hundred pounds should be levied on the plantations in the colony, to defray the charge of advancing the fortifications at Saybrook fort. A committee was appointed, at the same time, to bargain with Mr. Griffin for that purpose, and to make provision for the immediate completion of the fortifications in view. A letter was also dispatched, from the court, to Mr. Fenwick, desiring him, if his circumstances would permit, to make a voyage to England, to obtain an enlargement of the patent, and to promote other interests of the colony.

Hostility of the Narragansets.

Notwithstanding the unwearied pains the commissioners of the colonies, and the colonies themselves, had taken to prevent hostilities among the Indians, and to preserve the peace of the country, the perfidious Narragansets were continually waging war. Pessacus and the Narraganset Indians, in violation of all their treaties, had repeatedly invaded the Moheagan country and assaulted Uncas in his fort. They had killed and taken numbers of his men, and so pressed him, that both Connecticut and New-Haven were obliged to dispatch parties of men to his assistance, to prevent the enemy from completely conquering him and his country.

Governor Winthrop therefore called a special meeting

the colony for more than a century and an half. May the descendants ever inherit its virtues and honors!
* An old word, meaning the quantity of inhabited buildings.

of the commissioners, at Boston, on the 28th of June, 1645. Governor Winthrop and Mr. Herbert Pelham, were commissioners for Massachusetts. Mr. Thomas Prince and Mr. John Brown for Plymouth, Edward Hopkins and George Fenwick, Esquires, for Connecticut, governor Eaton and Mr. Stephen Goodyear for New-Haven.

Book I. 1645. Extraordinary meeting of the commissioners, June 28th. Messengers sent to the Narragansets, insulted.

Immediately on the meeting of the commissioners, they dispatched messengers into the Narraganset and Mohegan countries. They were charged to acquaint the sachems and Indians of the respective tribes, that if they would go to Boston, the commissioners would impartially hear and determine all their differences; and that, however the treaty might end, they should be allowed to go and return in safety. The sachems, at first, seemed to give some fair speeches; but finally determined, that they would neither go nor send to Boston. The Narragansets insulted and abused the messengers, and uttered haughty and threatening speeches against the English. One of the sachems declared, that he would kill their cattle and pile them in heaps; and that an Englishman should no sooner step out at his doors than the Indians would kill him. He declared that, whoever began the war, he would continue it; and that nothing should satisfy him but the head of Uncas. On the whole, the messengers were obliged to return without effecting any good purpose. By them Mr. Williams wrote to the commissioners, assuring them that an Indian war would soon break out; and that, as a preparative, the Narragansets had concluded a neutrality with Providence and the towns upon Aquidney island.

These reports roused the English spirit. The commissioners, considering that the Narragansets had violated all their treaties, killed a number of the Moheagans, taken others captive, destroyed their corn, and, with great armies, besieged Uncas in his fort; and besides, that they had highly insulted the united colonies and abused their messengers, determined that an immediate war with them was both justifiable and necessary.

However, as they wished to act with prudence as well as spirit, and to give general satisfaction in an affair of such moment, they desired the advice of the magistrates, elders, and a number of the principal military officers in the Massachusetts. These assembled, and were unanimously of the opinion, that their engagements obliged them to defend Uncas and the Moheagans: that the defence which they were obliged to give, according to the common acceptation of such engagements, extended not

152   HISTORY OF   Chap. VIII.

Book I. barely to the defence of Uncas and his men in their fort,
1645. but to his estate and liberties; and that the aid to be given must be immediate, or he would be totally ruined.

War with the Narragansets determined.

It was therefore determined, that a war with the Indians was just, that the case should be stated in short, and war, with the reasons of it, be proclaimed. A day of fasting and prayer was appointed on the fourth of September. It was resolved, That three hundred men should be forthwith raised, and sent against the enemy. Massachusetts were to furnish 190, Plymouth and Connecticut 40 each, and New-Haven 30. As the troops from Connecticut and New-Haven, who had assisted in defending Uncas, the former part of the summer, were about to return to their respective colonies, forty men were impressed in the Massachusetts, and marched in three days, completely armed and victualled. These were commanded by Humphry Atherton. Orders were dispatched to the troops to be raised in Connecticut and New-Haven, to join them at Moheagan. A commission was forwarded to captain Mason to take the command of all the troops, until the whole army should form a junction. The chief command of the army was given to major Edward Gibbons, of Massachusetts. He was instructed not only to defend Uncas, but to invade and distress the Narragansets and Nehanticks, with their confederates. He had instructions to offer them peace. If they would receive it upon honorable terms, he, with his officers, had power to make a treaty with them. If the enemy should flee from the army, and would neither fight nor make peace, the commander had orders to build forts in the Nehantick and Narraganset country; to which he might gather the enemy's corn and goods, as far as it should be in his power.

The Narragansets had sent a present to governor Winthrop, of Boston, desiring that they might have peace with the English, but wage war with Uncas, and avenge the death of Miantonimoh. The governor refused to receive the present upon such terms; but the messengers, by whom it was carried, urging that they might leave it until they could consult their sachems,' he suffered it to be left with him. The commissioners ordered, that it should be immediately returned. Captain Harding, Mr. Wilbore, and Benedict Arnold, were sent into the Narraganset country, to return the present, and to assure Pessacus, Canonicus, Janimo, and the other sachems of the Narraganset and Nehantick Indians, that they would neither receive their presents, nor give them peace, until they should make satisfaction for past injuries, and give security for their peace-

CHAP. VIII. CONNECTICUT.

able conduct for the future. They were to certify the Indians, that the English were ready for war; and that if war was their choice, they would direct their affairs for that purpose. At the same time, they had orders to assure them, that if they would make satisfaction for the damages which they had done, and give security for their peaceable conduct, in time to come, they should know, that the English were as desirous of the peace, and as tender of the blood of the Narragansets, as they had ever been.

The messengers prosecuted their journey with great dispatch, and brought back word, that Pessacus, chief sachem of the Narragansets, and others, were coming to Boston forthwith, vested with full powers to treat with the commissioners. The messengers, though sent on purpose to carry back the present, and to assure the Indians that the English would not receive it, returned with it to Boston. They also wrote to captain Mason, acquainting him that there were hopes of peace with the Indians.

The commissioners, therefore, while they acknowledged the pains and expedition with which they had accomplished their journey, censured them, for not attending to their instructions. Especially, they judged them worthy of censure, for bringing back the present, and for writing to captain Mason. The latter, they imagined, could have no other effect than to retard his operations.

The Indians, finding that an army was coming into the heart of their country, made haste to meet the commissioners, and ward off the impending blow. A few days after the return of their messengers, Pessacus, Meeksamo, the eldest son of Canonicus, and Wytowash, three principal sachems of the Narragansets, and Awashequen, deputy of the Nehanticks, with a large train, arrived at Boston.

They, at first, denied and excused many particulars which the commissioners charged upon them. They insisted on the old story of the ransom, and proposed to make a truce with Uncas, until the next planting time, or for a year. The commissioners assured them, that matters were now come to a crisis, and that they would accept of no such terms. They charged the Indian sachems with their perfidious breach of treaties, with the injuries they had done to Uncas, with their insults of the English, and with the great trouble and expense to which they had put them, to defend Uncas, and maintain the peace of the country. The Indians, finally, though with great reluctance, acknowledged their breach of treaties. One of the sachems presented the commissioners with a stick, signifying, by

Book I.

1645.

The Indians treat for peace.

BOOK I. that token, that he submitted the terms of war and peace into their hands, and wished to know what they required of the Indians.

1645.

The commissioners represented to them, that the charge and trouble which they had brought on the colonies was very great, besides all the loss and damages which Uncas had sustained. They charged all these, upon their infraction of the treaties which they had made with the colonies, and with Uncas. They assured the Indians, that though two thousand fathom of white wampum would, by no means, be equal to the expense to which they had put the colonies, entirely by their violation of their treaties; yet, to show their moderation, they would accept of that sum for all past damages. It was required, that they should restore to Uncas all the captives and canoes which they had taken from him; that they should submit all matters of controversy, between them and Uncas, to the commissioners, at their next meeting; and that they should maintain perpetual peace with the English, and all their subjects and allies. Finally, hostages were demanded, as a security for the performance of the treaty.* These, indeed, were hard terms. The Indians made many exceptions to them; but as they knew the English were gone into their country, and were fearful that hostilities would be commenced, even while the treaty was pending, they submitted to them. Some abatement was made, as to the times of payment at first proposed, and it was agreed that Uncas should restore to the Narragansets all captives and canoes which he had taken from them. This gave the Narragansets and Nehanticks some ease; but it was with great reluctance, that they finally signed the articles. Nothing but the necessity of the case, could have been a sufficient inducement.

Articles signed.

On the 30th of August, the articles were signed, and the Indians left several of their number, as hostages, until the children, who had been agreed upon for a permanent security, should be delivered.

The troops which had been raised were disbanded, and the day appointed for a general fast was celebrated as a day of general thanksgiving.

Designs to obtain patents.

New-Haven, this year, appointed Mr. Gregson their agent to the parliament in England, to procure a patent for the colony. The court at New-Haven, voted, that it was a proper time to join with Connecticut, in procuring a patent from parliament, for these parts.† It appears, that

* Records of the united colonies.
† Records of New-Haven.

CHAP. VIII.   CONNECTICUT.

both Connecticut and New-Haven, at this time, had it in contemplation to obtain charters from parliament, for their respective jurisdictions; but Mr. Fenwick, who had been desired to undertake a voyage, for this purpose, in behalf of Connecticut, did not accept the appointment, and Mr. Gregson was lost at sea. In consequence of these circumstances, and the state of affairs in England afterwards, the business rested until after the restoration.

This year Tunxis was named Farmington. At this time, there were in the colony of Connecticut eight taxable towns; Hartford, Windsor, Weathersfield, Stratford, Fairfield, Saybrook, South-Hampton and Farmington. In the colony of New-Haven were six; New-Haven, Milford, Guilford, Southhold, Stamford and Branford.

In 1646 there was an alteration in the act respecting juries. In 1644, an act passed authorizing the court of magistrates to increase or mitigate the damages given by verdict of the jury. It was now enacted, that whatever alterations should be made of this kind, at any time, should be made in open court, in the presence both of the plaintiff and defendant, or upon affidavit made, that they had been summoned to appear.

At this court the town of Fairfield made objections to that part of the act passed in 1644, which admitted of a jury of six. They insisted on twelve jurymen in all cases triable by a jury; but consented, that eight out of twelve should bring in a verdict. It does not appear, that a jury of six was ever empannelled, after this time. The laws were soon after revised, and ordained a jury of twelve in all cases which required a jury.

The commissioners of the united colonies met, this year, at New-Haven. The Dutch continuing their injurious conduct against the English, complaints were made to the commissioners, of the recent and repeated insults and damages which they had received from them. Instead of making them the least satisfaction for past injuries, they proceeded to new instances of insolence and abuse. Kieft wrote a most imperious letter to governor Eaton, charging him, and the people at New-Haven, with an unsatiable desire of possessing that which belonged to the Dutch nation. He affirmed, that contrary to ancient leagues, between the kings of England and the States General, contrary to the law of nations, and his protestations, they had, indirectly, entered upon the limits of New-Netherlands. He therefore protested against them, as breakers of the peace and disturbers of the public tranquillity. Indeed he proceeded so far as to threaten, that if the English, at

Book I.
1645.

Towns in Connecticut and New-Haven.

1646.

April 6.

Kieft's letter and protest.

BOOK I.
1646.

New-Haven, did not restore the places which they had usurped, and repair the losses which the Dutch had sustained, that they would, by such means as God should afford, recover them. He affirmed, that the Dutch would not view it as inconsistent with the public peace, but should impute all the evils, which might ensue, to the English.*

Governor Eaton's reply.

Governor Eaton replied to this letter, that the colony under his government had never entered upon any land, to which the Dutch had any known title : That, notwithstanding all the injuries received from the Dutch, and the very unsatisfying answers which their governor had given, from time to time, the colony, in his apprehensions, had done nothing inconsistent with the law of God, the law of nations, nor with the ancient leagues subsisting between England and Holland. He therefore assured him, that the colony would cheerfully submit all differences, between them and the Dutch, to an impartial hearing and adjudication, either in Europe or America.

Misdemeanors of the Dutch at Hartford.

The Dutch, at Hartford, maintained a distinct and independent government. They resisted the laws of the colony, and counteracted the natural rights of men. They inveigled an Indian woman who, having been liable to public punishment, fled from her master. It was supposed, that the Dutch kept her for the purpose of wantonness. Though her master demanded her, as his property, and the magistrates, as a criminal, on whom the law ought to have its course, yet they would not restore her. The Dutch agent at Hartford, in the heighth of disorder, resisted the guard. He drew his rapier upon the soldiers, and broke it upon their arms. He then escaped to the fort, and there defended himself with impunity.

Complaint to the commissioners.

The commissioners of Connecticut and New-Haven made complaint of these insults and misdemeanors to the commissioners of the united colonies, and laid open the whole conduct of the Dutch towards them. They represented, that in answer to their complaints of past injuries, they had, instead of satisfaction, received nothing but injury and abuse.

The commissioners write and send an express to the Dutch governor.

The commissioners, upon a deliberate view of the case, wrote to the Dutch governor, stating how they had written to him from time to time ; and, in consideration of the great worth of peace, had attempted to compromise the differences which had so long subsisted between the Dutch and their confederates. They observed to the governor, that he had returned nothing but an ignoramus, with an offen-

* Kieft's letter to governor Eaton, on the records of the united colonies.

sive addition, which they left to his review and better consideration. They stated the affair at Hartford, and observed, that had the Dutch agent been slain, in the haughty affront which he had given, his blood would have been upon his own head. They assured him, that his agent and the company at Hartford, had proceeded to an intolerable state of conduct: that they had forcibly taken away their cattle from authority, and made an assault upon a man, who had legally sought justice for damages which he had sustained: that they struck him, and, in a hostile manner, took his team and loading from him. The commissioners noticed the letter of the Dutch governor to the colony of New-Haven, and manifested their approbation of the answer which governor Eaton had given. They expressed their hopes, that it would give satisfaction. They concluded by observing, that, to prevent all inconveniences which might arise from any part of the premises, they had sent an express, by whom they wished to receive such an answer as might satisfy them of his concurrence with them, to embrace and pursue righteousness and peace.

Several of the English who had traded with the Dutch, had not been able to recover their just debts, and governor Kieft would not afford them that assistance which was necessary for the obtaining of justice. Mr. Whiting, of Connecticut, complained, that an action had been carried against him at Manhatoes, in his absence, and when he had no agent to exhibit his evidence, or plead his cause. He also made complaint, that, upon demanding a just debt, long since due from the Dutch, the governor neglected to give him that assistance which was necessary for the recovery of his right.

The commissioners wrote also to governor Kieft on this subject. They desired him to grant Mr. Whiting a review in the case specified, and proper assistance in the recovery of his debts from the Dutch. They assured him, that all the colonies would grant similar favours to the Dutch in all their courts.

By their express, the commissioners received two letters from the Dutch governor, in answer to what they had written, expressed in the same haughty and offensive strain, as his former letters. He denied that the woman, who had been detained by the Dutch at Hartford, was a servant, with many other facts which had been stated by the commissioners. Instead of submitting the affairs in dispute to a legal decision, either in Europe or America, he still threatened to avenge the injuries of which he complained, by force of arms. With respect to other matters of special

Book I.
1646.

Dutch letters and protest.

158   HISTORY OF   Chap. VIII.

Book I.
1646.

importance, he passed them without the least notice. He compared the commissioners to eagles which soar aloft, and always despise the little fly; but he assured them, that the Dutch, by their arms, would manfully pursue their rights. He then finished his letters in this remarkable manner:—
"We protest against all you commissioners, met at the red mount,* as against breakers of the common league, and, also, infringers of the rights of the lords, the states, our superiors, in that you have dared, without our express and special consent, to hold your general meeting within the limits of New Netherlands."

The commissioners' reply.

The commissioners made a short reply, assuring the Dutch governor, that they could prove the facts which they had stated to him in their letters; and that the woman whom the Dutch had detained, was a servant, and an important part of her master's property: that she had fled from civil justice, and, by the confession of Mr. David Provost, Dutch agent at Hartford, had been defiled. They insisted, that the conduct of the Dutch at Hartford, was intolerable, and complained, that he had given no orders to redress the grievances which they had mentioned. They also complained, that he had made no reply to so many important articles, concerning which they had written to him. With respect to the protest, with which he had closed his letter, they observed, that, though it was offensive, yet it agreed with the general strain of his writing; and that he had no more reason to protest against their boldness in holding their session at New-Haven, than they had to protest against his boldness in the protest which he had sent them. After all the insult which the commissioners received from the Dutch governor, their replies were cool and without threatening.†

Plot against Governor Hopkins, Haynes, &c.

This year a horrid plot was concerted among the Indians, for the destruction of a number of the principal inhabitants of Hartford. Sequassen, a petty sachem upon the river, hired one of the Waronoke Indians to kill governor Hopkins and governor Haynes, with Mr. Whiting, one of the magistrates. Sequassen's hatred of Uncas was insatiable, and, probably, was directed against these gentlemen, on account of the just and faithful protection which they had afforded him. The plan was, that the Waronoke Indian should kill them, and charge the murder upon Uncas, and by that means engage the English against him to his ruin. After the massacre of these gentlemen, Sequas-

---
* The Dutch called New-Haven the Red Mount, and the Red Hills, from the appearance of the rocks west and north of the town.
† Records of the United Colonies.

sen and the murderer were to make their escape to the Mohawks. Watohibrough, the Indian hired to perpetrate the murder, after he had received several girdles of wampum, as part of his reward, considering how Bushheag, the Indian who attempted to kill the woman at Stamford, had been apprehended and executed at New-Haven, conceived that it would be dangerous to murder English sachems. He also revolved in his mind, that if the English should not apprehend and kill him, he should always be afraid of them, and have no comfort in his life. He also recollected, that the English gave a reward to the Indians who discovered and brought in Bushheag. He therefore determined, it would be better to discover the plot, than to be guilty of so bloody and dangerous an action. In this mind he came to Hartford, a few days after he had received the girdles, and made known the plot. Nearly at the same time the Waranoke Indians did much damage to the people at Windsor, burning up their tar and turpentine, and destroying their tools and instruments, to the value of a hundred pounds or more. The magistrates at Hartford issued a warrant, and apprehended the Indian whom they supposed to be guilty; but the Indians rose and made an assault upon the officers, and rescued the criminal from justice.

<small>Book I.
1646.

Indians do damage at Windsor.</small>

Upon complaint and evidence of these misdemeanors, the commissioners sent messengers to Sequassen, demanding his appearance at New-Haven, and they ordered, that if he would not voluntarily appear, all means, consistent with the preservation of his life, should be used to take him. Messengers were also sent to Waranoke, to the Indians who had done the mischief at Windsor, with orders to seize the delinquents, and bring them off, if they judged they could do it with safety. Sequassen had art enough to keep out of their hands, and those who had done the damage could not be found. The messengers were insulted at Waranoke. The Indians boasted of their arms, primed and cocked their pieces in their presence, and threatened that if a man should be carried away, the Indians would generally rise and fight.

The commissioners, on the whole, judged it not expedient, in the state in which the Indians then were, to proceed any further than to resolve, that if any Indian or Indians, of what plantation soever, should do any damage to the English colonies, or to any of their inhabitants, that, upon due proof of it, they would, in a peaceable manner, demand satisfaction. But if any sagamore, or plantation of Indians, should hide, convey away, entertain, or protect such offender or offenders, that then the English would de-

<small>Resolution respecting the Indians.</small>

Book I. mand satisfaction of such Indian sagamore or plantation, and do themselves justice, as they might, upon all such 1646. offenders. At the same time, they declared, that they would keep peace and amity with all other Indians. This resolution was to be made known to the Waranoke Indians in particular.

The Indians, at particular times, were very mischievous, and gave much trouble to all the plantations. Sometime after the settlement of Milford, the Indians there set all the adjacent country on fire. It was supposed that their design was to burn the town: but the inhabitants were so fortunate as to stop the fires at the swamps and brooks which surround it on the west and north. By this means the town was preserved.

The Mohawks, though not hostile to the English, by coming down and murdering the Connecticut Indians, put the plantations in fear, and gave them not a little trouble. Some years after the settlement of Milford, they came into the town, and secreted themselves in a swamp,* about half a mile east of Stratford ferry, with a view to surprise the Indians at the fort. The English accidentally discovering them, gave notice of it to the Milford Indians. They at once set up the war whoop, and collected such numbers that they ventured to attack them. The Mohawks were overpowered, and several of them taken. One stout captive, the Milford Indians determined to kill, by famine and torture. They stripped him naked and tied him up in the salt meadows for the moschetoes to eat and torment to death. An Englishman, one Hine, finding him in this piteous condition, loosed and fed him, and enabled him to make his escape. This very much conciliated the Mohawks towards the English, and especially towards the family of the Hines, whom, it is said, they ever afterwards particularly noticed, and treated with uncommon friendship.

Perfidy of the Narragansets. The Narraganset and Nehantick Indians neglected to perform any part of the treaty which they had made the last year. They neither paid the wampum stipulated, nor met the commissioners, at New-Haven, to settle the differences between them and Uncas. They neither restored the captives nor canoes taken from him, nor made him any compensation for the damages which they had done him. They had attempted to deceive the English with respect to the hostages. Instead of the children of their sachems and chief men, whom they agreed to deliver, they made an attempt to impose upon them children of the lowest

* This is known by the name of Mohawk swamp to the present time.

CHAP. VIII. CONNECTICUT.

rank. Even to this time, they had not brought those whom they had promised. They were still intriguing with the Mohawks; and, by presents and various arts, attempting to engage them against the English colonies. The commissioners judged, that they had just occasion to avenge the injuries which they had received, and to seek a recompence by force of arms. However, that they might show their love of peace, and their forbearance towards these barbarians, they dispatched another message to them. In this a full representation was made of these particulars. They were assured, that the commissioners were apprised of their intrigues, and that, in the eyes of all the colonies, they had rendered themselves a perfidious people.

The war between the Dutch and Indians continuing, a great and general battle was fought between them in that part of Horseneck commonly known by the name of Strickland's plain. The action was long and severe, both parties fighting with firmness and obstinacy. The Dutch, with much difficulty, kept the field, and the Indians withdrew. Great numbers were slain on both sides, and the graves of the dead, for a century or more, appeared like a number of small hills.*

New-Haven having been exceedingly disappointed in trade, and sustained great damages at Delaware, and the large estates which they brought into New-England rapidly declining, this year, made uncommon exertions, as far as possible, to retrieve their former losses. Combining their money and labors, they built a ship, at Rhode-Island, of 150 tons; and freighted her, for England, with the best part of their commercial estates. Mr. Gregson, captain Turner, Mr. Lamberton and five or six of their principal men embarked on board. They sailed from New-Haven in January, 1647. They were obliged to cut through the ice to get out of the harbour. The ship foundered at sea, and was never heard of after she sailed. The loss of this ship, with the former losses which the company had sustained, broke up all their expectations with respect to trade, and as they conceived themselves disadvantageously situated for husbandry, they adopted the design of leaving the country. They were invited to Jamaica, in the West-Indies. They had also an invitation to Ireland. It seems they entered into treaties for the city of Galloway, which they designed to have settled, as a small province for themselves.† Nevertheless they were disappointed with respect to all these designs. Their posterity, who

BOOK I.
1646.

Battle on Strickland's plain.

Losses of New-Haven.

Attempts to remove.

* Manuscripts of the Rev. Stephen Monson.
† Magnalia, B. I. p. 25, 26.

V

BOOK I.
1647.
Election at Hartford, 1647.

they feared would be reduced to beggary, made respectable farmers, and flourished, with respect to worldly circumstances, no less than their neighbours.

At the election, this year, at Hartford, nine magistrates were chosen. Mr. Cosmore and Mr. Howe were elected for the first time. The other magistrates were the same as in the preceding years.

At this session of the general court, an explanation or addition was made to the tenth fundamental article. By this article, as it stood, it was the opinion of some, that no particular court could be holden, unless the governor and four magistrates were present. It was therefore decreed,† that the governor, or deputy governor, with two magistrates, should have power to keep a particular court, according to the laws established; and, that in case neither the governor, nor deputy governor should be present, or able to sit, if three magistrates should meet, and choose one of themselves moderator, they might keep a particular court, which to all intents and purposes, should be deemed as legal, as if the governor or deputy governor were present. All orders contrary to this were repealed.‡

Act against the use of tobacco.

As tobacco, about this time, was coming into use, in the colony, a very curious law was made for its regulation, or suppression. It was ordered, that no person under twenty years of age, nor any other, who had not already accustomed himself to the use of it, should take any tobacco until he had obtained a certificate from under the hand of an approved physician, that it was useful for him, and until he had also obtained a license from the court. All others, who had addicted themselves to the use of it, were prohibited from taking it, in any company, or at their labors, or in travelling, unless ten miles, at least, from any company; and though not in company, not more than once a day, upon pain of a fine of sixpence for every such offence. One substantial witness was to be a sufficient proof of the crime. The constables of the several towns were to make presentment to the particular courts, and it was ordered, that the fine should be paid without gainsaying.§

June 2.

At a court in June, it was ordered, that the fort and guns at Saybrook, should be delivered to captain John Mason, and that he should give Mr. Fenwick a receipt for the premises. At the desire of the people there, captain Mason was appointed to the chief command of the fort; and was authorized to govern all the soldiers and inhabitants of the town; to call them forth and put them in such array as

† The enacting style, before the charter, was, It is ordered, sentenced, and decreed. Sometimes one of the words only was used.
‡ Records of Connecticut, folio vol. i. p. 162, 163.
§ Records of Connecticut.

might be necessary for the general defence of the country. Orders were given, that the fortifications should be repaired, and that the country rate of Saybrook should be appropriated to that purpose.

This court granted to the soldiers of the respective train bands in the colony, the privilege of choosing their own officers, to be commissioned by the court.

The conduct of the Narraganset and Nehantick Indians was so treacherous and hostile that, in midsummer, an extraordinary meeting of the commissioners was called at Boston. The commissioners were, Thomas Dudley and John Endicot, Esquires, from Massachusetts; Mr. William Bradford and Mr. John Brown, from Plymouth; governor Hopkins and captain John Mason, from Connecticut; governor Eaton and Mr. Goodyear, from New-Haven. Thomas Dudley was chosen president.

The Narraganset and Nehantick Indians, had not only neglected the performance of every part of their treaties with the English, but were, by all their arts, plotting against them. By their wampum they were hiring all the Indian nations round about them to combine against the colonies. They had sent messengers and presents to the Mohawks, to engage them in the general confederacy. As this faithless conduct was the occasion of the meeting, the commissioners immediately dispatched messengers to Pessacus, Ninigrate, Webetomaug, and all their confederates, to declare to them their breach of covenant, and to demand their attendance at Boston. The messengers were instructed to assure them, that if they did not appear, they would send to them no more. Pessacus owned, that he had broken covenant, and said it was the constant grief of his spirit. He pretended he would gladly go to Boston, but he was unwell, and could not travel. This was a mere pretence, as there was no appearance of indisposition upon him. He excused himself for not keeping the treaty, because he was frighted into it by the sight of the English army, which was about to invade his country. He represented, that he was in fear, if he did not make it, the English would follow him home and kill him. He declared, however, that he would send his whole mind by Ninigrate, and that he would abide by whatever he should transact in the affair.

On the 3d of August, Ninigrate, with two of Pessacus's men, and a number of the Nehantick Indians, arrived at Boston. When Ninigrate came before the commissioners, he pretended great ignorance of the treaties between the English and the Indians. He declared, that he knew no cause why the Narragansets should pay so much wampum. He said they owed nothing to the English. The commissioners acquainted him, that it was on account of their breach of treaty, and the great charge which, by that means, they had brought on the colonies, that the Narragansets engaged to pay such a quantity. Well knowing his deceit, they charged him as being the very man, who had been the principal cause of all their trouble and expense, relative to the Indians. They declared to him, that he was the sachem who had threatened to pile their cattle in heaps, and to kill every Englishman who should step out at his doors. At so home a charge, which he could not deny, he was not a little chagrined. However, he excused the matter with as much art as possible. With respect to the wampum, he declared, that the Narragansets had not a sufficiency to pay the sum required. The commissioners knew that the Narragansets were a great nation, and that they could, at any time, upon short notice, pay a greater amount than they demanded. They considered the demand, not only as their just due, but as matter of policy, as far as was consistent with justice, to strip them of their wampum, to prevent their hiring the Mohawks, and other Indians, to join with them, in a general war against the colonies. They, therefore, insisted that the whole sum should be paid. They declared to him, that they were not satisfied with his answers. Ninigrate, after he had taken time to consult with his council, the other deputies, who were with him, answered, that he was determined to give the colonies full satisfaction. He desired ten days to send messengers to Narraganset, to collect the wampum due, and offered himself a hostage until their return. The messengers returned with no more than two hundred fathoms. Ninigrate imputed this to his absence. He desired liberty to return, promising, that if the whole sum should not be paid by the next spring, the commissioners might take his head, and seize his country. The commissioners agreed with him, that if within twenty days, he would deliver a thousand fathoms of wampum, and the remainder which was due by the next planting time, they would dismiss him. They also, for his encouragement, acquainted him, that although they might justly put the hostages to death, for their delays and breach of covenant, yet they would forthwith deliver them to him; and if they should find him punctual to his engagements, they would charge former defects to Pessacus. These terms he gladly accepted.

The commissioners from Connecticut, the last year,

CHAP. VIII. CONNECTICUT.

made complaint, that Mr. Pyncheon and the inhabitants at Springfield, refused to pay the impost which had been imposed by Connecticut for the maintenance of the fort at Saybrook. The commissioners judged, that the fort was of great consequence to the towns on the river; but, as the affair of the impost had not been laid before the general court of Massachusetts, and as the commissioners of that colony had no instructions respecting it, a full hearing had been deferred to this meeting.

Meanwhile, the general court of the Massachusetts had taken up the affair, and passed a number of resolutions respecting the impost. These are a curiosity, exhibiting a lively picture of human nature, and, in the course of conduct consequent upon them, will afford a general specimen of the manner in which the Massachusetts anciently treated her sister colonies. The resolutions were, at this meeting, laid before the commissioners, and were to the following effect.

Resolutions of the court of Massachusetts, respecting the impost.

1. That the jurisdiction at Hartford had not a legal power to force any inhabitant of another jurisdiction, to purchase any fort or lands out of their jurisdiction.

2. That it was injurious to require custom for the maintenance of a fort which is not useful to those of whom it was demanded.

3. That it was unequal for Connecticut to impose a custom upon their friends and confederates, who have no more benefit of the river, by the exporting or importing of goods, than strangers of another nation, who, though they lived in Hartford, paid none.

4. That the propounding and standing upon an imposition of custom, to be paid at the river's mouth, by such as were of our jurisdiction, hindered our confederation ten years, and there was never any paid to this day; and that now to impose it upon them, after their confederation, would put them upon new thoughts.

5. That it appeared to them very hard, that any of their jurisdiction should be forced to such a disadvantage, as would necessarily enslave their posterity, by imposing such rates and customs, as would either constrain them to depart from their habitations, or weaken their estates; especially as they were with the first who took possession of the river, and were at great charge of building, &c. which if they had foreseen, they would not have made a plantation at that place.

6. If Hartford jurisdiction shall make use of their power over any of ours; we have the same power to imitate them in the like kind, which they desired might be forborne on

Book I. both sides. These resolutions were signed by the secretary of the colony.

1647.

Gov. Hopkins' reply to the resolutions.

Mr. Hopkins replied, in behalf of Connecticut, that the first article laboured under a great mistake: that the imposition was neither to buy lands nor the fort. He observed also, that it was not material to what purpose an impost was applied, if it were lawful in itself, and did not exceed the bounds of moderation. With respect to the second article, he said, that it impeached all states and nations of injustice, no less than Connecticut: that their practice, in all similar cases, warranted the impost. He urged, that, for twelve years, the fort at Saybrook had been of special service to Springfield; and that it was so still, and might be for a number of years to come. He therefore insisted, that it was strictly just, that the inhabitants of that town should pay the impost. He said he was willing to risk the case, and have it decided on the principles of strict justice. The third article, he observed, was a mere presumption, and had no just foundation; besides, if it were founded, he argued, that the comparison was not equal. The whole of the fourth article, he said, was a mistake: that the confederation was completed in about five years from the first mentioning of it, and that it was not retarded by the means suggested, nor were they ever mentioned. With reference to the fifth article, he replied, that all taxes weakened estates, and if this were a ground of objection against the impost, then no tax or impost could ever be laid. He insisted, that the impost was just and moderate, and, therefore, could not enslave the inhabitants of Springfield. The towns in Connecticut, he observed, were settled before Springfield, and that town had been at no expense in making settlements, more than the towns in Connecticut. He said, if Connecticut, at any time, should become exorbitant in its impositions upon any of the colonies, they would find a remedy in the confederation. With reference to the last article, he declared his willingness, in all similar cases, to submit to the like imposition.

Determination of the commissioners.

The commissioners, upon a full hearing, determined, that it was of weighty consideration to all the plantations upon the river, that the mouth of it should be secured, and a safe passage for goods, up and down the river, be maintained, though at some expense; and, that as Springfield enjoyed the benefit, the inhabitants should pay the impost of two pence per bushel for corn, and a penny on the pound for beaver, or twenty shillings upon every hogshead. Nevertheless, out of respect and tenderness to the Massachusetts, it was resolved, that Springfield, or the general court,

CHAP. VIII. CONNECTICUT.

might have the liberty of exhibiting further reasons against the impost, if any should occur.

At this meeting, Mr. John Winthrop, of Pequot, laid claim to the whole country of the western Nehanticks, including a considerable part of the town of Lyme. He represented, that he obtained the title to this large tract partly by purchase, and partly by deed of gift, before the Pequot war. He petitioned the commissioners to this effect: "Whereas I had the land at Nehantick by deed of gift and purchase from the sachem, before the Pequot war, I desire the commissioners would confirm it unto me, and clear it of all claims of English and Indians, according to the equity of the case." As he had no deed nor writing respecting the land, he produced the testimony of three Nehantick Indians. They testified, that before the Pequot war, Sashions, their sachem, called all his men together, and told them, that he was determined to give his country to the governor's son, who lived at Pattaquasset,* and that his men gave their consent: that afterwards he went to Mr. Winthrop, at Pattaquasset, and when he came back, said that he had granted all his country to the governor's son; and also, that he had received coats for it, which they saw him bring home. Three Englishmen also testified, that they had heard the Indians report the same concerning the grant of the Nehantick† country to Mr. Winthrop. Thomas Stanton deposed, that he remembered Sashions, sachem of the Nehanticks, did give his country to Mr. John Winthrop, before the Pequot war, and that he was interpreter in that business.

The commissioners of Connecticut pleaded against the claim of Mr. Winthrop, that his purchase bore no date; that the tract pretended to be purchased or given, was not circumscribed within any limits; and that it did not appear, that the Indian, who granted the lands, had any right in them: that the grant was verbal, and, at most, could be but a vague business. They also urged, that it did not appear, but that Mr. Winthrop purchased the lands for the noblemen and gentlemen, in whose service he was, at that time, employed; and that, as the lands had been conquered, at the hazard and expense of Connecticut, before Mr. Winthrop made known his claim, whatever it was, it was then dormant, and of no validity. They further insisted, that, as they were not prepared to give a full answer, no decision might be made, until Connecticut should be fully heard with respect to the premises.

BOOK I.
1647.
Mr. Winthrop's claim to the Nehantick country.

Reply of Connecticut to his claim.

* This is sometimes spelt Pamaquasset, and was, I suppose, the Indian name of Saybrook.
† Some spelt it Neanticut.

Book I.
1647.

Settlement of accounts.

Congratulatory letter to the Dutch governor.

Saybrook fort burnt.

The commissioners declined any decision of the controversy; but it does not appear that Mr. Winthrop ever after prosecuted his claim. As it seems Mr. Winthrop, about this time, had a design of purchasing Long-Island, the commissioners took occasion to premonish him, that the Island was already under engagements for considerable sums of money, to a number of persons in Connecticut and New-Haven. They represented to him, that any title which might be derived from Mr. Cope, would be very precarious, as he had confessed a short time before his death.†

The commissioners, this year, brought in the number of polls in the several colonies, and made a settlement of their accounts. The whole expenditure of the confederates was 1043 pounds : 10 : 0. There was due to Connecticut, 155 pounds : 17 : 7, which the colony had expended in the general defence, more than its proportion. New-Haven had expended 7 pounds : 0 : 0 more than its proportion. This was exclusive of all the expense which these two colonies had borne in defending themselves against the Indians at Stamford and its vicinity, and in attempting to bring the murderers of the English to condign punishment. Massachusetts and Plymouth paid the balance to Connecticut and New-Haven.

On the 27th of May, Peter Stuyvesant, who, the last year, had been appointed governor of New-Netherlands, arrived at Manhadoes, and commenced his government of the Dutch settlements. The commissioners wrote him a long letter of congratulation. They complained also, that the Dutch sold arms and ammunition to the Indians, and even in the English plantations. They desired that an immediate stop might be put to so dangerous a trade. They made complaint also, that the Dutch had laid so severe an impost upon all goods, as greatly discouraged trading with them, while all the harbors in the united colonies were open and free to them. As the Dutch also imposed heavy fines or forfeitures for miscntries, or defect in commissions, the commissioners desired to be made particularly acquainted with their customs.

This winter, the fort and buildings at Saybrook unaccountably took fire, and, with some goods, were destroyed. Captain Mason, with his wife and child, narrowly escaped the conflagration. The damage was estimated at more than a thousand pounds.

† Records of the united colonies.

CHAPTER IX.

Settlement of New-London. Salaries first granted to civil officers. Troubles with the Narraganset Indians. Rhode-Island petitions to be united with the colonies in confederation. The Massachusetts resume the affair of the impost. Mr. Westerhouse complains of the seizure of his vessel by the Dutch, in the harbour of New-Haven. Murders committed by the Indians; resolutions respecting the murderers. Body of laws compiled. Debates relative to the settlement of Delaware. The Pequots revolt from Uncas, and petition the English. Resolution respecting them. Mr. Westerhouse petitions to make reprisals from the Dutch. Letter to the Dutch governor. Further altercations respecting the impost. Final issue of that affair. The conduct of the Massachusetts upon its decision, and the declaration of the commissioners respecting it. Their treatment of Connecticut respecting the line between the colonies. The court of Connecticut determine to avenge the death of John Whitmore, and detach men to take the murderer.

THE last year several persons began settlements at Pequot harbour. Lots were laid out to them, but part of them were soon discouraged, and left the plantation. This year Mr. Richard Blinman, who had been a minister in England, removed from Gloucester to this new settlement; in consequence of which a considerable addition was made to the number who had kept their station. By the next year, 1648, there was such an accession, that the inhabitants consisted of more than forty families. Some of the principal men were John Winthrop, Esq. the Rev. Mr. Blinman, Thomas Minot, Samuel Lothrop, Robert Allyn and James Avery. For their encouragement, the general court granted them a three years exemption from all colonial taxation. Mr. Winthrop was authorized to superintend the affairs of the plantation. The next year a court was appointed for the trial of small causes. The judges were Mr. Winthrop, Thomas Minot and Samuel Lothrop. The Indian name of the place was Nameaug, alias Towawog. In 1654, the whole tract, now comprised within the towns of New-London and Groton, was called Pequot, from the name of the harbour and original inhabitants. By this it was known for about four years. On the 24th of March, 1658, the assembly passed

BOOK I.
1648.
The act of assembly respecting its name.

an act respecting it, which is so curious, and expressive of the feelings of our ancestors towards their native country, as to render it worthy of publication.

"Whereas, it hath been the commendable practice of the inhabitants of all the colonies of these parts, that as this country hath its denomination from our dear native country of England, and thence is called New-England; so the planters, in their first settling of most new plantations, have given names to those plantations of some cities and towns in England, thereby intending to keep up, and leave to posterity, the memorial of several places of note there, as Boston, Hartford, Windsor, York, Ipswich, Braintree, Exeter; this court considering, that there hath yet no place in any of the colonies been named in memory of the city of London, there being a new plantation within this jurisdiction of Connecticut, settled upon that fair river Moheagan, in the Pequot country, being an excellent harbour and a fit and convenient place for future trade, it being also the only place which the English in these parts have possessed by conquest, and that upon a very just war, upon that great and warlike people, the Pequots, we therefore that we might thereby leave to posterity that we memory of that renowned city of London, from whence we had our transportation, have thought fit, in honor to that famous city, to call the said plantation New-London." The name of the river was also changed and called the Thames.*

Salary for the governor.

Until this time the governors and magistrates appear to have served the people for the honor of it, and the public good. The general court took the affair into their consideration, and granted the governor 30 pounds annually. The same sum was also voted for the deputy governor, who had presided the preceding year. These appear to have been the first salaries given to any civil officers in the colony, and to have been a compensation for the expense of the office, rather than for the service performed.

Election at Hartford, May 19th.

Upon the election at Hartford, Mr. Hopkins was chosen governor, and Mr. Ludlow deputy governor. Mr. Haynes supplied the vacancy made by the advancement of Mr. Ludlow, and Mr. Cullick was elected magistrate and secretary in the place of Mr. Whiting.

Commissioners meet Sept. 7.

In September the commissioners of the united colonies convened at Plymouth. They were John Endicot and Simon Bradstreet, from Massachusetts; William Bradford and John Brown from Plymouth; governor Hopkins and Roger Ludlow, from Connecticut; governor Eaton and John Astwood, from New-Haven.

* Records of Connecticut and New-London.

CHAP. IX. CONNECTICUT.

The Indians, both in the Nehantick and Narraganset country, and in the western parts of Connecticut, had been more perfidious and outrageous this year than at any time since the Pequot war. The Narragansets and Nehanticks, instead of performing the fair promises which they had made, the last year, and of paying the wampum, which had been so long due, hired the Mohawk and Pocomtock Indians to unite with them in an expedition for the total destruction of Uncas and the Moheagans. The Pocomtocks made preparations and assembled for the purpose. They waited several days for the arrival of the Mohawks, who were to have joined them at that place. The Narragansets and Nehanticks removed their old men, women and children into swamps and fastnesses, and prepared an army of 800 men, who were to form a junction with the Mohawk and Pocomtock Indians, in Connecticut, near the Moheagans.

The governor and council, apprised of their designs, dispatched Thomas Stanton, their interpreter, and others to Pocomtock. They found the Pocomtocks actually met in arms, and waiting for the arrival of the Mohawks. It was represented that the Mohawks had four hundred fire arms, and a plenty of ammunition. The Pocomtocks acknowledged that they had been hired by the Narragansets. Such a confederacy was alarming to the colony. What such an army of savages might effect could not be determined. It was dangerous to suffer them to march through the colony, and form a junction near the plantations. Several happy circumstances united their influence to frustrate this formidable combination. The early discovery of the designs of the enemy, by the people of Connecticut, and the precautions which were taken, had a great effect. The Pocomtocks and Mohawks were assured, that the English would defend Uncas against all his enemies, and would avenge all injuries which they should do him. The Mohawks had one or two of their sachems and a number of their men killed by the French. They therefore did not come on. The Pocomtock Indians did not choose to march without them; and the Narragansets, thus deserted, were afraid to proceed. Thus the expedition failed.

The Narragansets not only plotted against the united colonies, but committed many outrages against the people of Rhode-Island. They made forcible entries into their houses, struck and abused the owners, stole and purloined their goods. At Warwick especially, they were exceedingly troublesome. They killed, in that plantation, about a hundred cattle, exclusive of other injuries which they

Book I.
1648.
Perfidy of the Narraganset Indians.

Rhode-Island petitions for admittance to the confederation.

BOOK I.
1648.

Reply of the commissioners.

Messengers sent to the Narragansets.

Further debate relative to the impost.

did to the inhabitants. Indeed, the Rhode-Islanders were so harassed, that they made application, by their representatives, to the commissioners, to be admitted to the confederation of the united colonies.

The commissioners replied, that they found their present state to be full of confusion and danger, and that they were desirous of giving them both advice and help. They however observed, that as the plantation made at Rhode-Island, fell within the limits of the ancient patent granted to the colony of New-Plymouth, they could not receive them as a distinct confederate. They represented, that it was the design of the honourable committee of parliament, that the limits of that colony should not be abridged or infringed. They proposed, that if the Rhode-Islanders would acknowledge themselves to be within the limits of Plymouth colony, they would advise how they might be received on equitable terms, with a tender regard for their convenience; and that they would afford them the same advice and protection, which they did the other plantations within the united colonies.

The commissioners sent messengers again to the Narraganset and Nehantick Indians, to charge their treachery upon them, remonstrate against their conduct, and demand the arrearages of wampum which were yet unpaid. Their outrages against the inhabitants of Rhode-Island were particularly noticed, and the sachems were peremptorily charged to keep their men under better government. The colonies wished to exhibit all forbearance towards the Indians, and, if possible, to preserve the peace of the country. They chose rather to restrain the natives by policy and the arts of peace, than by the sword.

The general court of Massachusetts was, by no means, pleased with the determination of the commissioners, the last year, relative to the impost to be paid at Saybrook. A committee was, therefore, appointed to draft an answer to the observations and pleadings of governor Hopkins before the commissioners, at their former sessions.

The committee introduced their answer with a number of questions relative to the articles of confederation. Some were calculated to make nothing of them, and exhibit them in a point of light entirely contemptible. Others related to the power of the commissioners, and to the degree in which obedience was due to their determinations. They inquired whether a non-compliance with the orders of the commissioners would be a breach of the articles of confederation? They complained, that they had not a greater number of commissioners, as Massachusetts was much larger than the other colonies. They proposed, that they should have the privilege of sending three commissioners, and that the meetings of the confederates should be triennial. They then proceeded to a large reply to the arguments of governor Hopkins; and attempted to vindicate the reasons which they had given before against the impost. In addition to what they had formerly offered, they endeavoured to show, that if Springfield was benefitted by the fort at Saybrook, and ought to pay the impost on that account, that New-Haven, Stamford, and all the towns on that side of the river, ought to pay it no less; because they had been already benefitted, and might be hereafter. Since this was the case, as they pleaded, they objected against the commissioners of New-Haven, as disqualified to judge in the case. They, also, objected against the decision of the commissioners, because it was made, as they said, without a sight of the Connecticut patent. They insisted, that if the patent had been produced, there might have been some clause which would have helped their case. The committee pleaded a priority of possession. They affirmed, that the first possession of Saybrook fort was taken by Mr. John Winthrop, in November, 1635; and our possession was before that: for those who went from Watertown, Cambridge, Roxbury, and Dorchester, the summer before, took possession in our name and right; and had a commission of government from us, and some ordnance for their defence. And in this state they remained a good space. In fine they urged, that if the impost were lawful, it was not expedient; that they could view it in no other light than as a bone of contention, to interrupt their happy union and brotherly love. Indeed, they represented, that it laid them under temptations to help themselves in some other way. This was adopted by the general court.

Governor Hopkins and Mr. Ludlow insisted on the answers which had been given the last year, to the arguments of the general court of the Massachusetts. They attempted to show, that, notwithstanding all which had been urged, the arguments in favour of the impost remained unanswered, and in their full force. They observed, that whatever propositions might have been made by the Massachusetts, in 1638, with respect to the exemption of plantations under their government from an impost, nothing was ever granted upon that head: that affairs were now in a very different state from what they were at the time of the confederation. They urged, that now the charge of the fort and garrison at Saybrook, lay upon the colony; which was not the case at that time; and that nothing could be fairly plead-

Book I.
1648.

ed from the circumstances in which the colonies confederated.

With respect to priority of right, and the commission which had been mentioned, they observed, that the commission of government was taken, *salvo jure*, of the interest of the gentlemen who had the patent of Connecticut, this commission taking rise from the desire of the people that removed, who judged it inexpedient to go away without any frame of government, not from any claim of the Massachusetts jurisdiction over them by virtue of patent.

With reference to the decision of the commissioners, without seeing the Connecticut patent, they observed, that a copy of it was exhibited at the time of the confederation; that it had been well known to many; and that the Massachusetts in particular knew, that it had recently been owned by the honourable committee of parliament; and that equal respect and power had been given by it to all within its limits, as had been either to Massachusetts or Plymouth, within the limits of their respective patents.

As to the inexpediency of the impost, as tending to disturb the peace and brotherly love subsisting between the colonies, they replied, that it was their hope and earnest desire, that in all the proceedings of the confederation, truth and peace might embrace each other. But they insisted, that pleading for truth and righteousness ought, by no means, to disturb peace or brotherly affection. Indeed, they maintained, that things which were rational, and consistent with truth and righteousness, should never be an occasion of offence to any.

The commissioners of Connecticut, at this time, produced an authentic copy of their patent, and governor Hopkins offered to attest it upon oath. As this was the third year since the affair of the impost had been litigated before the commissioners, it was urged, that it might have a final issue, agreeable to truth and righteousness. Governor Hopkins and Mr. Ludlow disputed the southern boundary of Massachusetts, and claimed Springfield as lying within the limits described in the patent of Connecticut.

The commissioners judged, that the objections offered against the gentlemen from New-Haven, were insufficient, and the commissioners from Massachusetts gave them up. Upon the whole, after a full hearing and mature deliberation, the former order, in favour of Connecticut, was confirmed.*

Trouble with the Dutch.

Notwithstanding the congratulatory letter, which the commissioners addressed to Stuyvesant, the Dutch gover-

* Records of the united colonies.

nor, at their last session, he proved not the most comfortable neighbour. He gave no answer to the complaints which had been stated to him, in their letter. He transmitted no account of the customs laid upon the English merchants, nor of the cases in which the Dutch made seizures, so that it was extremely difficult to know on what terms they could trade, or how to escape fines, seizures, and confiscations.

By Stuyvesant's order, the Dutch seized a vessel of Mr. Westerhouse, a Dutch merchant and planter at New-Haven, while riding at anchor within the harbour. He preferred a complaint to the commissioners. He came in from Virginia, and gave evidence, that, when he sailed thence, he made a full payment of all the customs. The commissioners wrote to the Dutch governor on the subject, and remonstrated against such a flagrant insult to the united colonies, and against the injustice done to Mr. Westerhouse. They protested against the Dutch claim to all the lands, rivers, and streams, from Cape Henlopen to Cape Cod; and asserted their claim to all the lands and plantations in the united colonies, as anciently granted by the kings of England to their subjects, and since purchased by them of the Indians, the original proprietors.

At the same time, they assured him, that they expected satisfaction, both for the injury and affront, in taking a ship out of one of their harbours, upon such a challenge and title to the place, unjustly claimed without purchase, possession, or any other considerable ground. They represented to him in strong terms, the absolute necessity of a meeting for the adjustment of the differences between the Dutch and the united colonies. They professed themselves to be inclined to pursue all proper counsels for that purpose. As his letters to them, as well as to the governors of Massachusetts and New-Haven, had been expressed in such indeterminate language on the subject, they wished him to be more explicit. They avowed their determination, that, until such time as the Dutch should come to an amicable settlement of the points in controversy, neither their merchants nor mariners should enjoy any privilege, in any of the English plantations or harbours, either of anchoring, searching, or seizing, more than the English did at the Manhadoes. They declared, that if, upon search, they should find arms and ammunition on board any of the Dutch ships, for the mischievous purpose of vending them within the limits of the united colonies, to the Indians, they would seize them, until further inquiry and satisfaction should be made. In short, they avowed their purpose of

Book I.

1648.

Mr. Westerhouse complains of the seizure of his ship.

The commissioners remonstrate and protest.

Book I.
1648.

treating the Dutch mariners and merchants in the English harbours and plantations, in the same manner in which they treated the English. They declared, that, if the Dutch should proceed to seize any vessel or goods, within any of the harbours of the united colonies, whether of English, Dutch, or any other nation, admitted to be planters in any of the said colonies, they should be necessitated to vindicate their rights, and to repair the damages by all just means.*

Mr. Whitmore murdered in October.

Soon after the meeting of the commissioners, Mr. John Whitmore, of Stamford, was murdered by the Indians. He was a peaceable, worthy man, and one of the representatives of the town in the general court at New-Haven. He fell as he was seeking cattle in the woods. The sachem's son first carried the news into town, and reported that one Toquattoes had killed him, and had some of his clothes, of which he gave a particular description. From this circumstance, it was suspected, that he was either a principal or an accomplice in the crime. No such evidence, however, could be obtained as would warrant the apprehending him. The English took great pains to find the remains of Mr. Whitmore, but could make no discovery at that time. About two months after, Uncas, with several of his Indians, went to Stamford, and making inquiry concerning Mr. Whitmore's body, the sachem's son and one Kehoran, another of the natives who had been suspected, led Uncas, with his men, and a number of the English, directly to the place of his remains. Upon carrying them into town, the sachem's son and Kehoran fell a-trembling, and manifested such signs of guilt, that the Moheagans declared that they were guilty. But before they could be apprehended, they made their escape. The Indians at Stamford and its vicinity, either through fear of their sachem, or favour to his son, or from some other cause, charged the murder upon Toquattoes. But neither he, nor the other suspected persons, were delivered up, nor could the English bring them to any examination respecting the subject.

Murder at Long-Island.

About the same time it was reported, that the Indians upon Long-Island had, some years before, murdered a number of Englishmen, who were part of the crew of a vessel of one Mr. Cope, which had been cast away near the island. These instances of bloodshed gave great alarm to Connecticut and New-Haven, especially to Stamford, and the towns in that vicinity. Mrs. Whitmore, by letters and messengers, sued for justice against the murderers of her husband. The Indians grew haughty and

* Records of the united colonies.

insolent, and censured the conduct of the English. It was dangerous to suffer such crimes to be unpunished, as it would embolden the natives to be constantly massacreing the English. But as nothing could be done, in this case, except by an armed force, it was deferred to the consideration of the commissioners of the united colonies.

Book I.

1649.

At the general election in Connecticut, Mr. Haynes was chosen governor, and Mr. Hopkins deputy-governor. Mr. Ludlow took his place again among the magistrates. The other officers were as they had been the preceding year.

Election, May 17th, 1649.

In consequence of the burning of the old fort at Saybrook, a new one was begun the last year, at a place called the new fort hill. At this session of the assembly, orders were given for the erecting of a new dwelling-house in the fort, and for completing the works and buildings at Saybrook. The magistrates were empowered to impress suitable hands for carrying the business into effect, and appropriations were made for that purpose.

Whereas the commissioners of Massachusetts, in their pleadings before the commissioners of the united colonies, at their last session, had expressed their doubts, whether the act of Connecticut, imposing a duty upon certain articles exported from Connecticut river, had any respect to the inhabitants of Springfield, the general court declared, that they had particular respect to them, as under the government of the Massachusetts. They also resolved, that, in their best apprehensions, nothing was imposed on them more than was strictly just, or than had been imposed on themselves; and that they ought to submit to the impost. They declared, that the execution of the act, with respect to their brethren at Springfield, had been deferred, only that the judgment of the commissioners of the other colonies might be had on the premises. The assembly also resolved, that they were wholly unsatisfied that Springfield did fall within the true limits of the Massachusetts patent. They also expressed their earnest wishes, that the line might be speedily and fully settled, in righteousness and peace. It was ordered, that these resolutions should be laid before the commissioners at their next meeting.

Resolutions of the general court, in the May session.

Mr. Ludlow had, for several years successively, been desired by the general court to make a collection of the laws which had been enacted, and to revise, digest, and prepare a body of laws for the colony. He had now finished the work, and at this session a code was established.

Until this time, punishments, in many instances, had been uncertain and arbitrary. They had been left wholly to the discretion of the court. Defamation had, in some

X

BOOK I.
1649.

instances, been punished by fine, repeated scourging, and imprisonment.* For violation of the sabbath, there is an instance of imprisonment during the pleasure of the court. Unchastity between single persons was, sometimes, punished by setting the delinquent in the pillory, and by whipping him from one town to another. But, from this time, the laws, in general, became fixed, and the punishment of particular crimes was specified, so that delinquents might know what to expect, when they had the temerity to transgress.

The statute now required a jury of twelve men: that in cases in which they were doubtful with respect to law, they should bring in a *non liquet*, or special verdict; and that matter of law should be determined by the bench, as it is at the present time. But if, after the jury had been sent out repeatedly, the court judged they had mistaken the evidence, and brought in a wrong verdict, they were authorised, in civil cases, to impannel a new jury. The court, also, retained the power of lessening and increasing the damages given by the jury, as they judged most equitable.† All cases of life, limb, or banishment, were determined by a special jury of twelve able men, and a verdict could not be accepted unless the whole jury were agreed. Connecticut now had the appearance of a well regulated commonwealth.

Commissioners meet, July 23.

An extraordinary meeting of the commissioners was holden this year at Boston. The members were Thomas Dudley, Esq'r. Mr. Simon Bradstreet, William Bradford, Esq'r. Mr. John Brown, Edward Hopkins, Esq'r. Mr. Thomas Wells, Governor Eaton, and Mr. John Astwood.

The settlement of Delaware bay urged.

Governor Eaton, in behalf of the colony of New-Haven, proposed that effectual measures might be immediately adopted for the settlement of Delaware bay. The title which a number of merchants, at New-Haven, had to extensive tracts on both sides of the river, by virtue of fair purchases from the Indians, was laid before the commissioners. The fertility of the soil, the healthfulness of the country, the convenience of the several rivers, the great advantages of settlements, and a well regulated trade there, not only to New-Haven, but to all the New-England colonies, were strongly represented.

---

* In 1646, one Robert Bartlett, for defamation, was sentenced to stand in the pillory during the public lecture, then to be whipped, pay £5, and suffer six months imprisonment. This year one Daniel Turner, for the same crime, was sentenced to be whipped, and then imprisoned a month: at the month's end to go to the post again, and then to be bound to his good behaviour.
† Old Connecticut code, p. 37.

CHAP. IX.   CONNECTICUT.

The commissioners, after a full hearing and mature deliberation, were of the opinion, that the circumstances of the colonies were such, that it would not be prudent, at that time, by any public act, to encourage the settlement of those tracts. Besides the contest with the Dutch and the danger of involving the colonies in war, it was observed, that they had scarcely sufficient numbers of men at home for their own defence, and the prosecution of the necessary affairs of their respective plantations.

It was therefore recommended to the merchants and gentlemen at New-Haven, either to settle or make sale of the lands which they had, as should appear most expedient. The commissioners resolved, that if any persons in the united colonies should attempt, without their consent, to make settlements on the lands, or to do any thing injurious to the rights of the purchasers, that they would neither own nor protect them in their unjust attempts.*

The murder of Mr. Whitmore, and the other murders which the Indians had committed against the English, were fully considered. The commissioners therefore resolved, that the guilty should be delivered up; and if they were not, that the sachem, at Stamford, or his son, should be apprehended and kept in durance, until they should be secured, and justice have its course. They ordered, that search should be made with respect to the murders, said to be committed, at Long-Island, and, if evidence could be obtained, to apprehend the delinquents and bring them to justice.

Some time before the meeting of the commissioners, the Indians upon Long-Island perpetrated murder at Southold. They rose, in a hostile manner, for several days round the town. The inhabitants were obliged to arm and stand upon their defence against them for a considerable time; and afterwards to keep a strong and vigilant guard by night. The town was not only exceedingly alarmed and distressed, but put to great expense. They therefore made application to the commissioners for relief. But they would not consent, that the colonies in general should bear any of the charge, in such instances. They determined in this case, as they had done before with respect to other towns in the jurisdictions of Connecticut and New-Haven. The colonies and towns, which had suffered, had been obliged to bear all the expense of defending Stamford and other places, Uncas and the Moheagans, in all instances in which they had not been warranted, by the particular directions of the commissioners.

Records of the united colonies.

Margin notes: Book I. 1649. Advice of the commissioners respecting it. Resolutions respecting Indian murderers. Murder at Southold.

BOOK I.

1649.
Narragansets and Nehanticks continue their plots. Attempt to assassinate Uncas.

The Narraganset and Nehantick Indians still persisted in their murderous designs against Uncas, and in their perfidious conduct towards the colonies. The alarming aspect of affairs, with respect to them, was the occasion of this extraordinary meeting.

An Indian, hired by the Narraganset and Nehantick sachems to kill Uncas, going on board a vessel in the Thames, where he was, ran him through the breast with a sword. The wound, at first, was judged to be mortal; Uncas however finally recovered. At this meeting, he presented himself before the commissioners, and complained of the assault made upon him; and affirmed, that these sachems had hired the Mohawks and other Indians against him, as well as an assassin to kill him secretly. He complained also, that the Narragansets had neither restored his canoes nor his captives, as had been expressly demanded and stipulated. He prayed, that, as he had ever been friendly and faithful to the colonies, they would provide for his safety, avenge these outrages, and do him justice.

Ninigrate was examined before the commissioners on these points; and it was proved, by the confession of the Mohawks themselves, that the Narragansets had hired them against Uncas. The Indian, who had wounded Uncas, declared, that he had been hired by Pessacus and Ninigrate. Ninigrate made but a poor defence, either of himself or Pessacus. The commissioners dismissed him, entirely unsatisfied, and assured him, that unless he immediately complied with the terms on which they had formerly agreed, they should leave him to his own counsels.

The colonies were alarmed with the report, that one of the brothers of Sassacus, or his son, was about to marry the daughter of Ninigrate: and it was conjectured, that the Narraganset and Nehantick Indians were concerting a plan to collect the scattered remains of the Pequots, and to set them up as a distinct nation with the son, or brother of Sassacus, at their head. The commissioners viewed the colonies as upon the commencement of an Indian war, and gave directions, that they should be immediately prepared for any emergency.

Petition of the Pequots.

The Pequots, who had been given to Uncas, had now for more than two years revolted from him, and lived separately, as a distinct clan. In 1647, they complained to the commissioners, that Uncas and the Moheagans had abused them. They represented, that, though they had submitted and been faithful to him, assisted him in his wars, been esteemed as his men, and paid him tribute, he had nevertheless grossly injured them. They said, that he had required tribute of them, from time to time, upon mere pretences; and that since they had been put under him, they paid him wampum forty times. They alledged, that upon the death of one of his children, he gave his squaw presents, and ordered them to comfort her in the same way; and that they presented her with a hundred fathom of wampum: That Uncas was pleased, and promised that, for the future, he would esteem and treat them as Moheagans. They affirmed, that notwithstanding this engagement, the Moheagans wronged them in their plays, and deprived them of their just rights. Obachickquid, one of their chief men, complained that Uncas had taken away his wife and used her as his own. They proved, that Uncas had wounded some of them, and plundered the whole company. They prayed, that the English would interpose for their relief, and take them under their protection. The petition was presented in the behalf of more than sixty.

The commissioners found these charges so well supported, that they ordered Uncas to be reproved, and decreed, that he should restore Obachickquid his wife, and pay damages for the injuries he had done the Pequots. They also fined him a hundred fathom of wampum. Nevertheless, as it had been determined, by Connecticut, that the name of the Pequots should be extinguished, and that they should not dwell in their own country, it was resolved that they should return, and be in subjection to Uncas. He was directed to receive them without revenge, and to govern them with moderation, in all respects, as he did the Moheagans. They did not however return to Uncas; but annually presented their petition to the commissioners to be taken under the protection of the English, and to become their subjects. They pleaded, that though their tribe had done wrong, and were justly conquered, yet that they had killed no English people; and that Wequash had promised them, if they would flee their country, and not injure the colonies, that they would do them no harm. To ease them, as far as might be consistent with former determinations, the commissioners recommended it to Connecticut to provide some place for them, which might not injure any particular town, where they might plant and dwell together. At the same time, they were directed to be in subjection to Uncas; and it was again enjoined on him to govern them with impartiality and kindness.

Mr. Westerhouse renewed his complaint respecting the seizure of his vessel, in the harbour of New-Haven. He and peti-

BOOK I.
1649.
tion of Mr. Westerhouse.

alledged, that besides the loss of his vessel, and the advantages of trading, the prime cost of his goods was 2,000 pounds; and that, after repeated application to the Dutch governor, he had not been able to obtain the least compensation. He had therefore petitioned the government of New-Haven, that some Dutch vessel might be taken by way of reprisal. He now petitioned the commissioners for liberty to make reprisals, by way of indemnification, until he should obtain satisfaction.

Commission of reprisals not granted.

Though the commissioners declared against the injustice of the seizure, and regretted both the insult done to the united colonies, and the damages sustained by Mr. Westerhouse, yet they declined granting him a commission to make reprisals. They judged it expedient first to negotiate.

Commissioners write to the Dutch governor.

They therefore wrote to the Dutch governor, that Mr. Westerhouse had applied to them for a commission to make reprisals, and that they had not granted his petition, as they wished first to acquaint him with the motion, and to represent to him the equity of making reprisals, unless justice should be done him some other way. They again avowed their claim to all parts of the united colonies. They asserted the right of New-Haven to Delaware bay, and assured him, that it would not be given up. They complained of his letter, the last year, that it was, in various respects, unsatisfying; and that with regard to that dangerous trade of arms and ammunition carried on with the Indians, at fort Aurania and in the English plantations, it was wholly silent. They observed, that all differences, between them and the Dutch, might have been amicably settled, had it pleased him to attend the meeting of the commissioners, at Boston, according to the invitation which they had given him. As that was not agreeable to him, they avowed their designs of making provision for their own safety.

Resolution against vending arms to the natives.

To prevent the vending of arms and ammunition to the Indians in the united colonies, they passed the following resolve: "That after due application hereof, it shall not be lawful for any Frenchman, Dutchman, or person of any foreign nation, or any Englishman living among them, or under the government of any of them, to trade with any Indian or Indians within this jurisdiction, either directly or indirectly, by themselves or others, under the penalty of confiscation of all such goods and vessels as shall be found so trading, or the true value thereof, upon just proof of any goods or vessels so traded or trading."

The gentlemen from Massachusetts, at this meeting, a-

CHAP. IX.   CONNECTICUT.   183

gain brought on the dispute between them and Connecticut relative to the impost. They pretended, that Mr. Fenwick, some years before, had promised to join with them, in running the line, but that as he had not done it, and it had now been done by them, at their own expense, and to their satisfaction, it ought to be satisfactory to all others, who could make no legal claim to the adjacent lands. This they insisted that Connecticut could not, because they had no patent.

The commissioners from Connecticut denied the facts which had been stated. They insisted, that Mr. Fenwick never had agreed to run the line with them; and that their running the line, at their own expense, was not owing to any defect of his, nor on the part of Connecticut; for they ran the line a year before the dispute with Mr. Fenwick respecting Waranoke. Besides, they said, what he promised at that time, was not to run the line, but to clear his claim to that plantation. With respect to the patent, they acknowledged, they had not indeed exhibited the original, but a true copy, to the authenticity of which Mr. Hopkins could give oath. They observed, it was well known that they had a patent; that the original was in England, and could not then be exhibited; and that the Massachusetts insisting on this point was an entire bar to the amicable settlement of the line between the colonies. Mr. Hopkins insisted, that the southerly extent of the Massachusetts patent ought first to be mutually settled; then he proposed, that the line should be run by skilful men, mutually chosen, and at the mutual expense of the colonies. The commissioners from Connecticut indeed declared, that it was evident, beyond all doubt, that Springfield, at first, was settled in combination with Connecticut; and, that it had been acknowledged to be so even by the colony of Massachusetts. They affirmed, that when propositions were sent, by governor Winthrop, to the plantations upon the river, in 1637, relative to a confederation of the New-England colonies, Mr. Pyncheon, in prosecution of that design, was, in 1638, chosen and sent as a commissioner from Connecticut, to act in their behalf: That it was at this time, and never before, he suggested his apprehensions, that Springfield would fall within the limits of Massachusetts; and that this was received as a fact without any evidence of what had been alledged. They expressed it, as their full persuasion, that Mr. Pyncheon's representations and motion, at that time, originated from a pang of discontent which had overtaken him, in consequence of a censure laid upon him, by the general court

Book 1.
1649.
Further litigation respecting the impost. Objections of Massachusetts.
Reply of Connecticut.

Book I. of Connecticut.* They concluded by expressing their earnest wishes, that both the government of the Massachusetts and their commissioners would consider, that they did not comply with the advice of the commissioners relative to the present dispute; and that they insisted upon what they knew could not, at that time, be obtained. They charged them, with an unwillingness to submit the differences, subsisting between them and Connecticut, to the mature and impartial judgment of the commissioners of the other colonies, according to the true intent of the confederation. In a very modest and respectful manner, they referred it to the serious consideration of their brethren of the Massachusetts, whether their conduct was not directly contrary to the articles and design of the confederates, to which they all ought to pay a conscientious regard.†

1649.

Final decision of the commissioners. Act of Massachusetts.

The commissioners finally decided the controversy in favor of Connecticut. Upon this the gentlemen from Massachusetts produced an order of their general court, passed by way of retaliation, imposing a duty upon all goods belonging to any of the inhabitants of Plymouth, Connecticut or New-Haven, imported within the castle, or exported from any part of the bay.‡

This was very extraordinary indeed, as it was contrary to all the arguments from justice, liberty, expediency, or brotherly love, which they had pleaded against their sister colony. It was extravagant and unreasonable, as it respected Connecticut; as the impost at Saybrook affected the inhabitants of one of their towns only; and that solely upon the export of two or three articles; whereas their impost was upon the inhabitants of all the plantations in the colony; and upon all their imports, as well as exports. With respect to the other colonies, who had laid no kind of imposition on any of the inhabitants of Massachusetts, it was still more unjust and cruel.

The commissioners from Plymouth, Connecticut and New-Haven, in consequence of this extraordinary act, drew up the following declaration and remonstrance, addressed to the general court of Massachusetts.

Declaration of the commissioners.

"A difference between the Massachusetts and Connecticut, concerning an impost at Saybrook, required of Springfield, having long depended, the commissioners hoped, according to the advice at Plymouth, might, at this meeting, have been satisfyingly issued: but upon the pe-

* It seems the court had blamed him for a particular instance of his conduct, in trading with the Indians.
† Records of the united colonies.
‡ Hutchinson, vol. i. p. 154, 155.

rusal of some late orders made by the general court of the Massachusetts, they find, that the line on the south side of the Massachusetts jurisdiction is neither run, nor the place whence it should be run agreed: That the original patent for Connecticut, or an authentic exemplification thereof, (though Mr. Hopkins hath offered upon oath to assert the truth of the copy by himself presented,) is now required; and that a burthensome custom, is, by the Massachusetts, lately imposed not only upon Connecticut, interested in the impost at Saybrook, but upon Plymouth and New-Haven colonies, whose commissioners, as arbitrators, according to an article in the confederation, have been only exercised in the question, and that upon the desire of the Massachusetts, and have impartially, according to their best light, declared their apprehensions; which custom and burthen, (grievous in itself) seems the more unsatisfying and heavy, because divers of the Massachusetts deputies, who had a hand in making the law, acknowledge, and the preface imports it, that it is a return, or retaliation upon the three colonies for Saybrook: and the law requires it of no other English, nor of any stranger of what nation soever. How far the premises agree with the law of love, and with the tenor and import of the articles of confederation, the commissioners tender and recommend to the serious consideration of the general court for the Massachusetts. And in the mean time desire to be spared in all future agitations respecting Springfield."*

Governor Hutchinson observes, that this law was produced to the dishonor of the colony: That had the Massachusetts imposed a duty upon goods from Connecticut only, they might, at least, have had a colour to justify them; but that extending their resentment to the other colonies, because their commissioners had given judgment against them, admitted of no excuse. It was a mere exertion of power, and a proof of their great superiority, which enabled them, in effect, to depart from the union, whenever they found it to be for their interest. If it had been done by a single magistrate, it would have been pronounced tyrannical and oppressive. He observes that, in all ages and countries, communities of men have done that, of which most of the individuals, of whom they consisted, would, acting separately, have been ashamed.†

The Massachusetts treated Connecticut in the same ungenerous manner, with respect to the line between the colonies. In 1642, they employed one Nathaniel Woodward

Book I.

1649.

Manner of Massachusetts running the line.

* Records of the united colonies.
† Hutchinson, vol. i. p. p. 155, 156.

Book I.
1649.

and Solomon Saffery, whom Douglass calls two obscure sailors, to run the line between them and Connecticut. They arbitrarily fixed a boundary, as the exact point to which three miles south of every part of Charles river would carry them. Thence by water they proceeded up Connecticut river, and setting up their compass in the same latitude, as they supposed, declared, that the line struck the chimney of one Bissell's house, the most northern building then in the town of Windsor. This was a whole range of towns south of the true line between the colonies. Connecticut considered the boundary fixed as entirely arbitrary, and six or eight miles further south than it ought to have been. They imagined, that the error at Windsor was still greater, as no proper allowance had been made for the variation of the needle. They viewed the manner in which this had been effected, as contrary to all the rules of justice, and to the modes in which differences of that magnitude ought to be accommodated. The utmost extent of Narraganset river was their north line, and they were persuaded, that this would run so far north as to comprehend the town of Springfield, and other towns in the same latitude. Therefore, neither Connecticut, nor the commissioners of the united colonies, considered any boundary as properly settled, whence the line should be run, nor any line run between the colonies.

Connecticut wished to have the southern boundary of Massachusetts mutually settled and the line run, at the joint expense of the two colonies; but Massachusetts would neither consent to this, nor even allow that the copy of the Connecticut patent was authentic. For nearly seventy years they encroached upon this colony, and settled whole towns within its proper limits.

The general court of Connecticut adopted the recommendation of the commissioners, with respect to the prohibition of all trading of foreigners among the Indians of the united colonies. They made the penalty to be the confiscation of all vessels and goods employed in such trade.

The assembly's determination to arrest murderers.

The court also, after conferring with New-Haven, determined to avenge the blood of John Whitmore, of Stamford; and, considering all its circumstances, and the conduct of the Indians in the town, and bordering upon it, resolved, that it was lawful to make war upon them. It was ordered, that fifty men should be immediately drafted, armed, and victualled, for the purpose of bringing the murderers to condign punishment, or of arresting other Indians, until the delinquents should be delivered to justice.* These

* Records of Connecticut.

spirited measures appear to have had the desired effect. The Indians at Stamford, it seems, became peaceable, and there is nothing further upon the records respecting any trouble with them.

1650.

CHAPTER X.

Court of Election at Hartford. Grants to Captain Mason. The commissioners meet and dispatch Captain Atherton to the Narragansets. Their message to Ninigrate. The Dutch governor arrives at Hartford, and refers the differences between him and the colonies to arbitrators. Their determination, and the line is fixed between the English and Dutch plantations. Agreements with Mr. Fenwick occasion general uneasiness. Committees are appointed to explain and ascertain them. Towns are invited to attend the committees, by their deputies, at Saybrook. An act for the encouragement of Mr. Winthrop, in seeking and improving mines. Norwalk and Mattabeseck settled, and made towns. The colony of New-Haven make another attempt to settle at Delaware. The Dutch governor seizes the company, and frustrates the design. He pursues his former line of conduct towards the colonies. The resolutions of the commissioners relative to his conduct, to the settlement of Delaware, and the tribute to be paid by the Pequots. French commissioners from Canada. Their proposals. Reply to them. The Dutch governor and Indians concert a plan to extirpate the colonies. The commissioners meet, and dispatch agents to the Dutch governor. They determine upon war, unless he should manifest his innocence, and redress the grievances of the colonies. They determine on the number of men to be raised, and draw a declaration of the reasons of the war. The agents return unsuccessful. The commissioners meet again, and determine to make war upon the Dutch and Narraganset Indians. The general court of Massachusetts refuses to raise men, and prevents the war. Altercations between that general court and the commissioners, and between that and the general courts of Connecticut and New-Haven. The alarm and distress of the plantations in these colonies. Their general courts protest against the court of Massachusetts, as violators of the articles of

Book I.
1650.

confederation; and write to Cromwell and the parliament for assistance. The tumultuous state of the inhabitants in several of the towns.

Election, May 16th.

UPON the election at Hartford, Mr. Hopkins was chosen governor, and Mr. Haynes deputy governor. Mr. Clark was added to the magistrates. The court consisted of thirty-two members; the governors, ten assistants, and twenty deputies.

Grant to captain Mason.

The court had granted a thousand acres of land to captain Mason, for his good services in the Pequot war; five hundred to himself, and five hundred to be given to his five best officers and soldiers. It was now ordered, that the five hundred acres granted to the soldiers, should be laid out for them at Pequot, or in the Neanticut country. The next year the court made a grant of Chippachauge island, in Mystic bay, and a hundred and ten acres of land at Mystic, to the captain.

Commissioners meet, Sept. 5th.

The commissioners met this year at Hartford. The meeting consisted of Mr. Simon Bradstreet and Mr. William Hawthorne, Mr. Thomas Prince and Mr. John Brown, and of Governors Hopkins and Haynes, Eaton and Goodyear. Governor Hopkins was chosen president.

Captain Atherton sent to Narragansett.

As the Narragansets still neglected to pay the tribute which had been so many years due, the commissioners dispatched captain Atherton, of Massachusetts, with twenty men, to demand and collect the arrearages. He was authorised, if they should not be paid, upon demand, to seize on the best articles he could find, to the full amount of what was due; or on Pessacus, the chief sachem, or any of his children, and carry them off. Upon his arrival among the Narragansets, he found the sachem recurring to his former arts, putting him off with deceitful and dilatory answers, and not suffering him to approach his presence. In the mean time, he was collecting his warriors about him. The captain, therefore, marched directly to the door of his wigwam, where posting his men, he entered himself with his pistol in his hand, and seizing Pessacus by the hair of his head, drew him from the midst of his attendants, declaring, that if they should make the least resistance, he would dispatch him in an instant. This bold stroke gave him such an alarm, that he at once paid all the arrearages.

Ninigrate, sachem of the Nehanticks, continuing his perfidious practices, began to lay claim to the Pequot country, and appeared to be concerting a plan to recover it from the English. Captain Atherton, therefore, made him a visit, and, according to his instructions, assured him, that the

Chap. X. CONNECTICUT. 189

commissioners were no strangers to his intrigues, in marrying his daughter to the brother of Sassacus; in collecting the Pequots under him, as though he designed to become their head; and in his claims and attempts respecting the Pequot country. He remonstrated against his conduct, as directly opposite to all the covenants subsisting between him and the English colonies. He protested to him, that the colonies would never suffer him to accomplish his designs; either to possess any part of the country which they had conquered, or even to hunt within its limits. He demanded where the brother of Sassacus was? What numbers he had with him? And what were his designs? He insisted upon categorical answers, that the commissioners might order their affairs accordingly. Having, in this spirited manner, accomplished his business, he returned in safety.

Meanwhile, Stuyvesant, the Dutch governor, arrived at Hartford. He had been often invited to attend the meeting of the commissioners, with a view to the accommodation of the difficulties subsisting between him and the English colonies. He chose to treat by writing, and on the 13th* day of September, he introduced his correspondence with the commissioners. In his letter he complained of the encroachments made upon the West India company, and the injuries done them, both by Connecticut and New-Haven. He pretended, that the Dutch, in behalf of said company, had purchased the lands upon the river, of the native Americans, before any other nation had bought them, or laid any claim to them. He, therefore, demanded a full surrender of said lands, and such compensation as the nature of the case required. He also complained of the act prohibiting all foreigners to trade in the English colonies, and that the English sold goods so cheap to the natives, as to ruin the trade for other nations. He concluded with intimations of his willingness to settle a general provisional line, between the Dutch and English plantations, by a joint writing to their superiors in England and Holland, or by the decision of agents, mutually chosen and empowered for that purpose.

The commissioners, observing that his letter was dated at New-Netherlands, replied, that they would not treat, unless he would alter the name of the place where he wrote. He answered, that if they would not date at Hartford, he would not at New-Netherlands, but at Connecticut. They consented, that he should date at Connecticut, but claimed a right for themselves to date at Hartford. He gave

* 23d old style, as he dated.

Book I.
1650.

Sept. 11th, Stuyvesant arrives.

Correspondence commences.

Dispute respecting the place of dating.

190 HISTORY OF Chap. X.

Book I. up the right of dating at the Netherlands, and the treaty proceeded.

1650. Reply of the commissioners to the Dutch complaints. The commissioners replied to his complaints, to this effect: That their title to Connecticut river, and the adjacent country, had been often asserted, and made sufficiently evident, both to the Dutch and English; and that they hoped amply to prove their title to what they enjoyed, by patent, purchase, and possession. Consequently, they insisted, that they had made no encroachments on the honorable West India company, nor done them the least injury. They affirmed, that they knew not what the Dutch claimed, nor upon what grounds: That at some times they claimed all the lands upon the river, and at others, a part only: That their claim was founded sometimes upon one thing, and at other times upon another; and that it had been so various and uncertain, as to involve the whole affair in obscurity.

With respect to trade, they observed, that they had the same right to regulate it, within their jurisdiction, which the Dutch, French, and other nations had to regulate it, within their respective dominions: That their merchants had a right to deal with the natives on such terms as they pleased; and that they presumed they did not trade to their own disadvantage. They gave intimations that, if the then present treaty should succeed agreeably to their wishes, they might reconsider the act of trade, and repeal the prohibition respecting foreigners.

Statement of their own grievances. They then proceeded to a large and particular statement of the grievances they suffered from the Dutch; particularly representing those which have been already noticed in this history, with several other more recent injuries. Especially, that the Dutch agents had gone off from Hartford, without paying for the goods which they had taken up: That their successors had refused to make any settlement of their accounts; and that the Dutch governor had not obliged them to make payment: That the Dutch bought stolen goods, and would make no compensation to the English, whose property they were: And that they had, not only formerly, helped criminals to file off their irons and make their escape; but that they had been guilty of a recent instance of similar conduct. They alleged, that a Dutch servant had, lately, assisted a criminal, committed for a capital offence, to break gaol and make his escape; and that the Dutch called him to no account, for so gross a misdemeanor.

Arbitrators chosen. Various letters passed, and several days were spent, in these altercations. At length, the commissioners chose

Mr. Bradstreet, of Massachusetts, and Mr. Prince, of Plymouth, as arbitrators, to hear and compose all differences with respect to injury and damages; to make provisional boundaries, in all places where their respective limits were controverted, and to settle a just and free correspondence between the parties. The Dutch governor chose Thomas Willet and George Baxter for the same purpose. Both parties, in the most ample manner, authorised the arbitrators to hear and determine, in the most full and absolute manner, all differences between the two nations in this country.

The arbitrators, after a full hearing of the parties, came to the following determination, which they drew up in the form of an agreement.

"Articles of an agreement, made and concluded at Hartford, upon Connecticut river, September 19th, 1650, betwixt the delegates of the honored commissioners of the united English colonies, and the delegates of Peter Stuyvesant, governor general of New-Netherlands.

I. "Upon a serious consideration of the differences and grievances propounded by the two English colonies of Connecticut and New-Haven, and the answer made by the Dutch governor, Peter Stuyvesant, Esq. according to the trust and power committed to us, as arbitrators, and delegates betwixt the said parties: We find that most of the offences or grievances were things done in the time, or by the order and command of Mons. Kieft, the former governor, and that the present honorable governor is not prepared to make answer to them; we therefore think meet to respite the full consideration and judgment concerning them, till the present governor may acquaint the H. M.* States and West India company with the particulars, that so due reparation may accordingly be made."

II. "The commissioners, for New-Haven, complained of several high and hostile injuries which they, and others of that jurisdiction, have received from and by order of the aforesaid Mons. Kieft, in Delaware bay and river, and in their return thence, as by their former propositions and complaints may more fully appear; and besides the English right, claimed by patent, presented and showed several purchases they have made, on both sides the river and bay of Delaware, of several large tracts of land unto, and somewhat above the Dutch house or fort there, with the consideration given to the said sachems and their companies for the same, acknowledged and cleared by the hands of the Indians, who they affirmed were the true proprietors:

* H. M. High and Mighty.

Book I. and testified by many witnesses. They also affirmed, that, according to the best of their apprehensions, they have sustained 1000 pounds damage there, partly by the Swedish governor, but chiefly by order from Mons. Kieft. And therefore required due satisfaction, and a peaceable possession of the aforesaid lands, to enjoy and improve according to their just rights. The Dutch governor, by way of answer, affirmed and insisted on the title and right to Delaware, or the south river, as they call it, and to the lands there, as belonging to the H. M. States and West-India company; and professed he must protest against any other claim; but is not provided to make any such proof, as in such a treaty might be expected, nor had he commission to treat or conclude any thing therein. Upon consideration whereof, we, the said arbitrators or delegates, wanting sufficient light to issue or determine any thing in the premises, are necessitated to leave both parties *in statu quo prius*, to plead and improve their just interest, at Delaware, for planting or trading, as they shall see cause: Only we desire, that all proceedings there, as in other places, may be carried on in love and peace, till the right may be further considered and justly issued, either in Europe or here, by the two states of England and Holland."

III. " Concerning the seizing of Mr. Westerhouse's ship and goods, about three years since, in New-Haven harbour, upon a claim to the place, the honored governor, Peter Stuyvesant, Esq. professed, that what passed in writing that way was through error of his secretary, his intent not being to lay any claim to the place, and with all affirming, that he had orders to seize any Dutch ship, or vessel, in any of the English colonies or harbours, which should trade there without express license or commission. We therefore think it meet, that the commissioners of New-Haven accept and acquiesce in this answer."

" Concerning the bounds and limits betwixt the English United colonies, and the Dutch province of New-Netherlands, we agree as followeth."

I. " That upon Long-Island, a line run from the westernmost part of Oyster-Bay, and so a straight and direct line to the sea, shall be the bounds betwixt the English and Dutch there, the easterly part to belong to the English, and the westernmost to the Dutch."

II. " The bounds upon the main to begin at the west side of Greenwich bay, being about four miles from Stamford, and so to run a northerly line, twenty miles up into the country, and after, as it shall be agreed, by the two governments of the Dutch and New-Haven, provided the said line come not within ten miles of Hudson's river. And it is agreed, that the Dutch shall not, at any time hereafter, build any house or habitation within six miles of the said line; the inhabitants of Greenwich to remain (till further consideration thereof be had) under the government of the Dutch."

III. "The Dutch shall hold and enjoy all the lands in Hartford, that they are actually possessed of, known and set out by certain marks and bounds, and all the remainder of the said land, on both sides of Connecticut river, to be and remain to the English there."

"And it is agreed, that the aforesaid bounds and limits, both upon the island and main, shall be observed and kept inviolable, both by the English of the united colonies, and all the Dutch nation, without any encroachment or molestation, until a full and final determination be agreed upon, in Europe, by the mutual consent of the two states of England and Holland."

"And in testimony of our joint consent to the several foregoing conclusions, we have hereunto set our hands this 19th day of September, Anno Dom. 1650."

SIMON BRADSTREET,
THOMAS PRINCE,
THOMAS WILLET,
GEORGE BAXTER.

The Dutch governor promised also, and his agents, Messrs. Willet and Baxter, engaged for him, that Greenwich should be put under the government of New-Haven, to whom it originally belonged. It was also agreed, that the same line of conduct which had been adopted, with respect to fugitives, by the united colonies, in the eighth article of confederation, should be strictly observed between them and the Dutch, in the province of New-Netherlands. The Dutch governor also acquainted the commissioners, that he had orders from Europe to maintain peace and good neighbourhood with the English in America; and he proceeded so far as to make proposals of a nearer union and friendship, between the Dutch and the united colonies. The commissioners declined acting upon these proposals, without consulting their constituents; and recommended the consideration of them to their respective general courts.

While this settlement with the Dutch seemed to give a favorable aspect to the affairs of the colonies, there arose a great and general uneasiness in Connecticut, relative to the agreements which had been made with Mr. Fenwick, and to the state of the accounts between him and the colony.

General uneasiness respecting the agreements with Mr. Fenwick.

Z

Book I.
1650.

By the first agreement, besides the impost on several articles exported from the mouth of the river, for ten years, the people were obliged to pay one shilling annually for every milch cow and mare in the colony, and the same sum for every swine killed either for market or private use. Springfield refused to pay the impost; and it seems that Connecticut was obliged, by the conduct of Massachusetts, to repeal the act relating to the imposition. By reason of the controversy which arose between Connecticut and Massachusetts, and some other circumstances, several of the towns, during the two first years, paid but a small proportion of what had been stipulated. The colony therefore, on the 17th of February, 1646, made a new agreement with Mr. Fenwick. This was to the following effect:

That, instead of all former grants, he should receive from the colony, annually, one hundred and eighty pounds, for ten years. He was to collect what was due from Springfield, and to enjoy certain profits arising from the beaver trade. A hundred and seventy or eighty pounds was also to be paid to him from Saybrook and one or two newly settled towns. The whole amount appears to have been more than 2,000 pounds, which the colony paid for the right of jurisdiction, the ordnance, arms and stores at the fort.* As different apprehensions had arisen, respecting these agreements, and the state of affairs between Mr. Fenwick and the colony, the general court appointed committees to meet at Saybrook to ascertain them. To quiet the minds of the people, notice was given to every town of the time and place of the meeting of the committees, and each was authorized to send representatives to hear the disputes and report the issue, with the reasons of it, to their constituents. By these means the inhabitants obtained general satisfaction.

Feb. 5th, 1651.

May 15.

Mr. John Winthrop, at the election, was chosen into the magistracy. The assembly consisted of thirty four members; twelve magistrates and twenty two deputies.

Rhode-Island entertains fugitives.

The colony of Rhode-Island gave great trouble to her neighbours, by giving entertainment to criminals and fugitives. Connecticut found it so prejudicial to the course of justice and to the rights of individuals, that the court resolved to recommend the consideration of the affair to the commissioners of the united colonies.†

Mr. Winthrop imagined, that Connecticut contained

---

* See the agreements, Numbers V and VI.
† Augustus Hareiman, a Dutch trader, with his vessel, was seized by the people of Saybrook for illicit trade with the Indians. The court fined him 40 pounds and confiscated his vessel and cargo. They also made him give it in writing, under his hand, that he had been well treated.

mines and minerals, which might be improved to great advantage to individuals, as well as to the public emolument. Upon a motion of his, the assembly passed the following act.

"Whereas, in this rocky country, among these mountains and rocky hills, there are probabilities of mines of metals, the discovery of which may be of great advantage to the country, in raising a staple commodity; and whereas John Winthrop, Esquire, doth intend to be at charges and adventure, for the search and discovery of such mines and minerals; for the encouragement thereof, and of any that shall adventure with the said John Winthrop, Esquire, in the said business, it is therefore ordered by the court, that if the said John Winthrop, Esquire, shall discover, set upon, and maintain such mines of lead, copper or tin; or any minerals, as antimony, vitriol, black lead, allum, stone salt, salt springs, or any other the like, within this jurisdiction; and shall set up any work for the digging, washing and melting, or any other operation about the said mines or minerals, as the nature thereof requireth; that then the said John Winthrop, Esquire, his heirs, associates, partners or assigns, shall enjoy forever, said mines, with the lands, wood, timber and water, within two or three miles of said mines, for the necessary carrying on of the works, and maintaining of the workmen, and provision of coal for the same: provided it be not within the bounds of any town already settled, or any particular person's property; and provided it be not in, or bordering upon any place, that shall, or may, by the court, be judged fit to make a plantation of."

Though the eastern and middle parts of Norwalk had been purchased more than ten years, yet there had been only a few scattering inhabitants within its limits. But the last year, upon the petition of Nathan Ely and Richard Olmstead, the court gave liberty for its settlement, and ordained that it should be a town by the name of Norwalk. The western part of it was purchased on the 15th of February. The inhabitants, at this time, consisted of about twenty families. About four years after, the general court vested them with town privileges. The situation of the place is very agreeable; the harbor is pleasant and safe, and the lands rich, yielding plenteously. The air is uncommonly healthful and salubrious.*

*From the first settlement of the town, to 1732, a term of more than 90 years, there was no general sickness, except the measles, in the town. From 1715, to 1719, there died in that large town, twelve persons only. Out of one train band, consisting of a hundred men, there died no one person, from 1716, to 1730, during the term of fourteen years. Mrs. Has-

Book I.
1651.

Act to encourage the discovery of mines.

Settlement of Norwalk.

HISTORY OF — Chap. X.

Book I.
1651.
Settlement of Middletown.

The settlement of Mattabeseck commenced about the same time. The principal planters were from England, Hartford, and Weathersfield. The greatest number were from Hartford. There was a considerable accession from Rowley, Chelmsford, and Woburn, in Massachusetts. By the close of this year it became considerably settled. In November, 1653, the general court gave it the name of Middletown. Twenty years after, the number of shares was fixed at fifty-two. This was the whole number of the householders, at that period, within the town.

The agreement, made the last year, with the Dutch governor, and his professions of amity, encouraged the English to prosecute the settlement of the lands, which they had purchased in the vicinity of the Dutch.

Attempt to settle Delaware.

Fifty men from New-Haven and Totoket, made preparations to settle their lands at Delaware. This spring, they hired a vessel to transport themselves and their effects into those parts. They had a commission from governor Eaton; and he wrote an amicable letter to the Dutch governor, acquainting him with their design; assuring him, that, according to the agreement at Hartford, they would settle upon their own lands, and give no disturbance to their neighbours. A letter, of the same import, was also addressed to him from the governor of Massachusetts. But no sooner had governor Stuyvesant received the letters,

New-Haven people imprisoned by the Dutch governor.

than he arrested the bearers, and committed them close prisoners, under guard. Then sending for the master of the vessel to come on shore, that he might speak with him, he arrested and committed him. Others, as they came on shore, to visit and assist their neighbours, were confined with them. The Dutch governor desired to see their commission, promising it should be returned when he had taken a copy. But when it was demanded of him, he would not return it to them. Nor would he release the men from confinement, until he had forced them to give it under their hands, that they would not prosecute their voyage; but, without loss of time, return to New-Haven. He threatened, that, if he should afterwards find any of them at Delaware, he would not only seize their goods, but send them prisoners into Holland. He also caused a considerable part of the estate of the inhabitants of Southampton to be attached, and would not suffer them to remove it within the jurisdiction of the English. Captain Tapping, Mr. Fordham, and others, therefore complained, and petitioned to the commissioners for redress.

ford, relict of the first minister of the town, died Sept. 12th, 1730, aged 90 years. Manuscripts of the Rev. Moses Dickinson.

CHAP. X. CONNECTICUT.

They met this year at New-Haven. The members were Mr. Bradstreet and captain John Hawthorne, Mr. John Brown and Mr. Timothy Hatherly, governor Hopkins and Mr. Ludlow, governors Eaton and Goodyear. Governor Eaton was chosen president.

Jasper Crane and William Tuttle, in behalf of themselves, and many others, inhabitants of New-Haven and Totoket, presented a petition to the commissioners, complaining of the treatment which they had received from the Dutch governor, and representing, that they had sustained more than three hundred pounds damage, besides the insult and injury done to the united colonies. They showed, that the Dutch had seized, and were about to fortify, upon the very lands which they had bought of the original proprietors at Delaware: That, had it not been for the injustice and violence of the Dutch, the New-England colonies might have been greatly enlarged, by settlements in those parts; that the gospel might have been published to the natives, and much good done, not only to the colonies, at present, but to posterity. They also represented, that the Dutch were, by gifts and art, enticing the English to make settlements under their jurisdiction. They insisted, that suffering them thus to insult the English, and to seize on lands to which they could shew no just claim, would encourage them to drive them from their other settlements, and to seize on their lands and property, whenever they pleased; and that it would make them contemptible among the natives, as well as among all other nations. They pressed the commissioners, therefore, to act with spirit, and immediately to redress the injuries which had been done to them and the colonies.

The commissioners nevertheless, declined acting against the Dutch, without previously writing, and attempting to obtain redress by negotiation. They wrote to Stuyvesant, insisting that he had acted in direct contravention of the agreement at Hartford, and noticed that, in a letter to governor Eaton, he had threatened force of arms, and bloodshed, to any who should go to make settlements upon their lands, at Delaware, to which he was unable to show any claim. They represented to him, how deficient it appeared at Hartford, not only to the commissioners, but even to the arbitrators of his own choosing. They charged him with a breach of the engagement of Mr. Willet and Mr. Baxter, in his behalf, with respect to the restoration of Greenwich to the government of New-Haven. They remonstrated against his conduct, in imprisoning the people of New-Haven and Totoket, in detaining their commis-

BOOK I.
1651.
Commissioners meet at New-Haven. Sept. 14th. Petition respecting Delaware.

The commissioners remonstrate and protest against the Dutch governor.

198 HISTORY OF CHAP. X.

Book I.
1651.

sion, and frustrating their voyage; and also in beginning to erect fortifications upon the lands of the New-Haven people, at Delaware. They affirmed, that they had as good a right to the Manhadoes, as the Dutch had to those lands. They declared that the colonies had just cause to vindicate and promote their interests, and to redress the injuries which had been done to their confederates. They protested, that whatever inconveniences or mischief might arise upon it would be wholly chargeable to his unneighbourly and unjust conduct.

Resolution respecting the settlement of Delaware.

At the same time, for the encouragement of the petitioners, they resolved, that if, at any time, within twelve months, they should attempt the settlement of their lands, at Delaware, and, at their own charge, transport a hundred and fifty, or at least a hundred men, well armed, with a good vessel or vessels for such an enterprise, with a sufficient quantity of ammunition; and warranted by a commission from the authority at New-Haven, that then, if they should meet with any opposition from the Dutch or Swedes, they would afford them a sufficient force for their defence. They also resolved, that all English planters, at Delaware, either from New-Haven, or any other of the united colonies, should be under the jurisdiction of New-Haven.

Tribute demanded of the Pequots.

The Pequots among the Moheagans and Narragansets, and those who had removed to Long-Island, had, to this time, neglected to pay any part of the tribute, which had been stipulated, at Hartford, in 1638, upon condition, that the English would spare their lives and defend them from their enemies. The general court had given orders, that it should be collected forthwith, and had appointed captain Mason to go to Long-Island, and demand it of the Pequots there, as well as of those in other places.

They demand why it was required.

Uncas, with a number of the Moheagans, and of Ninigrate's men, therefore presented himself before the commissioners; and, in behalf of the Pequots, paid a tribute of about three hundred fathoms of wampum. He then, in their name, demanded, why this tribute was required? How long it was to continue? And whether it must be paid by the children yet unborn?

Answer of the commissioners.

The commissioners answered, that, by covenant, it had been annually due ever since the year 1638: That after a just war, in which the Pequots were conquered, the English, to spare, as far as might be, the blood of the guilty, accepted of a small tribute, as expressed in the covenant. They insisted, that they had a right to demand it as a just debt. They observed, that twelve years tribute was now due, reckoning only to the year 1650; but that, to show

CHAP. X. CONNECTICUT.

their lenity, and encourage the Pequots, if they would behave themselves well, and pay the tribute agreed upon, for ten years, reckoning from 1650, they would give them all which was due for past years; and that, at the expiration of the ten years, they and their children should be free. This, it seems, they thankfully accepted, and afterwards became as faithful friends to the English as the Moheagans. They assisted them in their wars with other Indians; especially, in that against Philip and the Narragansets.

Book I.
1651.

While the commissioners were at New-Haven, two French gentlemen, Monsieur Godfroy and Monsieur Gabriel Druillets, arrived in the capacity of commissioners from Canada. They had been sent by the French governor, Monsieur D'Aillebout, to treat with the united colonies. They presented three commissions, one from Monsieur D'Aillebout, another from the council of New-France, and a third to Monsieur Gabriel Druillets, who had been authorized to publish the doctrines and duties of christianity among the Indians.

French agents from Canada.

Present their commissions.

In behalf of the French in Canada, and the christianized Indians in Acadia, they petitioned for aid against the Mohawks and warriors of the six nations. They urged, that the war was just, as the Mohawks had violated the most solemn leagues, and were perfidious and cruel: That it was a holy war, as the Acadians were converted Indians, and the Mohawks treated them barbarously, because of their christianity. They insisted, that it was a common concern to the French and English nations, as the war with the six nations interrupted the trade of both, with the Indians in general.

Sue for aid against the six nations.

Monsieur Druillets appeared to be a man of address. He opened the case to the best advantage, displaying all his art, and employing his utmost ability to persuade the commissioners to engage in the war against the six nations. He urged, that, if they would not consent to join in the war, they would at least, permit the enlistment of volunteers, in the united colonies, for the French service; and grant them a free passage through the colonies, by land or water, as the case might require, to the Mohawk country. He also pleaded, that the christianized Indians might be taken under the protection of the united colonies. He made fair promises of the ample compensation which the French would make the colonies for these services. He represented, that, if these points could be gained, they would enter immediately upon a treaty, for the establishment of a free trade between the French and English in all parts of America.

Their address.

BOOK I.
1651.
Reply of the commissioners.

The reply of the commissioners exhibits policy and prudence; showing, that they were not ignorant of men, nor of the arts of negotiation. They answered, that they looked upon such Indians, as had received the yoke of Christ, with another eye, than upon those who worshipped the devil: That they pitied the Acadians, but saw no way to help them, without exposing the English colonies, and their own neighbouring Indians, to war: and that some of those Indians professed christianity no less than the Acadians. They observed, that it was their desire, by all just means, to keep peace with all men, even with these barbarians; and that they had no occasion for war with the Mohawks, who, in the war with the Pequots, had shown a real respect to the English colonies, and had never since committed any hostility against them. They declared their readiness to perform all offices of righteousness, peace, and good neighbourhood towards the French colony; yet, that they could not permit the enlisting of volunteers, nor the marching of the French and their Indians through the colonies, without giving grounds of offence and war to the Mohawks, and exposing both themselves and the Indians, whom they ought to protect. They observed, that the English engaged in no war, until they were satisfied that it was just, nor until peace had been offered on reasonable terms, and had been refused: that the Mohawks were neither in subjection to the English, nor in league with them; so that they had no means of informing themselves what they could say in their own vindication. They, also, assured the French ambassadors, that they were exceedingly dissatisfied with that mischievous trade, which the French and Dutch had carried on, and still continued, with the Indians, in vending them arms and ammunition, by which they were encouraged, and made insolent, not only against the christian Indians and catechumens, but against all christians in Europe, as well as America. But if all other difficulties were removed, they represented, they had no such short and convenient passage, by land or water, as might be had by Hudson's river to fort Aurania and beyond, in the possession of the Dutch. They concluded, by observing, that the honoured French deputies, as they conceived, had full powers to settle a free trade between the English and French colonies; but if, for reasons best known to themselves, it was designed to limit the English, by the same restraints and prohibitions to which the unprivileged French were subjected, not suffering them to trade, until they had obtained a particular license from the governor and company of New France, they must wait a

CHAP. X. CONNECTICUT.

more favourable opportunity for negotiation. Such an opportunity, whenever it should offer, they intimated they should readily embrace.*

The commissioners, apprehending that there was little prospect of obtaining a redress of their grievances from the Dutch, by remonstrance and negotiation, wrote to Mr. Winslow, agent for Massachusetts in England, on the subject. They represented the claims and rights of the colonies, and the injuries which they suffered from the Dutch. They insisted, that their conduct was a high affront, not only to the colonies, but to the honour of the English nation. They desired Mr. Winslow to inquire how the parliament and council of state esteemed the ancient patents, and how any engagements of the colonies against the Dutch, for the defence of their rights, would be viewed by the parliament. It was desired, that he would give them the earliest information on the subject.

The people at New-Haven persisted in their purpose of making, if possible, a permanent settlement upon their lands at Delaware. They were sensible, that such was the situation of their affairs, that a leader, who was not only a politician, but a man of known courage, military skill and experience, would be of great importance to the enterprise. They, therefore, made application to captain Mason, to remove with them to Delaware, and take on him the management of the company. They made him such offers, that it seems he had a design of leaving the colony, and putting himself at the head of the English settlements in those parts. But the general court at Connecticut, would by no means consent. They unanimously desired him to entertain no thoughts of changing his situation. This appears to have prevented his going, and to have frustrated the design.

The grand list of the colony appears this year, for the first time, upon the records. There are the lists of seven towns only. The others either paid no taxes, or their lists were not completed and returned. The amount of the whole, was 75,492l. 10s. 6d. It appears that the towns, at this period, were not, upon an average, more than equal to our common parishes at this day.

At the general election in Connecticut, in 1652, the former magistrates were re-elected.

The commencement of hostilities, the last year, between England and Holland, the perfidious management of the Dutch governor, with apprehensions of the rising of the Indians, spread a general alarm through the colony.

*Records of the united colonies.

BOOK I.
1651.
Letter to Mr. Winslow.

Capt. Mason invited to remove to Delaware.

List of the colony, Oct. 9th.

Election, May 20th, 1652.

BOOK I.
1652.
June 30th.

The assembly convened on the 30th of June, and adopted several measures for the common safety. Orders were given, that the cannon at Saybrook should be well mounted on carriages; that the fort should be supplied with ammunition; and that the inhabitants, who were scattered abroad, should collect their families into it, and hold themselves in the best state of readiness for their common defence.

Indians required to give up their arms, April, 1653.

The Indians in the vicinity of the several plantations, within the colony, were required to give testimony of their friendship and fidelity to the English, by delivering up their arms to the governor and magistrates. Those who refused, were to be considered as enemies.

Stuyvesant, the Dutch governor, made no satisfaction for past injuries; but added new insults and grievances to those which were past. He again revived the claims which he had renounced at Hartford; and though he restrained the Dutch from open hostility, yet he used all his arts with the Indians to engage them to massacre the English colonists.

April 19th, commissioners meet.

A discovery was made in March, that he was confederate with the Indians, in a plot for the extirpation of the English colonies. An extraordinary meeting of the commissioners was called upon the occasion. It consisted of Governor Endicott, Mr. William Hawthorne, William Bradford, Esq'r. Mr. John Brown, Mr. Ludlow, Captain Cullick, Governor Eaton, and Captain John Astwood. Gov. Endicott was chosen president.

Plot of the Dutch and Indians.

Upon a close attention to the reports which had been spread, and a critical examination of the evidence, all the commissioners, except those of the Massachusetts, were of the opinion, that there had been a horrid and execrable plot, concerted by the Dutch governor and the Indians, for the destruction of the English colonies. Ninigrate, it appeared, had spent the winter at the Manhadoes, with Stuyvesant, on the business. He had been over Hudson's river, among the western Indians; procured a meeting of the sachems; made ample declarations against the English; and solicited their aid against the colonies. He was brought back in the spring, in a Dutch sloop, with arms and ammunition from the Dutch governor. The Indians, for some hundreds of miles, appeared to be disaffected and hostile. Tribes, which before had been always friendly to the English, became inimical; and the Indians boasted, that they were to have goods from the Dutch, at half the price for which the English sold them, and powder as plenty as the sand. The Long-Island Indians testified to the

Evidence of it.

plot. Nine sachems, who lived in the vicinity of the Dutch, sent their united testimony to Stamford, "that the Dutch governor had solicited them, by promising them guns, powder, swords, wampum, coats, and waistcoats, to cut off the English." The messengers who were sent, declared, "they were as the mouth of the nine sagamores who all spake, they would not lie." One of the nine sachems, afterwards, came to Stamford, with other Indians, and testified the same. The plot was confessed by a Wampeag and a Narraganset Indian, and was confirmed by Indian testimonies from all quarters.* It was expected, that a Dutch fleet would arrive, and that the Dutch and Indians would unite in the destruction of the English plantations. It was rumoured, that the time for the massacre was fixed upon the day of the public election, when the freemen would be generally from home.

The country was exceedingly alarmed; especially Connecticut and New-Haven. They were greatly hindered in their ploughing, sowing, planting, and in all their affairs. They were worn down with constant watching and guarding, and put to great expense for the common safety.

Book I. 1653. Alarm and distress of the colonies.

Six of the commissioners were satisfied, that they had just grounds of war with the Dutch. They drew up a general declaration of their grievances, for the satisfaction of the people. They also stated the evidence they had of the conspiracy, which they supposed was then in hand. They determined, nevertheless, before they commenced hostilities against the Dutch, to acquaint the governor with the discovery which they had made, and to give him an opportunity of answering for himself.

In the mean time letters arrived from the Dutch governor, in which he appeared, with great confidence, absolutely to deny the plot which had been charged upon him. He offered to go or send to Boston to clear his innocence; or desired that some persons might be deputed and sent to the Manhadoes, to examine the charges and receive his answers. Other letters arrived at the same time confirming the evidence of the conspiracy, and representing, that the Indians were hastened to carry it into execution.

The commissioners determined to send agents to the governor; and with the utmost dispatch made choice of Francis Newman, one of the magistrates of New-Haven, captain John Leveret, afterwards governor of Massachusetts, and Mr. William Davis. They vested them with plenary powers to examine the whole affair, and to receive the governor's answer, according to his own proposals.

Agents dispatched to the Dutch governor.

* Records of the united colonies.

Stuyvesant, in his letters, pretended to express his admiration, that the English should give credit to Indian testimony. The commissioners, therefore, in their reply, charged him with making use of heathen testimony against New-Haven; and observed, that Kieft, his predecessor, had used Indian testimonies against the English in a strange manner, in a case of treason, and life or death. They also acquainted him with the bloody use which the Dutch governor and his council had made of the confession of the Japanese, against captain Towerson and the English christians at Amboyna, though it was extorted by torture.

They wrote to Monsieur Montague and captain Newton, who were of the Dutch governor's council, that his protestations of innocence gave them no satisfaction. They charged the fiscal,* as well as the governor, with the plot. They stated their grievances, demanded satisfaction for past injuries, and security for the future.

While their agents were employed at the Manhadoes, they determined on the number of men to be raised, in case of a war. For the first expedition they resolved to send out five hundred; and appointed captain Leveret to the chief command. They also determined, that, should they engage in war with the Dutch, the commissioners of the united colonies should meet at New-Haven, to give all necessary directions respecting the expedition, and to order the war in general.

Notwithstanding the fair proposals which governor Stuyvesant had made, he would submit to no examination, by the agents, any further than a committee of his own appointing should consent. Two of the committee were persons who had been complained of for misdemeanors, at Hartford; and one of them had been laid under bonds for his crimes. The agents conceived, that the very proposal of such persons as a committee was a high affront to them, to the united colonies, and to the English nation. Besides, the Dutch governor would not suffer the witnesses to speak unless they were previously laid under such restraints as would prevent all benefit from their evidence. The agents not only objected to the committee, and declined all connection with them, but remonstrated against the restraints proposed to be laid on the witnesses. Finding that nothing could be effected with respect to the design of their agency, they, in a spirited manner, demanded satisfaction for insults and injuries past, and security against future abuse, and took leave of the Manhadoes.

As they returned, they took various testimonies respect-

* That is, the treasurer.

ing the plot; some from the Indians, and others from the English, sworn before proper authority. Before their return, the commissioners were dispersed, and the general elections were finished. The courts at Connecticut and New-Haven voted their respective quotas of men, appointed their officers, and gave orders, that all necessary preparations should be made for the designed expedition.

[margin: Book I. 1653. Agents return.]

On the election at Hartford, the former officers were rechosen. The time of election, at New-Haven, had been changed from October to May; and this year was on the 25th of the month. The governors were the same as they had been for several years, Eaton and Goodyear. The magistrates were, Mr. William Fowler, Mr. John Astwood, William Leet, Esquire, Mr. Joshua Atwater, and Mr. Francis Newman. Mr. Atwater was treasurer, and Mr. Newman secretary.

[margin: Magistrates of New-Haven.]

Immediately, on the return of the agents, from the Manhadoes, the general court of Massachusetts summoned another extraordinary meeting of the commissioners, at Boston, about the last of May. The commissioners were all the same who composed the last meeting, except Mr. Bradstreet in the room of governor Endicott, who was obliged to attend the general court.

[margin: Commissioners meet again.]

The agents made report of the treatment which they had received from the Dutch, and of such evidence as they had taken of the plot on their return. The commissioners were also certified, that the Indians, on Long-Island, had charged the fiscal with the plot; and that captain Underhill, having reported what the Indians declared, was seized and carried by a guard of soldiers, from Flushing to the Manhadoes, where he was confined by the fiscal, until what he had reported, was affirmed to his face: then he was dismissed, without trial, and all his charges borne. No sooner had the agents taken their departure from the Manhadoes, than the captain, because he had been active in exhibiting the evidence of the Dutch and Indian conspiracy, notwithstanding all the important services he had rendered the Dutch, was ordered to depart. The commissioners received a letter from him, May 24th, representing the extreme danger in which he and all the English were, assuring them, that as necessity had no law, he had, like Jeptha, put his life in his hand, to save English blood; and that he was waiting their orders, with loyalty to them and the parliament, to vindicate the rights of the nation. The Dutch demanded, that all the English among them should take an oath of fidelity to them. This, in case of war, might have induced them to fight against their own nation.

[margin: Agents make report.]

Book I.
1653.

The people of Hampstead, at the same time, represented that they were in the utmost danger, and wrote, in the most pressing manner, for arms and ammunition, to defend themselves. Letters were also sent from Connecticut and New-Haven, with intelligence, that the Dutch governor, by presents of wampum, coats, and other articles, was exciting the Mohawks, and various Indian tribes, to rise and attack the English, both on Long-Island, and on the main.

A long letter from the Dutch governor was also received, in which, in general terms, he excused himself relative to the plot; but he gave no encouragement of the least satisfaction, in a single instance; or that the colonies should be more safe from injury and insult, for the future. Indeed, he still insulted them, renewing the claims, both to Connecticut and New-Haven, which he had given up at Hartford.

The commissioners are for war.

All the commissioners, excepting Mr. Bradstreet, voted for war against the Dutch. He was under the influence of the general court of Massachusetts, who were using all their arts to oppose the commissioners, and prevent open hostility. The commissioners, however, so strenuously urged the justice and necessity of an immediate war with the Dutch, and so spiritedly remonstrated against the conduct of the court, as violaters of the articles of union, that they appointed a committee of conference with them. They desired, that a statement of the case might be made, and the advice of the elders taken on the subject. The committee of the court were major Denison and captain Leveret.

The commissioners replied, that their former declaration, their letter to the Dutch governor, and the evidence before them, afforded clear and sufficient light in the affair. Nevertheless, they appointed captain Hawthorne, Mr. Bradford, and governor Eaton, a committee to confer with the gentlemen appointed by the court. Governor Eaton drew a state of the case, in behalf of the committee of the commissioners. The committee from the general court would not consent to it, but drew a statement of their own. Under the influence of the general court, and the different representation which their committee had made, the elders gave their opinion:

Advice of the elders.

"That the proofs and presumptions of the execrable plot, tending to the destruction of so many of the dear saints of God, imputed to the Dutch governor and the fiscal, were of such weight as to induce them to believe the reality of it; yet they were not so fully conclusive, as to clear up a present proceeding to war before the world; and to bear up their hearts with that fulness of persuasion, which was meet in commending the case to GOD, in prayer, and to the people in exhortations; and that it would be safest for the colonies to forbear the use of the sword; but advised to be in a posture of defence, and readiness for action, until the mind of GOD should be more clearly known, either for a more settled peace, or manifest grounds of war."

It seems, that the affair was very partially referred to the ministers, whether the evidence of the plot was so clear as to warrant a war; whereas, this was but one circumstance among many, which might render it just and necessary. These ought to have been considered, no less than the other. The deputies of the court concurred with the clergy.

In the mean time, all the commissioners, except Mr. Bradstreet, continued determined for war. Governor Eaton insisted, that the Dutch had, for many years, during a succession of governors, multiplied injuries and hostile affronts, with treachery and falsehood, against the English, to their very great damage: That these injuries had been fully and repeatedly represented to them, and satisfaction demanded; yet that nothing had been received in return, but dilatory, false, and offensive answers. He observed, that the governor and his associates had been formerly suspected and accused of instigating the Indians against the English; and that now a treacherous and bloody plot had been discovered, and charged upon him and his fiscal, by more witnesses than could have been expected; that by it the peace of the country had been disturbed, their own lives, the lives of their children, and all their connexions, had been in constant jeopardy: That though they had allowed the Dutch governor a fair opportunity of clearing himself, of making satisfaction, and securing the colonies for the future; yet that, by his conduct, he had increased the evidence of his guilt; and that he had given the colonies no security for their future peace and safety; nor had they the least reason to expect them. He insisted, that the English, under the jurisdiction of the Dutch, were in the most immediate danger, not only from them, but the Indians, through their instigation; because they would not submit to an oath to join with them in fighting against their own nation. He urged, that the insolence, treachery, and bitter enmity, which the Dutch had manifested against the nation of England, and all the English abroad, as they had opportunity, were sufficient to assure them that, as soon as the States General should be able to send a small fleet to the Manhadoes, the colonies could not be safe, ei-

Book I.

1653.

Governor Eaton's representation of the Dutch conduct.

Book I. ther in their persons or property, by land or sea. He fur-
1653.   ther insisted, that the state of the commonwealth of En-
gland, and of the colonies, was such as called for war; and that, if either of the colonies should refuse to join in it, against the common enemy, and if any of the plantations, through such refusal, should be destroyed, the guilt of such blood would lie upon them.*

Mr. Norris pleads for war. Some faithful people in the Massachusetts were entirely opposed to the conduct of their general court, and ventured to express their opinion. The Rev. Mr. Norris, of Salem, sent a writing to the commissioners, representing the necessity of a war. He urged, that if the colonies, in their then present circumstances, should neglect to engage in it, it would be a declaration of their neutrality in the contest;

May 30. might be viewed in that light by the parliament; and be of great and general disservice to their interests: That the spending of so much time in parlies and treaties, after all the injuries they had received, and while the enemy was insulting them, and fortifying against them, would make them contemptible among the Indians: That it was dishonoring God, in whom they professed to trust, and bringing a scandal among themselves. He insisted that, as their brethren had sent their moan to them, and desired their assistance, if they should refuse, the curse of the angel of the Lord against Meroz would come upon them. This, he said, he presented in the name of many pensive hearts.†

Declaration of the general Court of Massachusetts. But nothing could induce the Massachusetts to unite with their brethren, in a war against the Dutch. The general court, in direct violation of the articles of confederation, resolved, that no determination of the commissioners, though they should all agree, should bind the general court to join in an offensive war, which should appear to such general court to be unjust. This declaration gave great uneasiness to the commissioners, and to the sister colonies. Indeed, it nearly effected a dissolution of their union.

The commissioners, finding that the Massachusetts would not submit to their determination, nor afford any assistance to her confederates, dissolved.

Resolution of the general court at Connecticut, June 25th. In this important crisis, governor Haynes called a special court, on the 25th of June. The court resolved, that the fears and distresses of the English, bordering upon the Dutch, and the damages which they had sustained, should be forthwith represented to the magistrates in Massachusetts: That the opinion of the court, respecting the power

* Records of the united colonies.
† Records of the united colonies.

CHAP. X.   CONNECTICUT.   209

of the commissioners to make war, and the reasons of their opinion, should be communicated. They also determined, that their messengers should humbly pray, that war might be carried on against the Dutch, according to the determination of the commissioners. The messengers were instructed, to use their influence, that three magistrates might have power to call a meeting of the commissioners, at Hartford or New-Haven, to conduct the affairs of the war, as occasion might require. If this could not be obtained they were to desire that liberty might be given to enlist volunteers, in the Massachusetts, for the defence of the colonies.

Book I. 1653.

Governor Haynes and Mr. Ludlow, were appointed to confer with governor Eaton and his council on the subject. The court at New-Haven were no less clear and unanimous, in the opinion of the power of the commissioners to declare war and make peace, than the general court at Connecticut; and that all the colonies were absolutely bound by their determination. Both colonies united in sending the messengers, and in the purport of their message. But nothing more could be obtained, than the calling of another meeting of the commissioners, at Boston.

Confer with New-Haven.

They met on the 11th of September. The resolutions of the general courts of Connecticut and New-Haven were produced, expressing their entire approbation of the determination of the commissioners, and remonstrating against the declaration of the general court of Massachusetts, and the sense which they had put on the articles of confederation.

Commissioners meet, Sept. 11th.

The general court of Massachusetts returned an answer to this effect: that since their brethren of the other colonies had apprehensions different from theirs, they judged it might conduce most to peace to wave the point in controversy. At the same time, they intimated they had no occasion to answer them.

The commissioners refused to accept this as an answer. They insisted, that they had ample powers, from all the other colonies, to determine, in all affairs of peace and war; and that this was consistent with the grammatical, and true sense of the articles of confederation. They insisted, that it was totally inconsistent, not only with the articles of union, but with the welfare of the colonies, that they should be at so much expense and trouble, to meet and deliberate on the general interests of the confederates, if their determinations were to be annulled by one court and another.

Reject the answer of the general court of Massachusetts. Altercations between them.

The general court, on their part, insisted, that the deter-

B 2

minations of the commissioners, could not bind them to a war which they could not see to be just; and that it was inconsistent with the liberties of the colonies, that their decisions should compel them to action.

The commissioners replied, that no power could bind men to do that which was absolutely unlawful; but that their authority was as absolute, with respect to war and peace, as any authority could be; and that it was their province only to judge of the justice of the cause. They maintained, that it could be no infringement of the rights of the colonies, to be bound by the acts of their own agents, vested with plenary powers for those very acts. They represented the religious and solemn manner in which the confederation was made; that, by its express words, it was a perpetual league for them and their posterity, in which their eight commissioners, or any six of them, should have full power to determine all affairs of war and peace, leagues, aids, &c: That every article had been examined, not only by a committee of the four general courts, but by the whole court of Massachusetts, at the time when it was completed: That many prayers were addressed to heaven for its accomplishment, while it was under consideration; and that the carrying of it into execution, had been an occasion of abundant thanksgiving. They said, that after practising upon it for ten years, the colonies had experienced the most salutary effects, to the great and general advantage of all the confederates. In these views, they insisted, that the violation of it would be matter of great sin in the presence of God, and of scandal before men. They referred it to the serious consideration of the general court, whether they would not, in his sight who knew all hearts, be guilty of this sin and scandal?

The general court earnestly requested, that they would drop the dispute, and enter upon business. Their commissioners also pressed the same. But, with a spirit of magnanimity and firmness, becoming their character, they utterly refused; determining, to a man, after drawing a remonstrance against the Massachusetts, to return to their respective colonies, and leave the event with the supreme ruler.

No sooner had the general court intelligence of what was transacting, than they dispatched a writing to the commissioners, apparently retracting all which they had before advanced in opposition to them. It was, however, expressed artfully in doubtful language. Upon the reception of this, they proceeded to business.

Ninigrate, ever since the Pequot war, had been the

CHAP. X. CONNECTICUT.

common pest of the colonies. He had violated all his contracts with them; had fallen on the Long-Island Indians, who were in alliance with the English, and slain many of them; and carried others, men, women, and children, into captivity. By his hostilities, he gave alarm and trouble to the English plantations, on the island, in the neighbourhood of the Indians. When messengers had been sent to him, demanding that he would return the captives, and desist from war, he absolutely refused; and would give no account of his conduct. He had now spent the winter with the Dutch governor, in concerting measures against the English colonies; and had been beyond Hudson's river, spiriting up the Indians there, as well as in other quarters, to a general rising against them. The commissioners therefore declared war against him, and appointed the number of men and officers for the service. They also again resolved upon war against the Dutch. All the commissioners joined in these resolutions, except Mr. Bradstreet. But they were to no purpose. The general court refused to bear any part in the war against either.

Book I.
1653.
Conduct of Ninigrate.
War declared against him.

The commissioners protested against the members of the court of Massachusetts, as violators of the confederation. They pressed it as an indispensable duty, to avenge the blood of innocents, who had depended on them for safety, and had suffered on the account of their faithfulness to the colonies; to recover their wives and children from captivity; to protect their friends from the insults of barbarous and bloody men; and to vindicate the honor of themselves, and of the nation.*

Protest against the Massachusetts.

The Massachusetts nevertheless persisted in their opposition to the commissioners, and would bear no part in the war. Their desertion of their confederates was matter of great injury and distress to them; especially to Connecticut and New-Haven. They were not only obliged to put up with all former insults and damages from the Dutch; but after they had been at great expense already, in fortifying and guarding against the Dutch and Indians, and had been worn down with anxiety and watching, from the very opening of the spring, they were still left to their fears, and obliged to combine together for mutual defence, in the best manner of which they were capable.

They persist in their opposition to the commissioners.

Few instances occur in history, of so flagrant and obstinate a violation of a covenant, so solemnly made, as this of the general court of Massachusetts; especially, of a cove-

* Records of the united colonies, in which this controversy is recorded at large.

Book I.
1653.

nant made between christians of the same nation, and all professed brethren of the same faith. What interest the Massachusetts made by thus favoring the Dutch, is not known; but surely it is painful to relate the indelible stain, which the legislature of so ancient and respectable a colony have left, by this conduct, upon their honor, as men, and upon their morals, as christians.

Meetings of the general courts of Connecticut and New-Haven.

The general courts of Connecticut and New-Haven were convoked soon after the return of the commissioners. That at New-Haven convened on the 12th of October, and the court at Connecticut, on the 25th of November. Both considered the court of Massachusetts as having wilfully violated the articles of union. The general court at New-Haven expressly resolved, "that the Massachusetts had broken their covenant with them, in acting directly contrary to the articles of confederation."

They address letters to Cromwell and the parliament.

Both colonies therefore determined to seek redress from the commonwealth of England. Captain Astwood was appointed agent to the lord protector and parliament, to represent their state, and to solicit ships and men for the reduction of the Dutch. Connecticut and New-Haven conferred together, by their committees, and letters were sent, in the name of both the general courts, containing a complete statement of their circumstances. It was agreed, that the address to lord Cromwell should be concluded in the words following:

"That unless the Dutch be either removed, or so far, at least, subjected, that the colonies may be free from injurious affronts, and secured against the dangers and mischievous effects, which daily grow upon them, by their plotting with the Indians, and furnishing them with arms against the English; and that the league and confederation between the four united English colonies, be confirmed and settled according to the true sense, and, till this year, the continued interpretation of the articles, the peace and comfort of these smaller, western colonies, will be much hazarded, and more and more impaired. But as they conceive it their duty, thus fully to represent their afflicted condition to your excellency, so they humbly leave themselves, with the remedies, to your consideration and wisdom."

As governor Hopkins was now in England, he was desired to give all assistance in his power, to the agent whom they had agreed to send. Connecticut dispatched letters to the parliament, to general Monk, and Mr. Hopkins.

As Stamford was a frontier town, a guard of men was

CHAP. X.	CONNECTICUT.	

dispatched for its defence. Connecticut and New-Haven provided a frigate of ten or twelve guns, with forty men, to defend the coast against the Dutch, and to prevent Ninigrate and his Indians from crossing the sound, in prosecution of his hostile designs against the Indians in alliance with the colonies.*

<small>Book I.
1653.
Provide a frigate for their defence.</small>

The towns bordering upon the Dutch, on Long-Island, were in great distress and alarm. Captain Underhill sent to his friends at Rhode-Island, for assistance; and, with such Englishmen as he could obtain, made the best defence in his power. However, Hampstead and some other towns were continually harassed, and suffered much damage and insult from the Dutch.

Indeed, this was a year of uncommon alarm, expense, and distress to Connecticut and New-Haven. Early in the spring they were filled with the most terrible apprehensions of a sudden and general massacre. A great proportion of time was employed, by the magistrates and principal men, in meetings of the general courts, of the commissioners, of committees and officers to consult and provide for the general safety; in raising men and making preparations for war. The common people, at the same time, were called off from their labors and worn down with watching and guarding by night and day.

The Dutch, at New-Netherlands, waited only for a reinforcement from Holland to attack and reduce the English colonies. Of this, both they and the English were in constant expectation. It was reported, and feared, that when the signals should be given from the Dutch ships, the Indians would rise, fire the English buildings, and begin their work of destruction.

<small>Expectations of a Dutch fleet.</small>

Providence, however, combined a number of circumstances for the preservation of the exposed colonies. The defeat of the Dutch fleet by the English, and the spoil which they made upon their trade, prevented the arrival of the expected reinforcements; the Indians could not be united; many of the sachems said, the English had done them no injury, and they would not fight them. The early intelligence, received by the colonies, of the plans which they and the Dutch were concerting, and the constant watch and guard which the plantations maintained disconcerted them. By these means, a general attack upon them was prevented.

<small>Circumstances preserving the colonies.</small>

Another mischief however arose. Some of the towns, and many of the people, in the colonies of Connecticut and New-Haven, were so dissatisfied that the war was not

<small>Disturbance at Stamford and Fairfield.</small>

* Records of Connecticut and New-Haven.

Book I. prosecuted against the Dutch, according to the resolution of the commissioners, that they were with great difficulty restrained from open mutiny and rebellion. They imagined, that Connecticut and New-Haven were sufficient to subdue the Dutch, and ought to have undertaken an expedition against them.

1653.

Stamford and Fairfield, in particular, became very disorderly. The former complained, that the government was bad, and the charges unreasonable; and that they were neglected, and deprived of their just privileges. They pretended to set up for the government of England, for their liberties, as they called them, in opposition to the government of the colony. They sent to the general court at New-Haven desiring them to prosecute the war against the Dutch; resolved to raise a number of men among themselves; and prayed for permission to enlist volunteers in the several towns.

The town of Fairfield held a meeting on the subject, and determined to prosecute the war. They appointed Mr. Ludlow commander in chief. He was in the centre of the evidence against the Dutch; had been one of the commissioners, at the several meetings relative to the affair; had been zealous and active for the war; and conceiving himself and the town in imminent danger, unless the Dutch could be removed from the neighbourhood, too hastily accepted of the appointment. Robert Basset and John Chapman were the heads of this party. They attempted to foment insurrections, and, without any instructions from authority, to raise volunteers, for an expedition against the Netherlands.

The general court, at New-Haven, judged that the season was too far advanced to undertake the enterprise. They nevertheless determined to consult Connecticut, and to proceed or not, as 'the council there should judge most expedient.

It was now the latter part of November, and it was the general opinion, that ships and men could not be seasonably provided.

Deputy governor Goodyear and Mr. Newman were dispatched to Stamford to compose the minds of the people. They called a meeting of the town, and labored to quiet them; but could make no considerable impressions upon them, until they read an order of the committee of parliament, requiring, that the plantations should be in subjection to the authority of their respective jurisdictions. This appeared to have some good effect. But as the inhabitants had been at great expense, not only in watching and guarding the town, but in erecting fortifications about the meeting house, they insisted, that the colony should bear a part of the expense, and provide a guard during the winter.

The public burthens this year were great. The expenses of the colony of New-Haven were about 400 pounds. The court made some abatements in favour of Stamford; but Basset and Chapman were punished for attempting to make an insurrection in the colony, and others were bound, in large bonds, to their good behaviour.*

CHAPTER XI.

The death and character of Governor Haynes. The freemen of Connecticut meet, and appoint a moderator. Mr. Ludlow removes to Virginia. The spirited conduct of the people at Milford, in recovering Manning's vessel. The freemen add to the fundamental articles. Fleet arrives at Boston for the reduction of the Dutch. The colonies agree to raise men to assist the armament from England. Peace prevents the expedition. The general court at New-Haven, charge the Massachusetts with a breach of the confederation. They refuse to join in a war against Ninigrate, and oblige Connecticut and New-Haven to provide for the defence of themselves and their allies. Ninigrate continuing his hostile measures, the commissioners send messengers to him. His answer to them. They declare war, and send an army against him. The art of Massachusetts, and the deceit of Major Willard, defeat the designed expedition. The number of rateable polls, and the amount of the list of Connecticut. The Pequots are taken under their protection. Ninigrate persisting in his hostilities against the Indians upon Long-Island, the general court adopt measures for the defence of the Indians and the English inhabitants there. New-Haven perfect and print their laws. The answer of New-Haven to the protector's invitation, that they would remove to Jamaica. Reply of the commissioners to the Dutch governor. Uncas embroils the country. Deaths and characters of Governors Eaton and Hopkins. Settlement of Stonington. Mr. Winthrop cho-

---

* Records of New-Haven. The general court of Connecticut, at their session in November, ordered that 20 pounds should be paid to the support of a fellowship in Cambridge College.

BOOK I.
1654.

sen governor. The third fundamental article is altered by the freemen. Mr. Fitch, and his church and people, remove to Norwich. Final settlement of accounts with the heirs of Mr. Fenwick. Deputy governor Mason resigns the Moheagan lands to the colony.

Death of Governor Haynes.

THE colony sustained a great loss this year, in the death of Governor Haynes. He had been a father to it from the beginning; employed his estate, counsels, and labours, for its emolument, and bore a large share in its hardships and dangers. He was a gentleman from the

His character.

county of Essex, in England, where he had an elegant seat, called Copford Hall, worth a thousand pounds sterling a year. He came into New-England with the Rev. Mr. Hooker, in 1632, and settled with him, first at Cambridge, in Massachusetts. His distinguished abilities, prudence, and piety, so recommended him to the people, that, in 1635, he was chosen governor of Massachusetts. He was not considered, in any respect, inferior to Governor Winthrop. His growing popularity, and the fame of Mr. Hooker, who, as to strength of genius, and his lively and powerful manner of preaching, rivalled Mr. Cotton, were supposed to have had no small influence upon the general court, in their granting liberty to Mr. Hooker and his company to remove to Connecticut. There, it was judged, they would not so much eclipse the fame, nor stand in the way of the promotion and honour of themselves or their friends. Upon his removal to Connecticut, he was chosen governor of this colony. He appeared to be a gentleman of eminent piety, strict morals, and sound judgment. He paid attention to family government, instruction, and religion. His great integrity, and wise management of all affairs, in private and public, so raised and fixed his character, in the esteem of the people, that they always, when the constitution would permit, placed him in the chief seat of government, and continued him in it until his death.*

* The governor, by two wives, had eight children; five sons and three daughters. By his first, he had Robert, Hezekiah, John, Roger, and Mary; and by his second, Joseph, Ruth, and Mabel. When he came into New-England, he left his sons, Robert and Hezekiah, and his daughter Mary, at Copford Hall. Upon the commencement of the civil wars in England, Robert espoused the royal cause; but Hezekiah, declaring for the parliament, was, afterwards, promoted to the rank of major-general, under Cromwell. Upon the ruin of the king's affairs, Robert was put under confinement, and died without issue. Hezekiah enjoyed Copford Hall, under his father, until his decease. He then possessed it as a paternal inheritance, and it descended to his heirs. John and Roger, who came into this country with their father, some time before his death returned to England. Roger died on his passage, or soon after his arrival. John settled in the ministry, at or near Colchester, in the county of Essex, in England,

Mr. Hopkins was in England, and the colony had neither governor nor deputy governor present, to act in its behalf. The freemen, therefore, in February, convened at Hartford, and elected Mr. Thomas Wells moderator of the general court, until a governor should be chosen.

Book I. 1654. Feb. 16th.

About this time, there happened a great controversy between Uncas and the inhabitants of New-London, relative to their respective limits. It seems that the inhabitants carried the dispute so far, as to rise and take possession of his forts and many of his wigwams. The assembly interposed, and gave orders, that the Indians should not be injured, and that the people should be accountable for all damages which they had done them. A committee was appointed to fix the boundaries between New-London and Uncas, and to compose all differences between the parties.

Controversy with Uncas.

March 1st,

Nearly at the same time, the colony received an order from the parliament, requiring that the Dutch should be treated, in all respects, as the declared enemies of the commonwealth of England. In conformity to this order, the general court was convened, and an act passed sequestering the Dutch house, lands, and property of all kinds, at Hartford, for the benefit of the commonwealth; and the court, also, prohibited all persons whatsoever from improving the premises, by virtue of any former claim, or title, had, made, or given, by any of the Dutch nation, or any other person, without their approbation.

Order of parliament. Sequestration of the Dutch house at Hartford, April 6th.

In the proclamation for a general fast, this spring, the great breach made in the colony, by the death of the governor; the alienation of the colonies, on account of the violation of the articles of confederation; the spreading of erroneous opinions in the churches; the mortality which had been among the people of Massachusetts; and the calamitous state of the English nation; were particularized as matters of humiliation.

The colony was, this year, deprived of Mr. Ludlow, one of its chief magistrates. He was one of the most zealous for prosecuting the war against the Dutch, and no man was more displeased, that the colonies did not follow the determinations of the commissioners. He might apprehend himself to be particularly in danger at Fairfield. Besides, he had taken a very hasty and unadvised step, in

Mr. Ludlow leaves the colony.

Reasons of it.

where he left issue. Joseph was ordained pastor of the first church in Hartford. Mary married Mr. Joseph Cook, in England; Ruth, Mr. Samuel Wyllys, of Hartford; and Mabel, Mr. James Russell, of Charlestown, in Massachusetts; and all had issue. The Rev. Mr. Haynes, of Hartford, had one son, John, a gentleman of reputation, for some years one of the magistrates of the colony. He had sons, but they died without issue, and the name became extinct in this country.

BOOK I.
1654.

accepting the command of men to go against the Dutch, without any legal appointment. He had, doubtless, apprehensions of trouble on that account, or, at least, that the freemen would neglect him. For some, or all of these reasons, about this time, he removed with his family to Virginia.* He was clerk of the town of Fairfield, and carried off their records, and other public writings. He came from the west of England, with Mr. Warham and his company. In 1630, he was chosen into the magistracy of the Massachusetts company; and in 1634, deputy governor of that colony. He was twice elected deputy governor of Connecticut, and was every year magistrate or deputy governor, from his first coming into the colony, in 1635, until the time of his departure. He appears to have been distinguished for his abilities, especially his knowledge of the law, and the rights of mankind. He rendered most essential services to this commonwealth; was a principal in forming its original civil constitution, and the compiler of the first Connecticut code, printed at Cambridge, in 1672. For jurisprudence, he appears to have been second to none who came into New-England at that time. Had he possessed a happier temper, he would, probably, have been the idol of the people, and shared in all the honours which they could have given him.

Captain Manning apprehended.

Nearly at the same time, an affair happened, in which the people of Milford exhibited a noble spirit of zeal and enterprise. One captain Manning, master of a ten gun ship, had been apprehended for an unlawful trade with the Dutch, at the Manhadoes. While the affair was upon trial before the court at New-Haven, his men ran off with the ship from Milford harbour. The people completely armed and manned a vessel, with so much dispatch, that they pressed hard upon the ship before she could reach the Dutch island. The men, perceiving they must be taken, unless they immediately abandoned the ship, made their escape in their boat. The ship, thus left adrift, was recovered, and brought into Milford harbour, and, with all her goods, condemned as a lawful prize.

Court of election, May 18th.

At the general election, Mr. Hopkins, though in England, was chosen governor. Mr. Wells was appointed deputy governor. Mr. Webster, Mr. Mason, Mr. Winthrop, Mr. Cullick, Mr. Wolcott, Mr. Clark, Mr. Wyllys, son of George Wyllys, and Mr. John Talcott, were elected magistrates. Mr. Cullick was secretary, and Mr. Talcott treasurer.

* By the records of New-Haven, it appears, that he was shipping his family and effects on the 26th of April.

CHAP. XI.   CONNECTICUT.   219

At this court, the freemen passed the following resolution, as an addition to the fundamentals of their constitution:—"That the major part of the magistrates, in the absence of the governor and deputy governor, shall have power to call a general court; and that any general court, being legally called and met, the major part of the magistrates and deputies then met, in the absence of the governor and deputy governor, shall have power to choose unto, and from among themselves, a moderator, which being done, they shall be deemed as legal a general court, as if the governor, or deputy governor were present."

Book I.
1654.
Addition to the fundamental articles.

At the election in New-Haven, the only alteration in public officers, was the addition of Mr. Samuel Eaton, of New-Haven, to the magistrates, and the choice of Mr. Benjamin Fenn, in the room of captain John Astwood.

May 31. Election at New-Haven.

About the same time, in answer to the petitions of Connecticut and New-Haven, major Sedgwick and captain Leveret arrived at Boston, with a fleet of three or four ships, and a small number of land forces, sent by Oliver Cromwell, lord protector, for the reduction of the Dutch. On the 8th of June, governor Eaton received a letter from his highness, certifying, that he had sent ships and ammunition for the assistance of the colonies. With this came a letter from major Sedgwick and captain Leveret, requesting, that commissioners might be sent immediately from each of the governments, to consult with them on the objects of the designed expedition. Mr. William Leet and Mr. Jordan were appointed commissioners for New-Haven. They were authorised to engage, in behalf of that jurisdiction, to furnish all the men and provisions which it could spare. An embargo was laid on all provisions, and every measure adopted, that the utmost assistance might be given, in the enterprise. Such was the zeal of the general court, that they instructed their commissioners to engage the assistance of that colony, though no other, except Connecticut, should join with them.

June 9th.

On the 13th of June, the general court of Connecticut convened, at Hartford, and appointed major John Mason and Mr. Cullick commissioners. They were directed to proceed with the utmost dispatch to Boston; and, in behalf of Connecticut, to engage any number of men, not exceeding two hundred, but rather than the expedition should fail, four or five hundred.

June 13th.

The general court of Massachusetts was convoked on the 9th of June, but did not agree to raise any men themselves. They granted liberty, nevertheless, for major Sedgwick and captain Leveret to raise five hundred vol-

BOOK I.
1654.

unteers. The commissioners finally agreed upon 800 men, as sufficient for the enterprise. The ships were to furnish two hundred soldiers; three hundred volunteers were to be raised in Massachusetts; two hundred men were to be sent from Connecticut; and a hundred and thirty three from New-Haven. But while preparations were making with vigor and dispatch, the news of peace, between England and Holland, prevented all further proceedings relative to the affair.

The total defeat of the Dutch fleet, the loss of admiral Tromp and a great number of their merchantmen, made the Dutch in earnest for peace; and it was expeditiously concluded, on the 5th of April. The news of it arrived in America, almost as soon as the fleet. The commander in chief therefore employed his forces, with the Massachusetts volunteers, in dispossessing the French from Penobscot, St. John's, and the adjacent coast. This was doubtless one object of the expedition, and not undertaken without orders from the protector.

Transactions respecting the confederation.

It was not expected, that there would have been any meeting of the commissioners this year. Massachusetts had violated the articles of union, and the colonies had protested against them, as breakers of the most solemn confederation. The general court of Massachusetts had also represented, to the other colonies, that the articles needed explanation and emendation, that they might be consistent with the rights of the several general courts. Indeed, it had proposed a meeting of the commissioners for that purpose. The other colonies viewed the articles as perfectly intelligible, and consistent with the rights of the confederates. They therefore rejected the motion. The general court of New-Haven had voted, that there was no occasion for appointing commissioners that year.

But on the 5th of July, governor Eaton received a letter from the general court of the Massachusetss, waving an answer to the letter jointly written from the general courts of Connecticut and New-Haven, and lamely excusing their non-compliance with the resolution of the commissioners, on the account of their not being able to apprehend the justice of the war with the Dutch and Ninigrate. They complained of the other colonies, for treating them as violators of the confederacy. They professed themselves to be passionately desirous of its continuance, according to the genuine construction of the articles. They gave information, that they had chosen commissioners, and had determined to empower them as had been usual.

The general court, at New-Haven, replied, that they and

the other colonies had justly charged them with a violation of their covenant, and urged, that, according to their own interpretation of the articles, they stood responsible to them for the infraction; and that, according to the eleventh article of the confederation, they were to be treated by them according to the magnitude of their fault. They observed, that her sister colonies had not only condemned their conduct, but had sent messengers and taken proper pains to inform them, and adjust the difference between them; but that they had treated them in a very disagreeable manner, and their endeavours had been to no good purpose. They declared, nevertheless, that, if the combination might be again firmly settled, according to the original intention and grammatical sense of the articles, they would, without further satisfaction, forgetting what was past, cheerfully renew their covenant, and send their commissioners to meet, at any time and place, for that end. This was subscribed by the secretary, and sent to Hartford, to be subscribed by the general court of Connecticut; and to be transmitted, in the name of each of the colonies, to the Massachusetts. This, it seems, was harmoniously done.

<small>Book I. 1654.</small>

As the general court of the Massachusetts would not join with her confederates, against Ninigrate, he prosecuted the war against the Long-Island Indians, and it was supposed, that his design was to destroy, both those Indians and the Moheagans. For this purpose he had hired the Mohawks, Pocomtocks, and Wampanoags, afterwards called Philip's Indians, to assist him. By a collection of such numbers of Indians, from the westward, northward, and eastward, the general peace of the country would have been greatly endangered, and the Long-Island Indians, who had put themselves under the protection of the English, exposed to a total extirpation. They had been obliged, not only to fortify themselves, and to use every precaution for their own defence, but to suffer the loss of many of their people, who had been already either slain or captivated.

<small>Ninigrate continues hostile.</small>

The deputy governor, and council, of Connecticut, judged it an affair of such importance, to defend their allies, and provide for their own safety, that they determined to dispatch major Mason, with ammunition, and a number of men, to the assistance of the Indians upon the Island. The deputy governor and Mr. Clark acquainted governor Eaton with their views and determination, and desired that the colony of New-Haven would send lieutenant Seely, with a detachment of men, and with supplies of ammunition, to second their design. The court of New-Haven complied with the desire of Connecticut. Lieutenant See-

<small>Connecticut and New-Haven send aid to Montauket Indians.</small>

ly had orders to join major Mason at Saybrook. They were instructed to acquaint the Montauket Indians, that the colonies made them that present of ammunition, wholly for their own defence, and not to enable them to injure Ninigrate, or any other Indians, unless they should make an attack upon them: and that, while they continued faithful to the English, they would be their friends. It was ordered that, if Ninigrate should invade the Long-Island Indians, the English officers should use their endeavours to persuade them to peace, and to refer their differences to the decision of the commissioners. But if he would fight, they were commanded to defend themselves, and the Indians in alliance with the colonies, in the best manner they could.*

In September, the commissioners convened at Hartford. They consisted of the following gentlemen, Mr. Simon Bradstreet, Major Denison, Mr. Thomas Prince, Mr. John Brown, major Mason, Mr. John Webster, governor Eaton, and Mr. Francis Newman. Governor Eaton was chosen president. They immediately dispatched messengers to Ninigrate, demanding his appearance at Hartford, and the payment of the tribute so long due for the Pequots under him. On the 18th, Mr. Jonathan Gilbert returned, and made a report of Ninigrate's answer, in the words following:

"Concerning the Long-Island Indians, he answered, wherefore should he acquaint the commissioners, as the Long-Island Indians began with him, and had slain a sachem's son, and sixty of his men; and therefore he will not make peace with the Long-Islanders; but doth desire that the English will let him alone; and that the commissioners would not request him to go to Hartford; for he hath done no hurt. What should he do there? If our governor's son were slain, and several other men, would you ask counsel of another nation, how and when to right yourselves? And added, that he would neither go nor send to Hartford. Concerning the upland Indians,† his answer was, that they were his friends, and came to help him against the Long-Islanders, who had killed several of his men. Wherefore should he acquaint the commissioners of it? He did but right his own quarrel, which the Long-Islanders began with him." With respect to the tribute due for the Pequots, though he had never paid it, yet he pretended there was none due.

The commissioners, considering his perfidious conduct,

* Records of Connecticut and New-Haven.
† Thus he called the Pocomtocks and Wampanoags.

CHAP. XI. CONNECTICUT.

the last year, his present answer, and that lenity and forbearance had been an encouragement of his insolence and barbarity, ordered forty horsemen, and two hundred and seventy infantry to be raised, to chastise his haughtiness. The Massachusetts were to raise the forty horsemen, and a hundred and fifty-three footmen; Connecticut forty-five, and New-Haven thirty-one. Orders were given, that twenty horse, from Massachusetts, twenty-four men from Connecticut, and sixteen from New-Haven, should be immediately dispatched into the Nehantick country. The commissioners nominated major Gibbons, major Denison, or captain Atherton, to the chief command; leaving it, in complaisance, to the general court of Massachusetts, to appoint which of the three should be most agreeable to them. But rejecting these, who were men of known spirit and enterprise, they appointed major Willard. The commissioners instructed him to proceed with such troops, as should be found at the place of general rendezvous, by the 13th of October, directly to Ninigrate's quarters, and demand of him the Pequots, who had been put under him, and the tribute which was due. If Ninigrate should not deliver them, and pay the tribute, he was required to take them by force. He was instructed to demand of Ninigrate, a cessation from all further hostilities against the Long-Islanders. If he would not comply with these demands, he had express orders to subdue him. If a greater number of men should be found necessary, his instructions were to send for such a number, as he should judge sufficient to carry the expedition into effect. The place of rendezvous was at Thomas Stanton's, in the Narraganset country. When he arrived at the place appointed, he found that Ninigrate had fled into a swamp, at fourteen or fifteen miles distance from the army. He had left his country, corn, and wigwams, without defence, and they might have been laid waste, without loss or danger. Nevertheless, he returned, without ever advancing from his head quarters, or doing the enemy the least damage.

BOOK I.
1654.
Commissioners determine upon war with Ninigrate.

Massachusetts and major Willard defeat their design.

About a hundred Pequots took this opportunity to renounce the government of Ninigrate, and come off with the army. They put themselves under the protection and government of the English.

The commander pleaded, in excuse, that his instructions were equivocal, and the season for marching unfavorable. The commissioners, however, were entirely unsatisfied. They observed to him, "That, while the army was in the Narraganset country, Ninigrate had his mouth in the dust; and that he would have submitted to any reasonable terms,

Commissioners dissatisfied.

Book I.
1655.
Charge major Willard with neglect of duty.

which might have been imposed upon him." They charged the major with neglecting an opportunity of humbling his pride; and they referred it to his consideration, what satisfaction ought to be expected from him, and those of his council, who advised and joined with him in his measures.*

Governor Hutchinson has observed, that major Willard was a Massachusetts man, and although that colony had so far complied with the rest, as to join in sending out the forces, yet they were still desirous of avoiding an open war. This was the second time of their preventing a general war, contrary to the minds of six of the commissioners of the other colonies.†

The general court of Massachusetts had receded from their explanation of the articles of confederation, and the commissioners had a most amicable meeting. They were unanimous in the war against Ninigrate, and yet the Massachusetts, by private intrigue, defeated their designs. In which instance they acted the most honorable and consistent part, when, by an open infraction of the articles of union, they prevented a war, or when they supplanted their brethren, by secret treachery, the impartial world will judge.

The whole number of rateable persons, in the colony of Connecticut this year, was 775, and the grand list was 79,073 pounds.‡

Upon the election at Hartford, Thomas Wells, Esq'r. was chosen governor, and Mr. John Webster, deputy-governor. The magistrates elected were, Mr. Hopkins, Mr. Mason, Mr. Winthrop, Mr. Wolcott, Mr. Cullick, Mr. Clark, Mr. Wyllys, Mr. Talcott, Mr. John Cosmore, and Mr. Thomas Tapping. Mr. Cullick was secretary, and Mr. Talcott treasurer.

Election, May 17th.

At the general election in New-Haven, this year, there was no alteration of their officers.

* Records of the united colonies.
† Hutchinson, vol. i. p. 186, 187.
‡ By the number of persons, and the amount of the lists in each town, an idea may be formed of their proportion to each other.

Towns.	Persons.	Estates.
Hartford,	177	£ 19,609
Windsor,	165	15,833
Weathersfield,	113	12,602
Fairfield,	94	8,634
Saybrook,	53	4,437
Stratford,	72	7,956
Farmington,	46	5,519
Middletown,	31	2,172
Norwalk,	24	2,309
	775	79,073

The Pequots persevering, in their petitions, to be taken under the protection and government of the English, the commissioners, this year, granted their request. Places of residence were afterwards appointed for them, by the general court of Connecticut, about Pawcatuck and Mistic rivers. They were allowed to hunt on the lands west of the latter. They were collected together in these two places, and an Indian governor was appointed over them in each place. General laws were made for their government. Blasphemy, murder, witchcraft, and conspiracy against the colonies, were prohibited upon pain of death. Sabbath-breaking, adultery, and drunkenness, were prohibited under proper penalties. He who stole was required, on conviction, to pay double damages. They were prohibited to make war with other Indians, or to join with them in their wars, unless it were in their own just defence, without the consent of the commissioners of the united colonies. They were obliged to submit to the Indian governors, whom they should appoint over them, and pay them the same tribute which they had stipulated to pay to the English.*

After the return of major Willard and the troops under his command, from the Narraganset country, Ninigrate assumed his former haughtiness, and continued the war against the Indians upon Long-Island. Mr. Thomas James, minister of Easthampton, captain Tapping of Southampton, captain Underhill and others, wrote to the commissioners, that both the English and Indians on the Island were in a calamitous and distracted condition; and in imminent danger, on the account of his constant hostilities. They assured them, that the Indians, upon the Island, could not hold out much longer, but must submit themselves and their country to the Narragansets, unless they should have some speedy assistance. They intreated them to consult some effectual measures to prevent such calamity.

In consequence of this intelligence, they ordered, that a vessel, well armed and manned, should lie in the road between Neanticut and the Island, to watch the motions of Ninigrate; and, if he should attempt to pass the sound, to stave and destroy his canoes, and to make all the slaughter and destruction upon him, which should be in their power. Captain John Youngs was appointed to command this vessel of observation. He was authorised to draught men from Saybrook and New-London, as emergencies might require. An encouraging message was sent to the

* Records of the colonies.

D 2

Book I. Montauket sachem, acquainting him with the measures the English were taking for his defence. The commissioners sent him a supply of ammunition. Provision was also made, that South and East-Hampton, with all the adjacent towns, should be completely furnished with all articles necessary for war. Orders were given, that if the Indians could not maintain their ground, in any assault, they should flee towards some of the neighbouring towns; and that, if the enemy should pursue them within two miles of any of the settlements, the inhabitants should immediately repair to their assistance. Intelligence of these resolutions was dispatched to the Narragansets, as well as the Long-Islanders. All the united colonies were exceedingly offended at the conduct of major Willard, except the Massachusetts, under whose influence he was supposed to act. The general court at New-Haven, resolved, that he had not followed his instructions, in the expedition against Ninigrate; but that they were willing to suspend their judgment, with respect to the measures to be taken with him, until they should be certified of the opinions of the other confederates. Whatever their opinions or wishes were, major Willard was safe under the wing of the Massachusetts; and Connecticut and New-Haven had principally to bear the unhappy consequences of his perfidious conduct. They were obliged, the next year, at their own expense, to continue the commission of captain Youngs to cruise between the main and Long-Island, to prevent the designs of Ninigrate. They also found it necessary to furnish both men and provisions, for the defence of the Islanders.

1655.

Governor Eaton compiles a code for New-Haven.

Governor Eaton had been desired to perfect a code of laws for the colony of New-Haven. For his assistance in the compilation, he was requested, by the general court, to consult the Rev. Mr. Cotton's discourse on civil government in a new plantation, and the laws of Massachusetts. Having accomplished the work, and the laws having been examined and approved, by the elders of the jurisdiction, they were presented to the general court. They ordered, that 500 copies should be printed. The copy was sent to England, that the impression might be made under the inspection of governor Hopkins. He procured the printing of the laws, at his own expense, and sent them the number proposed, with some other valuable books, as a present. The laws were distributed to the several towns in the jurisdiction.

October 19th the court order them to be printed.

Death of Henry Wolcott, Esq.

This year, died Henry Wolcott, Esq'., in the 78th year of his age. He was the owner of a good estate in Somersetshire, in England. His youth, it is said, was spent in

CHAP. XI. CONNECTICUT. 227

gaiety and country pastimes; but afterwards, under the instructions of Mr. Edward Elton, his mind was entirely changed, and turned to the sincere love and practice of religion. As the puritans were then treated with great severity, he sold about 8,000 pounds worth of estate in England, and prepared for a removal into America. He came into New-England with Mr. Warham, in May, 1630, and settled first at Dorchester, in Massachusetts. In 1636, he removed to Windsor, and was one of the principal planters of that town. He was chosen into the magistracy in 1643, and continued in it until his death. He left an estate in England, which rented at about sixty pounds a year, which the family, for some time, enjoyed; but it was afterwards sold. After his decease, some one of his descendants was annually chosen into the magistracy, for a term of nearly eighty years, until the year 1754, when governor Wolcott left the chair.*

<small>Book I. 1655. His character.</small>

At the election in Connecticut, Mr. John Webster was chosen governor, and Mr. Wells deputy governor. This was the only alteration in the magistracy.

At New-Haven, the former governors and magistrates were rechosen. Mr. John Wakeman was appointed treasurer. The general court at New-Haven, took great pains to put the colony in a state of defence. Orders were given for the raising of a troop of sixteen horse, in the five towns upon the sea coast, with complete arms and furniture. For their encouragement, they were exempted from taxation, and from training with the foot, and were to enjoy all the privileges of troopers in Massachusetts. This was the first troop in any part of Connecticut. It was ordered, that all the common soldiers should be trained to shooting at a mark; that they should be furnished with ammunition for that purpose, at the public expense; and that prizes should be prepared for the best marksmen. The soldiers were directed to play at cudgels, and at the broad sword, that they might know how to defend themselves and their country.

<small>Election at New-Haven, May, 1656.

May 28th.

Troop of horse appointed.</small>

* Manuscripts from Windsor, found in the collection of the Rev. Mr Prince, at Boston.

The family have kept up the monument of their ancestor, and preserved their dignity to the present time. His Excellency, Oliver Wolcott, Esq'r. one of the sons of the former governor, Roger Wolcott, Esq'r. is the present governor of the state. His brother, the Hon. Erastus Wolcott, Esq'r. was, for some years, one of the magistrates of Connecticut, and, afterwards, one of the judges of the superior court. Oliver Wolcott, Esq'r. one of the sons of the present governor Wolcott, is secretary of the treasury of the United States. Some of the family have been members of the assembly, judges of the superior court, or magistrates, from the first settlement of the colony to this time, during the term of more than a century and a half.——A. D. 1797.

Book I. The protector, Oliver Cromwell, having conquered Jamaica, made it a favourite object to remove the people of New-England to that island. He artfully represented, that they had as clear a call for transporting themselves from New-England to Jamaica, as they had for emigrating from Old England to New, for the advancement of their interests; as the Lord's people were to be the head, and not the tail. He likewise represented, that it would have a tendency to the destruction of the man of sin. He wrote particularly to New-Haven on the subject, and sent them a copy of his instructions relative to the affair. These he had given to one captain Gookins, whom he had employed in the several plantations, to promote this, his favourite design. He and major Sedgwick dispatched letters also to New-Haven, on the same business.

1656.

Governor Eaton had, some time before this, laid them before the general court. The several plantations in the colony had been made acquainted with their contents, and the deputies had been desired to return their opinion to the court. After a long and serious debate, the court resolved, "That, though they could not but acknowledge the love, care, and tender respect of his highness, the Lord Protector, to New-England in general, and to this colony in particular, yet, for divers reasons, they cannot conclude that God calls them to a present remove thither."

The governor was desired to write to the lord protector, acknowledging his great care and love towards the colony.

Commissioners meet, Sept. 4th.

The commissioners of the united colonies, this year, held their meeting at Plymouth. They received a very plausible letter from Stuyvesant, the Dutch governor. He wrote with a great show of religion, expressing his joy that God had quenched the bloody war between the Dutch and the English, in Europe; and his warm desires, that it might redound to the great advantage of the subjects of the two nations, in these remote parts of the earth. He solicited a nearer union between the Dutch and the united colonies. At the same time, he certified them, that he had received a ratification of the agreement made at Hartford, in 1650, under the seal of the High and Mighty States of the United Belgick Provinces; and desired that time and place might be appointed for delivering and interchanging the ratifications.

Letter from the Dutch governor.

The governor was so well known to the commissioners, that neither the plausibility of his letter, nor the very christian manner in which it was written, made any deep impressions upon them. They replied, in short, that the peace was matter of joy to them, and they wished the continuance of it in Europe, and in all the plantations abroad. They gave assurances, that the preservation of it should be their constant endeavour. Nevertheless, they gave no intimations that they desired a nearer union, or to ratify the agreement. The Dutch governor had not observed it himself; they considered the Dutch as mere intruders, and were growing daily more able to defend themselves against their encroachments: they were, therefore, determined to do nothing further relative to the affair.

They observed to the governor, that he had made no reparation of the damages he had done the colonies, and that they had not heard that he designed to make any: that they heard he yet laid claim to Oyster bay, and that he had made no proper resignation of Greenwich. They desired him to be explicit on these points.*

The last year, complaints were made to the court at New-Haven, that the inhabitants of Greenwich were under little government, and demeaned themselves in a lawless manner. They admitted of drunkenness among themselves, and among the Indians, by reason of which, damages were done to themselves and to the towns in the vicinity, and the public peace was disturbed. They received children and servants, who fled from the correction of their parents and masters, and unlawfully joined persons in wedlock, with other misdemeanors. *Complaint against Greenwich.*

Upon this, the general court asserted their right to Greenwich, and ordered the inhabitants to submit to their jurisdiction. But they continued much in the same state, and sent a letter to the court in May, denying their jurisdiction, and refusing any subjection to the colony, unless they should be compelled to it, by the parliament. The court, therefore, resolved, that, unless they should appear before the court, and make their submission, by the 25th of June, Richard Crab and others, who were the most stubborn among them, should be arrested and punished, according to law. They, therefore, some time after, subjected their persons and estates to the government of New-Haven. *The inhabitants submit to New-Haven.*

Uncas, though friendly to the English, appears to have been a proud, mischievous sachem, who, by his haughty carriage and provoking language, was often embroiling the country, and bringing trouble upon himself and the colonies. He made an assault upon the Podunk Indians, at Hartford. He, or his brother, invaded the Norwootucks. He upbraided the Narragansets of their dead sachems, and challenged them to fight. Among other in-

* Records of the united colonies.

Book I.
1656.

stances of misconduct, he proved treacherous to the Montauket sachem, and joined with Ninigrate, in his perfidious practices. By these means, the country was so disquieted, that it was with great difficulty the commissioners maintained the general peace. They interposed, and obliged Uncas to make restitution to the Indians, whom he had injured. They prohibited his making war, without their consent and advice. They endeavored to quiet and conciliate the natives; but they found them, whether they were friends or foes, to be a troublesome people. After all their precautions, the country was still more alarmed the next year.

1657.

In April, the Indians committed a horrid murder at Farmington, and besides Mesapano, who was the principal actor, the Norwootuck and Pocomtock Indians were supposed to be accomplices.

The Montaukets, after all the trouble and expense, which the English had been at for their defence, became tumultuous, and did great damage to the inhabitants of Southampton.

April 9th. The general court at Hartford, gave orders that the Indians, who perpetrated the murder at Farmington, should be apprehended, and that the sachems of the Pocomtock and Norwootuck Indians should deliver up the delinquents among them.

Major Mason was ordered, with a detachment, to Long-Island, to bring the Indians there to a just and peaceable conduct, and adjust affairs between them and the English.*

May 21st.

At the general election in Connecticut, 1657, Mr. John Winthrop was elected governor, and Mr. Thomas Wells deputy-governor. Mr. Webster was chosen the first magistrate. The other officers were the same who had been appointed the last year. The freemen, at the election in New-Haven, made no alteration in their magistrates.

May 27th.

Wars among the Indians.

The general court at Hartford, this year, was uncommonly thin, consisting of twenty-two members only. The danger of the plantations, and of particular families, from the hostile state of the Indians, appears to have been the reason. The Montaukets, Moheagans, Narragansets, and Norwootucks, engaged in implacable wars with each other. They would pursue one another into the English plantations, and even into their houses, and kill each other in the presence of the families, to their great alarm and astonishment. Uncas was so pressed by the Narragansets, that Connecticut was obliged to send men to his fortress, to assist him in defending himself against them. The Nar-

* Records of Connecticut.

CHAP. XI. CONNECTICUT.

ragansets, in several instances, threatened and plundered the inhabitants of Connecticut.

Therefore, when the commissioners met, in September, they sent messengers to them, demanding that they should cease from war, until their grievances, and the grounds of their contentions, should be heard. They assured them, that they would hear and determine impartially, without favoring any of the parties. They represented to them the covenants which they had made with the English, and the entire inconsistency of their conduct, with those engagements. They also prohibited all fighting in the English plantations.

This year, the colony of New-Haven, and indeed all the New-England colonies, sustained a heavy loss in the death of governor Eaton.* He was a minister's son, born at Stony Stratford, in Oxfordshire; was educated an East India merchant, and was sometime deputy-governor of the company, trading to the East Indies. For several years, he was agent for the king of England at the court of Denmark. After his return, he was a merchant of great business and respectability, in the city of London.

Upon the Laudean persecution, he left his native country, and came into New-England with Mr. Davenport, his minister, in 1637. He was one of the original patentees of the Massachusetts, and soon after his arrival was chosen one of the magistrates of that colony. Upon the settlement of New-Haven, he was chosen governor of the colony, and was annually re-elected until his death. He is represented as comely and personable, and is said to have appeared upon the bench with a dignity and majesty, which admit of no description. The impartiality with which he administered justice, was most exemplary, and his authority was not to be opposed. The wisdom, gravity, and integrity of his administration, were viewed with universal admiration. In honor to his memory, and the good services which he had rendered the colony, his funeral charges were borne, and a handsome monument erected at the public expense.†

BOOK I.

1657.
Sept. 3d.

Death and character of Theophilus Eaton, Esq.

---

* He died January 7th, 1657, in the 67th year of his age.
† His private was not less amiable than his public character. In conversation, he was affable, courteous, and generally pleasant; but always grave and cautious. He was pious and strictly moral. His meekness, patience, and fortitude, were singular.

In the conduct of his family, he was strict, prudent, and happy. Though it sometimes consisted of not less than thirty persons, yet they were under the most perfect order and government. They were all assembled morning and evening, and the governor, after reading the scriptures, and making devout and useful observations upon them, prayed with great reverence and pertinency. On the sabbath, and other days of public devotion, he

BOOK I. Nearly at the same time, died his son-in-law, Edward Hopkins, Esquire, for a number of years governor of Connecticut. He conducted the affairs of government with great wisdom and integrity, and was universally beloved. He was a gentleman of exemplary piety, righteousness, and charity. In his family and secret devotions, he followed the example of governor Eaton. His charity was great and extensive. Besides the relief he dispensed to the poor, with his own hands, he gave considerable sums of money to others, to be disposed of to charitable purposes. When he went into England, on the occasion of his brother's death, who had been warden of the English fleet, he designed to return again to his family and friends, in New-England; but he was very soon particularly noticed, and made first warden of the fleet, in the room of his brother. He was then chosen commissioner of the admiralty and navy; and finally member of parliament. These unexpected preferments altered his designs, and determined him to send over for his family, and to spend the remainder of his days in his native country. He had been a consumptive man, attended with a cough, and spitting of blood, for more than thirty years. His constitution was now entirely wasted, and he died in the 58th year of his age.

1657.
Character of governor Hopkins.

His donations. His last will was highly expressive of that public spirit and charity, which had so distinguished him in life. His whole estate, in New-England, was given away to charitable purposes. He manifested his peculiar friendship to the family of Mr. Hooker, his pastor, at Hartford, by giving his relict, Mrs. Hooker, all the debts due from the family, to him; by giving to Mrs. Wilson, of Boston, Mr. Hooker's eldest daughter, his farm at Farmington, with all the houses, out-houses, and buildings upon it; and by legacies to several others of his descendants. All the remainder of his estate, in New-England, he bequeathed to his "father, Theophilus Eaton, Esquire, master John Davenport, master John Cullick, and master William Goodwin, in full as-

spent an hour or two with his family, in instructing them in the duties of faith and practice; and in recommending to them the reading and study of the scriptures, secret devotion, the sanctification of the sabbath, and a devout and constant attendance on all divine institutions. On these days he sang praises, as well as prayed with his family. He was greatly beloved by his domestics, as well as by the commonwealth. Indeed, there was no man, among the first planters of New-England, who had a more general acquaintance with public business, or who sustained a fairer character. His monument is kept up to the present time. Upon it are these expressive lines:

"Eaton, so meek, so wise, so fam'd, so just,
The Phœnix of our world here hides his dust:
This name forget, New-England never must.

surance of their trust and faithfulness, in disposing of it according to the true intent and purpose of him, the said Edward Hopkins, which was to give some encouragement, in those foreign plantations, for the breeding up of hopeful youths, in a way of learning, both at the grammar school and college, for the public service of the country, in future times." He also made a donation of five hundred pounds more, out of his estate in England, to the said trustees, in further prosecution of the same public ends, "for the upholding and promoting the kingdom of the Lord Jesus Christ, in those parts of the earth." This last donation was considered as made to Harvard college, and, by virtue of a decree in chancery, was paid in 1710. The interest given in New-England, was estimated at about 1,000l. sterling; and was appropriated to the support of the grammar schools in New-Haven, Hartford, and Hadley. The money originally belonged to New-Haven and Hartford; but as a considerable number of the people of Hartford afterwards removed to Hadley, and were principal settlers of that town, they received their proportion of the donation.

1657.

At a general court in Hartford, March 11th, 1658, a troop of thirty horsemen was established in Connecticut, and Richard Lord was appointed captain. This was the first in the colony.

1658. First troop in Connecticut.

This year there was a very considerable alteration with respect to governors and the council, both in Connecticut and New-Haven. At the election in Connecticut, Thomas Wells, Esquire, was elected governor, and John Winthrop, Esquire, deputy governor. To the magistrates last year, who were again re-chosen, there was an addition of Mr. Matthew Allen, Mr. Phelps, Mr. John Wells, Mr. Treat, Mr. Baker, Mr. Mulford, and Mr. Alexander Knowles. There appears to have been sixteen magistrates, and twenty-six deputies; in the whole, forty-two members.

Election at Hartford, May 20.

On the election at New-Haven, Mr. Francis Newman was chosen governor, and William Leet, deputy governor.* Mr. Jasper Crane was added to the magistrates, and Mr. William Gibbard was appointed secretary.

This year a considerable settlement was made between Pawca-Mistic and Pawcatuck rivers. This tract was called Pequot, and originally belonged to New-London. The first

Pawcatuck, afterwards

* Mr. Stephen Goodyear, who had been deputy governor, with governor Eaton, through almost his whole administration, died this year, in London, and was either there, or on his passage, at this election. He appears to have been a worthy man, and left a respectable family.

E 2

Book I. man who settled upon this tract, was William Cheesebrough, from Rehoboth, in 1649. A complaint was exhibited against him for carrying on an illicit trade with the Indians, for repairing their arms, and endangering the public safety. The general court of Connecticut declared, that they had a clear title to those lands, and summoned him before them. They reprimanded him for settling upon them without their approbation; for withdrawing himself from christian society and ordinances; and for unlawfully trading with and assisting the Indians. He confessed his faults; but pleaded, in excuse, that he had been encouraged by Mr. Winthrop, who claimed a right at Pawcatuck. He gave bonds for his good conduct, and was allowed to continue upon the land. The court promised him, that if he would procure a sufficient number of planters, they would give them all proper encouragement, in making a permanent settlement. About ten or twelve families, this year, made settlements in that quarter; and, finding that there was a controversy between Connecticut and the Massachusetts, with respect both to title and jurisdiction, they, on the 30th of June, entered into a voluntary contract to govern themselves, and conduct their affairs in peace, until it should be determined to which colony they should submit. The principal planters were George Denison, Thomas Stanton, Thomas Shaw, William, Elisha, and Samuel Cheesebrough, and Moses and Walter Palmer. These, with some others, were signers of the voluntary compact.

1658.
named Stonington, settled.

Cheesebrough reprimanded.

The planters agree to govern themselves.

Claim of Massachusetts.

Determination of the commissioners.

At the meeting of the commissioners, the Massachusetts claimed that tract of country, by virtue of the assistance which they afforded Connecticut in the conquest of the Pequots. The commissioners resolved, "That the determination did arise only from the several rights of conquest, which were not greatly different; yet that being tender of any inconvenience which might arise to those who were already possessed, either by commission from Massachusetts or Connecticut, in any part thereof, should they be put off their improvements; also, upon inquiry, finding, that the Pequot country, which extended from Nehantick to Wekapaug, about ten miles eastward from Mistic river, may conveniently accommodate two plantations, did, respecting things as they then stood, conclude, that Mistic river be the bounds between them, as to propriety and jurisdiction, so far as conquest may give title. Always provided, that such as are already accommodated, by commission of either of the said governments, or have grants of any tracts of land, on either side of the Mystic river, be not molested in any of their possessions or rights, by any other grants."

Upon the petition of the planters, the general court of the Massachusetts made them a grant of eight miles from the mouth of Mystic river towards Wekapaug, and eight miles northward into the country, and named the plantation Southerton. It continued under the government of Massachusetts until after Connecticut obtained a royal charter.

1658. Oct. 19th.

This was a year of great sickness and mortality in Connecticut, and in New-England in general. Religious controversies, at the same time, ran high, and gave great trouble to church and commonwealth. The Indians continued their wars with implacable animosity. The commissioners employed all their wisdom and influence to make peace; but they could not reconcile those bloodthirsty barbarians. The crops were light, and it was a year of fear, perplexity, and sorrow.*

John Winthrop, Esq'r. was chosen governor of Connecticut for the year 1659, and Thomas Wells, Esq'r. deputy governor. Captain Tapping and Mr. Robert Bond were elected magistrates, in the room of Mr. Knowles and Mr. Mulford.

Election at Hartford, May 19th, 1659.

At the election in New-Haven, the same governor and council were rechosen. Indeed, little alteration was made with respect to them, until the union of that colony with Connecticut.

At the October session, Cromwell bay, or Setauket, on Long-Island, at the desire of the inhabitants, was admitted as a member of the jurisdiction of Connecticut.

Oct. 6th.

In 1660, Mr. John Winthrop was rechosen governor. This was the first time that any governor had been elected to that office more than once in two years. Major Mason was advanced to the place of deputy governor. The magistrates were Mr. Henry Clark, Mr. Wyllys, Mr. Phelps, Mr. Allen, Mr. Treat, Mr. Gould, Mr. Tapping, Mr. Ogden, Mr. Bond, Mr. Daniel Clark, and Mr. Talcott. Mr. Daniel Clark was secretary, and Mr. Talcott treasurer.

Election, May 17th, 1660.

Mr. Webster and Mr. Wells appear now to be no more. They had been annually chosen into the magistracy, for about twenty years, and both had the honour of the chief seat of government.†

---

* In a proclamation for a general fast, the intemperate season, thin harvest, sore visitation by sickness, and the sad, prolonged differences in the churches, are particularized as matters of humiliation.

† Four or five governors of Connecticut, governor Haynes, governor Wyllys, governors Wells and Webster, lie buried at Hartford, without a monument. William Leet, Esq. governor of New-Haven and Con-

Book I.
1660.

Distress of Uncas.

Relieved by Thomas Leffingwell.

Norwich settled.

At this election, the freemen, having found by long experience, that the clause in the third fundamental article, incapacitating any person to be chosen governor more than once in two years, was prejudicial, rather than advantageous to the colony, resolved, that there should be liberty for the annual choice of the same person governor, or of any other whom they should judge best qualified to serve the commonwealth.

During the wars between Uncas and the Narragansets, they besieged his fort, near the bank of the Thames, until his provisions were nearly exhausted, and he found that he, and his men, must soon perish, by famine or sword, unless he could obtain speedy relief. In this crisis, he found means of communicating his danger to the scouts, who had been sent out from Saybrook fort. By his messengers, he represented the great danger the English, in those parts, would be in immediately, if they should suffer the Moheagans to be destroyed.

Upon this intelligence, one Thomas Leffingwell, an ensign at Saybrook, an enterprising, bold man, loaded a canoe with beef, corn, and pease, and, under cover of the night, paddled from Saybrook into the Thames, and had the address to get the whole into the fort. The enemy soon perceiving that Uncas was relieved, raised the siege. For this service, Uncas gave said Leffingwell a deed of a great part, if not of the whole town of Norwich. In June, 1659, Uncas, with his two sons, Owaneco and Attawanhood, by a more formal and authentic deed, made over unto said Leffingwell, John Mason, Esq. the Rev. James Fitch, and others, consisting of thirty-five proprietors, the whole township of Norwich, which is about nine miles square. The company, at this time, gave Uncas and his sons about seventy pounds, as a further compensation for so large and fine a tract.

Preparations were immediately made for its settlement; and, this spring, the Rev. James Fitch, with the principal part of his church and congregation, removed from Saybrook, and planted the town of Norwich. Three or four planters joined them from New-London, and two or three from the towns of Plymouth and Marshfield, in Massachusetts. In 1663, the general assembly ordered that the deed should be recorded. The limits were afterwards ascertained, and the town received a patent of the whole.

necticut, also lies interred there, in the same obscure manner. Considering their many and important public services, this is remarkable; but their virtues have embalmed their names, and will render them venerable to the latest posterity.

CHAP. XI. CONNECTICUT. 237

The Moheagans were a great defence, and of essential service to the town for many years. They kept out their scouts and spies, and so constantly watched their enemies, that they gave the earliest notice of their approach, and were a continual defence against them. For this purpose, in times of danger, they often moved and pitched their wigwams near the town, and were a great terror to the enemy. Once the hostile Indians came near to the town, upon the sabbath, with a design to make a descent upon it; but, viewing it from an eminence, and seeing the Moheagan huts, they were intimidated, and went off without doing the least damage.*

This year, the town of Huntington, upon Long-Island, was received as a member of the Connecticut jurisdiction.

This general court ordered, that grand jurors should be appointed in every town, to make presentment of all breaches of law, in their respective towns. The law required that the presentments should be made to the particular court, in May and October.

The accounts with the heirs of George Fenwick, Esq. had not been closed, nor discharges given, relative to the purchase made of the fort at Saybrook, and the old patent of Connecticut. This was an occasion of great uneasiness among the people. The three towns of Hartford, Windsor, and Weathersfield, presented petitions to the general court, praying that the accounts might be adjusted, and the colony discharged. In consequence of these, a large committee was appointed to make a complete settlement with the said heirs. They having prepared the accounts for a final adjustment, the general court, at their session in October, authorised them, in their behalf, to perfect and confirm the writings. The governor was authorised, in their name, to affix the public seal of the colony to those which were to be delivered to captain Cullick, and Elizabeth, his wife, heirs of the said George Fenwick, Esq. and to receive of them the writings, to be delivered to the court, in favour of the colony.

Accordingly, on the 7th of October, the colony discharged Mr. John Cullick, and Elizabeth, his wife, their heirs, &c.; and the said John, and Elizabeth, his wife, gave an ample discharge to the colony of Connecticut, from all sums of money due to the said Fenwick, his heirs or assigns, by virtue of the agreements made with Mr. Fenwick, or purchase of the river's mouth.†

*Manuscripts from Norwich, and Records of Connecticut.
† Mr. Cullick, who, for several years, had been one of the magistrates of Connecticut, and secretary of the colony, had now removed his residence to Boston.

BOOK I.
1660.

500 pounds due to the colony.

March 14, 1661, major Mason resigns the Moheagan lands.

Thus, after the term of sixteen years, from the first, and fourteen from the second agreement with Mr. Fenwick, the colony completed a settlement respecting the fort and lands holden by him; and became legally possessed of the tract conveyed to the lords and gentlemen severally named in the patent.

Upon a final adjustment of the accounts, it appeared, that Mr. Cullick and the heirs of Mr. Fenwick were indebted 500 pounds sterling to the colony, which had been paid them, more than what was due according to the original agreements with Mr. Fenwick.

John Mason, Esq. now deputy governor, had some time since been authorised, in behalf of the colony, to purchase of Uncas all the lands, which he had reserved for himself and the Moheagans, in the deed of 1640, under the name of planting grounds. Having effected the purchase, he made a surrender of the lands, in the presence of the general court. The following is a minute of the transaction.

"Hartford, session of the general court, March 14, 1660.*

"The jurisdiction power over that land, which Uncas and Wawequa have made over to major Mason, is by him surrendered to this colony. Nevertheless, for the laying out of those lands to farms, or plantations, the court doth leave it in the hands of major Mason. It is also ordered and provided, with the consent of major Mason, that Uncas and Wawequa, and their Indians and successors, shall be supplied with sufficient planting ground at all times, as the court sees cause, out of that land. And the major doth reserve to himself a competency to make a farm."

For want of form, and a more legal manner of conveyance, with respect to those lands, originated the memorable Mason case, or controversy, as it was called. It continued about seventy years, and was an occasion of great trouble and expense to the colony. A statement of it will be made in the progress of this history.

* This according to the present mode of dating was March 14, 1661.

CHAP. XII. CONNECTICUT. 239

BOOK I.

CHAPTER XII.

1660.

The general court of Connecticut declare their loyalty and submission to the king; determine to address his majesty, and apply for charter privileges. A petition to his majesty is prepared, and a letter addressed to lord Say and Seal. Governor Winthrop is appointed the colony's agent, to present their petition, and solicit a patent. Regicides condemned. Whalley and Goffe arrive at Boston, escape to New-Haven, and are kindly entertained, and kept from their pursuers. New-Haven falls into great trouble and danger on that account. New-Haven excuse themselves; decline sending an agent; but join with Massachusetts, in supporting one. The king proclaimed. Governor Winthrop obtains the charter of Connecticut. First governor and council under the charter. Representation of the constitution it ordains, and the privileges it conveys. Difficulties of the colony of New-Haven. Governor Leet's address. Charter of Connecticut arrives. Proceedings of Connecticut in consequence of the charter. They extend their jurisdiction to all places within the limits of their patent, and challenge New-Haven colony, as under their jurisdiction. Controversy between the two colonies. Settlement of Killingworth. Patent of the duke of York. Colonel Nichols and commissioners arrive, reduce all the Dutch settlements. Their extraordinary powers. Important crisis of Connecticut. The general court make a present to the commissioners. Answer to the propositions from his majesty, and reply to the duke of Hamilton's claim and petition. Boundaries between Connecticut and New-York. Union of Connecticut and New-Haven.

THE colony having purchased the patent, and the government of England having been settled in the king and parliament, the general court determined to make application for a charter under the royal signature. They avowed their allegiance to his majesty, king Charles the second; declared that all the inhabitants of this colony were his faithful subjects; and that it was necessary to petition him for his grace, and the continuance and confirmation of their rights and privileges. The court resolved, that the 500 pounds due from Mr. Cullick should be appropriated to the prosecution of their address, and application to his majesty for a patent.

March 14.

The court avow their allegiance to king Charles II.

Book I.
1661.
Prepare a petition for a charter.
May 16.

At the session in May, a petition to his majesty was presented by the governor, and approved by the general court. That it might, however, be made as perfect as possible, the governor and deputy governor, Mr. Wyllys, Mr. Allen, Mr. Warham, Mr. Stone, Mr. Hooker, Mr. Whiting, and the secretary, were appointed a committee for its emendation. They were authorised to methodize and make all such alterations, as they should judge expedient, provided the substance of it were retained. They were directed to write letters to any noble personages in England, to whom it might be expedient to make application, and to transact whatever might be necessary, respecting the petition and the procurement of a patent.

Gov. Winthrop appointed agent.

Governor Winthrop was appointed agent to present the petition to his majesty, and to transact all affairs in England, respecting the general welfare of the colony. He had particular instructions from the general court for the management of the business of his agency. He was especially directed to obtain the consent, and take the advice of the nobles and gentlemen, who had been interested in the old patent of Connecticut; and to engage the friendship and influence of all those, who might be active and serviceable, with respect to the interests of the colony.

Representations in the petition.

In the petition to his majesty, it was represented, that the greatest part of the colony had been purchased and obtained by great and valuable considerations; that some other part thereof had been obtained by conquest; and that it had, with great difficulty, at the sole endeavours, expense and charges of themselves and their associates, under whom they claimed, been subdued and improved, and thereby become a considerable enlargement and addition to his majesty's dominions and interests in New-England.* These were pleaded as reasons, with his majesty, to grant the tract and privileges for which the petitioners prayed.

Letter to lord Say and Seal.

At the same time, a letter was addressed to lord Say and Seal, representing the encouragements which their fathers, and some of their surviving associates, received from him, to transplant themselves into the inland parts of this vast wilderness, and their assurances of his patronage and favor.

Complaints against Mr. Fenwick.

They also complained, that Mr. George Fenwick, several years after he had taken possession of the entrance of Connecticut river, determining to return to England, proposed to sell the fort, at Saybrook, with all the buildings and appurtenances there, together with all the lands upon the river, as far eastward as Narraganset bay, with the right of jurisdiction, to the colony. They represented,

* Appendix No. VII.

CHAP. XII.   CONNECTICUT.

that this, at first, was strenuously opposed, by many of the inhabitants, as they imagined his lordship, and the other noble patentees, had very bountiful intentions towards them; and that such a procedure would be extremely contrary to their designs. Nevertheless, that afterwards, as some of those gentlemen, who had the greatest interest in the affections of their lordships, were removed by death; and as Mr. Fenwick pretended to be the only patentee; and threatened, that unless the colony would purchase the lands, on his own terms, he would either impose duties upon the people, or sell the premises to the Dutch, they finally agreed with him, and paid him 1,600 pounds for them. They intimated that this was the only way in which the peace and safety of the community could have been preserved. As a further matter of grievance, they complained, that, besides this great abuse, Mr. Fenwick had given them nothing under his hand, to oblige himself or his heirs to fulfil his engagements; and that they had nothing to secure them, in the enjoyment of their just rights and privileges, as a distinct commonwealth. They further made complaint of encroachments made upon them, on the north by the Massachusetts, and by them and others towards the Narragansets; and that they knew not how to support their claims, or ascertain their boundaries, without a patent. They intreat his lordship to consider their circumstances, counsel and assist their agent, and countenance their designs.*

The only alteration which had been made, at the election, this year, in Connecticut, was the choice of Mr. Thurston Rayner into the magistracy; but at New-Haven the alteration was very considerable.

Governor Newman dies.

Francis Newman, Esq. who had succeeded governor Eaton, in the chief seat of government, was now no more. He had been for many years secretary, under the administration of governor Eaton, and was well acquainted with the affairs of the colony. He is represented as a gentleman of piety and unblemished morals, happily imitating his predecessor both in public and private life.

Election at New-Haven, May 29th.

Upon the election, William Leet, Esq. was chosen governor, and Mr. Matthew Gilbert, deputy governor. Mr. Benjamin Fenn, Mr. Robert Treat, Mr. Jasper Crane, Mr. John Wakeman, and Mr. William Gibbard, were elected magistrates. The spirit of republicanism however was so high, at New-Haven, that several of them would not accept their appointments and take the oaths prescribed. Mr. Wakeman and Mr. Gibbard utterly refused. Mr.

* Letter to his lordship, No. VIII.

BOOK I.
1661.

Fenn was hardly prevailed with to accept his office. He at last took the oath, with this previous explanation, that it was only with reference to the particular laws of that colony; and that if any thing foreign should present, it should give no offence if he should decline acting. Mr. James Bishop was chosen secretary, and Mr. Robert Allen, treasurer.

An affair had happened at New-Haven, a few months before this, which now began to alarm the country, and soon gave great anxiety and trouble to that colony.

Regicides condemned.

Very soon after the restoration, a large number of the judges of king Charles the first, commonly termed regicides, were apprehended and brought upon their trials, in the Old Baily. Thirty nine were condemned, and ten executed as traitors. Some others, apprehensive of danger, fled out of the kingdom before king Charles II. was proclaimed. Colonels Whalley and Goffe made their escape to New-England. They were brought over by one captain Gooking, and arrived at Boston, in July, 1660. Governor Endicott and gentlemen of character, in Boston and its vicinity, treated them with peculiar respect and kindness. They were gentlemen of singular abilities, and had moved in an exalted sphere. Whalley had been a lieutenant general, and Goffe, a major general, in Cromwell's army. Their manners were elegant, and their appearance grave and dignified, commanding universal respect. They soon went from Boston to Cambridge, where they resided until February. They resorted openly to places of public worship on the Lord's day, and at other times of public devotion. They were universally esteemed, by all men of character, both civil and religious. But no sooner was it known, that the judges had been condemned as traitors, and that these gentlemen were excepted from the act of pardon, than the principal gentlemen in the Massachusetts began to be alarmed. Governor Endicott called a court of magistrates to consult measures for apprehending them. However, their friends were so numerous that a vote could not, at that time, be obtained to arrest them. Some of the court declared that they would stand by them, others advised them to remove out of the colony.

Whalley and Goffe arrive at Boston.

Retire to Cambridge.

Finding themselves unsafe at Cambridge, they came, by the assistance of their friends, to Connecticut. They made their route by Hartford, but went on directly to New-Haven. They arrived about the 27th of March, and made Mr. Davenport's house the place of their residence. They were treated with the same marks of esteem and generous friendship, at New-Haven, which they had received in the

Arrive at New-Haven, March 27.

Massachusetts. The more the people became acquainted with them, the more they esteemed them, not only as men of great minds, but of unfeigned piety and religion. For some time, they appeared to apprehend themselves as out of danger, and happily situated among a number of pious and agreeable friends. But it was not long before the news of the king's proclamation against the regicides arrived, requiring, that wherever they might be found, they should be immediately apprehended. The governor of Massachusetts, in consequence of the royal proclamation, issued his warrant to arrest them. As they were certified, by their friends, of all measures adopted respecting them, they removed to Milford. There they appeared openly in the day time, but at night often returned privately to New-Haven, and were generally secreted at Mr. Davenport's, until about the last of April.

Go to Milford.

In the mean time, the governor of Massachusetts received a royal mandate requiring him to apprehend them; and a more full and circumstantial account of the condemnation and the execution of the ten regicides, and of the disposition of the court towards them, and the republicans and puritans in general, arrived in New-England. This gave a more general and thorough alarm to the whole country. A feigned search had been made in the Massachusetts, in consequence of the former warrant, for the colonels Whalley and Goffe; but now the governor and magistrates began to view the affair in a more serious point of light; and appear to have been in earnest to secure them. They perceived, that their own personal safety, and the liberties and peace of the country, were concerned in the manner of their conduct towards those unhappy men. They therefore immediately gave a commission to Thomas Kellond and Thomas Kirk, two zealous young royalists, to go through the colonies, as far as the Manhadoes, and make a careful and universal search for them. They pursued the judges, with engagedness, to Hartford; and, repairing to governor Winthrop, were nobly entertained. He assured them, that the colonels made no stay in Connecticut, but went directly to New-Haven. He gave them a warrant and instructions similar to those which they had received from the governor of Massachusetts, and transacted every thing relative to the affair with dispatch. The next day they arrived at Guilford, and opened their business to deputy governor Leet. They acquainted him that, according to the intelligence which they had received, the regicides were then at New-Haven. They desired immediately to be furnished with powers, horses, and assistance to arrest them.

Kellond and Kirk commissioned to search the country.

Come to Guilford.

Book I.
1661.
Sentiments of governor Leet and his council.

Their conduct respecting the regicides.

But here they were very unwelcome messengers. Governor Leet, and the principal gentlemen in Guilford and New-Haven, had no ill opinion of the judges. If they had done wrong in the part they had acted, they viewed it as an error in judgment, and as the fault of great and good men, under peculiar and extraordinary circumstances. They were touched with compassion and sympathy, and had real scruples of conscience with respect to delivering up such men to death. They viewed them as the excellent in the earth, and were afraid to betray them, lest they should be instrumental in shedding innocent blood. They saw no advantage in putting them to death. They were not zealous therefore to assist in apprehending them. Governor Leet said, he had not seen them, in nine weeks, and that he did not believe they were at New-Haven. He read some of the papers relative to the affair with an audible voice. The pursuivants observed to him, that their business required more secrecy, than was consistent with such a reading of their instructions. He delayed furnishing them with horses until the next morning, and utterly declined giving them any powers, until he had consulted with his council, at New-Haven. They complained, that an Indian went off, from Guilford to New-Haven, in the night, and that the governor was so dilatory, the next morning, that a messenger went on to New-Haven, before they could obtain horses for their assistance. The judges were apprised of every transaction respecting them, and they, and their friends, took their measures accordingly. They changed their quarters, from one place to another in the town, as circumstances required; and had faithful friends to give them information, and to conceal them from their enemies.

On the 13th of March, the pursuivants came to New-Haven, and governor Leet arrived in town, soon after them, to consult his council. They acquainted him, that, from the information which they had received, they were persuaded, that the judges were yet in the town, and pressed him and the magistrates to give them a warrant and assistance, to arrest them, without any further delay. But after the governor and his council had been together five or six hours, they dispersed, without doing any thing relative to the affair. The governor declared, that they could not act without calling a general assembly of the freemen. Kellond and Kirk observed to him, that the other governors had not stood upon such niceties; that the honor and justice of his majesty were concerned, and that he would highly resent the concealment and abetting of such traitors and regicides. They demanded whether he, and his council, would own and honour his majesty? The governor replied, we do honour his majesty, but have tender consciences, and wish first to know whether he will own us.*

The tradition is, that the pursuivants searched Mr. Davenport's house, and used him very ill. They also searched other houses, where they suspected that the regicides were concealed. The report is, that they went into the house of one Mrs. Eyers, where they actually were; but she conducted the affair with such composure and address, that they imagined the judges had just made their escape from the house, and they went off without making any search. It is said, that once, when the pursuers passed the neck bridge, the judges concealed themselves under it. Several times they narrowly escaped, but never could be taken.

These zealous royalists, not finding the judges in New-Haven, prosecuted their journey to the Dutch settlements, and made interest with Stuyvesant, the Dutch governor, against them. He promised them, that, if the judges should be found within his jurisdiction, he would give them immediate intelligence, and that he would prohibit all ships and vessels from transporting them. Having thus zealously prosecuted the business of their commission, they returned to Boston, and reported the reception which they had met with at Guilford and New-Haven. *Kellond and Kirk return, and report.*

Upon this report, a letter was written by secretary Rawson, in the name of the general court of Massachusetts, to governor Leet and his council, on the subject. It represented, that many complaints had been exhibited in England against the colonies, and that they were in great danger. It was observed, that one great source of complaint, was their giving such entertainment to the regicides, and their inattention to his majesty's warrant for arresting them. This was represented as an affair which hazarded the liberties of all the colonies, and especially those of New-Haven. It was intimated, that the safety of particular persons, no less than that of the colony, was in danger. It was insisted, that the only way to expiate their offence, and save themselves harmless, was, without delay, to apprehend the delinquents. Indeed, the court urged, that not only their own safety and welfare, but the essential interests of their neighbours, demanded their indefatigable exertions to exculpate themselves. *Letter from the court of Massachusetts to governor Leet.*

Colonels Whalley and Goffe, after the search which had

* Report of Kellond and Kirk to governor Endicott; to which they gave oath, in the presence of the governor and his council.

246 HISTORY OF CHAP. XII.

BOOK I.
1661.
Regicides change their quarters.

been made for them at New-Haven, left Mr. Davenport's, and took up their quarters at Mr. William Jones's, son in law to governor Eaton, and, afterwards, deputy governor of New-Haven and Connecticut. There they secreted themselves until the 11th of May. Thence they removed to a mill in the environs of the town. For a short time, they made their quarters in the woods, and then fixed them in a cave in the side of a hill, which they named Providence Hill. They had some other places of resort, to which they retired as occasion made it necessary; but this was, generally, the place of their residence until the 19th of August.* When the weather was bad, they lodged, at night, in a neighbouring house. It is not improbable, that, sometimes, when it could be done with safety, they made visits to their friends at New-Haven.

They appear openly at New-Haven.

Indeed, to prevent any damage to Mr. Davenport, or the colony, they once, or more, came into the town openly, and offered to deliver up themselves to save their friends. It seems it was fully expected, at that time, that they would have done it voluntarily. But their friends neither desired, nor advised them, by any means, to adopt so dangerous a measure. They hoped to save themselves and the colony harmless, without such a sacrifice. The magistrates were greatly blamed for not apprehending them, at this time in particular. Secretary Rawson, in a letter of his to governor Leet, writes, "How ill this will be taken, is not difficult to imagine; to be sure not well. Nay, will not all men condemn you as wanting to yourselves?" The general court of Massachusetts further acquainted governor Leet, that the colonies were criminated for making no application to the king, since his restoration, and for not proclaiming him as their king. The court, in their letter, observed, that it was highly necessary that they should send an agent to answer for them at the court of England.

Governor Leet convenes the general court, Aug. 1st.

New-Haven's excuse.

On the reception of this intelligence, governor Leet convoked the general court, and laid the letters before them. After much debate, it was concluded to address a letter to the general court, exculpating the colony. With respect to the regicides, they declared, that they had neither disowned nor slighted the king nor his authority; and that the apprehending of them was not defeated by any delay of theirs, as they had made their escape before the king's

* About this time they removed to Milford, where they continued about two years. On the arrival of the king's commissioners in New-England, they retired again to their cave for a short time, and about the 13th of October, 1664, removed to Hadley. As the late Rev. President Stiles has written their history, no notice will be taken of it in this work, further than it is connected with the affairs of the colony.

CHAP. XII.   CONNECTICUT.

warrant arrived in the colony. They alledged, that the pursuers neglected their business, to attend upon the governor and his council, for which they had no authority. Besides, they pleaded scruples of conscience, and fear of unfaithfulness to the people, who had given them all their power, and to whom they were bound by solemn oath. Further, they insisted, that acting upon the warrant would have been owning a general governor, and dangerous to the liberties of the people. To him they said the warrant was directed, and though other magistrates were mentioned, yet they were considered only as officers under him.

With reference to the magistrates not arresting the judges, when they appeared openly in the town, they said, it was owing to a full persuasion that they would certainly surrender themselves, according to their promise. They affirmed, that they had used all diligence with those who had shown them kindness, to persuade them to deliver them up; that they were ignorant where they were, and that they did not believe that they were in the colony. They promised, that they would exert themselves to arrest and secure them, if an opportunity should present.

They excused themselves for not making an address or application to his majesty, because it was to them a new and unprecedented affair, and they were ignorant of the proper form. Indeed, they said they could not agree in one which might be acceptable. These they avowed to be the reasons of their omission, and not any disloyalty to his majesty. As the form in which the colony of Massachusetts made their submission to the king, had been laid before them, they declared, that it was to their satisfaction, and that, from their hearts, they acknowledged and said the same. They promised full subjection and entire allegiance to his majesty, king Charles II. Upon this submission and declaration, they supplicated for the same immunities and privileges with their sister colonies, and declared their expectations of the full enjoyment of them.

At the same time, they declined the making of any particular address to the king, on account of their inability to procure a proper agent to present it to his majesty. In their great distress, they desired the general court of Massachusetts to represent them to the king as cordially owning and complying with their address, as though it had been said and made by themselves. They expressed their opinion of the necessity of a general agent for New-England, to supplicate the royal favour, to defeat the designs of their enemies, and to procure for them all acts of indemnity and grace. They agreed to bear their proportionable part of

BOOK I.
1661.

New-Haven unite in sending a general agent.

BOOK I.
1661.
They proclaim the king, August 21st.
Gov. Winthrop's conduct in England.

the expense. The court immediately sent an agent to Boston, on this business. One great matter of complaint, against the colonies, had been their not proclaiming the king. But as he had now been proclaimed in all the other colonies, in New-England, the general court at New-Haven judged it expedient formally to proclaim him there.*

About this time, it seems, governor Winthrop took his passage for England. Upon his arrival, he made application to lord Say and Seal, and other friends of the colony, for their countenance and assistance.

Lord Say and Seal, appears to have been the only nobleman living, who was one of the original patentees of Connecticut. He held the patent in trust, originally, for the puritanic exiles. He received the address from the colony most favorably, and gave governor Winthrop all the assistance in his power.† The governor was a man of address, and he arrived in England at a happy time for Connecticut. Lord Say and Seal, the great friend of the colony, had been particularly instrumental in the restoration. This had so brought him into the king's favor, that he had been made lord privy seal. The earl of Manchester, another friend of the puritans, and of the rights of the colonies, was chamberlain of his majesty's household. He was an intimate friend of lord Say and Seal, and had been united with him in defending the colonies, and pleading for their establishment and liberties. Lord Say and Seal engaged him to give Mr. Winthrop his utmost assistance. Mr. Winthrop had an extraordinary ring, which had been given his grand father by king Charles the first, which he presented to the king. This, it is said, exceedingly pleased his majesty, as it had been once the property of a father most dear to him. Under these circumstances, the petition of Connecticut was presented, and was received with uncommon grace and favor.

Friendship of lord Say and Seal.

Favorable circumstances under which the petition was presented.

* The form was curious. It was expressed in the following words. "Although we have not received any form of proclamation, by order from his majesty or council of state, for proclaiming his majesty in this colony; yet, the court taking encouragement from what has been done in the rest of the united colonies, hath thought fit to declare publicly, and proclaim, that we do acknowledge his royal highness, Charles the second, king of England, Scotland, France, and Ireland, to be our sovereign lord and king: and that we do acknowledge ourselves, the inhabitants of this colony, to be his majesty's loyal and faithful subjects."

† Letter to governor Winthrop, in England, No. IX. His lordship ever retained his friendship for the colonies, and not only rendered great services to Connecticut, but to them all, in vindicating them against the complaints made against them, and in conciliating the favor of the king and his court towards them. In a letter of his, to the government of Massachusetts, he says, "I have not been wanting both to the king and council to advance your interest; more I cannot do, but pray the Lord to stand with you and for you."

Form of proclamation.

CHAP. XII. CONNECTICUT.

Upon the 20th of April, 1662, his majesty granted the colony his letters patent, conveying the most ample privileges, under the great seal of England. It confirmed unto it the whole tract of country, granted by king Charles the first unto the earl of Warwick, and which was, the next year, by him consigned unto lord Say and Seal, lord Brook and others. The patent granted the lands in free and common socage. The facts, stated and pleaded in the petition, were recognized in the charter, nearly in the same form of words, as reasons of the royal grant, and of the ample privileges which it conveyed.

It ordained, that John Winthrop, John Mason, Samuel Wyllys, Henry Clarke, Matthew Allen, John Tapping, Nathan Gould, Richard Treat, Richard Lord, Henry Wolcott, John Talcott, Daniel Clarke, John Ogden, Thomas Wells, Obadiah Bruen, John Clark, Anthony Hawkins, John Deming, and Matthew Canfield, and all such others as then were, or should afterwards be admitted and made free of the corporation, should forever after be one body corporate and politic, in fact and name, by the name of the GOVERNOR AND COMPANY OF THE ENGLISH COLONY OF CONNECTICUT IN NEW-ENGLAND IN AMERICA; and that by the same name, they and their successors should have perpetual succession. They were capacitated, as persons in law, to plead and be impleaded, to defend and be defended, in all suits whatsoever: To purchase, possess, lease, grant, demise, and sell lands, tenements, and goods, in as ample a manner, as any of his majesty's subjects or corporations in England. The charter ordained, that there should be, annually, two general assemblies; one holden on the second Thursday in May, and the other on the second Thursday in October. This was to consist of the governor, deputy governor, and twelve assistants, with two deputies from every town or city. John Winthrop was appointed governor, and John Mason, deputy governor, and the gentlemen named above, magistrates, until a new election should be made.

The company were authorised to have a common seal, to appoint judicatories, make freemen, constitute officers, establish laws, impose fines, assemble the inhabitants in marshal array for the common defence, and to exercise martial law in all cases, in which it might be necessary.

It was ordained by the charter, that all the king's subjects, in the colony, should enjoy all the privileges of free and natural subjects within the realm of England; and that the patent should always have the most favorable construction for the benefit of the governor and company.

Book I.

1662.

Charter granted.

Territory conveyed.

Reasons recognized.

Book I.
1662.

The charter did not come over until after the election. This was on the 15th of May, and the freemen made no alteration in their officers.

Many of the colony of New-Haven appear to have been exceedingly opposed to king Charles, and to the royal instructions which they had received. It had been with great difficulty, that the governor and council had managed the government in such a manner, as to keep peace among the people, and not incur the displeasure of the king and his council. Though they had done as little as possible, consistent with loyalty, in conforming to his majesty's orders, yet they had done more than was pleasing to all. There had been some insurrections and tumults, and the authority, in some instances, had not been well treated. Some complained, that they could not enjoy their privileges more amply; and that none but church members could be freemen of the corporation.

Governor Leet's conciliatory speech, May 20th.

Governor Leet, therefore, at the court of election, made a pacific speech to the freemen. He represented to them the great difficulties and dangers of the year past, and the divine goodness towards them, in the continuation of their civil and religious privileges. He acknowledged himself to be subject to many imperfections, yet professed, that, in his office, he had acted conscientiously, consulting the common safety and happiness. He declared his readiness to give the reasons of his conduct to any brother, or brethren, who would come to him, in an orderly manner. He acknowledged their kind affection and patience towards him, in covering and passing by his infirmities.

Upon this, the election proceeded, and he was chosen governor, and Matthew Gilbert deputy governor. The deputy governor's not apprehending the regicides, did not, in any measure, injure his popularity. No objection was made against either of the governors. Mr. William Jones and Mr. William Gibbard were chosen magistrates, for New-Haven; Mr. Benjamin Fenn and Mr. Robert Treat, for Milford; and Mr. Jasper Crane, for Branford. Several of the magistrates took the oath, this year, with the explanations and exceptions which they had made the last.

General election at Hartford, Oct. 9th, 1662.

Before the session of the general assembly of Connecticut, in October, the charter was brought over; and as the governors and magistrates, appointed by his majesty, were not authorised to serve after this time, a general election was appointed on the 9th of October. John Winthrop, Esq. was chosen governor, and John Mason, Esq. deputy governor. The magistrates were, Matthew Allen, Samuel Wyllys, Nathan Gould, Richard Treat, John Ogden,

CHAP. XII. CONNECTICUT.

John Tapping, John Talcott, Henry Wolcott, Daniel Clarke, and John Allen, Esquires, Mr. Baker, and Mr. Sherman. John Talcott, Esq. was treasurer, and Daniel Clarke, Esq. secretary.

Book I.

1662.

Upon the day of the election, the charter was publicly read to the freemen, and declared to belong to them and their successors. They then proceeded to make choice of Mr. Wyllys, Mr. Talcott, and Mr. Allen, to receive the charter into their custody, and to keep it in behalf of the colony. It was ordered, that an oath should be administered by the court, to the freemen, binding them to a faithful discharge of the trust committed to them.

The general assembly established all former officers, civil and military, in their respective places of trust; and enacted, that all the laws of the colony should be continued in full force, except such as should be found contrary to the tenor of the charter. It was also enacted, that the same colony seal should be continued.

Acts passed upon the reception of the charter, Oct. 9th, 1662.

The major part of the inhabitants of Southhold, several of the people at Guilford, and of the towns of Stamford and Greenwich, tendering their persons and estates to Connecticut, and petitioning to enjoy the protection and privileges of this commonwealth, were accepted by the assembly, and promised the same protection and freedom, which was common to the inhabitants of the colony in general. At the same time, it was enjoined upon them, to conduct themselves peaceably, as became christians, towards their neighbours, who did not submit to the jurisdiction of Connecticut; and that they should pay all taxes due to the ministers, with all other public charges then due. A message was sent to the Dutch governor, certifying him of the charter, granted to Connecticut, and desiring him, by no means, to trouble any of his majesty's subjects, within its limits, with impositions, or prosecutions from that jurisdiction.

The assembly gave notice to the inhabitants of Winchester, that they were comprehended within the limits of Connecticut; and ordered, that, as his majesty had thus disposed of them, they should conduct themselves as peaceable subjects.

The assembly resolved, that the inhabitants of Mistic and Pawcatuck should no more exercise any authority, by virtue of commissions from any other colony, but should elect their town officers, and manage all their affairs, according to the laws of Connecticut. It was also resolved, that this, and some other towns, should pay twenty pounds

The assembly extend their jurisdiction to Pawcatuck and Long-Island.

Book I. each, towards defraying the expense of procuring the charter.*

1662. Huntington, Setauket, Oyster-Bay, and all the towns upon Long-Island, were obliged to submit to the authority, and govern themselves agreeably to the laws of Connecticut. A court was instituted at Southhold, consisting of captain John Youngs, and the justices of South and East-Hampton. The assembly resolved, that all the towns, which should be received under their jurisdiction, should bear their equal proportion of the charge of the colony, in procuring the patent.

Appoint a committee to confer with New-Haven.
As the charter included the colony of New-Haven, Mr. Matthew Allen, Mr. Samuel Wyllys, and the Rev. Messrs. Stone and Hooker, were appointed a committee, to proceed to New-Haven, and to treat with their friends there, respecting an amicable union of the two colonies.†

The committee proceeded to New-Haven, and after a conference with the governor, magistrates, and principal gentlemen in the colony, left the following declaration, to be communicated to the freemen.

Committee's declaration.
"We declare, that through the providence of the Most High, a large and ample patent, and therein desirable privileges and immunities from his majesty, being come to our hand, a copy whereof we have left with you, to be considered, and yourselves, upon the sea coast, being included and interested therein, the king having united us in one body politic, we, according to the commission wherewith we are intrusted, by the General Assembly of Connecticut, do declare, in their name, that it is both their and our earnest desire, that there may be a happy and comfortable union between yourselves and us, according to the tenor of the charter; that inconveniences and dangers may be prevented, peace and truth strengthened and established, through our suitable subjection to the terms of the patent, and the blessing of GOD upon us therein."

The authority of New-Haven made the following reply.

New-Haven's reply.
"We have received and perused your writings, and heard the copy read of his majesty's letters patent to Connecticut colony; wherein, though we do not find the colony of New-Haven expressly included, yet to show our de-

---

* It appears, from the appropriations made, and taxes imposed, to pay the charges of governor Winthrop's agency, that the charter cost the colony about thirteen hundred pounds sterling.

† A thanksgiving was appointed by this assembly, through the colony, to celebrate the divine beneficence: especially, in granting them such a favorable reception with his majesty, and such ample civil and religious privileges, as had been conferred by their charter: and for God's gracious answer to the prayers of his people, in abating the sickness of the country, and giving them rain in the time of drought.

CHAP. XII. CONNECTICUT.

sire that matters may be issued in the conserving of peace and amity, with righteousness between them and us, we shall communicate your writing, and a copy of the patent, to our freemen, and afterwards, with convenient speed, return their answer. Only we desire, that the issuing of matters may be respited, until we may receive fuller information from Mr. Winthrop, or satisfaction otherwise; and that in the mean time, this colony may remain distinct, entire, and uninterrupted, as heretofore: which we hope you will see cause lovingly to consent unto; and signify the same to us with convenient speed."

On the 4th of November, the freemen of the colony of New-Haven, convened in general court. The governor communicated the writings to the court, and ordered a copy of the patent to be read. After a short adjournment, for consideration in an affair of so much importance, the freemen met again, and proceeded to a large discussion of the subject.

Book I.

1662.

Court meet at New-Haven, Nov. 4th.

The Rev. Mr. Davenport was entirely opposed to an union with Connecticut. He proceeded, therefore, to offer a number of reasons, why the inhabitants of New-Haven could not be included in the patent of that colony, and for which they ought by no means, voluntarily to form an union. He left his reasons in writing, for the consideration of the freemen. He observed that, he should leave others to act according to the light which they should receive.

Mr. Davenport opposes the union.

It was insisted, that New-Haven had been owned as a distinct government, not only by her sister colonies, by the parliament, and the protector, during their administration; but by his majesty, king Charles the second: That it was against the express articles of confederation, by which Connecticut was no less bound, than the other colonies; That New-Haven had never been certified of any such design, as their incorporation with Connecticut; and that they had never been heard on the subject. It was further urged, that, had it been designed to unite them with Connecticut, some of their names, at least, would have been put into the patent, with the other patentees; but none of them were there. Hence it was maintained, that it never could have been the design of his majesty, to comprehend them within the limits of the charter. It was argued, that for them to consent to an union would be inconsistent with their oath, to maintain that commonwealth, with all its privileges, civil and religious. Indeed, it was urged, that it would be incompatible both with their honor and most essential interests.

Reasons against it.

Governor Leet excused himself from speaking on the

Book I.
1662.

subject, desiring rather to hear the freemen speak their minds freely, and to act themselves, with respect to the union.

After the affair had been fully debated, the freemen resolved, that an answer to Connecticut should be drawn up under the following heads.

1. "Bearing a proper testimony against the great sin of Connecticut, in acting so contrary to righteousness, amity, and peace."

2. "Desiring that all further proceedings, relative to the affair, might be suspended, until Mr. Winthrop should return, or they might otherwise obtain further information and satisfaction."

3. "To represent, that they could do nothing in the affair, until they had consulted the other confederates."*

The freemen appointed all their magistrates and elders, with Mr. Law, of Stamford, a committee to draw up an answer to the General Assembly of Connecticut. They were directed to subjoin the weighty arguments, which they had against an union. If these should not avail, they were directed to prepare an address to his majesty, praying for relief.

The committee drew up a long letter, in which they declared, that they did not find any command in the patent, to dissolve covenants, and alter the orderly settlement of New-England; nor a prohibition against their continuance as a distinct government. They represented, that the conduct of Connecticut, in acting at first without them, confirmed them in those sentiments; and that the way was still open for them to petition his majesty, and obtain immunities, similar to those of Connecticut. They declared, that they must enter their appeal from the construction which Connecticut put upon the patent; and desired that they might not be interrupted, in the enjoyment of their distinct privileges. They solicited, that proceedings relative to an union might rest, until they might obtain further information, consult their confederates, and know his majesty's pleasure concerning them.

The committee then proceeded to represent the unreasonable and injurious conduct of Connecticut towards them, in beginning to exercise jurisdiction within their limits, before they had given them any intimations that they were included in their charter; before they had invited them to an amicable union; and before they had any representation in their assembly, or name in their patent. They urged, that, in such a procedure, they had encouraged divi

* Records of New-Haven.

CHAP. XII.   CONNECTICUT.

sion, and given countenance to disaffected persons: that they had abetted them in slighting solemn covenants and oaths, by which the peace of the towns and churches, in that colony, was greatly disturbed. Further, they insisted, that, by this means, his majesty's pious designs were counteracted, and his interests disserved: that great scandal was brought upon religion before the natives, and the beauty of a peaceable, faithful and brotherly walking exceedingly marred among themselves. The committee also represented, that these transactions were entirely inconsistent with the engagements of governor Winthrop, contrary to his advice to Connecticut, and tended to bring injurious reflections and reproach upon him. They earnestly prayed for a copy of all which he had written to the deputy governor and company on the subject. On the whole, they professed themselves exceedingly injured and grieved; and intreated the general assembly of Connecticut to adopt speedy and effectual measures to repair the breaches which they had made, and to restore them to their former state, as a confederate and sister colony.*

<small>BOOK I.
1662.</small>

Connecticut made no reply to this letter; but at a general assembly, holden March 11th, 1663, appointed the deputy governor, Messrs. Matthew and John Allen, and Mr. John Talcott, a committee to treat with their friends at New-Haven, on the subject of an union. But the hasty measures which the general assembly had taken, in admitting the disaffected members of the several towns, under the jurisdiction of New-Haven, to their protection, and to the privileges of freemen of their corporation, and in that way beginning to dismember that colony, before they had invited them to incorporate with them, had so soured their minds and prejudiced them, that this committee had no better success than the former.

<small>Assembly at Connecticut, March 11, 1663.</small>

In consequence of the claims of Connecticut, and of what had passed between the two colonies, governor Leet called a special assembly at New-Haven, on the 6th of May. It was then proposed to the court, whether, considering the present state of the colony, and the affairs depending between them and Connecticut, any alteration should be made, with respect to the time or manner of their election? The freemen resolved, that no alteration should be made. They then determined upon a remonstrance, or declaration, to be sent to the general assembly of Connecticut. In this they gave an historical account of the ends of their coming, with their brethren in the united colonies, into New-England, and of the solemn manner in

<small>General court at New-Haven, May 6th.</small>

<small>Remonstrance against Connecticut.</small>

* Letter to Connecticut, No. X.

which these colonies had confederated; and insinuated, that the conduct of Connecticut towards them, was directly contrary to the designs of the first planters of New-England, and to that express article of the confederation, that no one colony should be annexed to another, without the consent of the other colonies. They declared, that if, through the contrivance of Connecticut, without their knowledge or consent, the patent did circumscribe that colony, it was, in their opinion, contrary to brotherly love, righteousness, and peace. They also declared, that, notwithstanding the sense which Connecticut put upon their patent, they could not find one line or letter in it, expressing his majesty's pleasure, that they should become one with that colony. The court affirmed, that they were necessitated to bear testimony against the appointment of constables and other officers, in the towns under their jurisdiction, and the dismembering of their colony, by receiving their disaffected people under the protection of a legislature distinct from theirs, and in which they had no representation. They remonstrated against this, as distracting the colony, destroying the comfort, and hazarding the lives and liberties of their confederates; as giving great offence to their consciences, and as matter of high provocation and complaint before God and man. All this unbrotherly and unrighteous management, they represented as exceedingly aggravated, in that, notwithstanding their former representations and intreaties, in writing, notwithstanding their appeal to his majesty, and notwithstanding all their past distress and sufferings, they were still pursuing the same course. They still declared, that they appealed to his majesty; and that, exceedingly grieved and afflicted, they, in the sight of God, angels, and men, testified against such proceedings.*

Governor Winthrop writes to Connecticut, March 1663.

While these affairs were transacted in the colonies, the petition and address of New-Haven, to his majesty, arrived in England. Upon which governor Winthrop, who was yet there, by the advice of the friends of both colonies, agreed, that no injury should be done to New-Haven, and that the union and incorporation of the two colonies should be voluntary. Therefore, on the 3d of March, 1663, he wrote to the deputy governor and company of Connecticut, certifying them of his engagements to the agent of New-Haven; and that, before he took out the charter, he had given assurance to their friends, that their interests and privileges should not be injured by the patent. He represented, that they were bound by the assurances he

* No. XI.

CHAP. XII.   CONNECTICUT.

had given; and, therefore, wished them to abstain from all further injury and trouble of that colony. He imputed what they had done to their ignorance of the engagements which he had made. At the same time, he intimated his assurance, that, on his return, he should be able to effect an amicable union of the colonies.*

At the election in Connecticut, Mr. Howell and Mr. Jasper Crane were chosen magistrates, instead of Mr. John Allen and Mr. John Ogden.† Mr. John Allen was appointed treasurer.

Connecticut now laid claim to West-Chester, and sent one of their magistrates to lead the inhabitants to the choice of their officers, and to administer the proper oaths to such as they should elect. The colony also extended their claim to the Narraganset country, and appointed officers for the government of the inhabitants at Wickford.

Notwithstanding the remonstrance of the court at New-Haven, their appeal to king Charles the second, and the engagements of governor Winthrop, Connecticut pursued the affair of an union, in the same manner in which it was begun. At a session of the general assembly, August 19th, 1663, the deputy governor, Mr. Wyllys, Mr. Daniel Clarke, and Mr. John Allen, were appointed a committee to treat with their friends of New-Haven, Milford, Guilford, and Branford, relative to their incorporation with Connecticut. Provided they could not effect an union, by treaty, they were authorised to read the charter publicly at New-Haven, and to make declaration to the people there, that the assembly could not but resent their proceeding, as a distinct jurisdiction, since they were evidently included within the limits of the charter, granted to the corporation of Connecticut. They were instructed to proclaim, that the assembly did desire, and could not but expect, that the inhabitants of New-Haven, Milford, Guilford, Branford, and Stamford, would yield subjection to the government of Connecticut.

At the meeting of the commissioners, in September, New-Haven was owned by the colonies, as a distinct confederate. Governor Leet and Mr. Fenn, who had been sent from that jurisdiction, exhibited a complaint against Connecticut, of the injuries which they had done, by encroaching upon their rights, receiving their members under their government, and encouraging them to disown their authority, to disregard their oath of allegiance, and to refuse all attendance on their courts. They further complain-

Marginalia: Book I. 1663. Election at Hartford, May 14th, 1663. July 10th. Committee appointed again to treat with New-Haven, Aug. 19th, 1663. Commissioners meet at Boston, Sept. 3d, 1663. Complaint of New-Haven.

* Governor Winthrop's letter to Connecticut, No. XII.
† Mr. Crane was chosen magistrate, this year, in both colonies.

Book I.
1663.

Reply of Connecticut.

Determination of the commissioners.

Sept. 3d.

The Dutch governor complains of a breach of the articles of agreement in 1650.

Reply of Connecticut.

ed, that Connecticut had appointed constables in several of their towns, to the great disquiet and injury of the colony. They prayed, that effectual measures might be taken to redress their grievances, to prevent further injuries, and secure their rights as a distinct confederate.

Governor Winthrop and Mr. John Talcott, commissioners from Connecticut, replied, that, in their opinion, New-Haven had no just grounds of complaint; that Connecticut had never designed them any injury, but had made to them the most friendly propositions, inviting them to share with them freely in all the important and distinguishing privileges, which they had obtained for themselves; that they had sent committees amicably to treat with them; that they were still treating, and would attend all just and friendly means of accommodation.

The commissioners of the other colonies, having fully heard the parties, determined, that as the colony of New-Haven had been "owned, in the articles of confederation, as distinct from Connecticut, and having been so owned, by the colonies jointly in the present meeting, in all their actings, they may not, by any acts of violence, have their liberty of jurisdiction infringed, by any other of the united colonies, without breach of the articles of confederation; and that where any act of power hath been exerted against their authority, that the same ought to be recalled, and their power reserved to them entire, until such time, as, in an orderly way, it shall be otherwise disposed." With respect to the particular grievances, mentioned by the commissioners of New-Haven, the consideration of them was referred to the next meeting of the commissioners at Hartford.*

The extending of the claims of Connecticut to all the plantations upon Long-Island, to West-Chester, and the neighbouring towns, alarmed Stuyvesant, the Dutch governor. He, therefore, appeared before the commissioners at Boston, and complained of the infraction of the articles of agreement, concluded at Hartford, between the English and Dutch, and desired the commissioners to determine, whether they considered said articles as binding the parties or not.

As this complaint respected Connecticut more especially, governor Winthrop and Mr. Talcott replied, in behalf of their constituents. They pleaded, that, as it was an affair of great concernment, and as Connecticut had not been certified of any such complaint, and they had no instructions relative to the subject, the decision of it might be deferred until the next meeting of the commissioners.

* Records of the united colonies, vol. ii.

CHAP. XII.   CONNECTICUT.

The commissioners resolved, that, saving their allegiance to his majesty, and his claim to the lands in controversy, and the right of Connecticut colony, by virtue of their charter, they did, for themselves, esteem the articles of agreement, in 1650, to be binding, and that they would not countenance the violation of them. They advised the parties concerned, to refer all matters, respecting the subject, to the next meeting of the commissioners. In the mean time, they advised, that the articles of agreement should be observed, and that all persons in the places in controversy, should be acquitted from penalties and damages, on the account of their having resisted the authority of the Dutch.*

Connecticut was now attacked from all quarters. While the colony was without a royal grant, its neighbours made encroachments with impunity; and now, when it extended its claims, by virtue of regal authority, they all complained, and took all possible advantage of former encroachments and decisions, at times when they could plead no such authority. As all the united colonies, except Plymouth, were affected by the claims of the colony, so they were mutually interested in opposing and determining against them.

As Connecticut had now claimed Pawcatuck, or Southerton, and prohibited the exercise of any authority there, except such as was derived from the legislature of that colony, the inhabitants had exhibited three addresses to the general court of Massachusetts, petitioning for relief and protection.

The commissioners from Massachusetts, Mr. Bradstreet and Mr. Danforth, laid the complaints and petitions before the commissioners of the other colonies, and prayed for relief, according to the provision made, in such cases, in the articles of confederation.

The court of commissioners advised, that the affair should be respited for the present; that Connecticut should apply to the general court of the Massachusetts, for an amicable settlement: and that, if this should not be effected, the aggrieved party might make application to the commissioners, at their next meeting. In the mean time, they advised, that affairs at Southerton, should be managed according to their former decisions.

When the general assembly of Connecticut convened, in October, they paid particular attention to these great objects of general concernment. Notwithstanding all which

*Records of the united colonies, vol. II.

Book I. had happened relative to New-Haven, the following act passed.

1663.
Act respecting New-Haven.

"This court doth declare, that they can do no less, for their own indemnity, than to manifest their dissatisfaction with the plantations of New-Haven, Milford, Guilford, Stamford, and Branford, in their distinct standing from us, in point of government; it being directly opposite to the tenor of the charter, lately granted to our colony of Connecticut, in which these plantations are included. We do also expect their submission to our government, according to our charter, and his majesty's pleasure therein expressed; it being a stated conclusion with the commissioners, that jurisdiction right goeth with patent. And whereas, the aforesaid people of New-Haven, Milford, Guilford, Stamford, and Branford, pretend they have power of government, distinct from us, we do hereby declare, that our council will be ready to attend them, or a committee of theirs; and if they can rationally make it appear, that they have such power, and that we have wronged them according to their complaints, we shall be ready to attend them with due satisfaction."*

The assembly appointed a committee to draught a letter to the gentlemen at New-Haven, and to inclose to them the preceding resolution.

Agents from the Dutch.

Agents were sent to this assembly from the Manhadoes, to treat with the legislature, relative to the differences subsisting between them and the Dutch. A petition, at the same time, was presented from the English plantations upon Long-Island, in the vicinity of the Dutch, praying for the protection and privileges of the corporation of Connecticut. Upon which the assembly passed the following resolve:

"That, as they were solicitous to maintain the interests and peace of his majesty's subjects, and yet to attend all ways of righteousness, so that they might hold a friendly correspondence with their neighbours, at the Manhadoes, they would, for the present, forbear all acts of authority towards the English plantations on the west end of Long-Island, provided the Dutch would forbear to exercise any coercive power towards them; and this court shall cease from further attendance unto the premises, until there be a seasonable return, from the general Stevenson, to those propositions his messengers carried with them, or until there be an issue of the difference, between them and us. And, in case the Dutch do unjustly molest or offer violence unto them, we declare, that we shall not be willing to see

* Records of Connecticut.

CHAP. XII.   CONNECTICUT.   261

our countrymen, his majesty's natural born subjects, and his interests, interrupted or molested, by the Dutch or any others; but we shall address ourselves, to use such just and lawful means, as GOD shall, in his wisdom, offer to our hands, for their indemnity and safety, until his majesty, our sovereign lord the king, shall please to declare his royal pleasure for their future settlement."

BOOK I.

1665.

As governor Winthrop was now returned from England, the assembly embraced the first opportunity to present him with the thanks of the colony, for the great pains he had taken, and the special services he had rendered it, in procuring the charter.

The legislature, determining to secure, as far as possible, the lands within the limits of their charter, authorised one Thomas Pell to purchase of the Indian proprietors all that tract between West-Chester and Hudson's river, and the waters which made the Manhadoes an island; and resolved, that it should be added to West-Chester.

The towns on the west end of Long-island petitioning to be under the government of Connecticut, the assembly declared, that, as the lines of their patent extended to the adjoining islands, they accepted those towns under their jurisdiction.

It was resolved, in October, that Hammonasset should be a town. The same month, twelve planters, principally from Hartford, Windsor, and Guilford, fixed their residence there. It was afterwards named Killingworth. At the October session, 1703, the assembly gave them a patent, confirming to the proprietors all the lands within the limits of the town.*

October.

While these affairs were transacted in Connecticut, the colony of New-Haven persisted in their opposition to an incorporation with that government. On the 22d of October, their general court convened, and governor Leet acquainted the court, that, since the meeting of the commissioners, their committee had written to Connecticut to the following effect: That as the commissioners had unanimously established the confederation, and the distinct and entire jurisdiction of each confederate colony, they judged, that it would not be unacceptable to present to their general assembly our request, that they would act in conformity to the advice of the commissioners, and recal all former acts, inconsistent with their determinations. They insisted, that a compliance with their wishes would be no ob-

Oct. 22, the general court at New-Haven write to Connecticut.

---

* The name originally designed was Kennelworth, and thus it is written, for some years, on the records of the colony, but by mistake it was recorded Killingworth, and this name finally prevailed.

BOOK I.
1663.

struction to an amicable treaty; but that its tendency would be sooner to effect the union, which they desired: That it could, by no means, endanger their patent, nor any of their chartered rights; and that they had the countenance of all the confederates, to apologize for them in their present request, and in maintaining their rights, as a distinct jurisdiction. Governor Leet further certified the court, that their committee had desired an answer to their letter, before the present session of their general court, and previously to their answering the proposals made to them by Connecticut.

The freemen determine to hold no further treaty with that colony.

The freemen of the colony of New-Haven were not only opposed to an incorporation with Connecticut, but even to treating with them, under the then present circumstances.

The court, after a long and serious debate, considering, that the general court of Connecticut had not complied with their request, but still claimed a right of jurisdiction over them, and countenanced the malcontents in their several towns, were decidedly against any further treaty. The following resolution was adopted. "That no treaty be made, by this colony, with Connecticut, before such acts of power, exerted by them, upon any of our towns, be revoked and recalled, according to the honorable Mr. Winthrop's letter engaging the same, the commissioners' determination, and our frequent desires."

Order that rates shall be distrained.

The court ordered, that the magistrates, or other officers, where there were no magistrates, should issue warrants, according to law, to attach the personal estate of those who, upon legal demand, had refused, or should refuse to make payment of their rates. It was provided, that, in case of resistance and forcible rescue, violence should not be used to the shedding of blood, unless it were in a man's own defence. The court further determined to make application to his majesty for redress. The plan adopted by the court, as circumstances then were, was to petition the king for a bill of exemption from the government of Connecticut, and to leave the affair of procuring a patent, for that colony, to the wisdom of their agents in England, as they should judge to be most expedient.

A tax of 300 pounds was levied upon the colony, for the purpose of enabling them to prosecute the affair before his majesty in council.

A day of extraordinary fasting and prayer was appointed to supplicate divine mercy, for the afflicted people of God universally, and especially for themselves, that they might be directed to the proper means of obtaining an established and permanent enjoyment of their just rights and privileges.

CHAP. XII.   CONNECTICUT.

The affairs of the colony of New-Haven were now exceedingly embarrassed, and approaching to an important crisis. The colony was much in debt. Taxes had not been punctually collected. Many were disaffected with the government, and refused to pay any thing for its support. When the officers of New-Haven attempted to collect the taxes, which had been imposed, they repaired to Connecticut for protection; and, with too little appearance of justice, or brotherly affection, were protected, by its legislature. Indeed the colony was so reduced, that it could not pay the stated salaries of its principal officers. While the court expressed their ardent desires, were it in their power, to give the governors the full salary, which had been usual, yet, considering the low state of the colony, and the numbers withdrawn from them, they judged they were not able to give the governor more than forty pounds, and the deputy governor not more than ten.

Book I. 1663. Embarrassed state of New-Haven.

No sooner did the officers begin to distrain the rates of those who refused to pay, than it produced the most alarming and dangerous consequences. One John Rossiter of Guilford, and his son, bold and disorderly men, who had been punished for misdemeanors, by the authority of the colony of New-Haven, made a journey to Hartford, and obtained two of the magistrates of Connecticut, a constable, and several others, to come down to Guilford, on the night of the 30th of December. By firing a number of guns in the night, they greatly alarmed and disturbed the town. Some of the men, from Connecticut, were rough, and used high and threatening language. In such a crisis, governor Leet judged it expedient to send immediately to Branford and New-Haven, for assistance. Both the towns were alarmed, in the dead time of night, and forwarded men to the aid of the governor. The governor and magistrates conducted affairs with such moderation and prudence, that no mischief was done. The gentlemen from Connecticut remonstrated against collecting taxes from those, who had been taken under the protection of that colony, and desired New-Haven to suspend the affair for further consideration.

Alarm at Guilford, Branford, and New-Haven, Dec. 30th.

Governor Leet therefore convoked a special court, at New-Haven, on the 7th of January, 1664. He opened the public business, by acquainting the court, that it was the earnest desire of the magistrates from Connecticut, and of Mr. Rossiter and his son, that the act of the general court of New-Haven, relative to the distraining of taxes, might be suspended, until there could be another conference between the colonies; at which, they were in expec-

General court at New-Haven, Jan. 7th, 1664.

Book I.
1663.

Persists in its resolution not to treat with Connecticut.

Statement of New-Haven case.

tation, that all difficulties might be amicably settled. He also laid before the court the representations which the gentlemen from Connecticut had made of the great danger there would be, in carrying that act into execution, in direct opposition to the authority of Connecticut. It was desired, that the court would maturely consider the affair.

The court insisted, that all former treaties with Connecticut had been without any good effect; and persisted in the resolution, that, until the members, which had been so unrighteously taken from them, should be restored, they would hold no further treaty with that colony.* Mr. Davenport and Mr. Street were appointed to make a draught of their grievances, to be transmitted to the General Assembly of Connecticut. It was to be examined and approved by such a number of their committee, as could be convened upon the occasion. They drew up a long and sensible remonstrance, which they termed "NEW-HAVEN CASE STATED." The subject was introduced with a declaration to this effect: That it was their deep sense of the injuries, which the colony had suffered, by the claims and encroachments, which had been made upon their just prerogatives and privileges, which had induced them, unanimously, though with great reluctance, to declare their grievances unto them. They proceeded then, to declare, that they settled at New-Haven, with the consent of Connecticut; had purchased the whole tract of land, which they had settled upon the sea coast, of the Indians, the original proprietors of the soil; and had quietly possessed it nearly six and twenty years: That they had expended great estates, in clearing, fencing, and cultivating the lands, without any assistance from Connecticut; and had formed themselves, by voluntary compact, into a distinct commonwealth. They then proceeded to state a great variety of instances, in which Connecticut, the united colonies, the parliament, and protector, the king, and his council, had owned them as a distinct colony. They insisted that, notwithstanding, they had now procured a patent including New-Haven, not only without their concurrence, but contrary to their minds, previously expressed; contrary to the express articles of the confederation, and to their own engagements, not to include them in the charter. Further they affirmed, that Mr. Winthrop, before his departure for England, had, by his letters, given assurance, that it was not designed to include New-Haven in the patent; and that the magistrates of Connecticut had agreed, that, if the patent should include them, they should be at full liberty to incorporate

* Records of New-Haven.

CHAP. XII.   CONNECTICUT.

with them or not, as should be most agreeable to their inclinations. They alledged that, contrary to all the premises, to justice, to good faith, to brotherly kindness, to the peace and order of church and commonwealth, Connecticut, even in their first assembly, proceeded to the dismemberment of the colony of New-Haven, by receiving its members from Stamford, Guilford, and Southhold: That, after such dismemberment, they had preposterously pretended to treat with them relative to an union: And that, after a conference with the committee from Connecticut, and the reading of their charter, it did not appear that they were so much as mentioned, or that it had any reference to them. They declared that, in a full persuasion of his majesty's pleasure, to continue them a distinct jurisdiction, they had assured the committee of their design to appeal to him, and know his royal purpose: That, though they immediately sent their appeal; yet that, out of tender respect to the peace and honor of Mr. Winthrop, they advised their friends, in England, to acquaint him with their papers, that he might adopt some effectual expedient, to compromise the unhappy differences between the two colonies: And that it was on the account of Mr. Winthrop's engagements to their friends, that their rights and interests should not be disquieted nor injured, that the appeal to his majesty was then suspended.* From a statement of these, and some other facts and circumstances, they attempted to demonstrate their rights, as a distinct colony, and the injustice, unfaithfulness, ingratitude, and cruelty of Connecticut, in their claims upon them, and in the manner of their prosecuting them. Their beginning to dismember their colony, by receiving and protecting their subjects and malcontents, previous to any treaty with them; their appointing officers, creating animosities, and raising alarms in their several towns, were especially insisted on, as contrary to all their covenants, as brethren and confederates, and contrary to all order, peace, and justice.

The General Assembly of Connecticut, at their session in May, avowed their claim to Long-Island, as one of the adjoining islands mentioned in their charter, except some preceding right should appear, approved by his majesty. Officers were appointed, by the court at Hampstead, Jamaica, Newtown, Flushing, Oyster-Bay, and all the towns upon the west end of the island.

Upon the general election at New-Haven, the freemen proceeded to the choice of their civil officers, as had been

*Records of New-Haven.

Book I.

1664.

Assembly at Connecticut, May 12th.

General election at New-Haven, May 25th.

Book I. usual. Governor Leet was rechosen, and Mr. William Jones was elected deputy-governor. Matthew Gilbert, 1664. Esq. the former deputy-governor, Mr. Benjamin Fenn, Mr. Jasper Crane, Mr. Treat, and Mr. Nash, were appointed magistrates. The two last would not accept the office. The governor and deputy-governor were chosen commissioners for the next meeting at Hartford. The colony was now become so weak, and the affairs of it so embarrassed, by the claims and proceedings of Connecticut, that the general court either did no business, or judged it expedient to put nothing upon record.

In this situation of affairs, an event took place, which alarmed all the New-England colonies, and at once changed the opinions of the commissioners, and of New-Haven, with respect to their incorporation with Connecticut.

King Charles the second, on the 12th of March, 1664, gave a patent to his brother, the Duke of York and Albany, of several extensive tracts of land, in North America, the boundaries of which are thus described.

Duke of York's patent. "All that part of the main land of New-England, beginning at a certain place, called and known by the name of St. Croix, next adjoining to New-England in America, and from thence extending along the sea coast unto a certain place called Pemaquie or Pemaquid, and so up the river thereof, to the furthest head of the same, as it tendeth northward; and extending from thence to the river Kembequin, and so upwards by the shortest course to the river Canada, northward: and also, all that island or islands, commonly called by the general name or names of Meitowax, or Long-Island, situate and being toward the west of Cape Cod, and the narrow Highgansets, abutting upon the main land between the two rivers there called or known by the several names of Connecticut and Hudson's river, and all the land from the west side of Connecticut river to the east side of Delaware bay, and also all those several islands called or known by the names of Martin's Vineyard or Nantucks, otherwise Nantucket: together," &c.

The concern of the Duke of York for his property, the aversion both of his majesty and the duke to the Dutch, with the differences between them and the New-England colonies, made an expedition against the New-Netherlands a prime object of their attention. Though his majesty king Charles II. was an indolent prince, devoted to dissipation and pleasure, yet, under the influence of these motives, an armament was soon prepared, and a fleet dispatched to New-England, for the reduction of the Dutch settlements on the continent. Colonel Richard Nichols

Armament for the reduction of the Dutch settlements.

Chap. XII. CONNECTICUT.

was chief commander of the fleet and army. Colonel Nichols had not only a commission, for the reduction of the Dutch plantations, and the government of them, but he, with George Cartwrith, Esq. Sir Robert Carr, and Samuel Maverick, Esq. were appointed commissioners, by his majesty, and vested with extraordinary powers, for visiting the New-England colonies; hearing and determining all matters of complaint and controversy between them, and settling the country in peace.*

Colonel Nichols arrived at Boston, with the fleet and troops under his command, on the 23d of July, 1664. He immediately communicated his commission to the colonies, and his majesty's requisition of troops, to assist in the expedition against the Dutch. He then sailed for the New-Netherlands, and on the 20th of August, made a demand of the town and forts upon the island of Manhadoes. He had previously sent letters to governor Winthrop to join him, at the west end of Long-Island. Governor Winthrop, with several of the magistrates and principal gentlemen of Connecticut, joined him, according to his wishes.

Stuyvesant, the Dutch governor, was an old soldier, and had he been better prepared, and the people united, doubtless would have made a brave defence. But he had no intimations of the design, until the 8th of July, when he received intelligence, that a fleet of three or four ships of war, with three hundred and fifty soldiers on board, were about to sail from England, against the Dutch settlements. Upon this, he immediately ordered that the forts should be put into a state of defence, and sent out spies into several parts of Connecticut, with a view of obtaining further information. Indeed, the tradition has been, that the Dutch governor, apprehending the danger in which all the Dutch plantations would immediately be, on the arrival of the fleet, should the colonies unite against them, came to Hartford to negotiate a neutrality with Connecticut; and that he was there when he received the news of the arrival of the fleet at Boston. The story has been, that he made his departure in the night, and returned with the utmost expedition.

He was extremely opposed to a surrender of the fort and town. Instead of submitting to the summons at first sent him, he drew up a long statement of the Dutch claims, and their indubitable right to the country. He insisted that, had the king of England known the justice of their claims, he never would have adopted such measures against them. He concluded, by assuring colonel Nichols, that

*No. xiii. and his majesty's letter No. xiv.

Sidenotes: Book I. 1664. Commissioners with extraordinary powers. Colonel Nichols arrives at Boston, July 23d. Demands a surrender of the fort and town at the Manhadoes. Dutch governor opposed to a submission.

268　　　　　　　　HISTORY OF　　　　　　Chap. XII.

Book I. he should not submit to his demands, nor fear any evils, but such as God, in his providence, should inflict upon him.*

1664.

Colonel Nichols, in his first summons, had, in his majesty's name, given assurance, that the Dutch, upon their submission, should be safe, as to life, liberty, and property. Governor Winthrop also wrote a letter to the governor and council, advising them to surrender. But they were careful to secrete the writings from the people, lest the easy terms proposed, should induce them to surrender. The burgo-masters and people desired to know of the governor, what was the import of the writings he had received, and especially of the letter from governor Winthrop. The Dutch governor and his council giving them no intelligence, they solicited it still more earnestly. The governor, irritated at this, in a paroxysm of anger, tore the letter in pieces. Upon which the people protested against his conduct, and all its consequences.

The people oppose him.

While the governor and his council were thus contending with the burgo-masters and people, in the town, the English commissioners caused a proclamation to be published, in the country, encouraging the inhabitants to submit to his majesty's government. This promised to all the inhabitants, who would become subject to his majesty, "that they should be protected by his majesty's laws and justice, and peaceably enjoy whatever God's blessing, and their honest industry, had furnished them with, and all the other privileges with his majesty's English subjects."

The commissioners issue a proclamation.

The colonel, finding that the Dutch governor was determined, if possible, to keep his station, sent officers to Jamaica, Hampstead, and other towns, upon the island, to beat up for volunteers. Captain Hugh Hyde, who commanded the ships, had orders to proceed to the reduction of the fort.† Troops were raised in New-England, and ready to march upon the first notice. Two thirds of the inhabitants upon Long-Island were English subjects, and wished for the success of his majesty's arms. They were ready, if necessary, to afford their immediate assistance. In such circumstances, opposition would have been madness. The Dutch therefore, on the 27th of August, submitted on terms of capitulation. The articles secured them in the enjoyment of liberty of conscience in divine worship, and their own mode of discipline. The Dutch governor and people became English subjects, enjoyed their estates, and all the privileges of Englishmen. Upon the

The Dutch at New-Amsterdam, fort Orange, and Delaware, submit to his majesty's arms, and become English subjects.

* Smith's History of New-York, p. 12, 14.
† The same, p. 10, 22.

surrender of the town of New-Amsterdam, it was named New-York, in honor to the duke of York.

Part of the armament immediately sailed up the river, under the command of Carteret, to fort Orange, or Aurania. This surrendered on the 24th of September. This was named Albany, in honor to the duke of York and Albany. Sir Robert Carr proceeded with another division of the fleet to Delaware. He obliged the Dutch and Swedes to capitulate, and deliver up their respective garrisons, on the 1st of October. Upon this day, the whole of New-Netherlands became subject to the crown of England. The Dutch, who before had given so much trouble to the English colonists, from this time, commenced their loyal and peaceable fellow subjects.

The short time the commissioners tarried at Boston, before they proceeded upon their expedition against the Dutch, was sufficient to discover something of their extraordinary powers, and such a taste of the high and arbitrary manner in which they conducted, as spread a general alarm, and awakened, in the colonies, serious apprehensions for their liberties. Mr. Whiting, who was at Boston, and learned much of their temper, was sent back, in haste, to give information of the danger, in which, it was apprehended, the colonies all were; to advise New-Haven to incorporate with Connecticut, without delay; and to make a joint exertion for the preservation of their chartered rights. This was pressed, not only as absolutely necessary for New-Haven, but for the general safety of the country.

In consequence of this intelligence, a general court was convened at New-Haven, on the 11th of August, 1664. Governor Leet communicated the intelligence which he had received from their friends at Boston. He acquainted them that Mr. Whiting and Mr. Bull had made a visit to New-Haven, and in their own names, and in behalf of the magistrates of Connecticut, pressed their immediate subjection to their government. Further, the court was certified, that after some treaty with those gentlemen, their committee had given an answer, purporting, that, if Connecticut would, in his majesty's name, assert their claim to the colony of New-Haven, and secure them in the full enjoyment of all the immunities, which they had proposed, and engage to make a united exertion, for the preservation of their chartered rights, they would make their submission. After a long debate the court resolved, that, if Connecticut should come and assert their claim, as had been agreed, they would submit until the meeting of the com-

Book I.
1664.

News and advice from Boston.

General court at New-Haven, August 11th.

Book I.
1664.

Connecticut remonstrate against the sitting of the commissioners of New-Haven.

missioners of the united colonies. The magistrates and principal gentlemen of the colony, seem to have been sensible, not only of the expediency, but necessity of an incorporation with Connecticut. The opposition, however, was so general among the people, that nothing further could be effected.

The court of commissioners was so near at hand, that governor Winthrop and his council judged it not expedient to make any further demands upon New-Haven, until their advice could be known. However, when the general assembly met, early in September, they passed a remonstrance against the sitting of governor Leet and deputy governor Jones with the commissioners. In the remonstrance they declared, that New-Haven was not a colony, but a part of Connecticut, and avowed their claim to it as such. They insisted, that owning that as a colony, distinct from Connecticut, after his majesty had, by his letters patent, incorporated it with that colony, was inconsistent with the king's pleasure; would endanger the rights of all the colonies, and especially the charter-rights of Connecticut. The assembly, at the same time, declared, that they would have a tender regard to their honored friends and brethren, at New-Haven, and exert themselves to accommodate them, with all the immunities and privileges which were conveyed by their charter.

Court of commissioners meets Sept. 1st. Advise to a speedy union of Connecticut and New-Haven.

On the 1st of September, the court of commissioners met at Hartford. The commissioners from New-Haven were allowed their seats with the other confederates. The case of New-Haven and Connecticut was fully heard, and though the court did not approve of the manner, in which Connecticut had proceeded, yet they earnestly pressed a speedy and amicable union of the two colonies. They represented, that the divine honor, and the welfare of all the colonies, as well as their own, were greatly concerned in the event.

To remove all obstructions on their part, the commissioners recommended it to the general courts of Massachusetts and Plymouth, that, in case the colony of New-Haven should incorporate with Connecticut, they might then be owned as one colony, and send two commissioners to each meeting; and that the determinations of any four of the six, should be equally binding on the confederates, as the conclusions of six out of eight, had been before. It was also proposed to the court, that the meeting, which of course had been at New-Haven, should be at Hartford.*

* Records of the united colonies. It was determined, at this court, that their meetings, for the future, should be triennial.

CHAP. XII.   CONNECTICUT.

In compliance with the advice of the commissioners, governor Leet convened the general court at New-Haven, on the 14th of September, and communicated the advice which had been given, and papers from the committee of Connecticut, advising and urging them to unite. They referred it to their most serious consideration, whether, if the king's commissioners should visit them, they would not be much better able to vindicate their liberty and just rights, in union with Connecticut, under a royal patent, than in their then present circumstances. Many insisted, notwithstanding, "That to stand as God had kept them to that time was their best way." Others were entirely of the contrary opinion, and after the fullest discussion of the subject, no vote for union or treaty could be obtained.

New-Haven and Branford were more fixed and obstinate in their opposition to an incorporation with Connecticut, than any of the other towns in that colony. Mr. Davenport and Mr. Pierson seem to have been among its chief supporters. They, with many of the inhabitants of the colony, were more rigid, with respect to the terms of church communion, than the ministers and churches of Connecticut generally were. The ministers and churches in Connecticut were, a considerable number of them, in favor of the propositions of the general council, which met at Cambridge, in 1662, relative to the baptism of children, whose parents were not in full communion. The ministers and churches of New-Haven were universally and utterly against them. Mr. Davenport, and others in this colony, were also strong in the opinion, that all government should be in the church. No person in this colony could be a freeman, unless he were a member in full communion. But in Connecticut, all orderly persons, possessing a freehold to a certain amount, might be made free of the corporation. Those gentlemen, who were so strong in the opposition, were, doubtless, jealous that an union would mar the purity, order, and beauty of their churches, and have an ill influence on the civil administrations. The removal of the seat of government; the apprehension which some had of losing their places of trust and general influence; with strong prejudices and passions against Connecticut, on account of the injuries, which it was conceived it had done the colony, all operated in forming the opposition. Besides, it was a painful reflection, that, after they had been at so much pains and expense to form and support themselves as a distinct commonwealth, and had been so many years owned as one, their existence must cease and their name be obliterated.

[Marginalia: Book I. 1664. General court at New-Haven. No vote obtained for an union. Grounds of opposition to an union with Connecticut.]

Book I. This event, however, was hastening, and grew more and more urgent. Milford, at this time, broke off from them,

1664. and would no more send either magistrate or deputies to the general court. Mr. Richard Law, a principal gentleman at Stamford, also deserted them.

Assembly meets Oct. 13th. Important crisis with Connecticut.

In this state of affairs, the general assembly of Connecticut convened, on the 13th of October. This was an important crisis with the colony. In few instances, have so many important objects of consideration, at one time, presented themselves to a legislature. Their liberties were not only in equal danger with those of their sister colonies, from the extraordinary powers, and arbitrary dispositions and measures of the king's commissioners, but the duke of York, a powerful antagonist, had received a patent, covering Long-Island and all that part of the colony west of Connecticut river. The Massachusetts were encroaching upon them on their northern and eastern boundaries. William and Anne, the duke and dutchess of Hamilton, had petitioned his majesty to restore to them the tract of country granted to their father, James, marquis of Hamilton, in the year 1635; and his majesty had, on the 6th of May, 1664, referred the case to the determination of colonel Nichols and the other commissioners.* Besides, the state of affairs with New-Haven was neither comfortable nor safe.

Acts of the assembly, respecting the commissioners, Massachusetts & Rhode-Island.

In these circumstances, the legislature viewed it as a point of capital importance to conciliate the commissioners, and obtain the good graces of his majesty. For this purpose, they ordered a present of five hundred bushels of corn, to be made to the king's commissioners. A large committee was appointed to settle the boundaries between Connecticut and the duke of York. A committee, consisting of Mr. Allen, Mr. Wyllys, Mr. Talcott, and Mr. Newbury, was also appointed to settle the boundary line between this colony and Massachusetts, and between Connecticut and Rhode-Island. They were instructed not to give away any part of the lands, included within the limits of the charter.

Respecting New-Haven.

Mr. Sherman, Mr. Allen, and the secretary, were authorised to proceed to New-Haven, and, by order of the general assembly, "in his majesty's name, to require the inhabitants of New-Haven, Milford, Branford, Guilford, and Stamford, to submit to the government established by his majesty's gracious grant to this colony, and to receive their answer." They had instructions to declare all the freemen, in those towns, free of the corporation of Connecticut; and to make all others, in the respective towns men-

* No. XV.

CHAP. XII. CONNECTICUT.

tioned, qualified according to law, freemen of Connecticut. At the same time, they were directed to administer to them the freeman's oath.

Besides, they were authorised to make declaration, that the assembly did invest William Leet and William Jones, Esquires, Mr. Gilbert, Mr. Fenn, Mr. Crane, Mr. Treat, and Mr. Law, with the powers of magistracy; to govern their respective plantations agreeably to the laws of Connecticut, or such of their own laws, as were not inconsistent with the charter, until their session in May next. It was proclaimed also, that all other officers, civil and military, were established in their respective places; and that cognizance should not be taken of any case which had been prosecuted, to a final adjudication, in any of the courts of that colony.*

The gentlemen appointed to this service, on the 19th of November, went to New-Haven, and proceeded according to their instructions.

About the same time, Governor Winthrop, Mr. Allen, Mr. Gould, Mr. Richards, and John Winthrop, the committee appointed to settle the boundaries between Connecticut and New-York, waited on the commissioners upon York Island. After they had been fully heard, in behalf of Connecticut, the commissioners determined, "That the southern bounds of his majesty's colony of Connecticut, is the sea; and that Long-Island is to be under the government of his royal highness, the duke of York, as is expressed by plain words in the said patents respectively. We also order and declare, that the creek or river called Mamaronock, which is reputed to be about twelve miles to the east of West-Chester, and a line drawn from the east point or side, where the fresh water falls into the salt, at high water mark, north-north-west, to the line of Massachusetts, be the western bounds of the said colony of Connecticut; and the plantations lying westward of that creek, and line so drawn, to be under his royal highness's government; and all plantations lying eastward of that creek and line, to be under the government of Connecticut.†

In consequence of the acts of Connecticut, and the determination of the commissioners, relative to the boundaries of the colony, a general court was called at New-Haven, with the freemen, and as many of the inhabitants of the colony as chose to attend, on the 13th of December, 1664. The following resolutions were then unanimously passed.

1. "That, by this act or vote, we be not understood to

*Records of Connecticut. † No. XVI.

BOOK I.
1664.

Determination of his majesty's commissioners, Nov. 30th.

General court at New-Haven, Dec. 13th.

Book I.
1664.
Resolves of the court.

justify Connecticut's former actings, nor any thing disorderly done by their own people, on such accounts."

2. "That, by it, we be not apprehended to have any hand in breaking or dissolving the confederation."

3. "Yet, in loyalty to the king's majesty, when an authentic copy of the determination of his majesty's commissioners is published, to be recorded with us, if thereby it shall appear to our committee, that we are, by his majesty's authority, now put under Connecticut patent, we shall submit, by a necessity brought upon us, by the means of Connecticut aforesaid; but with a *salvo jure* of our former rights and claims, as a people, who have not yet been heard in point of plea."*

The members of the court, then present, the elders of the colony, with Mr. John Nash, Mr. James Bishop, Mr. Francis Bell, Mr. Robert Treat, and Mr. Richard Baldwin, were appointed a committee to consummate an union between the colonies.

Several letters passed between the committees of the two colonies, on the subject, in which the committee of New-Haven signified, that the officers in that colony would continue to act in their respective offices, and expressed their good designs and wishes towards Connecticut, and their loyalty to his majesty. They also represented their expectations, that the governor and company, according to their engagements, would give them all the advantages and privileges which they could do, consistent with the patent, and their desires still to continue the confederation.†

The committee of Connecticut, in answer to New-Haven, assured them of their willingness to bestow on them all the privileges granted in their charter, prepared ready to their hands. They acquainted them, that provision had been made for the continuance of the confederation, according to their wishes. They pleaded the necessity and importance of their incorporation with Connecticut, as they were nearly in the centre of the colony, as an apology for the measures which they had taken. They expressed their strong desires that New-Haven would cordially unite with them, and, by no means, view it as a matter of constraint: that mutual candour might be exercised; and that all reflections and past conduct, disagreeable to either of them, be entirely buried and for ever forgotten.‡

Session of assembly, April 20th, 1665.

The general assembly of Connecticut appointed no committee to meet with that chosen by the general court of New-Haven. Of this their committee complain, in their

* Records of New-Havens † No. XVII.
‡ Letter of Connecticut to New-Haven, No. XVIII.

last letter.* However, at a session of theirs, the 20th of April, 1665, they passed several resolves, for the further completion of the union.

It was resolved, that William Leet and William Jones, Esquires, Mr. Benjamin Fenn, Mr. Matthew Gilbert, Mr. Jasper Crane, Mr. Alexander Bryan, Mr. Law, and Mr. Robert Treat, should stand in the nomination for magistrates at the next election.

{Resolutions respecting New-Haven.}

The assembly, also, passed the following declaration: "That all acts of the authority of New-Haven, which had been uncomfortable to Connecticut, should never be called to an account, but be buried in perpetual oblivion."†

The king's commissioners presented the following propositions, or requisitions, from his majesty, to this assembly.

{His majesty's requisitions.}

1. "That all householders, inhabiting this colony, take the oath of allegiance, and that the administration of justice be in his majesty's name."

2. "That all men of competent estates and of civil conversation, though of different judgments, may be admitted to be freemen, and have liberty to choose, or to be chosen officers, both military and civil."

3. "That all persons, of civil lives, may freely enjoy the liberty of their consciences, and the worship of God in that way which they think best; provided that this liberty tend not to the disturbance of the public, nor to the hindrance of the maintenance of ministers, regularly chosen, in each respective parish or township."

4. "That all laws, and expressions in laws, derogatory to his majesty, if any such have been made, in these troublesome times, may be repealed, altered, and taken off the file."

The assembly answered in the manner following.

{The answer to them.}

1. "That according to his majesty's pleasure, expressed in our charter, our governor formerly appointed meet persons to administer the oath of allegiance, who have, according to their order, administered the said oath to several persons already; and the administration of justice among us hath been, is, and shall be, in his majesty's name."

2. "That our order for the admission of freemen is consonant with that proposition."

3. "We know not of any one that hath been troubled, by us, for attending his conscience, provided he hath not disturbed the public."

4. "We know not of any law, or expressions of law,

* No. XIX.   † Records of Connecticut.

Book I.
1665.

Answer to the duke of Hamilton's petition.

that are derogatory to his majesty among us; but if any such be found, we count it our duty to repeal, alter, and take them off the file; and this we attended, upon the receipt of our charter."

About this time, it seems, the council gave the following answer, for substance, to the commissioners, relative to the claim and petition of the duke of Hamilton: That the grant of Connecticut to the nobles and gentlemen, of whom they purchased, was several years prior to the marquis of Hamilton's: That with great difficulty they had conquered a potent and barbarous people, who spread over a great part of that tract of country, which he claimed; and that it was but a small compensation, for the blood and treasure which they had expended in conquering it, and defending it for his majesty's interest against the Dutch and other foreigners: That they had peaceably enjoyed that tract for about thirty years: That they had with great labor and expense cultivated the lands, to their own and his majesty's interest; and that his majesty, of his grace, had been pleased to confirm it to them, by his royal charter, in which these reasons had been recognized.*

They at the same time, solicited their honors, the commissioners, to present their humble acknowledgments to his majesty for his abundant grace, in the granting of their charter, and for his gracious letter, sent them by his commissioners, re-ratifying their privileges, civil and ecclesiastical.

Election, May 11th.

Colonies united in one assembly.

At the general election, May 11th, 1665, when the two colonies of Connecticut and New-Haven united in one, the following gentlemen were chosen into office. John Winthrop, Esq. was elected governor, John Mason, Esq. deputy governor, and Matthew Allen, Samuel Wyllys, Nathan Gould, John Talcott, Henry Wolcott, John Allen, Samuel Sherman, James Richards, William Leet, William Jones, Benjamin Fenn, and Jasper Crane, Esquires, magistrates. John Talcott, Esq. was treasurer, and Daniel Clark secretary.

A proportionable number of the magistrates were of the former colony of New-Haven; all the towns sent their deputies; and the assembly appears to have been entirely harmonious.

This assembly enacted, that Hastings and Rye should be one plantation, by the name of Rye.

County courts first instituted, May 11th.

By this assembly county courts were first instituted, by that name. It was enacted, that there should be two county courts holden annually, in New-Haven; one on the sec-

* No. XX.

CHAP. XII.   CONNECTICUT.

ond Thursday in June, the other on the third Thursday in November. The court was to consist of five judges, two magistrates, and three justices of the quorum. A similar court was appointed at New-London; and, the next October, that was made a distinct county.

Book I.
1665.

At the session in October, a county court was appointed, at Hartford, instead of the quarterly courts. This was to be holden annually in the months of March and September. The county courts had cognizance of all cases except those of life, limb, or banishment. In cases of more than twenty shillings, the law required that a jury should be impannelled.

At the same time, a superior court was appointed to be holden, at Hartford, the Tuesday before the session of the general assembly in May and October. This was to consist of eight magistrates, at least, and always to be attended with a jury. In this court were tried all appeals from the several county courts, and all capital actions, of life, limb, and banishment.

Superior court instituted, Oct. 12.

All the towns, formerly under the jurisdiction of New-Haven, were satisfied with the union of the colonies, except Branford. But Mr. Pierson and almost his whole church and congregation were so displeased, that they soon removed into Newark, in New-Jersey. They carried off the records of the church and town, and after it had been settled about five and twenty years, left it almost without inhabitants. For more than twenty years from that time, there was not a church formed in the town. People, from various parts of the colony, gradually moved into it, and purchased the lands of the first planters, so that, in about twenty years, it became re-settled. In 1685, it was re-invested with town privileges.

Branford dissatisfied with the union.

The union of the colonies was a happy event. It greatly contributed to the convenience, strength, peace, and welfare of the inhabitants of both, and of their posterity. Greater privileges New-Haven could not have enjoyed, had they been successful in their applications to his majesty. This must have been very expensive, and after much expense, they might have failed in their attempts and lost their liberties, or have been joined to Connecticut at last. Had they remained a distinct colony, the charges of government would have been greater than in their state of incorporation. Their situation, in so central a part of the colony, would have been extremely inconvenient, especially for Connecticut. It was, doubtless, his majesty's pleasure, and for his interest, that the colonies should be one; and their friends on both sides the water judged it

The union a happy event.

Reasons for it.

Book I. most expedient. It was what their own and the general good demanded. All these circumstances, Connecticut could plead, as an apology for their conduct. But after all, it will be difficult, if not impossible, to reconcile some parts of it, at least, with their pre-engagements, the rules of justice, and brotherly affection.

1665.

War was proclaimed, this year, in London, in the month of March, between England and Holland. His majesty had given intelligence to the colony, that De Ruyter, the Dutch admiral, had orders to visit New-York. The colony was alarmed, and put into a state of defence. But the admiral was diverted from the enterprise, and the year passed in peace.

In the proclamation for thanksgiving, in November, the people were excited to praise the SUPREME BENEFACTOR, for preventing the troubles which they had feared, and for the blessings of liberty, health, peace, and plenty.*

CHAPTER XIII.

A view of the churches of Connecticut and New-Haven, from their first settlement, until their union, in 1665. Their ministers. The character of the ministers and first planters. Their religious and political sentiments. Gathering of the churches of New-Haven and Milford. Installation of Mr. Davenport and Mr. Prudden. Church formed at Guilford. Number of ministers in Connecticut and New-Haven, before the union. Proportion of ministers to the people, before and at the time of the union. Harmony between the civil rulers and the clergy. Influence of the clergy, and the reasons of it. Their opposition to Antinomianism. Assisted in the compilation of Cambridge Platform. Ecclesiastical laws. Care to diffuse general knowledge; its happy influence. Attempts to found a college at New-Haven. No sectaries in Connecticut nor New-Haven, until after the union. Deaths and characters of several of the first ministers. Great dissensions in the church at Hartford, soon after Mr. Hooker's death; dissensions and controversies in the colony, and churches in general, relative to baptism, church-

---

* It was now thirty years since the settlement of the colony commenced, yet, after the defalcation of Long-Island, it consisted of nineteen towns only, which paid taxes. The grand list was no more than £153,620 : 16 : 5.

CHAP. XIII.   CONNECTICUT.   279

membership, and the rights of the brethren. A new generation arises, who had not all imbibed the spirit of their fathers. Grievances presented to the general court of Connecticut, on the account of the strictness of the churches, and that sober people were denied communion with them, and baptism for their children. The court of Connecticut send to the other general courts for advice. Laws against the Quakers. Massachusetts and Connecticut agree in appointing a synod at Boston. General court at New-Haven oppose the meeting of a synod, and decline sending their elders. Questions proposed for discussion. The synod meets and answers them; but it had no good effect on the churches. They would not comply with their decisions. Dissensions continued at Hartford; acts of the general court respecting them. Councils from Massachusetts. Difficulties in some measure composed. Divisions and animosities at Weathersfield. Act of the general court respecting the church there. Mr. Russel and numbers remove from Weathersfield and Hartford, and settle Hadley. Mr. Stow dismissed from the ministry at Middletown, by a committee of the general court. Synod at Boston. Its determination relative to baptism and the consociation of churches. Division in the synod, and in the churches, relative to these points. The court at Connecticut sent no elders to the council, nor took any part in the controversy, until some time afterwards.

CONNECTICUT, no less than other parts of New-England, was settled with a particular view to religion. It was the design of the first planters, to erect churches in the strictest conformity to scripture example; and to transmit evangelical purity, in doctrine, worship, and discipline, with civil and religious liberty, to their posterity. The attention which they paid to these interesting points, will be the principal subject of this chapter.

The first churches, though their numbers were small, and they had to combat all the hardships, dangers, and expense, of new settlements, commonly supported two able, experienced ministers. With the first three churches, settled in Connecticut, there were, at Hartford, the Rev. Mr. Hooker and Mr. Stone, at Windsor, Mr. Warham and Mr. Hewet, and at Weathersfield, Mr. Prudden, in 1638, while his people were making preparations to remove from New-Haven to Milford. To the garrison, at Saybrook fort, Mr. John Higginson, son of the Rev. Mr. Higginson, of Salem, preached three or four of the first years. At New-Haven, at first were Mr. Davenport and Mr. Samuel Eaton, broth-

First ministers of Connecticut and New-Haven.

er to governor Eaton. At Milford, Mr. Prudden was pastor, and the church invited Mr. John Sherman, afterwards minister of Watertown, in Massachusetts, to be their teacher; but he declined their invitation, and that church never had but one settled minister at the same time. The Rev. Mr. Whitfield was pastor of the church at Guilford, and about the year 1641, Mr. Higginson removed from Saybrook, and became teacher, as an assistant to Mr. Whitfield, in that church. After Mr. Prudden left Weathersfield, Mr. Henry Smith was elected, and ordained pastor of the church and congregation in that town. About the time that Mr. Higginson left Saybrook, the Rev. Mr. Thomas Peters became chaplain to colonel Fenwick, and the people there. Upon the removal of Mr. Eaton, from New-Haven, Mr. William Hook was installed teacher, as an asssistant of Mr. Davenport. The six first towns in Connecticut and New-Haven, enjoyed the constant labor of ten able ministers. This was as much as one minister to about fifty families, or to two hundred and sixty or seventy souls. As other towns settled, churches were gathered, and ministers installed or ordained. Mr. Jones was chosen pastor at Fairfield, Mr. Adam Blackman, at Stratford, and Mr. Richard Denton, at Stamford. Mr. Abraham Pierson was pastor of the church at Branford, and it seems one Mr. Bruey assisted him as a teacher for some time. Fourteen or fifteen of these ministers had been episcopally ordained in England, before they came into America.

The Rev. Mr. Richard Blynman, first pastor of the church at New-London, was also ordained in England. After he came into this country, he settled first, pastor of the church at Gloucester, in Massachusetts. From thence he removed to New-London in 1648.

From these reverend fathers, the ministers of Connecticut trace their ordinations; especially, from Mr. Hooker, Mr. Warham, Mr. Davenport, and Mr. Stone. Some or other of these assisted in gathering the churches, and ordaining the ministers settled in their day.

Their religious sentiments. With respect to their religious sentiments, and those of their followers, they were puritans. This was a name which first obtained in the reign of queen Elizabeth, in 1564. It was given as a name of reproach, to distinguish and stigmatize those who did not conform to the liturgy, ceremonies, and discipline, of the church of England. Fuller says, "it was improved to abuse pious people, who endeavoured to follow the minister with a pure heart, and labored for a life pure and holy."* When arminianism be-

* Fuller's ecclesiastical history, b. IX, p. 76.

CHAP. XIII.   CONNECTICUT.

gan to prevail, in the latter part of the reign of James the first, those who were calvinistic, were termed doctrinal puritans.† It was used finally, as a stigma for all christians, who were strict in morals, calvinistic in sentiment, and unconformed to the liturgy, ceremonies, and discipline of the established church.‡

This was truly the character of the first ministers and churches in this colony. They were strictly calvinistic, agreeing in doctrine with their brethren of the established church, and with all the protestant reformed churches. In discipline, they were congregationalists, and dissented from the national establishment. They firmly believed, that it was the sole prerogative of Christ, as king in Zion, to direct the mode of worship and discipline, in his own house. They were persuaded, that the scriptures were a perfect rule, not only of faith and manners, but of worship and discipline: and that all churches ought to be formed entirely after the pattern exhibited in the New Testament.

Some of the ministers of Connecticut were distinguished for literature, piety, and ministerial gifts. Mr. Hooker, Mr. Davenport, Mr. Stone, and some others, were men of great learning and abilities. They were all men of the strictest morals, serious, experimental preachers. Mr. Neal, after giving a catalogue of the ministers, who first illuminated the churches of New-England, bears this testimony concerning them. "I will not say that all the ministers mentioned, were men of the first rate for learning, but I can assure the reader, they had a better share of it, than most of their neighbouring clergy, at that time: they were men of great sobriety and virtue, plain, serious, affectionate preachers, exactly conformable to the doctrine of the church of England, and took a great deal of pains to promote a reformation of manners in their several parishes." They were mighty, and abundant in prayer. They not only fasted and prayed frequently with their people, in public, but kept many days of secret fasting, prayer, and self-examination, in their studies. Some of them, it seems, fasted and prayed, in this private manner, every week. Besides the exercises on the Lord's day, they preached lectures, not only in public, but from house to house. They were diligent and laborious in catechising and instructing the children, and young people, both in public and private.

They paid a constant attention to the religion of their

† Fuller, b. X, p. 100.
‡ Neal's history of the puritans, preface to vol. I, p. 7, and vol. I, p. 72. Second edition, quarto, London, 1754.

Book I. families. They read the scriptures, and prayed in them daily, morning and evening, and instructed all their domestics constantly to attend the secret, as well as private and public duties of religion. They were attentive to the religious state of all the families and individuals of their respective flocks.* As they had taken up the cross, forsaken their pleasant seats and enjoyments in their native country, and followed their Saviour into a land not sown, for the sake of his holy religion, and the advancement of his kingdom, they sacrificed all worldly interests to these glorious purposes.

The people who followed them into the wilderness, were their spiritual children, who imbibed the same spirit and sentiments, and esteemed them as their fathers in Christ.

General character and morals of the people.

Many of them were men of figure, as Haynes, Hopkins, Wyllys, Ludlow, Wolcott, Eaton, Gregson, Desborough, Leet, and others, who were governors and magistrates in their respective colonies. Many of them, especially their governors, magistrates, and leading men, were not less pious and exemplary than their ministers. The people in general were pious, and strictly moral. Instances of intemperance, wantonness, sabbath-breaking, fraud, or any other gross immorality, for many years, were rarely found among them. If any there were, they were commonly found among servants, or some of the lowest of the people.

Their sentiments relative to churches, church officers and discipline.

It was the opinion of the principal divines, who first settled New-England and Connecticut, that in every church, completely organized, there was a pastor, teacher, ruling elder, and deacons.† These distinct offices, they imagined, were clearly taught in those passages, Romans, xii, 7, 1 Corinth. xii, 28, 1 Timothy, v, 17, and Ephesians, iv, 11. From these they argued the duty of all churches, which were able, to be thus furnished.‡ In this manner were the churches of Hartford, Windsor, New-Haven, and other towns organized. The churches which were not able to support a pastor and teacher, had their ruling elders and deacons. Their ruling elders were ordained with no less solemnity, than their pastors and teachers. Where no teacher could be obtained, the pastor performed the duties, both of pastor and teacher. It was the general opinion, that the pastor's work consisted principally in exhortation, in working upon the will and affections. To this the whole force of his studies was to be directed; that, by his judi-

* See an account of the lives of many of them, in the Magnalia, b. III. Particular tracts and manuscripts characterize them in the same manner.
† Hooker's Survey, part II, p. 4 to 20.
‡ Ibidem, and Cambridge Platform, chap. vi, and vii.

cious, powerful, and affectionate addresses, he might win his hearers to the love and practice of the truth. But the teacher was *doctor in ecclesia*, whose business it was to teach, explain, and defend, the doctrines of christianity. He was to inform the judgment, and advance the work of illumination.*

The business of the ruling elder was to assist the pastor in the government of the church. He was particularly set apart to watch over all its members; to prepare and bring forward all cases of discipline; to visit and pray with the sick; and, in the absence of the pastor and teacher, to pray with the congregation, and expound the scriptures.†

The pastors and churches of New-England maintained, with the reformed churches in general, that bishops and presbyters were only different names for the same office; and, that all pastors, regularly separated to the gospel ministry, were scripture bishops.‡ They also insisted, agreeably to the primitive practice, that the work of every pastor, was confined, principally, to one particular church and congregation, who could all assemble at one place, whom he could inspect, and who could all unite together in acts of worship and discipline.§ Indeed, the first ministers of Connecticut and New-England, at first maintained, that all the pastor's office power was confined to his own church and congregation; and that the administering of baptism and the Lord's supper in other churches, was irregular.¶

With respect to ordination, they held, that it did not constitute the essentials of the ministerial office; but the qualifications for office, the election of the church, guided by the rule of Christ, and the acceptance of the pastor elect.** Says Mr. Hooker, "ordination is an approbation of the officer, and solemn setting and confirmation of him in his office, by prayer, and laying on of hands." It was viewed, by the ministers of New-England, as no more than putting the pastor elect into office, or a solemn recommending of him and his labors to the blessing of God. It was the general opinion, that elders ought to lay on hands in ordination, if there were a presbytery in the church, but if there were not, the church might appoint some other elders, or a number of the brethren to that service.††

Calling and ordination of ministers

* Survey, part II, p. 19, 20, 21, and Cambridge Platform, chap. vi.
† Hooker's Survey, part II, p. 13, 19, C. Plat. chap. vii.
‡ Hooker's Survey, and Cambridge Platform.
§ Cambridge Platform, chap. iii, and chap. ix.
¶ Hooker's Survey, part II, p. 62, 68.
** The same, part II, p. 75, 78, Cam. Platform, chap. ix.
†† These sentiments were not peculiar to the first ministers and churches

Book I.

Power of synods.

It was acknowledged that synods or general councils, were an ordinance of Christ, and in some cases, expedient and necessary: That their business was to give light and counsel in weighty concerns, and bear testimony against corruption in doctrines and morals. While it was granted, that their determinations ought to be received with reverence, and not to be counteracted, unless apparently repugnant to the scriptures, it was insisted, that they had no juridical power.† The churches of Connecticut originally maintained, that the right of choosing and settling their ministers, of exercising discipline and performing all juridical acts was in the church, when properly organized; and they denied all external or foreign power of presbyteries, synods, general councils, or assemblies. Hence they were termed congregational churches.

As to politics, the first settlers were republicans.

The fathers of Connecticut, as to politics, were republicans. They rejected with abhorrence the doctrines of the divine right of kings, passive obedience, and non-resistance. With Sidney, Hampden, and other great writers, they believed that all civil power and government was originally in the people. Upon these principles they formed their civil constitutions.

Confession of faith and solemn manner of covenanting.

The churches of New-Haven, Milford, and Guilford, were formed first, by the choice of seven persons, from among the brethren, who were termed the pillars. A confession of faith was drawn up, to which they all assented, as preparatory to their covenanting together in church estate. They then entered into covenant, first with God, to be his people in Christ, and then with each other, to walk together in the strict and conscientious practice of all christian duties, and in the enjoyment of all the ordinances and privileges of a church of Christ. The confessions of faith contained a summary of christian doctrine, and were strictly calvinistic. The covenants were full, solemn, and impressive, importing, that they avouched the Lord Jehovah, Father, Son, and Holy Ghost, to be their sovereign Lord and supreme Good; and that they gave themselves up to him, through Jesus Christ, in the way and on the terms of the covenant of grace. They covenanted with each other to uphold the divine worship and ordinances, in the churches of which they were members; to watch over each other as brethren; to bear testimony against all sin; and to teach all under their care to fear and serve the Lord. The other brethren joined themselves to the seven pillars, by

of New-England. Augustine, Chrysostom, Zanch, Bucer, Melancthon, Dr. Ames, Dr. Owen, and many other divines of great fame, were of the same opinion.

† Hooker's Survey, part IV. p. 45—48. C. Plat. chap. XVI.

CHAP. XIII.   CONNECTICUT.

making the same profession of faith, and covenanting in the same manner. The members, previously to their covenanting with each other, gave one another satisfaction with respect to their repentance, faith, and purposes of holy living.

It appears, that the churches of New-Haven and Milford were gathered to the seven pillars, on the 22d of August, 1639.* The tradition is, that soon after, Mr. Davenport was chosen pastor of the church, at New-Haven; and that Mr. Hooker and Mr. Stone came and assisted in his installation. *(margin: Churches of New-Haven and Milford, gathered Aug. 22d, 1639.)*

Mr. Prudden was installed pastor of the church, at Milford, April 8th, 1640, upon a day of solemn fasting and prayer. Imposition of hands was performed by Zechariah Whitman, William Fowler, and Edmond Tapp. They were appointed to this service by the other brethren of the church.† The installation was at New-Haven, and it seems that the hands of the brethren were imposed in the presence of Mr. Davenport and Mr. Eaton. *(margin: Installation of Mr. Prudden, April 18th, 1640.)*

Though the members of Mr. Whitfield's church were in the original agreement, at New-Haven, and engaged to embody into church estate, in the same manner as New-Haven and Milford churches did, yet they delayed the completion of the work for a considerable time. Probably, it was because their company were not yet all arrived. But in April, 1643, Mr. Whitfield, Mr. Higginson, Mr. Samuel Desborough, Mr. William Leet, Mr. Jacob Sheaf, Mr. John Mipham, and Mr. John Hoadly, were elected the seven pillars. On the 19th of June, all the other church members were gathered unto these seven persons. Mr. Higginson, who had been preaching about two years at Guilford, with Mr. Whitfield, was, at this time, elected teacher in that church. Mr. Whitfield had not separated from the episcopal church, when he came into New-England. As he came over in orders, and his church came generally with him, there are no intimations of his installation. *(margin: Guilford church gathered, April 1643.)*

The circumstance of the seven pillars in these three churches appears to have been peculiar to them. There are no intimations of it in the formation of any other churches. The churches in the other towns were gathered, by subscribing similar confessions of faith, and covenanting together in the same solemn manner, upon days of fasting and prayer. Neighbouring elders and churches were present on those occasions, assisted in the public solemnities, and gave their consent. When new members were

* Milford church records.   † Ibidem.

Book I. admitted to full communion, in any of the first churches of Connecticut, they gave satisfaction to the brethren of their sincere repentance towards God, and faith in the Lord Jesus Christ. They commonly made a relation of their religious experiences. They were then admitted to full communion, by a public profession of their faith, and by covenanting in the manner which has been represented.

Mr. Eaton continued but a short time at New-Haven, and then returned to England. Mr. William Hook succeeded him as teacher in the church.

Mr. Denton removes from Stamford. Mr. Bishop succeeds him.
Mr. Denton, after spending three or four years at Stamford, removed to Hampstead on Long-Island.

Upon his removal, the church sent two of their members to seek them a minister. They travelled on foot, through the wilderness, to the eastward of Boston, where they found Mr. John Bishop, who left England before he had finished his academical studies, and had completed his education in this country. They engaged him to go with them to Stamford. He travelled with them, on foot, so great a distance. The people were united in him, and he labored with them, in the ministry, nearly fifty years.

Church gathered and Mr. Fitch ordained at Saybrook, 1646.
Mr. Peters, after preaching three or four years, at Saybrook, returned to England. In 1646, a church was formed in that town, by the direction and assistance of the Rev. Mr. Hooker and some other ministers. At the same time, Mr. James Fitch, who had perfected his theological studies, under the direction of Mr. Hooker, was ordained their pastor. The tradition is, that though Mr. Hooker was present, yet that hands were imposed by two or three of the principal brethren, whom the church had appointed to that service.

On the 13th of October, 1652, a church was gathered at Farmington, and Mr. Roger Newton was ordained pastor.

The same year, Mr. Thomas Hanford began to preach at Norwalk, and some time after a church was formed in the town, and Mr. Hanford ordained pastor.

In 1660, Mr. Fitch and the greatest part of his church removed to Norwich. Mr. Thomas Buckingham succeeded him in the ministry at Saybrook. A council of ministers and churches assisted at his ordination, but the imposition of hands was performed by the brethren, as it had been before in the ordination of Mr. Fitch. The council considered it as an irregular proceeding, but the brethren were so tenacious of what they esteemed their right, that it could not be prevented without much inconvenience.*

These fifteen churches were the whole number, formed

* Manuscripts from Saybrook.

in the colony, and in which ministers had been installed, or ordained, at the time of the union. The settlements and churches upon Long-Island had been adjudged to the jurisdiction of New-York. There were several other towns which paid taxes, where churches were not formed nor pastors ordained. This was the case with Stonington, Middletown, Greenwich, and Rye. Nevertheless, at the two former, there was constant preaching. The general court would not suffer any plantation to be made which would not support an able, orthodox preacher.

At Stonington, Mr. Zechariah Brigden officiated about three years, until his death in 1663. To him succeeded Mr. James Noyes, the same year, who preached more than fifty-five years in the town, but he was not ordained until more than ten years after his first preaching to the people.

At Middletown, Mr. Nathaniel Collins was preaching, but not ordained. Mr. Stow also preached there, before, or with, Mr. Collins. Greenwich and Rye were but just come under the jurisdiction of Connecticut, and not in circumstances for the support of ministers. They had occasional preaching only, for a considerable time.

From this view, it appears, that the first towns and churches in Connecticut were remarkably instructed. Scarcely in any part of the christian church, have so many stars, of such distinguished lustre, shone in so small a firmament. At the time of the union, the colony contained about 1700 families, eight or nine thousand inhabitants, and they constantly enjoyed the instructions of about twenty ministers. Upon an average, there was as much as one minister to every eighty-five families, or to about four hundred and thirty souls. In some of the new plantations, thirty families supported a minister, and commonly there were not more than forty when they called and settled a pastor. In several of the first churches, there were not more than eight, nine, and ten male members. Exclusive of Hartford, Windsor, New-Haven, and Guilford, there appears to have been none, in which there were more than sixteen or seventeen male communicants, at their formation.

That the first churches and congregations, notwithstanding their poverty, hardships, dangers, and expense in settling in a wilderness, and in defending themselves against the savages and other enemies, should maintain such a number of ministers, strongly marks their character as christians, who desired the sincere milk of the word. It affords a striking evidence of their zeal for religion, and that the word and ordinances were indeed precious in those days.

Harmony between the legislature and clergy.

The most perfect harmony subsisted between the legislature and the clergy. Like Moses and Aaron, they walked together in the most endearing friendship. The governors, magistrates, and leading men, were their spiritual children, and esteemed and venerated them, as their fathers in Christ. As they had loved and followed them into the wilderness, they zealously supported their influence. The clergy had the highest veneration for them, and spared no pains to maintain their authority and government. Thus they grew in each other's esteem and brotherly affection, and mutually supported and increased each other's influence and usefulness.

Influence of the clergy.

Reasons of it.

Many of the clergy who first came into the country, had good estates, and assisted their poor brethren and parishioners in their straits, in making new settlements. The people were then far more dependent on their ministers, than they have been since. The proportion of learned men was much less then, than at the present time. The clergy possessed a very great proportion of the literature of the colony. They were the principal instructors of the young gentlemen, who were liberally educated, before they commenced members of college, and they assisted them in their studies afterwards. They instructed and furnished others for public usefulness, who had not a public education. They had given a striking evidence of their integrity and self denial, in emigrating into this rough and distant country, for the sake of religion, and were faithful and abundant in their labours. By their example, counsels, exhortations, and money, they assisted and encouraged the people. Besides, the people who came into the country with them, had a high relish for the word and ordinances. They were exiles and fellow sufferers in a strange land. All these circumstances combined to give them an uncommon influence over their hearers, of all ranks and characters. For many years, they were consulted by the legislature, in all affairs of importance, civil or religious. They were appointed committees, with the governors and magistrates, to advise, make drafts, and assist them in the most delicate and interesting concerns of the commonwealth. In no government have the clergy had more influence, or been treated with more generosity and respect, by the civil rulers and people in general, than in Connecticut.

Ministers of Connecticut condemn Antinomianism, in 1638.

The ministers and churches of Connecticut abhorred the Antinomian heresy, which so distracted the church at Boston, and some others in the Massachusetts. In the first

CHAP. XIII.   CONNECTICUT.

general council in New-England, Mr. Hooker and Mr. Davenport bore a noble testimony against the prevailing errors and spirit of that time.

In the next general council in New-England, ten years after, the ministers and churches of Connecticut and New-Haven were present, and united in the form of discipline which it recommended. By this platform of discipline, the churches of New-England, in general, walked for more than thirty years. This, with the ecclesiastical laws, formed the religious constitution of the colonies.

1648. Their elders adopt Cambridge platform.

In the platform, it is declared to be evident, "That necessary and sufficient maintenance is due to ministers of the word, from the law of nature and nations, the law of Moses, the equity thereof, and also the rule of common reason:" that it is matter of indispensable duty, a debt due, and not an affair of alms or free gift. "That not only members of churches, but all who are taught in the word, are to contribute unto him that teacheth in all good things: and that the magistrate is to see that the ministry be duly provided for."*

Opinion respecting the maintenance of ministers.

An early provision was therefore made, by law, in Massachusetts and Connecticut, for the support of the ministry. In Connecticut, all persons were obliged, by law, to contribute to the support of the church, as well as of the commonwealth. All rates respecting the support of ministers, or any ecclesiastical affairs, were to be made and collected in the same manner as the rates of the respective towns.† Special care was taken, that all persons should attend the means of public instruction. The law obliged them to be present at the public worship on the Lord's day, and upon all days of public fasting and prayer, and of thanksgiving, appointed by civil authority, on penalty of a fine of five shillings for every instance of neglect.‡ The congregational churches were adopted and established by law; but provision was made that all sober, orthodox persons, dissenting from them, should, upon the manifestation of it to the general court, be allowed peaceably to worship in their own way.§ It was enacted, "That no persons within this colony, shall in any wise embody themselves into church estate, without consent of the general court, and approbation of neighbouring elders." The laws, also, prohibited that any ministry, or church administration, should be entertained, or attended, by the inhabitants of any plantation in the colony, distinct and separate from

Ecclesiastical laws.

* Cambridge Platform, chap. xi.
† The first code of Connecticut, p. 52 and 59.
‡ Ibid. p. 22.   § Ibid. p. 21.

Book I. and in opposition to, that which was openly and publicly observed and dispensed, by the approved minister of the place; except it was by the approbation of the court and neighbouring churches.* The penalty for every breach of this act, was five pounds.

The court declared, that the civil authority established in the colony, "Had power and liberty to see the peace, ordinances, and rules of Christ, observed in every church, according to his word; and, also, to deal with any church member in a way of civil justice, notwithstanding any church relation, office, or interest." The law also provided, that no church censure should degrade or depose any man from any civil dignity, office, or authority, which he should sustain in the colony.†

Care to propagate knowledge and good morals.

In the grant of all new townships, special care was taken, by the legislature, that the planters should not be without a minister, and the stated administration of gospel ordinances.

Every town, consisting of fifty families, was obliged, by the laws, to maintain a good school, in which reading and writing should be well taught; and in every county town a good grammar school was instituted. Large tracts of land were given and appropriated, by the legislature, to afford them a permanent support.

The select men of every town were obliged, by law, to keep a vigilant eye upon all the inhabitants, and to take care that all the heads of families should instruct their children and servants to read the English tongue well, and that once every week they should catechise them in the principles of religion. The penalty for every instance of neglect, in this respect, was twenty shillings, for any family so neglecting. The select men were also authorised, to take care that all families should be well furnished with bibles, orthodox catechisms, and books on practical godliness. It was provided by the legislature, that the capital laws should be taught weekly in every family.‡

The colony of New-Haven, from the beginning, made provision for the interests of religion, learning, and the good conduct of the inhabitants, with no less zeal than Connecticut.

The care and piety of the first planters did not rest here; but they were careful, as soon as possible, in their circumstances, to found public seminaries, in which young men might be instructed in the liberal arts, prepared for the

* The first code of Connecticut, p. 21.
† Ibid. p. 22.
‡ Old code of Connecticut, p. 13.

CHAP. XIII.   CONNECTICUT.

ministry, and all places of importance, in civil or religious life.

As Connecticut and New-Haven were not able, of themselves, at first, to erect a college, they united with Massachusetts, and contributed to the support of that at Cambridge. Frequent contributions were made, both in Connecticut and New-Haven, for that purpose, and money was paid from the public treasury. For a course of years, the inhabitants educated their sons at that university.

By these means, knowledge, at an early period, was generally diffused among people of all ranks. This abundant public and private instruction, and constant attention to the morals, industry, and good conduct of the inhabitants, has been the means of that general illumination, which has always been observable among the people of this colony; and of that high degree of civil, ecclesiastical, and domestic peace and order, which, for so long a period, have rendered them eminent, among their neighbors. This has made it feasible to govern them by that free constitution and mild system of laws, by which they have ever been distinguished. To this, are owing the wisdom and steadiness of their elections, and the integrity and firmness of their public administrations. In this way they have been formed not only to virtue, but to industry, economy, and enterprise. Indeed, they have been rendered one of the happiest people upon the earth. *Happy effects of them.*

Cambridge platform, in connection with the ecclesiastical laws, was the religious constitution of Connecticut, for about sixty years, until the compilation of the Saybrook agreement.

The colony of New-Haven, sensible of the importance of public seminaries, and of the inconvenience of sending their sons to so great a distance as Cambridge for an education, at an early period, attempted the founding of a college. A proposal, for this purpose, was made to the general court, in 1654. The next year, at the session in May, it appeared, that New-Haven had made a donation of 300l. and that Milford proposed to give 100l. more, for the encouragement of the design. The court proposed it to the deputies of the other towns to enquire, and make report, what they would give. Mr. Davenport, who was the principal promoter of the affair, about the same time, wrote to governor Hopkins, who was then in England, upon the subject; and it seems, solicited his assistance. Soon after, some lands were given, by the people of New-Haven, for the further encouragement of so laudable an undertaking. Upon these favorable prospects, the legislature, in 1659, *Grammar school instituted, and college founded at New-Haven.*

Book I. proceeded to institute a grammar school at New-Haven. It was ordered, that 40l. annually, should be paid out of the public treasury, for its support. 100l. were also appropriated for the purchase of books for the school. In 1660, the donation of governor Hopkins having come into the possession, and being at the disposal of Mr. Davenport, he, on the 30th of May, surrendered it into the hands of the general court, for the purpose of founding a college. He proposed, that this donation should be united with the lands which had been already given, and with such other donations as might be made by the legislature, for the same purpose. The elders of the several churches in the colony, were nominated as trustees. As Mr. Davenport was the only surviving legatee of governor Hopkins, with respect to that part of the donation which had fallen to the share of New-Haven, he desired, that, for the better discharge of the trust, which had been reposed in him, he might have a negative upon the corporation, with respect to the disposal of that, whenever he could exhibit substantial reasons, that it was about to be applied to any purpose contrary to the design of the donor. The resignation was made in writing, in a formal manner, containing valuable sketches of history, and a complete plan of the college and grammar school, which it was designed to institute.*

The general court thankfully accepted the donation, upon the terms on which it had been surrendered. They appropriated the lands, which had been given, at New-Haven, to the support of the college; agreed to collect the money given by governor Hopkins; and besides all other grants previously made, enacted, that a hundred pounds stock should be paid in from the treasury of the colony, in such time and manner as the court should order. The court also ordained, that both the grammar school and college should be at New-Haven. One Mr. Peck was appointed master of the school; but this and the college were of short continuance. The troubles in which the colony was involved by the claims of Connecticut, and the defection of such numbers of their inhabitants, so impoverished and weakened it, that a support could not be obtained for the instructor. He became discouraged, and the court gave up the school. By the same means, the design of a college also miscarrried. After the union, the colony made further provision for a grammar school, and all the lands and money, which had been given for that and the college, were appropriated to its support. The school revived and has continued unto the present time.

* Appendix, No. xxi.

CHAP. XIII.   CONNECTICUT.   293

For a long course of years, there were no sectaries in Connecticut. The churches, in general, enjoyed great peace and harmony, during the continuance of the first ministers and principal members of whom they were composed. But many of these were considerably advanced in life when they came into the country, and in about four or five and twenty years after the first settlements, a considerable proportion of them were in their graves, some had returned to England, and others were far advanced in years. Before the union of the colonies, in 1665, almost all the first ministers were either dead, or removed.

Mr. Hewet, teacher in the church at Windsor, died September 4th, 1644.

The Rev. Thomas Hooker, the father and pillar of the churches in Connecticut, died July 7th, 1647, in the 61st year of his age.* He was born at Marshfield, in the county of Leicester, 1586. He appears to have been educated at Emmanuel college, Cambridge, in England. Afterwards he was promoted to a fellowship in the same college, where he acquitted himself with such ability and faithfulness, as commanded universal approbation and applause. While at college, in his youth, he was arrested with strong convictions of his sin and misery, and of the dreadfulness of the divine displeasure. His heart was afterwards humbled, and submitting to the terms of mercy, he received the spirit of adoption; and was enabled to exhibit a life of the most exemplary piety, self-denial, patience, and goodness. He was naturally a man of strong and lively passions; but obtained a happy government of himself. In his day, he was one of the most animated and powerful preachers in New-England. In his sermons, he insisted much on the application of redemption; was searching, experimental, and practical. Another circumstance, which rendered his public performances still more engaging and profitable, was his excellency in prayer. A spirit of adoption seemed to rest upon him. In conversation he was pleasant and entertaining, but always grave. He was exceedingly prudent in the management of church discipline. He esteemed it a necessary and important, but an extremely difficult, part of duty. He rarely suffered church affairs to be publicly controverted. Before he brought any difficult matter before the church, special care was taken to converse with the leading men, to fix them right, and to prepare the minds of the members; so that they might be harmonious, and that there might be no con-

BOOK I.

Death and character of Mr. Hooker.

* He possessed considerable property. His estate was appraised at £1336 : 15 : 0. His library only, at £300.

Book I. troversy with respect to any point, which he judged expedient for the church to adopt. He was affable, condescending, and charitable; yet his appearance and conduct were with such becoming majesty, authority, and prudence, that he could do more with a word, or a look, than other men could with severe discipline. It was not an uncommon instance, with him, to give away five or ten pounds at a time to poor widows, orphans, and necessitous people. At a certain time, when there was a great scarcity, at Southampton, upon Long-Island, Mr. Hooker, with some friends who joined with him, sent the people a small vessel, freighted with several hundred bushels of corn, for their relief. In family religion and government, he was strict and prudent. In his family was exhibited a lively and sincere devotion, and the very power of godliness. Not only his own children and domestics, but students, and other persons, who occasionally resided in his family, were instructed and edified, so that their acquaintance with it, was matter of their joy and devout thanksgiving. He died of an epidemical fever, which prevailed that year in the country. He had, for many years, enjoyed a comfortable assurance of his renewed estate, and when dying said, "I am going to receive mercy." He closed his own eyes, and appeared to die with a smile in his countenance.*

Mr. Henry Smith, first pastor of the church at Weathersfield, died in 1648, and was succeeded by the Rev. Jonathan Russell.

Death and character of Mr. Peter Prudden.

The Rev. Mr. Prudden departed this life in 1656, in the 56th year of his age. Before he came into New-England, he was a preacher in Herefordshire, and in the parts bordering upon Wales. His ministry was attended with uncommon success; and when he came into this country, it seems, that many good people followed him, that they might enjoy his pious and fervent ministrations. He had the character of a most zealous preacher, and of a man of an excellent spirit. He had a singular talent for reconciling contending parties, and maintaining peace among brethren and neighbors. His ministry was conducted with prudence, and his church enjoyed great harmony during his life, and rejoiced in his light.†

* His character may be seen more at large in the Magnalia, B. iii. p. 58—68.

† His estate in this country was appraised at £924: 18: 6. He left a landed interest in England, at Edgton, in Yorkshire, valued at £1500 sterling, which is still enjoyed by some of his heirs. He had two sons. One of them, John Prudden, was educated after his decease, and graduated at Cambridge, 1668. He settled in the ministry, at Newark, in New-Jersey. The other inherited the paternal estate; and their descendants are numerous, both in Connecticut and New-Jersey.

He was succeeded by Mr. Roger Newton, who removed from Farmington, and was installed at Milford, August 22d, 1660. Hands were imposed at his installation, by Zechariah Whitman, ruling elder, deacon John Fletcher, and Robert Treat, who were appointed to that service by the brotherhood.

Book I. Succeeded by Mr. Newton, 1660.

Mr. Samuel Hooker, son of the famous Mr. Hooker, of Hartford, succeeded Mr. Newton at Farmington. He was ordained in July, 1661.

Mr. Hooker ordained at Farmington.

These deaths were all before the charter. There were also a number of removals of some of the principal ministers. The Rev. Mr. Whitfield, after he had labored eleven years, with the people at Guilford, returned again to England. Some time in the year 1650, he took leave of his flock and congregation, and embarked for his native country. He was exceedingly beloved by his flock, and they accompanied him to the water's side with many tears. He had a large family of nine children, whom he supported principally out of his own estate, as most of his people were poor. He found that his estate was much exhausted, and that he must still labor under many and great inconveniences, if he continued in this country; and he had numerous and pressing invitations to return to England. A combination of these circumstances, at length, prevailed with him to leave his flock. He was one of the wealthiest clergymen, who came into Connecticut. Before he came into this country, he enjoyed one of the best church livings at Okely, in the county of Surrey, and had a fine interest of his own. His charity was happily proportioned to his opulence. While he was at Okely, he procured another pious and able preacher, that he might go abroad and give assistance unto other churches and poor people. While he was in England, his house was a place of resort for the distressed. Though he was, for twenty years, a conformist, yet his house was a place of refreshment for Mr. Cotton, Mr. Hooker, Mr. Goodwin, and other pious nonconformists. After he came into New-England, he expended much of his interest in assisting his poor people. He was a capital preacher, delivering himself with a peculiar dignity, beauty, and solemnity. After his return to England, he appears to have finished his life, in the ministry, at the city of Winchester.*

Removal of Mr. Whitfield, 1650.

His character.

* In consequence of Mr. Whitfield's estate and expenses, in purchasing and settling the plantation, and of Mr. Fenwick's gift of the eastern part of the township to him, a large portion of the best land in the town was allotted to him. On his return to England, he offered, upon very low terms, to sell all his lands to the town. But the people were poor, and imagined they should soon follow their pastor, and neglected to purchase.

Book I. Several of the principal men returned to England with Mr. Whitfield; particularly Mr. Samuel Desborough, Mr. Jordan, and others. Mr. Desborough, after his return, was made lord keeper of the great seal, and one of the seven counsellors of the kingdom of Scotland.

Mr. Higginson continued his ministry, as teacher in the church at Guilford, until about the year 1659, when, upon the death of his father, he returned to Salem, and succeeded him in the pastoral office, over the church in that town.

Mr. Hook removes, 1655. Mr. William Hook, who, for about fourteen years, had been teacher in the church at New-Haven, about the year 1655 returned to England. Mr. Eaton and Mr. Hook have been represented as men of great learning and piety, and as possessing excellent pulpit talents. A writer of Mr. Eaton's character, says, "He was a very holy man, a person of great learning and judgment, and a most incomparable preacher." He dissented from Mr. Davenport, with respect to his strict terms and form of civil government. His brother, governor Eaton, therefore, advised him to a removal. After his return, he became pastor of a church at Duckenfield, in the parish of Stockport, in Cheshire. Mr. Hook, after his return, was some time minister at Exmouth, in Devonshire; and then master of the Savoy, on the Strand, near London, and chaplain to the greatest man then in the nation. After the restoration, he was silenced for non-conformity, May 24th, 1662. On the 21st of March, 1667, he died in the vicinity of London. Mr. Eaton was a companion with him in tribulation; for soon after the restoration of king Charles the second, he was silenced, and suffered persecution for conscience sake.

Mr. Blynman removes, 1658. The Rev. Mr. Blynman, after he had labored about ten years in the ministry at New-London, in 1658, removed to New-Haven. After a short stay in that town, he took shipping and returned to England. He lived to a good old age; and, at the city of Bristol, happily concluded a long life, spent in doing good.

Mr. Nicholas Street succeeded Mr. Hook, as teacher in the church, at New-Haven, about the year 1659. And Mr. Blynman was succeeded in office at New-London, by Mr. Gershom Bulkley, from Concord, in Massachusetts.

Divisions in the church at Hartford. The first ministers in the colonies being thus dead, or removed, and a new generation risen up, who had not all imbibed the sentiments and spirit of their pious fathers, alterations were insisted on with respect to church member-

Mr. Whitfield, therefore, sold them to major Robert Thompson, in England, by whose heirs they have been holden, to the great damage of the town, to this time.

ship, discipline, and baptism; and great dissensions arose in the churches. They began first in the church at Hartford, not many years after Mr. Hooker's decease. The origin of them appears to have been a difference between the Rev. Mr. Stone and Mr. Goodwin, the ruling elder in the church, upon some nice points of congregationalism. It seems, that some member had been admitted, or baptism administered, which elder Goodwin conceived to be inconsistent with the rights of the brotherhood, and the strict principles of the congregational churches. Perhaps he imagined himself not to have been properly consulted and regarded. Not only this church became divided and inflamed with the controversy, but it spread into almost all the neighbouring churches. They interested themselves in the controversy, some taking one side, and some another, as their connections, prejudices, and particular sentiments led them. The whole colony became affected with the dispute, and the general court particularly interested themselves in the affair. The brethren in the church at Hartford, became so inflamed, and imbibed such prejudices and uncharitable feelings one towards another, that it was with great difficulty they could be persuaded to walk together. To prevent an entire division of the church, it appears, that about the years 1654 and 1655, several councils of the neighbouring elders and churches were called, to compose the differences between the parties. They laboured to satisfy them, with respect to the points in controversy. But the brethren at Hartford imagined, that all the elders and churches in Connecticut and New-Haven, were prejudiced in favour of one party or the other, and, therefore, they would not hear their advice. For this reason, it was judged expedient to call a council from the other colonies. Some time in the year 1656, it seems, a number of elders and churches from Massachusetts came to Hartford, and gave their opinion and advice to the church and the aggrieved brethren. But it appears, that, in the apprehension of the aggrieved, the church did not comply with the result. The state of the church, therefore, was no better than it was before, but the parties became more alienated and embittered. Elder Goodwin was joined by governor Webster, Mr. Whiting, Mr. Cullick, and other principal gentlemen at Hartford, who were leaders in what they imagined to be a defence of the true principles of congregationalism.

Meanwhile, there was a strong party in the colony of Connecticut, who were for admitting all persons of a regular life to a full communion in the churches, upon their

Book I. making a profession of the christian religion, without any inquiry with respect to a change of heart; and for treating all baptized persons as members of the church. Some carried the affair still further, and insisted, that all persons, who had been members of churches in England, or had been members of regular ecclesiastical parishes there, and supported the public worship, should be allowed to enjoy the privileges of members in full communion in the churches of Connecticut. They also insisted, that all baptized persons, upon owning the covenant, as it was called, should have their children baptized, though they came not to the Lord's table.

Numbers of them took this opportunity to introduce into the assembly a list of grievances, on account of their being denied their just rights and privileges by the ministers and churches. A dispute had arisen in the churches and congregations, relative to the choice of a pastor. It was urged, that it did not belong to the churches solely to choose the pastor for themselves and the congregation; but, as the inhabitants in general had an equal concern for themselves and their children, with the members of the church, in the qualifications of their pastor, and as they were obliged to contribute their proportion to his support, they had a just right to give their voice in his election. The denying them this right was considered as a great grievance. Many of the churches, and some or other of the members in all of them, it seems, maintained, that the choice of a pastor belonged to them solely, exclusive of the congregation: that there was no scripture example of any person's ever giving a suffrage, in the choice of a pastor, but members of the church: that pastors were ordained over the churches only, and were termed the elders, pastors, and angels of the churches. It appears, by the acts of the assembly, and the questions proposed, that these, and a number of other points, were now warmly agitated in the colony.

Different state of the country. The general state of the country was greatly altered from what it was at its first settlement. The people then were generally church members, and eminently pious. *Reason of the dissensions.* They loved strict religion, and followed their ministers into the wilderness, for its sake. But with many of their children, and with others who had since emigrated into this country, it was not so. They had made no open profession of religion, and their children were not baptized. This created uneasiness in them, in their ministers, and others. They wished for the honours and privileges of church members for themselves, and baptism for their children; but they were not persuaded that they were regenerated, and knew not how to comply with the rigid terms of the congregational churches. A considerable number of the clergy, and the churches in general, zealously opposed all innovations, and exerted themselves to maintain the first practice and purity of the churches. Hence the dissensions arose.

The general court, it seems, with a view to reconcile the church at Hartford, and to compose difficulties, which were generally rising in the colony, at their session in May, 1656, took the affair into their serious consideration. They appointed a committee, consisting of governor Webster, deputy governor Wells, Mr. Cullick, and Mr. Talcott, all of Hartford, to consult with the elders of the colony, respecting the grievances complained of; and to desire their assistance, in making a draft of the heads of them, that they might be presented to the general courts of the united colonies, for their advice. The general courts were desired to give their answers with as much expedition as possible. *The court of Connecticut send to the other general courts for advice, May 15th, 1656.*

While the churches were thus divided, they were alarmed by the appearance of the Quakers. A number of them arrived at Boston, in July and August, and had been committed to the common gaol. A great number of their books had been seized with a view to burn them. In consequence of their arrival, and the disturbance they had made, at Boston, the commissioners of the united colonies, at their court in September, recommended it to the several general courts, "That all quakers, ranters, and other notorious heretics, should be prohibited coming into the united colonies; and that, if any should come, or arise amongst them, they should be forthwith secured, and removed out of all the jurisdictions."* *Resolution of the commissioners respecting the Quakers.*

In conformity to this recommendation, the general court of Connecticut, in October, passed the following act:— "That no town within this jurisdiction, shall entertain any Quakers, Ranters, Adamites, or such like notorious heretics; nor suffer them to continue in them above the space of fourteen days, upon the penalty of five pounds per week, for any town entertaining any such person: but the townsmen shall give notice to the two next magistrates, or assistants, who shall have power to send them to prison, for securing them, until they can conveniently be sent out of the jurisdiction. It is also ordered, that no master of a vessel shall land any such heretics; but if they do, they shall be compelled to transport them again out of the colo- *Law of Connecticut against the Quakers, October, 1656.*

* Records of the united colonies.

ny, by any two magistrates or assistants, at their first setting sail from the port where they landed them; during which time, the assistant or magistrate shall see them secured, upon penalty of twenty pounds for any master of any vessel, that shall not transport them as aforesaid."*

The court at New-Haven passed a similar law. In 1658, both courts made an addition to this law, increasing the penalties and prohibiting all conversation of the common people with any of those heretics, and all persons from giving them any entertainment, upon the penalty of five pounds. The law however was of short continuance, and nothing of importance appears to have been transacted upon it, in either of the colonies.

Massachusetts and Connecticut appoint a general council.

Upon the representations made of the heads of grievance, which had been matter of complaint, to the general courts of the confederate colonies, the court of Massachusetts advised to a general council, and sent letters to the other courts, signifying their opinion. The general court of New-Haven wrote an answer to the grievances, and to the questions proposed respecting them. They supposed it sufficient. The general court of Connecticut, nevertheless, on the 26th of February, 1657, determined to have a general council. They appointed Mr. Warham, Mr. Stone, Mr. Blynman, and Mr. Russell, to meet the elders, who should be delegated from the other colonies, at Boston, the next June; and to assist in debating the questions proposed by the general court of Connecticut, or any of the other courts, and report the determination of the council to the general court.

Feb. 1657.

The church at Hartford continuing their contentions, the court directed the elders, who were going to Boston, to confer with the several ministers in the Massachusetts, who had been of the council, relative to the circumstances of that church, and to desire them to come to Connecticut, and give their assistance in council at Hartford. The court also directed the church there to send for the former council; and with the letters missive, to state the particulars, in the advice of the council, with which they were not satisfied. If this council should not be so happy as to give them satisfaction, then they were directed to invite Mr. Sherman of Watertown, and several other ministers from the Massachusetts, to make a visit at Hartford, and attempt the healing of the breach made in the church there.

Governor Webster and others dissent.

Governor Webster, Mr. Cullick, and Mr. Steel dissented from the resolution of the assembly, and declared, in

* Records of Connecticut.

CHAP. XIII. CONNECTICUT. 301

open court, that it did not appear to them, that the measures, adopted by the court, were any where directed by the divine word, or calculated to restore peace to the churches. They appear to have been of the aggrieved brethren at Hartford, and satisfied with the result of the former council, to which the church, in their apprehensions, did not submit. They doubtless judged it more agreeable to scripture and reason, and especially to the principles of congregational churches, to choose a council for themselves, when they should judge it expedient, than to have one imposed upon them, by legislative authority.

The general court, at New-Haven, were utterly opposed to a general council; and upon receiving a letter from the Massachusetts, inviting them to send a number of their elders to assist in the council, they, in a long letter, remonstrated against it, and excused themselves from sending any of their ministers. They represented, that the petition and questions, exhibited to the general court of Connecticut, were unwarrantably procured, and of dangerous tendency: That they heard the petitioners were confident that they should obtain great alterations both in civil government and church discipline: That they had engaged an agent to prove, "That parishes, in England, consenting to and continuing meetings to worship God, were true churches," and that the members of those parishes, coming into New-England, had a right to all church privileges; though they made no profession of a work of faith and holiness upon their hearts. They expressed their apprehensions, that a general council at that time, would endanger the peace and purity of the churches. They acquainted the general court of Massachusetts, that they had sent an answer to all the questions, proposed to the court of Connecticut; and that it was their opinion, that the legislature and elders of that colony were sufficient to determine all those points without any assistance from abroad. They observed that, on account of the removal of Mr. Whitfield and Mr. Hook, and the late death of Mr. Prudden, their elders could not be spared. With their letter, they sent the answers, which they had given to the questions to be debated, and they intreated the court and their elders seriously to consider them. They desired, that, as the court had formed their civil polity and laws upon the divine word, and as the elders and churches had gathered and received their discipline from the same, they would exert themselves to preserve them inviolable. They observed,

Book I.

Court of New-Haven oppose a council.

Book I. that, considering the state of affairs, in Connecticut, unless the general court of Massachusetts should firmly adhere to their then constitution, and the council should have the divine presence with them, their meeting might be of the most unhappy consequence to the churches. Considering how soon the church at Ephesus, though famous for her first love, declined and was forsaken of her Saviour, they insisted, that there was great occasion of watchfulness and prayer, lest the churches of New-England should decline after her example.*

The colonies of Connecticut and Massachusetts persisted in calling a general council.

The questions proposed for discussion, as they stand upon the records, are the following.

Questions proposed to the general council, June, 1657.

1. Whether federal holiness, or covenant interest, be not the proper ground of baptism?

2. Whether communion of churches, as such, be not warrantable by the word of God?

3. Whether the adult seed of visible believers, not cast out, be not true members, and subjects of church watch?

4. Whether ministerial officers are not as truly bound to baptize the visible disciples of Christ, providentially settled among them, as officially to preach the word?

5. Whether the settled inhabitants of the country, being members of other churches, should have their children baptized amongst us, without themselves first orderly joining in churches here?

6. Whether membership, in a particular instituted church, be not essentially requisite, under the gospel, to entitle to baptism?

7. Whether adopted children and such as are bought with money are covenant seed?

8. Whether things new and weighty may be managed, in a church, without concurrence of officers, and consent of the fraternity of the same church? And if things of common concernment, then how far the consent of neighbouring churches is to be sought?

9. Whether it doth not belong to the body of a town, collectively taken, jointly to call him to be their minister, whom the church shall choose to be their officer?

10. Whether the political and external administration of Abraham's covenant be not obligatory to gospel churches?

11. Unto whom shall such persons repair, that are grieved at any church process or censure; or whether they must acquiesce in the church's censure to which they belong?

* Records of New-Haven.

12. Whether the laying on of hands in ordination, belong to presbyters or brethren?

13. Whether the church, her invitation and election of an officer, or preaching elder, necessitates the whole congregation to sit down satisfied, as bound thereby to accept him as their minister, though invited and settled without the town's consent?

14. What is the gospel way to gather and settle churches?

15. From whom do ministers receive their commission to baptize?

16. Whether a synod hath a decisive power?

17. Whether it be not justifiable, by the word of God, that civil authority indulge congregational and presbyterian churches, and their discipline in the churches?*

It appears, by the records, that several other questions were proposed, but these are all which are to be found upon them. They stand in the same order in which they are here inserted.

The council convened at Boston, June 4th, 1657, and, after a session of a little more than a fortnight, gave an elaborate answer to twenty-one questions. The elders from Connecticut brought back an authentic copy of the result of the council, and presented it to the general court, at a session on the 12th of August. The court ordered, that copies should be sent forthwith to all the churches in the colony; and if any of them should have objections against the answers which had been given, they were directed to transmit them to the general court, at the session in October.

Council at Boston, June 4th, 1657.

The answers were, afterwards, printed in London, under the title of "A disputation concerning church members and their children." Several of the questions involve each other. The principal one was that respecting baptism and church membership. An answer to this, in effect, answered a considerable part of the other questions. With respect to this, they asserted, and learned pains were taken to prove, "That it was the duty of infants, who confederated in their parents, when grown up unto years of discretion, though not fit for the Lord's supper, to own the covenant they made with their parents, by entering thereinto, in their own persons; and it is the duty of the churches to call upon them for the performance thereof; and if, being called upon, they shall refuse the performance of this great duty, or otherwise continue scandalous, they are liable to be censured for the same by the church. And in case they understand the ground of religion, and are not scandalous, and

Answer to the question respecting baptism, and church membership.

* Records of Connecticut.

solemnly own their covenant in their own persons, wherein they give up themselves and their children unto the Lord, and desire baptism for them, we see not sufficient cause to deny baptism unto their children."†

The answer to this question was, in effect, an answer to the other respecting the right of towns to vote in the election of ministers; for if they were all members of the church by baptism, and under its discipline, they, doubtless, had a right to vote with the church in the election of their pastor. Indeed, there was no proper ground of distinction between them and the church. Hence, it seems, the answer to that question was to this effect, "That though it was the right of the brotherhood to choose their pastor, and though it was among the arts of antichrist to deprive them of this power, yet they ought to have a special regard to the baptized, by the covenant of God, under their watch."

The decisions of the council do not appear to have had any influence to reconcile, but rather to inflame the churches.

A number of ministers, and the churches pretty generally, viewed this as a great innovation, and entirely inconsistent with the principles on which the churches of New-England were originally founded, and with the principles of congregationalism.

The church at Hartford, and the aggrieved brethren, instead of being satisfied and reconciled, appeared to be thrown into a state of greater alienation and animosity. The aggrieved soon after withdrew from Mr. Stone and the church, and were about forming an union with the church at Weathersfield. Among the aggrieved were governor Webster, Mr. Goodwin, ruling elder in the church, Mr. Cullick, and Mr. Bacon, principal men both in the church and town. Mr. Stone and the church were proceeding with them in a course of discipline.

1658.

In this state of their affairs, the general court, interposed, and passed an act, prohibiting the church at Hartford, to proceed any further in a course of discipline of the members, who had withdrawn from their communion, and those members to join with the church at Weathersfield, or any other church, until further attempts should be made, for their reconciliation with their brethren. By the act it appears, that the churches in the colony were generally affected with the dispute at Hartford, and viewed it as a common cause, with respect to all the congregational churches. It exhibits, in so strong a point of light, the

† Magnalia, B. V. p. 63.

| CHAP. XIII. | CONNECTICUT. | 305 |

authority, which the general court imagined they had a right to exercise over the churches, and the spirit of those times, as to merit a place in this history. It is in the following words.

BOOK I.

"This court orders, in reference to the sad difficulties that are broken out in the several churches in this colony, and in special, betwixt the church at Hartford and the withdrawers; and to prevent further troubles and sad consequences, that may ensue from the premises to the whole commonwealth, that there be, from henceforth, an utter cessation of all further prosecution, either on the church's part at Hartford, towards the withdrawers from them; and, on the other part, that those, that have withdrawn from the church, at Hartford, shall make a cessation in prosecuting their former propositions to the church at Weathersfield, or any other church, in reference to their joining there, in church relation, until the matters, in controversy betwixt the church at Hartford and the withdrawn members, be brought to an issue, in that way the court shall determine."

Act of the general court of Connecticut, March 11, 1659.

The court, having desired the elders of the colony to meet them, and assist in adopting some measures by which the divisions in the churches, and especially in that at Hartford, might be healed, adjourned about a fortnight.

It met again on the 24th of March. Whether the elders met with them, or not, does not appear; but the advice of the assemby, at this time, was that Mr. Stone, with the church and brethren who had withdrawn, should meet together; and, in a private conference, if possible, agree upon some terms by which they might be reconciled. Governor Wells and deputy governor Winthrop were appointed to meet with them, and employ their wisdom and influence to make peace.

Advice of the court. March 24.

It seems, that the church did not comply with this advice; or if there were any meeting of the parties, nothing was done to effect an accommodation. It appears, that Mr. Stone viewed the withdrawn brethren as in the hands of the church at Hartford, and the matters to be determined as not lying before any council or the general court. And he would not admit, that he, or the church, had counteracted the advice of the former council. He therefore, at the session in May, petitioned, that the subsequent propositions might be entered upon the records of the colony, and that the withdrawn brethren, or some person whom they should appoint, would dispute them with him in the presence of the court.

May 20th, 1658.

BOOK I.

1. "The former council, at Hartford, June 26, is utterly cancelled and of no force.

2. "There is no violation of the last agreement, (made when the reverend elders of the Massachusetts were here,) either by the church of Christ at Hartford, or their teacher.

3. "The withdrawn brethren have offered great violence to the forementioned agreement.

4. "The withdrawn brethren are members of the church of Christ at Hartford.

5. "Their withdrawing from the church is a sin exceeding scandalous and dreadful, and of its own nature destructive to this and other churches.

6. "The controversy between the church of Christ at Hartford, and the withdrawn persons, is not in the hands of the churches, to be determined by them.*

"SAMUEL STONE."

It does not appear that the court gave their consent, that the propositions should be disputed before them, or that they enacted any thing, at this court, respecting the affairs of the church, or the brethren who had withdrawn.

August 18th. But at a session, in August, they insisted, that the church and aggrieved brethren should meet together, according to their former advice, and debate their difficulties among themselves, and that the points in controversy should be clearly stated.

At this time, a complaint was exhibited against governor Webster, Mr. Cullick, elder Goodwin and others, who had withdrawn from their brethren. But the court would not hear it at that time. It ordered, that, if the church and brethren would not agree to meet together and debate their differences among themselves, each party should choose three as indifferent elders as could be found; who should afford all the light and assistance in their power, towards settling the differences according to the divine oracles; and that both parties should peaceably submit to their advice. If either of the parties should refuse to make choice of three gentlemen, for the design proposed, the court determined to choose for them. The church rejected the proposal, and the court chose Mr. Cobbett, Mr. Mitchel, and Mr. Danforth, for them. For a reserve, if either should fail, Mr. Brown was chosen. The aggrieved brethren chose Mr. Davenport, Mr. Norton, and Mr. Fitch; and as a reserve, Mr. Street. The council were to meet on the 17th of September.

The church, it seems, would not send for the council, and so it did not convene.

* Records of Connecticut.

CHAP. XIII.   CONNECTICUT.   307

At a session of the general court, the next year, March 9th, 1659, it was determined, that, as its past labors, to promote unanimity, at Hartford, had been frustrated, by the non-compliance of the parties, the secretary, in the name of the court, should desire the elders, who had been formerly appointed, to meet at Hartford on the 3d of June succeeding, and afford their assistance in healing the breach, which had been made there. It was also enacted, that the church, at Hartford, and the brethren who had withdrawn, should jointly bear the expenses of the former council, and of making provision for that which had been then appointed.

<small>Book I.
Resolution of the court respecting a council, March 9, 1659.</small>

The council consisted of the elders and churches of Boston, Cambridge, Charlestown, Ipswich, Dedham, and Sudbury. They convened according to appointment, and were abundant in their labors to soften the minds and conciliate the affections of the parties; and though they did not effect a reconciliation, yet they brought the brethren much nearer together than they had been, and left the church and town in a better state than they had enjoyed for years before.

<small>June 3, 1659.
Council at Hartford.</small>

On the 15th of June, the court convened, and perceiving the good effects of this council, desired the same gentlemen to meet again, at Hartford, on the 19th of August. Upon the choice and desire of the brethren who had withdrawn, the Rev. John Sherman, and the church at Watertown, and the elder and church at Dorchester, were also invited to come with them.

The general court, in this state of the controversy, ordered the heads of the complaint, which had been exhibited against the withdrawn brethren, to be drawn up and sent to them, and they were required to appear before the court, in October, and answer to them. The church agreed to the whole council, and the brethren aggrieved, to seven of them. The general court ordered, that both parties should submit to the judgment of the council, and that it should be a final issue.

The council convened again, at Hartford, and so far composed the difficulties which had so long subsisted, as to prevent a separation at that time. Some of the capital characters were soon removed into the land of silence, where all animosities are forgotten. Mr. Cullick removed to Boston, and a considerable number removed to Hadley. By these means, the church was restored to a tolerable state of peace and brotherly affection; but it was viewed, by some of its own members, and others, as having, in some degree, departed from the strict principles of the

BOOK I. first congregational churches in New-England; and seems, afterwards, to have divided nearly on the same grounds.

Nature of the controversy. Doctor Mather, in his Magnalia, represents, that it was difficult, even at the time of the controversy, to find what were the precise points in dispute. Indeed, what the particular act or sentiment in Mr. Stone or the church was, which gave elder Goodwin disgust, and began the dissension, does not fully appear. Nothing however is more evident, from the questions propounded, which it appears were drawn by the very heads of the parties, and by the gentlemen chosen by the disaffected brethren, and rejected by the church, than that the whole controversy respected the qualifications for baptism, church membership, and the rights of the brotherhood. Mr. Stone's ideas of congregationalism appear to have bordered more on presbyterianism, and less on independence, than those of the first ministers in the country in general. His definition of congregationalism, was, "That it was a speaking Aristocracy in the face of a silent Democracy."

Controversy at Hartford remarkable in its day. The Hartford controversy was, for its circumstances, duration, and obstinacy, the most remarkable of any in its day. It affected all the churches, and insinuated itself into all the affairs of societies, towns, and the whole commonwealth. Doctor Mather, in his figurative manner of description, says, "From the fire of the altar, there issued thunderings, and lightnings, and earthquakes, through the colony." This was considered as much more remarkable, as the church, at Hartford, had been famous for its instruction, light, gifts, peace, and brotherly love. It had been viewed as one of the principal churches in New-England. Its dissensions were a ground of great sorrow to all the good people in the country. Extraordinary were the pains taken, by the principal characters in New-England, to heal them.

Letter from the commissioners of the united colonies. The commissioners of the united colonies, in September 1656, wrote them a friendly and pacific letter on the subject. They say, "We have, with much sorrow of heart, heard of your differences, and that the means attended hitherto, for composing them, have proved ineffectual. We cannot but be deeply sensible of the sad effects and dreadful consequences of dissensions, heightened and increased in a church of such eminence for light and love." They represented to them, that though all the churches sympathized with them, yet they themselves would be sure, in the the first place, to feel the smart. They most earnestly exhorted them not only to be exceedingly cautious of all further provocations, but to employ all their wisdom and ex-

CHAP. XIII.   CONNECTICUT.

ertions for a reconciliation. They intreated them, not to suffer any discouragements to prevail with them, to make a separation and scatter abroad.*

The churches in Connecticut and New-Haven laboured to harmonize their views and affections, and to make peace. The ministers in Massachusetts were so affected with their circumstances, that they offered to make a journey to Connecticut, to attempt their reconciliation. The long and repeated journeys they made, and the indefatigable labours they employed to compose their difficulties, exhibited a noble spirit of benevolence, and a zeal for the peace and prosperity of Zion. They not only merited the grateful acknowledgments of the people at Hartford, but of the colony in general.

The proclamation for a public thanksgiving in November, recognized the success of the council, in composing the difficulties at Hartford, as an event demanding public joy and praise.

The church at Weathersfield interested themselves in the dispute at Hartford, and became divided and contentious. Some of the brethren exhibited a complaint to the court against Mr. Russell, for joining with the church in excommunicating one of the brethren, as it was alledged, without giving him a copy of the complaint exhibited against him, and without acquainting him with his crime. The general court ordered, that Mr. Russell should be reproved, for acting contrary to the usage of the churches. The brethren were divided with respect to their church state. Some insisted, that they were no church, because they had never been gathered according to gospel order; or if they had been a church, that the members of it had moved away in such a manner, as had destroyed its very existence. Many were inviolably attached to Mr. Russell, while others strenuously opposed him.

In this state of affairs, the general court appointed the elders and churches of Hartford and Windsor, a council to hear the difficulties which had arisen in the church and town. But the parties could not be reconciled. Mr. Russell removed to Hadley, where he and a number of his warm friends from Hartford and Weathersfield, planted a new town and church. The general court resolved, that a church had been regularly gathered at Weathersfield, by the consent of the general court, and approbation of neighbouring elders; and that, though divers of the members had removed to other places, yet the brethren there were the true and undoubted church of Weathersfield, and so to

1660.

Mr. Russell removes to Hadley.

* Records of the united colonies.

Book I. be accounted, notwithstanding any thing which did appear. Thus terminated the controversy; and Mr. Bulkley, in 1666, removed from New-London, and succeeded Mr. Russell in the pastoral office. The same year, Mr. Simon Bradstreet, from Charlestown, came to New-London, and took the pastoral charge of the church there.

Mr. Samuel Stow dismissed from Middletown. About the time of Mr. Russell's removal from Weathersfield, the minds of the people at Middletown became alienated from Mr. Stow, who appears to have been the first minister in that town. A committee of ministers and civilians, appointed by the general court, dismissed him, on account of the evil temper of the people towards him.

Many of the ministers and of the people, in the country, were for extending baptism, according to the determination of the general council, in 1657; but the churches were so generally and warmly opposed to it, that it could not be effected without a synod. As this and the consociation of churches were favourite points, which a large number of the clergy and principal civilians in Massachusetts and Connecticut, wished to carry, the general court of Massachusetts appointed a synod of all the ministers in that colony, to deliberate and decide on those points. The questions proposed, were,

1. Who are the subjects of baptism?
2. Whether, according to the word of God, there ought to be a consociation of churches?

Synod, 1662. The council met at Boston, in September, 1662. Their answer to the first question, was substantially the same with that given by the council, in 1657.

Its resolutions. They declared, "That church members, who were admitted in minority, understanding the doctrine of faith, and publicly professing their assent thereunto, not scandalous in life, and solemnly owning the covenant before the church, wherein they give up themselves and children to the Lord, and subject themselves to the government of Christ in his church, their children are to be baptized." They further resolved, "That the members of orthodox churches, being sound in the faith, and not scandalous in life, and presenting due testimony thereof, these occasionally coming from one church to another, may have their children baptized in the church whither they came, by virtue of communion of churches." They, also, gave their opinion in favour of the consociation of churches.

They are opposed. However, the council were not unanimous; several learned and pious men protested against the determination relative to baptism. The Rev. Charles Chauncey, president of Harvard college; Mr. Increase Mather, afterwards

Chap. XIII.   CONNECTICUT.

doctor in divinity; Mr. Mather, of Northampton; and others, were warmly in the opposition. President Chauncey wrote a tract against the resolution respecting baptism, entitled Antisynodalia. Mr. Increase Mather, also, wrote in opposition to the council. Mr. Davenport, and all the ministers in the colony of New-Haven, and numbers in Connecticut, were against the resolutions. Mr. Davenport wrote against them. The churches were more generally opposed to them than the clergy.

The general court of Connecticut took no notice of the synod, nor of the dispute, but left the elders and churches at liberty to act their own sentiments. They were attempting to form an union with New-Haven; and, as the ministers and churches of that colony were unanimous in their opposition to the synod, they, probably, judged it impolitic, at that time, to act any thing relative to these ecclesiastical points.

While the churches were agitated with these disputes, another of their original lights was extinguished. Mr. Stone expired July 20th, 1663. He had his education at Emmanuel college, in the university of Cambridge. He was eminently pious and exemplary; abounded in fastings and prayer, and was a most strict observer of the christian sabbath. Preparatory to this, he laboured to compose himself on Saturday evening, to the most heavenly views and exercises, and was careful not to speak a word which was not grave, serious, and adapted to the solemnity. He spent much time, on this evening, in the instruction of his family, commonly delivering to them the sermon which he designed to preach on the morrow, or some other, which might be best calculated for their instruction and edification. His sermons were doctrinal, replete with sentiment, concisely and closely applied. He was esteemed one of the most accurate and acute disputants of his day. He was celebrated for his great wit, pleasantry, and good humour. His company was courted by all gentlemen of learning and ingenuity, who had the happiness of an acquaintance with him.

Book I.

Death of Mr. Stone, July 20th, 1663.

His character.

All the ministers who illuminated the first churches in Connecticut and New-Haven, except Mr. Warham and Mr. Davenport, had now finished their course, or returned to England; and most of their brethren, who composed the first churches, slept with them in the dust. The first governors and magistrates were no more.

The next year, the general court of Connecticut came to a resolve, with a view to enforce the resolution of the synod, upon the churches in Connecticut. It was in the words following.

BOOK I.

Resolve of the general court respecting baptism and church membership. Oct. 13, 1664.

"This court understanding, by a writing presented to them, from several persons of this colony, that they are aggrieved, that they are not entertained in church fellowship, this court, having duly considered the same, desiring, that the rules of Christ may be attended, do commend it to the ministers and churches in this colony, to consider, whether it be not their duty to entertain all such persons, who are of an honest and godly conversation, having a competency of knowledge in the principles of religion, and shall desire to join with them in church fellowship, by an explicit covenant; and that they have their children baptized: and that all the children of the church be accepted and accounted real members of the church; and that the church exercise a due christian care and watch over them: and that when they are grown up, being examined by the officer, in the face of the church, it appear in the judgment of charity, that they be duly qualified to participate in that great ordinance of the LORD's supper, by their being able to examine themselves and discern the LORD's body, such persons be admitted to full communion.

"The court desireth the several officers of the respective churches would be pleased to consider, whether it be not the duty of the court to order the churches to practice according to the premises, if they do not practice without such order. If any dissent from the contents of this writing, they are desired to help the court, with such light as is with them, the next session of this assembly."

The secretary was directed to send a copy of this resolution to all the ministers and churches in the colony.

The elders and churches, who would not comply with the proposed innovation, had not only to combat the arguments and influence of the synod, but the influence of the uneasy people in the congregations, and of the general court; but it was but slowly, and with great difficulty, that the practice of owning the covenant, and baptizing the children of parents who did not enter into full communion, and attend both the sacraments, was introduced. But few churches, for many years, admitted the practice, and some never did. It appears that, notwithstanding the influence of the general court, and the resolutions of the synods, or general councils, a majority of the churches in Connecticut were against it. They imagined, that such a latitude in baptism, and admission of members to communion, would subvert the very design for which the churches of New-England were planted.

Discipline continues nearly the same.

The discipline and usages of the Connecticut churches continued yet, for some time, nearly in the same situation in which they had been from the beginning. The clergy and churches were strict in the admission of members to full communion. Those who were admitted, generally made a public relation of their christian experiences, by which they gave satisfaction to the church of their repentance, faith, and sincere friendship to the REDEEMER.

The elders and churches were exceedingly strict, with respect to those whom they ordained; examining them not only in the three learned languages and doctrinal points of theology, with respect to cases of conscience, and their ability to defend christianity and its doctrines against infidels and gainsayers, but with respect to their own experimental, heart religion. All those, who were to be ordained over any church, previously to their separation to the sacred office, satisfied the brotherhood of their spiritual birth, and were admitted to their communion and fellowship. None were ordained, or installed over any church, until after they had been admitted to its full communion and fellowship.

They were also strict in the formation of churches; none could be formed, nor any minister ordained, without liberty from the general court, and the approbation of the neighboring elders and churches.

From the preceding view, it appears, that before the union there were fifteen churches in Connecticut, exclusive of those which had been formed upon Long-Island. There had been thirty-one ministers in the colony; of whom about twenty-five or six had been installed or ordained. Twenty-one were ministering to the people at the time of the union; nineteen of whom had been installed or ordained. The other two, Mr. Noyes and Mr. Collins, were afterwards settled in the ministry, in the towns where, for some years, they had been laboring.

CHAPTER XIV.

Conduct of the king's commissioners. Counties and county courts regulated. Governor Winthrop's estate freed from taxation. Towns settled. Controversy with Rhode-Island. The grounds of it. Courts appointed in the Narraganset country. Laws revised and printed. War with the Dutch. Claims and conduct of major Edmund Andross, governor of New-York. Protest against him. Conduct of captain Thomas Bull. Proclamation respecting the insult received from major Andross. Philip's war. Captains Hutchinson and Lothrop surprised and slain. Treachery of the Springfield Indians. Hadley attacked by the enemy. The assembly make provision for the defence of Connecticut. Expedition against the Narraganset Indians. The reasons of it. The great swamp fight. Loss of men. Courage exhibited, and hardships endured. Captain Pierce and his party cut off. Nanuntenoo taken. Success of captains Denison and Avery. Captain Wadsworth and his party slain. Death and character of governor Winthrop. Success of major Talcott. Attack upon Hadley. The enemy beaten and begin to scatter. They are pursued to Housatonick. Sachem of Quabaug and Philip killed. Number of the enemy before the war. Their destruction. Loss of the colonies. Connecticut happy in preserving its own towns and assisting its neighbors.

AFTER the reduction of the Dutch settlements, colonel Nichols fixed his residence at New-York, to manage the affairs of government. Sir Robert Carr, Cartwrith, and Maverick, the other commissioners, soon went to Boston, and proceeded upon the business of their commission. After they had communicated their instructions to the general court, and made a number of requisitions inconsistent with the chartered rights of the colony, and some inconsistent with the rights of conscience and of the churches, they went from Boston to Narraganset. They held courts at Warwick and Southerton, and spent a considerable time in hearing the complaints of the Indians, in determining the titles of the English to their lands; and, without any color of authority from their commission, undertook to make a new province. They determined, that the deed of the Rhode-Islanders, from the Indians, was of no force. Captain Atherton, and others, had made a large purchase of the Indians, in Narraganset, east of Pawcatuck river, and the planters had put themselves under the government of Connecticut. The commissioners determined, that captain Atherton's deed was not legal, because there was no mention of the sum which he had paid. However, as it appeared that considerable had been paid the Indians for the lands, the commissioners ordered the natives to pay to the purchasers a certain quantity of wampum, and ordered the planters to move off from the lands. As the Narraganset sachems had, in 1644, made their subjection to the king of England, acknowledging themselves to be his subjects, they declared that the country belonged to his majesty, and that, in future, it should be called THE KING'S PROVINCE. They determined, that no person, of what colony soever, should presume to exercise any authority within that tract, except those who should be authorised by them, until his majesty's pleasure should be known. They further decreed, that the king's province should extend westward to the middle of Pawcatuck river, and northward as far as the south line of Massachusetts. In the plenitude of their power, they also ordered, that the Pequots, to whom the General Assembly of Connecticut had, agreeable to a resolution of the commissioners of the united colonies, assigned a tract of land on the east of Pawcatuck, should be removed and settled in some other place, which the assembly should appoint, west of that river.* It appears that they came to these important decisions, without giving Connecticut notice, or ever hearing what reasons the colony had to offer against them.

When they had finished their business in Narraganset, they returned to Boston. There they proceeded in the most arbitrary manner, giving the general court of Massachusetts and the whole colony unspeakable trouble. They undertook the protection of criminals against the commonwealth; and summoned the members of the general court before them to answer for judgments which they had given in their legislative and executive capacity. They received complaints against the colony, from Indians and other disaffected persons; and undertook to judge in cases which had been previously prosecuted to a final adjudication, according to law. Indeed, they did not content themselves with determining civil matters only, they made requisitions respecting the church. They demanded, that all persons of orthodox opinions, competent knowledge, and

* Records of Connecticut, in their book of patents, letters, determinations, &c.

Book I. civil lives, should be admitted to the Lord's supper, and their children to baptism.†

1665. While the general court of Massachusetts expressed entire loyalty to his majesty, they firmly maintained their charter rights, and remonstrated against the proceedings of the commissioners. At this firm conduct, they were highly disgusted, and made a very unfavorable representation of the colony to his majesty, much to its disadvantage.

They came to no determination with respect to the claim of duke Hamilton, but returned the answer of Connecticut to the king, and made a very friendly report to him of the manner in which they had been received by the colony of Connecticut, and of the loyalty and attachment of the people to his royal person. In consequence of it, the king sent a most gracious letter to the colony. In this, he says, " We cannot but let you know how much we are pleased. Although your carriage doth of itself most justly deserve our praise and approbation, yet it seems to be set off with more lustre, by the contrary deportment of the colony of Massachusetts. We shall never be unmindful of this your loyal and dutiful behaviour."‡

Election May 11th, 1666. At the general election, May 11th, 1666, the former governor and council were re-elected.

Counties made and the county courts regulated. The general assembly, at this session, proceeded to ascertain the limits of the counties and the business of the county courts. It was enacted, that the towns upon the river, from the north bounds of Windsor, with Farmington, to thirty miles island, should be one county, to be called the county of Hartford. That from Pawcatuck river, with Norwich, to the west bounds of Hammonasset, should be one county, by the name of the county of New-London; and that from the east bounds of Stratford to the western boundary of the colony, be another county, to be known by the name of the county of Fairfield. The county courts were to consist of one magistrate, at least, and of two justices of the quorum. If three magistrates were present they were authorised to proceed to business, though the justices were absent. The probation of wills and all testamentary matters, which before had been transacted in the court of magistrates, were referred to the county courts, with the liberty of appeal to the superior court.

May 1667. In 1667, no alteration was made with respect to the governor and council, but governor Winthrop, at first, declined his office. The assembly appointed a committee, and

† Hutchinson's Hist. vol. i. p. 230—256
‡ No. XXII.

CHAP. XIV. CONNECTICUT.

desired to know the reasons of his desire to leave the chair. They reported the reasons to the assembly. It seems that the expense of his office was such, in his opinion, that he could not, consistently with his duty to himself and family, continue in it, without some further allowance from the colony. The assembly continued their earnest desire, that he would accept the trust to which he had been chosen. To enable him to support his office with dignity, the legislature freed all his estate, in the colony, from taxation, and granted him a hundred and ten pounds out of the public treasury. Upon these encouragements, in connection with the desire and unanimity of the freemen, he consented to accept his appointment.

Book I.

1667.

About the year 1664, settlements commenced on the east side of Connecticut river, upon the tract, on that side, which originally belonged to the town of Saybrook. In May, 1667, the inhabitants were so increased, that the assembly made them a distinct town by the name of Lyme. The Indian name for the eastern part of the town was Nehantick.

Lyme made a town, May, 1667.

At the election in 1668, the freemen elected Mr. Alexander Bryan, Mr. James Bishop, Mr. Anthony Hawkins, and Mr. Thomas Wells, magistrates, instead of Mr. Matthew Allen, Mr. Sherman, Mr. Crane, and Mr. Clark.

May 14th, 1668.

In this and the next year, several new settlements were made and new towns incorporated.

On the 20th of May, 1662, a purchase was made of the Indians, of a township of land termed thirty miles island. The Indian name of the tract, east of the river, since called East-Haddam, was Machemoodus. The original proprietors were twenty eight. They began their settlements on the west side of the river, and the inhabitants were so increased that, in the session in October, 1668, the plantation was vested with town privileges, and named Haddam. The extent of the town was six miles east and west of the river.

Haddam made a town, Oct. 1668.

About the same time a settlement was made at Massacoe. In April, 1644, the general court of Connecticut gave liberty to governors Hopkins and Haynes to dispose of the lands upon Tunxis river, called Massacoe, to such of the inhabitants of Windsor as they should judge expedient. In 1647, the court resolved, that Massacoe should be purchased by the country, and a committee was appointed to dispose of it to such of the inhabitants of Windsor as they should choose. A purchase of the lands was made of the Indians, and settlements began under the town of Windsor. The plantation, at first, was considered as an ap-

Massacoe purchased, and made a town, by the name of Symsbury.

Book I.
1670.

Wallingford incorporated.

May 12th, 1670.

Alteration of the mode of election.

Dispute with Rhode-Island respecting boundaries.

pendix, or part of that town. In the session in May, 1670, it was enacted, that Massacoe should be a distinct town, by the name of Symsbury. The limits granted were ten miles northward from the north bounds of Farmington, and ten miles westward from the western bounds of Windsor.

At the same time, New-Haven Village was incorporated and made a town, by the name of Wallingford. The purchase of the town was made by governor Eaton, Mr. Davenport, and other planters of New-Haven, in December, 1638. The settlement was projected in 1669. A committee was appointed, by the town of New-Haven, vested with powers to manage the whole affair of the settlement. This committee held the lands in trust, and acted in all the affairs of the town, as trustees, until May, 1672, when they resigned their trust to the town.

At the general election, May, 1670, William Leet, Esq. was chosen deputy governor, and major Mason, who for many years had been deputy governor, was chosen the first magistrate.

Until this time, the great body of the freemen had annually convened at Hartford, upon the day of election, to make choice of the governor, magistrates, and civil officers, appointed by charter, to be elected on that day. But the freemen were now become so numerous, and it had been found to be so expensive and inconvenient, that it was judged necessary to alter the mode of election. The assembly resolved, " That henceforth all the freemen of this jurisdiction, without any further summons, from year to year, shall or may upon the second Thursday in May yearly, in person or in proxy, at Hartford, attend and consummate the election of governor, deputy governor, and assistants, and such other public officers as his majesty hath appointed, by our charter, then yearly to be chosen." A law was then made regulating the freemen's meetings and the mode of election, for substance nearly the same with the law respecting the election at the present time.

While the colony was thus extending its settlements, and regulating its internal police, great troubles arose respecting the boundaries between Connecticut and Rhode-Island. From year to year Connecticut had appointed committees to settle the boundary line between the colonies, but all their attempts had been unsuccessful.

In 1668, the assembly appointed Mr. Wyllys, and Mr. Robert Thompson, of London, by petition or otherwise, to represent the affair to his majesty, and obtain a resolution respecting the boundary line. Nothing decisive, however, was effected. Meanwhile, the conduct of Rhode-Island was such, that the General Assembly of Connecticut declared it to be intolerable, and contrary to the settlement made by his majesty's commissioners. The assembly, therefore, in May, 1670, appointed Mr. Leet, the deputy-governor, John Allen, and James Richards, Esquires, captain John Winthrop, and captain Benjamin Newbury, a committee to meet at New-London, the June following, to treat with such gentlemen, from Rhode-Island, as should be sent, properly authorised to act in the affair; and concerning the injuries which the inhabitants of that colony had done to the people of Connecticut. They were not only vested with plenary powers to compromise these difficulties, but, in case the commissioners from Rhode-Island would not agree to some equitable mode of settlement, to reduce the people of Squamacuck and Narraganset to obedience to this colony. They were also authorised to hold courts in the Pequot and Narraganset country, and to hear and determine all cases of injury, which had been done to the inhabitants of Connecticut, according to law. Instructions were also given them to appoint all officers, necessary for the peaceable government of that part of the colony.

The commissioners of the two colonies met at New-London, but could effect no settlement of the controversy. The commissioners from Rhode-Island, insisted that Pawcatuck river was their boundary, according to the express words of their charter. Those from Connecticut, insisted that their charter, which was prior to that of Rhode-Island, bounded them easterly upon Narraganset bay and river, and that the Pequot country, which they had conquered, extended ten miles east of Pawcatuck; that, therefore, they had a right to that part, both by charter and conquest.

As no agreement could be effected, the committee from Connecticut, went into the Narraganset country, and read the charter at Wickford, and the plantations east of Pawcatuck river, and, in the name of the General Assembly of Connecticut, demanded the submission and obedience of the people to its authority and laws. They also appointed officers for the good government of the people.*

Both colonies had something plausible to plead. The case, truly stated, is this. The old patent of Connecticut, to lord Say and Seal, lord Brook, and their associates, bounded the tract conveyed eastward, by Narraganset bay and river. The charter granted in April, 1662, gave the same boundaries as the old patent in 1631. Pawcatuck

* Records of Connecticut.

BOOK I.
1670.

Mr. Winthrop and Mr. Clark submit their differences to arbitrators

river was never known by the name of Narraganset river, and it made no bay; consequently the mouth of it, and the sea there, could not be called Narraganset bay. But when Mr. John Clark was in England, as agent for the colony of Rhode-Island, in 1663, there arose much difficulty between him and Mr. Winthrop, respecting the boundaries between the two colonies. They were advised, by their friends, to submit the controverted points to arbitrators, in England, to which they consented. William Breereton, Esq. major Robert Thompson, capt. Richard Deane, capt. John Brookhaven, and doctor Benjamin Worseley, were mutually chosen to hear and determine the differences between them. They came to the following determination:

Their determination, April, 1663.

"FIRST, That a river there commonly called and known by Pawcatuck river, shall be the certain bounds between those two colonies, which said river shall, for the future, be also called alias Narragance or Narraganset river."

"SECONDLY, If any part of that purchase at Quinebaug doth lie along upon the east side of the river, that goeth down by New-London, within six miles of the said river, that then it shall wholly belong to Connecticut colony, as well as the rest which lieth on the western side of the aforesaid river."

"THIRDLY, That the proprietors and inhabitants of that land about Mr. Smith's trading house, claimed or purchased by major Atherton, capt. Hutchinson, lieut. Hudson, and others, or given unto them by Indians, shall have free liberty to choose to which of those colonies they will belong."

"FOURTHLY, That propriety shall not be altered nor destroyed, but carefully maintained through the said colonies."

To this the two agents, John Winthrop and John Clark, Esquires, interchangeably set their hands and seals, as an agreement finally terminating the controversy between them. This was signed on the 7th of March, 1663.

In consequence of this agreement, the charter of Rhode-Island, granted July 8th, 1663, bounded that colony westward by Pawcatuck river, and ordained, with particular reference to the agreement, which is recognized in the charter, that this river should be called alias Narragance or Narraganset river; and that the same shall be holden by the colony of Rhode-Island, "any grant, or clause in a late grant, to the governor and company of Connecticut colony in America, to the contrary thereof, in any wise notwithstanding.

The proprietors, mentioned in the agreement, made

CHAP. XIV. CONNECTICUT.

choice of the government of Connecticut, July 3d, 1663, and were taken under the jurisdiction and protection of this colony.

Connecticut insisted, that Mr. Winthrop's agency was finished before the agreement with Mr. Clark, and that he had never received any instructions from the colony authorizing him to enter into any such compact. It was also pleaded, that his Majesty could not re-grant that which he had previously granted to Connecticut. Rhode-Island insisted on the agreement between Mr. Winthrop and Mr. Clark, and on the limits granted in the charter of that colony. Hence arose a controversy between the colonies, which continued more than sixty years.

Governor Winthrop, at the session in October, again proposed a resignation of his office, and desired the consent and approbation of the general assembly. The assembly were utterly opposed to it, and could, by no means, be persuaded to give their consent. Through the influence of the houses, he was persuaded to keep the chair, and means were adopted to give him satisfaction. The assembly, at the next session, granted a hundred and fifty pounds salary. Grants were several times made him of valuable tracts of land. These considerations, with the great unanimity and esteem of the freemen, prevailed with him to continue in office until his death.

In 1671 the former officers were all re-chosen.

During the term of eighteen or twenty years, attempts had been making to settle a township at Paugasset. About the year 1653, it appears that governor Goodyear, and several other gentlemen in New-Haven, made a purchase of a considerable tract there. About the year 1654, it seems that some few settlements were made. The next year, at the session in October, the planters presented a petition to the general court, at New-Haven, to be made a distinct town, and to order their affairs independently of the other towns. The court granted their petition; gave them liberty to purchase a tract sufficient for a township; released them from taxes; and appointed Richard Baldwin moderator to call meetings, and conduct the affairs of the plantation. At the next court, however, Mr. Prudden, and the people of Milford, made such strong remonstrances against the act, that the court determined the people at Paugasset should continue, as they had been, under the town of Milford, unless the parties should come to an agreement, respecting the incorporation of the inhabitants there into a distinct township. In 1657 and 1659 a purchase was made of the lands of the chief sagamores, Wetanamow and Ras-

BOOK I.
1671.

May, 1671.
Settlement of Derby.

kenute. The purchase appears to have been confirmed afterwards by Okenuck, the chief sachem. Some of the first planters were Ed. Wooster, Ed. Riggs, Richard Baldwin, Samuel Hopkins, Thomas Langdon, and Francis French. They preferred a petition to the general assembly of Connecticut, praying for town privileges, in 1671. The assembly determined that their south bounds should be the north line of Milford, and that they should extend their limits twelve miles northward, to a place called the notch. For their encouragement, it was promised, that, as soon as there should be thirty families in the plantation, they should be vested with town privileges. About four years after, Oct. 1675, they renewed their application. They represented that they then consisted of twelve families, and that eleven more were about moving directly into the plantation: that they had procured a minister, built him a house, and made provision for the enjoyment of divine ordinances. Upon these representations, the assembly made them a town, by the name of Derby.

Major John Mason, who, for many years, had been deputy governor, and rendered many important services to the colony, being far advanced in years, and visited with many infirmities, about this time, excused himself from the service of the commonwealth. At the next election, May 9th, 1672, Mr. John Nash was chosen magistrate, to fill the vacancy made by his resignation.*

Until this time, the colony had kept their laws in manuscript, and had promulgated them, by sending copies to be publicly read in the respective towns. This year, the first code of Connecticut was published. It was printed at Cambridge, in Massachusetts. It consisted of between seventy and eighty pages, in small folio, printed, and of nearly the same number of blank pages. It is a great curiosity. The preface is written in the most religious manner, sufficiently solemn for an introduction to a body of sermons. It is thus introduced, " To our beloved brethren and neighbours, the inhabitants of Connecticut, the

* John Mason, Esq. was bred to arms in the Dutch Netherlands, under Sir Thomas Fairfax. He came into New-England with Mr. Warham and his company, in 1630. Five years after, he removed to Connecticut, and was one of the first planters of Windsor. In 1642 he was chosen magistrate; in which office he continued until May, 1660, when he was chosen deputy governor. In this office he continued ten years. At the desire of the inhabitants of Saybrook, and for the defence of the colony, he removed to that town in 1647. From thence he removed to Norwich, in 1659, where he died, in 1672 or '73, in the 73d year of his age. He was tall and portly, full of martial fire, and shunned no hardships or dangers in the defence and service of the colony. He was a gentleman not only of distinguished heroism, but of strict morals and great prudence.

general court of that colony wish grace and peace in our Lord Jesus." It recognizes the design of the first planters, "who," as the court express it, "settled these foundations," for the maintaining of "religion according to the gospel of our Lord Jesus;" which it declares "ought to be the endeavour of all those, that shall succeed, to uphold and encourage unto all generations." The assembly enacted, that every family should have a law book. In the blank pages, all the laws enacted after 1672 were inserted, in writing, until the year 1699, when the book was filled up.

<small>Book I.
1672.</small>

At the election, May 8th, 1673, Robert Treat, Esq. was chosen into the magistracy.

At this court, Richard Smith was appointed a commissioner at Narraganset, and vested with the powers of magistracy through that country. A court of commissioners was instituted there, and Mr. Smith was appointed the chief judge. This court had cognizance of all cases not exceeding twenty pounds, provided that all such as exceeded forty shillings should be tried by a jury. A commissioner* was appointed at Pettyquamscot.

<small>Court of election, May 8th, 1673.</small>

As war had been declared in England, the last year, against the Dutch, the colony was put into a state of defence. It was ordered that a troop of horse should be raised in each county. This year, the colony was more thoroughly alarmed, and experienced the benefit of being in a good state of preparation. On the 30th of July, a small Dutch fleet, under the command of commodores Cornelius Everste and Jacob Benkes, arrived at New-York. One John Manning, who commanded the fort and island there, treacherously delivered them up to the enemy, without firing a gun, or attempting the least resistance. The inhabitants of New-York and New-Jersey generally submitted to the Dutch without opposition. About the same time, the Dutch captured a vessel of Mr. Sillick's of this colony, near one of the harbours of the western towns.

<small>War with the Dutch.</small>

Upon this emergency, a special assembly was convoked, at Hartford, on the 7th of August. Orders were immediately issued, that the respective troops, in the colony, with five hundred dragoons, should forthwith be ready for service; and that all the trainbands should be complete in their arms. The same day, Mr. James Richards and Mr. William Roswell, were dispatched, with a letter from the assembly, to the Dutch commodores, to know their further intentions. The assembly remonstrated against their conduct in capturing Mr. Sillick's vessel, and in demanding

<small>The assembly meet, and send messengers to the Dutch commodores.</small>

* Commissioner was a name for a justice of the peace.

Book I.
1673.

the submission of his majesty's English subjects, upon Long-Island, and that they should take the oath of allegiance to the States General. They acquainted the Dutch commanders, that the united colonies were, by his majesty, constituted the defenders of the lives and liberties of his subjects, in these parts of his dominions, and assured them that they would be faithful to their trust.

The assembly appointed the governor, deputy governor, and a number of the council, a committee of war, to act as emergencies should require.

The Dutch commanders returned a soldier-like answer to the messengers and letter from Connecticut, purporting, that they had a commission to do all damages, in their power, to their enemies, by land and sea: that they had summoned the towns upon Long-Island to submit to them; and that, unless they should comply, they would reduce them to their subjection by force of arms: that as the vessel they had taken was their enemy's it was strange to them that any questions were proposed concerning it: and that while they doubted not of the faithfulness of the united colonies in defending their majesty's subjects, they should not be less zealous and faithful in the service of the States General.*

On the 11th of August, the committee of war met at Hartford. They appear to have apprehended an immediate invasion. They gave orders, that the whole militia of the colony should be ready to march at an hour's warning, to any place which might be attacked. They made such arrangement of the dragoons, and sent such assistance to their friends upon Long-Island, as prevented an invasion of any part of the colony, and the plunder and destruction of the English upon the island.

Assembly meet Oct. 9th.

On the meeting of the assembly, in October, letters were sent to Massachusetts and Plymouth, to solicit their united assistance against the Dutch, and to know their opinion relative to proclaiming war, and engaging in offensive operations against them. Mr. John Banks was sent express to the Dutch commanders, with a spirited remonstrance against the conduct of the Dutch, who had threatened the towns on the Island with destruction, by fire and sword, unless they would submit and swear allegiance to the States General. They had sent ships and an armed force towards the east end of the island, to subdue the people; but had been prevented. The assembly assured them, that they knew how to avenge themselves upon their plantations, and not only so, but upon their head quarters, if the

* Letter on file.

CHAP. XIV.   CONNECTICUT.

colonies should rise, and warned them of the consequences of injuring the English towns upon the island.

Connecticut, upon consulting their confederates, found it to be the general opinion to act offensively against the Dutch. A special assembly was called on the 26th of November, and war was immediately proclaimed against them. It was determined, that an expedition should be undertaken against New-York. This, it seems, was in conjunction with the other confederates. Major Treat was appointed to command the troops from Connecticut.

The Dutch not only threatened the English towns on the island with destruction, but, it seems, made several descents upon it, with a view to attack them: however, by the assistance of the troops from Connecticut, they were, in all instances, repulsed, and driven from the island.* Before suitable preparations could be made for an attack upon the Dutch, at their head quarters, the season was too far advanced for military operations. Early in the spring, the news of a general pacification between England and Holland, prevented all further proceedings of this kind. The whole militia of the colony, at this time, amounted to no more than 2,070 men. One quarter, it seems, were mounted as dragoons, and employed for the defence of the colony, and of his majesty's English subjects upon Long-Island.

The only alteration made by the election in 1674, was the choice of Thomas Topping, Esq. instead of Mr. Hawkins.

As the inhabitants of Long-Island had been protected and governed, the latter part of the last year, by Connecticut, they made application, at this assembly, for the further enjoyment of its protection and government. The legislature accepted them, and appointed officers in the several English towns, as they had done at their session the preceding October.

Upon the application of the town of Wickford, and other plantations in Narraganset, the legislature took them under the government of this colony. A court was instituted at Stonington, for the government of the people in Narraganset, that they might not live in dissolute practices, to the dishonour of God, of the king and nation, and to the scandalizing of the very heathens.

The legislature, in 1672, granted liberty to Mr. Sherman, Mr. William Curtiss, and their associates, to make a plantation at Pomperaug. Such a number of settlements had been made there, in about two years, that the assembly,

Pomperaug settled and named Woodbury.

BOOK I.
1674.

* Records of Connecticut, and letters on file.

Book I. in May, 1674, enacted that it should be a town, by the name of Woodbury.

1675. Scarcely had the colonies recovered from one calamity and danger, before new and more terrible scenes of alarm and destruction presented themselves. Not only Connecticut, but all the New-England colonies, were now verging upon a most distressful and important period, in which their very existence was endangered.

Major Andross appointed governor of New-York. Upon the pacification with the Dutch, the duke of York, to remove all doubt and controversy respecting his property in America, took out a new patent from the king, June 29th, 1674, granting the same territory described in the former patent. Two days after, he commissioned major, afterwards Sir Edmund Andross, to be governor of New-York, and all his territories in these parts. The major was a mere tool of the duke, and a tyrant over the people. Mr. Smith, in his history of New-York, observes, "That he knew no law but the will of his master; and that Kirk and Jefferies were not fitter instruments than he to execute the despotic projects of James the second."

His claims upon Connecticut, 1675. Notwithstanding the priority of the patent of Connecticut to the duke of York's, and the determination of his majesty's commissioners about ten years before, he set up the duke's claim to all that part of the colony which lies to the westward of Connecticut river, and he threatened the colony with an invasion.

War with Philip. At the same time, Philip, sachem of the Wampanoags, commenced hostilities against the colonies, and involved *The reasons of it.* them in a most bloody and destructive war. It had been supposed, that the Indians, for several years, had been concerting a general conspiracy against the plantations in New-England, with a view of extirpating the English from the country. They viewed themselves as a free and independent people. Their sachems were men of high and independent spirits. They considered themselves as sovereign princes, and claimed to be the original proprietors and lords of the land. They viewed the English as intruders and usurpers. While, therefore, they saw them, in almost every quarter, extending their settlements over the dominions of their ancestors, they could not but kindle into resentment, and adopt counsels to prevent the loss of their liberties and country. Though they had entered into treaties with the colonies, and acknowledged themselves to be subjects of the king of England, yet it is by no means probable, that, by these treaties and acknowledgments, they designed to give up their independence, or any of their natural rights. They viewed themselves rather as allies,

CHAP. XIV.   CONNECTICUT.

than as subjects of England. To be called to an account for their conduct, and to be thwarted in their designs, by the colonies, or to be holden as amenable to them for their actions, was a treatment which their haughty spirits could not brook. These were general reasons for which they might wish for the destruction of their English neighbors. But beside these, there were others, which had more immediate influence upon Philip. John Sausaman, a christian Indian, who had once been a subject of Philip, made a discovery of his plots against the English. Philip, fired with resentment, procured the murder of Suasaman. The murderers were discovered, tried by the English laws, and executed. Philip, enraged at the execution of his subjects, conscious of his own guilt, and probably apprehensive for his personal safety, armed his own warriors, the Wampanoags, and such strange Indians as he could engage to embark in his measures, and, with the most hostile appearances, began to march up and down the country.

As the colonies, for some time, had been apprised, that the Indians were forming designs against them, they, by treaties, and such other means as appeared to be wise and politic, had been attempting to prevent the storm. Notwithstanding, it now burst upon them with uncommon fury. Its destruction was wide and dreadful.

Philip's numbers daily increasing, gave him fresh courage, and increased his insolence. On the 20th of June, 1675, his Indians commenced hostilities upon Swanzey, one of the frontier towns of New-Plymouth, bordering on the territories of Philip, whose chief seat was at Mount Hope.* They insulted the English, rifled their houses, and killed their cattle. Four days after, they killed nine, and wounded seven of the inhabitants. The troops of that colony marched immediately to the defence of the town. In four days, they were reinforced with several companies from Boston. On the 29th, the troops were drawn forth against the enemy. They instantly fled before them, for a mile or two, and took refuge in a swamp. The next day, major Savage arrived with more troops and a general command from Boston. He marched the army into the Indian towns, to surprise their head quarters, and give them battle upon their own grounds. The troops found the enemy's towns, and even the seat of Philip, deserted with marks of the utmost precipitation. As the Indians fled, they marked their route with the burning of buildings, the scalps, hands, and heads of the English, which they had

Book I.
1675.

The Indians commence hostilities, June 20th.

* Mount Hope is an eminence in the eastern part of the town of Bristol, in Rhode-Island.

taken off and fixed upon poles by the way side. As they could not come up with the enemy, they returned to their head quarters, at Swanzey.

Troops dispatched to Stonington and the seaport towns.

In consequence of the war with Philip, the commissioners of the united colonies met at Boston, and governor Winthrop, who was one of the commissioners for Connecticut, was gone there, to attend the business of the country. Deputy-governor Leet and the council, upon receiving intelligence of the war, dispatched troops to Stonington, to defend that part of the colony against the enemy.

At the same time, it was discovered that major Andross was about to make a hostile invasion of the colony, and to demand a surrender of its most important posts to the government of the duke of York. Detachments from the militia were, therefore, sent, with the utmost expedition, to New-London and Saybrook. Captain Thomas Bull, of Hartford, commanded the party sent to Saybrook.

Major Andross appears with an armed force at Saybrook.

About the 8th or 9th of July, the people of that town were surprised by the appearance of major Andross, with an armed force, in the sound, making directly for the fort. They had received no intelligence of the affair, nor instructions from the governor and council, how to conduct themselves upon such an emergency. They were, at first, undetermined whether to make any resistance or not; but they did not hesitate long. As the danger approached, and their surprise abated, the martial spirit began to enkindle; the fort was manned, and the militia of the town drawn out for its defence.* At this critical juncture, captain Bull with his company arrived, and the most vigorous exertions were made, for the defence of the fort and town.

Demands the fort.

On the 11th, major Andross, with several armed sloops, drew up before the fort, hoisted the king's flag on board, and demanded a surrender of the fortress and town. Captain Bull raised his majesty's colors in the fort, and arranged his men in the best manner. They appeared with a good countenance, determined and eager for action. The major did not like to fire on the king's colors, and perceiving that, should he attempt to reduce the town by force, it would be a bloody affair, judged it expedient not to fire upon the troops. He, nevertheless, lay all that day, and part of the next, off against the fort.

Assembly meet, July 9th.

The critical state of the colony had occasioned the meeting of the assembly, at Hartford, on the 9th of July. They immediately proceeded to draw up a declaration, or protest, against the major, in the words following.

* Letter from the Rev. Mr. Buckingham to the governor and council, on the subject.

CHAP. XIV. CONNECTICUT.

Book I.

1675.
Protest against Andross, July 10th.

"Whereas, we are informed that major Edmund Andross is come with some considerable force into this his majesty's colony of Connecticut, which might be construed to be in pursuance of his letter to us, to invade or intrude upon the same, or upon some part of our charter limits and privileges, and so to molest his majesty's good subjects, in this juncture, when the heathen rage against the English, and by fire and sword have destroyed many of his majesty's good subjects, our neighbors of Plymouth colony, and still are carrying their heads about the country, as trophies of their good success; and yet are proceeding further in their cruel designs against the English; in faithfulness to our royal sovereign, and in obedience to his majesty's commands, in his gracious charter to this colony, we can do no less than publicly declare and protest against the said major Edmund Andross, and these his illegal proceedings, as also against all his aiders and abettors, as disturbers of the peace of his majesty's good subjects in this colony; and that his and their actions, in this juncture, tend to the encouragement of the heathen to proceed in the effusion of christian blood, which may be very like to be the consequence of his actions, and which we shall unavoidably lay at his door, and use our utmost power and endeavour, (expecting therein the assistance of Almighty God) to defend the good people of this colony from the said major Andross his attempts; not doubting but his majesty will countenance and approve our just proceedings therein, they being according to the commission we have received from his majesty, in his gracious charter to this colony; by which power and trust, so committed unto us, we do again forewarn and advise the said major Andross, and all his aiders and abettors, to forbear and desist such forenamed unjust and unwarrantable practices, as they expect to answer the same, with all such just damages and costs as may arise or accrue thereby. And we do further, in his majesty's name, require and command all the good people, his majesty's subjects, of this colony of Connecticut, under our present government, utterly to refuse to attend, countenance or obey the said major Edmund Andross, or any under him, in any order, instruction, or command, diverse from or contrary to the laws and orders of this colony here established, by virtue of his majesty's gracious charter, granted to this colony of Connecticut, as they will answer the contrary at their peril."

"God save the King."

This was voted unanimously. It was sent by an express to Saybrook, with instructions to captain Bull to pro-

BOOK I.
1675.

Major Andross comes on shore.

Is forbidden to read his commission.

Sails for Long-Island.

Declaration of the general assembly.

pose to major Andross the reference of the affair in dispute to commissioners, to meet in any place in this colony which he should choose. Early in the morning of the 12th of July, the major desired that he might have admittance on shore, and an interview with the ministers and chief officers. He probably imagined, that if he could read the duke's patent and his own commission, it would make an impression upon the people, and that he should gain by art that which he could not by force of arms. He was allowed to come on shore with his suit. Meanwhile, the express arrived with the protest, and instructions from the assembly. Captain Bull and his officers, with the officers and gentlemen of the town, met the major, at his landing, and acquainted him that they had, at that instant, received instructions to tender him a treaty, and to refer the whole matter in controversy to commissioners, capable of determining it according to law and justice. The major rejected the proposal, and forthwith commanded, in his majesty's name, that the duke's patent, and the commission which he had received from his royal highness, should be read. Captain Bull commanded him, in his majesty's name, to forbear reading.* When his clerk attempted to persist in reading, the captain repeated his command, with such energy of voice and manner, as convinced the major it was not safe to proceed. The captain then acquainted him that he had an address from the assembly to him, and read the protest. Governor Andross, pleased with his bold and soldier-like appearance, said, "What is your name?" He replied, "My name is Bull, Sir." "Bull!" said the governor, "It is a pity that your horns are not tipped with silver." Finding he could make no impression upon the officers or people, and that the legislature of the colony were determined to defend themselves, in the possession of their chartered rights, he gave up his design of seizing the fort. He represented the protest as a slender affair, and an ill requital of his kindness. He said, however, he should do no more. The militia of the town guarded him to his boat, and going on board he soon sailed for Long-Island.

The general assembly considered this as a great abuse and insult of the colony, and, upon receiving an account of the major's conduct, came to the following resolution.

"This court orders, that this declaration shall forthwith be sent forth to the several plantations, sealed with the seal of the colony, and signed by the secretary, to be there published."

* Captain Bull's letter to the assembly.

CHAP. XIV.   CONNECTICUT.

"Forasmuch as the good people of his majesty's colony of Connecticut have met with much trouble and molestation from major Edmund Andross, his challenge and attempts to surprise the main part of said colony, which they have so rightfully obtained, so long possessed, and defended against all invasions of Dutch and Indians, to the great grievance of his majesty's good subjects in their settlements, and to despoil the happy government, by charter from his majesty granted to themselves, and under which they have enjoyed many halcyon days of peace and tranquillity, to their great satisfaction, and to the content of his majesty, graciously expressed by letters to them, so greatly engaging their loyalty and thankfulness, as makes it intolerable to be put off from so long and just settlement under his majesty's government by charter. Hereupon, for the prevention of misrepresentations into England, by the said major Andross against us, for our refusal, and withstanding his attempts, made with hostile appearances to surprise us at Saybrook, while we were approaching towards a savage Indian enemy that had committed much outrage and murder, by fire and sword, upon our neighbours about Plymouth; this court have desired the honorable John Winthrop and James Richards, Esquires, or either of them, (intending a voyage to England upon their own occasions,) to take with them the narrative and copies of all the transactions betwixt us, and to give a right understanding for clearing our innocence, and better securing our enjoyments as occasion shall offer." *Book I. 1675.*

As the Narraganset Indians were considered as abettors of Philip, harbouring the old men and women whom he had sent off to them, and as the colonies feared that they would proceed to open hostilities, unless it could be prevented by some vigorous measures, it was determined to march the army, which had been rendezvoused at Swanzey, immediately into their country, and to treat with them sword in hand. Captain Hutchinson was dispatched commissioner, from the general court of Massachusetts, to conduct the treaty.* On the 15th of July, a treaty was concluded between the united colonies and the six Narraganset sachems, and the sunk squaw or old queen of Narraganset. Perpetual peace was stipulated between the parties. It was also agreed, that all stolen goods should be returned; that neither Philip nor any of his subjects should be harboured by the Narragansets; but if any of them should enter upon their lands they should kill and destroy

The army marches to Narraganset.

Treaty with the Narragansetts.

---

* Major Wait Winthrop and Mr. Richard Smith were commissioners from Connecticut.

Book I. them, until a cessation of hostilities should be concluded between Philip and the united colonies: that the commissioners should give to any of the Narraganset Indians, who should bring in Philip alive, forty coats, and twenty for his head: that two coats should be given for every subject of Philip delivered alive to the English, and one for his head. On the part of the Narragansets, hostages were delivered, as a security, for the faithful performance of the treaty. This, at best, was a forced business, rather calculated to irritate, than to reconcile a free and haughty people. The conditions were imposed by the army.

1675.

Fight at Pocasset Neck, July 18th.

On the 17th of July, the troops returned to Taunton. Upon intelligence, that Philip and his warriors were in a swamp at Pocasset, the Massachusetts and Plymouth forces formed a junction, and on the 18th, attacked them with firmness and resolution. The enemy had chosen an advantageous retreat. As the army entered the swamp, they retired deeper and deeper into it, until the troops were led into such an hideous thicket, that it was impossible for them to keep their order. It was so thick and dark, as the night approached, that the men were in danger, not only from the enemy, but from one another. They fired at every bush which appeared to shake. The action was continued until night, when the English retreated. The attempt was unhappy. Sixteen brave men were killed, and Philip and his men, after they had been reduced to the greatest distress, and were upon the point of surrendering themselves, made their escape. A fine army was collected. Philip was enclosed in a swamp and neck of land, and could not at that time have made his escape, by any other means than by defeating, or fighting his way through the army, had the English conducted with prudence and fortitude. They might have renewed the attack upon him next morning, and had the day before them to finish their work, and put an end to the war; but, instead of this, they left a few companies to guard the swamp, which was upon Pocasset neck, and starve out the enemy. Philip, about six or eight days after, found means to rid himself from the danger. He either waded across an arm of the sea, at low water, or passed over it with his warriors upon rafts. He and his warriors triumphed, and were blown up with still greater courage and insolence. The Indians in general were encouraged, so that soon after there was a general rising of them against the English throughout New-England, for an extent of nearly three hundred miles.

As the Indians had lived promiscuously with the English, in all parts of the country, they were generally as well

CHAP. XIV.   CONNECTICUT.   333

acquainted with their dwellings, fields, and places of worship, as themselves. They were perfectly acquainted with their roads, times, and places of resort. They were at hand, to watch all their motions, to attack them at every difficult pass, and in every unguarded moment. Except some of the thickest settlements, and the centre of the towns, the country was a vast wilderness. This enabled the enemy, not only in small skulking parties, but in great bodies, to make their approaches undiscovered, almost into the very midst of them; and under covert of the night, to creep into their barns, gardens, and out houses; to conceal themselves behind their fences, and lie in wait for them on the roads and in their fields. Sometimes they concealed themselves before their very doors. No sooner did they open them, in the morning, than they were instantly shot dead. From almost every quarter, they were ready to rise upon them. At midnight, in the morning, or whenever they could obtain an advantage, they were ready to attack them. While the English were hunting them in one place, they would be slaying the inhabitants, and plundering and burning in another. In a short time, they would plunder and burn a town, kill and captivate the inhabitants, and retire into swamps and fastnesses, where it was dangerous to pursue, difficult to discover, and impossible to attack them, but at the greatest disadvantage.

Book I.

1675.

Advantages of the Indians.

Notwithstanding every precaution and exertion of the colonies, they continued plundering, burning, killing, and captivating, in one place and another, and kept the whole country in continual fear and alarm. There was no safety to man, woman, nor child; to him who went out, nor to him who came in. Whether they were asleep or awake—whether they journeyed, laboured, or worshipped, they were in continual jeopardy. The inhabitants of Massachusetts, Plymouth, and Rhode-Island, especially, were killed, plundered, and their towns and buildings burned, in a most distressing and terrible manner.

Danger and distress of the colonies.

Beside other damages, not so considerable, captain Hutchinson, who had been sent with a party of horse, to treat with the Nipmuck Indians, was drawn into an ambush, near Brookfield, and mortally wounded. Sixteen of his company were killed. The enemy then rushed in upon the town, and burnt all the dwelling-houses, except one, which was defended by the garrison, until it was reinforced, two days after, by major Willard. The enemy then drew off, having burned twenty dwelling-houses, with all the barns and out houses, and killed all the cattle and horses which they could find. In September, Hadley,

Captain Hutchinson surprised, and Brookfield burnt, Aug. 2d.

A Complete History of Connecticut, Civil and Ecclesiastical

1675.

Hadley, Deerfield, and Northfield attacked.

Deerfield, and Northfield, on Connecticut river, were attacked, and numbers of the inhabitants killed and wounded. Most of the buildings in Deerfield were burnt, and Northfield was soon after abandoned to the enemy. There were a number of skirmishes, about the same time, in that part of the country, in which the English, on the whole, were losers.

Captain Beers and his party killed, Sept. 12th.

Captain Beers was surprised near Northfield, by a large body of the enemy, and he and twenty of his party were killed.

The officers who commanded in that quarter, finding that, by sending out parties, they sustained continual loss and disappointment, and effected nothing of importance, determined to collect a magazine at Hadley, and garrison the town. At Deerfield, there were about three thousand bushels of wheat in stack. It was resolved to thresh this out, and bring it down to Hadley. While captain Lothrop, with a chosen corps of young men, the flower of the county of Essex, was guarding the teams employed in this service, seven or eight hundred Indians suddenly attacked

Captain Lothrop and his party killed, Sept. 18th.

him. Though he fought with great bravery, yet he fell, with nearly his whole party. Many of the teamsters were also cut off. Ninety or an hundred men were killed on the spot. Captain Mosely, who was stationed at Deerfield, marched to reinforce captain Lothrop, but he arrived too late for his assistance. Captain Mosely was then obliged to fight the whole body of the enemy, for several hours, until the brave major Treat, of Connecticut, with about a hundred and sixty Englishmen and Moheagan Indians, marched up to his assistance, and put the enemy to flight.* The fall of captain Lothrop, and such a fine body of men, was a heavy loss to the country; especially to the county of Essex, filling it with great and universal lamentation.

During the term of about forty years, the Indians in the vicinity of Springfield had lived in the greatest harmony with the English, and still made the strongest professions

Indian treachery.

of friendship; yet, about this time, they conspired with Philip's warriors for the destruction of that town. At the distance of about a mile from it they had a fort. The evening before they made their assault, they received into it about three hundred of Philip's warriors. The same

---

* The commissioners, about the middle of September, ordered 1000 men to be raised for the general defence. Of these 500 were to be dragoons, with long arms. Connecticut was required to raise 315 men, for her proportion. A considerable part of this force was employed by Connecticut, under major Treat, for the defence of the upper towns. Captain Watts had been sent with a company to Deerfield, some time before.

CHAP. XIV.   CONNECTICUT.

evening, one Toto, a Windsor Indian, discovered the plot, and dispatches were immediately sent off, from Windsor to Springfield, and to major Treat, who lay at Westfield, with the Connecticut troops, to apprise them of the danger. But the people at Springfield were so strongly persuaded of the friendship of those Indians, that they would not credit the report. One lieutenant Cooper, who commanded there, was so infatuated, that, as soon as the morning appeared, instead of collecting his men and preparing for the defence of the town, he, with another bold man, rode out, with a design to go to the fort, and discover how the matter was. He soon met the enemy, who killed his companion, by his side, and shot several balls through his body. As he was a man of great strength and courage, he kept his horse, though mortally wounded, until he reached the first garrisoned house, and gave the alarm. The enemy immediately commenced a furious attack upon the town, and began to set fire to the buildings. The inhabitants were in the utmost consternation. They had none to command them, and must soon have all fallen a bloody sacrifice to a merciless foe, had not major Treat appeared for their relief. Upon receiving intelligence of the designs of the enemy, he marched, without loss of time; but meeting with considerable hindrance in crossing the river, for want of boats, his arrival was not in such season as to prevent the attack. He soon drove off the enemy, saved the inhabitants, and a considerable part of the town. Great damage, however, was done in a very short time. Thirty dwelling houses, besides barns and out houses, were burned. Major Pyncheon and Mr. Purchas sustained each the loss of a thousand pounds.* Mr. Pelatiah Glover, minister of the town, lost his house, with a large and excellent library.

Book I.

1675.

Springfield attacked and partly burned.

In this stage of the war, the General Assembly of Connecticut convened, October 14th. The court, sensible of the good conduct of major Treat, in defending the colony, and the towns on Long-Island against the Dutch, and in relieving captain Mosely and Springfield, returned him public thanks, appointed him to the command of all the troops to be raised in the colony, to act against the enemy, and desired his acceptance of the service.

Upon intelligence from the Rev. Mr. Fitch, that a large body of the enemy were approaching the town of Norwich, major Treat was directed to march forthwith, for the defence of that part of the colony. But soon after, his or-

* Major Pyncheon was at Hadley, but did not come down, with the troops there, in season to prevent this great damage. He had, until this time, the chief command in that part of the country, but he soon after resigned it, that he might take care of his own affairs.

BOOK I.

1675.
Assault upon Hadley, Oct. 19th.

ders were countermanded, and he marched for Northampton. Here he arrived in season to render his country another piece of important service. The enemy had been so elated with their various successes, that, having collected about eight hundred of their warriors, they made a furious attack upon Hadley. Almost every part of the town was assaulted at the same instant. But the town was defended by officers and men of vigilance and spirit, so that the enemy every where met with a warm reception. Several parties of the Massachusetts troops, who were in the neighboring garrisons, flew to their assistance, and major Treat, advancing with his usual dispatch from Northampton, soon attacked them, with his whole force, and they were put to a total flight. They sustained such loss, and were so disheartened, that, from this time, the main body of them left that part of the country, and held their general rendezvous in Narraganset. Small numbers, however, remained, doing damage as they had opportunity, and keeping the people in constant fear and alarm.

The enemy routed.

Rendezvous in Narraganset.

The assembly adopt measures for the common safety

From the intelligence communicated to the general assembly of Connecticut, during the October session, it appeared that the enemy had designs upon almost all the frontier towns in the colony. Each county was therefore required to raise sixty dragoons, complete in arms, horses, and ammunition, for the immediate defence of the colony, wherever their services might be necessary. Captain Avery was appointed to the command of forty Englishmen from the towns of New-London, Stonington, and Lyme, with such a number of Pequots as he should judge expedient, for the defence of that part of the country, and the annoyance of the enemy, as occasion should present. Captain John Mason was appointed to command another party of twenty Englishmen, and the Moheagan Indians. These parties were ordered to post themselves in the best manner to guard the eastern towns, and to act conjointly or separately, as emergencies should require. An army of one hundred and twenty dragoons was appointed to act against the enemy, under the command of major Treat. It was ordered that all the towns should be fortified, and that every town should provide the best places of defence of which it was capable, for the security of the women and children, who were directed to repair to them upon the first intimations of danger. The inhabitants of the towns on the frontiers, who were few in number, and most exposed, were advised to remove their best effects, and people unable to defend themselves, to retire into the more populous parts of the colony, where they would be in a more probable state of safety.

CHAP. XIV.   CONNECTICUT.   337

The Narragansets, in direct violation of the treaty, which they had made with the colonies, gave a friendly reception to Philip's men and other hostile Indians. The commissioners of the united colonies were satisfied, that some of them had been in actual service, in the assaults which had been made upon the English. Their young men had returned wounded to Narraganset. It was supposed, that the Narraganset sachems could muster two thousand warriors, and that they had a thousand muskets. It was judged that, if they should all engage, in the spring, in open hostilities, and scatter, as they might, into all parts of the country, all the force, which the colonies could bring into the field, would not be sufficient to defend the plantations against the united exertions of the enemy. In the summer and fall past, one company of brave men after another had been cut off, and future prospects were not more favorable. The commissioners of the united colonies therefore resolved, that an army of a thousand men should be raised, for a winter campaign, to attack the enemy at their head quarters, in the Narraganset country. The colony of Massachusetts furnished a corps of five hundred and twenty seven men, consisting of six companies of foot and a troop of horse, commanded by major Appleton. Plymouth furnished one hundred and fifty-eight men, consisting of two companies, under the command of major Bradford and captain Gorham. The proportion of Connecticut was three hundred and fifteen men, but they sent into the field three hundred English men and 150 Moheagan and Pequot Indians. These were divided into five companies, commanded by captains Seely, Gallup, Mason, Watts, and Marshall. This corps was commanded by major Treat. The honorable Josiah Winslow, Esq. governor of New-Plymouth, was appointed commander in chief. The orders of the commissioners to Connecticut were issued at Boston, the 12th of November. They required, that the best officers and firmest men should be appointed, and armed and clothed in the best manner. It was required, that the troops should rendezvous at New-London, Norwich, and Stonington, by the 10th of December, ready to receive orders from the commander in chief.

The commissioners were sensible, that an expedition, at this season, would be most distressful and hazardous. Such is the extremity of the weather, in this climate, that they were not without apprehensions; the whole army might perish, should the troops be obliged to lie uncovered a single night in the open field. It did not escape their deliberations, that the snow often fell so deep, that it would be ex-

BOOK I.
1675.
The Narragansets treacherous.
Reasons of the expedition against them.

Number of men.

Danger of the expedition.

S 2

BOOK I.
1675.

tremely difficult, if not impossible, to send any succours to the army, in case of any misfortune; but they considered this as the only probable expedient of defeating the enemy, and preventing the desolating of the country. They observed, "It was a humbling providence of God, that put his poor people to be meditating a matter of war at such a season." They appointed the second of December to be observed as a solemn fast, to seek the divine aid.*

The Connecticut troops arrived at Pettyquamscot, on the 17th of December. Here had been a number of buildings, in which the troops expected to have been covered and kindly entertained; but the enemy, a day or two before, had killed ten men and five women and children, and burned all the houses and barns. The next day, they formed a junction with the Massachusetts and Plymouth forces. Though the evening was cold and stormy, the troops were obliged to remain uncovered in the open field. The next morning, at the dawning of the day, they commenced their march towards the enemy, who were in a swamp at about fifteen miles distance. The troops from Massachusetts, headed by captains Mosely and Davenport, led the van; their rear was brought up by major Appleton and captain Oliver. General Winslow, with the Plymouth companies, formed in the centre; and the troops of Connecticut formed in the rear of the whole, brought up by major Treat. This was the line of march.†

Saturday, Dec. 18.

Line of march, Lord's day, Dec. 19th.

The troops proceeded with great spirit, wading through the snow, in a severe season, until nearly one o'clock, without fire to warm or food to refresh them, except what had been taken on the way. At this time, they had arrived just upon the seat of the enemy. This was upon a rising ground, in the centre of a large swamp. It was fortified with palisades, and compassed with a hedge without, nearly of a rod's thickness. The only entrance, which appeared practicable, was over a log, or tree, which lay up five or six feet from the ground. This opening was commanded in front by a kind of log house, and on the left by a flanker. As soon as the troops entered the skirts of the swamp, they discovered an advanced party of the enemy, upon whom they immediately fired. The enemy returned the fire, and retired before them, until they were led to the very entrance by the blockhouse. Without reconnoitering the fort, or waiting for the army to march up and form for the attack, the Massachusetts troops, led on by their officers, with great courage, mounted the tree and entered the fort,

Situation of the enemy.

Attack upon the fort.

* Letters of the commissioners to Connecticut.
† Hubbard's Narrative, p. 104.

CHAP. XIV.   CONNECTICUT.

but they were so galled from the blockhouse, and received such a furious and well directed fire from almost every quarter, that, after every exertion of skill and courage, of which they were capable, they were obliged to retreat out of the fort. The whole army pressed forward with the utmost courage and exertion, but such were the obstructions from the swamp and the snow, that it was a considerable time before the men could all be brought up to action. By reason of this, and the sharpness of the fire from the flanker and block-house, a sufficient number of men were not able to enter the fort to support those brave officers and men, who so courageously began the assault. Captains Johnson and Davenport, and many brave men of the Massachusetts, were killed. The Connecticut troops, who formed in the rear, coming up to the charge, mounted over the log before the blockhouse, the captains leading and spiriting up the men in the most undaunted manner. About the same time that the main body of the Connecticut troops were forcing their way by the blockhouse, a few bold men ran round to the opposite part of the fort, where they found a narrow spot where there were no palisades, but a high and thick hedge of trees and brush. The sharpness of the action in the front had drawn off the enemy from this part, and climbing over unobserved, they ran down between the wigwams, and poured a heavy and well directed fire upon the backs of the enemy, who lay wholly exposed to their shot.* Thus assaulted, in front and rear, they were driven from the flanker and block-house. The captains crying out, they run, they run, the men pressed so furiously upon them, that they were forced from that part of the fort. The soldiers without rushed in, with great spirit, and the enemy were driven from one covert and hiding place to another, until the middle of the fort was gained; and after a long and bloody action they were totally routed and fled into the wilderness. As they retired, the soldiers set fire to the wigwams, about six hundred of which were instantly consumed. The enemy's corn, stores, and utensils, with many of their old men, women, and children, perished in the conflagration. It was supposed, that three hundred warriors were slain, besides many wounded, who afterwards died of their wounds and with the cold. Nearly the same number were taken, with three hundred women and children. From the number of wigwams in the fort, it is probable that the whole number of the Indians was nearly

Book I.

1675.

Dec. 19

The enemy defeated and their wigwams burnt.

* Manuscripts of the Rev. Mr. Ruggles. He observes, "It is a pity things so curious and remarkable, and wherein the hand of Providence so evidently appeared, as in taking the fort at Narragansett, should be lost. They deserve to be recorded in history."

Book I.
1675.

March to head quarters.

Courage exhibited, and hardships endured.

State of the army on the 20th.

four thousand. Those who were not killed in battle, or did not perish in the flames, fled to a cedar swamp, where they spent the night, without food, fire, or covering.

It was, nevertheless, a dearly bought victory. Six brave captains fell in the action, and eighty men were killed or mortally wounded. A hundred and fifty were wounded, who afterwards recovered. After the fatiguing march, and hard fought battle of three hours, in which the troops had been exercised, the army, just at the setting of the sun, having burnt and destroyed all in their power, left the enemy's ground, and, carrying about two hundred dead and wounded men, marched back, sixteen or eighteen miles, to head quarters. The night was very cold and stormy. The snow fell deep, and it was not until midnight, or after, that the army got in. Many of the wounded, who otherwise might have recovered, died with the cold, and the fatigue and inconveniences of such a distressing march.* After lying the preceding night in the open field, and after all the exertions of so long and sharp an action, the army marched, through snow and a pathless wilderness, in less than twenty-four hours, more than thirty miles. The courage exhibited by every part of the army, the invincible heroism of the officers, the firmness and resolution of the soldiers, when they saw their captains falling before them, and the hardships endured, are hardly credible, and rarely find a parallel in ancient or modern ages. The cold was extreme, and the snow fell so deep that night, that it was difficult, the next day, for the army to move. Many of the soldiers were frozen, and their limbs exceedingly swollen. Four hundred were disabled and unfit for duty. The Connecticut troops were more disabled than those of the other colonies. They had endured a tedious march from Stonington to Pettyquamscot; and as the buildings there were all destroyed, they endured great hardships before their junction with the troops of the other colonies. They had sustained a much greater loss in the action, in proportion to their numbers, than the troops of the other colo-

* It appears, by the letters from the army, that twenty men only were killed in the action. This was the whole number dead, when the army began their march for head quarters. Eight were left on the ground, and twelve carried off by the army. Ten or twelve died on the march, and several next morning, so that on the 20th of December, thirty-four were buried in a grave. Four died the next day, and two the day after. Forty only were dead on the 22d. Though the best surgeons which the country could furnish, were provided, yet the season was so severe, and the accommodations, after all the exertions which could be made, so poor, that, by the end of January, twenty more were in their graves. The number mentioned, as killed, in the ancient histories, included all who were killed or died afterwards of their wounds.

CHAP. XIV.   CONNECTICUT.

nies.† Of the five Connecticut captains, three, Seely, Gallup, and Marshall, were killed, and captain Mason received a wound, of which he died about nine months after. Marshall was killed as he ascended the tree before the log house. The fire of the enemy was dreadful, when the Connecticut men were entering, and after they first entered the fort, until the men who came in upon the backs of them, began to fire their large muskets, loaded with pistol bullets, upon the enemy, where they stood together in the closest manner. This at once disconcerted them, and checked their fire, in that quarter. Gallup and Seely, leading and animating their men, in this dreadful moment, soon fell. The enemy made an obstinate defence, after the men gained the fort the second time, taking the advantage of their block-houses, wigwams, and every covert of which they could avail themselves. Some of the soldiers expended all their ammunition before the action was terminated, and were obliged to seek new supplies.

The troops from Connecticut had sustained such a loss of officers, and were so disabled, that major Treat judged

† The whole number killed and wounded, was about two hundred. From the returns and letters before me, it appears, that of the Massachusetts, there were one hundred killed and wounded, of whom thirty-one were killed or died of their wounds. Among these were captains Johnson, Davenport, and Gardiner. They had, also, a lieutenant Upham mortally wounded, who died afterwards at Boston. Plymouth sustained the loss of twenty killed and wounded; eight or nine, it seems, were killed, or died of their wounds afterwards. Of the three hundred Englishmen from Connecticut, eighty were killed and wounded; twenty in captain Seely's, twenty in captain Gallup's, seventeen in captain Watts's, nine in captain Mason's, and fourteen in captain Marshall's company. Of these about forty were killed, or died of their wounds. About half the loss in this bloody action, fell upon Connecticut. The legislature of the colony, in a representation of the services they had performed in the war, say, "In that signal service, the fort fight, in Narraganset, as we had our full number, in proportion with the other confederates, so all say they did their full proportion of service. Three noble soldiers, Seely, courageous Marshall, and bold Gallup, died in the bed of honour; and valiant Mason, a fourth captain, had his death's wound. There died many brave officers, and sentinels, whose memory is blessed; and whose death redeemed our lives. The bitter cold, the tarled swamp, the tedious march, the strong fort, the numerous and stubborn enemy they contended with, for their God, king and country, be their trophies over death. He that commanded our forces then, and now us, made no less than seventeen fair shots at the enemy, and was thereby as oft a fair mark for them. Our mourners, over all the colony, witness for our men, that they were not unfaithful in that day." It is the tradition, that major, afterwards governor Treat, received a ball through the brim of his hat, and that he was the last man who left the fort, in the dusk of the evening, commanding the rear of the army. The burning the wigwams, the shrieks and cries of the women and children, and the yelling of the warriors, exhibited a most horrible and affecting scene, so that it greatly moved some of the soldiers. They were in much doubt then, and, afterwards, often seriously inquired, whether burning their enemies alive could be consistent with humanity, and the benevolent principles of the gospel. Manuscripts of the Rev. Mr. Thomas Ruggles.

BOOK I.
1675.

it absolutely necessary to return to Connecticut, where he might recruit them, and cover them with more convenience, than could possibly be done in that part of the country. The wounded men, who were not able to travel, were put on board vessels and carried to Rhode-Island. The Connecticut troops, in their march from Stonington to Pettyquamscot, killed six and captivated seven of the enemy. On their return home, they killed and captivated about thirty more.

The Massachusetts and Plymouth troops kept the field the greatest part of the winter, ranged the country, captivated numbers of the enemy, brought in considerable quantities of corn and beans, and burned more than 200 wigwams; but achieved nothing brilliant or decisive. In the whole, in the fort and in the country, the English burned between eight and nine hundred wigwams, and destroyed almost the whole of the enemy's provisions. This was much more distressing, and had a greater influence in their total ruin, than was at first imagined.

Meanwhile, much pains were taken to make peace, and various messages passed between the English and the Indians, on that subject; but they would not accept of any overtures which the colonies thought proper to make to them.

1676.

As the enemy had lost their dwellings and principal stores, in Narraganset, the great body of their warriors moved off to the northward, to the Nipmuck country, and into the wilderness, north of Brookfield. They were not, however, idle. The latter part of January, they drove off, from one man, at Warwick, as they took leave of their country, sixteen horses, fifty neat cattle, and two hundred sheep.

Lancaster burnt. Feb. 10th.
Medfield assaulted. Feb. 20th.

In February, the Narraganset and Nipmuck Indians fell upon Lancaster, and plundered and burned the greatest part of the town. They either killed or captivated forty of the inhabitants.* Some days after, they made an assault on Medfield, killed twenty men, and laid nearly half of the town in ashes.

March was a month of still greater disasters. The towns of Northampton and Springfield, of Chelmsford, Groton, Sudbury, and Marlborough, in Massachusetts, and of Warwick and Providence, in Rhode-Island, were assaulted; and some of them partly, and others entirely, destroyed. Many of the inhabitants were killed, and others led away into a miserable captivity.

* The enemy set fire to the garrison house, and the women and children were all captivated, among whom was the wife and family of Mr. Rowlandson, minister of the town.

CHAP. XIV. CONNECTICUT.

Captain Pierce, about the same time, with fifty Englishmen and twenty friendly Indians, was drawn into an ambush, and surrounded by a great body of the enemy, who slew every Englishman, and the greatest part of the Indians. This was a great loss to so small a colony as Plymouth, to whom captain Pierce and his company belonged. Two days after, the enemy fell upon Rehoboth, in the vicinity of Swanzey, where hostilities first began, and burned forty dwelling houses, besides barns and out houses.

Captain Wadsworth, a brave officer, with fifty men, marching, ten days before, to the relief of Sudbury, was surrounded by a numerous body of the enemy, and fell with his whole party. Massachusetts, at this time, was in great distress and sorrow. It was feared by many, that the whole colony would be depopulated. But it was now full tide with the enemy, they soon received an important check, and began rapidly to decline.

In February, 1676, a number of volunteers from Connecticut, belonging principally to New-London, Norwich, and Stonington, formed themselves into companies, under major Palms, captain George Denison, captain James Avery, and captain John Stanton, for the annoyance of the enemy. They engaged a number of Moheagans, Pequots, and Narragansets, to be associates with them, for the sake of plunder, and other considerations. The Moheagans were commanded by Onecho, one of the sons of Uncas; the Pequots, by Cassasinamon, their chief; and the Narragansets, consisting of about twenty men, by Catapazet. These latter were Ninigrate's men, who, in time past, had given the colonies so much trouble; but at this time they remained quiet, and would not join the other Narraganset sachems.*

These companies began to range the Narraganset country, and harass the enemy, the latter part of February, and continued making their incursions from that time until the enemy were driven from those quarters. As soon as one company returned, another went out immediately, so as to keep the enemy in continual alarm. Their success was admirable.

Captain Denison, of Stonington, on the 27th of March, began a very successful incursion into the country.

Nanuntenoo, or Canonchet, the head sachem of all the Narragansets, son of Miantonimoh, inheritor of all his

* The principal seat of Ninigrate was at Westerly, which formerly belonged to Stonington. He put himself under the English, and he, and his Indians, were the only ones who were not destroyed, or driven from that part of the country.

BOOK I.
1676.

Nanuntte-
noo sur-
prised and
taken.

pride, and of his insolence and hatred towards the English, had ventured down from the northern wilderness to Seaconk, near the seat of Philip, to procure seed corn, to plant the towns which the English had deserted, upon Connecticut river. He had been aiding in the slaughter of captain Pierce and his men just before. After captain Denison and his party had wearied themselves for several days, in hunting the enemy, they came upon their tracks near Blackston's river, and soon discovered, by a squaw whom they took, that Nanunttenoo was in a wigwam, not far distant. The captain made dispositions immediately to surprise him. While he was boasting of that great feat of cutting off captain Pierce, and diverting himself with the story, the English came upon him. Some of his party, discovering them, ran off with great precipitation; but one more faithful than the rest, entered the wigwam and acquainted him with his danger. He instantly fled with all his might. Catapazet, from the manner of his running, suspecting it was Nanunttenoo, gave chase with as much eagerness as he fled. The other Indians, who were most light of foot, joined in the pursuit. They pressed him so hard, that he soon threw off his blanket, and then his silver laced coat, which had been given him at Boston. The pursuers, perceiving that they were not mistaken with respect to the person, employed their utmost exertions to seize him. At length, plunging through the river, his foot slipped, upon a smooth stone, and he fell and wet his gun. One Monopoide, a Pequot, outrunning the other Indians, leaped through the river after him, and soon laid hold upon him. Though he was a man of goodly stature, and of great strength and courage, yet he made no resistance. One Robert Stanton, a young man, was the first Englishman who came up to him. He asked him several questions; but this haughty sachem, looking with disdain upon his youthful countenance, replied, in broken English, "You too much child; no understand matters of war—Let your captain come; him I will answer." This party, in about sixteen days, killed and took nearly fifty of the enemy, without the loss of a single man. This success was more important on account of the capture of the chief sachem, and a number of counsellors and war captains.

Nanunttenoo would not accept of life when offered upon the condition that he should make peace with the English; nor would he so much as send one of his counsellors to make a single proposal for that purpose. When he was made acquainted that it was determined to put him to death, he said, "He liked it well; that he should die before his

CHAP. XIV.   CONNECTICUT.   345

heart was soft, or he had spoken any thing unworthy of himself." The Moheagan sachem, his counsellors, and the principal Pequots, shot him at Stonington. Those brave volunteer captains and their flying parties had, at this time, killed and captivated forty-four of the enemy, and before the end of April, seventy-six more, about a hundred and twenty in one month. Among these was another sachem, a grandson of Pomham, who was esteemed the best soldier and most warlike of all the Narraganset sachems. They made, in the spring, summer, and fall, ten or twelve expeditions, in which they killed and captivated two hundred and thirty of the enemy, took fifty muskets, and brought in one hundred and sixty bushels of their corn. They drove all the Narraganset Indians out of their country, except those at Westerly under Ninigrate.* In all these expeditions they had not one man killed or wounded.† Governor Hutchinson observes, that "the brave actions of the Connecticut volunteers have not been enough applauded. Denison's name ought to be perpetuated."

Book I. 1676.

While Connecticut had the honor and happiness of giving a check to the war, the colony sustained a heavy loss in the death of governor Winthrop. He had been chosen one of the commissioners from Connecticut, the May preceding, to the court of the commissioners of the united colonies. Upon the meeting of this court, early in the spring, he went to Boston, where he was taken sick and died, April 5th, 1676, in the 71st year of his age. He was honorably interred, at Boston, in the same tomb with his father.

Death of Gov. Winthrop, April 5th.

He was the eldest son of the honorable John Winthrop, Esq. the first governor of Massachusetts. His birth was at Groton in England, 1605. His father gave him a liberal education, at the university of Cambridge, in England; and afterwards supported him some years at the university of Dublin, in Ireland. As travelling was considered a great accomplishment to a young gentleman, he travelled into France, Holland, Germany, Italy, and Turkey. With these advantages he returned to England, not only a great scholar, rich in experience and literature, but a most accomplished gentleman. While he collected the literature and excellencies of the various nations and countries through which he passed, he cautiously avoided their errors and vices. He was a puritan of distinguished piety and morals. After his return from his travels, he came into New-England, with his father's family, in 1631, and was

His character.

* Declaration of the volunteers, sworn before governor Saltonstall.
† Hubbard's Narrative, from p. 125 to 131.

T 2

BOOK I.
1676.

chosen one of the magistrates of the colony of Massachusetts. He afterwards went into England; and in 1635, returned with a commission to erect a fort at the mouth of Connecticut river, and to be governor of that part of the country. In 1651, he was chosen one of the magistrates of Connecticut. In 1657, he was elected governor, and the next year deputy governor. In 1659, he was again chosen governor; from which time he was annually rechosen to that office, until his death. He was one of the greatest chymists and physicians of his age, a member of the royal society of philosophical transactions, and one of the most distinguished characters in New-England. He rendered many important services to the colony, was exceedingly beloved in life, and died greatly and universally lamented.

Election, May 11th, William Leet, Esq. chosen governor.

At the election, May 11th, William Leet, Esq. was chosen governor, and Robert Treat, Esq. deputy governor. Captain John Mason was chosen magistrate, to fill the vacancy made by the advancement of major Treat, to the office of deputy governor. No alteration was made with respect to the other officers.

The assembly raise an army.

The assembly voted three hundred and fifty men, who, with the friendly Indians, were to be a standing army, to defend the country and harass the enemy. Major John Talcott was appointed to the chief command. The Rev. Gershom Bulkley, of Weathersfield, was appointed surgeon, and Mr. James Fitch, chaplain. Mr. Bulkley was viewed as one of the greatest physicians and surgeons then in Connecticut. The assembly ordered that the surgeon and chaplain should be of the council of war.

Major Talcott commander.

Major Talcott, on his appointment to the command of the army, resigned the office of treasurer, and William Pitkin, Esq. was appointed to that office, by the assembly.

The first general rendezvous of the army, this year, was at Norwich. From thence major Talcott marched, the beginning of June, with about two hundred and fifty English soldiers and two hundred Moheagan and Pequot Indians, up towards the Wabaquasset country, scouring the woods through that long tract. They found the country every where deserted. The fort and wigwams at Wabaquasset were deserted. Nothing more could be done there, than demolish the Indian fortress and destroy about fifty acres of corn which the enemy had planted. On the 5th of June, the army marched to Chanagongum, in the Nipmuck country. There they killed nineteen Indians, and took thirty-three captives.* The army then marched to Qua-

* Major Talcott's letter to the committee of war, June 8, 1676.

CHAP. XIV.   CONNECTICUT.   347

haug, or Brookfield, and thence to Northampton. This was a long march, in which the troops suffered greatly for want of provisions. It has ever since, in Connecticut, been known by the name of the long and hungry march. Major Talcott expected to have met with the Massachusetts forces at Brookfield, or in that vicinity, but they did not arrive.

On the 12th of June, four days after the arrival of the Connecticut troops at Northampton, about seven hundred Indians made a furious attack upon Hadley; but major Talcott, with his party, soon appeared for the relief of the garrison, and drove off the enemy. His seasonable arrival was, providentially, a happy circumstance, which probably saved Hadley, and other towns upon the river.

Some time after, the Massachusetts forces arrived, and, in conjunction with major Talcott and his soldiers, scoured the woods on both sides the river, as far as the falls at Deerfield. The enemy, by this time, had made their escape from that part of the country. The army broke up their fisheries, destroyed their fish and other stores, recovered some stolen goods, and returned, without effecting any thing very important.

After major Talcott had spent about three weeks in service upon the river, he left that quarter, and marched through the wilderness, towards Providence and the Narraganset country. On the 1st of July, the army came near a large body of the enemy, and took four. Two days after, major Talcott surprised the main body of them, by the side of a large cedar swamp. He made such a disposition of his men, and attacked them so suddenly, that a considerable number were killed and taken on the spot; others escaped to the swamp. The troops compassed the swamp, and, after an action of two or three hours, killed and took 171. Thirty-four warriors were killed in the action, and also Magnus, the sunk squaw, or old queen of Narraganset; 90 of the captives were killed, and between 40 and 50 women and children preserved alive.

The same day, the troops marched to Providence, and compassed the neck there, and afterwards, Warwick neck; in which places they killed and captured 67. Eighteen were killed. In these several rencontres, 238 were killed and taken, with about 30 arms.*

About the 5th of July, the army returned to Connecticut. In their route, they took 60 more of the enemy. From about the beginning of April to the 6th of July, the Con-

*Major Talcott's letter to the council of war, July 4th, 1676.

Marginal notes: Book I. 1676. Hungry march. July 3d.

Book I. necticut volunteers, and the troops under major Talcott, killed and captivated about 420 of the enemy.†

1676.

The enemy, about this time, fell into a state of division, fear, and astonishment. They found that, 'by attempting to destroy their English neighbours, they had utterly ruined themselves. A complication of evils conspired for their destruction. The destruction of their fort and principal stores, in the dead of winter, the burning of their wigwams, and bringing off their corn and beans, in all parts of the country, put them to inexpressible hardships and distresses. They had been able to plant but little, in the spring; what they had planted, the English had destroyed; they had been driven from the sea and rivers, and cut off from almost every kind of subsistence. They had been obliged to lie in swamps and marshes; to feed on horse flesh, and other unwholesome food; all which gendered infirmity and death; so that they became debilitated and disheartened by fatigue, famine, disease, and mortality.‡ They could not keep together in any considerable bodies, for want of sustenance. They were pursued and hunted from swamp to swamp, and from one lurking place to another; so that, in July and August, they began to come in to the English, in large bodies, and surrender themselves to the mercy of their conquerors.

Distressed condition of the enemy.

The enemy fly to the westward.

Major Talcott pursues and surprises them.

Major Talcott, after his return from Narraganset, having recruited his men a short time in Connecticut, took his station at Westfield. While he lay there, a large body of the enemy was discovered fleeing to the westward. Major Talcott pursued them, and on the third day, about half way between Westfield and Albany, discovered them lying on the west side of Housatonick river, entirely secure. It was judged too late in the day to attack them to any purpose. The army, therefore, retreated, and lay upon their arms, in great silence, during the night. Towards morning, the troops were formed in two divisions. One was ordered to pass the river below the enemy, and to advance and compass them in on that side. The other party, creeping silently up to the east bank of the river, were to lie prepared instantly to fire, when they should receive the signal from the other division, who, when they had reached their ground, were to fire a single gun. But this well contrived plan was in some measure disconcerted. An Indian had left his companions in a dead sleep, and proceeded down

† Hubbard's Narrative, p. 131, 164, 166. Hutchinson's history, vol. i. p. 305, 306.
‡ Some of the captives reported, that more died by sickness, than the sword.

CHAP. XIV.   CONNECTICUT.

the river to catch fish. As the division on the west side of the river was advancing to surround the enemy, he discovered them, and roared out, "Awanaux, Awanaux." Upon this, one of the party fired, and killed him on the spot. The other division, on the east bank of the river, supposing this to be the signal gun, discharged upon the enemy, as they were rising in surprise, or lay upon the ground, and killed and wounded a great number of them. Those who were not killed, or disabled by wounds, instantly fled, leaving their camp, baggage, provisions, and many of their arms. As the division on the west side, had not advanced to the ground designed, before the alarm was given, the enemy made their escape with much less damage, than otherwise they could have done. The troops pursued them some distance, but the woods were so extremely thick, that they soon disappeared, and the army returned. The sachem of Quabaug or Brookfield was killed, and 44 other Indians were killed and taken. Among the killed were 25 warriors.*

Book I.
1676.
Sachem of Brookfield killed.

Several brave captains and officers in the Massachusetts, in July and August, were very successful. Captain Church, of Plymouth, afterwards major Church, a famous partisan, took several small parties of the enemy. The Indians, who were taken or came in to the English to save their own lives, betrayed their friends, and led the English captains to their haunts and hiding places. Thus assisted, the Massachusetts and Plymouth soldiers hunted Philip from week to week, and from place to place. They killed and captured his brother, his counsellors, and chief men, his wife and family ; but his mind continued firm and unbroken. In the midst of all this misfortune and distress, he would hear no proposals of peace. At length, on the 12th of August, captain Church, led by one of Philip's men, whom he had disaffected, by shooting his brother, only for proposing to him to make peace with the colonies, surprised this famous sachem, in a swamp, near Mount Hope. As he was flying to make his escape, the Indian who had been guide to the party, shot him through the heart. Thus fell a brave enemy, who had defended himself and his country, and what he imagined to be his own, and the just rights of his countrymen, to the last extremity.

Philip killed, Aug. 12th.

The Indians in this part of the country, now generally submitted to the English, or fled and incorporated with distant and strange nations. After this time, very little damage was done.

* Manuscripts of the Rev. Thomas Ruggles and Hubbard's Narrative.

BOOK I.
1676.

Connecticut offered the same conditions to the enemy, upon their submission, which had been given to the Pequots: That they should have life, liberty, protection, and ground to plant. Some principal incendiaries and murderers, however, were excepted. They disdained to accept the terms, and generally fled their country. The Nipmucks, Nashawas, Pocomtocks, the Hadley and Springfield Indians, fled to the French and their Indians, in Canada. About 200 of them, after their surprise at Housatonick river, fled to the Moheaganders, upon Hudson's river, incorporated and became one with them.

When Philip began the war, he, and his kinswoman, Wetamoe, had about 500 warriors, and the Narragansets nearly 2000. The Nipmuck, Nashawa, Pocomtock, Hadley, and Springfield Indians, were considerably numerous. It is probable, therefore, that there were about 3000 warriors combined for the destruction of the New-England colonies, exclusive of the eastern Indians. The war terminated in their entire conquest, and almost total extinction. At the same time, it opened a wide door to extensive settlement and population.

Losses in the war.

This, however, in its connection with the war with the eastern Indians, which commenced about the same time, was the most impoverishing and distressing, of any which New-England has ever experienced, from its first settlement to the present time. The war with the eastern Indians continued until the spring of the year 1678. The enemy killed and captivated great numbers of the people, captured nearly twenty fishing vessels, with their crews, and rioted in plunder and devastation, until most of the settlements in those parts were swept away, and the country was reduced to their domination.*

About 600 of the inhabitants of New-England, the greatest part of whom were the flower and strength of the country, either fell in battle, or were murdered by the enemy. A great part of the inhabitants of the country were in deep mourning. There were few families or individuals who had not lost some near relative or friend. Twelve or thirteen towns, in Massachusetts, Plymouth, and Rhode-Island, were utterly destroyed, and others greatly damaged. About 600 buildings, chiefly dwelling houses, were consumed with fire.† An almost insuperable debt was con-

* Dr. Belknap's hist. vol. i. p. 157, 159.
† This statement of the loss of lives, towns, and buildings, is made from an accurate enumeration of the various numbers mentioned, in the ancient histories, of the lives lost, and of the towns and buildings burned. But as there were, doubtless, many persons killed, and others who died of their wounds, not mentioned in those accounts, they must have exceeded the

tracted by the colonies, when their numbers, dwellings, goods, cattle, and all their resources, were greatly diminished.

Connecticut, indeed, had suffered nothing, in comparison with her sister colonies. Her towns and inhabitants had been preserved from the ravages of the enemy; but about a seventh part of the whole militia was out upon constant service, besides the volunteers. A large proportion was obliged to watch and guard the towns at home. The particular towns were necessitated to fortify themselves with an inclosure of pallisades, and to prepare and fortify particular dwellings for garrison houses, which might, in the best manner, command the respective towns; and to which the aged people, women, and children might repair, and be in safety, in the time of danger. For three years after the war commenced, the inhabitants paid eleven pence on the pound, upon the grand list, exclusive of all town and parish taxes. After the war was finished, they had a considerable debt to discharge. The colony, nevertheless, was highly distinguished and favoured in many respects. The numerous Indians within it, were not only peaceable, but the Moheagans and Pequots were of great service in the war. They were not only a defence to the eastern towns, but especially advantageous in discovering and harassing the enemy, and in preventing a surprise by them. Connecticut had not one party of men surprised and cut off during the war; nor did the colony sustain any considerable loss of men, at any time, except in taking the fort in Narraganset. At the same time, the legislature and people were happy, in giving seasonable and powerful assistance to their confederates, and in repeatedly rescuing whole towns and parties, when in the most imminent danger.

number here stated. The histories of those troubles, rarely mention the barns, stores, and out houses burned; and sometimes there is notice of the burning of part of a town, and of the buildings in such a tract, without any specification of the number. All the buildings in Narraganset, from Providence to Stonington, a tract of about fifty miles, were burned, or otherwise destroyed, by the enemy, but the number is not mentioned. The loss of buildings must, therefore, have been much greater than has been mentioned.

The militia of Connecticut, in 1675, amounted to 2,250 men. Of these, the commissioners required 315, as their proportion of the 1,000 men then to be raised.

If the proportion was just, there were about 7,150 of the militia of the united colonies. Reckoning every fifth man a soldier, and five persons to every family, there were 7,150 families, and 35,750 inhabitants, at that time in the united colonies. According to this estimation, about one fencible man in eleven was killed, and every eleventh family was burnt out; or an eleventh part of the whole militia, and of all the buildings of the united colonies were swept away by this predatory war. This greatly exceeded the loss in the late war with Great-Britain, in proportion to the numbers and wealth of the United States.

CHAPTER XV.

Measures adopted to discharge the public debt, and settle the country in peace. The reasons of the colony's claim to Narraganset. The former settlers and owners of land there apply to Connecticut for protection. Major Treat goes to the upper towns upon Connecticut river, to treat with the Indians. Fasts appointed through New-England. Act concerning the conquered lands in Narraganset. Navigation act grievous to the colonies. Governor Leet takes the oath respecting trade and navigation. Answers to queries from the lords of trade and plantations. Protest against Sir Edmund Andross's claim to Fisher's Island. Character of Governor Leet. Commissioners appointed, by his majesty, to examine and make report, concerning all claims to the Narraganset country, or king's province. They report in favour of Connecticut. Answers to the renewed claim of the Duke of Hamilton, and opinions on the case. Connecticut congratulates the arrival of Colonel Dungan, governor of New-York, and agree with him respecting the boundary line between that colony and Connecticut. Petition to King James II. Settlement of Waterbury. Quo warrantos against the colony. The assembly petition his majesty to continue their charter privileges. Sir Edmund Andross made governor of New-England. Arrives at Hartford, and takes the government, by order of his majesty. The oppression and cruelty of his administration. Distressed and sorrowful state of the people.

CONNECTICUT had now conquered the Narraganset country, and, in conjunction with the other confederates, terminated the war in this part of New-England. Oct. 12th. The legislature, therefore, addressed themselves to discharge the public debt; to settle the friendly Indians in a state of peace among themselves, and with the colonies; and to extend their settlements in the Narraganset country, as well as in other parts of their jurisdiction. To discharge the public debt, they levied a tax of eight pence on the pound, upon the whole list of the colony, in October annually, during the term of two years. They appointed a committee to hear all affairs, which the Moheagans, Pequots, and Narragansets, under Ninigrate, or Ninicraft, had to lay before them; and to do whatever they should judge expedient to promote peace among them, and to preserve their friendship and attachment to the English. For their encouragement, the legislature granted liberty for them to hunt, in all the conquered lands, during their pleasure. They were also authorised to kill and destroy any of the enemy, who should return to their country, without submitting to the colony and accepting the terms which had been offered them.

Book I.

1677.

At the election, in May, 1677, there was no alteration in the legislature, excepting the choice of Andrew Leet, Esq. into the magistracy, instead of captain John Mason, who died, the September before, of the wounds he had received in taking the Narraganset fort. The same governor, deputy governor, and magistrates were re-elected for several years successively. A committee was appointed, by the assembly, to settle all affairs of government in the Narraganset country, and to report what places there were there adapted to the purpose of planting new towns.

Court of election, May 10, 1677.

As the Rhode-Islanders had deserted the country, in the war, and had done nothing in the defence of it, and as the Connecticut volunteers had driven the enemy entirely from that extensive tract, the legislature determined to plant and govern it, as part of this colony.

Determination of Connecticut to settle and govern Narraganset.

For various reasons they viewed the act of his majesty's commissioners, determining that Rhode-Island and Narraganset should be a province for the king, as a mere nullity. Their commission gave them no power to make new colonies. It required that colonel Nichols should always be one of the council, that any of its acts might be valid; but he was not present at that determination. Further, colonel Nichols, with two or three of his council, afterwards reversed that judgment.

Reasons of their determination.

In the same point of light they viewed the agreement with Mr. Clark, as it was after Mr. Winthrop had obtained the Connecticut charter, and sent it to the colony, at which time his agency was terminated. Further, that agreement was entirely alien from the business of his agency, and without any instructions or authority from the colony. The agreement with Mr. Clark was considered as a nullity, in another point of light, as the charter to Rhode-Island recognized and had reference to one article of the agreement only, and as Rhode-Island had never submitted to one of the other articles. In direct contravention of them, they had invaded the property of the settlers named in it, wantonly carried off the productions of their lands and fruits of their labors, driven off their cattle, forced the inhabitants from their possessions, burned their fences,

Book I. and even pulled down their houses.* They had claimed jurisdiction over them, after they had, in the year 1663, chosen to belong to Connecticut, and formally put themselves under the government of that colony. They had not regarded the agreement even with respect to the boundaries, but attempted to extend their limits beyond what was expressed in the charter. Besides, when his majesty had previously granted that tract to Connecticut, there remained, in law and reason, no further right in him to that country. He had nothing there further to grant. Therefore he could grant nothing there to Rhode-Island. Connecticut well knew that Pawcatuck never was called Narraganset river, and that the Narragansets never extended their claims so far westward; but that Pawcatuck, and the country some miles to the east of it, belonged to the Pequots.† For these reasons, the legislature considered their title and claim to this part of the colony as clear and just, as to any other part of it whatever.

1677.

Mr. Hutchinson and others petition for protection.

Elisha Hutchinson, William Hudson, and others, their associates, claiming a large tract in the Pequot and Narraganset country,‡ applied to the general assembly for their assistance and protection, against Rhode-Island, in the re-settlement of their lands. The assembly determined to extend their protection and government to them.

Oct. 11.

At the session in October, the upper towns, upon Connecticut river, sent messengers to the assembly, acquainting them, that there were considerable bodies of Indians collected together in their vicinity; and that they made proposals of peace. The messengers solicited the assembly to send major Treat, the deputy governor, with a detachment of forty men, to Northampton, to treat with them, or to defend those towns, as occasion might require. The assembly complied with the request, and the deputy governor proceeded immediately to Northampton. He was instructed, in the first place, to use his utmost endeavours for the redemption of the captives, with money, goods, or by any other means in his power. The terms of peace, which he was authorized to propose, were life and liberty, upon the submission of the Indians to the English, in the

---

* Prayer of the inhabitants to the general court of Connecticut, on file, representing the outrages of the Rhode-Islanders.

† Case of Connecticut, with respect to Narraganset, stated, in which these articles are largely insisted on.

‡ It appears, by the report of the committee, appointed to view and make report concerning the state of Narraganset, that the gentlemen mentioned above, major Atherton, and their associates, owned a tract of more than 5,000 acres, only on what was called Boston neck, and that large tracts were owned by other purchasers. Indeed the principal part of Narraganset was owned by them.

several places where they should be settled. He was directed to assure the Indians of protection and safety during the treaty. It does not appear, that many of the northern Indians accepted the terms proposed, or ever returned to their former places of abode. Little more appears to have been effected by the treaty, than the redemption of some of the captives.

The colonies, at this time, had many enemies, and the most injurious complaints and unfavorable representations were made of them in England. Edward Randolph, especially, whom the people of New-England represented as going about to destroy them, was indefatigable in his complaints against them, and in aggravating whatever he imagined might serve to their disadvantage. He came over to Boston, in 1676, and annually, in person or by writing, made complaints against them. He generally returned to England in the fall, and in the spring or summer, came over fraught with new mischief. He busied himself, among other affairs, in complaining of the colonies for their opposition to the acts of trade and navigation. Unhappily for Great-Britain and the colonies, they were suffering under an arbitrary prince, inimical to the civil and religious rights of his subjects. His ear was open to complaints against those, who did not cheerfully submit to his despotic impositions; and he readily promoted those who made them. The colonies knew how affairs were conducted in England, and were deeply apprehensive of the danger they were in, of a total deprivation of their liberties.

The commissioners of the united colonies, in these views, recommended a general fast to the confederate colonies to humble themselves for their offences, and to pray for the divine favor, in the continuation of their just rights and privileges.

In consequence of this recommendation, the general assembly of Connecticut appointed the third Tuesday in November a public fast, in union with their confederates, to humble themselves, and pray for the purposes recommended.

The general assembly, at their session in May, 1679, to prevent the people of Rhode-Island, and other intruders, from taking up lands in Narraganset, enacted, that none of the conquered lands should be taken up, or laid out into farms, without special and express order from them.*

The Rhode-Islanders, in the time of danger, deserted the country and bore no part in the war. However, as

* Records of Connecticut.

Book I. soon as the inhabitants, who had settled under Connecticut, began to return to their former settlements, to build 1679. upon their lands, and cultivate their farms, under the government of this colony, the legislature of Rhode-Island began to usurp authority and practice their former vexations.

John Cranston, Esq. governor of Rhode-Island, held a court in Narraganset, in September, and made attempts to introduce the authority and officers of Rhode-Island, into that part of Connecticut. The general assembly therefore, in October, protested against his usurpation, and declared his acts to be utterly void. They also prohibited all the inhabitants to receive any office from the legislature of Rhode-Island, or to yield obedience to its authority.*

May 13, 1680, Gov. Leet took the navigation oath.

The acts of trade and navigation were exceedingly grievous to the colonies. They viewed them as utterly inconsistent with their chartered rights. This made them extremely unwilling to submit to them. Massachusetts never would fully submit; but as it was matter of great and continual complaint against the colonies, and as his majesty insisted on the respective governors taking the oath, respecting trade and navigation, it was judged expedient, that governor Leet should take it, in the presence of the assembly. It was accordingly administered to him, at the session in May, 1680.

This assembly ordered, that a letter should be written to the general court of Massachusetts, desiring their concurrence in mutually settling the line between that colony and Connecticut. It was requested, that the court would appoint a committee fully authorised for that purpose, to join with one from Connecticut vested with similar powers. If the general court of the Massachusetts should refuse to comply with this proposal, then the governor and his council, with such as they should appoint to that service, were authorised to run the line without them.

Answers to queries, July 15, 1680.

The lords of trade and plantations having transmitted a number of queries to the governor and company, the governor and council were desired to answer them. By their answers, it appears, that there were twenty-six towns in the colony:† that the militia, including horse and foot, consisted, in 1679, of 2,507 men: that the annual exports were about 9,000l.: that there were in the colony about twenty small merchants, trading to Boston, New-York, Newfoundland, and the West-Indies: and that its shipping consisted of four ships, three pinks, eight sloops, and

---

* Records of Connecticut.
† Rye and Bedford appear to have been included in this number.

other small vessels, amounting in the whole to twenty-seven, the tonnage of which was only 1,050. The number of inhabitants is not mentioned, but, from the number of the militia, it must have been nearly 12,000. To one of the enquiries, the following answer is given: "If so be Hartford, New-London, New-Haven, and Fairfield, might be made free ports, for fifteen or twenty years, it would be a means to bring trade there, and much increase the navigation and wealth of this poor colony."*

About this time, Sir Edmund Andross, governor of New-York, asserted his right of jurisdiction over Fisher's Island, as included in the duke of York's patent.

Upon this claim, the legislature of the colony asserted, "that the said island was a part, and member of this colony of Connecticut, and under the government thereof; and that they have ever exercised, and shall, and will exercise government there, as occasion shall require; and do hereby declare, and protest against sir Edmund Andross, and all other persons, their claims, or exercise of any authority or government, on, or over the said island."

At the election, in 1683, major Robert Treat was chosen governor, and James Bishop deputy-governor. The former magistrates were generally re-chosen; but by reason of several vacancies which had been made, captain Robert Chapman, captain James Fitch, Mr. Samuel Mason, and Mr. Joseph Whiting, were elected magistrates. The change of governors was occasioned by the death of governor Leet, who, after faithfully serving the colonies, for many years, had now finished his course.‡

---
* Connecticut book of patents, letters, &c.

‡ The governor, William Leet, Esq. was bred a lawyer in England, and was, for a considerable time, clerk of a bishop's court. In this service he became acquainted with the conduct of the bishops towards the puritans, with the pleas, and serious conversation and conduct of the latter, when arraigned before them. He observed the great severity which the court exercised towards them, for going to hear good sermons in the neighbouring parishes, when they had none at home, and what light matters they made of wantonness, and other instances of gross sin, and how much better persons guilty of such crimes were treated, than the puritans. This brought him to a serious consideration of the affair, and to acquaint himself more thoroughly with the doctrines and discipline of the puritans. In consequence of this he became a puritan, left the bishop's court, and, in 1638, came into New-England, with Mr. Whitfield and his company. He was one of the seven pillars of his church. In 1643, he was chosen magistrate for the colony of New-Haven, and was annually re-elected, until May, 1658. He was then chosen deputy-governor of that colony, in which office he continued until he was elected governor in 1661. He continued chief magistrate of that colony, until the union in 1665. He was then chosen one of the magistrates of Connecticut. In 1669, he was elected deputy-governor, and was annually re-elected, until 1676, when he was chosen governor of Connecticut. During the term of forty years, he was magistrate, deputy-governor, or governor of one or other of the colonies.

BOOK I.
1683.

Commission to Edward Cranfield, &c. April 7th, 1683.

As there had been long disputes relative to the Narraganset country, and as the king, in consequence of the act of his commissioners, in 1665, claimed it as his province, commissioners were appointed to hear and determine all titles and claims respecting that tract. On the 7th of April, 1683, his majesty king Charles II. granted a commission to Edward Cranfield, Esq. lieutenant-governor of New-Hampshire, William Stoughton, Joseph Dudley, Edward Randolph, Samuel Shrimpton, John Fitz Winthrop, Edward Palms, Nathaniel Saltonstall, and John Pynchon, jun. Esquires, or any three of them, of whom Edward Cranfield, or Edward Randolph was to be of the quorum, "to examine and enquire into the respective claims and titles, as well of his majesty, as of all persons and corporations whatsoever, to the immediate jurisdiction, government, or propriety of the soil of a certain tract of land, within his majesty's dominion of New-England, called the king's province, or Narraganset country; and to call before them any person, or persons, and to search records, as they shall find requisite, and the proceedings therein, with the opinions upon the matters that shall be examined by them, to state, and with all convenient speed, report thereof to make to his majesty."

The commissioners convened on the 22d of August, 1683, at the house of Richard Smith, in the Narraganset country. They summoned all persons and corporations, in whatever place, who were concerned in the title or government of that country, to appear before them, and to produce all charters, deeds, records, letters, and orders, from his majesty and council, or of any of his commissioners, to the respective colonies, governors, or governments, which might give information on the subject. At the time and place appointed, the records represent, "that there was the greatest appearance of the most ancient English and Indians, then living, to testify the truth of their knowledge," respecting the matters then to be determined.

The commissioners, having fully heard every thing respecting the claims and title to that part of New-England, adjourned to Boston, and there made a report to his majesty, in an ample manner, declaring, that the government of it belonged to Connecticut. The report, so far as it respects this colony, and can reflect light on the subject, is as followeth.

In both colonies he presided in times of the greatest difficulty, yet always conducted himself with such integrity and wisdom, as to meet the public approbation. After he was chosen governor of Connecticut, he removed to Hartford, where he died full of years and good works. He left a numerous offspring. One of his sons, Andrew Leet, Esq. was some years one of the magistrates of the colony.

CHAP. XV. CONNECTICUT.

"In humble obedience to your majesty's commands, we, your majesty's commissioners, have seriously considered the several claims before us. We find, that your majesty, by your letters patent, dated at Westminster, the three and twentieth of April, in the fourteenth year of your majesty's reign, granted to the governor and company of Connecticut, and their successors, all that part of your dominions in New-England, bounded on the east by Narraganset bay, where the said river falls into the sea, and on the north by the line of the Massachusetts plantation, and on the south by the sea."

Book I.

1683. Report relative to the Narraganset country, Oct. 20th, 1683.

"We have also had information, that, some time after your majesty's grant, and said patent was sent to your colony of Connecticut, the said country of the Narraganset was likewise, by patent, granted by your majesty to the governor and company of Rhode-Island plantation, and is, by charter, bounded by a river called Pawcatuck, which, by said charter, is for ever to be accounted and called the Narraganset river: And this latter grant of your majesty to Rhode-Island, seems to be founded upon advice submitted to by John Winthrop, Esq. said to be agent for Connecticut colony, and Mr. John Clark, agent for Rhode-Island; to which Connecticut plead, that Mr. Winthrop's agency for them ceased, when he had obtained and sent the patent to them; and that no submission, or act of his, could invalidate, or deprive them of any of the benefits graciously granted by your majesty's charter: and that, notwithstanding the seeming boundaries, set by said articles, signed by Mr. Winthrop and Mr. Clark, it is in the same articles provided, that the proprietors and inhabitants of the Narraganset country should choose to which of the two governments to belong, and that they unanimously chose and subjected to the government of Connecticut."

"With humble submission, we cannot see any cause to judge, that the said Pawcatuck river anciently was, or ought to be, called or accounted the Narraganset river."

I. "Because it lies some miles within the Pequot country, a nation, till extirpated by the English, often, or always, at war with the Narragansets, and to which territories the Narragansets never pretended."

II. "Because Pawcatuck river falls into the sea many miles westward of any part of Narraganset bay, which is the river anciently called Narraganset river, both because it, on the eastward, washes and bounds the whole length of the Narraganset country; and for that Plymouth colony, which hath now been planted near three score years, have ever since bounded themselves according to the sense and

BOOK I.
1683.

meaning, or limitation of their patent, by the same bay, called Narraganset river, towards the south."

"Thus, after most strict and impartial inquiry and examination, having stated, we most humbly lay before your majesty the several original claims and pretensions offered to us with respect to the propriety, both of jurisdiction and soil, in your majesty's province, or Narraganset country; and, in further obedience to your said commission, have seriously weighed and considered all evidences, pleas, proofs, and allegations, &c. and with most humble submission and reservation of your majesty's right, offer our opinions, that by virtue of your said letters patent, granted to Connecticut, jurisdiction in, and through the said province, or Narraganset country, of right belongs to the colony of Connecticut; and that propriety of soil, as derived from Mr. Winthrop and major Atherton, is vested upon the heirs and assigns of said Mr. Winthrop, the heirs of Thomas Chiffinch, Esq. major Atherton, Mr. Richard Smith, Mr. Simon Lynde, Mr. Elisha Hutchinson, Mr. John Saffin, Mr. Richard Wharton, and partners."

"Finally, we hold it our duty humbly to inform your majesty, that so long as the pretensions of the Rhode-Islanders to the government of the said province continue, it will much discourage the settlement and improvement thereof; it being very improbable, that either the aforenamed claimers, or others of like reputation and condition, will remove their families, or expend their estates under so loose and weak a government."

"Your majesty's most loyal and obedient subjects.
"EDWARD CRANFIELD,
"WILLIAM STOUGHTON,
"SAMUEL SHRIMPTON,
"JOHN PYNCHEON, jun.
"NATHANIEL SALTONSTALL."

"Boston, Oct. 20th, 1683."

Edward Randolph, Esq. claims duke Hamilton's lands.

Connecticut had no sooner gained their point against the claims of his majesty and Rhode-Island, than they were obliged to answer to a new antagonist. Edward Randolph, Esq. on the 30th of June, 1683, had received a power of attorney from William and Ann, duke and duchess of Hamilton, and James, earl of Aran, son and heir of William and Ann, and grandson of James, marquis of Hamilton, to sue for and recover their right and interest in lands, islands, houses, and tenements, in New-England. He appeared before the commissioners at Boston, and, in the name of the said duke, duchess, and earl, claimed the lands which they supposed had been granted to their ancestor, in the deed of 1635.

This renewed claim of that tract of country, occasioned answers from the proprietors of the lands, and from Connecticut, with several opinions on the case.

It may be proper to communicate the substance of these to the public.

Mr. Saffin, in November, gave the following answer, in behalf of the proprietors.

"The ends aimed at and propounded in the king's charter to the great council of Plymouth, was the propagation of the gospel among the heathen, and the enlargement of his majesty's empire, by plantation; and whatsoever grants were made by said council, were founded upon those considerations; which being not pursued, rendereth all grants of land void. *Qui sentit commodum, incommodum sentire debet et onus.** And it doth not appear, that his grace, (as other patentees,) did transport any person, or plant any colony, nor used any other means, either to instruct the natives, or purchase their right in the lands, or appointed any agent to take possession, in order to the improvement of the same. But it is probable, that the duke, understanding a former patent was granted, by the council of Devon, to the lords Say and Brook, &c. in and about the year 1631, and purchased and improved by the colony of Connecticut, might divert him from any procedure therein. The copy of said patent, as we have been informed, when exhibited by John Winthrop, Esq. before the king in council, the then lord chancellor, Hyde, declared, the lords Say and Brook's title to be good and unquestionable; and upon that interest, we presume, it was, that Connecticut made application to his majesty, and that their charter was granted; the lords Say and Brook, and partners, having expended nine thousand pounds in settlement of the lands claimed by his grace; and had made considerable improvements and fortifications upon the lands, in several places, divers years before the date of duke Hamilton's grant.

"Our present gracious sovereign, &c. hath, by his royal letters, manifested his approbation of the purchase, possession, and improvement of his loyal subjects, the proprietors here. The said proprietors have been necessarily engaged in a bloody war with the Indians, in their late rebellion.

"We further humbly offer, that, in regard that the copy of the duke's deed, presented by Mr. Randolph, in behalf of his grace, seems to have no signification of any hand or seal affixed to it, nor mention made of any witnesses, said

Book I.

1683.

Mr. Saffin's answer.

---

* He who enjoys the benefit of a grant, ought to bear its disadvantage and burthen.

BOOK I.
⁓⁓⁓
1683.

Answer of Connecticut to duke Hamilton.

to be the original instrument, (yet affirmed to be a true copy thereof,) it may be presumed the said original deed was never completed according to law."

The governor and council of Connecticut answered, December 13th, 1683, in the manner following.

"As to the substance of the duke's claim, so far as it concerns us, it is preceded, some years, by a grant from the right honourable, Robert, earl of Warwick, to the lord Say, and other persons of honour and credit, March 19th, 1631, whereas his grace's deed was made four years after, viz. on the 20th of April, 1635.

"By virtue of his majesty's grant to lords Say, Brook, &c. they, and their assigns, our predecessors, did, at their own proper charge, about the year 1634, begin to enter upon the said lands, and so have continued ever since, in actual possession and improvement thereof, without challenge or claim from duke Hamilton: which improvement hath been with great cost, hazard, and labour of his majesty's subjects; yet by the blessing of God, and his majesty's grace, hath, in a good measure, answered the ends of those grants or patents; as the propagating the christian religion, and the increase and enlargement of his majesty's empire: of all which, his grace, duke Hamilton, hath, in these parts, done nothing that we know of."

"His present majesty, understanding the condition of his subjects in this colony, upon our humble address, April 23d, 1662, was graciously pleased to grant us a charter, for holding the lands therein granted firm, to us and our successors, for ever; and in his letters, dated April 23d, 1664, sent to us by his majesty's honourable commissioners, he is pleased to call his grant a renewing of our charter, which must relate to that grant made by the earl of Warwick, in the year 1631; for we had no other, before his majesty's grant and confirmation aforesaid.

"Under these securities and encouragements, we laid out our estates, labors, &c. and suddenly after our first settling we were engaged in a bloody war, anno 37, with the Pequots, which was chargeable and expensive to us. Also, in the year 1675, a great people, who inhabited the Narraganset country, rose up against his majesty's subjects, who were planted in these parts, slew many of them, burnt their houses, and destroyed their cattle, whereby we were engaged in another bloody war, which was the cause of great expense of blood and treasure, (his grace duke Hamilton being no partaker with us in any of those expenses, or helper of us therein,) and by the assistance of Almighty God, and countenance of his majesty, in both these forementioned wars, we overcame our enemies, that rose up against us, without which all our grants would have been of little benefit to us.

"It is required by his majesty's good laws, as in the twenty-first of king James, 10th, that the duke, and all others, should have sued out his claims: The reason of which law, as it is very great, so it is pleadable on our account; for it being latent unto us, for near fifty years, would prove our ruin, if thereupon our property be altered. Had the duke's grace, or his predecessors timeously set his claim, in competition with lord Say's patent, that we had purchased, the people had known how to have applied themselves; but after half a century's settlement, as aforesaid, we hope his majesty will be pleased to secure the same to his good subjects here.

"We desire, that we may have a more fit opportunity to make a more full answer, and to present our proofs.

"Per order of the governor and council,
"signed per me,
"JOHN ALLEN, Secretary."

Some years after, several opinions, by gentlemen learned in the law, were given on the case, both as it respected the duke of Hamilton and the colony of Rhode-Island.

Sir Francis Pemberton, having largely stated the case between Connecticut and the duke of Hamilton, says, "Marquis Hamilton, nor his heirs, or any deriving from him, have ever had possession or laid out any thing upon the premises, nor made any claim, in said country, until the year 1683, which was about forty-eight years after said grant, the said heir by his attorney, claimed the said lands, at Boston, in New-England, which is above seventy miles from the premises, and in another country."

"The heir of said marquis Hamilton, after threescore and two years, demands the said premises, or a quit rent. I am of the opinion, that the heir of M. H. after such purchases and so long quiet enjoyment of them, &c. ought not to recover any of the lands or grounds or quit-rents out of them.

"I am of opinion, that these purchasers, by virtue of their purchases, and so long and uninterrupted possession under them, have an undoubted right and title to these grounds and lands, and the buildings and improvement of them, and ought not now, after so much money laid out upon them, and such enjoyment of them, to be disturbed in their possession of them.

"FRANCIS PEMBERTON."

Mr. Trevor, having stated the case between Connecticut

Book I. and Rhode-Island, gives his opinion to the lords of trade and plantations, in the words following. "I am humbly of opinion, that this grant to Rhode-Island is *void in law*, because the country of Narraganset bay was granted before to Connecticut, and that therefore the government of Narraganset bay doth, of right, belong to Connecticut, and not to Rhode-Island: all which is humbly submitted to your honor's great wisdom.

1683. Opinion of Mr. Trevor.

"THOMAS TREVOR.

"October 28, 1696."

The aspects of Providence upon the colony, this year, were exceedingly gloomy. Besides the dangers which threatened them, with respect to their civil and religious privileges, the people were visited with great sickness and mortality. The instances of death among the clergy were uncommonly numerous, and many churches were made to sit in widowhood. The fruits of the field were also diminished, and the inhabitants in various ways impoverished and distressed.

The general assembly, in October, considered the divine dispensations so afflictive as to demand their deepest humiliation. A general fast was appointed, and the people called upon to repent and humble themselves.*

Committee to congratulate the duke's governor, and to agree upon boundaries, Nov. 14th.

Colonel Dungan having lately arrived at New-York, the assembly, in November, appointed major Nathan Gould, captain John Allen, and Mr. William Pitkin, a committee, to congratulate him upon his arrival at his seat of government; and to agree with him upon a settlement of boundaries between the colonies. The committee were instructed not to exceed his demands of twenty miles east of Hudson's river: To examine his powers to treat, and if they were only conditional, to treat with him upon the same terms. They were directed to insist upon this, that there was no mistake with respect to the rise of the line at Memoronock. If they should be obliged to give up jurisdiction at any place, they were instructed to preserve property inviolably to the proprietors; and to insist on the former line, unless it should, in any place, approach near-

---

* The proclamation is introduced in these words, "Whereas it is evident to all who observe the footsteps of Divine Providence, that the dispensations of God, towards his poor wilderness people, have been very solemn, awful, and speaking, for many years past; and particularly towards ourselves in this colony, this present year, by occasion of general sickness in most places, and more than ordinary mortality in some, as also excessive rains and floods in several plantations, shortening us in our enjoyments; and considering also the holy hand of God, in bereaving so many churches and congregations of a settled ministry, whereby they are left, and have been, some of them, a long time, as sheep without a shepherd, as if the Lord intended, for our sins, to quench the light of our Israel."

Chap. XV. CONNECTICUT.

er to Hudson's river than the distance of twenty miles. In fine, they were required to make his honor sensible, that the former line was legal and firm, and that the present settlement was solely for the purpose of promoting peace and a good correspondence between his majesty's colony of Connecticut and the duke's territories, and their successive governors.

As the colony had been certified, by letters from his majesty, of a conspiracy against himself and the duke of York, the assembly addressed him on the subject. They declared, in the strongest terms, their utmost abhorrence of all plots against his royal person and government: That they prayed for kings and all men, and especially for his majesty, and all in authority under him: That they feared God and honored the king. In such suppliant language as follows, they prayed for the continuance of their chartered rights.

"Most dread sovereign, we humbly pray the continuance of your grace and favor in the full enjoyment of those former privileges and liberties you have, out of your princely grace and bounty, bestowed upon us, in your royal charter, granted this corporation, that our poor beginnings may prosper, under your shadow, to the glory of God, and the enlargement of your majesty's dominions."*

The committee appointed to agree with colonel Dungan, with respect to the line of partition between Connecticut and New-York, came to an agreement respecting it, November 28th, 1683. It was agreed, "That the line should begin at Byram river, where it falleth into the sound, at a point called Lyon's point, to go as the said river runneth to the place where the common road, or wading place, over the said river is; and from the said road or wading place, to go north northwest into the country, as far as will be eight English miles from the foresaid Lyon's point; and that a line of twelve miles, being measured from the said Lyon's point, according to the line or general course of the sound eastward, where the said twelve miles endeth, another line shall be run from the sound, eight miles into the country, north north-west, and also, that a fourth line be run, (that is to say,) from the northernmost end of the eight miles line, being the third mentioned line, which fourth line, with the first mentioned line, shall be the bounds where they shall fall to run; and that from the easternmost end of the fourth mentioned line, (which is to be twelve miles in length,) a line parallel to Hudson's river,

Book I.

1683.

Address and petition to his majesty, Charles II.

Agreement relative to the boundary line between Connecticut and New-York, Nov. 28, 1683.

* The number of persons giving in their lists, Oct. 1683, was 2,735, and the grand list was £159,395.

Book I. in every place twenty miles distant from Hudson's river, shall be the bounds there, between the said territories or province of New-York, and the said colony of Connecticut, so far as Connecticut colony doth extend northwards; that is to the south line of the Massachusetts colony: only it is provided, that in case the line from Byram brook's mouth, north north-west eight miles, and the line, that is then to run twelve miles to the end of the third forementioned line of eight miles, do diminish or take away land within twenty miles of Hudson's river, that then so much as is in land diminished of twenty miles of Hudson's river thereby, shall be added out of Connecticut bounds unto the line aforementioned, parallel to Hudson's river, and twenty miles distant from it; the addition to be made the whole length of the said parallel line, and in such breadth, as will make up quantity for quantity, what shall be diminished as aforesaid."

1683.

May 8, 1684. The assembly, in the session of May, 1684, approved of this agreement, and appointed major Nathan Gould, Mr. Jehu Burr, and Mr. Jonathan Selleck, to lay out the lines according to the stipulation. The lines accordingly were run, and on the 24th of February, 1685, were ratified by governor Dungan and governor Treat.

Law made against pirates, July 5, 1684. Great complaints had been made, in England, against the colonies for harbouring pirates; and that no laws had been made against them. A letter had been written to the governor and company, by Lyonel Jenkins, Esq. complaining of this neglect, and demanding, in his majesty's name, that a law should forthwith be made against piracy. A special assembly was consequently called on the 5th of July, and a law enacted against it, and a copy of it forwarded immediately to his majesty's secretary of state.

May 14, 1685. At the election, 1685, Giles Hamlin was chosen into the magistracy, in the place of Mr. Topping, who seems now to have been dead.

A letter to king James. The legislature, at this session, addressed a letter of condolence to his majesty, king James II. on account of the demise of his brother, king Charles II. and congratulating him on his peaceful accession to the throne of his ancestors. They presented him with the strongest assurances of their loyalty and attachment to his royal person and government. At the same time, sensible of their danger, under a prince of his character, they most humbly besought him to continue to them their civil and religious privileges, and that he would preserve to them the peaceable enjoyment of their property.

Upon the petition of a number of the inhabitants of

Farmington, presented to the assembly in 1673, a committee was appointed to view Mattatock, and report to the assembly, whether a plantation might not be made in that tract. In May, 1674, the committee reported, that Mattatock was a place sufficient to accommodate thirty families. Upon this report, a committee was appointed to settle a plantation there. Some time after the settlement commenced. The number of sharers was about twenty-eight. May 13th, 1686, they appear to have been vested with town privileges, by the name of Waterbury.*

In the last years of the reign of king Charles the second, the rights of the nation were violated, and a great number of corporations in England and Wales were obliged to resign their charters. Indeed, he, and his officers, seemed to sport with the liberty, property, and lives of his subjects. King James the second began his reign in the most flagrant violation of the laws of his three kingdoms. His reign grew more intolerable, from year to year, until he became the general abhorrence of the nation. He proceeded in the same lawless and cruel manner with the colonies, vacating their charters, and governing them by the worst measures and the worst men.

In July, 1685, a quo warranto was issued against the governor and company of Connecticut, requiring their appearance before him, within eight days of St. Martin's, to show by what warrant they exercised certain powers and privileges.

The governor, having received intelligence of the measures adopted against the colony, on the 6th of July, 1686, called a special assembly, to consult what might be done for the preservation of the just rights of the colony.

The assembly, after most serious deliberation, addressed a letter, in the most suppliant terms, to his majesty, beseeching him to pardon their faults in government, and continue them a distinct colony, in the full enjoyment of

* Several misfortunes attended the plantation, which very greatly impoverished it, and prevented its population. In February, 1691, the town was nearly ruined by an inundation. The rain fell in great abundance, and the frost came out of the ground very suddenly, which rendered it uncommonly soft. At the same time, the river rose to an unusual height, overflowed the meadows, and ran with such rapidity and violence, that it tore away a great part of them. Other parts were covered with earth and stone, so as to be greatly damaged. Numbers of the inhabitants were so discouraged, that they left the town, and it did not recover its former state for some years.

In 1712, on the 15th of October, began a great sickness in the town, which continued until the 12th of September, 1713, and was so general, that there were scarcely a sufficient number well to attend the sick, and bury the dead. Between twenty and thirty persons died of the sickness. Manuscripts of Mr. Southmayd.

Book I.

1686.

Quo warrantos arrive, July 21st.

Special assembly, July 28th.

Mr. Whiting appointed agent.

Another quo warranto, Dec. 28th.

their civil and religious privileges. Especially, they besought him to recal the writ of quo warranto, which they heard had been issued against them, though it had not yet arrived. They pleaded the charter which they received of his royal brother, and his commendation of them, for their loyalty, in his gracious letters, and his assurances of the continuance of their civil and religious rights. They made the strongest professions of loyalty, and of their constant supplications to the Supreme Ruler, that he would save and bless his majesty.

On the 21st of July, 1686, two writs of quo warranto were delivered to governor Treat. They had been brought over by Edward Randolph, that indefatigable enemy of the colonies. The time of appearance before his majesty, was past before the writs arrived.

Upon the reception of the writs, and a letter from Richard Normansel, one of the sheriffs of London, the governor immediately convoked another special assembly, which met on the 28th of July. The assembly appointed Mr. Whiting to be their agent, to present their petition to the king. He was instructed to acquaint his majesty with the time of the colony's receiving the quo warrantos, and of the impossibility of its making its appearance before his majesty, at the time appointed: fully to represent the great injury which the colonists would sustain, by the suspending their charter rights; and especially by a division of the colony. If Connecticut could not be continued a distinct government, he was instructed to supplicate his majesty to continue to them the enjoyment of their property, their houses and lands, and especially their religious privileges.

On the 28th of December, another writ of quo warranto was served on the governor and company, bearing date October 23d, requiring their appearance before his majesty within eight days of the purification of the blessed Virgin. Though the writs gave no proper time for the appearance of the colony, and, consequently, no time at all; yet they declared all its chartered rights vacated, upon its not appearing, at time and place. The design of the king and his corrupt court was to re-unite all the colonies to the crown. James the second was an obstinate, cruel tyrant, and a bigoted Roman catholic; destitute of all the principles of true honour, faith, justice, or humanity. He wantonly trampled on the constitution, laws, and liberties of the nation; and, with his ministers and officers, in an unrighteous and merciless manner, shed the blood of his subjects, and wreaked his vengeance on all who made the

CHAP. XV.   CONNECTICUT.

least opposition to his lawless proceedings. The most humble petitions, arguments from reason, charters, the most solemn compacts and royal promises, from justice, humanity, or any other consideration, which a subject could plead, had no weight or influence with him. Nearly fifty corporations in England had been deprived of their charters. The city of London, and the corporation of Bermudas, had stood trial with his majesty, and their charters had been taken from them. The charter of Massachusetts had been vacated, and Rhode-Island had submitted to his majesty. A general government had been appointed over all New-England, except Connecticut. By the commission, instituting this general government, Connecticut was totally excluded from all jurisdiction in the Narraganset country, or king's province.*

The governor and company of Connecticut, however, in these discouraging circumstances, spared no pains, nor omitted any probable means for the preservation of their chartered rights.

A special assembly was called on the 26th of January, 1687, after the reception of the third writ of quo warranto, to deliberate on the measures to be adopted, in the then present circumstances of the colony. Little more, however, was done, than to desire the governor and council to transact all business, which they should judge necessary and expedient, further to be done for the preservation of their privileges.

The election in May proceeded regularly, but the assembly did nothing important. Fear and hesitation appear to have attended the legislature. They knew not what course to steer, with safety, either to themselves, or their constituents. They, with the colony in general, were in great fear and distress, lest, after all their expense, hardships, and dangers, in settling and defending the country, and all their self-denial and sufferings for the sake of enjoying the worship and ordinances of Christ, according to the gospel, they should not only be deprived of all their civil and religious liberties, but even of their houses and lands. There was no security for any thing under a prince like James the second. He had, indeed, in his letters,

Book I.
1686.

Special assembly, Jan. 26th, 1687.

May 12th.
Fear and distress of the colony.

---

* This general commission was granted by king James II. in the first year of his reign, Oct. 8th, 1685. Joseph Dudley, Esq. was appointed president of the commissioners. On the 28th of May, 1686, the president issued a proclamation, discharging all the inhabitants of Rhode-Island, and the Narraganset country, from all obedience either to Connecticut or Rhode Island; and prohibiting all government of either in the king's province. At the same time, the president required the entire submission of all the inhabitants to the commissioners, and the officers whom they should appoint. Proclamation on file.

W 2

Book I. promised them* the preservation of all their liberties; yet, without any fault on their part, he was arbitrarily wresting 1687. them from their hands. It is difficult to conceive, and much more to express, the anxiety of our venerable ancestors in this terrible crisis of their affairs.

Mr. Whiting exerted himself in England, to procure all the influence, and make all the opposition he possibly could, against a general governor of the colonies, and especially to prevent the suspension of the government of Connecticut, according to charter; but he found his utmost exertions to be in vain. He wrote to the governor, January 15th, 1687, that if the governor and council would defend their charter at law, they must send over one or more from among themselves. A special assembly was called upon the reception of the agent's letter, which convened on the 15th of June, to deliberate on the expediency of sending another agent. The prospects appeared so unfavourable, that it was determined not to send another. Mr. Whiting was thanked for his services, in favour of the colony, and desired to continue them.

Agent Whiting writes to the governor.

Special assembly, June 15th.

Decline sending another agent.

Mr. Dudley, while president of the commissioners, had written to the governor and company, advising them to resign the charter into the hands of his majesty, and promising to use his influence in favour of the colony. Mr. Dudley's commission was superseded by a commission to Sir Edmund Andross to be governor of New-England. He arrived at Boston, on the 19th of December, 1686. The next day his commission was published, and he took on him the administration of government. Soon after his arrival, he wrote to the governor and company, that he had a commission, from his majesty, to receive their charter, if they would resign it; and he pressed them, in obedience to the king, and as they would give him an opportunity to serve them, to resign it to his pleasure. At this session of the assembly, the governor received another letter from him, acquainting him, that he was assured, by the advice which he had received from England, that judgment was, by that time, entered upon the quo warranto against their charter, and that he soon expected to receive his majesty's commands respecting them. He urged them, as he repre-

---

* In his letter to governor Treat, June 26th, 1685, he says: "As we cannot doubt of the ready and dutiful assurances and expressions of loyalty and obedience, from our good subjects under your government, since our accession to the crown, so shall we, at all times, extend our royal care and protection to them, in the preservation of their rights, and in the defence and security of their persons and estates; which we think fit that you signify unto the inhabitants of that our colony." Letter of king James II. on

CHAP. XV.   CONNECTICUT.   371

sented it, that he might not be wanting in serving their welfare, to accept his majesty's favour, so graciously offered them, in a present compliance and surrender. Colonel Dungan also used his influence to persuade them to resign, and put themselves under his government.* But the colony insisted on their charter rights, and on the promise of king James, as well as of his royal brother, to defend and secure them in the enjoyment of their privileges and estates; and would not surrender their charter to either. However, in their petition to the king, in which they prayed for the continuance of their chartered rights, they desired, if this could not be obtained, and it should be resolved to put them under another government, that it might be under Sir Edmund's, as the Massachusetts had been their former correspondents and confederates, and as they were acquainted with their principles and manners. This was construed into a resignation, though nothing could be further from the design of the colony.

The assembly met, as usual, in October, and the government continued according to charter, until the last of the month. About this time, Sir Edmund, with his suit, and more than sixty regular troops, came to Hartford, when the assembly were sitting, demanded the charter, and declared the government under it to be dissolved. The assembly were extremely reluctant and slow with respect to any resolve to surrender the charter, or with respect to any motion to bring it forth. The tradition is, that governor Treat strongly represented the great expense and hardships of the colonists, in planting the country; the blood and treasure which they had expended in defending it, both against the savages and foreigners; to what hardships and dangers he himself had been exposed for that purpose; and that it was like giving up his life, now to surrender the patent and privileges, so dearly bought, and so long enjoyed. The important affair was debated and kept in suspence, until the evening, when the charter was brought and laid upon the table, where the assembly were sitting. By this time, great numbers of people were assembled, and men sufficiently bold to enterprise whatever might be necessary or expedient. The lights were instantly extinguished, and one captain Wadsworth, of Hartford, in the most silent and secret manner, carried off the charter, and secreted it in a large hollow tree, fronting the house of the Hon. Samuel Wyllys, then one of the magistrates of the colony. The people appeared all peaceable and orderly. The candles were officiously re-lighted; but the patent was

*Letters of Dudley, Andross, and Dungan, on file.

Book I.
1687.

Sir Edmund Andross comes to Hartford, and demands the charter.

Governor Treat remonstrates against surrendering it.

It is carried off by captain Wadsworth.

Book I. gone, and no discovery could be made of it, or of the person who had conveyed it away. Sir Edmund assumed the government, and the records of the colony were closed in the following words.

1687.

"At a general court at Hartford, October 31st, 1687, his excellency, Sir Edmund Andross, knight, and captain-general and governor of his majesty's territories and dominions in New-England, by order from his majesty, James the second, king of England, Scotland, France, and Ireland, the 31st of October, 1687, took into his hands the government of the colony of Connecticut, it being, by his majesty, annexed to Massachusetts, and other colonies under his excellency's government."

"FINIS."

Sir Edmund assumes the government.

Sir Edmund appointed officers civil and military, through the colony, according to his pleasure. He had a council, at first, consisting of about forty persons, and afterwards, of nearly fifty. Four of this number, governor Treat, John Fitz Winthrop, Wait Winthrop, and John Allen, Esquires, were of Connecticut.

The oppressive government of Sir Edmund Andross.

Sir Edmund began his government with the most flattering professions of his regard to the public safety and happiness. He instructed the judges to administer justice, as far as might be consistent with the new regulations, according to the former laws and customs. It is, however, well observed, by governor Hutchinson, that "Nero concealed his tyrannical disposition more years, than Sir Edmund and his creatures did months." He soon laid a restraint upon the liberty of the press; and then, one far more grievous upon marriage. This was prohibited, unless bonds were previously given, with sureties, to the governor. These were to be forfeited, in case it should afterwards appear, that there was any lawful impediment to the marriage. Magistrates only were allowed to join people in the bands of wedlock. The governor not only deprived the clergy of the perquisite from marriages, but soon suspended the laws for their support, and would not suffer any person to be obliged to pay any thing to his minister. Nay, he menaced the people, that, if they resisted his will, their meeting-houses should be taken from them, and that any person who should give two pence to a non-conformist minister, should be punished.

The fees of all officers, under this new administration, were exorbitant. The common fee for the probate of a will was fifty shillings. The widow and fatherless, how distant soever, were obliged to appear at Boston, to transact all business relative to the settlement of estates.* This

* Hutchinson's Hist. Vol. I. p. 358.

was a grievous oppression of the poor people; especially, of the fatherless and widow.

Sir Edmund, without an assembly, nay, without a majority of his council, taxed the people at pleasure. He and Randolph, with four or five others of his creatures, who were sufficiently wicked to join with him, in all his oppressive designs, managed the affairs of government, as they pleased. But these were but the beginnings of oppression and sorrow. They were soon greatly increased and more extensively spread.

In 1688, Sir Edmund was made governor of New-York, as well as of New-England, and the same kind of government was exercised in that department.† As the charters were now either vacated, surrendered, or the government under them suspended, it was declared, that the titles of the colonists to their lands were of no value. Sir Edmund declared, that Indian deeds were no better than "the scratch of a bear's paw." Not the fairest purchases and most ample conveyances from the natives, no dangers, disbursements nor labors, in cultivating a wilderness, and turning it into orchards, gardens, and pleasant fields, no grants by charter, nor by legislatures constituted by them, no declarations of preceding kings, nor of his then present majesty, promising them the quiet enjoyment of their houses and lands, nor fifty or sixty years undisturbed possession, were pleas of any validity or consideration with Sir Edmund and his minions. The purchasers and cultivators, after fifty and sixty years improvement, were obliged to take out patents for their estates. For these, in some instances, a fee of fifty pounds was demanded. Writs of intrusion were issued against persons of principal character, who would not submit to such impositions, and their lands were patented to others. Governor Hutchinson observes, with respect to Massachusetts, that "men's titles were not all questioned at once. Had this been the case, according to the computation then made, all the personal estate in the colony would not have paid the charge of the new patents."‡

The governor, and a small number of his council, in the most arbitrary manner, fined and imprisoned numbers of the inhabitants of Massachusetts, and denied them the benefit of the act of habeas corpus. All town meetings were prohibited except one in the month of May, for the elec-

Book I.

1687.

† The same, p. 371. It is strange, that Mr. Smith, in his history of New-York, takes no notice of this, nor gives any account of Sir Edmund's administration.
‡ Hutchinson's Hist. vol. I. p. 359.

tion of town officers, to prevent the people from consulting measures for the redress of their grievances. No person indeed was suffered to go out of the country, without leave from the governor, lest complaints should be carried to England against his administration. At the same time, he so well knew the temper and views of his royal master, that he feared little from him, even though complaints should be carried over against him. Hence he and his dependants oppressed the people, and enriched themselves without restraint.

The most humble petitions were presented to his majesty, from corporations of various descriptions, beseeching him, that the governor's council might consist of none but men of considerable property in lands; that no act might be passed to bind the people, but by a majority of the council; and that he would quiet his good subjects in the enjoyment of all property in houses and lands.* But, in the reign of James the second, petitions so reasonable and just could not be heard. The prince, at home, and his officers abroad, like greedy harpies, preyed upon the people without control. Randolph was not ashamed to make his boast, in his letters, with respect to governor Andross and his council, "that they were as arbitrary as the great Turk." All New-England groaned under their oppression. The heaviest share of it, however, fell upon the inhabitants of Massachusetts and New-Plymouth. Connecticut had been less obnoxious to government, than Massachusetts, and as it was further removed from the seat of government, was less under the notice and influence of those oppressors.

Governor Treat was a father to the people, and felt for them, in their distressed circumstances. The other gentlemen, who were of the council, and had the principal management of affairs, in Connecticut, were men of principle, lovers of justice and of their fellow subjects. They took advantage of Sir Edmund's first instructions, and as far as they possibly could, consistently with the new regulations, governed the colony according to the former laws and customs. The people were patient and peaceable, though in great fear and despondency. They were no strangers to what was transacted in the neighbouring colonies, and expected soon fully to share with them, in all their miseries. It was generally believed, that Andross

* Sir Edmund, with all his vigilance, could not prevent the carrying over of complaints against him. Mr. Increase Mather, got on board a ship, and sailed to England, for this very purpose, and delivered the complaints, which he carried over, into his majesty's hands.

CHAP. XVI. CONNECTICUT.

was a papist; that he had employed the Indians to ravage the frontiers, and supplied them with ammunition; and that he was making preparations to deliver the country into the hands of the French. All the motives to great actions, to industry, economy, enterprise, wealth, and population, were in a manner annihilated. A general inactivity and languishment pervaded the whole public body. Liberty, property, and every thing, which ought to be dear to men, every day, grew more and more insecure. The colonies were in a state of general despondency, with respect to the restoration of their privileges, and the truth of that divine maxim, "when the wicked beareth rule the people mourn," was, in a striking manner, every where exemplified.

CHAPTER XVI.

Revolution in New-England. Connecticut resume their government. Address to king William. Troops raised for the defence of the eastern settlements in New-Hampshire and the province of Maine. French and Indian war. Schenectady destroyed. Connecticut dispatch a reinforcement to Albany. Expedition against Canada. The land army retreats, and the enterprise proves unsuccessful. Leisler's abuse of major general Winthrop. The assembly of Connecticut approve the general's conduct. Thanks are returned to Mr. Mather, agent Whiting, and Mr. Porter. Opinions respecting the charter, and the legality of Connecticut's assuming their government. Windham settled. The Mohawk castles are surprised and the country alarmed. Connecticut send troops to Albany. Colonel Fletcher, governor of New-York, demands the command of the militia of Connecticut. The colony petition king William on the subject. Colonel Fletcher comes to Hartford, and, in person, demands that the legislature submit the militia to his command; but they refuse. Captain Wadsworth prevents the reading of his commission, and the colonel judges it expedient to leave the colony. The case of Connecticut relative to the militia stated. His majesty determines in favor of the colony. Committees are appointed to settle the boundary line between Connecticut and Massachusetts. General Winthrop returns and receives public thanks. Congratulation of the earl of

BOOK I.   *Bellemont, appointed governor of New-York and Massachusetts. Dispute with Rhode-Island continues. Committee to settle the boundaries. Expenses of the war. Vexatious conduct of governor Fletcher. Peace, joy and thanksgiving.*

1689.

SCARCELY any thing could be more gloomy and distressful, than the state of public affairs, in New-England, at the beginning of this year. But in the midst of darkness light arose. While the people had prayed in vain to an earthly monarch, their petitions had been more successfully presented to a higher throne. Providence wrought gloriously for their and the nation's deliverance. On the 5th of November, 1688, the prince of Orange landed at Torbay, in England. He immediately published a declaration of his design, in visiting the kingdom. A copy of this was received at Boston, by one Mr. Winslow, a gentleman from Virginia, in April, 1689. Governor Andross and his council were so alarmed with the news, that they ordered Mr. Winslow to be arrested and committed to gaol for bringing a false and traitorous libel into the country. They also issued a proclamation commanding all the officers and people to be in readiness to prevent the landing of any forces, which the prince of Orange might send into that part of America. But the people, who sighed under their burthens, secretly wished and prayed for success to his glorious undertaking. The leaders in the country determined quietly to wait the event; but the great body of the inhabitants had less patience. Stung with past injuries, and encouraged at the first intimations of relief, the fire of liberty re kindled, and the flame, which, for a long time, had been smothered in their bosoms, burst forth with irresistible violence.

Revolution in New-England.

On the 18th of April, the inhabitants of Boston and the adjacent towns rose in arms, made themselves masters of the castle, seized Sir Edmund Andross and his council, and persuaded the old governor and council, at Boston, to resume the government.

Government resumed at Connecticut, May 9, 1689.

On the 9th of May, 1689, governor Robert Treat, deputy governor James Bishop, and the former magistrates, at the desire of the freemen, resumed the government of Connecticut. Major general John Winthrop was, at the same time chosen into the magistracy, to complete the number appointed by charter. The freemen voted, that, for the present safety of that part of New-England called Connecticut, the necessity of its circumstances so requiring, " they would re-establish government, as it was before, and at

CHAP. XVI.   CONNECTICUT.

the time, when Sir Edmund Andross took it, and so have it proceed, as it did before that time, according to charter; engaging themselves to submit to it accordingly, until there should be a legal establishment among them."

The assembly having formed, came to the following resolution: "That whereas this court hath been interrupted, in the management of the government in this colony of Connecticut, for nineteen months past, it is now enacted, ordered, and declared, that all the laws of this colony, made according to charter, and courts constituted for the administration of government, as they were before the late interruption, shall be of full force and virtue, for the future, and until this court shall see cause to make further and other alterations, according to charter." The assembly then confirmed all military officers in their respective posts, and proceeded to appoint their civil officers, as had been customary at the May session.

It was expected, that it might soon be necessary to transact matters of the highest importance, respecting the most essential rights of the colony. The deputies therefore resolved, that if occasion should require any thing to be acted, respecting the charter, the governor should call the assembly, and not leave the affair with the council.

Book I. 1689.

Resolve of the deputies.

Upon the 26th of May, a ship arrived at Boston with advice that William and Mary were proclaimed king and queen of England. The joyful news soon reached Connecticut. A special assembly was called, which convened on the 13th of June. On the same day, William and Mary, prince and princess of Orange, were proclaimed with great ceremony and joy. Never was there greater or more general joy in New-England, than upon the accession of William and Mary to the throne of Great-Britain. The bands of oppression were now loosed, the fears of the people dissipated, and joy brightened in every countenance.

The legislature addressed his majesty, in the most loyal and dutiful manner. They represented, that the Lord, who sitteth king upon the floods, had separated his enemies from him, as he divided the waters of Jordan before his chosen people; and that, by the great actions which he had performed, in rescuing the nation from popery and despotism, God had begun to magnify him, as he did Joshua, in the sight of all Israel. In strong terms, they declared, that it was because the Lord loved his people, that he had exalted him to be king over them, to execute justice and judgment. They most humbly presented their grateful acknowledgments to him, for his zeal for the welfare of the nation, and for the protestant interest. At the

Address to his majesty king William.

X 2

Book I.
1689.

same time, they represented to his majesty the charter privileges, which they had obtained, and the manner in which Sir Edmund Andross had suppressed their government by charter: That they had never surrendered it, and that there had been no enrolment of any surrender of it, or act, in law, against it: And that, to avoid the inconveniences of having no government, and for their defence against their enemies, they had, at the desire of the freemen, resumed the government according to their ancient form. They humbly prayed for his majesty's directions, and his gracious confirmation of their charter rights.* The court ordered, that Mr. Whiting should present their address to his majesty.

Revolution at New-York.

Meanwhile a revolution had been made at New-York. One captain Jacob Leisler had assumed the government of that province, and kept the fort and city in behalf of king William. He had written to Connecticut and solicited assistance in defending the province. The assembly appointed major Gould and captain James Fitch to proceed to New-York, and confer with Leisler and his council relative to the defence of the frontiers. The committee, with captain Leisler, were authorized to determine the number of men to be employed and the measures to be adopted for that purpose. In consequence of their determination, the governor and council dispatched captain Bull, with a company, to Albany, for the defence of that part of the country, and to assist in a treaty with the Five Nations, with a view to secure their friendship and attachment, as far as possible, to the English colonies. Connecticut also sent a detachment of men to assist captain Leister in the defence of the fort and city of New-York.

While the French and Indians were threatening the northern frontiers, the eastern Indians were carrying on their depredations in the eastern parts of New-England. In September, a special assembly was called on that account. Commissioners were appointed to consult with the commissioners of the other colonies, relative to the war in those parts. As it was imagined the Indians there had been injured, by governor Andross and his officers, the commissioners were instructed to enquire into the grounds of the war with them; and if it should appear that they had been injured, to use their utmost influence, that justice might be done them, and the country quieted in that way. But if they found the war to be just and necessary, they were authorized to engage the colony's full proportion of men, unless it should amount to more than two hundred. Two

* Appendix No. XXIII.

companies were afterwards appointed to that service, under the command of captains George Denison and Ebenezer Johnson.

At the session in October, it was resolved, that by reason of the great expense of the colony, in defending his majesty's subjects, in other parts, it was necessary to withdraw the aid which they had sent to New-York.

At this general court, the law respecting the choice of the governors and magistrates was enacted nearly in the words in which it now stands; but it instituted a mode of nomination different from the present. This was to be made on the third Tuesday in March annually, and the votes were to be carried to Hartford by the constables of the county towns, and on the last Tuesday in the month were, by them, to be sorted and counted in the council chamber. The nomination was then transmitted to the several towns.

While the revolution delivered the nation from vassalage and popery, it involved it in an immediate war with France, and the colonies in a French and Indian war. A large number of troops and a considerable fleet were sent from France, in 1689, with a special view to the reduction of New-York. The enterprise was frustrated by the distressed condition to which the incursions of the Mohawks had reduced Canada.

Count Frontenac, to raise the depressed spirits of the Canadians, sent out several parties of French and Indians against the settlements in New-York and New-England. A detachment of between two and three hundred French and Indians, under the command of D'Aillebout, De Mantel, and Le Moyn, were dispatched from Montreal against the frontiers of New-York. They were furnished with every thing necessary for a winter's campaign. After a march of two and twenty days, in the dead of winter, they reached Schenectady, on Saturday, the 8th of February, 1690. They had been reduced to such straits that they had thoughts of surrendering themselves prisoners of war. But their scouts, who had been a day or two in the village, entirely unsuspected, returned with such accounts of the security of the inhabitants, as determined them to make an attack upon them. They found the gates open and unguarded. They entered them about eleven o'clock, and that they might invest every house, at the same time, they divided into small parties of six or seven men. The inhabitants were in a profound sleep, and unalarmed until the enemy had broken open their doors, and they were on the verge of destruction. Never were a poor people more

Book I.
1689.
Oct. 10.

Destruction of Schenectady, Feb. 8, 1690.

Book I.
1690.

dreadfully surprised. Before they had time to rise from their beds, the enemy began the perpetration of the most inhuman barbarities. No tongue, says colonel Schuyler, in his letter to the colonies, can express the cruelties which were committed. The inhabitants were instantly slain, and the whole village was in flames. Pregnant women were ripped open, and their infants cast into the flames or dashed against the posts of the doors. Sixty persons perished in the massacre, and twenty were captivated. The rest of the inhabitants escaped in their shirts, in a most stormy and severe night, and through a deep snow, which fell at the same time. Twenty five of the fugitives lost their limbs, in the flight, through the sharpness of the frost. Captain Bull's lieutenant, one of his sergeants, and three other men were killed, and five captivated. The enemy killed all the cattle and horses, which they could find, except about fifty of the best horses, which they carried off, loaded with the plunder of the village.

When the news of this destruction reached Albany, the next morning, an universal fear and consternation seized the inhabitants. The country became panick struck, and many entertained thoughts of destroying the town and abandoning that part of the country to the enemy. Indeed, the whole province of New-York was in deplorable circumstances. Leisler, who had assumed the government, was a weak, imprudent man, and there was a violent opposition both to him and his measures, especially at Albany. Government was nearly dissolved. The people would not suffer the officers, posted at Albany and Schenectady, to keep a regular watch, or to maintain any kind of military order. Captain Bull had remonstrated against their conduct, and threatened to withdraw his troops, unless they would submit to order. The bad weather only had prevented him from withdrawing the detachment from Schenectady. The people had been warned of their danger, and that an expedition had been undertaken by the enemy against that part of the country; but they imagined, that it was impracticable for any men to march hundreds of miles, with their arms and provisions, through the snow, in the depth of winter. This infatuation and disorder was the occasion of their destruction.*

Destruction of Salmon Falls, March 18, 1690.

A second party of the enemy, which count Frontenac had detached from the three rivers, under the command of the sieur Hartel, an officer of distinguished character in Canada, on the 18th of March, fell upon Salmon Falls. This was a plantation on the river which divides New-

* Colonel Schuyler's and captain Bull's letters on file.

Hampshire from the province of Maine. This party consisted of about fifty men, nearly half Indians. They commenced the attack at break of day, in three different places. Though the people were surprised, yet they flew to their arms, and defended themselves with a bravery which even their enemies applauded. But they were finally overpowered by numbers, and the whole settlement was pillaged and burned. Six and thirty men were killed, and fifty-four, principally women and children, carried into captivity.

These depredations filled the country with fear and alarm. The most pressing letters were sent to Connecticut for immediate assistance. A special assembly was called on the 11th of April. Letters were laid before the assembly from Massachusetts, soliciting that soldiers might be sent from Connecticut, to guard the upper towns upon Connecticut river; and that there might be a general meeting of commissioners from the several colonies, at Rhode-Island, to consult the common defence. There were also letters from captain Leisler, at New-York, and from colonel Schuyler, and other principal gentlemen at Albany, urging, that captain Bull and the soldiers there might be continued, and that reinforcements might be forwarded for the defence of that place and the adjacent country. It was also urged, that Connecticut would unite with the other colonies, in raising an army for the reduction of Canada.

The assembly determined, that there was a necessity of their utmost exertions to prevent the settlement of the French, at Albany. It was resolved, that two companies, of a hundred men each, should be raised and sent forward for that purpose. The colony also gave assistance to the frontier towns of Massachusetts upon the river.

For the defence of Connecticut, it was ordered, that a constant watch should be kept in the several towns, and that all the males in the colony, except the aged and infirm, should keep watch in their turns. If the aged and infirm were more than fifty pounds in the list, they were obliged to procure a man, in their turns, to watch and guard in their stead.

Though the colony had received no instructions from king William, confirming their charter, or directing the mode of government, yet at the general election, the freemen proceeded, as had been usual, to the choice of their officers. Robert Treat, Esq. was re-chosen governor, and James Bishop, Esq. deputy-governor. Samuel Wyllys, Nathan Gould, William Jones, John Allen, Andrew Leet, James Fitch, Samuel Mason, Samuel Talcott, John Burr,

Book 1. 1690.

Special assembly, April 11th.

Reinforcement sent to Albany.

Provision for the safety of the colony.

Court of election, May 8th.

BOOK I. William Pitkin, Nathaniel Stanley, and Daniel Witherell, Esquires, were chosen magistrates.

1690. Glastenbury made a distinct town.

At this session of the assembly, that part of Weathersfield which lay on the east side of Connecticut river, was made a distinct town, by the name of Glastenbury.

The proposed meeting of commissioners, was holden at New-York, instead of Rhode-Island, on the 1st of May, 1690. The commissioners from Connecticut, were Nathan Gould and William Pitkin, Esquires. It appears, that, at this meeting, the commissioners conceived the plan of an expedition against Canada. They ordered, that eight hundred and fifty men should be raised for that purpose. The quotas of the several colonies were fixed, and general rules adopted for the management of the army. A small vessel was sent express to England, the beginning of April, carrying a representation of the exposed state of the colonies, and of the necessity of the reduction of Canada. A prayer was also sent to his majesty, for a supply of arms, ammunition, and a number of frigates, to attack the enemy by water, while the colonial troops made an invasion by land. But the affairs of the nation were such, at that time, that no assistance could be given to the colonies. New-York and the New-England colonies, however, determined to prosecute their original plan of attacking Canada. It was proposed, with about eight or nine hundred Englishmen, and five or six hundred Indians, to make an attack upon Montreal;* while a fleet and army, of eighteen hundred or two thousand men, were to proceed up the St. Lawrence, and, at the same time, make an attack upon Quebec. It was hoped, by this means, so to distract and divide the enemy, that the whole country might be reduced to his majesty's government. It was expected, that a powerful assistance would be given by the five nations, who had, but a few years before, so exceedingly harassed and distressed the whole French colony. Jacob Milborn, son in law to Leisler, was commissary, and it was expected, that New-York would furnish provisions, and make preparations for the army to pass the waters to Montreal.

General Winthrop arrives with the land army at Wood creek.

John Winthrop, Esq. was appointed major-general and commander in chief of the land army. He arrived, with the troops under his command, near the falls at the head of Wood creek, early in the month of August. About the same time, the fleet sailed from Nantasket for Quebec. It consisted of between thirty and forty vessels, great and small. The largest carried forty-four guns, and two hun-

* Determination of the commissioners at New-York, and colonel Schuyler's letter, on file.

dred men. Sir William Phipps, governor of Massachusetts, had the chief command. The fleet had a long passage, and did not arrive before Quebec until the 5th of October.

When the land army arrived at the place appointed for the rendezvous of the Indians from the five nations, instead of finding that powerful body, which they expected, and which the Indians had promised, there were no more than seventy warriors from the Mohawks and Oneidas. A messenger was sent to the other nations, to know what they designed; whether they would join the army and go forward, or not. The messenger returned, and reported that they wished for some delay; and they never came on to join the army. When the general had advanced about a hundred miles, he found that there were not canoes provided sufficient to transport one half of the English soldiers across the lake. Upon representing to the Indians, that the army could not pass into Canada, without a much greater number of canoes, they replied, that it was then too late in the season to make canoes, as the bark would not peel. In short, they artfully evaded every proposal which the council of war made for the service; and, finally, told the general and his officers, that they looked too high, and advised them only to attack Chambly, and the out settlements, on this side of the St. Lawrence.* There was another insuperable difficulty arose. Milborn, commissary of the army, had not made a sufficient provision for the carrying on and supplying of provisions for the army, so that it was necessitated to retreat to Albany for subsistence. This was determined by a council of war. At the same time, about a hundred and forty of the sprightliest young men, English and Indians, were dispatched into Canada, to make all the diversion possible in favour of the fleet. However, the retreat of the army, and the late arrival of the armament before Quebec, defeated the expedition.

Book I. 1690.

Army obliged to retreat.

Means of defeating the enterprise.

Count Frontenac, who had advanced with all his force to Montreal, to defend the country against the army advancing towards the lake, no sooner received intelligence, by his scouts, that it was retreating, than he returned, with all possible dispatch, to Quebec. Though but two or three days before Sir William Phipps arrived before the town, there were not more than two hundred Frenchmen in the city, and, according to their own historians, it would have surrendered upon the first summons, yet, afterwards, the count was able to employ his whole force in its defence.

* Proposals made to the Indians and their answers, with colonel Schuyler's, and the recorder of Albany's letter, on file.

BOOK I.
1690.

On the 8th of October, the troops landed and advanced towards the town. The ships, the next day, were drawn up before it, and cannonaded it with all their force; but they were not able to do any great injury to the town, while they were considerably damaged by the enemy's fire from their batteries. On the 11th, the troops were re-embarked. Though they had advanced and maintained their ground with spirit, yet they received such accounts of the strength of the enemy, as very much discouraged them. Soon after, tempestuous weather came on, the ships were driven from their anchors, and the whole fleet scattered. Thus, for want of a sufficient preparation for the advancing of the land army, and in consequence of the too late sailing of the fleet, an otherwise well concerted plan was defeated.

Leisler's madness and abuse of general Winthrop.

Though general Winthrop had acted in perfect conformity to the agreement of the commissioners, at New-York, and to the instructions which had been given him, and though he had retreated and taken all his measures by the advice of his officers, in repeated councils of war, yet Leisler, Milborn, and their party, were filled with the utmost rage and madness at the retreat. It was ordained by the commissioners, that, in all matters of great importance, the general should be governed by a council of war, consisting of himself and his officers; and Leisler was the first signer to the instructions and orders given. It was impossible to pass the lake without boats and canoes. It would have been madness to have crossed it, if there had been canoes, when they had found, that, by all the means and exertions in their power, they could not procure provisions for the army on this side of the lake. Leisler, however, took the advantage of the general, after the army had crossed Hudson's river, and lay encamped on this side of it, to arrest and confine him, that he might try him by a court martial of his own appointment. He was some days under the arrest. But when he was brought upon trial, the Mohawks, who were in the camp, crossed the river and brought him off, with great triumph, and to the universal joy of the army. Leisler, Milborn, and their party, were so enraged with some of the principal gentlemen in Albany, who were of the general's council, that they were obliged to flee to Connecticut for safety. Mr. Livingston and others resided some time at Hartford. Leisler confined the commissary of the Connecticut troops, so that the army suffered for want of his assistance.

He is rescued by the Mohawks.

This was viewed, by Connecticut, as an entirely lawless proceeding; not only highly injurious to general Win-

CHAP. XVI.   CONNECTICUT.

throp and the colony, but to all New-England. The governor and council remonstrated against his conduct, and demanded the release of general Winthrop and their commissary. They certified him, that it belonged not to him to judge of the general's conduct, but to the colonies in general; that it was inconsistent with the very instructions which he had subscribed with his own hand; and that, if he proceeded in his unprecedented and violent measures, they would leave him and New-York to themselves, without any further aid from Connecticut, let the consequences be what they might.* They observed, that he needed friends and assistance, but was pursuing measures not only to make the powerful friends of general Winthrop, but all New-England, his enemies; and, that the character of the general was too good, and too well known, to be drawn into question or disrepute by his conduct towards him.

At the general court, in October, a narrative of the conduct of the general was exhibited, attested by the officers of the army, and by numbers of the principal gentlemen of Albany. Attested answers of the Indians to the several councils of war, with such other evidence as the assembly judged proper to examine, were heard. Upon a full examination of the affair, the assembly resolved: "That the general's conduct, in the expedition, had been with good fidelity to his majesty's interest, and that his confinement, at Albany, on the account thereof, deserved a timely vindication, as being very injurious and dishonorable to himself, and the colonies of New-England, at whose instance he undertook that difficult service." The court appointed two of the magistrates in their name, "To thank the general for his good service to their majesties, and to this colony, and assure him, that, on all seasonable occasions, they would be ready to manifest their good sentiments of his fidelity, valor, and prudence."† The assembly made him a grant of forty pounds, as a present, which they desired him to accept, as a further testimonial of their entire approbation of his services.

Besides the troops employed in the expedition against Canada, Connecticut maintained a company upon the river, for the defence of the towns in the county of Hampshire. Upon an alarm in the winter, the governor and council dispatched a company to Deerfield, for the protection of that and the neighboring towns.

At the election, May, 1691, all the former officers were re-elected.

BOOK I.

1690.
The governor and council remonstrate against Leisler's conduct.

Oct. 9th.

General Winthrop's conduct approved.

May 14th, 1691.

* Appendix No. XXIV.   † Records of the colony.

BOOK I.
~~~
1691.

On the account of the death of the deputy-governor, James Bishop, Esq.* a special assembly was convened, on the 9th of July, 1691; when William Jones, Esquire, was chosen deputy-governor, and captain Caleb Stanley, magistrate.

The Rev. Increase Mather, of Boston, was a most faithful friend to the liberties of his country; and though he was agent for the Massachusetts, yet he was indefatigable in his labors, and, as opportunity presented, performed essential services for the other colonies. At the accession of William and Mary he had prevented the bill for establishing the former governors of New-England. He had united all his influence with Mr. Whiting for the benefit of Connecticut. One Mr. James Porter, who was in London, had been very serviceable to the colony. The assembly, therefore, ordered, that a letter of thanks should be addressed to those gentlemen, for the good services which they had rendered the colony. They were, also, desired to use their influence to obtain, from his majesty, a letter approving of their administration of government, according to charter, as legal; and expressing his determination to protect them in the enjoyment of their civil and religious privileges.

The violation of the charters, in England, had been declared illegal and arbitrary. The charter of the city of London, and those of other corporations, in Great Britain, had been restored. The case of Connecticut, respecting their charter, had been stated, and the opinions of gentlemen, learned in the law, had been given relative to the legality of the government assumed by the colony. They are thus expressed.

Opinions relative to the charter of Connecticut.

"Query, Whether the charter belonging to Connecticut, in New-England, is by means of their involuntary submission to Sir Edmund Andross's government, void in law, so as that the king may send a governor to them, contrary to their charter privileges, when there has been no judgment entered against their charter, nor any surrender thereof upon record?"

* James Bishop, Esq. died June 22d, 1691. He appears to have been a gentleman of good ability and distinguished morals. The time of his coming over to America is uncertain. His first appearance upon the public records, was about the year 1648. In 1661, he was chosen secretary of the colony of New-Haven; in which office he continued until the union of the colonies of Connecticut and New-Haven. In May, 1668, he was chosen one of the magistrates of Connecticut, in which office he continued until May 10th, 1683, when he was elected deputy-governor. To this office he was annually re-elected until his death. His family has continued respectable to the present time. Samuel Bishop, Esq. chief judge of the court of common pleas, for the county of New-Haven, and mayor of the city, is one of his descendants.

"I am of opinion, that such submission, as is put, in this case, doth not invalidate the charter, or any of the powers therein, which were granted under the great seal; and that the charter not being surrendered under the common seal, and that surrender duly enrolled of record, nor any judgment of record entered against it, the same remains good and valid in law; and the said corporation may lawfully execute the powers and privileges thereby granted, notwithstanding such submission, and appointment of a governor as aforesaid.

"EDWARD WARD.

"2d August, 1690.
"I am of the same opinion. J. SOMERS.
"I am of the same opinion; and as this matter is stated there is no ground of doubt.

"GEO. TREBY."

_{Book I.}
_{1691.}

The people at the eastward, in New-Hampshire and the province of Maine, had been extremely distressed by the war, and a very great proportion of them driven from their settlements. It had also been found exceedingly difficult to persuade men to keep garrison for the defence of that part of the country. The general court of Connecticut, therefore, appointed a contribution, through the colony, for the encouragement of the soldiers, who should keep garrison there, and for the relief of poor families, which had kept their stations, or been driven from them by the ravages of the enemy. The clergy were directed to exhort the people to liberal contributions for these charitable purposes.*

Distressed circumstances of the eastern people.

Contribution for their relief.

At the election, May, 1692, William Jones, Esq. was chosen deputy governor by the freemen. Mr. Caleb Stanley and Mr. Moses Mansfield were chosen magistrates. Governor Winthrop and the other magistrates were the same they had been the year before.

Court of election, May.

The French, the last year, while the troops were employed in the expedition against Canada, made a descent upon Block-Island, plundered the houses, and captivated most of the inhabitants. This greatly alarmed the people of New-London, Stonington, and Saybrook. Detachments of the militia were sent to the seaport towns for their defence. The assembly therefore, about this time ordered, that New-London should be fortified; and that the fortifications at Saybrook should be repaired.

The French make a descent upon Block-Island.

The country had been alarmed with reports, that a large body of French and Indians were about to cross the lakes

* The number of persons, this year, ratable in the colony was 3,109, and the grand list £183,159.

Book I.
1692.

and come down upon the frontiers. Consequently it was ordered, that scouts, from the several counties should range the country, and make discovery of the enemy as they made their approach. Officers were also appointed to command such parts of the militia as it might be necessary to detach, in case of an invasion.

Settlement of the town of Windham, May 12, 1692.

Upon the 29th of February, 1675, Joshua, sachem of the Moheagans, son of Uncas, by his last will, gave unto captain John Mason, James Fitch, and others, to the number of fourteen, commonly called Joshua's legatees, the tract containing the town of Windham. It was, the next year, surveyed and laid out into distinct lots. In May, 1692, it was vested with town privileges. By Joshua's will, the lands in the town of Mansfield, no less than those in Windham, were given. The settlements, at both places, commenced about 1686, nearly at the same time. Canterbury originally belonged to the town of Windham, though it was some years after made a distinct town. The township of Windham comprises a fine tract of land, nearly ten miles square. Its situation is pleasant, and it is now one of the principal towns in the state.*

Enterprise against the Mohawk castles.

Count Frontenac, finding that he could not, with all his arts, accomplish a peace with the five nations, determined on the destruction of the Mohawks, who, of all the Indians, had been by far the most destructive to the settlements in Canada. He collected an army of six or seven hundred French and Indians, and, having supplied them with every thing necessary for a winter campaign, sent them against the Mohawk castles. They began their march from Montreal on the 15th of January, 1693. After suffering incredible hardships, they fell in with the first Mohawk castle, about the 6th of February. The Mohawks were entirely secure, not having the least intimation of their approach. The enemy took four or five men at this castle, and proceeded to the second. At this they were equally successful. A great part of the inhabitants were at Shenectady, and the rest were perfectly secure. When they advanced to the third castle, they found about forty warriors, collected at a war dance, as they designed the next day to go upon an enterprise against their enemies. A conflict ensued, in which the French, after losing about thirty men, were victorious, and the third castle

* Mr. John Cates, one of the first planters, a gentleman from England, who died July 16th, 1697, by his last will, gave a generous legacy, in plate, to the church. He also gave two hundred acres of land for the use of a school, and two hundred more for the use of the poor of the town forever. Windham was made a county town in May, 1726. The grand list, in 1768, was about £30,000, and the number of inhabitants 3,500.

CHAP. XVI.　　　　　CONNECTICUT.

was taken. The French, in this descent, captivated nearly three hundred of the allied Indians, principally women and children. The brave colonel Schuyler, of Albany, at the head of a party of volunteers, of about two hundred English and Dutch, pursued them. On the 15th of February, he was joined with about three hundred Indians, and, with this force, he fell in with the enemy, whom he found in a fortified camp. They made three successive sallies upon the colonel, and were as often repulsed. He kept his ground, waiting for provisions and a reinforcement from Albany. Meanwhile, the enemy, taking advantage of a severe snow storm, on the night of the 18th, marched off for Canada. The next day, captain Sims, with eighty regular troops, arrived with provisions for the army, and the day following the colonel resumed the pursuit. The French, however, luckily finding a cake of ice across the north branch of Hudson's river, made their escape. Nevertheless, they were so pressed, that they suffered most of their captives to escape. They all, except nine or ten, returned. Colonel Schuyler lost eight of his party, four christians, and four Indians. He had fourteen wounded. According to the report of the captives, the enemy lost forty men, three of whom were French officers, and two were Indian leaders; and they had thirty wounded. The Indians found about thirty corpses of the enemy, whom they scalped, and afterwards roasted and ate them, as they were exceedingly pinched for want of provisions.*

Book I.

1693.

While these affairs were transacting, dispatches were sent to Connecticut, acquainting governor Treat, that the French had invaded his majesty's territories, and taken the fortresses of his allies. A demand was made of two hundred men, complete in their arms, to march forthwith to Albany.

A special assembly was called on the 21st of February, 1693, and it was ordered, that one hundred and fifty men should be sent immediately to Albany, or any other place where the governor should judge to be most for his majesty's interest. Fifty of the troops marched for Albany the next day.

Special assembly, Feb. 21st.

Scarcely had the assembly dispersed, before another express arrived, from Sir William Phipps, requiring a corps of a hundred English men, and fifty Indians, to assist in the defence of the eastern settlements, in the province of Maine and Massachusetts. On the 6th of March, another special assembly was convened, and the legislature granted

Special assembly, March 6.

* Governor Fletcher's letter, on file.

Book I. a captain's company of sixty English men, and about forty Indians, under the command of captain William Whiting.

1693.
Election,
May 11th.
Major general Fitz John Winthrop was chosen magistrate at the election, which was the only alteration made among the magistrates this year.

The general court ordered a letter to be addressed to the governor of Massachusetts, once more desiring him and that colony amicably to join with Connecticut in running the partition line between the two colonies. William Pitkin, Esq. Mr. Samuel Chester, and captain William Whiting, were appointed a committee to run the line. They had instructions to begin, according to the express words of the patent of Massachusetts, three miles south of every part of Charles river, and thence to run to the westernmost bounds of Symsbury.

Colonel Fletcher challenges the command of the militia.
Colonel Benjamin Fletcher, governor of New-York, who had arrived at the seat of his government, August 29th, 1692, had received a commission entirely inconsistent with the charter rights and safety of the colonies. He was vested with plenary powers of commanding the whole militia of Connecticut and the neighboring provinces. He insisted on the command of the militia of Connecticut. As this was expressly given to the colony, by charter, the legislature would not submit to his requisition. They, however, judged it expedient to refer it to the freemen, whether they would address a petition to his majesty, praying for the continuance of the militia in the power of the colony, according to their charter, and for the continuance and preservation of all their chartered rights and privileges. There were 2,180 persons, or suffrages for addressing his majesty, and the freemen declared, that they would bear their proportionable charge with the rest of the colony, in prosecuting the affair to a final issue.

The legislature refuse to submit the militia to his command.

Petition his majesty, and appoint an agent.
At a special assembly, September 1st, 1693, the court appointed a petition to be drafted, to be presented to his majesty, king William, on the subject. Major-general Fitz John Winthrop was appointed agent to present the petition, and employ his best endeavours for the confirmation of all the chartered privileges of the colony. He was desired, as soon as possible, to take his passage to England, and, upon his arrival there, to lay the business, as expeditiously as might be, before his majesty, and prosecute the affair to an issue, with all convenient dispatch.

Instructions to the agent.
He was instructed to make a full representation of the great hardships, expense, and dangers of the inhabitants, in planting and defending the colony; and that these had been borne wholly by themselves, without any assistance

from the parent country: That it would endanger and ruin the colony, if the militia should be taken from it, and commanded by strangers at the distance of New-York and Boston: That it would wholly incapacitate them to defend themselves, their wives, and children: That before they could obtain instructions, from such a distance, upon any sudden emergency, the colony might be depopulated and ruined: That a stranger, at a distance, might not agree with the governor and council in employing the militia for the defence of the property, lives, and liberties of the subjects; and that the life and support of the laws, and the very existence of their civil constitution depended on the militia. He was also instructed further to represent the state of the militia of Connecticut, with respect to its difference from that of the militia of England: That, from the scattered state and small number of the inhabitants, it had been necessary, that all males, from sixteen years of age, should belong to the militia, and be made soldiers, so that if the militia were taken from the colony, there would be none left but magistrates, ministers, physicians, aged and infirm people, to defend their extensive sea coasts and frontiers; and that giving the command of the militia to the governor of another colony, was, in effect, to put their persons, interests, and liberties entirely into his power. The agent was, also, directed to represent the entire satisfaction of the colony with the present government, and the great advantages resulting from it: That giving the command of the militia to the governor of another province, would exceedingly endanger, if not entirely destroy, that general contentment, and all the advantages thence arising to his majesty and his subjects: That out of three thousand freemen in the colony, two thousand and two hundred actually met, and gave their suffrages for the present address; and that the greatest part of the other eight hundred were for it, but were, by their particular occasions, prevented from attending at the respective meetings, when the suffrages were taken: That the inhabitants were universally for the revolution; and that, in the whole colony, there were not more than four or five malcontents. The agent was charged to assure his majesty, that the militia should be improved with the utmost prudence and faithfulness, for his majesty's service, in the defence of the frontiers of Massachusetts and New-York; and to lay before him what the colony had already done; especially for the province of New-York, in their late distressed condition: That for its defence, and the securing of the five nations, in his majesty's interest, they had expended more than three thousand pounds, and lost a number of their men. Further, general Winthrop was directed, so far as might be judged expedient, to plead the rights granted in the charter, especially that of commanding the militia, and the common usage, ever since the grant of the charter, for a long course of years.

Sir William Phipps, governor of Massachusetts, had, on his appointment to that office, received a commission of the same tenor of governor Fletcher's. As the colony had not fully complied with his requisitions, it was expected that the agent would be interrogated upon that head. He was instructed, in that case, to reply, that Sir William never came into the colony, nor acted upon his commission, any further, than to give a copy of it, and to inquire who were the officers of the militia: That the governor and company had a prior commission, by charter, and that they could by no means give it up, until the affair had been laid before his majesty.

Assembly, Oct. 12th. The colony wished to serve his majesty's interest, and, as far as possible, consistently with their chartered rights, to maintain a good understanding with governor Fletcher. William Pitkin, Esq. was, therefore, sent to New-York, to treat and make terms with him respecting the militia, until his majesty's pleasure should be further known. But no terms could be made with him short of an explicit submission of the militia to his command.

Colonel Fletcher comes to Hartford, and demands the command of the militia, Oct. 26th. On the 26th of October, he came to Hartford, while the assembly were sitting, and, in his majesty's name, demanded their submission of the militia to his command, as they would answer it to his majesty; and that they would give him a speedy answer in one word, Yes, or No. He subscribed himself his majesty's lieutenant, and commander in chief of the militia, and of all the forces by sea or land, and of all the forts and places of strength in the colony of Connecticut.* He ordered the militia of Hartford under arms, that he might beat up for volunteers. It was judged expedient to call the trainbands in Hartford together; but the assembly insisted, that the command of the militia was expressly vested, by charter, in the governor and company; and that they could, by no means, consistently with their just rights and the common safety, resign it into any other hands. They insinuated, that his demands were an invasion of their essential privileges, and subversive of their constitution.

Declaration by col. Bayard. Upon this, colonel Bayard, by his excellency's command, sent a letter into the assembly, declaring, that his

* Governor Fletcher's letter, on file.

CHAP. XVI.   CONNECTICUT.

excellency had no design upon the civil rights of the colony; but would leave them, in all respects, as he found them. In the name of his excellency, he tendered a commission to governor Treat, empowering him to command the militia of the colony. He declared, that his excellency insisted, that they should acknowledge it an essential right, inherent in his majesty, to command the militia; and that he was determined not to set his foot out of the colony until the had seen his majesty's commission obeyed: That he would issue his proclamation, showing the means he had taken to give ease and satisfaction to his majesty's subjects of Connecticut, and that he would distinguish the disloyal from the rest.*

The assembly, nevertheless, would not give up the command of the militia; nor would governor Treat receive a commission from colonel Fletcher.

The trainbands of Hartford assembled, and, as the tradition is, while captain Wadsworth, the senior officer, was walking in front of the companies, and exercising the soldiers, colonel Fletcher ordered his commission and instructions to be read. Captain Wadsworth instantly commanded, "Beat the drums;" and there was such a roaring of them that nothing else could be heard. Colonel Fletcher commanded silence. But no sooner had Bayard made an attempt to read again, than Wadsworth commands, "Drum, drum, I say." The drummers understood their business, and instantly beat up with all the art and life of which they were masters. "Silence, silence," says the colonel. No sooner was there a pause, than Wadsworth speaks with great earnestness, "Drum, drum, I say;" and turning to his excellency, said, "If I am interrupted again I will make the sun shine through you in a moment." He spoke with such energy in his voice and meaning in his countenance, that no further attempts were made to read or enlist men. Such numbers of people collected together, and their spirits appeared so high, that the governor and his suit judged it expedient, soon to leave the town and return to New-York.

The assembly granted 500 pounds, to support major general Winthrop in his agency at the court of Great-Britain.

On the 7th of February, 1694, a special assembly was called, in consequence of a letter from king William relative to the fortifying of Albany. In compliance with his majesty's requisition, the assembly granted 600 pounds, to be paid into the hands of colonel Fletcher, for the defence

* Colonel Bayard's letter on file.

of Albany. A rate of one penny on the pound was levied to raise the money.*

1694. For the defence of the plantations in New-York, and the towns upon the river, in the county of Hampshire, the assembly ordered, that the commissioned officers, who were the nearest to the places, which should, at any time, be attacked, should dispatch immediate succours to them. Provision was also made that the several detachments of the militia should be furnished with all articles necessary for their marching, in any emergency, upon the shortest notice.

Statement of the case of Connecticut respecting the command of the militia. Major general Winthrop made a safe arrival in England, and presented the petition, with which he had been entrusted, to his majesty. A statement of the case of Connecticut was drawn and laid before the king. In this, besides the facts stated in the instructions of Mr. Winthrop, it was alledged, that in the charter, granted by king Charles, the command of the militia was, in the most express and ample manner, given to the colony; and that the governor had always commanded it for the common safety: That in the charter there was a clause for the most beneficial construction of it for the corporation; and another of non obstante to all statutes repugnant to said grant. It was stated, that whoever commanded the persons in a colony would also command their purse, and be the governor of the colony: That there was such a connection between the civil authority and the command of the militia, that one could not subsist without the other: That it was designed to govern the colonies, in America, as nearly as might be, in conformity to the laws of England. And that the king, and his lieutenants could not draw out all the militia of a county; but a certain part only, in proportion to its numbers and wealth. It was therefore pleaded, that governor Fletcher's commission ought to be construed with the same restriction: That were not the command of the king and his lieutenants restricted, by acts of parliament, the subjects could not be free; and that, for the same reason, governor Fletcher's command ought to be restrained, by the laws of Connecticut, so far as they were not repugnant to the laws of England. It was further stated, that it was impossible for governor Fletcher so well to judge of the dispositions and abilities of each town and division in Connecticut, or be so much master of the affections of the people, in time of need, as those who dwelt among them and had been chosen to command them; and therefore he could not be so well qualified for the local and ordinary command

* The rateable polls in the colony were, at this time, about 2,347, and the grand list £137,646.

CHAP. XVI. CONNECTICUT.

of the militia; nor serve the interests of his majesty, or the colony, in that respect, so satisfactorily and effectually as its own officers.*

His majesty's attorney and solicitor general, gave their opinion in favor of Connecticut's commanding the militia; and on the 19th of April, 1694, his majesty in council determined according to the report which they had made.† The quota of Connecticut, during the war, was fixed at one hundred and twenty men, to be at the command of governor Fletcher, and the rest of the militia to be commanded, as had been usual, by the governor of Connecticut.

Upon the solicitations of governor Fletcher and Sir William Phipps, agents and a number of troops were sent to attend a treaty with the Five Nations. The expense of it to the colony was about 400 pounds.

A committee was appointed again, in the May session, to run the partition line between Connecticut and Massachusetts. Massachusetts was invited to join with them, but as the court refused, the committee of Connecticut, by the direction of the assembly, ran the line without them. In October, 1695, the general assembly renewed their application to the general court of Massachusetts, intreating them to unite amicably in running the boundary line, or to agree to it, as it had been run by Connecticut. They acquainted them how it ran, what encroachments they had made upon the colony, and how they injured it, by declining a mutual and friendly settlement of the line. However they insisted upon the old line, run by Woodward and Saffery, and would take no measures to accommodate the difference.

At the court of election, May, 1696, Eleazar Kimberly was chosen secretary. Upon the requisition of governor Fletcher, a company of sixty men were ordered to Albany, under the command of captain William Whiting. Forty dragoons were also forwarded to the county of Hampshire, for the security of the inhabitants in that part of Massachusetts.

About this time, the town of Danbury was incorporated. The whole number of families was twenty four.

At the general court, May, 1697, colonel Hutchinson and captain Byfield were sent from Boston, to solicit the raising of such a number of troops as should enable Massachusetts to attack the eastern enemy, at their head quarters. The legislature judged themselves unable to furnish such a number, as would be necessary for that purpose, in addi-

*Statement on file. † Appendix No. XXIV.

Book I.
1698.

tion to the troops they must raise for the defence of their own frontiers, of New-York, and the county of Hampshire. The court agreed to furnish a party of about sixty Englishmen and forty Indians, to range the woods, near the walk of the enemy, and to defend the frontiers of the county of Hampshire.

January 22d, 1698.

At a general assembly, January 22d, 1698, an alteration was made in the constitution of the county court. It was enacted, that it should consist of one chief judge and four justices of the quorum, in each county, appointed by the assembly.

Major-general Winthrop, on his return, receives the thanks of the legislature.

Major-general Fitz John Winthrop, having returned from his successful agency at the court of Great-Britain, was received with great joy, by the legislature and the people in general. The assembly presented him with their thanks for the good services he had rendered to the government; and as a further testimonial of the high sense which they entertained of his merit, fidelity, and labours for the public, they voted him a gratuity of three hundred pounds.

Earl of Bellomont appointed governor of Massachusetts and New-York.

On the 18th of June, 1697, Richard, earl of Bellomont, received his commission to be governor of New-York and Massachusetts; and was, at this time, every day expected at New-York. The general court of Connecticut were desirous of honouring his majesty, by an exhibition of all proper respect and complaisance to his governor; and, at the same time, they wished to conciliate the good graces of so important a character. They, therefore, appointed general Winthrop, major Jonathan Sillick, and the Rev. Gurdon Saltonstall, upon the first notice of his arrival at New-York, to wait upon him, and, in the name of the general assembly of Connecticut, to congratulate his excellency upon his safe arrival at the seat of government. The earl arrived at New-York the 2d of April, 1698. The committee appointed to wait on him, were gentlemen of a good appearance and elegant manners; and they presented their congratulations with such dignity and address, as not only did honour to themselves and the colony, but highly pleased his excellency. Mr. Saltonstall was particularly noticed by the earl, as appearing the most like a nobleman of any person he had ever seen before in America.

Congratulated by Connecticut.

Notwithstanding the determination of lieutenant-governor Cranfield, and his majesty's commissioners, and the report to his majesty concerning the right of Connecticut to the Narraganset country, the controversy between Connecticut and Rhode-Island still continued. It was not the king's pleasure to confirm the judgment and report of his commissioners. The Rhode-Islanders, though they had violated every article of the agreement between Mr. Winthrop and Mr. Clark, yet were ready to plead it against Connecticut, whenever it would suit their turn. A letter from the lords of trade and plantations was laid before the assembly, advising Connecticut to a settlement of boundaries with that colony. Upon this recommendation, the general court appointed major James Fitch, captain Daniel Witherell, and the Rev. James Noyes, commissioners to treat with Rhode-Island, and, by all means in their power, to attempt an amicable settlement.

{1698. Committee appointed to settle boundaries.}

The peace of Riswick, September 11th, 1697, once more delivered Great-Britain and her colonies from the calamities of war. The Americans rejoiced at the return of peace. Connecticut had been happy in the preservation of her frontiers, in the loss of few men, and in the effectual aid which she had given to her sister colonies. Nevertheless, the war had been very expensive, and exceedingly vexatious. The whole amount of taxes, during the war, was about twenty pence on the pound. By the close of the year 1695, the colony had expended 7,000l. in the defence of Albany, and the frontiers of the county of Hampshire, in Massachusetts; exclusive of the expedition against Canada, under major-general Winthrop. This cost the colony more than 3,000l. The expense of the troops sent to the eastward, to the defence of that part of New-England, is also excluded. It is probable that the remaining years of the war cost about 2,000l. The whole expense of the war probably considerably exceeded 12,000l.*

{Peace. Expense and vexations of the war.}

The expense of Mr. Winthrop's agency, and the trouble respecting the militia, were very considerable.

Governor Fletcher made the colony much unnecessary trouble and expense. Upon almost every rumour of danger, he would send on his expresses to Connecticut; and the governor and council, and sometimes the assembly, were obliged to meet, and dispatch troops to one place and another. Often, by the time they had marched, orders would come to recal them. By the time they were returned, some new and groundless alarm would be made, and pressing orders sent on for them forthwith to march again. In this manner, he almost wore out the governor and council with meetings, and beyond measure harassed the militia, and occasioned great trouble, and expense of time and money, both to the soldiers and officers. The whole colony was so troubled with his vexatious management, that the

* The accounts, to the close of the year '95, are particularly stated. After that time, they do not appear to be ascertained.

BOOK I.
1698.

governor wrote to Mr. Winthrop, while he was in England, desiring him to represent his conduct to his majesty, and pray for relief.

But the clouds were now dissipated. The successful agency of general Winthrop, his safe return to the arms of his country, the blessings of peace, and the appointment and arrival of the earl of Bellomont to the government of the neighbouring provinces, united their influence to diffuse universal joy. The legislature appointed a day of public thanksgiving, and the people, with glad hearts and voices, celebrated the beneficence and glories of their COMMON BENEFACTOR.

CHAPTER XVII.

General Winthrop is elected governor. The assembly divide and form into two houses. Purchase and settlement of several towns. The boundary line between Connecticut and New-York surveyed and fixed. Attempts for running and establishing the line between Massachusetts and Connecticut. Owaneco and the Moheagans claim Colchester and other tracts in the colony. Attempts to compose all differences with them. Grant to the volunteers. The assembly enacts, that the session in October, shall, for the future, be in New-Haven. An act enlarging the boundaries of New-London, and acts relative to towns and patents. Measures adopted for the defence of the colony. Appointment of king's attorneys. Attempts to despoil Connecticut of its charter. Bill for re-uniting the charter governments to the crown. Sir Henry Ashurst petitions against, and prevents the passing of the bill. Governor Dudley, Lord Cornbury, and other enemies conspire against the colony. They exhibit grievous complaints against it. Sir Henry Ashurst defends the colony, and defeats their attempts. Quakers petition. Moheagan case. Survey and bounds of the pretended Moheagan country. Dudley's court at Stonington. The colony protest against it. Dudley's treatment of the colony. Judgment against it. Petition to her majesty on the subject. New commissions are granted. Act in favour of the clergy. State of the colony.

Court of election.
May 12th, 1698.

AT the election in 1698, there was a considerable alteration in the legislature. Major-general Fitz John

Winthrop, by his address, and the success of his agency in England, had rendered himself so popular, that he was elected governor. The former governor, Treat, who had, for many years, presided, and who had grown old in the service of the colony, was elected deputy-governor; William Jones, Esq. who, for a number of years, had been deputy-governor, was left out of the council.* Mr. Joseph Curtis was chosen magistrate, to fill the vacancy made by the preferment of general Winthrop.

Book I. 1698.

Until the session in October, 1698, the assembly consisted of but one house, and the magistrates and deputies appear to have acted together. But, at this time, it was enacted, that the General Assembly should consist of two houses: That the governor, or, in his absence, the deputy-governor and magistrates, should compose the first, which should be called the upper house: That the other should consist of the deputies, regularly returned from the several towns in the colony, which should be called the lower house. This house was authorised to choose a speaker to preside, and when formed, to make such officers and rules as they should judge necessary for their own regulation. It was also enacted, that no act should be passed into a law of this colony, nor any law, already enacted, be repealed, nor any other act, proper to this General Assembly, be passed, except by the consent of both houses.

Oct. 13th, 1698, the assembly made two houses.

At the general court, in October, an act passed, regulating the county court. It ordained, that it should consist of one chief judge, and two justices of the quorum.

In 1699, the governor and deputy-governor were re-elected. Richard Christopher was chosen into the magistracy, and captain Joseph Whiting, treasurer.

May 11th, 1699.

At this session, the lower house, for the first time, formed separately, and chose Mr. John Chester speaker, and captain William Whiting clerk. This assembly passed

---

* Deputy-governor Jones was son in law to governor Eaton. He brought over a good estate from England, and made a settlement at New-Haven. He was, for the term of about six and thirty years, either magistrate or deputy-governor of the colony of New-Haven or Connecticut. In 1662, he was chosen magistrate for the colony of New-Haven. Two years after, he was elected deputy-governor. Upon the union, in 1665, he was chosen one of the magistrates of Connecticut, in which office he served until July 9th, 1691, when the assembly elected him deputy-governor. In May, 1692, he was chosen to the same office by the freemen. He was annually re-chosen, until May 12th, 1698. At that period he was about 74 years of age, and retired from public business. He died October 17th, 1706, aged 82 years. The General Assembly was sitting at New-Haven, at the time of his decease, and voted, "That in consideration of the many good services, for many years done by that honored and religious gentleman, Mr. William Jones, then deceased, a sum should be paid out of the treasury towards defraying the charges of his funeral."

BOOK I. an act exempting the clergy from taxation. Several acts were also passed, relative to the settlement of new townships.

1698.
Purchase and settlement of Plainfield.

In June, 1659, governor Winthrop obtained liberty of the assembly, to purchase a large tract at Quinibaug. Soon after he made a purchase of Allups, alias Hyemps, and Mashaushawit, the native proprietors, of the lands comprised in the townships of Plainfield and Canterbury, lying on both sides of Quinibaug river. There were a small number of families on the lands, at the time of the purchase; but the planters were few, until the year 1689, when a number of people, chiefly from Massachusetts, made a purchase of the heirs of governor Winthrop, and began settlements in the northern part of the tract. At their session, in May, 1699, the General Assembly vested the inhabitants with town privileges. The next year, it was named Plainfield.

Grant and settlement of Colchester.

The legislature, in the October session, 1698, enacted, that a new plantation should be made at Jeremy's farm. It was determined, that it should be bounded southerly on Lyme, westerly on Middletown, and easterly on Norwich and Lebanon. This was most commonly termed the plantation at twenty mile river. The settlement began about 1701. In 1703, the assembly gave the planters a patent, confirming to them the whole tract. Some of the principal planters, were the Rev. John Bulkley, Samuel Gilbert, Michael Tainter, Samuel Northam, John Adams, Joseph Pomeroy, and John Loomis.

Cogingchaug, Durham granted and settled.

At the same session, a plantation was granted, upon the petition of the inhabitants of Guilford, at a place called Cogingchaug. It was bounded northerly on Middletown, easterly on Haddam, westerly on Wallingford, and southerly on Guilford. The petitioners were thirty-one, but few of them moved on to the lands. For this reason, the settlement went on very slowly. The two first planters, were Caleb Seward and David Robinson, from Guilford. Some others afterward removed from the same town, and made settlements there. May 11th, 1704, it was named Durham. But the whole number of inhabitants was very small. In 1707, the number of families was no more than fifteen. The inhabitants held meetings, and acted as a town, but were not incorporated with town privileges, until May, 1708. After this time, the plantation increased rapidly. There was a great accession of inhabitants from Northampton, Stratford, Milford, and other towns.

Committees were again appointed, at the session in October, to attempt a settlement of the boundaries between

Massachusetts and Connecticut, and between this colony and Rhode-Island. However, like all former ones, they were unsuccessful.

1700.

March 28th, 1700, his majesty, king William, in council, was pleased to confirm the agreement made between Connecticut and New-York, in 1683, respecting the boundary line between the two colonies. New-York neglected, however, to run the line. Connecticut, therefore, about twelve years after, applied to governor Hunter, to appoint commissioners to complete the running of the line, and mark it with proper bounds. He laid the affair before the legislature of New-York: but, as they would adopt no measures for that purpose, and, as there was no appearance that they designed it, Connecticut presented a petition to his majesty king George the first, praying that he would issue his royal commands to his government of New-York, that they should forthwith appoint commissioners, in concert with Connecticut, to complete the running of the line, and the erecting of proper monuments. In consequence of this, the legislature of New-York, in 1719, passed an act empowering their governor to appoint commissioners to run the line parallel to Hudson's river, to re-survey the former lines, and to distinguish the boundary. In May, 1725, the commissioners and surveyors of the two colonies, met at Greenwich, and, having agreed upon the manner in which the work should be accomplished, the survey was executed, in part, immediately, and a report of what they had done, was made to the respective legislatures of Connecticut and New-York. On the 14th of May, 1731, a complete settlement was made. By the partition line, finally established, Connecticut ceded to New-York a tract of 60,000 acres, as an equivalent for lands which New-York had surrendered to Connecticut, lying upon the sound. This tract, from its figure, has been called the Oblong.

King William establishes the agreement in 1683.

The line between Connecticut and New-York run and fixed.

In 1700, the governor and council were all re-elected. Many acts of violence, since the last session of the assembly, had been committed against the inhabitants of Windsor and Simsbury, by the people of Enfield and Suffield. They had made encroachments two miles upon the land of those towns, beyond all former instances. Great animosities subsisted between those towns on the account of the encroachments and damages, which the inhabitants of Connecticut suffered by them.

Court of election, May, 1700.

To compose these difficulties, if possible, the assembly appointed William Pitkin, Esq. Mr. John Chester, and Mr. William Whiting, a committee, with plenary powers,

Attempts to settle the line between

BOOK I.
1700.
Massachusetts and Connecticut.

to address the general court of Massachusetts, and to represent to them the readiness of the legislature of Connecticut, to join with them in any just measures, for an amicable settlement of the boundary line. The court of Massachusetts appointed colonel Hutchinson, Mr. Taylor, Mr. Authrum, and Mr. Prout, a committee, but with limited powers, to find the southernmost line of Massachusetts, run by Nathaniel Woodward and Solomon Saffery. The general court, also, on the 5th of June, passed an act, in answer to the proposal made by Connecticut, in which they insisted on the line run by Woodward and Saffery. These were termed skilful and approved artists. The court also, in their act, insisted, that all grants, made by them to the inhabitants of Woodstock, or of any other place, should remain good and valid to the grantees, though the places should be found south of the line of Massachusetts. To these hard terms the committee conceded, upon the condition, that all the grants made by Connecticut, to the inhabitants of Windsor and Simsbury, should be acknowledged as valid, and the land granted be reserved to the proprietors. But the court of Massachusetts would not concede even this. No accommodation could therefore be effected.

The general court of Massachusetts determined to rely upon, and maintain the line run by their sailors, in 1642. They insisted that it had been the boundary between the colonies, for nearly sixty years : that the colony of Connecticut was bounded on the south line of Massachusetts, which they said was not an imaginary, but well known line. They pleaded, that Mr. Winthrop, when he procured the charter, knew that to be the line, and that no other could be intended.

Connecticut, on the other hand, maintained, that the south line of Massachusetts, according to the express words of their charter, was a line running due west from a point, or station, three miles south of every part of Charles river; and that the station fixed by Woodward and Saffery was too far south. It was also insisted, that, even allowing Woodward's and Saffery's station to be right, a due west line from it would run far north of Bissell's ferry house at Windsor. The committee, appointed by the court of Massachusetts, reported, that the line would run north of Bissell's house; yet the court of Massachusetts would not run the line, nor come to any accommodation; but insisted on the line as it had been run by them, in 1642, and on Connecticut's ceding their rights to all the lands which

CHAP. XVII.   CONNECTICUT.

they had granted, whether they lay north or south of said line.*

Though Colchester held their lands from the colony, which claimed by virtue of Uncas's deed in 1640, major Mason's purchase, in behalf of the colony, and surrender of the lands in the presence of the general assembly, and by virtue of Joshua's will; and though the inhabitants had deeds from Owaneco, and the Moheagan sachems, covering the whole tract, yet they met with great difficulties, in the settlement of the town, from Owaneco and the Moheagans, who were made uneasy, and stirred up to mischief, by designing men. The Masons, Daniel Clark, Nicholas Hallam, major Palms, major Fitch, and others, about this time, conceived the plan of obtaining a large tract of land, comprising Colchester, part of Lyme, and New-London, Plainfield, Canterbury, and Windham, for themselves. They imagined, that the surrender of major Mason, in the general assembly, was not legal, and that the circumstances of those early transactions were so far obliterated from the memory of the living, that they should be able to recover, in law, all the lands made over, by Uncas, to major Mason, acting as agent of the colony in 1659.

The legislature, though they viewed their title to the lands in the colony legal and indubitable, yet judged it expedient, rather than to have any difficulty with the Indians, to treat with them, and make them easy.

The governor and council were appointed a committee for these purposes. They were instructed to obtain a quit claim of the Indians upon reasonable terms, and to advise the inhabitants, with respect to their settlements. Captain Samuel Mason, who was one of the magistrates, was particularly desired to use his influence with the Indians to promote the design, and quiet the planters.

From the first settlement of the colony, it had been customary to make grants of land to officers, soldiers, and others, who had been specially serviceable to the colony. Grants had been made to major Mason, to his officers and soldiers, in the Pequot war. This encouraged the volunteers, who had performed such signal feats in the Narraganset war, to make application to the assembly, for the grant of a new township, as an acknowledgment of their good services. Upon the petition of captain Thomas Leffingwell, of Norwich, and Mr. John Frink, of Stonington, in behalf of themselves and other volunteers, the general assembly, in October, 1696, granted them a township six miles square, to be taken up in the conquered lands. A

Book 1. 1700.

Grant of Voluntown Oct. 10th

* Records of Connecticut, acts and letters on file.

BOOK I.
1701.

committee having surveyed the lands and made their report to the assembly, four years after, a township was confirmed to the petitioners, by the name of Voluntown. It was bounded by a due north line, from the pond at the head of Pawcatuck river, to Greenwich path, thence west to the bounds of Preston, thence bounded by Preston and Stonington to Pawcatuck river, and thence by the river to the pond, the first mentioned bounds. Nineteen years after, the assembly granted an addition of a considerable tract on the north part of the township.

Court of election, May 8th, 1701.

In 1701, governor Winthrop and deputy governor Treat were re-chosen. The magistrates were Andrew Leet, James Fitch, Samuel Mason, Daniel Witherel, Nathaniel Stanley, Moses Mansfield, John Hamlin, Nathan Gould, William Pitkin, Joseph Curtis, John Chester, and Josiah Rossiter, Esquires. Joseph Whiting, Esq. was re-elected treasurer, and Eleazar Kimberly, secretary.

Ever since the union of the colonies, the assembly had convened at Hartford, both in May and October; but, at this session, an act passed, that the assembly, in October, should be holden, at the usual time, in New-Haven. It was also enacted, that the court of magistrates, which had been commonly holden at Hartford, in October, should, for the future, be holden at New-Haven, on the first Tuesday of the same month. A respectable committee was appointed again, this year, to make a settlement of the boundary line with Rhode-Island, and committees were appointed, from year to year, for the same purpose, but all attempts, for a long time, were unsuccessful.

May 14th, 1702.

The election in 1702, made no alteration in the legislature.

Mansfield made a town.

The inhabitants of Windham having agreed upon a division of that town, on the 30th of January, 1700, the assembly, at this session, confirmed the agreement, and enacted that Windham should be divided into two towns, and that the town at the north end should be called Mansfield. The next May, the assembly vested them with distinct town privileges. Patents were granted, at the same time, to both townships. The Indian name of Mansfield, was Nawbesetuck. Settlements were made here soon after they commenced at Windham.

Danbury made a town.

Danbury had been surveyed for a town in 1693, soon after a plantation was made upon the lands. Some of the principal planters were James Beebe, Thomas Taylor, Samuel and James Benedict, John Hoit, and Josiah Starr. The general court at this session, gave them a patent, granting them a township extending eight miles in length,

CHAP. XVII. CONNECTICUT.

north and south, and six miles in breadth, according to the original survey.

In October, the general assembly was holden at New-Haven.

The colony having received intelligence of the demise of king William, and a gracious letter from queen Anne, voted, that a letter should be addressed to her majesty, congratulating her upon her happy accession to the throne of her ancestors, and expressing their thanks for the favorable notice she had taken of the colony.

The only alteration made, by the election, in May, 1703, was the choice of Peter Burr, Esq. into the magistracy.

At this assembly, an addition was made to the town of New-London of all that tract, lying north of the former bounds, included in a line drawn from the northeastern corner of Lyme, to the southwestern corner of Norwich, as it goes down to trading cove. A patent was, at the same time, given to the inhabitants, confirming this and all other parts of the town to them forever.

At the same session, it was enacted, that all the townships in this colony, to which the assembly had given patents, should remain a full and clear estate, with all the privileges and immunities therein granted, in fee simple to the proprietors, their heirs and assigns forever. It was also enacted, that all lands sequestered, and given to public or private uses, should remain forever, for the ends for which they had been given.

Queen Anne, the emperor of Germany, and the States General, in May, 1702, declared war against France and Spain. Consequently the American colonies were again involved in a French and Indian war. The legislature, at the session in October, found it necessary to adopt measures for the safety of the country. A requisition was made, by governor Dudley, and the general court of Massachusetts, of a detachment of a hundred men, to assist them in the war against the eastern Indians. Soldiers were detached and sent forth for the defence of the western towns in Connecticut. A committee of war was appointed to send troops into the county of Hampshire, in Massachusetts, and to the frontier towns in this colony, as emergencies should require.

At this assembly, it was enacted, that the town of Plainfield should be divided, and that the inhabitants on the west side of the river should be a distinct town, by the name of Canterbury. It seems, that the settlement of this tract commenced about the year 1690. The principal settlers, from Connecticut, were major James Fitch and Mr.

Book I.
1703.

Solomon Tracy, from Norwich, Mr. Tixhall Ellsworth and Mr. Samuel Ashley, from Hartford; but much the greatest number was from Newtown, Woburn, Dorchester, Barnstable, and Medfield, in Massachusetts. Among these were John, Richard, and Joseph Woodward, William, Obadiah, and Joseph Johnson, Josiah and Samuel Cleaveland, Elisha Paine, Paul Davenport, and Henry Adams.

Special assembly, March 15th, 1704.

On the 15th of March, 1704, a special assembly was convened to provide for the common safety. To prevent mischief from the friendly Indians, and preserve them from being corrupted and drawn away by the enemy, both the civil and military officers, in the respective towns, were directed to take special care of them; to keep them within their own limits, and not to suffer them, upon their peril, to remove from the places which should be assigned them, nor to hold any correspondence with the enemy, or any foreign Indians, nor by any means to harbor them. A premium of ten pounds was proposed, as an encouragement to every friendly Indian, who should bring in and deliver up one who was an enemy.

Orders for the common safety.

Orders were given, requiring every particular town, in the colony, to convene and determine upon the manner of fortifying and defending themselves. In case of any sudden attack or invasion, the commissioned officers, in the several towns, were authorised to detach and send forth any number of soldiers, not exceeding half the militia, to repel and pursue the enemy. It was resolved, that a grand scout should be employed by the committee of war, upon the frontiers, for the discovery and annoyance of the enemy. Until this could be sent forth, it was determined, that small scouts, from the frontier towns, should be constantly kept out, to discover and give notice of the motions of the enemy. It was ordered, that the hundred men, solicited by the Massachusetts, should be raised forthwith, to act against the eastern Indians, and that governor Dudley should be requested to call them out immediately. A detachment of sixty men was ordered for the public service, principally with a view to the defence of the county of Hampshire. These were to be under the command of the committee of war in Connecticut, and the commanding officer in that county.

Election May 11th, 1704.

At the court of election, May, 1704, the former governors and magistrates were re-chosen. John Allen, Esq. was chosen magistrate, to fill the vacancy made by the death of Moses Mansfield, Esq.

Committees were appointed in the several counties to meet together, to consult and determine upon the best measures for the general defence and safety.

CHAP. XVII.   CONNECTICUT.

As the deserting or giving up of any place, would encourage the enemy, disserve her majesty's interests, and the welfare of the colony, it was enacted, that if any persons or families, in any of the frontier towns, should desert their habitations or places of residence, without leave from the assembly, they should forfeit their freehold of lands and tenements in that place. It was further enacted, that if any male person, of the age of sixteen years, should so remove from any frontier town, he should pay a fine of ten pounds, and that the fine should be applied to the defence of the town from which he had removed.

Good policy required, that as great a number of the friendly Indians as possible, should be employed in the public service. Gentlemen were, therefore, appointed to enlist them as volunteers. Good encouragements were given for this purpose. Indians were the best troops to scout and range the woods; and in proportion as they offered themselves, Englishmen, whose labours were much more useful, were kept at home.

Besides the hundred men dispatched to the eastward, four hundred were raised for the defence of this colony, and of the county of Hampshire. They were required to be always ready. That they might be completely ready, both in summer and winter, to march immediately, upon any emergency, it was ordered, that they should be furnished with snow shoes, that they might travel and run upon the snow. A number of men in every town were obliged to prepare themselves in this manner.*

For the maintenance of good morals, the suppression of vicious and disorderly practices, and the preservation of the common peace, the assembly ordered, that a sober, religious man, be appointed by the county court, in each of the counties, to be an attorney for her majesty, to prosecute all criminal offenders.

Appointment of king's attorneys.

The colony, at this time, was in the most critical situation. It was not only in danger, and put to great expense, by reason of the war, to defend itself, but to still greater, to defend the neighbouring colonies of Massachusetts and New-York. It was continually harassed by the demands of Joseph Dudley, Esq. governor of Massachusetts, and of lord Cornbury, governor of New-York and the Jerseys, for men and money, as they pretended for the defence of their respective governments.

Critical state of the colony.

At the same time, the colony had a number of powerful enemies, who, by misrepresentation and every other artifice in their power, were seeking to deprive them both of

Arts of its enemies, Dudley and Cornbury.

* Records of the colony.

Book I.

1704.

BOOK I.
1704.

their lands and all their chartered rights and privileges. Governor Dudley, lord Cornbury, and their instruments, combined together to despoil the colony of its charter, and subject it entirely to their government. It appears, from the letters and acts on file, that Dudley wished to unite all New-England under his own government. At the same time, it seems, he flattered lord Cornbury, that, if they could effect the re-union of all the charter governments to the crown, he should not only have the government of the southern colonies, but of Connecticut. Dudley was a man of great intrigue and duplicity, well versed in court affairs, and had powerful connections in England. He had been connected with Sir Edmund Andross in the government of New-England, and was an enemy to all the chartered rights of the colonies. While he was soliciting the government of Massachusetts, he had a view to the government of all New-England. As he had conceived this plan as early as the latter part of the reign of king William, he opposed whatever he suspected would operate against it, and prevent the suspension of all government by charter. When he found, therefore, that Sir Henry Ashurst was appointed agent for Connecticut, about the beginning of the present century, he opposed his undertaking the agency with all his influence, because he knew his friendship to the colonies, and that he was a powerful man. He united all his influence with the court party, and the enemies to the liberties of the colonies, to vacate all the charters in America. He so far succeeded, that, in the latter part of the reign of king William, a bill was prepared for re-uniting all the charter governments to the crown. Early in the reign of queen Anne, it was brought into parliament. It imported, that the charters given to the several colonies in New-England, to East and West New-Jersey, Pennsylvania, Maryland, Carolina, the Bahama and Lucay islands, were prejudicial and repugnant to the trade of the kingdom, and the welfare of his majesty's subjects in the other plantations, and to his majesty's revenue arising from the customs. It also further alledged, that irregularities, piracies, and unlawful trade, were countenanced and encouraged by the authority in the chartered colonies. It therefore enacted, "That all and singular, the clauses, matters, and things, contained in any charters, or letters patents, granted by the great seal of England, by any of his royal predecessors, by his present majesty, or the late queen, to any of the said plantations, or to any persons in them, should be utterly void, and of none effect. It further enacted, that all such power, authority, privileges, and jurisdictions,

Attempts to vacate the charter.

Bill for re-uniting it to the crown.

CHAP. XVII. CONNECTICUT. 409

should be, and were re-united, annexed to, and vested in his majesty, his heirs and successors, in right of the crown of England, to all intents and purposes, as though no such charters or letters patent had been had or made.*

Book I.
1704.

Sir Henry Ashurst, viewing the act as unjust, and subversive of the civil and religious rights of the colony, preferred a petition to the lords spiritual and temporal in parliament assembled, representing that said bill would do great injustice to the inhabitants of Connecticut: That it would make void the charter granted to the colony by king Charles the second: That the government was, by said charter, granted to them, and was so interwoven with their property, that it could not be taken away, without exposing them to the utmost confusion, if not to utter ruin: That the inhabitants had never been accused of mal-administration, piratical or unlawful trade; and that their case was different from his majesty's other plantations in America. He, therefore, humbly prayed to be heard, by his council, at the bar of the house, in their behalf.† In consequence of this, it was granted, May 3d, 1701, that the petitioner should be heard against the bill.

Petition against the bill.

Sir Henry was a faithful man, had honourable connections, and his influence at court was very considerable. He raised all the opposition to the passing of the bill in his power. Representations were made, not only of the ample rights and privileges granted to Connecticut, by charter, but that they were granted for important considerations, and particular services performed: That the inhabitants, at great expense and danger, had purchased, subdued, and planted an extensive country; had defended it against the Dutch, French, and other enemies of the nation; had enlarged his majesty's dominions, and increased commerce: That the charter not only gave the inhabitants powers of government, but secured the title of their lands and tenements; and that, in these views, the passing of the bill would be an act of great injustice; would be ruinous to the colony, and prejudicial to the general interest. It was insisted, that it would be still more arbitrary and unjust, as the colony had not been even accused of mal-administration, piratical or illegal practices, or so much as heard on the subject. It was pleaded, that the colony had ever been loyal and obedient, and if any irregularities, or inadvertencies should finally be found in the government, it would, on the first notice of it, undoubtedly be reformed. At the same time, the taking away of so many charters, was, at once, calculated to destroy all confidence in the

Reasons against its passing.

* Copy of the bill on file.   † Petition on file.

B 3

BOOK I.
1704.

crown, in royal patents and promises; to discourage all further enterprise, in settling and defending the country; to create universal discontent and disaffection in the colonies; and to produce effects much more prejudicial to the nation, than any of those which were then matter of complaint. It would, also, afford a precedent most alarming to all the chartered corporations in England. These various considerations operated so powerfully against the bill, that it could not be carried through the houses.

It miscarries.

Enemies of the colony not discouraged.

Governor Dudley and lord Cornbury, however, were not discouraged. They determined to make a more open and powerful opposition to the charter rights of Connecticut. And they determined, as much had been made of this argument, that Connecticut had never been accused of mal-administration, piracy, or any illegal trade, to remove it out of the way, by a direct impeachment of the colony of high misdemeanors. They were both powerful enemies. Governor Dudley was not only a man of great intrigue, but had a party at court, who were men of art and influence. Lord Cornbury was nearly related to her majesty, queen Anne, and had many noble connections, whose weight with her royal person and the court, was not inconsiderable. Exclusive of these, the colony had enemies among themselves. Nicholas Hallam, major Palms, captain Mason, Daniel Clark, and others, had either appealed to England against the colony, or were scheming to possess themselves of large tracts of land, and, for that purpose, were encouraging the Moheagan controversy. Hallam had appealed to England against the colony, and lost his case. The king, in council, had established the judgment given against him in the courts of Connecticut. Major Palms, who had married the daughter of John Winthrop, Esq. the first governor of Connecticut, under the charter, had imagined himself injured by the administrators on the governor's estate, and had brought an action against them. Losing his case before the courts in this colony, he had appealed to England. He was particularly irritated against the colony, and against his brother in law, Fitz John Winthrop, Esq. then governor of the colony. These malcontents all united their influence, by the grossest misrepresentations, and all other means in their power, to injure the colony in its most essential interests.

They are powerful.

Unite their influence against the colony.

Lord Cornbury was poor, and not unwilling, by any means, to get money. He had made a demand of four hundred and fifty pounds upon the colony, for the defence of New-York. Connecticut judged, that it was not their duty to comply with his demand, as their expenses already were as great as the colony was able to bear.

CHAP. XVII. CONNECTICUT.

Dudley and Cornbury, therefore, proceeded to draw up articles of complaint against the colony. Dudley employed one Bulkley to write against the government. He drew up a large folio book, which he termed the Doom or Miseries of Connecticut. In this, he not only exceedingly misrepresented and criminated the colony, but expatiated on the advantages of a general governor of New-England, and highly recommended the government of Sir Edmund Andross.*

Among other complaints, the principal articles particularly charged, were, summarily, these: That the governor did not observe the acts of trade and navigation, but encouraged illegal commerce and piracy: That the colony was a receptacle of pirates, encouraged and harboured by the government: That the government harboured and protected soldiers, seamen, servants, and malefactors, who made their escape from other parts, and would not deliver them up, when demanded. It was, also, charged against the colony, that it harboured great numbers of young men, from Massachusetts and New-York, where they were obliged to pay taxes for the expenses of the war, and induced them to settle there, principally, because it imposed no taxes for that purpose: That the colony would not furnish their quota for the fortification of Albany and New-York, and the assistance of Massachusetts Bay, against the French and Indians: And that, if any of her majesty's subjects, of the other colonies, sued for debt, in any of the courts of the colony, no justice could be done them, if the debt were against any of its inhabitants. It was also charged, that Connecticut, under the colour of their charter, made capital laws; tried murders, robberies, and other crimes, and punished with death and banishment; and that their courts of judicature were arbitrary and unjust: That the legislature would not suffer the laws of England to be pleaded in their courts, unless it were to serve a turn for themselves: That they had refused to grant appeals to her majesty, in council, and had given great vexation to those who had demanded them: That the government had refused to submit to her majesty, and to his royal highness's commission of vice admiralty, and for commanding its militia; and had defeated the powers which had been given to the governors of her majesty's neighbouring colonies, for that purpose. Finally, it was charged, that the legislature had made a law, that christians, who were not of their communion, should not meet to worship God, without license from their assembly, which law extended even to the

BOOK I.

1701.

Complaints against the colony.

* Letter of Sir Henry Ashurst, on file.

Book I.
1704.

Moheagan affair.

Petition to her majesty in fa-

church of England, as well as to christians of other denominations tolerated in England.

While governor Dudley was thus attempting the ruin of the colony, in the court of England, he kept up the appearance of the most entire friendship towards it, in this country; and in a letter, of about the same date with his complaints, thanked the legislature for the great supplies which they had given him and the colony.

The general assembly had appointed the most respectable committees, and taken great pains to compromise all difficulties with Owaneco and the Moheagans; and though they had made repeated purchases and obtained ample deeds of their lands, yet, rather than have any uneasiness among the Indians, they offered Owaneco such a sum of money, to make him easy, as was entirely satisfactory to him; but Mason and the other malcontents, who wished to possess the Indian lands, would not suffer him to accept it, and frustrated all attempts for an accommodation.

While Mason and other enemies were practising their arts, in Connecticut, Hallam, assisted by Dudley and his party, with other malcontents, on both sides of the water, was making grievous complaints, in England, of the injustice and cruelty of the colony towards Owaneco, in driving him from his lands, and depriving the Moheagans even of their planting grounds. It was pretended, that, in the late grant and patent to the town of New-London, the legislature had conveyed away all his lands in that quarter, whereas particular care was taken, both in the grant and patent, to secure all the property and privileges of the Moheagans. The assembly had taken the most faithful and tender care of them, from the first settlement of the colony to that time. According to their agreement with major Mason, then deputy governor of the colony, when he resigned the Moheagan land to the assembly, they granted him a farm of five hundred acres, and it was laid out to him at a place called, by the Indians, Pomakuk. They had also reserved a fine tract of land, of between four and five thousand acres, to the Moheagans to plant on, which was much more than sufficient for that purpose. But the representations, which these evil minded men were constantly making to Owaneco and his people, at some times, made them uneasy, and some of them probably imagined, that they were really injured. At the same time, the affair was so represented in England, as made impressions on the minds of many very unfavorable to the colony.

In this situation of affairs, Hallam, assisted by the malcontents in England and America, preferred a complaint

CHAP. XVII. CONNECTICUT. 413

and petition to her majesty, queen Anne, representing, that the sachems of the Moheagan tribe of Indians were the original and chief proprietors of all the lands in the colony: That they were a great people, and had received and treated the first planters in a peaceable and friendly manner: That, for an inconsiderable value, they had granted their lands to them, reserving to themselves a small parcel only for planting ground; and that the general assembly of Connecticut had passed an act by which they had taken that from them, which, until that time, they had always enjoyed. For these reasons, it was prayed, that her majesty would appoint commissioners to examine into all these matters, and into all the other injuries and violences which had been done to the Moheagans, and to determine respecting them according to equity.

Her majesty, imposed upon and deceived by these representations, and not waiting to give the colony an opportunity to be heard, on the 19th of July, 1704, granted a commission to Joseph Dudley, Esq. the great enemy of the colony, Thomas Povey, Esq. lieutenant governor of Massachusetts, major Edward Palms, and others, to the number of twelve, authorizing them to hear and determine the whole affair, reserving liberty to either to appeal to her majesty in council.

At the session in May, a respectable committee was appointed, with ample powers, to examine into all the complaints of Owaneco and the Moheagan Indians, and to report to the assembly in October. The committee appointed time and place, and attempted to accomplish the business, for which they had been appointed; but captain Mason, whom Owaneco had chosen for his guardian, had art enough to frustrate the design. He made a journey to Boston, at the very time, and Owaneco would do nothing without him. In the mean time, the commission was granted by the queen, and the colony were unhappily drawn into a long and expensive controversy.

The Masons claimed the lands purchased by their ancestor, deputy governor John Mason, by virtue of a deed given to him by Uncas, in 1659, while he acted as agent of the colony, and denied the legality of the surrender which he had made of them, in the general assembly, the next year. They insisted, that it respected nothing more than the jurisdiction right, and that the title to the soil was vested in their family, as guardians or overseers of the Indians. While they pretended great concern for the Indians, their sole object was to hold all those lands, included in said deed, for themselves and others, who had united with them in prosecution of the affair against the colony.

Book I.
1704.
vor of the Moheagans.

Her majesty appoints commissioners to hear the case.

BOOK I.
~~~
1705.

Hearing of the complaints against Connecticut before her majesty, 1705.

Sir Henry Ashurst, wishing to preserve the important privileges of the colony, had taken pains to postpone the hearing of the complaints against it, as far as possible, that the governor and company might have intelligence concerning them, and send their answer; but, on the 12th of February, 1705, the hearing came on, before her majesty in council. Governor Dudley and Lord Cornbury had spared no pains to carry their point before her majesty. Dudley had been careful to procure and lay before her an opinion of the attorney general, in king William's reign, " that he might send a governor to Connecticut." Further, to prepare the way for the decision which he wished, he procured another opinion of the attorney and solicitor general, respecting the case of Connecticut, as it then appeared, " that if it were as governor Dudley had represented, there was a defect in the government: That the colony was not able to defend itself, and in imminent danger of being possessed by the queen's enemies: And that, in such case, the queen might send a governor, for civil and military government; but not to alter the laws and customs."

Her majesty had directed Sir Henry to appear and show reasons, if any he had, why she should not appoint a governor over the colony. He considered every thing dear to it at stake, and therefore made exertions in some measure proportionate to the magnitude of the cause. Lord Paget, a man of great influence, was his brother by marriage, and he was related to, or intimately connected with other principal characters at court. He made all the interest, and obtained all the influence which he possibly could, either by himself or his connections, in favor of the colony. He obtained two of the best council in England; both parliament men, possessing an estate of a thousand pounds a year. He stood firm against all the charges of Dudley, lord Cornbury, Congreve, and others, against the colony, and by his counsel, for an hour and an half, defended it against all the art and intrigue of its adversaries, and all the law learning and eloquence of the attorney and solicitor general.*

Pleadings in vindication of the colony.

As Connecticut was entirely ignorant of the charges brought against it, and no information or evidence could be thence obtained, Sir Henry and his council were necessitated to employ such means as were in their power. They amply stated the rights and privileges granted by the royal charter, the territory it conveyed, and the powers with which it vested the governor and company. They

* Letter of Sir Henry Ashurst, February 15th, 1705, on file.

CHAP. XVII.   CONNECTICUT.

showed, that these patents were confirmed by a non ob- Book 1.
stante, and always to be construed in the most favorable
light for the grantees. It was demonstrated, that the leg- 1705.
islature were vested with ample powers to make laws,
criminal and capital, as well as civil; to inflict banishment,
death, and all other capital punishments, in all capital cases, no less than in others. It was also represented, that
the governors, or commanders in chief, were, by charter,
vested with plenary powers to assemble in martial array,
and put in warlike posture the inhabitants of the colony,
for their defence, and to commission others, for the like
purposes. It was also clearly shown, that, by charter, they
had the same right to fish, trade, and do all other business,
and enjoy all other privileges, by land and sea, which any
other of her majesty's subjects had a right to do, or enjoy.
It was, therefore, urged, that all those matters, charged
against the colony, respecting their making capital laws,
and inflicting capital punishments, whether death or banishment, were no crimes; but things which the legislature
not only had a right, but were bound in faithfulness to do,
as circumstances might require. For the same reason, it
was also insisted, that the colonies claiming a right to command their own militia, and defeating the designs of the
governors of the other colonies, who wished to command
it, were no crimes. It was insisted, that doing them was
no more than defending themselves in the enjoyment of their
legal rights.

With respect to the irregularity and injustice of the courts
in Connecticut, it was observed, that general charges deserved no reply: That it did not appear, that what was
charged was any thing more than mere hearsay and clam-
or. But it was pleaded, that, on the contrary, they had
substantial evidence of the justice of the courts in Connecticut. That several appeals had been made, to her
majesty, from the judgment of those courts: That these
had been different cases, and in every instance, the judgments given by the courts in Connecticut, had been approved by her majesty, and the lords committee of council.
This, it was said, was a notable evidence of their justice;
and that, so far as appeared, there had been no injustice
or irregularity in any one court in the colony.

With respect to governor Dudley's complaint, that Connecticut did not furnish the men which he demanded, and
that of lord Cornbury, that it did not comply with his demands for money, it was answered, that it did not appear,
from the charter, that the colony was obliged to comply
with those requisitions: That the governors of other colo-

nies had no right to command the legislature and people of Connecticut: and that they were under no obligations to obey them, any further than it should be required by her majesty. It was further observed, with respect to the money, that it appeared from his lordship's letter, that the general assembly of Connecticut had taken the requisition into their consideration, and had determined to know her majesty's pleasure, before they gave away their money. It was affirmed, that there was nothing disloyal in such a determination: That the colony had a right to grant, or not to grant their money, as they judged it expedient or not: That they had a right to know the purpose for which they granted it; and that their referring it to her majesty's pleasure, was an implication of their obedience to it, whenever it should be known.

With reference to Connecticut's harboring deserters, malefactors, pirates, and the like, it was observed, that it was a general charge of little weight, and deserved no answer. It was affirmed to be a common thing, even in England, for soldiers and others to go from one country into another, and not to be found; yet it might not be any crime or fault in the country where they secreted themselves. As to captain Matthews finding two soldiers at Stamford, and sending for major Silleck to secure them, it did not appear that there was the least fault in the major. It was evident, from his lordship's letter, that he went to Stamford, that the soldiers were brought, and that, while the major and Matthews were conversing together, in a private room, they made their escape. It was said, it might be more the fault of Matthews than of Silleck; for it did not appear that Matthews was kept there by any force or constraint, but was examining into the affair, or talking generally upon the subject.

With relation to the complaint of lord Cornbury, in his letter of June, 1703, "that he labored under great misfortunes, in relation to the neighboring provinces: That the coast of Connecticut is opposite to two thirds of Long-Island; by which means they filled all that part of the island with European goods, cheaper than their merchants could, because they paid duties, and those of Connecticut paid none; nor would they be subject to the acts of navigation; by which means there had been no trade between the city of New-York and the east end of Long-Island, from whence the greatest part of the whale oil came; and that it was difficult to persuade those people that they belonged to that province," it was replied, that there appeared to be no fault in Connecticut in this respect. It was maintained,

Chap. XVII. CONNECTICUT.

that the inhabitants had a right to trade where they pleased, if it were not repugnant to the laws of England. It also was pleaded, that there was no evidence, that they had been guilty of any illegal trade or practices; and that they were a poor people, and carried on little trade.

Book I.

1705.

In a letter of the same date with the former, his lordship had observed, "that he was satisfied this vast continent, which might be made very useful to England, if right measures were taken, would never be so, till all the propriety and charter governments were brought under the crown." To this it was replied, that this might, or it might not be the case: that the same, as circumstances might be, might be said of all the charters in England. It was however insisted, that the words sounded harsh, and had an ill relish.

It was, however, much insisted on, that the attorney and solicitor general had reported, "that her majesty might appoint a governor for Connecticut." To this, the council for the colony answered, that the report was hypothetical, founded on the supposition that the colony was not able to defend itself, and was in danger of falling into the hands of her majesty's enemies; but that there was no evidence of these facts. It did not appear, they said, that Connecticut was in a more defenceless state, or in greater danger of becoming a prey to her majesty's enemies, than any of the other colonies. It was pleaded, that the attorney and solicitor general had not reported, that either of these was the case, and therefore their opinion could not be made a plea for sending a governor to Connecticut.

Further, it was strenuously maintained, that it was an essential right of every individual and corporation, to be heard before they were condemned; and that the governor and company of Connecticut ought to be heard upon the articles exhibited against them, before any judgment be formed respecting them. It was observed, that governors, who, by enlarging their own territories, might increase their honors and profits, were apt to complain: that they were under peculiar temptations, especially at such a distance, where it was so difficult to make enquiry and obtain the truth: that there was more reason to suspect the governors complaining, than the governor of Connecticut, who acted with a council and an assembly. It was therefore affirmed, that there was every reason, that the colony should be heard in its own defence. If either the governor of New-England or New-York were impeached, and the same complaints made against them, said the counsel, which they have brought against Connecticut, her majesty would do nothing with respect to them, until they had been heard.

C 3

HISTORY OF   CHAP. XVII.

Book I. 1705. It would be contrary to all law and reason; much more so, to treat a whole colony in this manner, in a case in which their charter might be forfeited, and their fortunes ruined. It was observed, that governors appointed during pleasure, often committed barbarous acts to enrich themselves; and that they had nothing to lose but their office; whereas the colony of Connecticut was of great substance, and had every thing to lose: that even in ordinary cases, in which the character and property of one man only were concerned, nothing was determined, but upon sufficient evidence, given upon oath, and that it could never be reasonable to condemn a colony upon mere suggestions: that it might appear, upon a full examination, that the governor of Connecticut was much better qualified to govern, than the governor of New-York or Massachusetts. It was therefore pleaded, that the articles of complaint might be sent to the governor and company of Connecticut, and that they might have an opportunity to answer for themselves: that there could be no danger in this; and if any irregularities should be found, in the management of their government, they would most certainly reform and obey her majesty's commands.*

Her majesty's determination respecting Connecticut, Feb. 12, 1705. Upon this full hearing, it was determined, that the lords of trade should draw out the principal articles of complaint, and send a copy of them to the governor of Connecticut, and to the two principal complainants, governor Dudley, and lord Cornbury, and that Connecticut should send their answer, with evidence respecting the several articles, legally taken, and sealed with the public seal of the colony. Governor Dudley and lord Cornbury were also directed to transmit their evidence of the articles charged, publicly and legally taken.

Frustrates the designs of Dudley and Cornbury. By this means, Dudley, Cornbury, and their abettors were caught in their own snare, their selfishness and duplicity were made to appear, in a strong point of light, and their whole scheme at once totally ruined. They were totally unable to support the charges which they had brought against the colony. At the same time, the legislature of Connecticut could produce the most substantial evidence, that the very reverse of what had been pretended, was true. They had the last, and this year between five and six hundred men in actual service. Four hundred of this number had been employed, principally in the defence of Massachusetts and New-York. The committee of war, consisting of the governor, most of the council, and

Facts respecting the colony.

---
* Case of Connecticut stated, and pleadings before her majesty, February 12th, 1705, on file.

other principal men in the colony, had met, with officers and commissioners from Massachusetts, and most harmoniously united with them in opinion, and measures for the common defence. The legislature were not only able to prove these facts from the records of the colony, and from the resolutions of the committee of war, but, what was still more confounding to governor Dudley, to produce a letter of his, under his own hand and signature, acknowledging their generous and prompt assistance in the war, and thanking them for the aid which they had given him.* They produced substantial evidence, that when they had scarcely two thousand pounds, in circulating medium, in the whole colony, they had, in three years, expended more than that sum, in the defence of her majesty's provinces of Massachusetts and New-York. They were able to evince, that they had shewn the utmost loyalty and attachment to the queen; been punctual in their observance of the acts of trade and navigation; had not been pirates themselves, nor at any time harboured pirates, deserters, servants, or criminals among them.

With respect to appeals to her majesty, the legislature affirmed, that they had not refused to admit them, only in cases in which proper security, or sufficient bondsmen had not been offered. In the appeals of major Palms, which seem to have been the only instances of which complaint had been made, the court judged, that the security offered was insufficient. The men, who offered themselves to be bound, appeared to have little or no property. As to the vexations complained of, these respected the obtaining of copies of the judgments of the courts in his case. It seems he applied to the assembly for them, but the assembly declined giving them, insisting, that it was not their province to give copies of the doings of other courts. He was therefore referred to the courts in which the judgments had been given.

In the appeals of major Palms, and in all other instances, the judgments of the courts in Connecticut were finally established. Upon a full examination of the complaints, they appeared not only groundless, but invidious. The loyalty, justice, and honor of the colony appeared more conspicuous than they had done before: but it was some time before the evidence of the true state of the case could be collected and transmitted to England.

Meanwhile Dudley and Cornbury never lost sight of

* They were able to produce letters of thanks, from the commanding officers, ministers, and principal gentlemen in the county of Hampshire, for the assistance which they had given them. Those letters are now on file.

Book I.
1705.

Quakers petition to her majesty.

She revokes the act against them.

their object, but vigorously prosecuted the design of subverting the government. There had been, nearly fifty years before, a law enacted against the quakers, but it does not appear, that it had ever been acted upon, in Connecticut, and was, at that time, become obsolete. It appears, by a letter of the governor's, to Sir Henry Ashurst, that he did not know of one person, then in the colony, who was acknowledged to be a quaker. But governor Dudley, by some means, obtained a copy of the law, and procured a publication of it in Boston. The knowledge of it was communicated to the quakers in England, and they were spirited up to petition for a repeal of the law of Connecticut against the quakers. A petition, about the beginning of April, was preferred to her majesty, on the subject, reciting said law, and representing, that it was calculated to extirpate their friends from that part of her majesty's dominion, and praying that she would disallow the said law. Sir Henry Ashurst presented a petition to the lords of trade and plantation, to whom the petition of the quakers had been referred, praying them to advise her majesty to come to no determination on the subject, until the colony should have notice of the petition, and have time to send their answer. He represented, that the law was made against Adamites and Ranters: That it was become obsolete, and quakers lived as peaceably in Connecticut, as in any of her majesty's plantations. He represented to their lordships, that there had been more complaints exhibited against this poor colony, in three or four years, without any crime proved, than had been before from the time of its first settlement, which made him believe, that there were disaffected persons, who were attempting, by all means, to make them weary of their charter government: That before the appointment of a certain governor for New-England, the colony had enjoyed uninterrupted peace, for many years, and would have done to that time, had it not been for his misrepresentations. He assured them, that he had been informed, that governor Dudley had, about two years before, ordered the act against the quakers to be printed, in Boston, on purpose, that the quakers, in England, might join with his other instruments in clamors against Connecticut, to deprive it of its charter privileges.*

Her majesty, upon the advice of the lords of trade and plantations, declared the act against the quakers null and void, without giving the colony a hearing.

Sir Henry Ashurst, writing to the colony soon after, says, " You see how you are every way attacked."

* Petition on file.

CHAP. XVII.   CONNECTICUT.   421

The enemies of the colony in Connecticut and New-England were no less active than those on the other side of the water. As they had obtained a commission for the trial of the case between Connecticut and the Moheagans, they spared no pains to carry their point. On the 5th of July, 1705, captain John Chandler, in behalf of Owaneco, captain Samuel Mason, Hallam, and others, who interested themselves in recovering the lands from the colony, began the survey of the Moheagan country, and having accomplished the work, drew a map of it, with a view to the trial, before Dudley's court, which was approaching. The governor sent an officer and prohibited his entering upon the survey; but the party gave large bonds to indemnify him, and he proceeded notwithstanding. The boundaries, as surveyed and reported by Chandler, captain John Parke, Edward Culver, and Samuel Sterry, who assisted him, were, on the south from a large rock, in Connecticut river, near eight mile island in the bounds of Lyme, eastward, through Lyme, New-London, and Groton, to Ah-yo-sup-suck, a pond in the northeastern part of Stonington; on the east, from this pond northward, to Mah-man-suck, another pond, thence to Egunk-sank-a-poug, whetstone hills; from thence to Man-hum-squeeg, the whetstone country. From this boundary, the line ran southwest, a few miles, to Ac-quiunk, the upper falls in Quinibaug river. Thence the line ran, a little north of west, through Pomfret, Ashford, Willington, and Tolland, to Mo-she-nup-suck, the notch of the mountain, now known to be the notch in Bolton mountain. From thence the line ran southerly, through Bolton, Hebron, and East-Haddam, to the first mentioned bounds. This, it appears, was the Pequot country, to the whole of which the Moheagans laid claim, after the conquest of the Pequot nation, except some part of New-London, Groton, and Stonington, which had been the chief seat of that warlike tribe. The Moheagans claimed this tract as their hereditary country, and the Wabbequasset territory, which lay north of it, they claimed by virtue of conquest.

On the 23d of August, 1705, the court of commissioners, appointed by her majesty, to examine into the affair of the Moheagan lands, convened at Stonington. Writs had been previously issued, summoning the governor and company, with the claimers of lands in controversy, and all parties concerned, to attend at time and place. The court consisted of Joseph Dudley, Esq. president, Edward Palms, Giles Sylvester, Jahleel Brenton, Nathaniel Byfield, Thomas Hooker, James Avery, John Avery, John Morgan, and Thomas Leffingwell.

Book I.

1705.

Survey of the Moheagan country.

Boundaries.

Dudley's court, August 23, 1705.

BOOK I. It seems that the governor and general assembly of Connecticut had not been served with a copy of the commission, by which the court was instituted, and viewed it as a court of enquiry only, to examine and make report to her majesty, and not to try and determine the title of the lands in dispute. The committee, appointed by the assembly, to appear before the court, were conditionally instructed. Provided the court was instituted for enquiry only, they were to answer and show the unreasonableness of the Moheagan claims, and the false light in which the affair had been represented; but if the design was to determine with respect to the title of the colony, they were directed to enter their protest against the court, and withdraw. All inhabitants of the colony, personally interested in any of the lands in controversy, were forbidden to plead or make any answer before the court.

1705.

Instructions to the colony's committee.

Governor Winthrop addressed the following letter to the president.

Governor Winthrop's letter to the court.

"New-London, August 21st, 1705.

"SIR,

"I understand, by your excellency's letter of July 30th, your intentions to be at Stonington, on the 23d inst. to hear the complaints of Owaneco against this government. I have, therefore, in obedience to her majesty's commands, directed and empowered William Pitkin, John Chester, Eleazar Kimberly, Esquires, major William Whiting, Mr. John Elliot, and Mr. Richard Lord, to wait on your excellency, and show the unreasonableness of those complaints, and the unpardonable affront put upon her majesty, by that false representation, and the great trouble to yourself thereby; and I conclude, in a short hearing, your excellency will be able to represent to her majesty, that those complaints are altogether groundless. The gentlemen shall assist your excellency's enquiry, in summoning such persons as you shall please to desire, and all things else, reserving the honor and privileges of the government."

When the committee came before the court, they perceived that they determined to try the title of the colony to the lands, and judicially to decide the whole controversy. They resolved, therefore, not to make any answer or plea before them, but to protest against their proceedings. The protest is entered as followeth:

"To his Excellency, Joseph Dudley, Esquire, captain-general and governor in chief of her majesty's colony of Massachusetts Bay, &c.

"We, the commissioners of her majesty's colony of

CHAP. XVII. CONNECTICUT.

Connecticut, are obliged, by our instructions from this government, to certify your excellency, that, in obedience to her majesty's commands to this colony, we are ready to show the injustice of those complaints against the government, made by Owaneco, to her majesty, in council, if your excellency sees good that the complaints be produced, (provided the commissioners, mentioned in her majesty's commission, with your excellency, be qualified to act as members of the court of inquiry constituted thereby,) that so your excellency and commissioners may, upon inquiry, be enabled to make such a true and just report of the matters of fact, mentioned in said complaints to her majesty, as you shall see meet. But if your excellency, (as appears to us,) does construe any expressions in the said commission, so as to empower the said commissioners, by themselves, to inquire and judicially determine concerning the matter in controversy, mentioned in the said complaint, concerning the title of land or trespass, and do resolve to proceed accordingly, as we cannot but judge it to be contrary to her majesty's most just and legal intentions, in said commission; so we must declare against and prohibit all such proceedings, as contrary to law and to the letters patent under the great seal of England, granted to this her majesty's colony, and contrary to her majesty's order to this government, concerning the said commission and complaint, as well as to the known rights of her majesty's subjects, throughout all her dominions, and such as we cannot allow of. We only add, that it seems strange to us, that your excellency should proceed in such a manner, without first communicating your commission to the general assembly of this her majesty's colony.

"WILLIAM PITKIN, &c.

"August 24th, 1705."

Book I. 1705. Protest against the proceedings of the court.

The inhabitants who had deeds of the lands in controversy, made default, as well as the colony: but the court proceeded to an *ex parte* hearing. Owaneco, Mason, Hallam, and their council, produced such papers and evidence, and made such representations as they pleased, without any person to confront them. After such a partial hearing, of one day only, the court determined against the colony, and adjudged to Owaneco and the Moheagans a tract of land called Massapeag, lying in the town of New-London; and another tract, of about eleven hundred acres, in the northern part of the town, which the assembly had granted as an addition to that township, in 1703. The court, also, adjudged to them a tract in the town of Lyme, two miles in breadth, and nine miles in length, with the

Judgment and proceedings of the court.

Book I. whole tract contained in the town of Colchester. The court ordered Connecticut immediately to restore all those lands to Owaneco, and filed a bill of cost against the colony of 573l. 12s. 8d.* Thus a cause of such magnitude, in which the essential interests of a whole colony, and the fortunes of hundreds of individuals, were concerned, was carried wholly by intrigue and the grossest misrepresentations. The commission was granted by her majesty, wholly upon an *ex parte* hearing, upon the representation of the enemies of the colony; and the men who carried on the intrigue, were appointed judges in their own case. Without hearing the case, contrary to all reason and justice, they gave judgment against the colony, and hundreds of individuals. They gave away lands holden by conquest, purchase, ancient deeds from the original proprietors, well executed and recorded, by charter, acts, and patents from the assembly, and by long possession. The chief judge had been using all his art and influence to ruin the colony, and was now supposed to be scheming for a portion of its lands, as well as for the government. Major Palms had been a long time in controversy with the colony, was exceedingly embittered against it, and against the governor, his brother in law. Others of the commissioners were supposed to be confederate with Mason and Clarke, and interested in the lands in controversy. Hallam, Clarke, and several of the commissioners were witnesses in the case. They were witnesses and judges in their own cause, heard themselves, and no others. Owaneco was placed, in state, on the right hand of the president, and the colony were treated worse than criminals, with dishonour and contempt.†

After the court had given judgment against the colony, on the 24th of August, they spent three days in hearing such complaints as Owaneco, Mason, and other persons interested in the lands, or inimical to the colony, were pleased to make. When they had heard all the complaints and misrepresentations which they had to make, they represented to her majesty, that Owaneco complained he was disseised of a tract of land, containing about seven thousand acres, called Mamaquaog, lying northward of Windham; of another tract called Plainfield, and considerable skirts and parcels of land, encroached upon and taken in, by the towns of Lebanon, Windham, and Canterbury. The court prohibited all her majesty's subjects from entering upon, or improving any of those lands, until a further

* Moheagan case, in print.
† Petition to her majesty, printed in Moheagan trial.

CHAP. XVII.   CONNECTICUT.   425

hearing and determination of the case. Further, in the plenitude of their power, they appointed captain John Mason to be trustee, or guardian, to Owaneco and his people, and to manage all their affairs. They represented, from the evidence of major James Fitch and captain John Mason, that the colony had left the Indians no land to plant on, and that they consisted of a hundred and fifty warriors, one hundred of whom had been in the actual service of the country that very year.*

These Indians were enlisted and sent out by the colony of Connecticut, and went as cheerfully into service this year, as they had done at any time before. This gave demonstrative evidence, that there was no general uneasiness among the Moheagans. Had there been, two thirds of their warriors would not have enlisted into the service of the government. Indeed, Owaneco himself was not uneasy only at turns, when the Masons, Clarke, Fitch, Hallam, and others, made him so; who were scheming to deprive him and the Moheagans of their lands.

So far was it from being true, that Connecticut had injured them, or taken their lands from them, they had treated them with great kindness, defended them by their arms, and at their own expense, and prevented their being swallowed up by their enemies. They had left them a fine tract of land, of between four and five thousand acres, between New-London and Norwich; and both in the grant and patent to New-London, there was an express reservation of all the rights and property of the Indians.† The colony had not only reserved lands for the Moheagans, but for all other Indians in it, to plant upon. They suffered them to hunt, fish, and fowl, in all parts of it, and even to build their wigwams, and cut such wood and timber as they needed, in any of their uninclosed lands.

Dudley's court, having finished such business as was agreeable to its wishes, adjourned until the next May; but it never met again. Before that time, the intrigue and duplicity of governor Dudley and the malcontents, became so evident, that all their designs were frustrated.

The assembly, at their session in October, appointed a committee to examine into all matters respecting the Indians, and the complaints which had been made against the colony, and, as soon as possible, to transmit a particular and full answer to their agent. They were instructed fully to acquaint him with a true statement of the Mohea-

Book I.

1705.

The assembly appoint a committee to represent the affair to their agent.

* Proceedings and judgment of the court in print, Moheagan case, p. 26 to 67.
† Records of the colony, and Moheagan case, in print.

D 3

Book I. gan case, and of the whole management of Dudley and his court. They were to represent, that Dudley, Palms, and others of the commissioners, were interested, and parties in the cause, and to insist, that the manner in which the commission was procured, to governor Dudley, major Palms, and others, was matter of intrigue, and the whole process arbitrary and illegal.

1705.

Sir Henry Ashurst petitions her majesty.

Sir Henry Ashurst, on receiving the papers relative to the case, presented a petition to her majesty, representing the title of the colony to all the lands in controversy, by conquest, purchase, royal charter, long possession and improvement: That Uncas, when the English became first acquainted with him, was a revolted Pequot, expelled his country, and had not a sufficient number of men to make a hunt; and that the lands reserved to him, were not reserved to him in consequence of any right of his, but was a matter of mere permission: That Joseph Dudley, Esq. Hallam, Palms, the Averys, Morgan, and Leffingwell, had grants of several parts of the controverted lands, and, in their own names, or in the name of John Mason, were attempting to set up their titles to them: That Dudley and Hallam, by misrepresentation, had obtained a commission from her majesty, by surprise, under the great seal of England, directed to the said Dudley, Palms, the two Averys, Morgan, Leffingwell, and others, most of whom were of Dudley's and Hallam's denomination, and under his influence; and that in the court, thus instituted, they were the accusers, parties, and judges: That they had assumed to themselves jurisdiction, in a summary way, to try her majesty's petitioners' titles to their lands, and to evict and disseise them of their freeholds, properties, and ancient possessions, without any legal process, or so much as the form of a trial. This, it was represented, tended to the destruction of all the rights of the colony, and was directly contrary to divers acts of parliament, made and provided in such cases. The agent, therefore, in behalf of the colony, appealed from the judgment of said court to her majesty, in council, and prayed that the case might be heard before her.*

Connecticut always gets her case.

In consequence of this petition, her majesty, some time after, appointed a commission of review. The affair was kept in agitation nearly seventy years. It was always, upon a legal hearing, determined in favour of the colony. The final decision was by king George the third, in council.

Adjudication of the court of review, 1743.

The commissioners of review, in 1743, not only determined the title of the lands to be in the colony of Connecticut, but " That the governor and company had treated the

* Petition in print, Moheagan case, p. 153—157.

CHAP. XVII.   CONNECTICUT.

said Indians with much humanity, at all times; and had, at all times, provided them with a sufficiency, at least, of lands to plant on; and that no act, or thing, appeared, either before the judgment of Joseph Dudley, Esq. or since, by which they, the said governor and company, had taken from the Indians, or from their sachem, any tracts of land, to which the Indians or their sachem had any right, by reservation, or otherwise, either in law or equity."*

The proceedings of the several courts of review, and the pleadings before them and his majesty, in council, will most properly be noticed in the time of them, and will not be anticipated in this volume.

The agent of the colony petitioned her majesty, in its behalf, to hear the complaints exhibited by governor Dudley and his accomplices, that it might have an opportunity of demonstrating how false and groundless they were. He also prayed, that as Dudley had surprised her, to grant a commission of high powers to the subversion of the rights of her loyal subjects, and contrary to her gracious intentions towards them, and had abused her name and authority to serve his own dark designs, that her majesty would, in some exemplary manner, discountenance the said Dudley and his abettors.

However, it does not appear, that Dudley, or lord Cornbury, were ever obliged to bring forward any evidence in support of the charges which they had exhibited, or that her majesty, by any public act, discountenanced their intrigue and falsehood. They had such powerful friends at court, that they seem to have palliated, and kept the affair, as far as possible, out of public view; and it seems to have been passed by without any further examination.

There was no alteration made in the legislature, at the May, election in 1706.

1706.

The assembly adopted the same measures, for the defence of Connecticut and the neighbouring colonies, which they had done the year preceding. The same officers were appointed, and the same number of men sent into the field.

The colony had assurances from their agent, Sir Henry Ashurst, that they had a clear right to command their own militia; that the governors of the neighbouring colonies had no right to command their men, or money; and that this was the opinion of the best council in the nation. He assured them, that they were under no obligations to them, to do any thing more, than to furnish such quotas as her majesty should require.

* Judgment, in print, Moheagan case, p. 140.

	HISTORY OF	Chap. XVII.

Book I. 1706.
Connecticut had done much more than this, both in the reign of king William and queen Anne. Nevertheless, notwithstanding the abusive treatment of governor Dudley, lord Cornbury, and their associates in mischief, and the great expense which had been brought upon them, not only by the war, but in consequence of the defence which their agent had been obliged to make for them, in England, such was their zeal for her majesty's service, and their concern and good will for their sister colonies, that they exerted themselves no less for their defence, than if they had been under the command of their respective governors. It was declared to her majesty, that had this been the case they could have done no more.

Act for the encouragement of the clergy, Oct. 1706.
At the session in October, the assembly passed the following act in favor of the clergy, "That all the ministers of the gospel that now are, or hereafter shall be settled in this colony, during the continuance of their public service in the gospel ministry, shall have their estates, lying in the same town where they dwell, and all the polls belonging to their several familes exempted, and they are hereby exempted and freed from being entered in the public lists and payment of rates." By virtue of this act, for the encouragement of the clergy of this colony, they have always, from that to the present time, been exempted from taxation.*

The colony, at this period, was in very low circumstances. Its whole circulating cash amounted only to about two thousand pounds. Such had been its expense in the war, and in defending itself against the attempts of its enemies, in England and America, that the legislature had been obliged to levy a tax, in about three years, of more than two shillings on the pound, on the whole list of the colony. The taxes were laid and collected in grain, pork, beef, and other articles of country produce. These commodities were transported to Boston and the West-Indies, and by this means money and bills of exchange were obtained, to pay the bills drawn upon the colony, in England, and to discharge its debts at home. These low circumstances, these misrepresentations, abuse, and dangers, from their enemies, our venerable ancestors endured with an exemplary patience and magnanimity. Under the pressure of all this expense and danger, they cheerfully supported the gospel ministry and ordinances, in their respective towns and parishes. They contemplated their dangers and deliverances with wonder and thanksgiving,

* The legislature had before released their persons from taxation, but not their families and estates.

rejoiced in the enjoyment of their privileges, and in the divine care and beneficence.

CHAPTER XVIII.

The country is alarmed. Means of defence. The assembly decline the affording of any assistance in the expedition against Port Royal. Grant assistance to the frontier towns. New townships granted and settled. The Rev. Gurdon Saltonstall chosen governor. Act empowering the freemen to choose the governor from among themselves at large. Acts relative to the settlement of the boundary line with Massachusetts. Garrisons erected in the towns on the frontiers. Expedition against Canada. First emission of paper money. Address to her majesty. Loss of the colony at Wood Creek. Expedition against Port Royal. Expedition against Canada under the command of admiral Walker and general Nicholson. Fleet cast away and the enterprise defeated. The colony petition her majesty, and send the only pilot from Connecticut, to England, to represent to her majesty the loss of the fleet truly as it was. Acts respecting the superior court. Settlement of the boundary line between Massachusetts and Connecticut. Reasons why the colony consented to such a settlement. Return of peace. The colony happy in the the preservation of their frontiers. Towns settled under Massachusetts. State of the colony. Observations.

SUCH reports of the preparations of the French and Indians, to make a descent upon some part of New-England, were spread abroad, about the beginning of the year 1707, as gave a general alarm to the country. On the 6th of February, 1707, a council of war, consisting of the governor, most of the council, and a considerable number of the chief military officers in the colony, convened at Hartford. A letter was received from deputy governor Treat, and another from major Schuyler at Albany, giving intelligence, that the French, and Indians in their interest, were about to make a descent upon New-England. Information was also communicated, that suspicions were entertained, that the Pohtatuck and Owiantuck Indians designed to join the French and Indians from Canada.

BOOK I.

1707.
Measures adopted for the common safety.

The committee resolved, that the western frontier towns, Simsbury, Waterbury, Woodbury, and Danbury, should be fortified with all possible dispatch. As Waterbury had sustained great losses, by inundations, it was resolved, for their encouragement to fortify their houses well, that the governor and council would use their influence with the assembly, that their country rates should be abated. It was resolved, that each of these four towns should keep a scout of two faithful men, to be sent out every day, to discover the designs of the enemy, and give intelligence should they make their appearance near the frontier towns.

To prevent damages from the Pohtatuck and Owiantuck Indians, captain John Minor and Mr. John Sherman were appointed to remove them to Stratford and Fairfield. If by reason of sickness or any other cause they could not be removed, it was ordered, that a number of their chief men should be carried down to those towns, and kept as hostages to secure the fidelity of the rest.

Special assembly, April 2d.

On the second of April, a special assembly was convened in consequence of letters from governor Dudley. He had proposed to send an army of a thousand men against L'Acadia, and requested Connecticut to join with Massachusetts in the expedition.

The assembly will not join in the expedition to L'Acadia.

After the affair had been maturely considered, the assembly determined not to comply with the proposal. The reasons given were, that they had not been consulted, nor had opportunity to consent to the expedition: That they did not understand that the neighbouring colonies, who were equally interested in the expedition, with themselves, were called upon, or had consented to do any thing; and, that the vast expense of defending the county of Hampshire and their own frontiers, incapacitated them to join in the enterprise.

Court of election, May 8, 1707.

At the general election this year, the governor and council were all re-elected.

Hebron made a town.

Upon the petition of John Pratt, Robert Chapman, John Clark, and Stephen Post, appointed a committee in behalf of the legatees of Joshua Uncas,* the assembly granted a township which they named Hebron. The settlement of the town began in June, 1704. The first people who made settlements in the town were William Shipman, Timothy Phelps, Samuel Filer, Caleb Jones, Stephen

* By the last will of said Uncas, all the lands in Hebron were bequeathed to Thomas Buckingham, Esq. William Shipman and others, called the Saybrook legatees, except about 2,600 acres at the northeast corner, and about 4,000 acres at the south end of the town. There were also about 500 within the parish of Marlborough. These lands were claimed by Mason.

Post, Jacob Root, Samuel Curtis, Edward Sawyer, Joseph Youngs, and Benoni Trumbull. They were from Windsor, Saybrook, Long-Island, and Northampton. The settlement, at first, went on but slowly; partly, by reason of opposition made by Mason and the Moheagans, and partly, by reason of the extensive tracts claimed by proprietors, who made no settlements. Several acts of the assembly were made, and committees appointed to encourage and assist the planters. By these means they so increased in numbers and wealth that in about six or seven years they were enabled to erect a meeting-house and settle a minister among them.

At the session in October, the assembly granted a township to Nathan Gould, Peter Burr, captain John Wakeman, Jonathan Sturges, and other inhabitants of the town of Fairfield, bounded southerly on Danbury, easterly on New-Milford, and westerly upon the colony line. It extended fourteen miles northward from Danbury. It was afterwards named New-Fairfield. The war, for several years, prevented all attempts for the settlement of this tract.

As the frontier towns had exhibited much zeal in fortifying themselves agreeably to the directions of the governor and council, the assembly made them a liberal compensation.

About this time the colony sustained a great loss in the death of the honorable Fitz John Winthrop, Esq.† and a special assembly was convoked on the 17th of December, by deputy governor Treat, at New-Haven, for the purpose of electing another governor. The assembly ordered, that the votes of both houses should be mixed before they were sorted and counted, and that the majority of votes should determine the choice. Upon counting the votes, the Reverend Gurdon Saltonstall was declared to be chosen governor.

Four of the magistrates, the speaker of the house, with three of the other deputies, were appointed a committee to acquaint him with the choice, and solicit his acceptance of

---

† He was the son of the honorable John Winthrop, Esq. the first governor of Connecticut, under the charter. His birth was at Ipswich, in Massachusetts, 1638. Upon the assumption of the charter, May, 1689, he was chosen into the magistracy. In 1690, he was appointed major general of the land army designed against Canada. On the dispute relative to the command of the militia, he was sent agent, for the colony, to the British court, 1694. After his return, May, 1698, he was chosen governor, and was annually re-chosen during his life. He died November 27th, 1707, in the 69th year of his age.

He appears to have been a popular gentleman, and to have sustained a character without blemish.

BOOK I. the important trust to which he had been chosen. A letter
         was addressed to him by the assembly, desiring him to ac-
1707.   cept of the choice which they had made, and, with the
         committee appointed to wait on him, to answer the letters
         of their agent, and transact whatever the exigencies of the
         government might require. A letter was also addressed to
         his church and congregation at New-London, acquainting
         them with the call, which the assembly imagined Mr. Sal-
         tonstall had to leave the ministry, and to dispose them to
         submit to such a dispensation.

The magistrates, upon Mr. Saltonstall's acceptance of the trust to which he had been chosen, were directed to administer to him the oath of the governor, and the oath respecting trade and navigation.

January 1st, 1708. On the first of January, 1708, governor Saltonstall accepted of his office, and took the oaths appointed by law.

This assembly repealed the law which required, that the governor should always be chosen from among the magistrates in nomination, and gave liberty for the freemen to elect him from among themselves at large.

Election, May 13th, 1708. At the election, May 13th, 1708, governor Saltonstall was chosen governor by the freemen. Nathan Gould, Esq. was elected deputy-governor.* The former magistrates were re-chosen, and Mr. John Haynes, for the first time, was elected one of the council. The former treasurer and secretary were re-chosen.

A township was granted, in the course of this session, at Pohtatuck, afterwards named Newtown.

Act for quieting the inhabitants of Windsor and Suffield, and fixing the line between Massachu- Connecticut, for a long course of years, had been at great trouble and expense, in attempting the settlement of the boundary line between this colony and Massachusetts. The inhabitants of Windsor and Simsbury had been often exceedingly injured, in their persons and property, by the people of Suffield and Enfield, especially by the former. They had not only encroached upon their lands and cut down their timber, but often seized upon their tar

---

*The honorable Robert Treat, Esq. being, at this period, eighty-six years of age, retired from the scene of public action. He had been three years a magistrate, and thirty-two years governor, or deputy-governor of the colony. He was elected magistrate, May, 1673, deputy-governor, 1676, and governor, in 1683. To this office he was annually elected, fifteen years, until 1698: he was then chosen deputy-governor until the year 1708. He died about two years after, July 12th, 1710, in the 85th year of his age. Few men have sustained a fairer character, or rendered the public more important services. He was an excellent military officer; a man of singular courage and resolution, tempered with caution and prudence. His administration of government was with wisdom, firmness and integrity. He was esteemed courageous, wise, and pious. He was exceedingly beloved and venerated by the people in general, and especially by his neighbours, at Milford, where he resided.

CHAP. XVIII.   CONNECTICUT.   433

and turpentine, and even upon their persons, and forcibly carried them off to Suffield. In consequence of these outrages, great animosities had arisen between the inhabitants of those towns, and many lawsuits had been commenced. The assembly, as far as possible, to prevent and terminate these evils, enacted, that commissioners should be appointed, with full powers to run the line, with such commissioners as Massachusetts should appoint for that purpose. They were directed to take care that the line should be run by skilful artists, with good instruments; and to take their station three miles south of every part of Charles river, whence Mr. James Taylor and the commissioners of this colony ran the line in 1702. They were instructed to run a due west line from that station, and to make and set up fair marks and monuments in the line between the colonies. And to prevent all further contention, it was enacted, that the inhabitants of Windsor, Simsbury, Suffield, and Enfield, should not make any improvement on the contested lands, until the line should be run and settled. It was also enacted, that all suits should continue and rest, until the county court at Hartford, in October, and then to cease. It was provided, nevertheless, that the court of Massachusetts should give the same orders to the people of that province, who claimed upon the line, and should immediately unite with Connecticut in settling the boundary between the colonies. Otherwise, it was determined, that all causes, bonds, and the like should be, and remain as though this act never had been passed.

[margin: Book I. 1708. Massachusetts and Connecticut, May 13th, 1708.]

Further, it was enacted, that, upon running the line, all the most ancient grants, made to the proprietors, by either government, should give title and property to the settlers on either side of the line. It was determined, that unless the court of Massachusetts would agree to the running of the line in this manner, a petition should be addressed to her majesty, praying her to give orders, that the divisional line might be run.

The assembly, at this session, ordered that a township should be laid out east of Woodstock, eight miles in length, and six in breadth. The inhabitants were vested with the privileges of a distinct town, by the name of Killingly.*

[margin: Killingly made a town.]

The affairs of the war were conducted this year in the same manner as they had been the preceding. Colonel William Whiting commanded a body of horse and infantry

* At this session, the assembly ordered, "that the ministers of the gospel preach a sermon to the freemen, on the day appointed by law to choose their civil rulers, in the towns where they meet, proper for their direction in the work before them." This seems to have been the origin of preaching freemen's meeting sermons in Connecticut.

E 3

BOOK I.
1709.

Court of election, May 12th, 1709.

Expedition against the French.

in the county of Hampshire, and scouting parties and garrisons were maintained on the frontiers of the colony.

At the session in October, it was enacted, that two garrisons should be maintained, at the public expense, at Simsbury, and two at Waterbury. Garrisons were to be kept at Woodbury and Danbury, as the council of war should judge expedient.

At the election in 1709, Mr. Saltonstall was re-chosen governor, and Nathan Gould, deputy-governor. The magistrates were Daniel Witherel, Nathaniel Stanley, John Hamlin, William Pitkin, John Chester, Joseph Curtis, Josiah Rossiter, Richard Christopher, Peter Burr, John Allen, John Haynes, and Samuel Eells, Esquires. Captain Joseph Whiting was treasurer, and Caleb Stanley secretary.

A letter was laid before this assembly from her majesty, relative to an expedition against the enemy. The design was the reduction of the French in Canada, Acadia, and Newfoundland. The letters from the earl of Sunderland, advising that her majesty would dispatch a squadron of ships to Boston, by the middle of May, with five regiments of regular troops, required Connecticut to raise 350 men. The governments eastward of Connecticut, were required to raise 1200 men, and furnish them with transports, flat bottomed boats, pilots, and provisions for three months service. With this force, it was designed to make an attack upon Quebec. At the same time, it was proposed to raise 1500 men in the governments of Connecticut, New-York, New-Jersey, and the southern colonies. This corps was to proceed by the way of the lakes, and make a descent upon the island of Montreal.

The legislature of Connecticut voted and raised their quota, with cheerfulness and expedition. Colonel Whiting was appointed to command them. The assembly also voted an address of thanks to her majesty for her royal care and favor to the colonies, in devising means for the removal of an enemy, by whom the colonies had been so great and repeated sufferers.

All the colonies except Pennsylvania furnished their quotas. The troops, with provisions, transports, and articles necessary for the enterprise, were ready in season. The provincials, from the eastern colonies, were ready to sail for Quebec by the 20th of May. Francis Nicholson, who had been lieutenant-governor of New-York, under Andross, and afterwards lieutenant-governor of Virginia, was appointed to command the troops by land, and march as far as Wood Creek. There he was to wait until the ar-

CHAP. XVIII.   CONNECTICUT.

rival of the fleet expected at Boston, and then to advance, so that the attack upon Quebec and Montreal might be made at the same time. The colonies made great exertions for the public service. Besides their quotas, independent companies were raised and sent on to the army. More than a hundred batteaux, and an equal number of birch canoes, were constructed for crossing the lake. Three forts, several block houses, and stores for provisions were erected. But the armament expected from England did not arrive. The defeat of the Portuguese, and the straits to which the allies were reduced, occasioned the sailing of the fleet, designed for America, to Portugal; and the expedition was defeated. No intelligence arriving from England, and a great mortality prevailing among the troops, general Nicholson, early in the fall, returned to Albany. This fruitless undertaking was a capital loss and expense to the colonies. One quarter or more of the troops died. Connecticut only sustained the loss of ninety men.

Book I. 1709.

This expedition occasioned the first emission of paper money in Connecticut.

At a special assembly, on the 8th of June, it was enacted, "That to assist in the expedition, for want of money otherwise to carry it on, there be forthwith imprinted a certain number of bills of credit on the colony, in suitable sums, from two shillings to five pounds, which, in the whole, shall amount to the sum of 8000l. and no more." It was enacted, that the bills should be issued from the treasury as money, but should be received in payments at one shilling on the pound better than money. One half only was to be signed and issued at first, and the other was to remain unsigned, until it should be found necessary to put it into circulation. Taxes were imposed for the calling in of one half of it within the term of one year, and the other at the expiration of two years.

First emission of bills of credit, June, 1709.

The expectations of the people, in the spring, had been wrought up to a high degree of assurance, that Canada would be reduced before the close of the campaign. Joy brightened in every countenance, with the pleasing prospect, that a period would immediately be put to all the encroachments and ravages of a merciless enemy. Every heart was gladdened at the prospect of the enlargement of the British empire, and the augmentation of the national commerce. When, therefore, from such harmonious and general exertion, and such uncommon expense, they experienced nothing but loss and disappointment, the chagrin and depression were proportionably great.

Expectations of the country disappointed.

However, the importance of driving the French from

Book I.
1709.

Convention of governors.

Canada, and the necessity of immediate exertions to preserve the friendship and keep up the spirit of the five nations, without which, the frontiers would become a field of blood, induced the colonies to keep the object still in view. A congress of governors was appointed and met at Rehoboth, the beginning of October, to deliberate on the subject. General Nicholson, colonel Vetch, and others, met with them. An address was agreed upon to her majesty, representing the great harmony and exertions of the colonies in her majesty's service; the importance of reducing the French in North-America to her majesty's obedience; praying her majesty to grant the colonies an armament, with their assistance, adequate to the design.

Assembly, Oct. 13th, 1709.

When the general assembly convened in October, governor Saltonstall communicated the transactions of the governors of the several colonies, and the address, which they had prepared, to her majesty. The assembly approved the address, and determined on a similar one themselves. Governor Saltonstall was appointed agent to make a voyage to England, and present it in person to her majesty. Provision was also made for the expense of his agency.

Notwithstanding the war, the colony made progress in settlement. In 1708, John Belden, Samuel Keeler, Matthew Seymour, Matthias St. John, and other inhabitants of Norwalk, to the number of twenty-five, purchased a large tract, between that town and Danbury, bounded west on the partition line between Connecticut and New-York.

Ridgefield purchased, and made a town.

The purchase was made of Catoonah, the chief sachem, and other Indians, who were the proprietors of that part of the country. The deed bears date September 30th, 1708. At this session, it was ordained that it should be a distinct township, by the name of Ridgefield.

Election, May 11th, 1710.

The only alteration made, by the election, in 1710, was the choice of Matthew Allen, Esq. in the place of Daniel Witherell, Esq.

Measures adopted to obtain an armament from England.

New-York, as well as Connecticut and the other New-England colonies, had made great exertions, the last campaign, for the reduction of Canada. New-York, by means of the great influence of colonel Schuyler, had been able to bring six hundred of the Indians of the five nations into the field. The colonel was extremely discontented at the late disappointment. No man had more extensive views of the importance of expelling the French from this northern continent, and more zeal in the cause than he. So powerful was the influence which the affair had upon his mind, that he determined to make a voyage to England, at his own private expense, and to carry with him five sachems of the

CHAP. XVIII. CONNECTICUT.

five nations, that by their representations, the more sensible impressions might be made upon her majesty and the British court. The assembly of New-York had determined to address her majesty on the subject; and no sooner was the house apprised of his design, than they unanimously resolved, that he should present their address to her sacred majesty. Accordingly, colonel Schuyler went to England, and presented the address. The Indian sachems were, also, introduced to the queen. They represented their long war, in conjunction with her children, against her enemies, the French: That they had been a strong wall of defence to her colonies, to the loss of their best warriors; and that they mightily rejoiced, when they heard their great queen had resolved to send an army to Canada. They said, that, in token of their friendship, they had, with one consent, hung up the kettle, and taken up the hatchet, and assisted general Nicholson; but when they found, that their great queen, by some important affairs, had been diverted from her design of subduing the French, it made them sorrowful, lest the enemy, who hitherto had dreaded them, should now imagine they were unable to make war upon them. They represented, that the reduction of Canada was of great weight to them, that they might hunt freely. They insisted, that if their great queen should be unmindful of them, they, and their families, must forsake their country, and seek other habitations, or they must stand neuter; neither of which suited their inclinations. In hope of their great queen's favour, they referred the affair to her gracious consideration.

General Nicholson went to England, in the fall of 1709, on the same business, to solicit a force against Canada. Governor Saltonstall, for some reason, did not accept of the agency to which he had been appointed. The address of Connecticut, it seems, was sent to be presented by another hand. In consequence of these united applications, great encouragements were given, that an expedition would be again undertaken against Canada. In July, advice arrived in New-England, that lord Shannon, with a fleet destined for that service, was under sailing orders. Nicholson, who sailed with several ships of force, and some transports, from England, in the spring, came over with that expectation. However, it finally proved, that the reduction of Port Royal and Nova-Scotia was the only object.

In consequence of a letter from her majesty, requiring the assistance of her subjects in this colony, in the expedition, a special assembly was convoked on the 14th of August. Beside the loss of lives the last year, many of

Book I.
1710.

Address of the Indian kings to queen Anne.

Special assembly, Aug. 14th.

Book I. the soldiers then in service, remained in a sickly and weak condition. The enemy insulted the frontier towns, and the colony was obliged to keep a large number of men in pay for their defence. Nevertheless, such was the obedience of the legislature to her majesty's commands, and their zeal for her service, that they cheerfully voted three hundred men for the expedition. Vessels and sailors were procured, and all necessary provision was made for the transportation and support of the troops. In about a month, they were raised and transported to Boston.

1710.

Expedition against Port Royal.

On the 18th of September, a fleet of thirty-six ships of war and transports, sailed from Nantasket for Port Royal. There were fourteen transports in the pay of Massachusetts, five in the pay of Connecticut, two of New-Hampshire, and three of Rhode-Island. The chief command was given to general Nicholson. On the 24th, the fleet and army arrived at Port Royal. The troops landed without opposition, and made an easy conquest. On the 21st of October, the engineers opened three batteries, of two mortars and twenty-four cohorns in the whole. At the same time, a bomb ship, called the Star bomb, plied the enemy with her shells. The next day Monsieur Subercase capitulated, surrendering the fort and country to the crown of Great-Britain.

It surrenders, Oct. 22d.

General Nicholson left a sufficient garrison, under the command of colonel Vetch, his adjutant general, who had been appointed to the government of the country. In this expedition, the Mary galley, commanded by captain Taye, a transport in the service of Connecticut, ran aground, and was lost. Twenty-six men were drowned.* Fourteen or fifteen were lost in the expedition, while the troops were investing and besieging the fort. This was the whole loss sustained in the enterprise. From this time the name was changed, and the port was named Annapolis Royal.

General Nicholson, animated with his late success, in the fall made a second voyage to England, to solicit another expedition against Canada.

The country in general had no expectations, that he would succeed in his design. They could not imagine, that queen Anne's tory ministry would attempt any thing of this nature for New-England. Contrary, however, to all expectation, the affair was resumed. In June, general Nicholson arrived, at Boston, with the news, that a fleet might soon be expected from England, and with her majesty's orders that the several governments of New-Eng-

June 8th, 1711.

* This transport was hired of one Mr. Vryling, of Boston, and the colony paid him about 1,000l. for the loss of his vessel.

CHAP. XVIII. CONNECTICUT.

land, New-York, New-Jersey, and Pennsylvania should have their respective quotas in immediate readiness for the expedition.

Consequently a general meeting of the governors of the several colonies was immediately appointed at New-London. Sixteen days after the arrival of general Nicholson, the fleet arrived at Boston. But it was very extraordinary that the fleet had neither pilots nor provisions. Ten weeks provisions were demanded for the army. It had been suspected before this, that the reduction of Canada was not really designed by the ministry. These circumstances increased the suspicion. It was much doubted, whether, in the then state of the country, it were possible, in so short a time, as was necessary, to procure such a quantity of provisions, as had been demanded. There was, at the same time, a strong suspicion, that if the expedition should miscarry, it was designed to throw the whole blame upon New-England. Whether these suspicions were well grounded or not, it is certain, that they had great influence, together with the zeal which the colonies had for the service, to draw forth their utmost exertions.

When the fleet arrived at Boston, the governors were met in convention, at New-London, concerting measures for prosecuting the expedition with the utmost harmony and dispatch. The general courts of Massachusetts and Connecticut were in actual session. The general assembly of Connecticut convened on the 19th of June. A letter was communicated from her majesty and another from general Nicholson respecting the expedition. The assembly resolved, that three hundred and sixty men should be raised forthwith, as the quota of this colony in the expedition. It was also resolved, that four months provisions should be immediately procured, and that a suitable vessel should be provided to transport them to Albany, and to accommodate the sick and convey them back to Connecticut.

The assembly also addressed a letter to her majesty, returning her their most humble and dutiful acknowledgments, for that great expression of her royal care for her colonies and their peace and welfare, which she had manifested in the appointment of the present expedition against the common enemy. They particularly thanked her majesty for her royal bounty towards the colony, in furnishing the troops with clothing, arms, and ammunition, by which they were better enabled to bear the annual expenses of the war. They represented to her majesty, in a strong point of light, the horrible manner in which the en-

Book I.
1711.
June 24th, fleet arrives.

Suspicions of the country.

Conduct of the assembly respecting the expedition, June 19, 1711.

BOOK I.
1711.

emy carried on the war; lying in ambush, killing and scalping single persons, upon the frontiers, surprising and cutting off families, stealing captives, torturing and enslaving them. They promised a hearty concurrence with the royal requisitions, and a zealous performance of whatever might contribute to the success of the expedition.

To animate the general, and ingratiate themselves with him, the legislature appointed a committee to return him their thanks, for the good services he had rendered to her majesty's plantations in North America; and especially to Connecticut, in his former good conduct of the troops under his command. They thanked him, not only for his important services in the reduction of Port Royal and Nova-Scotia, but for the great pains he had taken since, in making a voyage to England, and representing to her majesty the true state and interest of the colonies, and by that means obtaining her orders for the then present expedition.

Universal harmony and exertion.

A punctual compliance with her majesty's orders was universally recommended by the governors in convention and by the several legislatures. Not only the several colonies but individuals exerted themselves beyond what had been known upon any other occasion.

The armament sails from Boston, July 30th.

In a little more than a month, from the arrival of the fleet, the new levies and provisions, for that and the army, were ready. Upon the 30th of July, the whole armament sailed from Boston for Canada. It consisted of fifteen men of war, twelve directly from England, and three which had before been stationed in America; forty transports, six store ships, and a fine train of artillery, with all kinds of warlike stores. The land army on board consisted of five regiments from England and Flanders, and two regiments raised in Massachusetts, Rhode-Island, and New-Hampshire; amounting in the whole to nearly seven thousand men. The fleet was commanded by Sir Hovenden Walker; and the army by brigadier Hill, brother to Mrs. Masham, then the queen's favorite. The land force was about equal to that which, under general Wolfe, afterwards reduced Quebec, though, at that time, it was not half so strong, as when it was reduced by that famous general.

Upon the same day on which the fleet sailed from Boston, general Nicholson began his journey for Albany, where, a few days after, he appeared at the head of four thousand men, from the colonies of Connecticut, New-York, and New-Jersey. The troops from Connecticut were commanded by colonel William Whiting, who was an experienced officer, and had commanded them the last year, at Port Royal. The New-York and New-Jersey troops were commanded by colonels Schuyler and Ingoldsby. Connecticut, besides victualling its own troops, furnished New-York with two hundred fat cattle and six hundred sheep. Thus, in about five weeks, the colonies had raised two considerable armies and furnished them with provisions. More than this could not have been expected.

Admiral Walker arrived in the mouth of the St. Lawrence, on the 14th of August. That he might not lose the company of the transports, as was pretended, he put into the bay of Gaspe, on the 18th, where he continued until the 20th of the month. On the 22d, two days after he sailed from the bay, the fleet appeared to be in the most hazardous circumstances. It was without soundings, without sight of land; the sky was darkened with a thick fog, and the wind high at east south-east. In this situation the ships brought to, with their heads to the southward. This was done with an expectation that the wind would drive them into the midst of the channel. But instead of this, about midnight, the seamen discovered that they were driven upon the north shore among rocks and islands, upon the verge of a total shipwreck. Eight or nine of the British transports were cast away, on board of which were about seventeen hundred officers and soldiers. Nearly a thousand men were lost. The admiral and general were in the most imminent danger, and saved themselves by anchoring. Such was the violence of the storm that they lost several anchors. Upon this disaster, the admiral bore away for Spanish river bay; but the wind shifting to the east it was eight days before all the transports arrived. In the same time, as the wind was, they might have easily arrived at Quebec. It was there determined, by a council of land and naval officers, that as they had but ten weeks provision, and could not expect a supply from New-England, to make no further attempt. The admiral sailed directly for England, and arrived at Portsmouth on the 9th of October. Here the fleet suffered another surprising calamity. The Edgar, a 70 gun ship, blew up, having on board four hundred men, besides many persons who were just come on board to visit their friends. As the cause of this event was wholly unknown, jealous minds were not without suggestions, that even this, as well as the other disaster, was the effect of horrid design.

The admiral and English officers, to exculpate themselves, laid the blame wholly upon the colonies, that they

Shipwreck, Aug. 22.

Book I. 1711.

Book I. were delayed so long for provision and the raising of the provincials, and that they had such unskilful pilots. The admiral declared, that it was the advice of the pilots that the fleet should come to in the manner it did, but the pilots, from New-England, declared, upon oath, that they gave no such advice. If any such was given it must have been by the French pilots on board, either through mistake or upon design. Charlevoix represents, that the French pilots warned the admiral of his danger, but that he did not sufficiently regard them.

1711. The blame imputed to the colonies.

The whigs, in England, generally censured the ministry for their conduct respecting the expedition. Lord Harley represented the whole affair as a contrivance of Bolingbroke, More, and the Lord Chancellor, Harcourt, to cheat the public out of twenty thousand pounds. Lord Harcourt was pleased to say, "No government was worth serving, that would not admit of such jobs." Another English writer observes, "That if the ministry were sincere in the prosecution of the war, they were certainly the most consummate blunderers that ever undertook the government of a state."*

General Nicholson had not advanced far before he received intelligence of the loss sustained by the fleet, and the army soon after returned.

The Marquis De Vaudreuil, governor of Canada, received intelligence of the arrival of the fleet from England, and of the preparations making in the colonies for the invasion of Canada, and had omitted nothing in his power to put it into a state of defence. No sooner was he apprised of so many ships wrecked and so many bodies with red coats driven on shore, and that the river was clear of ships, than he ordered the whole strength of Canada towards Montreal and lake Champlain. At Chambly he formed a camp of three thousand men to oppose general Nicholson. Had the general crossed the lake, it might have been difficult for him to have returned in safety.

Very providential it was, that all the provincial transports, except a small victualler, were preserved. The crew of the victualler were saved, and not a provincial lost. The loss and disappointment, nevertheless, were exceedingly grievous to the colonies. Many pious people, after so many attempts had been blasted, gave up all expectations of the conquest of Canada. They imagined it was not the design of providence, that this northern continent should ever wholly belong to any one nation.†

---

* Rider's Hist. of England, vol. xxxii. p. 189, 190.
† Hutchinson, vol. ii. p. 193—196. Smith's Hist. of New-York, p. 130, 131.

CHAP. XVIII. CONNECTICUT.

Upon the return of general Nicholson's army, and the report of Vaudreuil's force, the country were not only chagrined with disappointment, but alarmed with fear. They were apprehensive, that the enemy, in different parties, by different routes, would, with redoubled fury, harass and desolate the country. *Book I. 1711.*

To return to the affairs of Connecticut, the history of which has been in some measure interrupted with the general account of the war, it should be observed, that Joseph Talcott was this year chosen into the magistracy in the stead of Josiah Rossiter, Esq. An important alteration was also made, at the session in May, respecting the superior court. Until this time, it had been holden at two places only, Hartford and New-Haven, and at two terms annually. This was found to be an affair of expense and inconvenience. It was therefore resolved, that the superior court should sit twice annually, in each of the counties, and that all actions should be tried in the county in which they originated. *Superior court made circular, May, 1711.*

When the assembly met in October, an address was prepared to be presented to her majesty representing the exertions of the colony in her service, condoling her on the disappointment with respect to the expedition, and praying for the continuance of her favor to the colony. *Oct. 11th.*

At the session in May, 1708, the assembly made a grant of a township at a place called Pohtatuck, from a river of that name upon which part of it lies. At this session it was incorporated and named Newtown. *Newtown incorporated.*

A township had been given, several years before this time, by Joshua, sachem of the Moheagans, lying north of Lebanon and west of Mansfield, to certain honorable legatees in Hartford. The donation was approved by the assembly. The legatees conveyed their right to William Pitkin, Joseph Talcott, William Whiting, and Richard Lord, to be a committee to lay out said township and make settlements on the lands. On the 9th of May, 1706, the general assembly authorized those gentlemen to act as a committee for those purposes. October 11th, 1711, this committee was re-appointed, with one Nathaniel Rust, who had already settled upon the lands, more effectually to carry into execution the design of their former appointment. The township, at the same session, was named Coventry. Nathaniel Rust and some others settled in the town about the year 1700; but the settlement of it has generally been dated from 1709. In the spring of this year, a number of good householders, from Northampton and other places, moved into the town, and the inhabitants were so increas- *Coventry settled and incorporated.*

BOOK I.
1711.

Special assembly, Nov. 3d, 1711.

ed, in about two years, that they were incorporated with the privileges of other towns. The planters were from a great variety of places, but principally from Northampton and Hartford.

In consequence of letters from governor Dudley, of Boston, and from general Nicholson, relative to the unsuccessfulness of the late expedition, a special assembly was called, November 3d, 1711. The design of it was to consult the best means of acquainting her majesty truly how the affair was; what exertions the colonies had made, and that it was not through any fault of theirs that the enterprise was frustrated. It was judged best, that the colonies should make a joint representation, and that the pilots should be sent to England, to be examined and declare before her majesty what they knew concerning the shipwreck. The assembly determined, that the affair was of great importance to the colonies; and that John Mayhew, of New-London, who was the only pilot from Connecticut, should, forthwith, proceed to Great-Britain, with the pilots from Massachusetts. It was also resolved jointly, with the other colonies, to petition her majesty for another armament, in the spring, to assist them in the reduction of Canada. In the petition from Connecticut, the legislature lamented the miscarriage of the expedition, and the fatal consequences of it to these colonies. They represented it would put them to great expense to employ such a number of men as were necessary to defend such extensive frontiers as theirs were; and that, after all their exertions, one family and town after another would be swept away by the enemy. They expressed their apprehensions, that unless another expedition should be undertaken against the enemy, they would, in the spring, send out a greater number of scalping and plundering parties, than they had done in the preceding years of the war; and that her majesty's subjects would be greatly distressed. It was also suggested, that there was danger that the enemy would draw off many of the Indians who dwelt among them, as well as the Indians of the Five Nations, and engage them against the colonies. It was also urged, that the colonies were of great importance to her majesty's interest, and that it would be impolitic to suffer the enemy to possess so large a proportion of her majesty's dominions in North America, as they actually inhabited and claimed. It was insisted, that, by the smiles of providence on her majesty's arms, the settlements in Canada might be easily reduced to her majesty's obedience. They prayed her to revive the expedition, and promised a cheerful obedience to her commands, in contributing their proportion to the common service.†

The petitions were sent over seasonably, and the pilots were a considerable time in London, waiting to be examined, and give information, relative to the loss of the transports, and the miscarriage of the expedition. However, no examination was ever made concerning the failure of the enterprise. It did not appear that much had been expected from it in England, nor that people were discontented at the issue, or interested themselves very greatly in the affair. The court shewed no disposition to make any further attempt upon Canada.

The election in 1712, made little or no alteration with respect to public officers. Nothing very material appears to have been transacted this year. The legislature made the usual provision for the defence of this colony and the county of Hampshire. *[margin: Election, May 8th, 1712.]*

Nathan Gould, Esq. the deputy governor, was appointed chief judge of the superior court. William Pitkin, Richard Christopher, Peter Burr, and Samuel Eells, Esquires, were appointed assistant judges. In the absence of the deputy governor, William Pitkin was appointed chief judge; and in case either of the other judges were absent, any one of the magistrates was authorized to sit in his stead. Until this time, the judges of the superior court had been allowed nothing more than the fees of it. An act was, therefore, passed at the October session, that the judges, for the time being, upon laying their accounts before the assembly, should be allowed an honourable compensation for their expenses and services. *[margin: Regulation of the superior court, May, 1712.]*

About this time, the inhabitants of New-Milford were incorporated and vested with town privileges.* *[margin: New-Milford incorporated, Oct. 9th.]*

At the election in May, 1713, Mr. John Sherman, who had been some time speaker of the lower house, was chosen into the magistracy.

In October, 1687, a grant of lands, commonly called the Mashamoquet purchase, was made by the general assembly, to major James Fitch, lieutenant William Ruggles, Mr. John Gore, Mr. John Pierpont, Mr. John Chandler, Mr. Benjamin Sabin, Mr. Samuel Craft, Mr. John Grosvenor, Mr. Joseph Griffin, Mr. Samuel and John Ruggles, and Mr. Nathan Wilson. The most of these planters were from Roxbury, in Massachusetts. Some of them moved *[margin: Pomfret incorporated, May, 1713.]*

† Petition on file.
* About this time, William Patridge, Esq. of Newbury, and Jonathan Belcher, of Boston, opened a copper mine at Simsbury; and for their encouragement, the assembly exempted the miners, operators, and labourers, from military duties, for the term of four years.

Book I.
1713.

Settlement of the line with Massachusetts.

Reasons of settling it without an appeal to her majesty.

on to the lands in 1686, before the grant was made. At the session in May, 1713, the inhabitants were incorporated and vested with town privileges. The name was changed from Mashamoquet to Pomfret.

In 1706, the assembly of Connecticut determined, that, unless the province of Massachusetts would accept of the terms which they had proposed, relative to the line between them, they would make application to her majesty, desiring that orders might be given, that Massachusetts forthwith should mutually join with Connecticut in running and settling the boundary line between the colonies. Massachusetts, at that time, would not consent to run the line as it had been proposed. They would not grant that there had been any mistake in running it; but if there had been, they insisted, that, as it was run so long before the charter was granted to Connecticut, and they had been in possession of the lands in controversy for sixty-six years, and several towns and plantations had been settled upon them, it was not then reasonable to draw it into question. The assembly of Connecticut, therefore, in 1709, approved a letter, addressed to the lords of trade, giving reasons why the line run by Woodward and Saffery ought not to be established; and it seems to have been the determination of the legislature to have appealed to her majesty with respect to the partition line; but several circumstances finally prevented. Governor Dudley, who was a man of uncommon intrigue and duplicity, had many friends and great influence at court. Connecticut had no such friends, or influence with the court party. Sir Henry Ashurst, their agent for many years, appears now to have been no more; and they had not yet sufficient time to fix upon and have proof of the fidelity and ability of another in his place. The colony was poor, and had been put to great expense, in defending itself against the complaints of governor Dudley, lord Cornbury, and other enemies, and against the claims of Mason and his party. The ministry were high tories, and inimical to all charter governments. The legislature were apprehensive that their enemies were again concerting measures to deprive them of all the privileges which they had so dearly bought. Massachusetts also, in some good measure, agreed to part of the terms proposed in 1706. It was, therefore, in full view of these circumstances, judged most expedient to make the best settlement which could be obtained, without an appeal to her majesty.

Upon the 13th of July, 1713, commissioners, fully empowered from each of the colonies, came to an agreement, which was adopted by each court. They were both careful to secure the property to the persons to whom they had made grants of lands, and to maintain the jurisdiction over the towns which they had respectively settled. It was, therefore, expressly stipulated, as a preliminary, that the towns should remain to the governments, by which they had been settled; and that the property of as many acres as should appear to be gained by one colony from the other, should be conveyed out of other unimproved land, as a satisfaction or equivalent. With respect to about two miles, claimed by Windsor upon the town of Suffield, concerning the validity of which there had been a long contest, it was agreed, that, if the tract fell within the line, it should belong to Connecticut.

Book I. 1713. Settlement of boundaries with Massachusetts.

On running the line, it was found, at Connecticut river, to run ninety rods north of the north-east bounds of Suffield; and it appeared that Massachusetts had encroached upon Connecticut 107,793 acres, running a due west line from Woodward's and Saffery's station. Massachusetts made a grant of such a quantity of land to Connecticut, and it was accepted as equivalent. The whole was sold, in sixteen shares, in 1716, for the sum of 683l. New-England currency.* The money was applied to the use of the college.

Notwithstanding the long and expensive controversy of Connecticut with the colony of Rhode-Island, relative to the Narraganset country, and notwithstanding the king's commissioners, and attornies of the greatest fame, determined, that the title was, undoubtedly, in the governor and company of this colony, yet it was judged expedient to give up the claim. Lands were of so little value, and controversies before king and council so expensive, and the event so uncertain, that the legislature determined rather to comply with governor Winthrop's and Clark's agreement, than to prolong the controversy. The court party, both in king William's and queen Anne's reign, appeared reluctant to establish the charter limits of Connecticut at Narraganset river and bay; otherwise they would have advised to establish the judgment of the king's commissioners; and the king, or queen, would have adopted the same opinion, and established the boundary according to the charter. The court, probably, were influenced by political principles. The establishment of the eastern boundary

Settlement with Rhode-Island.

---

* This was a little more than a farthing per acre, and shows of what small value land was esteemed at that day. It affords, also, a striking demonstration, that, considering the expense of purchasing them of the natives, and of defending them, they cost our ancestors five, if not ten times their value.

BOOK I.
1713.

of Connecticut at Narraganset river and bay, would have ruined Rhode-Island, by reducing them to limits too small for a colony. Connecticut was, doubtless, fully sensible of these dispositions of the sovereigns and court of Great-Britain, and it, probably, operated as a strong motive to induce them to give up their claim.

In October, 1702, a committee was appointed to make a complete settlement of the boundary line between the colonies, reserving to all persons concerned, their entire property in lands and buildings, according to the agreement of governor Winthrop and Mr. Clark. On the 12th of May, 1703, the committees from the two colonies agreed, "That the middle channel of Pawcatuck river, alias Narraganset river, as it extends from the salt water upwards, till it comes to the mouth of Ashaway river, where it falls into the said Pawcatuck river, and from thence to run a straight line till it meet with the south-west bounds or corner of Warwick grand purchase, which extends twenty miles due west from a certain rock, lying at the outmost point of Warwick neck, which is the south-easterly bounds of said purchase; and from the said south-west bounds, or corner of said purchase, to run upon a due north line, till it meet with the south line of the province of Massachusetts Bay, in New-England: This to be, and for ever remain to be the fixed and stated line between the said colonies of Connecticut and Rhode-Island. Always provided, and it is hereby intended, that nothing in the aforementioned agreement, or any clause thereof, shall be taken or deemed to be the breach or making void of the fourth article in the agreement made between the agents of the said colonies of Connecticut and Rhode-Island, viz. John Winthrop, Esq. and Mr. Daniel Clark, for maintaining property, dated April 7th, 1663, but that the same shall be kept and justly performed, according to the true intent and meaning thereof; and that all former grants and purchases, granted by, or made within either of the colonies, and all other ancient grants confirmed by the authority of Connecticut colony within the township of Westerly, in the colony of Rhode-Island, shall be duly preserved and maintained, as fully and amply, to all intents and purposes, as if they were lying or continued within the bounds of the colony, by the authority of which it was granted or purchased."*

Notwithstanding this agreement, Rhode-Island, about this time, disowned its authenticity, pretending that their

* Agreement on file, signed with the hands of the commissioners, and sealed with nine seals.

commissioners were not empowered to conclude fully and finally upon such settlement. The cause was heard by the king in council, some years after, and decided according to the agreement of the commissioners as stated above.

September 27th, 1728, the line was finally ascertained and distinguished by proper monuments and boundaries. Roger Wolcott, James Wadsworth, and Daniel Palmer, on the part of Connecticut, and William Wanton, Benjamin Ellery, and William Jenks, in behalf of Rhode-Island, were the committees for the running and final fixing of the line.

No colony, perhaps, had ever a better right to the lands comprised in its original patent than Connecticut, yet none has been more unfortunate with respect to the loss of territory. King Charles the second, in favor of his brother the duke of York, granted a great part of the lands contained within its original limits to him, and the legislature, for fear of offending those royal personages and losing their charter, gave up Long-Island and agreed to the settlement of the boundary line with the king's commissioners. For the reasons which have been suggested they lost a considerable tract on the north and on the east. Indeed, considering the enemies and difficulties with which they had to combat, it is admirable that they retained so much territory, and so nobly defended their just rights and liberties.

The peace of Utrecht was signed by the plenipotentiaries of Great-Britain and France, March 30th, 1713. Official accounts of the pacification and orders for immediately proclaiming the peace were received by the governor of Connecticut, on the 22d of August. The governor having called together the deputy governor and council, they, on the 26th, made a formal proclamation of peace between the two nations.

Upon the pacification with France, the Indians buried the hatchet, and peace, with her olive branch, once more gladdened the colonies.

Connecticut had not been less fortunate in this, than in former wars. A single town had not been lost, nor had any considerable number of the inhabitants fallen by the hands of the enemy. In Philip's, king William's, and queen Anne's wars, Connecticut lost only the buildings and part of the effects of one town. The inhabitants of Simsbury, when consisting of about forty families, as the tradition is, supposing themselves in danger of a surprise, by the enemy, buried a considerable part of their effects, and generally removed back to Windsor. The enemy, find-

Book I.
1713.

ing the town nearly deserted, fell upon it, burned the buildings, and captivated several of the inhabitants. When the people moved back, such an alteration had been made, by the burning of the buildings and the growth of weeds and bushes, that the particular spot in which they had buried their effects, could not be found, and they were never recovered. This, most probably, was in the spring of 1676, when the Narraganset and other Indians appeared in strong parties upon the river above.

State of the colony at the commencement of peace.

The expense of this war was very considerable. Some years the colony paid a tax of about seven pence and eight pence on the pound, on the whole list of the colony. Besides, it was found necessary to emit, at several times, from June, 1709, to October, 1713, 33,500l. in bills of credit. Provision had been made, by acts of assembly, for the calling in of the whole, within the term of about

Amount of bills of credit.

seven years from the termination of the war. Twenty thousand pounds only were in circulation in October, 1713. The emissions were all in the same form, and, by a law of the colony, the bills of each were, to be received, in all payments at the treasury, at five per cent. better than money, or more than expressed on the face of the bill. In all other payments, it was enacted, that they should be received as money. So small was the sum, and such was the advance at which the bills were received at the treasury, that they appear to have suffered little or no depreciation. As some of the small bills had been altered, and the sum expressed made greater than in the original ones, the assembly passed an act for calling them all in, and emitting 20,000l. in new bills, which the treasurer was directed to issue.

After pursuing the history of the colony nearly eighty years, from the commencement of its first settlements, it appears, that, notwithstanding the many wars, numerous hardships, and difficulties, which it had almost continually to combat, its progress in numbers, plantations, husbandry, wealth, and commerce, were considerable.

Within the colony, and under its jurisdiction, were thirty-eight taxable towns, and forty sent deputies.

COUNTIES and TOWNS, October 8th, 1713.

Number of towns, and the time of settlement or incorporation.

County of HARTFORD.	Time of Settlement.		
Hartford,	1635	Haddam,	1668
Weathersfield,	1634	Glastenbury made a town,	1690
Windsor,	1635	Waterbury,	1686
Farmington,	1644	Windham,	1692
Middletown,	1651	Plainfield,	1689
Simsbury,	1650	East-Haddam,	1713
		Canterbury,	1703

CHAP. XVIII.　　　CONNECTICUT.

Mansfield,	1703*	Guilford,	1639	
Colchester,	1699	Branford,	1644	
Hebron,	1704*	Wallingford,	1670	1713.
Killingly,	1708*	East-Haven,	1607	
Coventry,	1709*	Derby,	1675	
County of	Time of	Durham,	1699	
NEW-LONDON.	Settlement.	New-Milford,	1712*	
New-London,	1648	County of	Time of	
Saybrook,	1639	FAIRFIELD.	Settlement.	
Norwich,	1660	Fairfield,	1639	
Lyme,	1667	Stratford,	1639	
Stonington,	1658	Greenwich,	1640	
Killingworth,	1663	Stamford,	1641	
Preston,	1686	Norwalk,	1651	
Lebanon incorpora-		Woodbury incorpora-		
ted,	1697	ted,	1674	
Voluntown,	1700	Danbury,	1693	
Pomfret incorporated,	1713*	Newtown incorpora-		
County of	Time of	ted,	1711*	
NEW-HAVEN.	Settlement.	Ridgefield incorpora-		
New-Haven,	1638	ted,	1709*	
Milford,	1639			

It was customary with the assembly, from the first settlement of the colony, to release the infant towns two, three, or four years, at first, from all taxes to the commonwealth; and especially this was the universal practice, while they were building meeting-houses and settling ministers. For these reasons, the eight towns marked with asterisks, at this time, appear to have been released from public taxation.

Attempts had been made for the settlement of Ashford; two families moved on to the lands in 1710, and began settlements, but it was not incorporated until October, 1714. The assembly had, also, appointed committees, and passed several acts respecting the settlement of New Fairfield, but it does not appear to have been incorporated at this time. Exclusive of the towns on Long-Island, and some others in New-York, and the town of Westerly, in Rhode-Island, Connecticut had settled forty-five towns under its own jurisdiction. Forty of them sent deputies. The house of representatives, when full, consisted of eighty members.

The grand list of the colony was 281,083l. The militia consisted of a regiment in each county, and amounted to nearly four thousand effective men. The number of inhabitants was about seventeen thousand. *List of the colony, number of militia and inhabitants.*

The shipping consisted of two brigantines, about twenty *Shipping.*

BOOK I. sloops, and some other small vessels. The number of seamen did not exceed a hundred and twenty.

1713. Towns granted and settled by Massachusetts. There were three considerable towns in the colony under the government of Massachusetts, Suffield, Enfield, and Woodstock. Suffield and Enfield were part of Springfield, which was purchased by Mr. Pyncheon and his company, of the natives, the original proprietors of the soil. This township, like Windsor, was of great extent. At first it was supposed to belong to Connecticut, and it always would have done had not the boundary line been fixed contrary to the expectations of the first planters. In 1670, a grant of Suffield was made to major John Pyncheon, Mr. Elizur Holyoke, Mr. Thomas Cooper, Mr. Benjamin Cooly, George Cotton, and Rowland Thomas, by the general court of Massachusetts, as a committee to lay it out and plant a township. And about that time it was settled, and incorporated with town privileges.

Enfield was settled by people from Massachusetts, about the year 1681. A grant of the township, which is six miles square, was made to several planters about two years before. The planters came on with numbers and strength. They brought with them two young gentlemen, one Mr. Whittington for a schoolmaster, and Mr. Welch, a candidate for the ministry, to be their preacher. In the year 1769, the number of families in the town was 214, and the number of inhabitants was 1,360. The town was named after one of the same name in England.*

Courts in Connecticut.

Courts and judges. The general court, or assembly, in May and October. The sessions at this period, generally, did not exceed ten or twelve days. The expense of government was very inconsiderable. The expense of the two sessions annually hardly amounted to 400 pounds. The salary of the governor was 200 pounds, and that of the deputy governor fifty pounds. The whole expense of government, probably did not exceed eight hundred pounds annually.†

The Superior court, which was made circular in 1711. At the May session, 1711, it was enacted, that there should be one superior court of judicature over the whole colony: That this court should be holden annually, within and for the county of Hartford on the third Tuesdays in March and September: Within and for the county of New-Haven on the second Tuesdays in March and September: Within and for the county of Fairfield, at Fairfield, on the first

---

* With respect to Woodstock there are no records or minutes.
† The expense of government in Connecticut did not generally amount to the salary of a king's governor.

CHAP. XVIII.   CONNECTICUT.

Tuesdays in March and September; and within and for the county of New-London on the fourth Tuesdays in said months.

This court consisted of one chief judge and four other judges, three of whom made a quorum. The judges of the court were all magistrates. William Pitkin, Esq. was chief judge. Richard Christopher, Peter Burr, Samuel Eells, and John Haynes, Esquires, were assistant judges. The wages of the chief judge were ten shillings a day, while on the public service. The other judges were allowed the fees, by law, payable to the bench.

The inferior, or county courts. At the session in May, 1665, counties were first made. From that time each county had a court of its own. This, after a few years, from its first institution, consisted of a chief judge and four justices of the quorum. The business of these courts has been already sufficiently noticed.

In each county there was a court of probates, consisting of one judge and a clerk. In this all testamentary affairs were managed. From this court appeals might be had to the county court. One of the magistrates of the county was commonly judge of this court. It met frequently, business was done with ease and dispatch, and with little expense to the fatherless and widow.

The manufactures of Connecticut at this time, were very inconsiderable. There was but one clothier in the colony. The most he could do was to full the cloth which was made. A great proportion of it was worn without shearing or pressing.*

The trade of the colony was not considerable. Its foreign commerce was indeed next to nothing. The only articles exported directly from it to Great-Britain were turpentine, pitch, tar, and fur. But these more generally were sent directly to Boston or New-York, and were traded for such European goods as were consumed in the colony. Its principal trade was with Boston, New-York, and the West-Indies. To the two former the merchants traded in the produce of the colony, wheat, rye, barley, indian corn, peas, pork, beef, and fat cattle.

To the West-Indies the merchants exported horses, staves, hoops, pork, beef, and cattle. In return they received rum, sugar, molasses, cotton wool, bills of exchange, and sometimes small sums of money. But little more was imported, than was found necessary for home consumption.

At this period there was not a printer in the colony.

* Answer to questions from the lords of trade and plantations, 1710.

Book I.
1713.

For this reason a great proportion of the laws were only in manuscript. The assembly had now desired the governor and council to procure a printer to settle in the colony. It was determined soon to revise and print the laws which made the assembly more urgent in the affair at that time. The council obtained Mr. Timothy Green, a descendant of Mr. Samuel Green of Cambridge in Massachusetts, the first printer in North-America. The assembly for his encouragement agreed that he should be printer to the governor and company and that he should have fifty pounds, the salary of the deputy governor, annually. He was obliged to print the election sermons, the proclamations for fasts and thanksgivings, and laws which were enacted at the several sessions of the assembly. In 1714, he came into Connecticut, and fixed his residence at New-London. He and his descendants were, for a great number of years, printers to the governor and company of Connecticut.*

At the period to which the history is brought down, almost all that part of the colony on the east side of Connecticut was settled. Ashford, Tolland, Stafford, Bolton, and two or three other towns have been settled in that part of the colony, and the greatest part of the county of Litchfield since. The settlement of these has been attended with little difficulty in comparison with what was experienced in the planting and defending of the former.

Who can contemplate the hardships, labors, and dangers of our ancestors, their self-denial, magnanimity, firmness, and perseverance, in defending their just rights, and the great expense, though they were poor, at which they maintained and transmitted the fairest inheritance to us, and not highly esteem and venerate their characters? If they had some imperfections, yet had they not more excellencies, and did they not effect greater things, for themselves and posterity, than men have generally done? Is it possible to review the sufferings, dangers, expense of blood and treasure, with which our invaluable liberties, civil and religious, have been transmitted to us, and not to esteem them precious? Not most vigilantly and vigorously defend them? Shall we not at all hazards, maintain and perpetuate them? Can we contemplate the sobriety, wisdom, integrity, industry, economy, public spirit, peaceableness, good order, and other virtues, by which this republic hath arisen from the smallest beginnings, to its present strength, opulence, beauty and respectability, and not admire those virtues? Not be convinced of their high importance to soci-

* The first printer in this colony was Thomas Short. He was recommended to the colony by Mr. Green. He came to New-London about the year 1709. In 1710, he printed Saybrook Platform, and soon after died.

ety? Shall we not make them our own? And by the constant practice of them, hand down our distinguished liberties, dignity, and happiness, to the latest ages?

CHAPTER XIX.

A View of the churches of Connecticut, from 1665 to 1714, continued from Chapter XIII. The general assembly appoint a synod to determine points of religious controversy. The ministers decline meeting under the name of a synod. The assembly alter the name, and require them to meet as a general assembly of the ministers and churches of Connecticut. Seventeen questions were proposed to the assembly to be discussed and answered. The assembly of ministers and churches meet and discuss the questions. The legislature declare that they had not been decided, and give intimations that they did not desire that the ministers and churches of Connecticut should report their opinion upon them. They express their desires of a larger council from Massachusetts and New-Plymouth. The Rev. Mr. Davenport removes to Boston. Dissension at Windsor. Mr. Bulkley and Mr. Fitch are appointed by the assembly to devise some way in which the churches might walk together, notwithstanding their different opinions relative to the subjects of baptism, church communion, and the mode of church discipline. The church at Hartford divides, and Mr. Whiting and his adherents are allowed to practise upon congregational principles. The church at Stratford allowed to divide, and hold distinct meetings. Mr. Walker and his hearers, upon advice, remove and settle the town of Woodbury. Deaths and characters of the Rev. Messrs. John Davenport and John Warham. General attempts for a reformation of manners. Religious state of the colony in 1680. Attempts for the instruction and christianizing of the Indians in Connecticut. Act of the legislature respecting Windsor. The people there required peaceably to settle and support Mr. Mather. Owning or subscribing the covenant introduced at Hartford. College founded, and trustees incorporated. Worship according to the mode of the church of England performed, in this colony, first at Stratford. Episcopal church gathered there. Act of assembly requiring the ministers and churches of Connecticut to meet and form a religious con-

BOOK I.
1666.

stitution. *They meet and compile the Saybrook Platform. Articles of discipline. Act of the legislature adopting the Platform. Associations; consociations. General association. Its recommendations relative to the examination of candidates for the ministry, and of pastors elect previous to their ordination. Ministers, churches, and ecclesiastical societies in Connecticut, in 1713. Degree of instruction. The whole number of ministers in the colony, from its first settlement to that period.*

ALTHOUGH the legislature of Connecticut, during the controversy respecting the union of the colonies, judged it expedient to transact nothing relative to the religious controversies then in the country, yet, as soon as the union was well established, they entered seriously upon measures to bring them to a final issue. For this purpose, they passed the following act.

Oct. 11th, 1666.

Act appointing a synod.

"This court doth conclude, to consider of some way or means to bring those ecclesiastical matters, that are in difference in the several plantations, to an issue, by stating some suitable accommodation and expedient thereunto. And do therefore order, that a synod be called to consider and debate those matters; and that the questions presented to the elders and ministers that are called to this synod, shall be publicly disputed to an issue. And this court doth confer power to this synod, being met and constituted, to order and methodize the disputation, so as may most conduce, in their apprehension, to attain a regular issue of their debates."

The court ordered, that all the preaching elders, or ministers, who were or should be settled in this colony, at the time appointed for the meeting of the synod, should be sent to, to attend as members of it. It was also ordered by the legislature, that Mr. Mitchell, Mr. Brown, Mr. Sherman, and Mr. Glover, of Massachusetts, should be invited to assist as members of the synod. It was also ordered, that, upon the meeting of a majority of the preaching elders in the colony, they should proceed as a synod. Further, it was enacted, that the questions proposed by this assembly, should be the questions to be disputed by the synod. The meeting of the synod was appointed on the third Wednesday in May, 1667. The secretary was directed to transmit to all the ministers in this colony, and those invited from the Massachusetts, a copy of this act of assembly, and of the questions to be disputed.

It seems, that the ministers had objections to meeting as a synod, and to the order of the assembly vesting them

CHAP. XIX.   CONNECTICUT.

with synodical powers. Numbers of the ministers and churches appear to have been too jealous for their liberties to admit of the authority of synods appointed by the assembly. The legislature, to ease this difficulty, in their May session, judged it expedient to alter the name of the council, and to call it an assembly of the ministers of Connecticut, called together by the general court, for the discussing of the questions stated, according to their former order.

Book I.
1667.
Name of the council altered, May 5th, 1667.

The assembly of ministers convened at the time appointed, and having conversed on the questions, and voted not to dispute them publicly, adjourned until the fall, determining then to meet again, and make their report, should it be the desire of the legislature. The questions were the same which had been exhibited ten years before.* The same points of controversy still subsisted. The churches continued in their former strict method of admitting members to their communion, and maintained their right to choose their ministers, without any controul from the towns or parishes of which they were a part. It does not appear, that one church in the colony had yet consented to the baptism of children, upon their parents owning the covenant, as it was then called. It was insisted, as necessary to the baptism of children, that one of the parents, at least, should be a member in full communion with the church, and in regular standing.

The assembly of ministers meet.

It seems, that the assembly's particularly inviting the gentlemen from the Massachusetts, in their name, to attend the general assembly of ministers and churches, was to enlighten and soften the minds of the ministers of Connecticut in those points, and to obtain a majority in the assembly for a less rigid mode of proceeding. Mr. Mitchell was the most powerful disputant of his day, in New-England, in favour of the baptism of children, upon their parents owning the covenant, though they neglected to obey and honour Christ, in attending the sacrament of the Lord's Supper. It appeared, however, that this party were not able to carry any point in the assembly, and that the questions were not likely to be determined according to the wishes of the majority of the legislature. Measures were, therefore, adopted to prevent the meeting and result of the assembly, at their adjournment in the fall.

Design of inviting ministers from the Massachusetts.

In September, the commissioners of the united colonies met at Hartford, and they interposed in the affair. They resolved, "That when questions of public concernment, about matters of faith and order, do arise in any colony, that the decision thereof should be referred to a synod, or

Resolution of the commissioners, Sept. 1667.

* See chapter xii. p. 316, 317.

H 3

458 HISTORY OF CHAP. XIX.

BOOK I.
1667.

council of messengers of churches, indifferently called out of the united colonies, by an orderly agreement of all the general courts; and that the place of meeting be at, or near Boston." This vote was, doubtless, obtained by the art of those gentlemen, among the civilians and ministers, who wished to prevent the meeting of the assembly of ministers, and their resulting upon the questions.

Application of Messrs. Warham, Hooker, and Whiting.

The reverend elders Warham, Hooker, and Whiting, in a writing under their hands, represented to the assembly, at their session in October, that it was the desire of the assembly of ministers, that there might be a more general meeting of ministers from Massachusetts, to assist in the consideration and decision of the questions proposed. It was also represented to the assembly, that though they and others were for disputing the questions publicly, and offered to do it, yet the major part of the assembly refused the offer.

Representations of Messrs. Bulkley and Haynes.

The Rev. Mr. Bulkley and Mr. Haynes, on the other hand, in a letter addressed by them to the assembly, represented, that the assembly had authorized a major part of the ministers to methodize the proceedings of the assembly, and that a majority were against a public disputation of the questions: That it was viewed as what would dishonour God, disserve the peace and edification of the churches, and the general interests of religion; and it was judged most expedient to deliberate upon and decide the questions among themselves, as was usual in councils, without a public disputation. They therefore observed, that whatever fair offers were made them to dispute the questions publicly, they could not consistently do it, as it was contrary to a major vote of the assembly of the ministers, and, in their opinion, would disserve the interest of the churches. With respect to the present application, made by Messrs. Warham, Hooker, and Whiting, they observed, that it appeared strange to them, as a considerable number of the ministers were positively against it, and others were neuter, and not in the vote for a more general council; and that it was the vote of the assembly of ministers, to meet again on the third Wednesday in October. They assured the legislature, that they were ready and determined to obey all their lawful commands; and they desired information from them, whether the assembly of ministers should meet again, according to adjournment, or not? The general assembly voted, that the questions had not been decided, and desired the several churches and plantations in the colony, to send their teaching elders, at their own expense, to sit in council, with such of the elders of Mas-

CHAP. XIX. CONNECTICUT.

sachusetts and Plymouth as should be appointed, to consider and determine the points in controversy. The assembly desired, that the general court of Massachusetts might be certified of the affair, and would appoint time and place for the meeting of a synod, if they should judge it expedient.

Whether the assembly really wished to have a general council, or whether this was only a matter of policy to prevent a determination of the questions contrary to their wishes, is not certain. No general council, however, was called; nor does it appear, that any motion was made afterwards for that purpose. Indeed, the legislature seem to have fallen under the conviction, that the clergy and churches would not give up their private opinions, in faith and practice, to the decisions of councils; that honest men would think differently, and that they could not be convinced and made of one mind by disputing. No further attempts were ever made by them, to bring those points to a public discussion.

While these affairs were transacting in Connecticut, a remarkable transaction took place in the first church at Boston, the most considerable church in New-England. Their pastor, the Rev. Mr. Wilson, was one of the synod in 1662, and one who had adopted its determinations relative to the subjects of baptism. His church also appeared to have consented to the practice of admitting persons to own their covenant and bring their children to baptism. Nevertheless, after Mr. Wilson's decease, they elected the Rev. Mr. Davenport, of New-Haven, for their pastor, as the only gentleman worthy to succeed the distinguished lights which had illuminated that golden candlestick. He had publicly written against the synod, and was one of the most strict and rigid ministers, with respect to the admission of members to full communion, the subjects of baptism, and with respect to church discipline, in New-England. He had now arrived nearly to seventy years of age, yet, in 1667, upon the application of the church and congregation at Boston, he accepted their invitation, and the next year removed to that capital. He had been about thirty years minister at New-Haven, and was greatly esteemed and beloved by his flock. This circumstance, with his advanced period of life, made his removal very remarkable. His church and people were exceedingly unwilling that he should leave them, and, it seems, never formally gave their consent. The affair, on the whole, was unhappy. It occasioned a separation from the first church in Boston; and the church and congregation at New-Ha-

Book I.

1667.

The church at Boston choose Mr. Davenport for their pastor.

He removes to Boston.

BOOK I. ven, for many years, remained in an uncomfortable state, unable to unite in the choice of any person to take the pastoral charge of them.

1667.
Contentions at Windsor.

The town of Windsor had, for many years, been almost in perpetual controversy, relative to the settlement of a minister. After Mr. Warham became advanced in years, he wished for a colleague, to assist him in ministerial labors. Various young gentlemen were invited to preach in the town; but such as one part of the people chose for the minister, the other would violently oppose. Sometimes one party would appear with great zeal for one candidate, and the other would strive with equal engagedness for another. In such case advice had been given, that both the persons, for whom they were thus contending, should leave the town, and that application should be made to some other candidate. Much heat and obstinacy, however, continued between the parties, and all attempts to unite them were unsuccessful. It seems, that their passions were so inflamed, that, upon occasion of their meetings, their language and deportment were unbrotherly and irritating. One Mr. Chauncey was now preaching in the town, and parties were warmly engaged for and against him. The general assembly, in this state of their affairs, enacted, "That all the freemen and householders in Windsor and Massacoe should meet at the meeting-house, on Monday morning next, by sun an hour high, and bring in their votes for a minister, to Mr. Henry Wolcott: That those who were for Mr. Chauncey to be the settled minister of Windsor, bring in a written paper, and those who were not for him to give in a paper without any writing upon it: That the inhabitants during the meeting forbear all discourse and agitation of any matter, which may serve to provoke and disturb each other's spirits, and when the meeting is over return to their several occasions."

Act of assembly respecting the inhabitants, Oct. 10th, 1667.

Mr. Wolcott reported to the assembly the state of the town, that there were eighty six votes for Mr. Chauncey and fifty five against him. The assembly, upon the petition of the minor party, and a full view of the state of the town, gave them liberty to settle an orthodox minister among themselves, and to the church and majority of the town to settle Mr. Chauncey, if they judged it expedient. It was enacted, that the minority should pay Mr. Chauncey until they should obtain another minister to preach and reside in the town. Mr. Chauncey was not finally ordained, but the affair was carried so far that a separation was soon after made in the church, and a distinct church was formed by the minority. The town continued in an unhappy state of division, for about sixteen years from this time.

CHAP. XIX. CONNECTICUT. 461

The legislature, having given over all further attempts to compose the divisions in the colony, by public disputation and the decisions of general councils, determined to pursue a different course. They conceived the design of uniting the churches in some general plan of church communion and discipline, by which they might walk, notwithstanding their different sentiments, in points of less importance. With this view, an act passed authorizing the Rev. Messrs. James Fitch, Gershom Bulkley, Joseph Elliot, and Samuel Wakeman, to meet at Saybrook, and devise a way in which this desirable purpose might be effected. This appears to have been the first step towards forming a religious constitution. From this time it became more and more a general object of desire and pursuit, though many years elapsed before the work could be accomplished.

Book I.
1668.
Attempt for a plan of union among the churches.

Notwithstanding the divisions in the church at Hartford, some years since, had been so far composed and healed, that it had been kept together until this time, yet there were really different sentiments among the brethren and between the ministers, relative to the qualifications of church members, the subjects of baptism, and the mode of discipline. Mr. Whiting and part of the church were zealous for the strictly congregational way, as it has been called, practised by the ministers and churches, at their first coming into New-England. Mr. Haynes and a majority of the congregation were not less engaged against it. The difference became so great, that it was judged expedient, both by an ecclesiastical council and the assembly, that the church and town should be divided. An ecclesiastical council having first advised to a division, the general assembly, in October, 1669, passed the following act.

Church of Hartford divided into two churches.

"Upon the petition presented by Joseph Whiting, &c. to this court, for a distinct walking in congregational church order, as hath been settled according to the council of the elders, the court doth commend it to the church at Hartford to take some effectual course, that Mr. Whiting, &c. may practise the congregational way, without disturbance, either from preaching or practice, diversely to their just offence; or else to grant their loving consent to their brethren to walk distinct, according to such their congregational principles; which this court allows liberty in Hartford to be done. But if both these be refused and neglected by the church, then these brethren may, in any regular way, relieve themselves without offence to this court."*

Act of assembly respecting it.

* Parties ran high at this time in the colony; four assistants and fourteen deputies dissented, and desired their dissent and names to be recorded.

BOOK I. The next February, Mr. Whiting and his adherents resolved and covenanted in the manner following, and formed the second church in Hartford.

1670. Declaration of the brethren forming the second church.

"Having had the consent and countenance of the general court, and the advice of an ecclesiastical council to encourage us in embodying as a church by ourselves, accordingly upon the day of completing our distinct state, (viz. February 12th, 1669*) this paper was read before the messengers of the churches and consented to by ourselves. Viz.

"The holy providence of the Most High so disposing, that public opposition and disturbance hath, of late years, been given, both by preaching and practice, to the congregational way of church order, by all manner of orderly establishments settled, and for a long time unanimously approved and peaceably practised in this place, all endeavours also (both among ourselves and from abroad) with due patience therein, proving fruitless and unsuccessful to the removing of that disturbance; We, whose names are after mentioned, being advised by a council of the neighbouring churches, and allowed also by the honorable general court, to dispose ourselves into a capacity of distinct walking, in order to a peaceable and edifying enjoyment of all God's holy ordinances, Do declare, that according to the light we have hitherto received, the forementioned congregational way (for the substance of it) as formerly settled, professed and practised, under the guidance of the first leaders of this church of Hartford, is the way of Christ; and that as such we are bound in duty carefully to observe and attend it, until such further light, (about any particular points of it) shall appear to us from the scripture, as may lead us, with joint or general satisfaction, to be otherwise persuaded. Some main heads or principles of which congregational way of church order are those that follow. Viz.

1. "That visible saints are the only fit matter, and confederation the only form of a visible church.

2. "That a competent number of visible saints, (with their seed) embodied by a particular covenant, are a true, distinct, and entire church of Christ.

3. "That such a particular church, being organized, or having furnished itself with those officers which Christ hath appointed, hath all power and privileges of a church belonging to it.

"In special,

1. "To admit or receive members.
2. "To deal with, and if need be, reject offenders.

* This, according to the present mode of dating, was February, 1670.

CHAP. XIX.   CONNECTICUT.   463

3. "To administer and enjoy all other ecclesiastical or- [Book I.
dinances within itself.

4. "That the power of guidance, or leading, belongs 1670.
only to the eldership, and the power of judgment, consent,
or privilege, belongs to the fraternity, or brethren in full
communion.

5. "That communion is carefully to be maintained between the churches of Christ according to his order.

6. "That counsel, in cases of difficulty, is to be sought
and submitted to according to God."

Having made this declaration, the brethren proceeded to
covenant in the following manner:

"Since it hath pleased God, in his infinite mercy, to
manifest himself willing to take unworthy sinners near unto himself, even into covenant relation to and interest in
him, to become a God to them, and avouch them to be his
people, and accordingly to command and encourage them
to give up themselves and their children also to him;

"We do, therefore, this day, in the presence of God, his
holy angels, and this assembly, avouch the LORD JEHO-
VAH, the true and living God, even God the FATHER, the
SON, and the HOLY GHOST, to be our God, and give up
ourselves and ours also unto him, to be his subjects, and
servants; promising through grace and strength in CHRIST
(without whom we can do nothing) to walk in professed
subjection to him as our LORD and LAWGIVER, yielding
universal obedience to his blessed will, according to what
discoveries he hath made, or shall hereafter make, of the
same to us; in special, that we will seek him in all his holy ordinances, according to the rules of the gospel, submitting to his government in this particular church, and
walking together therein, with all brotherly love and mutual watchfulness, to the building up of one another in
faith and love unto his praise. All which we promise to
perform, the LORD helping us, through his grace in JESUS
CHRIST."

Nearly at the same time, when the contentions commen- Controver-
ced in the church at Hartford, the people at Stratford fell sy and di-
into the same unhappy state of controversy and division. the church
During the administrations of Mr. Blackman, their first at Strat-
pastor, the church and town enjoyed great peace, and con- ford.
ducted their ecclesiastical affairs with exemplary harmony.
However, he was far advanced in years, and about the
year 1663 became very infirm, and unable to perform his
ministerial labors. The church, therefore, applied to Mr. Mr.
Israel Chauncey, son of the president Charles Chauncey, Chauncey
of Cambridge, to make them a visit and preach among ordained.

them. A majority of the church and town chose him for their pastor, and in 1665 he was ordained.* But a large and respectable part of the church and town were opposed to his ordination. To make them easy, it was agreed, that if, after hearing Mr. Chauncey a certain time, they should continue dissatisfied with his ministry, they should have liberty to call and settle another minister, and have the same privileges in the meeting house as the other party. Accordingly, after hearing Mr. Chauncey the time agreed upon, and not being satisfied with his ministerial performances, they invited Mr. Zechariah Walker to preach to them, and finally chose him for their pastor. He was ordained to the pastoral office in a regular manner, by the Rev. Mr. Haynes and Mr. Whiting, the ministers of Hartford, sometime about the year 1667, or 1668. Both ministers performed public worship in the same house. Mr. Chauncey performed his services at the usual hours, and Mr. Walker was allowed two hours in the middle of the day. But after some time, it so happened, that Mr. Walker continued his service longer than usual. Mr. Chauncey and his people coming to the house and finding that Mr. Walker's exercises were not finished, retired to a private house, and there performed their afternoon devotions. They were, however, so much displeased, that the next day they went over to Fairfield, and exhibited a complaint to major Gould, one of the magistrates, against Mr. Walker. The major, upon hearing the case, advised to pacific measures, and that Mr. Walker should be allowed three hours for the time of his public exercises.

In May, 1669, the general assembly advised the town to grant Mr. Walker full three hours for his exercises, until the next assembly in October. In the mean time, the parties were directed to call an able council to give them advice and assistance, and if possible to reconcile them. All attempts for a reconciliation, however, were unsuccessful. The parties became more fixed in their opposition to each other, and their feelings and conduct more and more unbrotherly. At length, Mr. Chauncey and the majority excluded Mr. Walker and his hearers the meeting house, and they convened and worshipped in a private dwelling.

Governor Winthrop, affected with the unhappy controversy and animosities subsisting in the town, advised, that Mr. Walker and his church and people should remove, and

* His ordination was in the independent mode. It has been the tradition, that Elder Brinsmade laid on hands with a leathern mitten. Hence it has been termed the leathern mitten ordination.

CHAP. XIX.   CONNECTICUT.

that a tract of land, for the settlement of a new township, Book I.
should be granted for their encouragement and accommodation. Accordingly, Mr. John Sherman,* Mr. William 1670.
Curtiss, and their associates, were authorized to begin a
plantation at Pomperaug. Consequently, Mr. Walker and
his people removed and settled the town of Woodbury,
about the years 1673 and 1674. This gave peace to the
town of Stratford, and Mr. Walker and his church and congregation walked in harmony among themselves and with
their sister churches.

The tradition is, that Mr. Walker and his church were
not so independent, in their principles, as the church of
Stratford; and that Mr. Walker was a more experimental,
pungent preacher, than Mr. Chauncey. Mr. Chauncey
was learned and judicious. They both became sensible
that their conduct towards each other, during the controversy at Stratford, had not, in all instances, been brotherly,
and, after some time, made concessions to each other, became perfectly reconciled, and conducted towards each
other with brotherly affection.

During these transactions, those venerable fathers, who Death and
had been singularly instrumental in planting, and had long character
illuminated the churches of Connecticut and New-Eng- of Mr. Da-
land, the Rev. John Davenport and the Rev. John War- 1670.
ham, finished their course. Mr. Davenport died at Boston, of an apoplexy, March 15th, 1670, in the 73d year of
his age. He was born in the city of Coventry, in War-
wickshire, 1597. His father was mayor of the city. At
about fourteen years of age, he was supposed to become
truly pious, and was admitted into Brazen Nose college, in
the university at Oxford. When he was nineteen, he became a constant preacher in the city of London. He appears, from his early life, to have been a man of public
spirit, planning and attempting to serve the general welfare of the church. About the year 1626, he united with
Dr. Gouge, Dr. Sibs, and Mr. Offspring, the lord mayor
of London, the king's sergeant at law, and with several
other attorneys and citizens, in a design of purchasing im-
propriations, and, with the profits of them, to maintain a
constant, able, and laborious ministry, in those parts of
the kingdom, where the poor people were destitute of the
word and ordinances, and such a ministry was most needed, and would be of the greatest utility. Such incredible

---

* Mr. Sherman was son of the Rev. John Sherman, of Watertown, he
was some years speaker of the lower house, and afterwards one of the
magistrates of this colony. He was one of Mr. Walker's principal hearers.

Book I. progress was made in this charitable design, that all the church lands, in the hands of laymen, would have been 1670. soon honestly recovered to the immediate service of the reformed religion. But bishop Laud, viewing the undertaking with a jealous eye, lest it might serve the cause of non-conformity, caused a bill to be exhibited in the exchequer chamber, by the king's attorney-general, against the feoffees, who had the management of the affair. By this means, an act of court was procured, condemning the proceedings, as dangerous to the church and state. The feoffments and contrivances made to the charitable design, were declared to be illegal, the company was dissolved, and the money was confiscated to the use of his majesty. But as the affair met with general approbation, and multitudes of wise and devout people extremely resented the conduct of the court, the crime was never prosecuted. Laud, however, watched Mr. Davenport with a jealous eye, and as he soon after discovered inclinations to non-conformity, he marked him out as an object of his vengeance. Mr. Davenport, therefore, to avoid the storm, by the consent of his people, resigned his pastoral charge in Coleman-street. He hoped, by this means, to enjoy a quiet life; but he found his expectations sadly disappointed. He was so constantly harassed by one busy and furious pursuivant after another, that he was obliged to leave the kingdom, and retire into Holland. In 1633, he arrived at Amsterdam, and, at the desire of the people, who met him on his way, became colleague pastor with the aged Mr. Paget. After about two years, finding that he could not conscientiously administer baptism in that loose way, to all sorts of children, practised in the Dutch churches, he desisted from his ministry at Amsterdam. While he was in this city, he received letters from Mr. Cotton, at Boston, acquainting him, that the order of the churches and commonwealth was then so settled, in New-England, by common consent, that it brought into his mind the new heaven and the new earth, wherein dwelleth righteousness. He, therefore, returned to London, and having shipped himself, with a number of pious people, came into New-England; and, as has been related, settled at New-Haven. He was a preacher of the gospel about fifty-four years, nearly thirty of which were spent at New-Haven. He was eminently pious, given to devotion in secret and private; and it was supposed that he was abundant in ejaculatory prayer. He is characterized as a hard student and universal scholar; as a laborious, prudent, exemplary minister; as an excellent preacher, speaking with a gravity,

CHAP. XIX. CONNECTICUT.

energy, and agreeableness, of which few of his brethren were capable. It is said, he was acquainted with great men, and great things, and was great himself.*

1670.

The Rev. John Warham survived Mr. Davenport but a short time. He expired on the 1st of April, 1670. He was about forty years minister in New-England; six at Dorchester, and thirty-four at Windsor. He was distinguished for piety and the strictest morals; yet, at times, was subject to great gloominess and religious melancholy. Such were his doubts and fears, at some times, that when he administered the Lord's supper to his brethren, he did not participate with them, fearing that the seals of the covenant did not belong to him. It is said, he was the first minister in New-England who used notes in preaching; yet he was applauded by his hearers, as one of the most animated and energetic preachers of his day. He was considered as one of the principal fathers and pillars of the churches of Connecticut.

After the close of the war with Philip and the Narraganset Indians, the general assembly recommended it to the ministers through the colony, to take special pains to instruct the people in the duties of religion, and to stir up and awaken them to repentance, and a general reformation of manners. They, also, appointed a day of solemn fasting and prayer, to supplicate the divine aid, that they might be enabled to repent, and sincerely amend their ways. The same measures were recommended, at the May session, the next year, and the people were called to humiliation and prayer, under a deep sense of the abounding of sin and the dark aspects of Providence.

Oct. 1676. Recommendation of a reformation of manners.

The general court, about three years after, for the more effectual preservation and propagation of religion to posterity, recommended it to the ministry of this colony, upon the Lord's day, to catechise all the youth in their respective congregations, under twenty years of age, in the assembly of divines, or some other orthodox catechism. To continue and increase unity in religious sentiments among the people, and that they might have the advantage of participating in the variety of ministerial gifts, it was also recommended to the ministers, to attend a weekly lecture in each county, on Wednesday, in such manner as they should judge most subservient to these purposes.†

May, 1680. Catechising recommended.

County lectures recommended.

The religious state of the colony, at this time, is given

* Magnalia, B. III. p, 51—57. He left a respectable family, and his descendants have supported its dignity to the present time. Some of them have been in the ministry, and others magistrates of this colony.
† Records of the colony.

Book I. in an answer to the queries of the lords of trade and plantations. It is to the following effect.

1676.
Religious state of the colony.

"Our people, in this colony, are some of them strict congregational men, others more large congregational men, and some moderate presbyterians. The congregational men, of both sorts, are the greatest part of the people in the colony. There are four or five seventh day men, and about so many more quakers."

"Great care is taken for the instruction of the people in the christian religion, by ministers catechising of them, and preaching to them twice every sabbath day, and sometimes on lecture days; and by masters of families instructing and catechising their children and servants, which they are required to do by law. In our corporation are twenty-six towns, and twenty-one churches. There is in every town in the colony a settled minister, except in two towns newly begun." In some towns there were two ministers; so that there were, on the whole, then about the same number of ministers as of towns. There was about one minister, upon an average, to every four hundred and sixty persons, or to about ninety families.

Attempts to christianize the Indians.

While settlements and churches were forming in various parts of the colony, and the English inhabitants were providing for their own instruction, some pains were taken to instruct and christianize the Connecticut Indians. A law was made, obliging those under the protection of the government to keep the christian sabbath. The Rev. Mr. Fitch was particularly desired to teach Uncas and his family christianity. A large bible, printed in the Indian language, was provided and given to the Moheagan sachems, that they might read the scriptures. When the council of ministers met at Hartford, in 1657, the famous Mr. Elliot, hearing of the Podunk Indians, desired that the tribe might be assembled, that he might have an opportunity of offering Christ to them for their Saviour.

By the influence of some principal gentlemen, they were persuaded to come together, at Hartford, and Mr. Elliot preached to them in their own language, and labored to instruct them concerning their CREATOR and REDEEMER. When he had finished his sermon, and explained the matter to them, he desired an answer from them, whether they would accept of Jesus Christ for their Saviour, as he had been offered to them? But their chief men, with great scorn and resentment, utterly refused. They said the English had taken away their lands, and were attempting now to make them servants.

Mr. Stone and Mr. Newton, before this time, had both

been employed, at the desire of the colony, to teach the Indians in Hartford, Windsor, Farmington, and that vicinity; and one John Minor was employed as an interpreter, and was taken into Mr. Stone's family, that he might be further instructed and prepared for that service. Catechisms were prepared by Mr. Elliot and others, in the Indian language, and spread among the Indians. The Rev. Mr. Pierson, it seems, learned the Indian language and preached to the Connecticut Indians. A considerable sum was allowed him by the commissioners of the united colonies; and a sum was also granted by them, for the instruction of the Indians in the county of New-Haven.* The ministers of the several towns, where Indians lived, instructed them, as they had opportunity; but all attempts for christianizing the Indians, in Connecticut, were attended with little success. They were engaged, a great part of their time, in such implacable wars among themselves, were so totally ignorant of letters and the English language, and the English ministers, in general, were so entirely ignorant of their dialect, that it was extremely difficult to teach them. Not one Indian church was ever gathered, by the English ministers, in Connecticut. Several Indians, however, in one town and another, became christians, and were baptized and admitted to full communion in the English churches. Some few were admitted into the church at Farmington,† and some into the church at Derby. One of the sachems of the Indians at Naugatuck falls, was a member of the church at Derby, and it has been said that he was a sober well conducted man. Some few of the Moheagans have professed christianity, and been, many years since, admitted to full communion in the north church in New-London.

The gospel, however, hath had by far the most happy effect upon the Quinibaug, or Plainfield Indians, of any in Connecticut. They ever lived peaceably with the English, and about the year 1745, in the time of the great awakening and reformation in New-England, they became greatly affected with the truths of the gospel, professed christianity, and gave the strongest evidence of a real conversion to God. They were filled with the knowledge of salvation, and expressed it to admiration. They were entirely reformed as to their manner of living. They became temperate, and abstained from drinking to excess, which it

---
* Records of the united colonies.
† There was an Indian school formerly kept in this town, at the expense of the society for propagating christian knowledge among the Indians. The number of Indian scholars was sometimes fifteen or sixteen.

Book I. had before been found utterly impossible to effect by any other means. They held religious meetings, and numbers of them formed into church state and had the sacraments administered to them.‡

1680.

Upon the assembly's granting liberty to the minor party in Windsor to call and settle an orthodox minister, they immediately called one Mr. Woodbridge to preach among them. Mr. Chauncey and Mr. Woodbridge continued to preach, one to one party, and the other to the other, from 1667 to 1680. Several councils had been called to advise and unite the parties, but it seems none had judged it expedient to ordain either of the gentlemen; but after a separation of about ten years, a council advised, that both ministers should leave the town, and that the churches and parties should unite, and call and settle one minister over the whole. As the parties did not submit to this advice, it seems, that another council was called three years afterwards, May, 1680, which gave the same advice, but the parties did not comply. The general assembly therefore interposed and passed the following act.

Act of assembly relative to Windsor, Oct. 14th, 1680.

"This court, having considered the petition of some of Windsor people and the sorrowful condition of the good people there, and finding, that notwithstanding all means of healing afforded them, they do remain in a bleeding state and condition, do find it necessary for this court to exert their authority towards issuing or putting a stop to the present troubles there; and this court do hereby declare, that they find all the good people of Windsor obliged to stand to, and rest satisfied with the advice and issue of the council they chose to hear and issue their matters; which advice being given and now presented to the court, dated January, 1677, this court doth confirm the same, and order that there be a seasonable uniting of the second society in Windsor with the first, according to order of council, by an orderly preparation for their admission; and if there be objection against the life or knowledge of any, then it be according to the council's advice heard and issued by Mr. Hooker and the other moderator's successor; and that both the former ministers be released: And that the committee appointed to seek out for a minister, with the advice of the church and town collectively, by their major vote, do vigorously pursue the procuring of an able, orthodox minister, qualified according to the advice of the governor and council, and ministers, May last; and all the good people of Windsor are hereby required to be aiding

‡ Manuscripts from Plainfield. These Indians were numerous at the time when the town was settled, amounting to 4 or 500.

and assisting therein, and not in the least to oppose and hinder the same, as they will answer the contrary at their peril."*

<small>Book I.
1682.</small>

In consequence of this act, Mr. Samuel Mather was invited to preach to the people, and about two years after, was ordained to the pastoral office over the whole town. The two parties were generally united in him, and to complete the union of the town and churches, the assembly enacted, "That the people at Windsor should quietly settle Mr. Mather and communicate to his support: That such as, on examination, should satisfy Mr. Mather of their experimental knowledge, should upon proper testimony of their good conversation, be admitted on their return from the second church."†

<small>Act of assembly respecting Windsor, May, 1682.</small>

Both churches, and the whole town, were united under Mr. Mather, and their ecclesiastical affairs were, under his ministry, conducted with harmony and brotherly affection.

Notwithstanding the result of the synod, in 1662, and the various attempts which had been made to introduce the practice of what has been generally termed owning the covenant, it does not appear to have obtained in the churches of this colony until the year 1696. It appears first to have been introduced by Mr. Woodbridge, at Hartford. The covenant proposed, bearing date, February, 1696, is for substance as follows,

"We do solemnly, in the presence of God and this congregation, avouch God, in Jesus Christ, to be our God, one God in three persons, the Father, the Son, and the Holy Ghost; and that we are by nature children of wrath, and that our hope of mercy with God, is only through the righteousness of Jesus Christ, apprehended by faith; and we do freely give up ourselves to the Lord, to walk in communion with him, in the ordinances appointed in his holy word, and to yield obedience to all his commandments, and submit to his government. And whereas, to the great dishonor of God, scandal of religion, and hazard of the damnation of many souls, drunkenness and uncleanness are prevailing amongst us, we do solemnly engage before God, this day, through his grace, faithfully and conscientiously to strive against these evils and the temptations leading thereunto."

<small>Covenant owned, Feb. 1696.</small>

Sixty nine persons, male and female, subscribed this in February; on the 8th of March, one fortnight after, eighty three more subscribed. In about a month, the number of subscribers amounted to one hundred and ninety two;

---
* Records of the colony.
† Records of the colony.

Book I. which appears to have been nearly the whole body of young people in that congregation.

1696. The like practice was, about the same time, or not many years after, introduced into the other church, and the practice of owning the covenant by people, and offering their children to baptism, was gradually introduced into other churches.

The practice of the ministers and churches at Hartford, in some respects, was different from that in other churches. The ministers, Mr. Woodbridge and Mr. Buckingham, with their deacons, went round among the young people and warned them, once every year, to come and publicly subscribe, or own the covenant. When such persons as had owned or subscribed it came into family state, they presented their children to baptism, though they made no other profession of religion, and neglected the sacrament of the Lord's supper and other duties peculiar to members in full communion. In other churches, the covenant was owned by persons, sometimes before marriage, but more generally not until they became parents, and wished to have baptism administered to their children.

The practice of making a relation of christian experiences, and of admitting none to full communion, but such as appeared to be christians indeed, yet prevailed; and the number of church members, in full communion, was generally small. In those churches where the owning of the covenant was not practised, great numbers of children were unbaptized.

Design of founding a college in Connecticut, 1698.

Reasons for it.

While the inhabitants and churches, in Connecticut, were constantly increasing, and the calls for a learned ministry, to supply the churches, became more and more urgent, a number of the ministers conceived the purpose of founding a college in Connecticut. By this means, they might educate young men, from among themselves, for the sacred ministry, and for various departments in civil life, and diffuse literature and piety more generally among the people. The clergy, and people in general, by long experience, found the great inconvenience of educating their sons at so great a distance as Cambridge, and in carrying so much money out of the colony, which otherwise might be a considerable emolument to this commonwealth. A well founded college might not only serve the interests of the churches in this government, but in the neighbouring colonies, where there were no colleges erected; might not only prevent a large sum of money annually from being carried abroad, but bring something considerable into it, from the extensive country around them. Colleges had

CHAP. XIX. CONNECTICUT. 473

been anciently considered as the schools of the church; BOOK I.
and not only the prophets had been encouragers and heads
of them; but the apostles and their immediate successors 1698.
had taken great care to establish schools, wherever the gospel had been preached, for the propagation of the truth,
and to transmit the religion of the Redeemer to all succeeding ages. The ministers therefore conceived it to be
entirely in character, and as happily corresponding with
the great design of the first settlement of New-England and
Connecticut, for them to be the planners and founders of a
college.

The design was first concerted, in 1698, by the Rev.
Messieurs Pierpont of New-Haven, Andrew of Milford, and
Russell of Branford. These were the most forward and active, in carrying the affair into immediate execution. The
design was mentioned to principal gentlemen and ministers
in private conversation, at occasional meetings of the clergy, and in councils. In this way the affair was so far ripen-
ed, that ten of the principal ministers in the colony were
nominated and agreed upon to stand as trustees, to found,
erect, and govern a college. The gentlemen thus agreed
upon were the Reverend Messieurs James Noyes of Ston- 1699.
ington, Israel Chauncey of Stratford, Thomas Bucking- Gentlemen nominated
ham of Saybrook, Abraham Pierson of Killingworth, Sam- for trus-
uel Mather of Windsor, Samuel Andrew of Milford, Timo- tees.
thy Woodbridge of Hartford, James Pierpont of New-Haven, Noadiah Russell of Middletown, and Joseph Webb of
Fairfield.

In 1700, these gentlemen convened at New-Haven, and College
formed themselves into a body or society, to consist of founded, 1700.
eleven ministers including a rector, and determined to
found a college in the colony of Connecticut. They had
another meeting, the same year, at Branford, and then
founded the university of Yale college. The transaction
was in this manner. Each gentleman gave a number of
books, and laying them upon a table, pronounced words to
this effect, " I give these books for the founding of a college in this colony." About forty volumes in folio were
thus given. The trustees took possession of them, and appointed Mr. Russell of Branford, to be keeper of their library.

Various other donations, both of books and money, were
soon after made, by which a good foundation was laid for a
public seminary. But doubts arising whether the trustees were vested with a legal capacity for the holding of
lands, and whether private donations and contributions
would be sufficient to effect the great design which they

K 3

Book I. had in view, it was, upon the best advice and mature deliberation, determined to make application to the legislature for a charter of incorporation. The draught was made by the honorable judge Sewall and Mr. secretary Addington of Boston. This was presented to the general assembly with a petition signed by a large number of ministers and other principal characters in the colony praying for a charter. The petition represented, "That from a sincere regard to, and zeal for, upholding the Protestant religion, by a succession of learned and orthodox men, they had proposed that a collegiate school should be erected in this colony, wherein youth should be instructed in all parts of learning, to qualify them for public employments in church and civil state; and that they had nominated ten ministers to be trustees, partners or undertakers for the founding, endowing and ordering the said school." The gentlemen were particularly named, and it was desired, that full liberty and privilege might be granted to them for that end.

1700.

To facilitate the design, the honorable James Fitch, Esq. of Norwich, one of the council, before the petition was heard, made a formal donation under his hand, predicated on "the great pains and charge the ministers had been at in setting up a collegiate school; and therefore to encourage a work so pleasing to God, and beneficial to posterity, he gave a tract of land, in Killingly, of about 600 acres; and all the glass and nails which should be necessary to build a college house and hall."

The founders of college incorporated by act of assembly, Oct. 1701.

The general assembly, at their session in October, 1701, incorporated the trustees nominated, granting them a charter, and vesting them with all powers and privileges necessary for the government of a college, the holding of lands, and the employment of all money and estates which might be given for the benefit of the college. The charter ordained that the corporation should consist of ministers only, and that none should be chosen trustees under the age of forty years. Their number was not, at any time, to exceed eleven nor be less than seven. The assembly made them an annual grant of one hundred and twenty pounds, equal to about sixty pounds sterling.

Nov. 11th, first meeting of the corporation. Rector chosen.

The trustees, animated with their charter privileges and the countenance of the legislature, met the next November, at Saybrook, and chose the Rev. Abraham Pierson of Killingworth, rector of the college, and the Rev. Samuel Russell was chosen a trustee to complete the number of the corporation. They also made rules for the general government and instruction of the collegiate school.

It was ordered, "That the rector take special care, as of the moral behaviour of the students at all times, so, with industry, to instruct and ground them well in theoretical divinity; and to that end, shall neither by himself, nor by any other person whomsoever, allow them to be instructed in any other system or synopsis of divinity, than such as the trustees do order and appoint: But shall take effectual care, that said students be weekly (at such seasons as he shall see cause to appoint) caused memoriter to recite the assembly's catechism in Latin, and Dr. Ames's Theological Theses, of which, as also Ames's Cases of Conscience, he shall make, or cause to be made, from time to time, such explanations as may, through the blessing of God, be most conducive to their establishment in the principles of the Christian Protestant religion."

Book I. 1701. Orders respecting the college.

"The rector shall also cause the scriptures daily, except on the sabbath, morning and evening, to be read by the students at the times of prayer in the school, according to the laudable order and usage of Harvard college, making expositions upon the same: And upon the sabbath, shall expound practical theology, or cause the non graduated students to repeat sermons: And in all other ways, according to the best of his discretion, shall, at all times, studiously endeavour, in the education of the students, to promote the power and purity of religion, and the best edification of these New-England churches."

At this meeting, it was debated where to fix the college. Though the trustees were not fully satisfied or agreed on the most convenient place, yet they fixed upon Saybrook, until, upon further consideration, they should have sufficient reason to alter their opinion. They desired the rector to remove himself and family to Saybrook. Until that could be effected, they ordered, that the scholars should be instructed, at or near the rector's house, in Killingworth. The corporation made various attempts to remove the rector to Saybrook, but his people were entirely opposed to it, and such other impediments were in the way that it was not effected. The students continued at Killingworth during his life. The library, for that reason, was removed from Branford, to the rector's house.

College appointed to be at Saybrook, but the rector does not remove.

The ministers had been several years in effecting their plan, and a number of young men had been preparing for college, under the instructions of one and another of the trustees. As soon as the college became furnished with a rector and tutor, eight of them were admitted and put into different classes, according to the proficiency which they had respectively made. Some, in a year or two, became qualified for a degree.

BOOK I. The first commencement was at Saybrook, September 13th, 1702. The following gentlemen appear, at this time, to have received the degree of master of arts, Stephen Buckingham, Salmon Treat, Joseph Coit, Joseph Moss, Nathaniel Chauncey, and Joseph Morgan. Four of them had been previously graduated at Cambridge. They all became ministers of the gospel, and three of them, Mr. Buckingham, Mr. Moss, and Mr. Chauncey, were afterwards fellows of the college.

1702.
First commencement in Connecticut.

To avoid charge and other inconveniences, for some years at first, the commencements were private. Mr. Nathaniel Lynde of Saybrook, was pleased generously to give a house and land for the use of the college, so long as it should be continued in that town. For the further encouragement and accommodation, in 1703, there was a general contribution through the colony, to build a college house at Saybrook, or any other place wherever it should finally be judged most convenient to fix the college.*

* This year, that venerable man, the Reverend James Fitch, pastor of the church in Norwich, finished his course, at Lebanon, in the 80th year of his age. His history and character are given in the inscription upon his monumental stone.

In hoc Sepulchro depositæ sunt Reliquiæ Viri vere Reverendi D. Jacobi Fitch; natus fuit apud Boking, in Comitatu Essexiæ, in Anglia, Anno Domini 1622, Decem. 24. Qui, postquam Linguis literatis optime instructus fuisset, in Nov-Angliam venit, Ætate 16 ; et deinde Vitam degit, Hartfordiæ, per Septennium, sub Instructione Virorum celeberrimorum D. Hooker & D. Stone. Postea Munere pastorali functus est apud Saybrook per Annos 14. Illinc cum Ecclesiæ majori Parte Norvicum migravit; et ibi exteros Vitæ Annos transegit in Opere Evangelico. In Senectute, vero, præ Corporis infirmitate necessarie cessabit ab Opere publico; tandemque recessit Liberis, apud Lebanon ; ubi Semianno fere exacto obdormivit in Jesu, Anno 1702, Novembris 18, Ætat. 80.

Vir Ingenii Acumine, Pondere Judicii, Prudentia, Charitate, sanctis Laboribus, et omni moda Vitæ sanctitate, Peritia quoque et Vi concionandi nulli secundus.

In English to this effect.

In this grave are deposited the remains of that truly reverend man, Mr. JAMES FITCH. He was born at Boking, in the county of Essex, in England, the 24th of December, in the year of our Lord, 1622. Who, after he had been most excellently taught the learned languages, came into New-England, at the age of sixteen ; and then spent seven years under the instruction of those very famous men, Mr. Hooker and Mr. Stone. Afterwards, he discharged the pastoral office, fourteen years, at Saybrook. Thence he removed, with the major part of his church, to Norwich ; where he spent the other years of his life in the work of the gospel. In his old age, indeed, he was obliged to cease from his public labors, by reason of bodily indisposition ; and at length retired to his children, at Lebanon ; where, after spending nearly half a year, he slept in Jesus, in the year 1702, on the 18th of November, in the 80th year of his age.

He was a man, as to the smartness of his genius, the solidity of his judgment, his charity, holy labors, and every kind of purity of life, and also as to his skill and energy of preaching, inferior to none.

During the term of about seventy years from the settlement of Connecticut, the congregational had been the only mode of worship in the colony. But the society for propagating the gospel in foreign parts, in 1704, fixed the Rev. Mr. Muirson as a missionary at Rye. Some of the people at Stratford had been educated in the church of England mode of worship and administering of the ordinances, and others were not pleased with the rigid doctrines and discipline of the New-England churches, and they made an earnest application to Mr. Muirson to make a visit at Stratford, and preach and baptize among them. About the year 1706, upon their invitation, he came to Stratford, accompanied with colonel Heathcote, a gentleman zealously engaged in promoting the episcopal church. The ministers and people, in that and the adjacent towns, it seems, were alarmed at his coming, and took pains to prevent their neighbors and families from hearing him. However, the novelty of the affair, and other circumstances, brought together a considerable assembly; and Mr. Muirson baptized five and twenty persons, principally adults. This was the first step towards introducing the church worship into this colony. In April, 1707, he made another visit to Stratford. Colonel Heathcote was pleased to honor him with his company, as he had done before. He preached, at this time, at Fairfield as well as Stratford; and in both towns baptized a number of children and adult persons. Both the magistrates and ministers opposed the introduction of episcopacy, and advised the people not to attend the preaching of the church missionaries; but the opposition only increased the zeal of the church people. Mr. Muirson, after this, made several journies to Connecticut, and itinerated among the people. But there was no missionary, from the society, fixed in Connecticut, until the year 1722, when Mr. Pigot was appointed missionary at Stratford. The churchmen at first, in that town, consisted of about fifteen families, among whom were a few husbandmen, but much the greatest number were tradesmen, who had been born in England, and came and settled there. Some of their neighbors joined them, so that Mr. Pigot had twenty communicants. and about a hundred and fifty hearers. In 1723, Christ Church in Stratford was founded, and the Rev. Mr. Johnson, afterwards Dr. Johnson, was appointed to succeed Mr. Pigot.*

The first plan of the college was very formal and mi-

* Manuscripts from Stratford, and Dr. Humphreys' History of the Incorporated Society's Missionaries.

Book I. nute, drawn in imitation of the ancient protestant colleges and universities in France. It was proposed, that it should be erected by a general synod of the consociated churches of Connecticut. It was designed, that it should be under the government of a president and ten trustees, seven of whom were to be a quorum: That the synod should have the nomination of the first president and trustees, and have a kind of general influence in all future elections, that the governors might be preserved in orthodox sentiments. It was designed also, that the synod should agree upon a confession of faith, to which the president, trustees, and tutors should, upon their appointment to office, be required to give their consent; and that the college should be called the school of the church. Indeed, it was proposed, that the churches should contribute to its support.

1706.

Proposal for a general synod, 1703.

Though this plan was not formally pursued, yet at a meeting of the trustees, at Guilford, March 17th, 1703, they wrote a circular letter to the ministers, proposing "to have a general synod of all the churches in the colony of Connecticut, to give their joint consent to the confession of faith, after the example of the synod in Boston, in 1680." As this proposal was universally acceptable, the churches and ministers of the several counties met in a consociated council, and gave their assent to the Westminster and Savoy confessions of faith. It seems, that they also drew up certain rules of ecclesiastical union in discipline, as preparatory to a general synod, which they had still in contemplation.

Customary meetings of ministers.

The Cambridge platform, which, for about sixty years, had been the general plan of discipline and church fellowship in New-England, made no provision for the general meeting of ministers, or for their union in associations or in consociations, yet, at an early period, they had a general meeting, both in Connecticut and Massachusetts, and began to form into associations. Their annual meetings were at the times of the general election at Boston and Hartford. At this time, they had handsome entertainments made for them at the public expense.* In these general meetings, they went into consultations respecting the general welfare of the churches, the supplying them with ministers, providing for their stated enjoyment of divine ordinances, and the preservation of their peace and order. The general interests of literature were consulted, and advice given in cases in which it was requisite. Sometimes

* The legislature have continued this generosity to the present time. A genteel entertainment is made not only for the clergy of Connecticut, but of the neighboring colonies, who are present on the occasion.

CHAP. XIX. CONNECTICUT.

measures were adopted to assist the poor and afflicted, in particular instances of distress. The affair of civilizing and christianizing the Indians, came under their serious deliberations. Sometimes they consulted measures, and gave general directions respecting candidates for the ministry, and the orderly manner of introducing them into the churches.

The ministers of particular neighborhoods, in various parts of the country, held frequent meetings, for their mutual assistance, and to instruct and advise the churches and people, as circumstances required. This particularly was the practice in Connecticut.

The venerable Mr. Hooker was a great friend to the meeting and consociation of ministers and churches, as a grand mean of promoting purity, union, and brotherly affection, among the ministers and churches. During his life, the ministers in the vicinity of Hartford, had frequent meetings at his house. About a week before his death, he observed, with great earnestness, "We must agree upon constant meetings of ministers, and settle the consociation of churches, or else we are undone." Soon after his decease, ministers in various parts of New-England, and especially in Connecticut, began to establish constant meetings, or associations, in particular vicinities, and agreed on the business to be done, and the manner in which they would proceed.

Mr. Hooker's conduct and opinion.

Book I.
1703.

They did not, however, all adopt the same mode. Some of the meetings, or associations, fasted and prayed, and discussed questions of importance for mutual instruction and edification. A moderator was chosen to conduct the business of the meetings with order and decency, to receive all communications which might be made from the churches, or other similar meetings, and to call the associated brethren together on particular emergencies. These meetings were always opened and concluded with prayer.

Some of the associations were very formal and particular in covenanting together, and in fixing the business which should be transacted by them. They covenanted to submit to the counsels, reproofs, and censures of the associated brotherhood; and that they would not forsake the association, nor neglect the appointed meetings, without sufficient reasons. They engaged, that in the meetings they would debate questions immediately respecting themselves and their conduct: That they would hear and consider all cases proposed to them from neighboring churches or individuals: answer letters directed to them from particular

Book I.
1703.

churches or persons; and discuss any question, which had been proposed at a preceding meeting. In some of these associations, it was agreed to meet statedly once in six weeks or two months.* As the design was for their own mutual improvement and the advancement of christianity in general, the associations attended a lecture in the parishes in which they convened for the instruction and edification of the people. In Connecticut, after the resolution of the assembly, in 1680, the ministers had county meetings every week.

But these associations and meetings were merely voluntary, countenanced by no ecclesiastical constitution, attended only by such ministers, in one place and another, as were willing to associate, and could bind none but themselves. The churches might advise with them if they chose it, or neglect it at pleasure. There was no regular way of introducing candidates to the improvement of the churches, by the general consent either of themselves or the elders. When they had finished their collegiate studies, if they imagined themselves qualified, and could find some friendly gentleman in the ministry to introduce them, they began to preach, without an examination or recommendation from any body of ministers or churches. If they studied a time with any particular minister or ministers, after they had received the honors of college, that minister, or those ministers introduced them into the pulpit at pleasure, without the general consent and approbation of their brethren. Many judged this to be too loose a practice, in a matter of such immense importance to the divine honor, the reputation of the ministry, and the peace and edification of the churches. Degrees at college were esteemed no sufficient evidence of men's piety, knowledge of theology, or ministerial gifts and qualifications.

Besides, it was generally conceded, that the state of the churches was lamentable, with respect to their general order, government, and discipline. That for the want of a more general and energetic government, many churches ran into confusion; that councils were not sufficient to relieve the aggrieved and restore peace. As there was no general rule for the calling of councils, council was called against council, and opposite results were given upon the same cases, to the reproach of councils and the wounding of religion. Aggrieved churches and brethren were discouraged, as in this way their case seemed to be without remedy. There was no such thing, in this way, as bringing their difficulties to a final issue.†

* Magnalia, B. V. p. 63.
† Wise's vindication. p. 165. Boston edition, 1772.

For the relieving of these inconveniences, there were many, in the New-England churches, not only among the clergy, but other gentlemen of principal character, who earnestly wished for a nearer union among the churches. A great majority of the legislature and clergy in Connecticut, were for the association of ministers, and the consociation of churches. The synod, in 1662, had given their opinion fully in favor of the consociation of churches. The heads of agreement drawn up and assented to, by the united ministers, in England, called presbyterian and congregational, in 1692, had made their appearance on this side of the Atlantic; and, in general, were highly approved. The VII. article of agreement, under the head of the ministry, makes express provision for the regular introduction of candidates for the ministry. The united brethren say, "It is expedient, that they who enter on the work of preaching the gospel, be not only qualified for the communion of saints; but also, that, except in cases extraordinary, they give proof of their gifts and fitness for the said work, unto the pastors of the churches of known abilities, to discern and judge of their qualifications; that they may be sent forth with solemn approbation and prayer; which we judge needful, that no doubt may remain concerning their being called unto the work; and for preventing, as much as in us lieth, ignorant and rush intruders." In these articles, it is also agreed, " that in so great and weighty a matter, as the calling and choosing a pastor, we judge it ordinarily requisite, that every such church consult and advise with the pastors of the neighboring congregations."

In this state of the churches, the legislature passed an act, at their session in May, 1708, requiring the ministers and churches to meet and form an ecclesiastical constitution. The apprehensions and wishes of the assembly will, in the best manner, be discovered by their own act, which is in the words following:

"This assembly, from their own observation, and the complaint of many others, being made sensible of the defects of the discipline of the churches of this government, arising from the want of a more explicit asserting of the rules given for that end in the holy scriptures; from which would arise a permanent establishment among ourselves, a good and regular issue in cases subject to ecclesiastical discipline, glory to Christ, our head, and edification to his members; hath seen fit to ordain and require, and it is by the authority of the same ordained and required, that the ministers of the several counties in this government shall meet together, at their respective county towns, with such

Act appointing a synod, May 13th, 1708.

Book I.
1708.

messengers, as the churches to which they belong shall see cause to send with them, on the last Monday in June next; there to consider and agree upon those methods and rules for the management of ecclesiastical discipline, which by them shall be judged agreeable and conformable to the word of God, and shall, at the same meeting, appoint two or more of their number to be their delegates, who shall all meet together at Saybrook, at the next commencement to be held there; where they shall compare the results of the ministers of the several counties, and out of and from them, to draw a form of ecclesiastical discipline, which, by two or more persons delegated by them, shall be offered to this court, at their session at New-Haven, in October next, to be considered of and confirmed by them: And the expense of the above mentioned meetings shall be defrayed out of the public treasury of this colony."

"A true copy of the record.

"Test. ELEAZER KIMBERLY, Secretary."

According to the act of the assembly, the ministers and churches of the several counties convened, at the time appointed, and made their respective drafts for discipline, and chose their delegates for the general meeting at Saybrook, in September.

The ministers and messengers chosen for this council, and its result, will appear from their minutes.

"At a meeting of delegates from the councils of the several counties of Connecticut colony, in New-England, in America, at Saybrook, Sept. 9th, 1708,

PRESENT,

Names of the synod, Sept. 9th, 1708.

From the council of Hartford county:—The Rev. Timothy Woodbridge, Noadiah Russell, and Stephen Mix. Messenger, John Haynes, Esq.

From the council in Fairfield county:—The Rev. Charles Chauncey and John Davenport. Messenger, deacon Samuel Hoyt.

From the council in New-London county:—The Rev. James Noyes, Thomas Buckingham, Moses Noyes, and John Woodward. Messengers, Robert Chapman, deacon William Parker.

From the council of New-Haven county:—The Rev. Samuel Andrew, James Pierpont, and Samuel Russell.

"The Rev. James Noyes and Thomas Buckingham being chosen moderators. The Rev. Stephen Mix and John Woodward being chosen scribes.

"In compliance with an order of the general assembly, May 13th, 1708, after humble addresses to the throne of grace for the divine presence, assistance, and blessing up-

CHAP. XIX. CONNECTICUT.

on us, having our eyes upon the word of God and the constitution of our churches, We agree that the confession of faith owned and assented unto by the elders and messengers assembled at Boston, in New-England, May 12th, 1680, being the second session of that synod, be recommended to the honourable general assembly of this colony, at the next session, for their public testimony thereunto, as the FAITH of the churches of this colony."*

"We agree also, that the heads of agreement assented to by the united ministers, formerly called presbyterian and congregational, be observed by the churches throughout this colony."

"And for the better regulation of the administration of church discipline, in relation to all cases ecclesiastical, both in particular churches and councils, to the full determining and executing the rules in all such cases, it is agreed,"

"I. That the elder, or elders of a particular church, with the consent of the brethren of the same, have power, and ought to exercise church discipline, according to the rule of God's word, in relation to all scandals that fall out within the same. And it may be meet, in all cases of difficulty, for the respective pastors of particular churches, to take advice of the elders of the churches in the neighbourhood, before they proceed to censure in such cases."

"II. That the churches which are neighbouring to each other, shall consociate, for mutual affording to each other such assistance as may be requisite, upon all occasions ecclesiastical. And that the particular pastors and churches, within the respective counties in this government, shall be one consociation, (or more, if they shall judge meet,) for the end aforesaid."

"III. That all cases of scandal, that fall out within the circuit of any of the aforesaid consociations, shall be brought to a council of the elders, and also messengers of the churches within the said circuit, i. e. the churches of one consociation, if they see cause to send messengers, when there shall be need of a council for the determination of them."

"IV. That, according to the common practice of our churches, nothing shall be deemed an act or judgment of any council, which hath not the act of the major part of the elders present concurring, and such a number of the messengers present, as makes the majority of the council: provided that if any such church shall not see cause to send any messengers to the council, or the persons chosen by

* This was the Savoy confession, with some small alterations.

Book I.
1709.

them shall not attend, neither of these shall be any obstruction to the proceedings of the council, or invalidate any of their acts."

"V. That when any case is orderly brought before any council of the churches, it shall there be heard and determined, which, (unless orderly removed from thence,) shall be a final issue; and all parties therein concerned shall sit down and be determined thereby. And the council so hearing, and giving the result or final issue, in the said case, as aforesaid, shall see their determination, or judgment, duly executed and attended, in such way or manner, as shall, in their judgment, be most suitable and agreeable to the word of God."

"VI. That if any pastor and church doth obstinately refuse a due attendance and conformity to the determination of the council, that hath the cognizance of the case, and determineth it as above, after due patience used, they shall be reputed guilty of scandalous contempt, and dealt with as the rule of God's word in such case doth provide, and the sentence of non-communion shall be declared against such pastor and church. And the churches are to approve of the said sentence, by withdrawing from the communion of the pastor and church, which so refused to be healed."

"VII. That, in case any difficulties shall arise in any of the churches in this colony, which cannot be issued without considerable disquiet, that church, in which they arise, (or that minister or member aggrieved with them,) shall apply themselves to the council of the consociated churches of the circuit, to which the said church belongs; who, if they see cause, shall thereupon convene, hear, and determine such cases of difficulty, unless the matter brought before them, shall be judged so great in the nature of it, or so doubtful in the issue, or of such general concern, that the said council shall judge best that it be referred to a fuller council, consisting of the churches of the other consociation within the same county, (or of the next adjoining consociation of another county, if there be not two consociations in the county where the difficulty ariseth,) who, together with themselves, shall hear, judge, determine, and finally issue such case, according to the word of God."

"VIII. That a particular church, in which any difficulty doth arise, may, if they see cause, call a council of the consociated churches of the circuit to which the church belongs, before they proceed to sentence therein; but there is not the same liberty to an offending brother, to call the council, before the church to which he belongs proceed to

CHAP. XIX. CONNECTICUT.

excommunication in the said case, unless with the consent of the church."

"IX. That all the churches of the respective consociations shall choose, if they see cause, one or two members of each church, to represent them in the councils of the said churches, as occasion may call for them, who shall stand in that capacity till new be chosen for the same service, unless any church shall incline to choose their messengers anew, upon the convening of such councils."

"X. That the minister or ministers of the county towns, or where there are no ministers in such towns, the two next ministers to the said town, shall, as soon as conveniently may be, appoint time and place for the meeting of the elders and messengers of the churches in said county, in order to their forming themselves into one or more consociations, and notify the time and place to the elders and churches of that county who shall attend at the same, the elders in their persons, and the churches by their messengers, if they see cause to send them. Which elders and messengers, so assembled in council, as also any other council hereby allowed of, shall have power to adjourn themselves, as need shall be, for the space of one year, after the beginning or first session of the said council, and no longer. And that minister who was chosen at the last session of any council, to be moderator, shall, with the advice and consent of two more elders, (or, in case of the moderator's death, any two elders of the same consociation,) call another council within the circuit, when they shall judge there is need thereof. And all councils may prescribe rules, as occasion may require, and whatever they judge needful within their circuit, for the well performing and orderly managing the several acts, to be attended by them, or matters that come under their cognizance."

"XI. That if any person or persons, orderly complained of to a council, or that are witnesses to such complaints, (having regular notification to appear,) shall refuse, or neglect so to do, in the place, and at the time specified in the warning given, except they or he give some satisfying reason thereof to the said council, they shall be judged guilty of scandalous contempt."

"XII. That the teaching elders of each county shall be one association, (or more, if they see cause,) which association, or associations, shall assemble twice a year, at least, at such time and place as they shall appoint, to consult the duties of their office, and the common interest of the churches, who shall consider and resolve questions and

Book I. cases of importance which shall be offered by any among themselves or others; who also shall have power of examining and recommending the candidates of the ministry to the work thereof.

1708.

"XIII. That the said associated pastors shall take notice of any among themselves, that may be accused of scandal or heresy, unto or cognizable by them, examine the matter carefully, and if they find just occasion shall direct to the calling of the council, where such offenders shall be duly proceeded against."

"XIV. That the associated pastors shall also be consulted by bereaved churches, belonging to their association, and recommend to such churches such persons, as may be fit to be called and settled in the work of the gospel ministry among them. And if such bereaved churches shall not seasonably call and settle a minister among them, the said associated pastors shall lay the state of such bereaved church before the general assembly of this colony, that they may take order concerning them, as shall be found necessary for their peace and edification."

"XV. That it be recommended as expedient, that all the associations in this colony do meet in a general association, by their respective delegates, one or more out of each association, once a year, the first meeting to be at Hartford, at the general election next ensuing the date hereof, and so annually in all the counties successively, at such time and place, as they the said delegates shall in their annual meetings appoint."

The confession of faith, heads of agreement, and these articles of discipline having unanimously passed, and been signed by the scribes, were presented to the legislature the succeeding October, for their approbation and establishment. Upon which they passed the following adopting act.

At a general court holden at New-Haven, October 1708.

Act of assembly adopting the Saybrook platform, Oct. 1708.

"The reverend ministers, delegates from the elders and messengers of this government, met at Saybrook, September 9th, 1708, having presented to this assembly a Confession of Faith, and Heads of Agreement, and regulations in the administration of church discipline, as unanimously agreed and consented to by the elders and churches in this government; this assembly doth declare their great approbation of such an happy agreement, and do ordain, that all the churches within this government, that are, or shall be, thus united in doctrine, worship, and discipline, be, and for the future shall be owned and acknowledged established by law; provided always, that nothing herein shall be intended or construed to hinder or prevent any society or church, that is or shall be allowed by the laws of this government, who soberly differ or dissent from the united churches hereby established, from exercising worship and discipline, in their own way, according to their consciences.

"A true copy, Test,
"ELEAZER KIMBERLY, Secretary."

Though the council were unanimous in passing the platform of discipline, yet they were not all of one opinion. Some were for high consociational government, and in their sentiments nearly presbyterians; others were much more moderate and rather verging on independency; but exceedingly desirous of keeping the unity of the spirit in the bond of peace, they exercised great christian condescension and amicableness towards each other.

As it was stipulated, that the heads of agreement should be observed through the colony, this was an important mean of reconciling numbers to the constitution, as these did not carry points so far as the articles of discipline. These did not make the judgments of councils decisive, in all cases, but only maintained, that particular churches ought to have a reverential regard to their judgment, and not to dissent from it without apparent grounds from the word of God. Neither did these give the elders a negative in councils over the churches; and in some other instances they gave more latitude than the articles of discipline. These therefore served to reconcile such elders and churches, as were not for a rigid consociational government, and to gain their consent. Somewhat different constructions were put upon the constitution. Those who were for a high consociational government, construed it rigidly according to the articles of discipline, and others by the heads of agreement; or, at least, they were for softening down the more rigid articles, by construing them agreeably to those heads of union.

Notwithstanding the Savoy confession was adopted, as the faith of the Connecticut churches, yet, by adopting the heads of agreement, it was agreed, that with respect to soundness of judgment in matters of faith, it was sufficient. "That a church acknowledge the scriptures to be the word of God, the perfect and only rule of faith and practice, and own either the doctrinal part of those commonly called the articles of the church of England, or the confession or catechisms, shorter or longer, compiled by the assembly at Westminster, or the confession agreed on at the Savoy, to be agreeable to the said rule."

BOOK I.
1709.

The Saybrook platform, thus unanimously recommended by the elders and messengers of the churches, and adopted by the legislature, as the religious constitution of the colony, met with a general reception, though some of the churches were extremely opposed to it.*

Feb. 1st, 1709.

Associations and consociations formed.

The elders and messengers of the county of Hartford met in council, at Hartford, the next February, and formed into two distinct consociations and associations for the purposes expressed in the constitution. The ministers and churches of the other three counties afterwards formed themselves into consociations and associations. There were therefore, soon after, five consociations and the same number of associations in the colony. The associations met annually, by a delegation of two elders from each association, in a general association. This has a general advisory superintendency over all the ministers and churches in the colony. Its advice has generally been acceptable to the ministers and churches, and cheerfully carried into execution. The meeting of the general association was anciently in September; but the time of meeting, after some years, was altered, and for more than sixty years has been on the third Tuesday in June.

General association.

The corporation of college having now obtained a confession of faith, adopted by the churches and legislature of the colony, adopted it for college, and the trustees and officers of the college, upon their introduction to office, were required to give their assent to it, and to the Westminster confession and catechisms.

Death and character of President Pierson.

But before this could be effected, Mr. Pierson, the president, was no more. He died on the 5th of March, 1707, to the unspeakable loss and affliction both of the college and the people of his charge. He had his education at Harvard college, where he was graduated, 1668. He appears first to have settled in the ministry at Newark in New-Jersey. Thence he came to Killingworth, and was installed in 1694. He had the character of a hard student, good scholar, and great divine. In his whole conduct, he was wise, steady, and amiable. He was greatly respected as a pastor, and he instructed and governed the college with general approbation.

Upon the death of rector Pierson, the Rev. Mr. Andrew

* Though Messrs. Andrew, Pierpont, and Russell, were influential characters, yet it is observable, that the churches, in that county, sent no messengers to the synod; and the tradition is that the church and people of Norwich were so offended with their minister, Mr. John Woodward, for consenting to it, that they never would forgive him and be reconciled; but made such opposition to his ministry, that, by the advice of council, he resigned it and left the town.

CHAP. XIX.   CONNECTICUT.

was chosen rector pro tempore. The senior class were removed to Milford, to be under his immediate instruction, until the commencement. The other students were removed to Saybrook, and put under the care and instructions of two tutors. Mr. Andrew moderated at the commencements and gave general directions to the tutors. Mr. Buckingham also, who was one of the trustees, and resided at Saybrook, during his life, had a kind of direction and inspection over the college. In this state it continued, without any material alteration, until about the year 1715.

Book I.

1700. Students removed to Saybrook.

The ministers of Connecticut were exceedingly attentive to the morals and qualifications of those, whom they recommended to the improvement of the churches, or ordained to the pastoral office. The general association, in 1712, at a meeting of theirs, at Fairfield, agreed upon the following rules, and recommended them to the consideration of the several associations for their approbation and concurrence.

Sept. 12, 1712.

"Rules agreed upon for the examination of candidates for the ministry.

"Agreed upon, that the person to be examined concerning his qualifications for the evangelical ministry, shall be dealt with, in his examinations, with all candor and gentleness.

Directions respecting candidates for the ministry.

"1. That he be able to give satisfaction, to the association examining him, of his skill in the Hebrew, Greek, and Latin tongues.

"2. That he be able to give satisfaction, to the association examining him, of his skill in Logic and Philosophy.

"3. He shall be examined what authors, in divinity, he hath read; and also concerning the main grounds or principles of the christian religion; and shall therein offer just matter of satisfaction to the association examining him; and shall give his assent to the confession of faith publicly owned and declared to be the confession of the faith of the united churches of this colony.

"4. That if the life and conversation of the person to be examined be not well known to the association examining him, then said person shall offer sufficient evidence to said association of his sober and religious conversation.

"5. That the person to be examined shall publicly pray, and also preach, in the presence of the association examining him, from some text of scripture which shall be given him by said association, and at such time and place as they shall appoint, in order to prove his gifts for the ministerial work.

M 2

BOOK I.

1712.
Respecting ministers to be ordained.

"Rules relating to the ordination of a person to the work of the ministry.

"Agreed, 1. In case of ordination, those who are to ordain ought to be satisfied, that the person to be ordained is apt to teach, and of his inclination to the work of the ministry.

"2. That they shall be satisfied with his prudence and fitness for the management of so great a trust, as that of the work of the ministry.

"3. The persons to ordain shall be satisfied, that his preaching and conversation be acceptable to the people over whom he is to be ordained.

"4. That he shall be able to explain such texts of scripture as shall be proposed to him.

"5. That he shall be able to resolve such practical cases of conscience as shall be proposed to him.

"6. That he shall shew, to the satisfaction of the pastors to ordain him, his competent ability to refute dangerous errors, and defend the truth against gainsayers.

"7. That he shall give his consent to the church discipline of this colony as established by law; yet the pastors to ordain are not to be too severe and strict with him to be ordained, upon his sober dissent from some particulars in said discipline."

Such has been the pious care of the venerable fathers of the churches in Connecticut, to preserve in them a learned, orthodox, experimental ministry. The associations have examined all candidates for the ministry and recommended them to the churches previously to their preaching in them. In their examinations, they have carefully enquired into their knowledge in divinity, their experimental acquaintance with religion, their ministerial gifts and qualifications, and have paid a special attention to their morals, and good character. Hence these churches have been distinguished and singularly happy in a learned, pious, laborious, and prudent ministry.

Donations made to the college.

About this time a very valuable addition of books was made to the college library, at Saybrook. In 1713, Sir John Davie, of Groton, who had an estate descended to him in England, with the title of baronet, gave a good collection. The next year a much greater donation was made by the generosity and procurement of Jeremiah Dummer, Esq. of Boston. He was then in London, in the capacity of an agent for several of the New-England colonies. He sent over above 800 volumes. About 120 of them were procured at his own charge. The rest were from principal gentlemen in England, through his solicitation and influence. Particularly from Sir Isaac Newton, Book 1. Sir Richard Blackmore, Sir Richard Steele, Doctors Burnet, Halley, Bentley, Kennet, Calamy, and Edwards; and from the Rev. Mr. Henry and Mr. Whiston. These severally gave a collection of their own works, and governor Yale put in about 40 volumes. The library now consisted of about nine hundred volumes. 1713.

From 1702 to 1713 inclusively, forty six young gentlemen were graduated, at Saybrook. Of these, thirty four became ministers of the gospel, and two were elected magistrates. Notwithstanding the infant state of the college, numbers of them, through their native strength of genius and the instructions of those excellent tutors, Mr. John Hart and Mr. Phineas Fisk, became excellent scholars, and shone not only as distinguished lights in the churches, but made a figure in the republic of letters. Seven of them afterwards were fellows of the college, at New-Haven; and another of them was that excellent man, the Reverend Jonathan Dickinson, president of the college in New-Jersey. *Number graduated at the college before the year 1714.*

The number of ordained ministers in the colony, this year, exclusive of those in the towns under the government of Massachusetts, was forty three. Upon the lowest computation there was as much as one ordained minister to every four hundred persons, or to every eighty families. It does not appear, that there was one bereaved church in the colony. Besides, there were a considerable number of candidates preaching in the new towns and parishes, in which churches were not yet formed. At or about this time, Mr. Thomas Towsey began to preach at Newtown, Mr. Joseph Meacham at Coventry, Mr. John Bliss at Hebron, and Mr. John Fisk at Killingly, at which places churches were soon after gathered and those gentlemen ordained. Several other candidates were preaching in other places. *Number of ordained ministers in 1713.*

A Catalogue of the ministers of Connecticut, from 1630, to 1713, inclusively.

COUNTY OF HARTFORD.

Minister's Names.	Names of towns.	Ordained or Installed.	Died or Removed.
Thomas Hooker		Oct. 11, 1633	July, 1647
Samuel Stone*		do. do.	July 20, 1663
Joseph Haynes			May 24, 1679
Samuel Whiting	Hartford		
Mr. Foster	1st church		
Timothy Woodbridge		Nov. 18, 1685	April 30, 1732
Samuel Whiting	2d do.	1669	1709
Tho's Buckingham			Nov. 19, 1731
John Warham			April 1, 1670
Ephraim Hewet	Windsor	1639	Sept. 4, 1644
Samuel Mather		1682	March 19, 1726
Timothy Edwards*	2d church	May, 1694	Jan. 27, 1758
Henry Smith			1641
Jonathan Russell			
Gershom Bulkley†	Weathersfield	Inst. 1666	Dis. 1667 / Died 1713
Joseph Rowlandson‡		Inst.	
John Woodbridge		Inst. 1679	
Stephen Mix		Ord. 1694	Aug. 28, 1738
Roger Newton		Oct. 19, 1652	Removed, 1657
Samuel Hooker	Farmington	July 1661	Nov. 6, 1697
Samuel Whitman		Dec. 10, 1706	
William Burnham	Kensington 2d ch	Dec. 10, 1712	
Nathaniel Collins	Middletown*†	Nov. 4, 1668†	Dec. 18, 1684
Noadiah Russell		Oct. 4, 1688	
Timothy Stevens	Glastenbury	Oct. 1693	April 16, 1725
Joseph Peck	Waterbury	Aug. 26, 1669†	June 7, 1699
John Southmayd		May 30, 1705	
Dudley Woodbridge	Simsbury	March 3, 1696	Aug. 3, 1710
Timothy Woodbridge		1712	Aug. 28, 1742
Jeremiah Hobart§	Haddam	Nov. 14, 1700‡	Died Nov. 6, 1715

As the gathering, or forming of the churches, as far as can be found, was universally on the day of ordination, no column is made to certify the time of their formation; but wherever this mark † is set after the figures expressing the time of ordination, it gives notice that the church was formed at the same time.

* Mr. Edwards was nearly sixty-four years in the ministry, and able to preach until he was about 84 years of age.

† Mr. Bulkley was son of the Rev. Peter Bulkley, of Concord, in Massachusetts, and a gentleman of a very eminent character. It is thus given upon his monument: "Who was of rare abilities, extraordinary industry, excellent in learning, master of many languages, exquisite in his skill in divinity, physic and law, and of a most exemplary and christian life." By reason of infirmity he resigned the ministry many years before his death.

‡ Mr. Rowlandson, the fourth minister of Weathersfield, removed from Lancaster, in Massachusetts, after that town was burnt by the Indians, in 1676.

*† Mr. Samuel Stow preached some years at Middletown, but as he was dismissed before the church was gathered, he is not reckoned in the list of its ministers.

§ The Rev. Mr. Hobart was first ordained at Topsfield, in Massachusetts. Thence he removed to Long-Island, and afterwards to Haddam, where he died in the ministry, at a very advanced age. Before him, Mr. Nicholas Noyes preached thirteen

CHAP. XIX. CONNECTICUT.

Minister's Names	Names of Towns	When ordained, or installed	Died, or removed
Samuel Whiting	Windham	Dec. 4, 1700‡	Sept. 27, 1725
John Bulkley	Colchester	Dec. 20, 1703‡	June, 1731
Stephen Hosmer	East-Haddam	May 3, 1704‡	
Joseph Coit	Plainfield	Jan. 6, 1706‡	Dismissed, 1748
Eleazar Williams	Mansfield	Oct. 18, 1710‡	
Nathaniel Chauncey	Durham	Feb. 7, 1711‡	Died Feb. 1, 1756
Samuel Easterbrook	Canterbury	June 13, 1711	D. June 26, 1727

COUNTY OF NEW-HAVEN.

Minister's Names	Names of Towns	When ordained, or installed	Died, or removed
John Davenport	New-Haven	Inst. 1639	Removed, 1668
William Hook	New-Haven	Ord. 1644	1656
Nicholas Street*	New-Haven	Ord. 1659	Di. Ap. 22, 1674
James Pierpont	New-Haven	July 2, 1685	Di. Nov. 22, 1714
Peter Prudden	Milford	April 18, 1640	1656
Roger Newton	Milford	In. Au. 22, 1660	June 7, 1683
Samuel Andrew	Milford	Nov. 18, 1685	Jan. 24, 1738
Henry Whitfield	Guilford		Removed, 1650
John Higginson	Guilford		Removed, 1659
Joseph Elliot	Guilford	1664	May 24, 1694
Thomas Ruggles	Guilford	Nov. 20, 1695	June 1, 1728
John Hart	E. Guilford 2d S.	Nov. 1707	March, 1732
Abraham Pierson	Branford	1644	Removed, 1665
Samuel Russell	Branford	March, 1687‡	June 25, 1731
John Bowers	Derby		
John James	Derby		
Joseph Moss	Derby		
Samuel Street	Wallingford‡	1674	Jan. 16, 1717
Samuel Whittelsey	Wallingford‡	May, 1710	April 15, 1752
James Hemingway	East-Haven	1707‡	Oct. 7, 1754

COUNTY OF NEW-LONDON.

Minister's Names	Names of Towns	When ordained, or installed	Died, or removed
Richard Blynman	New-London	1648	
Gershom Bulkley	New-London		Removed, 1666
Simon Bradstreet†	New-London	Oct. 5, 1670	Died, 1683
Gurdon Saltonstall	New-London	Nov. 25, 1691	Rem. Jan. 1707
Eliphalet Adams	New-London	Feb. 1709	Died, April, 1753

years in the town; but during this time no church was formed; and he left the town, and was afterwards ordained to the pastoral office in a church at Salem, in Massachusetts.

* After the removal of Mr. Davenport, Mr. Street continued the only instructor of the church until his death; and after his decease the church and people were eleven years without a pastor. A great variety of preachers were invited into the town, but none could unite them until Mr. Pierpont was called. Under his ministry they enjoyed great peace, and were edified.

‡ The committee of New-Haven for settling the town of Wallingford, for the safety of the church, obliged the undertakers, and all the successive planters, to subscribe the following engagement, viz. "He or they shall not by any means disturb the church, when settled there, in their choice of minister or ministers, or other church officers; or in any of their other church rights, liberties or administrations; nor shall withdraw due maintenance from such ministry." This shows how strongly the churches in this part of the colony were, at that time, opposed to towns and parishes having any thing to do in the choice of a minister, or in any church affairs.

† There seems to have been no church formed in New-London until the ordination of Mr. Bradstreet, and it is probable that neither Mr. Blynman nor Mr. Bulkley were installed or ordained in the town.

HISTORY OF

Minister's Names.	Names of Towns.	When ordained, or installed.	Died, or removed
James Fitch	Saybrook		
Thomas Buckingham	Saybrook		
James Noyes‡	Stonington	Sept. 10, 1674†	D. Dec. 30, 1719
James Fitch	Norwich	1660	1702
John Woodward	Norwich	Dec. 6, 1699	Dis. Sept.13, 1716
John Woodbridge		1666	Rem. to W. 1679
Abraham Pierson	Killingworth	Inst. 1694	Died May 5, 1707
Jared Elliott		Oct. 26, 1709	April 22, 1765
Ephraim Woodbridge	Groton	Nov. 8, 1714	1724
Moses Noyes	Lyme	1693†	
Samuel Pierpont§	Lyme	Dec. 10, 1724	March, 1723
Salmon Treat	Preston	Nov. 16, 1698	Res. Mar.14, 1744
Joseph Parsons	Lebanon	Nov. 27, 1700	Dismissed 1708
Samuel Wells	Lebanon	Dec. 5, 1711	1722

COUNTY OF FAIRFIELD.

Mr. Jones†			
Samuel Wakeman	Fairfield	Sept. 30, 1665	March 8, 1692
Joseph Webb		Aug. 15, 1694	Sept. 19, 1732
Adam Blackman	Stratford	1640†	Died, 1665
Israel Chauncey	Stratford	1665	March 14, 1722
Timothy Cutler		Jan. 11, 1709	R. to Y. C. 1719
Zachariah Walker	2d church		R. to Woodbury
Richard Denton‖	Stamford	1641	Removed, 1644
John Bishop	Stamford	1644	Died, 1691
John Davenport		1694	D. Feb. 5, 1731
Thomas Hanford	Norwalk	1654	
Stephen Buckingham	Norwalk	Nov. 17, 1697	Res. Feb.21, 1727
Joseph Morgan	Greenwich		
Seth Shove	Danbury	Oct. 15, 1697†	Oct. 3, 1735
Zachariah Walker	Woodbury	May 3, 1670	
John Bowers¶	Rye		

Ministers within the boundaries of Connecticut, but under the jurisdiction of Massachusetts, in 1713.

Nathaniel Collins**	Enfield		1697†	Res. died, 1757
Benjamin Ruggles	Suffield	May,	1698†	Sept. 5, 1708
Josiah Dwight	Woodstock			

Within the boundaries of the colony, including those under the jurisdiction of Massachusetts, there were forty-six churches, which had been illuminated with about ninety ministers. The churches enjoyed peace, and increased in numbers, knowledge and beauty.

‡ The Rev. Mr. Noyes preached at Stonington more than ten years before his ordination. It appears by the church records, that he preached in the town 55 years and 6 months.

§ Mr. Pierpont, returning from a visit which he had made his friends, at New-Haven, was drowned in Connecticut river, March, 1725. He attempted to cross the river in a canoe, but an unexpected gust of wind arose, by which it was overset. His body wafted to Fisher's Island, where it was taken up and buried.

† Mr. Jones was episcopally ordained in England, and came into this country at an early period, but as the first records of Fairfield were burnt, no particular account can be given of his installation, or the time of his death.

‖ Mr. Denton died at Hampstead, upon Long-Island, about the year 1663, where he left posterity.

¶ Mr. Bowers removed from Derby, and settled at Rye, about the year 1686. Mr. Webb then preached at Derby about twelve years, but was not ordained.

** Mr. Collins, after laboring more than twenty years at Enfield, resigned his ministry in that place, but preached to other congregations, and continued in it until his death.

APPENDIX.

ORIGINAL PAPERS

ILLUSTRATING THE PRECEDING HISTORY.

NUMBER I.

The old patent of Connecticut, 1631.

To all people, unto whom this present writing shall come, Robert, Earl of Warwick, sendeth greeting, in our LORD GOD everlasting.

KNOW ye, that the said Robert, Earl of Warwick, for divers good causes and considerations him thereunto moving, hath given, granted, bargained, sold, enfeoffed, alienated, and confirmed, and by these presents doth give, grant, bargain, sell, enfeoff, aliene, and confirm, unto the right honorable William, Viscount Say and Seal, the right honorable Robert, Lord Brook, the right honorable Lord Rich, and the honorable Charles Fiennes, Esq. Sir Nathaniel Rich, Knt. Sir Richard Saltonstall, Knt. Richard Knightly, Esq. John Pym, Esq. John Hampden, John Humphrey, Esq. and Herbert Pelham, Esq. their heirs and assigns, and their associates forever, all that part of New-England, in America, which lies and extends itself from a river there called Narraganset river, the space of forty leagues upon a straight line near the sea shore towards the southwest, west and by south, or west, as the coast lieth towards Virginia, accounting three English miles to the league; and also all and singular the lands and hereditaments whatsoever, lying and being within the lands aforesaid, north and south in latitude and breadth, and in length and longitude of and within, all the breadth aforesaid, throughout the main lands there, from the western ocean to the south sea, and all lands and grounds, place and places, soil, wood, and woods, grounds, havens, ports, creeks and rivers, waters, fishings, and hereditaments whatsoever, lying within the said space, and

APPENDIX.

every part and parcel thereof. And also all islands lying in America aforesaid, in the said seas, or either of them, on the western or eastern coasts, or parts of the said tracts of lands, by these presents mentioned to be given, granted, bargained, sold, enfeoffed, aliened, and confirmed, and also all mines and minerals, as well, royal mines of gold and silver, as other mines and minerals whatsoever, in the said land and premises, or any part thereof, and also the several rivers within the said limits, by what name or names soever called or known, and all jurisdictions, rights, and royalties, liberties, freedoms, immunities, powers, privileges, franchises, preeminencies, and commodities whatsoever, which the said Robert, Earl of Warwick, now hath or had, or might use, exercise, or enjoy, in or within any part or parcel thereof, excepting and reserving to his majesty, his heirs, and successors the fifth part of all gold and silver ore, that shall be found within the said premises, or any part or parcel thereof: To HAVE and to HOLD the said part of New-England in America, which lies and extends and is a-butted as aforesaid. And the said several rivers and every part and parcel thereof, and all the said islands, rivers, ports, havens, waters, fishings, mines, minerals, jurisdictions, powers, franchises, royalties, liberties, privileges, commodities, hereditaments and premises, whatsoever with the appurtenances, unto the said William, Viscount Say and Seal, Robert, Lord Brook, Robert, Lord Rich, Charles Fiennes, Sir Nathaniel Rich, Sir Richard Saltonstall, Richard Knightly, John Pym, John Hampden, John Humphrey and Herbert Pelham, their heirs and assigns and their associates; to the only proper and absolute use and behoof of them the said William, Viscount Say and Seal, Robert, Lord Brook, Robert, Lord Rich, Charles Fiennes, Sir Nathaniel Rich, Sir Richard Saltonstall, Richard Knightly, John Pym, John Hampden, John Humphrey, and Herbert Pelham, their heirs and assigns, and their associates for ever more. In witness whereof the said Robert, Earl of Warwick, hath hereunto set his hand and seal, the nineteenth day of March, in the seventh year of the reign of our sovereign Lord Charles, by the Grace of God, King of England, Scotland, France and Ireland, defender of the faith, &c. Annoq. Domini, 1631.

Signed, sealed, and delivered, in the presence of
 WALTER WILLIAMS.
 THOMAS HOWSON.

         ROBERT WARWICK. *A Seal.*

APPENDIX.

NUMBER II.

Mr. Winthrop's commission to erect a fort at the mouth of Connecticut river, with articles of agreement between him and their lordships Say and Seal, Brook, &c. 1635.

KNOW all men, by these presents, that we, Arthur Hasselring, Baronet, Sir Richard Saltonstall, Knt. Henry Lawrence, Henry Darley, and George Fenwick, Esquires, in our own names, and in the name of the right honorable Viscount Say and Seal, Robert, Lord Brook, and the rest of our company, do ordain and constitute John Winthrop, Esq. the younger, governor of the river Connecticut, with the places adjoining thereunto, for, and during the space of one whole year, after his arrival there, giving him, from and under us, full power and authority, to do and execute any such lawful act and thing, both in respect of the place and people, as also of the affairs we have, or shall have there, as to the dignity or office of a governor doth, or may appertain. In witness whereof we have hereunto put our hands and seals, this 18th day of July, 1635.

RICHARD SALTONSTALL,	ARTHUR HASSELRING,
HENRY LAWRENCE,	GEORGE FENWICK,
HENRY DARLEY.	

Five seals appendant, impressed in one large piece of wax.

Articles made between the right honorable the lord Viscount Say and Seal, Sir Arthur Hasselring, Baronet, Sir Richard Saltonstall, Knight, Henry Lawrence, Henry Darley, and George Fenwick, Esquires, on the one part, and John Winthrop, Esq. the younger, of the other, the 7th July, 1635.

First, That we, in our names, and the rest of the company, do by these presents appoint John Winthrop, the younger, governor of the river Connecticut, in New-England, and of the harbour and places adjoining, for the space of one year, from his arrival there. And the said John Winthrop doth undertake and covenant for his part, that he will, with all convenient speed, repair to those places, and there abide as aforesaid for the best advancement of the company's service.

Secondly, That so soon as he comes to the bay, he shall endeavour to provide able men to the number of fifty, at the least, for making of fortifications, and building of houses at the river Connecticut, and the harbour adjoining, first for their own present accommodations, and then such houses as may receive men of quality, which latter houses we would have to be builded within the fort.

APPENDIX.

Thirdly, That he shall employ those men, according to his best ability, for the advancement of the company's service, especially in the particulars abovementioned, during the time of his government; and shall also give a true and just account of all the monies and goods committed to his managing.

Fourthly, That for such as shall plant there now, in the beginning, he shall take care that they plant themselves either at the harbour, or near the mouth of the river, that these places may be the better strengthened for their own safety, and to that end, that they also set down in such bodies together, as they may be most capable of an entrenchment; provided that there be reserved unto the fort, for the maintenance of it, one thousand or fifteen hundred acres, at least, of good ground, as near adjoining thereunto as may be.

Fifthly, That forasmuch as the service will take him off from his own employment, the company do engage themselves, to give him a just and due consideration for the same. In witness whereof we have interchangeably hereunto subscribed our names.

W. SAY and SEAL, GEORGE FENWICK,
HENRY LAWRENCE, ARTHUR HASSELRING,
RICHARD SALTONSTALL, HENRY DARLEY.

NUMBER III.

The original constitution of Connecticut, formed by voluntary compact, 1639.

FORASMUCH as it hath pleased the Almighty GOD, by the wise disposition of his divine providence, so to order and dispose of things, that we the inhabitants and residents of Windsor, Hartford, and Weathersfield, are now cohabiting, and dwelling in and upon the river Connecticut, and the lands thereunto adjoining, and well knowing where a people are gathered together, the word of GOD requireth that, to maintain the peace and union of such a people, there should be an orderly and decent government established according to GOD, to order and dispose of the affairs of the people at all seasons, as occasion should require; do therefore associate and conjoin ourselves to be as one public STATE or COMMONWEALTH; and do, for ourselves and our successors, and such as shall be adjoined to us at any time hereafter, enter into combination and confederation together, to maintain and preserve the liberty and purity of the gospel of our LORD JESUS, which we now profess, as also the discipline of the churches, which, according to the truth of said gospel, is now practised amongst us; as also in our civil affairs to be guided and governed according to such

APPENDIX.

laws, rules, orders, and decrees, as shall be made, ordered, and decreed, as followeth:

I. It is ordered, sentenced, and decreed, that there shall be yearly two general assemblies or courts, the one on the second Thursday of April, the other the second Thursday of September following: The first shall be called the COURT of ELECTION, wherein shall be yearly chosen, from time to time, so many magistrates and other public officers, as shall be found requisite, whereof one to be chosen governor for the year ensuing, and until another be chosen, and no other magistrate to be chosen for more than one year; provided always, there be six chosen besides the governor, which being chosen and sworn according to an oath recorded for that purpose, shall have power to administer justice according to the laws here established, and for want thereof according to the rule of the word of God; which choice shall be made by all that are admitted freemen, and have taken the oath of fidelity, and do cohabit within this jurisdiction, having been admitted inhabitants by the major part of the town where they live, or the major part of such as shall be then present.

II. It is ordered, sentenced, and decreed, that the election of the aforesaid magistrates shall be in this manner; every person present and qualified for choice, shall bring in (to the persons deputed to receive them) one single paper, with the name of him written on it whom he desires to have governor, and he that hath the greatest number of papers shall be governor for that year: And the rest of the magistrates or public officers to be chosen in this manner; the secretary for the time being, shall first read the names of all that are to be put to choice, and then shall severally nominate them distinctly, and every one that would have the person nominated to be chosen shall bring in one single paper written upon, and he that would not have him chosen shall bring in a blank, and every one that has more written papers than blanks, shall be a magistrate for that year, which papers shall be received and told by one or more that shall be then chosen, by the court, and sworn to be faithful therein; but in case there should not be six persons as aforesaid, besides the governor, out of those which are nominated, then he or they which have the most written papers, shall be a magistrate or magistrates for the ensuing year, to make up the aforesaid number.

III. It is ordered, sentenced, and decreed, that the secretary shall not nominate any person new, nor shall any person be chosen newly into the magistracy, which was not propounded in some general court before, to be nominated the next election: And to that end it shall be lawful for each of the towns aforesaid, by their deputies, to nominate any two whom the

APPENDIX.

conceive fit to be put to election, and the court may add so many more as they judge requisite.

IV. It is ordered, sentenced, and decreed, that no person be chosen governor above once in two years, and that the governor be always a member of some approved congregation, and formerly of the magistracy within this jurisdiction, and all the magistrates freemen of this commonwealth; and that no magistrate or other public officer, shall execute any part of his or their office before they are severally sworn, which shall be done in the face of the court if they be present, and in case of absence, by some deputed for that purpose.

V. It is ordered, sentenced, and decreed, that to the aforesaid court of election, the several towns shall send their deputies, and when the elections are ended they may proceed in any public service, as at other courts; also, the other general court in September, shall be for making of laws, and any other public occasion which concerns the good of the commonwealth.

VI. It is ordered, sentenced, and decreed, that the governor shall, either by himself or by the secretary, send out summons to the constables of every town, for the calling of those two standing courts, one month at least, before their several times; and also, if the governor and the greatest part of the magistrates see cause, upon any special occasion, to call a general court, they may give order to the secretary so to do, within fourteen days warning; and if urgent necessity so require, upon a shorter notice, giving sufficient grounds for it to the deputies when they meet, or else be questioned for the same. And if the governor, or major part of the magistrates, shall either neglect or refuse to call the two general standing courts, or either of them, as also at other times when the occasions of the commonwealth require, the freemen thereof, or the major part of them, shall petition to them so to do; if then it be either denied or neglected, the said freemen, or the major part of them, shall have power to give order to the constables of the several towns to do the same, and so may meet together and choose to themselves a moderator, and may proceed to do any act of power which any other general courts may.

VII. It is ordered, sentenced, and decreed, that after there are warrants given out for any of the said general courts, the constable or constables of each town, shall forthwith give notice distinctly to the inhabitants of the same, in some public assembly, or by going or sending from house to house, that at a place and time by him or them limited and set, they meet and assemble themselves together, to elect and choose certain deputies to be at the general court then following, to agitate

APPENDIX.

the affairs of the commonwealth, which said deputies shall be chosen by all that are admitted inhabitants in the several towns, and have taken the oath of fidelity; provided, that none be chosen a deputy for any general court which is not a freeman of this commonwealth: The aforesaid deputy shall be chosen in manner following; every person that is present and qualified, as before expressed, shall bring the names of such, written on several papers, as they desire to have chosen, for that employment; and those three or four, more or less, being the number agreed on to be chosen, for that time, that have the greatest number of papers written for them, shall be deputies for that court; whose names shall be indorsed on the back side of the warrant, and returned into the court with the constable or constables hand unto the same.

VIII. It is ordered, sentenced, and decreed, that Windsor, Hartford, and Weathersfield, shall have power, each town, to send four of their freemen as their deputies, to every general court; and whatsoever other towns shall be hereafter added to this jurisdiction, they shall send so many deputies as the court shall judge meet; a reasonable proportion to the number of freemen that are in said towns, being to be attended therein; which deputies shall have the power of the whole town to give their votes, and allowance to all such laws and orders, as may be for the public good, and unto which the said towns are to be bound.

IX. It is ordered, sentenced, and decreed, that the deputies thus chosen, shall have power and liberty to appoint a time and a place of meeting together, before any general court, to advise and consult of all such things as may concern the good of the public; as also to examine their own elections, whether according to the order; and if they or the greatest part of them find any election to be illegal, they may seclude such for the present from their meeting, and return the same and their reasons to the court; and if it prove true, the court may fine the party or parties so intruding upon the town, if they see cause, and give out a warrant to go to a new election in a legal way, either in part or in whole; also the said deputies shall have power to fine any that shall be disorderly at their meeting, or for not coming in due time or place, according to appointment; and they may return said fine into the court, if it be refused to be paid, and the treasurer to take notice of it, and to estreat or levy the same as he doth other fines.

X. It is ordered, sentenced, and decreed, that every general court (except such as, through neglect of the governor and the greatest part of the magistrates, the freemen themselves do call,) shall consist of the governor, or some one chosen to moderate the court, and four other magistrates at least, with the major part of the deputies of the several towns legally chosen; and in case the freemen, or the major part of them, through neglect or refusal of the governor and major part of the magistrates, shall call a court, that shall consist of the major part of the freemen that are present, or their deputies, with a moderator chosen by them; in which said general court shall consist the SUPREME POWER of the COMMONWEALTH, and they only shall have power to *make laws or repeal them, to grant levies, to admit freemen, to dispose of lands undisposed of*, to several towns or persons, and also shall have power to *call* other courts, or magistrate, or any other person whatsoever, into question for any misdemeanor; and may for just causes displace or deal otherwise, according to the nature of the offence; and also may deal in any other matter that concerns the good of this commonwealth, except election of magistrates, which shall be done by the whole body of freemen; in which court the governor or moderator shall have power to order the court, to give liberty of speech, and silence unreasonable and disorderly speaking, to put all things to vote, and in case the vote be equal to have a casting voice; but none of these courts shall be adjourned or dissolved without the consent of the major part of the court.

XI. It is ordered, sentenced, and decreed, that when any general court, upon the occasions of the commonwealth, have agreed upon any sum or sums of money to be levied upon the several towns within this jurisdiction, that a committee be chosen to set out and appoint what shall be the proportion of every town to pay, of the said levy, provided the committee be made up of an equal number out of each town. 14th January, 1638.*

NUMBER IV.

The fundamental articles, or original constitution of the colony of New-Haven, June 4th, 1639.

THE 4th day of the 4th month, called June, 1639, all the free planters assembled together in a general meeting, to consult about settling civil government, according to God, and the nomination of persons that might be found, by consent of all, fittest in all respects for the foundation work of a church, which was intended to be gathered in Quinipiack. After solemn invocation of the name of God, in prayer for the presence and help of his spirit and grace, in those weighty businesses, they were reminded of the business whereabout they met, (viz.) for the establishment of such civil order as might be most pleas-

* This as we now date was 1639.

ing unto God, and for the choosing the fittest men for the foundation work of a church to be gathered. For the better enabling them to discern the mind of God, and to agree accordingly concerning the establishment of civil order, Mr. John Davenport propounded divers queries to them publicly, praying them to consider seriously in the presence and fear of God, the weight of the business they met about, and not to be rash or slight in giving their votes to things they understood not; but to digest fully and thoroughly what should be propounded to them, and without respect to men, as they should be satisfied and persuaded in their own minds, to give their answers in such sort as they would be willing should stand upon record for posterity.

This being earnestly pressed by Mr. Davenport, Mr. Robert Newman was intreated to write, in characters, and to read distinctly and audibly, in the hearing of all the people, what was propounded and accorded on, that it might appear, that all consented to matters propounded, according to words written by him.

Query I. Whether the scriptures do hold forth a perfect rule for the direction and government of all men in all duties which they are to perform to God and men, as well in families and commonwealth, as in matters of the church? This was assented unto by all, no man dissenting, as was expressed by holding up of the hands. Afterwards it was read over to them, that they might see in what words their vote was expressed. They again expressed their consent by holding up their hands, no man dissenting.

Query II. Whereas, there was a covenant solemnly made by the whole assembly of free planters of this plantation, the first day of extraordinary humiliation, which we had after we came together, that as in matters that concern the gathering and ordering of a church, so likewise in all public officers which concern civil order, as choice of magistrates and officers, making and repealing laws, dividing allotments of inheritance, and all things of like nature, we would all of us be ordered by those rules which the scripture holds forth to us; this covenant was called a plantation covenant, to distinguish it from a churh covenant, which could not at that time be made, a church not being then gathered, but was deferred till a church might be gathered, according to God: It was demanded whether all the free planters do hold themselves bound by that covenant, in all businesses of that nature which are expressed in the covenant, to submit themselves to be ordered by the rules held forth in the scripture?

This also was assented unto by all, and no man gainsayed it: and they did testify the same by holding up their hands, both when it was first propounded, and confirmed the same by holding up their hands when it was read unto them in public. John Clark being absent, when the covenant was made, doth now manifest his consent to it. Also, Richard Beach, Andrew Law, Goodman Banister, Arthur Halbridge, John Potter, Robert Hill, John Brocket, and John Johnson, these persons, being not admitted planters when the covenant was made, do now express their consent to it.

Query III. Those who have desired to be received as free planters, and are settled in the plantation, with a purpose, resolution and desire, that they may be admitted into church fellowship, according to Christ, as soon as God shall fit them thereunto, were desired to express it by holding up hands. Accordingly all did express this to be their desire and purpose by holding up their hands twice, (viz.) at the proposal of it, and after when these written words were read unto them.

Query IV. All the free planters were called upon to express, whether they held themselves bound to establish such civil order as might best conduce to the securing of the purity and peace of the ordinance to themselves and their posterity according to God? In answer hereunto they expressed by holding up their hands twice as before, that they held themselves bound to establish such civil order as might best conduce to the ends aforesaid.

Then Mr. Davenport declared unto them, by the scripture, what kind of persons might best be trusted with matters of government; and by sundry arguments from scripture proved that such men as were described in Exod. xviii. 2, Deut. i. 13, with Deut. xvii. 15, and 1 Cor. vi. 1, 6, 7, ought to be intrusted by them, seeing they were free to cast themselves into that mould and form of commonwealth which appeared best for them in reference to the securing the peace and peaceable improvement of all Christ his ordinances in the church according to God, whereunto they have bound themselves, as hath been acknowledged.

Having thus said he sat down, praying the company freely to consider, whether they would have it voted at this time or not. After some space of silence, Mr. Theophilus Eaton answered, it might be voted, and some others also spake to the same purpose, none at all opposing it. Then it was propounded to vote.

Query V. Whether free burgesses shall be chosen out of the church members, they that are in the foundation work of the church being actually free burgesses, and to choose to themselves out of the like estate of church fellowship, and the power of choosing magistrates and officers from among themselves, and the power of making and repealing laws, according to the word, and the dividing of inheritances, and deciding of differences that may arise, and all the businesses of like nature are to be transacted by those free burgesses? This was put to vote and agreed unto by lifting up of hands twice, as in the former it was done. Then one man stood up and expressed his dissenting from the rest in part; yet granting, 1. That magistrates should be men fearing God. 2. That the church is the company where, ordinarily, such men may be expected. 3. That they that choose them ought to be men fearing God: only at this he stuck, that free planters ought not to give this power out of their hands. Another stood up and answered, that nothing was done, but with their consent. The former answered, that all the free planters ought to resume this power into their own hands again, if things were not orderly carried. Mr. Theophilus Eaton answered, that in all places they choose committees in like manner. The companies in London choose the liveries by whom the public magistrates are chosen. In this the rest are not wronged, because they expect, in time, to be of the livery themselves, and to have the same power. Some others intreated the former to give his arguments and reasons whereupon he dissented. He refused to do it, and said, they might not rationally demand it, seeing he let the vote pass on freely and did not speak till after it was past, because he would not hinder what they agreed upon. Then Mr. Davenport, after a short relation of some former passages between them two about this question, prayed the company that nothing might be concluded by them on this weighty question, but what themselves were persuaded to be agreeing with the mind of God, and they had heard what had been said since the voting; he intreated them again to consider of it, and put it again to vote as before. Again all of them, by holding up their hands, did show their consent as before. And some of them confessed that, whereas they did waver before they came to the assembly, they were now fully convinced, that it is the mind of God. One of them said that in the morning before he came, reading Deut. xvii. 15, he was convinced at home. Another said, that he came doubting to the assembly, but he blessed God, by what had been said, he was now fully satisfied, that the choice of burgesses out of church members, and to instruct those with the power before spoken of, is according to the mind of God revealed in the scriptures. All having spoken their apprehensions, it was agreed upon, and Mr. Robert Newman was desired to write it as an order whereunto every one that hereafter should be admitted here as planters, should submit, and testify the same by subscribing their names to the order: Namely, that church members only shall be free burgesses, and that they only shall choose magistrates and officers among themselves, to have power of transacting all the public civil affairs of this plantation; of making and repealing laws, dividing of inheritances, deciding of differences that may arise, and doing all things and businesses of like nature.

This being thus settled, as a fundamental agreement concerning civil government, Mr. Davenport proceeded to propound something to consideration about the gathering of a church, and to prevent the blemishing of the first beginnings of the church work, Mr. Davenport advised, that the names of such as were to be admitted might be publicly propounded, to the end that they who were most approved might be chosen; for the town being cast into several private meetings, wherein they that lived nearest together gave their accounts one to another of God's gracious work upon them, and prayed together and conferred to their mutual edification, sundry of them had knowledge one of another; and in every meeting some one was more approved of all than any other; for this reason, and to prevent scandals, the whole company was intreated to consider whom they found fittest to nominate for this work.

Query VI. Whether are you all willing and do agree in this, that twelve men be chosen, that their fitness for the foundation work may be tried; however, there may be more named, yet it may be in their power who are chosen, to reduce them to twelve, and that it be in the power of those twelve to choose out of themselves seven, that shall be most approved of by the major part, to begin the church?

This was agreed upon by consent of all, as was expressed by holding up of hands, and that so many as should be thought fit for the foundation work of the church, shall be propounded by the plantation, and written down and pass without exception, unless they had given public scandal or offence. Yet so as in case of public scandal or offence, every one should have liberty to propound their exception, at that time, publicly against any man, that should be nominated, when all their names should be writ down. But if the offence were private, that men's names might be tendered, so many as were offended were intreated to deal with the offender privately, and if he gave not satisfaction, to bring the matter to the twelve, that they might consider of it impartially and in the fear of God.

APPENDIX.

NUMBER V.

The first agreement with George Fenwick, Esq. 1644.

Articles of agreement made and concluded betwixt George Fenwick, Esq. of Saybrook fort, on the one part, and Edward Hopkins, John Haynes, John Mason, John Steele, and James Boosy, for and on the behalf of the jurisdiction of Connecticut river, on the other part, the 5th of December, 1644.

THE said George Fenwick, Esq. doth, by these presents, convey and make over to the use and for the behoof of the jurisdiction of Connecticut river aforesaid, the fort at Saybrook, with the appurtenances hereafter mentioned, to be enjoyed by them forever. Two demiculvering cast pieces, with all the shot thereunto appertaining, except fifty, which are reserved for his own use; two long saker cast pieces, with all the shot thereunto belonging; one murderer, with two chambers and two hammered pieces; two barrels of gun powder, forty muskets, with bandoleers and rests, as also four carabines, swords, and such irons as are there for a draw bridge; one sow of lead, and irons for the carriages of ordnance, and all the housing within the palisado.

It is also provided and agreed, betwixt the said parties, that all the land upon the river of Connecticut shall belong to the said jurisdiction of Connecticut, and such lands as are yet undisposed of shall be ordered and given out by a committee of five, whereof George Fenwick, Esq. aforesaid is always to be one.

It is further provided and agreed, that the town of Saybrook shall be carried on according to such agreements, and in that way which is already followed there, and attended betwixt Mr. Fenwick and the inhabitants there.

It is also provided and agreed, betwixt the said parties, that George Fenwick, Esq. shall have liberty to dwell in, or make use of, any or all the housing belonging to the said fort, for the space of ten years; he keeping those which he makes use of in sufficient repair, (extraordinary casualties excepted;) and in case he remove his dwelling to any other place, that he should give half a year's warning thereof, that provision may be made accordingly; only it is agreed, that there shall be some convenient part of the housing reserved for a gunner, and his family to live in, if the jurisdiction see fit to settle one there.

It is further provided and agreed, betwixt the said parties, that George Fenwick, Esq. shall enjoy to his own proper use, these particulars following:

APPENDIX.

1st. The house near adjoining to the wharf, with the wharf and an acre of ground thereunto belonging; provided, that the said acre of ground take not up above eight rods in breadth by the water side.

2d. The point of land, and the marsh lying under the barn already built by the said George Fenwick.

3d. The island commonly called six mile island, with the meadow thereunto adjoining, on the east side the river.

4th. The ground adjoining to the town field, which is already taken off and inclosed with three rails, by the said George Fenwick; only there is liberty granted to the said jurisdiction, if they see fit, to build a fort upon the western point, whereunto there shall be allowed an acre of ground for a house lot.

5th. It is also provided and agreed, that the said George Fenwick, Esq. shall have free warren in his own land, and liberty for a floater for his own occasions; as also the like liberty is reserved for any others of the adventurers, that may come unto these parts, with a double house lot in such place where they make choice to settle their abode.

All the forementioned grants (except before excepted) the said George Fenwick, Esq. doth engage himself to make good to the jurisdiction aforesaid, against all claims that may be made, by any other to the premises by reason of any disbursements made upon the place.

The said George Fenwick doth also promise, that all the lands from Narraganset river to the fort of Saybrook, mentioned in a patent granted by the earl of Warwick to certain nobles and gentlemen, shall fall in under the jurisdiction of Connecticut, if it come into his power. For, and in regard of the premises, and other good considerations, the said Edward Hopkins, John Haynes, John Mason, John Steele, and James Boosy, authorized thereunto, by the general court for the jurisdiction of Connecticut, do, in behalf of the said jurisdiction, promise and agree, to and with the said George Fenwick, Esquire, that for and during the space of ten full and complete years, to begin from the first of March next ensuing the date of these presents, there shall be allowed and paid to the said George Fenwick, or his assigns, the particular sums hereafter following.

1st. Each bushel of corn, of all sorts, or meal, that shall pass out of the river's mouth, shall pay two pence per bushel.

2d. Every hundred of biscuit that shall in like manner pass out of the river's mouth, shall pay six pence.

3d. Each milk cow, and mare, of three years or upwards, within any of the towns or farms upon the river, shall pay twelve pence per annum during the foresaid term.

APPENDIX.

4th. Each hog or sow, that is killed by any particular person, within the limits of the river, and the jurisdiction aforesaid, to be improved either for his own particular use, or to make market of, shall in like manner pay twelve pence per annum.

5th. Each hogshead of beaver, traded out of this jurisdiction, and passed by water down the river, shall pay twenty shillings.

6th. Each pound of beaver, traded within the limits of the river, shall pay two pence. Only it is provided, that in case the general trade with the Indians, now in agitation, proceed, this tax upon beaver, mentioned in this, and the foregoing articles, shall fall.

7th. The said committee, by the power aforesaid, consent and agree, to and with the said George Fenwick, Esq. that he, the said George Fenwick, and his heirs, shall be free of any impositions or customs, that may hereafter, by the jurisdiction, be imposed at the fort.

It is agreed that the aforesaid payments shall be made in manner following: What shall be due from the grain that is exported, shall be paid in grain, according to the proportion of the several kinds of grain that do pass away, at the common current price; neither attending such prices on the one hand, that the court may set; nor yet on the other hand, such as corn may be sold at, through the necessities of men: And in case of any difference, then the price shall be set by two good men, the one chosen by Mr. Fenwick, and the other by the court. What shall be due otherwise, shall be paid in beaver, wampum, barley, wheat or pease; the former consideration for the price, to be herein also attended. And it is provided and agreed, that a strict order and course shall be taken in observing what grain is put aboard any vessel that goeth down the river, from any of the towns: and due notice being taken thereof, every boat or vessel shall be enjoined to take a note of some person deputed by the court in each town, what quantities and kinds of grain are aboard the said vessel; and to deliver to Mr. Fenwick, or his assigns, at Saybrook, so much as will be due to him according to the forementioned agreements. And likewise, for the other payments, due care shall be taken, that they be made at the place aforesaid, in as convenient a way as may comfortably be attended, and that all indirect courses be prevented, whereby the true intent and meaning of these agreements may be evaded. In witness whereof the parties before mentioned have hereunto put their hands, the day and year abovesaid. EDWARD HOPKINS, JOHN HAYNES,
JOHN MASON, JOHN STEELE,
GEORGE FENWICK. JAMES BOOSY.*

* Records of the colony of Connecticut, folio vol. II. pp. 59, 60, 61 and 62.

APPENDIX.

NUMBER VI.

The second agreement with George Fenwick, Esquire, February 17th, 1646.

IT was agreed betwixt Edward Hopkins, on the behalf of George Fenwick, Esq. and John Cullick, John Talcott, John Porter, and Henry Clark, James Boosy, and Samuel Smith, on the behalf of the jurisdiction of Connecticut, that the agreement formerly made with Mr. Fenwick, shall be afterwards, and what was to be received by him according to that, reduced to the terms hereafter expressed:—viz.—There shall yearly, for ten years, be paid to Mr. Fenwick, or his assigns, one hundred and eighty pounds per annum, to be paid every year before the last of June, as it shall be required by the assigns of the said George Fenwick, either to such vessels as shall be appointed, or to such house or houses, in Weathersfield or Hartford, as he shall direct and order. To be paid one third in good wheat, at 4s. per bushel; one third in pease, at 3s. per bushel; one third in rye or barley, at 3s. per bushel: And if rye or barley be not paid, then to pay it in wheat and pease, in an equal proportion; and this present year some Indian corn shall be accepted; but as little as may be. Also, there is to be received by the said George Fenwick what is due from Springfield, for the aforesaid term of ten years. As also, what else may be due upon the beaver trade, according to the former agreement with him. Also, whereas the town of Saybrook is to pay in this sum of 180l. for this year, 10l. when that town increaseth, so as they pay a greater proportion, in other rates, in reference to what these towns, Windsor, Hartford, Weathersfield, and Farmington do pay, they shall increase their pay to Mr. Fenwick accordingly. Also, whereas Mattabeseck may hereafter be planted, they shall pay unto Mr. Fenwick in the same proportion they pay other rates to these towns. These four towns being accounted at one hundred and seventy pounds.*

EDWARD HOPKINS,
JOHN CULLICK,
JOHN TALCOTT,

* Records of the colony of Connecticut, folio vol. ii. p. 63.

APPENDIX.

NUMBER VII.

Petition to his majesty, King Charles II. 1661, for charter privileges.

The humble petition of the General Court, at Hartford upon Connecticut, in New-England, to the high and mighty Prince Charles the second, humbly shewing:—

THAT whereas your petitioners have not had, for many years past, since their possession and inhabiting these western and inland parts of this wilderness, any opportunity, by reason of the calamities of the late sad times, to seek for, and obtain such grants, by letters patent from your excellent majesty, their sovereign lord and king, as might assure them of such liberties and privileges, and sufficient powers, as might encourage them to go on through all difficulties, hazards, and expenses, in so great a work of plantation, in a place so remote from the christian world, and a desert so difficultly subdued, and no way improveable for subsistence, but by great cost and hard labour, with much patience and cares.

And whereas, besides the great charge that hath been expended by our fathers, and some of their associates yet surviving, about the purchases, building, fortifying, and other matters, of culturing and improving to a condition of safety and subsistence, in the places of our present abode, among the heathen, whereby there is a considerable and real addition to the honour and enlargement of his majesty's dominion, by the sole disbursements of his majesty's subjects here; of their own proper estates, they have laid out a very great sum for the purchasing a jurisdiction right of Mr. George Fenwick, which they were given to understand was derived from true royal authority, by letters patent, to certain lords and gentlemen therein nominated, a copy whereof was produced before the commissioners of the colonies, and approved by them, as appears by their records, a copy whereof is ready to be presented at your majesty's command, though, either by fire at a house where it had been sometimes kept, or some other accident, is now lost; with which your poor subjects were rather willing to have contented themselves, in those afflicting times, than to seek for power or privileges from any other than their lawful prince and sovereign.

May it, therefore, please your most gracious and excellent majesty, to confer upon your humble petitioners, who unanimously do implore your highness's favour and grace therein, those liberties, rights, authorities, and privileges, which were granted by the aforementioned letters patent, to certain lords

APPENDIX.

and gentlemen, so purchased as aforesaid, or which were enjoyed from those letters patent, granted to the Massachusetts plantation, by our fathers, and some of us yet surviving, when there, in our beginning inhabiting; and upon which those large encouragements, liberties, and privileges, so great a transplantation from our dear England was undertaken, and supposed to be yet our inheritance, till the running of that western line, the bounded limits of those letters patent, did, since our removal thence, determine our lot to be fallen without the limits of that so bounded authority.

May it please your majesty graciously to bestow upon your humble supplicants such royal munificence, according to the tenor of a draft or instrument, which is ready here to be tendered, at your gracious order.

And whereas, besides those many other great disbursements as aforesaid, in prosecution of this wilderness work, your poor petitioners were forced to maintain a war against one nation of the heathens, that did much interrupt the beginnings of your servants, by many bloody and hostile acts, whereby divers of our dear countrymen were treacherously destroyed, and have, also, been ever since, and are still, at much charge in keeping such a correspondence of peace and amity with the divers sorts of the heathen nations, that are round about your plantations, thus far extended into the bowels of the country, besides the maintenance of all public charges for church and civil affairs, which are very great in respect of our great poverty.

May it please your most excellent majesty, out of your princely bounty, to grant such an immunity from customs, as may encourage the merchants to supply our necessities in such commodities as may be wanting here, for which we have neither silver nor gold to pay; but the supply in that kind may enable, in due time, to search the bowels of the earth for some good minerals, whereof there seems to be fair probabilities, or produce some such other staple commodities, as may, in future time, appear to be good effects of your majesty's goodness and bounty. If your poor colony may find this gracious acceptance with your majesty, as to grant their humble desire, whereby they may be encouraged to go on cheerfully and strenuously in their plantation business, in hope of a comfortable settlement for themselves and their posterity, that under your royal protection they may prosper in this desert; they shall, as is their acknowledged duty, ever pray for your great tranquillity and perpetual happiness; and humbly craving leave, they subscribe themselves your majesty's loyal subjects and servants, the general court of the colony of Connecticut, in New-England, per their order signed.*

Jan. 7th, 1661.'   DANIEL CLARK, Sec'ry.

* Old Book of Patents, Letters, &c. p. 12—14.

APPENDIX.

NUMBER VIII.

The letter of Connecticut to Lord Say and Seal, June 7, 1661.

RIGHT HONORABLE,

THE former encouragements that our fathers, and some of their yet surviving associates, received from your honor to transplant themselves and families into these inland parts of this vast wilderness, where (as we have been given to understand) your honor was, and as we conceive and hope are still interested, by virtue of patent power and authority, doth not only persuade us, but assure us of your patronage and favor, in that which may come within your power, wherein our comfort and settlement, and the well being of our posterity and the whole colony, both in civil and ecclesiastical policy, is so deeply concerned: Honorable Sir, not long after that some persons of note amongst us, and well known to yourself, whose names in that respect we forbear to write, had settled upon this river of Connecticut, and some plantations up the river were possessed, and in some measure improved, Mr. George Fenwick took possession of Saybrook fort, there residing for certain or several years; at length he was moved, for ends best known to himself, to return to England, and thereupon propounded by himself, our agent, the sale of the fort, with the housing there, and several appurtenances, together with all the lands on the river, and so to the Narraganset Bay, with jurisdiction power to this colony, which was exceedingly opposed by several amongst us, whom some of us have heard to affirm that such a thing would be very distasteful to your honor, with the rest of the noble patentees, who had very bountiful intentions to this colony; nevertheless, though there was a stop for the present, yet in some short time (God removing some from us by death, that were interested in the hearts and affections of several of those nobles and gentlemen the patentees in England) the business of purchase was revived by Mr. Fenwick, and expressions to this purpose given out by him, or his agents, or both; that he had power to dispose of the premises, the rest of the patenters deserting, it fell into his hands by agreement, and in case the towns on the river refused to comply with such terms as he proposed for the purchasing of the said fort, &c. it was frequently reported that he purposed either to impose customs on the river or make sale thereof to the Dutch our noxious neighbours; at last, for our peace, and settlement, and security, (as we hoped) we made, by our committee, an agreement with the said Mr. Fenwick, a copy whereof is ready to be presented unto your honor, which cost this riv-

P 3

APPENDIX.

er one thousand six hundred pounds, or thereabouts, wherein your honor may see the great abuse that we received at Mr. Fenwick's hands, he receiving a vast sum from a poor people, and we scarcely at all advantaged thereby, nay, we judge our condition worse than if we had contented ourselves with the patronage of the grand patentees, for we have not so much as a copy of a patent to secure our standing as a commonwealth, nor to ensure us of the continuance of our rights and privileges and immunities which we thought the jurisdiction power and authority, which Mr. Fenwick had engaged to us, and we paid for at a dear rate, nor any thing under his hand to engage him and his heirs, to the performance of that which was aimed at and intended in our purchase: the lands up the river, for a long tract, the Massachusetts colony doth challenge, and have run the line, which, as they say, falls into one of our towns: on the other side towards Narraganset, we know not how to claim, being destitute of patent and a copy to decide the bounds. Be pleased, noble sir, to consider our condition, who have taken upon us this boldness to address to his majesty, our sovereign lord, and to petition his grace and favor towards us, in granting us the continuance of his protection and the continuance of those privileges and immunities, that we have hitherto enjoyed in this remote western part of the world; and likewise for a patent whereby we may be encouraged and strengthened in our proceedings. Right honorable, our humble request to yourself is, that you would be pleased to countenance our enterprise, and so far to favor us as to counsel and advise our agent, who is to represent this poor colony and to act in our behalf, John Winthrop, Esq. our honored governor, whom we have commissioned and also directed to await your honor's pleasure for advice and counsel, both respecting our petition to the king's majesty, as also respecting the case forementioned, that if there be any relief for us, we may not lose such a considerable sum of money, and be exposed to further expense for the obtaining a patent. If we may find this favor with your honor to afford your advice and counsel, and helpfulness to bring to pass our desires, we shall still acknowledge your enlarged bounty and favorable respect to us and ours, and ever pray an inundation of mercies may flow in upon your lordship from the AUTHOR and FOUNTAIN of blessing. With all due respects, we subscribe, sir, your lordship's humble servants, the general assembly of the colony of Connecticut. Per their order signed,

Per DANIEL CLARK, Secretary.*

* Old book of letters, &c. p. 9—11.

APPENDIX.

NUMBER IX.

Letter of Lord Say and Seal to Governor Winthrop, December 11th, 1661.

Mr. Winthrop,

I RECEIVED your letter, by Mr. Richards, and I would have been glad to have had an opportunity of being at London myself to have done you and my good friends, in New-England, the best service I could; but my weakness hath been such, and my old disease of the gout falling upon me, I did desire leave not to come up this winter, but I have wrote to the Earl of Manchester, lord chamberlain of his majesty's household, to give you the best assistance he may; and indeed he is a noble and worthy lord, and one that loves those that are godly. And he and I did join together, that our godly friends of New-England might enjoy their just rights and liberties; and this colonel Crowne, who, I hear, is still in London, can fully inform you. Concerning that of Connecticut, I am not able to remember all the particulars; but I have written to my lord chamberlain, that when you shall attend him, (which I think will be best for you to do, and therefore I have inclosed a letter to him, in yours) that you may deliver it, and I have desired him to acquaint you where you may speak with Mr. Jesup, who, when we had the patent, was our clerk, and he I believe, is able to inform you best about it, and I have desired my lord to wish him so to do. I do think he is now in London. My love remembered unto you, I shall remain,

Your very loving friend,

W. Say and Seal.

NUMBER X.

Letter of New-Haven to Connecticut, November 5th, 1662.

Honored Gent.

WE have heard both the patent and that writing read, which those gentlemen (who said they were sent from your general assembly) left with our committee, and have considered the contents according to our capacities. By the one we take notice of their declared sense of the patent, and also of your desire of our uniting with yourselves upon that account; by the other, we understand, that his majesty hath been graciously pleased (at your earnest petition) to grant liberty to the colony of Connecticut, to acquire, have, possess, purchase, &c. whatever lands, &c. you have gained or shall gain by lawful means, within the precincts or lines therein mentioned: And

APPENDIX.

also, of his abundant grace, to allow and establish you to be one body politic for managing all your public affairs and government, in a religious and peaceable manner, to the intents and purposes by his majesty, and the adventurers therein professed, over all persons, matters, and things, so gained by purchase or conquest, at your own proper costs and charges, according as yourselves informed you had already done. Now whatever is so yours, we have neither purpose nor desire to oppose, hurt, or hinder in the least; but what ourselves (by like lawful means) have attained, as to inheritances, or jurisdiction, as a distinct colony, upon our most solemn and religious covenants, so well known to his majesty, and to all, we must say, that we do not find in the patent any command given to you, nor prohibition to us, to dissolve covenants, or alter the orderly settlements of New-England, nor any sufficient reason, why we may not so remain to be as formerly; also your beginning to procure, and proceeding to improve the patent without us, doth confirm this belief; but rather it seems that a way is left open to us to petition for the like favor, and to enter our appeal from your declared sense of the patent, and signify our grievances. Yet, if it shall appear (after a due and full information of our state) to have been his majesty's pleasure so to unite us, as you understand the patent, we must submit according to GOD; but, for the present, we cannot answer otherwise than our committee hath done, and likewise to make the same request unto you, that we may remain distinct as formerly, and may be succoured by you as confederates; at least, that none occasion be given by yourselves for any to disturb us in our ancient settlements, until that, either by the honored Mr. Winthrop, by our other confederates, or from his majesty, we may be resolved herein: All which means are in our thoughts to use, except you prevent, for the gaining of a right understanding, and to bring a peaceable issue or reconcilement of this matter; and we wish you had better considered than to act so suddenly, to seclude us from patent privileges at first, if we are included, as you say, and to have so proceeded since, as may seem to give advantage unto disaffected persons to slight or disregard oath and covenants, and thereby to rend and make division, manage contention and troubles in the townships and societies of this colony, and that about religious worships, as the inclosed complaint may declare, which seems to us a great scandal to religion before the natives, and prejudicial to his majesty's pious intention, as also to hold forth a series of means very opposite to the end pretended, and very much obscured from the beauty of such a religious and peaceable walking among English brethren, as may either invite the natives to the christian faith, or unite our spirits in this juncture; and this occasion given before any conviction tendered, or publication of the patent among us, or so much as a treaty with us in a christian, neighbourly way. No pretence for our dissolution of government, till then could rationally be imagined. Such carriage may seem to be against the advice and mind of his majesty in the patent; as also of your honored governor, and to cast reflection upon him, when we compare these things with his letters to some here; for the avoiding whereof, we earnestly request that the whole of what he hath written to yourselves, so far as it may respect us in this business, may be fully communicated to our view in a true copy or transcript of the same. We must profess ourselves grieved hereat, and must desire and expect your effectual endeavours to repair these breaches, and restore us to our former condition as confederates, until that by all, or some of these ways intimated, we may attain a clear resolution in this matter. Unto what we have herein propounded, we shall add, that we do not, in the least, intend any dislike to his majesty's act, but show our sense of your actings, first and last, so much to our detriment, and to manifest the consequent effects to God's dishonour, as also to give you to know how we understand the patent, hoping that you will both candidly construe, and friendly comply, with our desires herein, and so remove the cause of our distraction and sad affliction, that you have brought upon this poor colony; then shall we forbear to give you further trouble, and shall pray to the God of spirits to grant us all humility, and to guide us by his heavenly wisdom to a happy issue of this affair, in love and peace. Resting,

    Gentlemen, your very loving
        friends and neighbours,
           The Freemen of the colony of New-Haven.
Per James Bishop, Secretary, in the name, and by order and
   consent of the committee and freemen of New-Haven
   colony.

NUMBER XI.

New-Haven's remonstrance against Connecticut, May 6th, 1663.

GENTLEMEN,

THE professed grounds and ends of your and our coming into these parts are not unknown, being plainly expressed in the prologue to that solemn confederation entered into by the four colonies of New-England, printed and published to the world, viz. to advance the kingdom of our LORD JESUS CHRIST, and to enjoy the liberties of the gospel in purity with peace, for which we left our dear native country, and were willing to undergo the difficulties we have since met with, in this wilderness, yet fresh in our remembrance; being the only ends we still pursue, having hitherto found by experience so much of the presence of God with us, and of his goodness and compassion towards us in so doing, for these many years. Yet, considering how unanswerable our returns have been to God, how unfruitful, unthankful, and unholy, under so much means of grace, and such liberties, we cannot but lament the same, judge ourselves, and justify God, should he now at last (after so long patience towards us) bring desolating judgments upon us, and make us drink of the dregs of that cup of indignation, he hath put into the hands of his people in other parts of the world, or suffer such contentions (in just displeasure) to arise among us, as may hasten our calamity, and increase our wo; which we pray the Lord in mercy to prevent. And whereas, in the pursuance of the said ends, and upon other religious and civil considerations, as the security of the interest of each colony, within itself in ways of righteousness and peace, and all and every of the said colonies from the Indians and other enemies, they did judge it to be their bounden duty, for mutual strength and helpfulness, for the future, in all their said concernments to enter into a consociation among themselves, thereupon fully agreed and concluded by and between the parties or jurisdictions, in divers and sundry articles, and at last ratified as a perpetual confederation by their several subscriptions: Whereunto we conceived ourselves bound to adhere, until with satisfaction to our judgments and consciences, we see our duty, with the unanimous consent of the confederates, orderly to recede, leaving the issue unto the most wise and righteous God. As for the patent, upon your petition, granted to you by his majesty, as Connecticut colony, so far, and in that sense we object not against it, much less against his majesty's act in so doing, the same being a real encouragement to other of his subjects to obtain the like favor, upon their humble petition to his royal highness, in the protection of their persons and purchased rights and interests, is also a ground of hope to us. But if the line of your patent doth circumscribe this colony by your contrivement, without our cognizance, or consent, or regard to the said confederation on your parts, we have, and must still testify against it, as not consistent (in our judgment) with brotherly love, righteousness and peace: And that this colony (for so long time a confederate jurisdiction, distinct from yours and the other colonies) is taken in under the administration of the said patent, in your hands, and so its former being dissolved, and distinction ceasing, there being no one line or letter in the patent, expressing his majesty's pleasure that way. Although it is your sense of it, yet we cannot so apprehend; of which we having already given our grounds at large in writing, we shall not need to say much more; nor have we met with any argumentative or rational convictions from you, nor do we yet see cause to be of another mind.

As for your proceedings upon pretence of the patent towards us, or rather against us, in taking in sundry of the inhabitants of this colony under your protection and government, who, as you say, offered themselves, from which a good conscience, and the obligation under which most of them stood to this colony, should have restrained them, without the consent of the body of this colony first had, and in concurrence with them, upon mature deliberation and conviction of duty yet wanting, we cannot but again testify against as disorderly in them, and which admission, on your parts, we conceive, your christian prudence might have easily suspended, for prevention of that great offence to the consciences of your confederate brethren, and those sad consequences which have followed, disturbing the peace of our towns, destroying our comforts, hazard of our lives and liberties, by their frequent threats and unsufferable provocations, hath been, and is, with us, matter of complaint, both to God and man; especially when we consider, that thus you admitted them and put power into their hands, before you had made any overture to us, or had any treaty with us, about so weighty a business, as if you were in haste to make us miserable, as indeed, in these things, we are at this day.

And seeing upon the answer returned to your propositions made by you afterwards, of joining with you in your government, finding ourselves already so dismembered, and the weighty grounds and reasons we then presented to you, we could not prevail so far with you, as to procure a respite of your further proceedings, until Mr. Winthrop's return from England, or the grant of any time that way, which was thought but reasonable by some of yourselves, and the like seldom denied in war to very enemies, we saw it then high time and necessary (fearing these beginnings) to appeal unto his majesty, and so we did, concluding according to the law of appeals, in all cases and among all nations, that the same, upon your allegiance to his majesty, would have obliged you to forbear all further process in this business; for our own parts resolving (notwithstanding all that we had formerly suffered) to sit down patient under the same, waiting upon God for the issue of our said appeal. But seeing that, notwithstanding all that we had presented to you by word and writing—notwithstanding our appeal to his majesty—notwithstanding all that we have suffered, (by means of that power you have set up, viz. a constable at Stamford,) of which informations have been given you,

APPENDIX.

yet you have gone further, to place a constable at Guilford, in like manner, over a party there, to the further disturbance of our peace and quiet, a narrative whereof, and of the provocations and wrongs we have met with at Stamford, we have received, attested to us by divers witnesses, honest men. We cannot but, on behalf of our appeal to his majesty, whose honour is highly concerned therein, and of our just rights, but (as men exceedingly afflicted and grieved) testify in the sight of God, angels, and men, against these things. Our end therein being not to provoke or further any offence, but rather as a discharge of duty, on our parts, as brethren and christian confederates, to call upon you, to take some effectual course to ease and right us, in a due redress of the grievances you have caused by these proceedings; and that after you had complimented us with large offers of patent privileges, with desire of a treaty with us for union of our colonies; and you know, as your good words were kindly accepted, so your motion was fairly answered by our committee. That in regard we were under an appeal to his majesty, that being limited by our freemen, not to conclude any thing for altering our distinct colony state and government, without their consent, and without the approbation of the other confederate colonies, they were not in present capacity so to treat; but did little suspect such a design on foot against us, the effect whereof quickly appeared at Guilford, before mentioned.

But we shall say no more at this time, only tell you, whatever we suffer by your means, we pray the Lord would help us to choose it, rather than to sin against our consciences, hoping the righteous God will, in due time, look upon our affliction, and incline his majesty's heart to favour our righteous cause.

Subscribed in the name, and by order of
the general court of New-Haven colony.
Per JAMES BISHOP, Secretary.
New-Haven, May 6th, 1663.

NUMBER XII.

Governor Winthrop's letter to Connecticut, March 3d, 1663.

GENTLEMEN,

I AM informed by some gentlemen, (who are authorized to seek remedy here,) that since you had the late patent, there hath been injury done to the government of New-Haven, and, in particular, at Guilford and Stamford, in admitting of several of the inhabitants there unto freedom with you, and appointing officers, which hath caused divisions in the said towns, which

APPENDIX.

may prove of dangerous consequence, if not timely prevented; though I do hope the rise of it is from misunderstanding, and not in design of prejudice to that colony, for whom I gave assurance to their friends that their rights and interests should not be disquieted, or prejudiced by the patent, but if both governments would, with unanimous agreement, unite in one, their friends judged it for advantage to both: And further I must let you know, that testimony here doth affirm, that I gave assurance before authority here, that it was not intended to meddle with any town or plantation that was settled under any other government: had it been any otherwise intended, or declared, it had been injurious, in taking out the patent, not to have inserted a proportionable number of their names in it. Now, upon the whole, having had serious conference with their friends, authorized by them, and with others who are friends to both, to prevent a tedious and chargeable trial, and uncertain event here, I promised them, to give you speedily this representation, how far you are engaged. If any injury have been done, by admitting of freemen, or appointing officers, or other unjust intermeddling with New-Haven colony, in one kind or other, without the approbation of the government, that it be forthwith recalled, and that, for the future, there will be no imposing in any kind upon them, nor admitting of any members without mutual consent; but that all things be acted as loving neighbouring colonies, as before such patent granted, and unto this I judge you are obliged, I having engaged to their agent here, that this will be by you performed, and they have thereupon forborne to give you or me any trouble; but they do not doubt, but upon future consideration, there may be such a right understanding between both governments, that an union and friendly joining may be established, to the satisfaction of all; which, at my arrival, I shall also endeavour (God willing) to promote. Not having more at present, in this case, I rest, Your humble servant,

JOHN WINTHROP.

London, March 3d, 1662.*

* This, according to the present way of dating, was March 3d, 1663.

NUMBER XIII.

His majesty's commission to Colonel Nichols, Sir Robert Carr, knight, and others, for the settlement of boundaries, &c. April 26th, 1664.

CHARLES R.

Charles the second, by the grace of God, king of England, Scotland, France, and Ireland, defender of the faith, &c.

To all to whom these presents shall come, Greeting.

WHEREAS we have received several addresses from our subjects of several colonies of New-England, all full of duty and affection, and expressions of loyalty and allegiance to us, with their humble desires to us, that we would renew their several charters, and receive them into our favourable opinion and protection: And several of our colonies there, and other our loving subjects, have, likewise complained of differences and disputes arisen upon the limits and bounds of their several charters and jurisdictions, whereby unneighbourly and unbrotherly contentions have and may arise, to the damage and discredit of the English interest; and that all our good subjects residing there, and being planters within the several colonies, do not enjoy the liberties and privileges granted unto them by our several charters, upon confidence and assurance of which they transported themselves and their estates into those parts: And we having received some addresses from the great men and natives of those countries, in which they complain of breach of faith, and acts of violence and injustice, which they have been forced to undergo from our subjects, whereby not only our government is traduced, but the reputation and credit of the christian religion brought into prejudice and reproach, with the Gentiles and inhabitants of those countries, who know not God, the reduction of whom to the true knowledge and fear of God, is the most worthy and glorious end of these plantations. Upon all which motives, and as an evidence and manifestation of our fatherly affection towards all our subjects in those several colonies of New-England, (that is to say,) of the Massachusetts, Connecticut, New-Plymouth, Rhode-Island, and Providence plantations, and all other plantations which are in that tract of land known under the appellation of New-England; and to the end that we may be truly informed of the state and condition of our good subjects there, that so we may the better know how to contribute to the further improvement of their happiness and prosperity:

Know ye, therefore, that we, reposing especial trust and confidence in the fidelity, wisdom, and circumspection of our

APPENDIX.

trusty and well beloved colonel Richard Nichols, Sir Robert Carr, knight, George Cartwright, Esq. and Samuel Maverick, Esq. of our especial grace, certain knowledge, and mere motion, have made, ordained, constituted, and appointed, and do by these presents make, ordain, constitute, and appoint the said colonel Richard Nichols, Sir Robert Carr, knight, George Cartwright, and Samuel Maverick, Esquires, our commissioners; and do hereby give and grant unto them, or any three or two of them, or of the survivors of them, (of whom we will the said colonel Richard Nichols, during his life, shall be always one, and upon equal division of opinions, to have the casting and decisive voice,) in our name, to visit all and every the several colonies aforesaid, and also full power to hear and receive, and to examine and determine all complaints and appeals, in all causes and matters, as well military as criminal and civil, and proceed in all things for the providing for and settling the peace and security of the said country, according to their good and sound discretions, and to such instructions as they or the survivors of them have, or shall, from time to time, receive from us in that behalf, and from time to time, as they shall find expedient, to certify us or our privy council, of their actings or proceedings touching the premises; and for the doing thereof, or any other matter or thing relating thereunto, these presents, or the enrolment thereof, shall be unto them, and every of them, a sufficient warrant and discharge in that behalf. In witness whereof, we have caused these our letters to be made patent. Given at the court at Whitehall, the 26th day of April, 1664, and in the sixteenth year of our reign. BARKER.

NUMBER XIV.

His majesty's gracious letter to the governor and company of Connecticut, accompanying the commission, April 23d, 1664.

CHARLES R.

TRUSTY and well beloved, we greet you well, having, according to the resolution we declared to Mr. John Winthrop, at the time when we renewed your charter, now sent these persons of known abilities and affections to us, that is to say, colonel Richard Nichols, Sir Robert Carr, knight, George Cartwright, Esq. and Samuel Maverick, Esq. our commissioners, to visit those our several colonies and plantations in New-England, to the end that we may be the better informed of the state and welfare of our good subjects, whose prosperity is very dear to us; we can make no question but that they shall find that reception from you which may testify your respect to

APPENDIX.

us, from whom they are sent for your good. We need not tell you how careful we are of your liberties and privileges, whether ecclesiastical or civil, which we will not suffer to be violated in the least degree; and that they may not be is the principal business of our said commissioners, as likewise to take care that the bounds and jurisdictions of our several colonies there may be clearly agreed upon; that every one may enjoy what of right belongeth unto them, without strife or contention; and especially that the natives of that country, who are willing to live peaceably and neighbourly with our English subjects, may receive such justice and civil treatment from them, as may make them the more in love with their religion and manners; so not doubting of your full compliance and submission to our desire, we bid you farewell. Given at our court at Whitehall, the 23d day of April, 1664, in the sixteenth year of our reign.

By his majesty's command,

HENRY BENNIT.

NUMBER XV.

The Duke and Duchess of Hamilton's petition to King Charles second, and his majesty's reference of the case to his commissioners, May 6th, 1664.

To the King's most excellent majesty.
The humble petition of William, Duke of Hamilton, and Anne, Duchess of Hamilton; Sheweth,

THAT whereas in the eleventh year of the reign of your royal father, of ever blessed memory, the council established at Plymouth in the county of Devon, for planting, ordering and governing of New-England in America (according to the power given them in the eighteenth year of the reign of the late king James, by his letters patent, bearing date the third day of November) did for a competent sum of money and other valuable considerations, bargain and sell unto the petitioners' father, by the name of James, Marquis Hamilton, his heirs and assigns, all that part and portion of the main lands in New-England, lying and beginning at the middle part of the mouth of the river Connecticut, to proceed along the sea coast to be accounted about sixty miles, and so up to the westward arm of the river into the land northwestward till sixty miles be finished, and so to cross southwestward till sixty miles, all which part and portion of lands were to be called by the name of the county of New-Cambridge, with several other lands and privileges as by the said deed of feoffment doth more fully appear, a copy whereof is hereunto annexed. Since which time and

APPENDIX.

by reason of the late unhappy war several persons have possessed themselves of the best and most considerable parts of the said lands, without any acknowledgment of your petitioners' right. Your petitioners therefore most humbly pray, that your majesty will be graciously pleased to recommend the premises to your majesty's commissioners for New-England, and that care may be taken that your petitioners may be restored to their just right, and that nothing be done to their prejudice.

At the court at Whitehall, the 6th May, 1664.

His majesty is graciously pleased to refer this petition to the commissioners now employed by his majesty to settle the affairs of New-England, who are to examine the allegations thereof, and upon due consideration had, to preserve and restore to the petitioners their just right and interest, or otherwise to report their opinions thereupon to his majesty, who will then declare his further pleasure, for the honorable petitioners' just satisfaction.*

HENRY BENNIT.

NUMBER XVI.

The determination of his majesty's commissioners, relative to the boundaries of his royal highness the Duke of York's patent and of the patent of Connecticut, November 30th, 1664.

BY virtue of his majesty's commission, we have heard the differences about the bounds of the patents granted to his royal highness the Duke of York, and his majesty's colony of Connecticut—and having deliberately considered all the reasons alledged by Mr. Allen, senior, Mr. Gould, Mr. Richards, and captain Winthrop, appointed by the assembly held at Hartford, the 13th day of October, 1664, to accompany John Winthrop, Esq. the governor of his majesty's colony of Connecticut, to New-York, and by Mr. Howell and captain Young, of Long-Island, why the said Long-Island should be under the government of Connecticut; which are too long here to be recited: WE do declare and order, that the southern bounds of his majesty's colony of Connecticut, is the sea; and that Long-Island is to be under the government of his royal highness the Duke of York; as is expressed by plain words in the said patents respectively. And also by virtue of his majesty's commission and by the consent of both the governor and the gentlemen above named, we also order and declare, that the creek or river called Momoronock, which is reputed to be about twelve miles to the east of West-Chester, and a line drawn

* Old Book of Letters, &c. p. 138.

from the east point or side, where the fresh water falls into the salt, at highwater mark, north-northwest to the line of the Massachusetts, be the western bounds of the said colony of Connecticut, and the plantations lying westward of that creek, and line so drawn, to be under his royal highness's government; and all plantations lying eastward of that creek, and line to be under the government of Connecticut. Given under our hands at Fort James, in New-York, on Manhattans Island, this 30th day of Nov. 1664.

RICHARD NICHOLS,
GEORGE CARTWRIGHT,
SAMUEL MAVERICK.

We underwritten, on behalf of the colony of Connecticut, have assented unto this determination of his majesty's commissioners, in relation to the bounds and limits of his royal highness the duke's patent, and the patent of Connecticut.*

JOHN WINTHROP,
MATTHEW ALLEN,
NATHAN GOULD,
JAMES RICHARDS,
JOHN WINTHROP.

November 30, 1664.

NUMBER XVII.

Letter of New-Haven to Connecticut, December 14, 1664.

HONORED GENTLEMEN,

WE have been silent hitherto, as to the making of any grievance known unto the king's commissioners, notwithstanding what may be with us of such nature, from the several transactions that have been among us, and are desirous so to continue the managing of these affairs in ways consistent with the ancient confederation of the united colonies, choosing rather to suffer, than to begin any motion hazardful to New-England settlements; in pursuance whereof (according to our promise to your gentlemen, sent lately to demand our submission, though in a divided if not dividing way, within our towns, severally seeking to bring us under the government of yourselves already settled, wherein we have had no hand to settle the same, and before we had cleared to our conviction, the certain limits of your charter, which may justly increase the scruple of too much haste in that and former actings upon us) the generality of our undivided people have orderly met this 13th of the tenth month (64) and by the vote endorsed, have prepared for this answer to be given of our submission, which being done by

* Old Book, &c. p. 2.

us, then for the accommodation of matters betwixt us in an amicable way, by a committee impowered to issue with you on their behalf, and in the behalf of all concerned, according to instructions given to the said committee. We never did, nor even do intend to damnify your moral rights or just privileges, consistent with our like honest enjoyments, and we would hope that you have no further step towards us, not to violate our government interest, but to accommodate us with that we shall desire, and the patent bear, as hath been often said you would do; and surely you have the more reason to be full with us herein, seeing that your success for patent bounds with those gentlemen now obtained, seems to be debtor unto our silence before them, when as you thus by single application and audience issued that matter: you thus performing to satisfaction, we may still rest silent, and according to profession, by a studious and cordial endeavour with us to advance the interest of Christ in this wilderness, and by the Lord's blessing thereupon, love and union between us may be greatly confirmed, and all our comforts enlarged, which is the earnest prayer of, gentlemen, your loving friends and neighbours, the committee, appointed by the freemen and inhabitants of New-Haven colony, now assembled.

JAMES BISHOP, Secretary.

New-Haven, Dec. 14, 1664.

NUMBER XVIII.

Letter of Connecticut to New-Haven, in answer to the preceding letter, December 21st, 1664.

Hartford, Dec. 21st, 1664.

HONORED GENTLEMEN,

WE have received yours, dated the 14th of this instant, signed by James Bishop, &c. wherein you are pleased to mention your silence hitherto, as to the making any grievance known to his majesty's commissioners, notwithstanding what may be with you, &c. we can say the same, though we had fair opportunities to present any thing of that nature; as for your desire to manage affairs consistent with the confederation, the present motion will, we hope, upon a candid review, not appear any ways dissonant therefrom; for besides the provision made in one of the articles of confederation for two colonies uniting in one, there was special provision, as you well know, made at the last session of the commissioners to that purpose, conjoined with pathetical advice and counsel, to an amicable union. Our too much forwardness, with New-Haven, &c. is not so clear, seeing those plantations you inhabit are much about the center of our patent, which our charter limits, as also the inclosed determination of his majesty's honorable commissioners, will, to your conviction, be apparent; that our success for patent bounds with the king's commissioners is debtor to your silence, seems to us strange, when your non-compliance was so abundantly known to those gentlemen, yea, the news of your motions, when Mr. Joseph Allen was last with you, was at New-York, before our governor's departure thence; notwithstanding your silence, and yet so good an issue obtained, we desire such reflections may be buried in perpetual silence, which only yourselves necessitating thereunto, shall revive them, being willing to pursue truth and peace as much as may be with all men, especially with our dear brethren in the fellowship of the gospel, and fellow-members of the same civil corporation, accommodated with so many choice privileges, which we are willing, after all is prepared to your hands, to confer upon you equal with ourselves, which we wish may at last produce the long desired effect of your free and cordial closure with us, not attributing any necessity imposed by us, further than the situation of those plantations in the heart of our colony, and therein the peace of posterity in these parts of the country is necessarily included, and that after so long liberty to present your plea when you have seen meet. Gentlemen, we desire a full answer as speedily as may be, whether those lately empowered, accept to govern according to their commission, if not, other meet persons to govern may by us be empowered in their room; thus desiring the Lord to unite our hearts and spirits in ways well pleasing in his sight, which is the prayer of your very loving friends, the council of the colony of Connecticut.

Signed by their order, by me,

JOHN ALLEN, Secretary.

NUMBER XIX.

The final reply of New-Haven to Connecticut.

New-Haven, Jan. 5, 1664–5.

HONORED GENTLEMEN,

WHEREAS by yours, dated December 21st, 1664, you please to say, that you did the same as we, not making any grievances known to the commissioners, &c. unto that may be returned, that you had not the same cause so to do from any pretence of injury, by our intermeddling with your colony or government interest, unto which we refer that passage for our expressing desires to manage all our matters in confederacy with the confederation, we hope you will not blame us. How

APPENDIX.

dissonant or consonant your actings with us have been, we leave to the confederation to judge, as their records may show—that article, which allows two colonies to join, doth also, with others, assert the justness of each colony's distinct rights, until joined to mutual satisfaction, and the provision made in such case the last session, we gainsay not, when the union is so completed, and a new settlement of the confederation, by the respective general courts, accomplished. Their pathetical advice for an amicable union, we wish may be so attended—in order thereunto, we gave you notice of a committee prepared to treat with you, for such an accommodation, unto which you gave us no answer, but instead thereof, sent forth your edict from authority upon us, before our conviction for submission was declared to you. The argument from our intermixt situation, is the same now as it was before our confederating and ever since, and affords no more ground now to disannul the government than before. We might marvel at your strange, why we should think your success should be debtor to our silence, and that because the news of our non-compliance was with the commissioners, as if the mere news of such a thing contained the strength of all we had to say or plead. Gentlemen, we intreat you to consider, that there is more in it than so, yea, that still we have to alledge things of weight, and know where and how, if we chose not rather to abate and suffer, than by striving to hazard the hurting yourselves or the common cause. We scope not at reflections, but conviction and conscience satisfaction, that so brethren in the fellowship of the gospel might come to a cordial and regular closure, and so to walk together in love and peace, to advance Christ his interest among them, which is all our design: But how those high and holy ends are like so to be promoved between us, without a treaty for accommodation we have cause to doubt; yet that we may not fail in the least to perform whatever we have said, we now signify, that having seen the copy of his majesty's commissioners' determination (deciding the bounds betwixt his highness the Duke of York, and Connecticut charter) we do declare submission thereunto according to the true intent of our vote, unto which we refer you. As to that part of yours concerning our magistrates and officers acceptance, their answer is, that they having been chosen by the people here to such trust and sworn thereunto, for the year ensuing, and until new be orderly chosen, and being again desired to continue that trust, they shall go on in due observance thereof according to the declaration left with us by Mr. John Allen and Mr. Samuel Sherman, bearing date November 19th, 1664; in hopes to find that in a loving treaty for accommodating matters to the ends professed by you; unto which our committee stands ready to attend, upon notice from you; that so truth and peace may be maintained. So shall we not give you further trouble, but remain, gentlemen, your very loving friends and neighbours. the committee appointed by the freemen and inhabitants of New-Haven colony.

Signed per their order, per me,

JAMES BISHOP, Secretary.

NUMBER XX.

The answer of Connecticut to the claim and petition of the Duke and Duchess of Hamilton. March 25th, 1665.

THE king's commissioners had written to the colony, requesting, "That they might have something in writing to return to the king, concerning the grant of sixty miles square on the eastern side of Connecticut river, to James, Marquis of Hamilton, from the council of Plymouth in Devon, 1631, and to know in what particulars it was desired, that they should be solicitors to his majesty for the advantage of the colony," which they declared they would cordially endeavour.

In consequence of which the following answer was given.

To the Honorable Sir Robert Carr, knight, George Cartwright, Esq. and Samuel Maverick, Esq. his majesty's honorable commissioners.

IN answer to Duke Hamilton's petition, respecting a grant of land of sixty miles square, on the east side the river Converticu.

1. We are wholly ignorant of any river within the extent of our charter, that is known under such an appellation, and therefore cannot conceive that any part or tract of land, under this government, is concerned in this demand.

2. Yet upon supposition that it may be conceived to intend Connecticut river, we humbly conceive that the original patent grant, from royal authority to the Lord Say and other nobles and gentlemen, which we purchased at a dear rate, is lately ratified and confirmed by our gracious sovereign, under the broad seal of England (the most absolute and unquestionable security of the English subjects) in which grants the lands forementioned are comprised. The grant to Connecticut was precedent to that of Duke Hamilton's several years, which gives us to conclude, that priority of title will be settled by priority of grant.

3. A considerable tract of this land which the duke's petition refers to (if as before supposed, it be determined Connecticut) was possessed by a people most malignantly spirited against his majesty's English subjects, and at our first settling

APPENDIX.

here, when we were weak and few, they grew very insolent against us, making invasion upon us, murdering many of our people, thereby necessitating us to a hazardous undertaking, to cast ourselves into the arms of God's providence, in endeavouring to suppress those bloody heathen; and through divine benediction we found a good success; and though that wilderness land would not afford any considerable recompence for the loss of lives and great expenses, yet our peace attained by that conquest did greatly rejoice us.

4. We have had peaceable possession this thirty years, free from the least claim of any other, that we heard of, to this day; which persuades us that if the duke's highness had ever reason, by virtue of his grant, to make claim, yet that right pretended is extinct in law many years since.

His majesty, our gracious sovereign, was pleased of his abundant favor and grace, to his subjects of this colony, so far to declare his free reception of the reasons forementioned, of our purchase made, and conquest recovered, and likewise of our improvement and labor bestowed upon those lands, as to insert them as motives to that late renewal of our charter.

We humbly crave, that as it hath been his majesty's royal pleasure to manifest his tender affection to, and care of his subjects' welfare in these his colonies of New-England, in sending over his honorable commissioners to compose and issue those things that might be of ill consequence between the several colonies, so likewise that it be well pleasing to his majesty, that this his colony of Connecticut might be freed from further trouble or inconvenience by this claim, that we understand hath been presented by the Marquis Hamilton.

And whereas, your honors are pleased so far to exercise your thoughts about the promotion of the welfare of his majesty's subjects in this his colony, as to vouchsafe us so favorable a tender to be solicitors in our behalf to his majesty our gracious sovereign, in any particulars wherein we may be advantaged, we crave your honors' assistance as followeth.

1. That his majesty would be graciously pleased to silence the claim of Duke Hamilton, if any be by him pretended or presented, to any tract of land lying or being within the precincts of our charter (renewed and established to us by our royal sovereign) and possessed and improved by several poor people, whose progress in their labors and endeavours for their subsistence (at the best very mean) will be impeded and obstructed through fear of the event of such claims.

2. Whereas, the colony is at a very low ebb in respect of traffick, and although, out of a respect to our relation to the English nation, and that we might be accounted a people under the sovereignty and protection of his majesty the king of

APPENDIX.

England, we presumed to put the name or appellation of New-London upon one of our towns, which nature hath furnished with a safe and commodious harbour, though but a poor people, and discapacitated in several respects to promote traffick; we humbly crave of our gracious sovereign, that he would be pleased out of his princely bounty, to grant it be a place of free trade for seven, ten, or twelve years, as his royal heart shall incline to confer as a boon upon his poor, yet loyal subjects.

3. We request of your honors, 1. That you will please to represent unto his majesty our allegiance, with our ready acknowledgment of his princely grace in the late renewal of our charter. 2. His more abundant grace in re-ratifying our privileges both civil and ecclesiastic, in his late gracious letter sent to us by your honors. 3. Our ready compliance with his majesty's royal will and pleasure therein expressed. 4. Our christian moderation to men of different persuasions. 5. We humbly implore the continuance of the shines of his royal favor upon our mean beginnings, that so we may flourish under the benign aspect of our lord the king.*

NUMBER XXI.

The Reverend Mr. John Davenport's resignation of Governor Hopkins's donation to the general court of New-Haven, May 4th, 1660.

Quod felix faustumque sit!

On the 4th day of the fourth month, 1660, John Davenport, pastor of the church of Christ at New-Haven, presented to the honorable general court at New-Haven, as followeth;

MEMORANDUM,

I. That, sundry years past, it was concluded by the said general court, that a small college, such as the day of small things will permit, should be settled in New-Haven, for the education of youth in good literature, to fit them for public services, in church and commonwealth, as it will appear in the public records.

II. Thereupon, the said John Davenport, wrote unto our honored friend, Edward Hopkins, Esq. then living in London, the result of those consultations. In answer whereunto, the said Edward Hopkins wrote unto the said John Davenport, a letter, dated the 30th of the second month, called April, 1656, beginning with these words,

MOST DEAR SIR,

The long continued respects I have received from you, but

* This is an attested copy, in the old letter book, p. 128, 129, 130.

APPENDIX.

especially, the speakings of the Lord to my heart, by you, have put me under deep obligations to love and a return of thanks beyond what I have or can express, &c. Then after other passages (which being secrets hinder me from shewing his letters) he added a declaration of his purpose in reference to the college about which I wrote unto him, 'That which the Lord hath given me in those parts, I ever designed, the greatest part of it, for the furtherance of the work of Christ in those ends of the earth, and if I understand that a college is begun and like to be carried on, at New-Haven, for the good of posterity, I shall give some encouragement thereunto.' These are the very words of his letter. But,

III. Before Mr. Hopkins could return an answer to my next letter it pleased God to finish his days in this world: Therefore, by his last will and testament (as the copy thereof transcribed and attested, by Mr. Thomas Yale, doth shew) he committed the whole trust of disposing his estate in these countries (after some personal legacies were paid out) unto the public uses mentioned, and bequeathed it to our late honored governor, Theophilus Eaton, Esq. his father in law, and to the aforesaid John Davenport, and joined with them, in the same trust, captain John Cullick, and Mr. William Goodwin.

IV. It having pleased the most high to afflict this colony greatly by taking from it to himself, our former ever honored governor, Mr. Eaton, the surviving trustees and legatees met together, to consider what course they should take for the discharge of their trust, and agreed that each of them should have an inventory of the aforesaid testator's estate in New-England, in houses and goods and lands, (which were prized by some in Hartford intrusted by captain Cullick and Mr. Goodwin) and in debts, for the gathering in whereof some attorneys were constituted, empowered and employed by the three surviving trustees, as the writing in the magistrates' hand will shew.

V. Afterwards, at another meeting of the said trustees, they considering that by the will of the dead, they are joined together in one common trust, agreed to act together, with mutual consent, in performance thereof; and considering, that by the will of the testator, two of New-Haven were joined with two of Hartford, and that Mr. Hopkins had declared his purpose to further the college intended at New-Haven, they agreed that one half of that estate which should be gathered in, should be paid unto Mr. Davenport for New-Haven, the other half to captain Cullick and Mr. Goodwin, to be improved for the uses and ends fore noted where they should have power to perform their trust, which, because they would not expect to have at Hartford, they concluded it would be best done by them in that new plantation unto which sundry of Hartford

APPENDIX.

were to remove, and were now gone: yet they agreed that out of the whole 100l. should be given to the college at Cambridge, in the bay; the estate being 1000l. as captain Cullick believed it would be, which we now see cause to doubt, by reason of the sequestrations laid upon that estate, and still continued by the general court at Hartford, whereupon some refuse to pay their debts, and others forsake the purchases they had made, to their great hindrance of performing the will of the deceased, according to the trust committed to them, and to the great endamagement of the estate.

VI. The said John Davenport acquainted the other two trustees with his purpose, to interest the honored magistrates and elders of this colony in the disposal of that part of the estate, that was by their agreement to be paid thereunto, for the promoving the college work in a gradual way, for the education of youth in good literature, so far as he might, with preserving in himself, the power committed to him for the discharge of his trust: they consented thereunto. Accordingly, on the election day, it being the 30th day of the third month, he delivered up unto the hands of the honored governor and magistrates the writings that concern this business: (viz. the copy of Mr. Hopkins his last will and testament, and the inventory of his estate in New-England, and the appraisement of his goods, and the writings signed by the surviving trustees for their attornies, and some letters between the other trustees and himself,) adding also his desire of some particulars for the well performing the trust as followeth:

1. He desireth of New-Haven town,

First, That the rent of the oyster shell fields, formerly separated and reserved for the use and benefit of a college, be paid from this time forward, towards the making of some stock for disbursements of necessary charges towards the college till it be set up, and afterwards to continue for a yearly rent as belonging to it, under the name and title of college land.

Secondly, That if no place can be found more convenient, Mrs. Eldred's lot be given for the use of the college, and of the colony grammar school, if it be in this town, else only for the college.

Thirdly, That parents will keep such of their sons constantly to learning in the schools, whom they intend to train up for public serviceableness, and that all their sons may learn, at least, to write and cast up accounts competently, and may make some entrance into the latin tongue.

Fourthly, That if the colony settle 40l. per annum, for a common school, and shall add 100l. to be paid towards the building or buying of a school house and library in this town, seeing thereby this town will be freed from the charges which

APPENDIX.

they have been at hitherto to maintain a town school, they would consider what part of their former salary may be still continued for future supplies towards a stock for necessary expenses about the college or school.

2. He humbly desireth the honored general court of the colony of New-Haven,

First, That the 40l. per annum formerly agreed upon, to be paid by the several plantations, for a common grammar school, be now settled in one of the plantations which they shall judge fittest, and that a school master may forthwith be provided to teach the three languages, Latin, Greek, and Hebrew, so far as shall be necessary to prepare them for the college, and that if it can be accomplished, that such a school master be settled by the end of this summer, or the beginning of winter. The payments from the several plantations may begin from this time.

Secondly, That if the common school be settled in this town, the honored governor, magistrates, elders, and deputies, would solemnly and together visit the grammar school once every year, at the court for elections, to examine the scholars' proficiency in learning.

Thirdly, That for the payments to be made by the plantations, for the school, or out of Mr. Hopkins' estate, towards the college, one be chosen by themselves, under the name and title of steward, or receiver, for the school and college, to whom such payments may be made, with full power given him by the court to demand what is due, and to prosecute in case of neglect, and to give acquittances in case of due payments received, and to give his account yearly to the court, and to dispose of what he receiveth in such provisions as cannot be well kept, in the best way for the aforesaid uses according to advice.

Fourthly, That unto that end a committee of church members be chosen to meet together and consult and advise, in emergent difficult cases, that may concern the school or college, and which cannot be well delayed till the meeting of the general court, the governor being always the chief of that committee.

Fifthly, The said John Davenport desireth, that while it may please God to continue his life, and abode in this place, (to the end that he may the better perform his trust) in reference to the college, that he be always consulted in difficult cases, and have the power of a negative vote, to hinder any thing from being acted which he shall prove by good reason to be prejudicial to the true intendment of the testator, and to the true end of this work.

Sixthly, That certain orders be speedily made for the

APPENDIX.

school, and when the college shall proceed, for it also; that the education of youth may be carried on suitably to Christ's ends, by the counsel of the teaching elders in this colony; and that what they shall conclude with consent, being approved by the honored magistrates, be ratified by the general court.

Seventhly, Because it is requisite that the writings which concern Mr. Hopkins his estate be safely kept; in order thereunto, the said John Davenport desireth that a convenient chest be made, with two locks and two keys, and be placed in the house of the governor, or of the steward, in some safe room, till a more public place (as a library or the like) may be prepared; and that one key be in the hands of the governor, the other in the steward's hands. That in this chest all the writings now delivered by him to the magistrates may be kept; and all other bills, bonds, acquittances, orders, or whatsoever writings that may concern this business be put and kept there; and that some place may be agreed on where the steward or receiver may lay up such provisions as may be paid in, till they may be disposed of for the good of the school or college.

Eighthly, Because our sight is narrow and weak, in viewing and discerning the compass of things that are before us, much more in foreseeing future contingencies, he further craveth liberty for himself and other elders of this colony, to propound to the honored governor and magistrates what hereafter may be found to be conducible to the well carrying on of this trust, according to the ends proposed, and that such proposals may be added unto these, under the name and title of USEFUL ADDITIONALS; and confirmed by the general court.

Lastly, He hopeth he shall not need to add, what he expressed by word of mouth, that the honored general court will not suffer this gift to be lost from the colony, but as it becometh fathers of the commonwealth, will use all good endeavours to get it into their hands, and to assert their right in it for the common good; that posterity may reap the good fruit of their labors, and wisdom, and faithfulness; and that JESUS CHRIST may have the service and honor of such provision made for his people; in whom I rest.

JOHN DAVENPORT.

NUMBER XXII.

Letter of his majesty king Charles II. to Connecticut, April 10th,
1666.

CHARLES R.

TRUSTY and well beloved, we greet you well, having received so full and satisfactory an account from our commissioners, both of the good reception you have given them, and also of your dutifulness and obedience to us, we cannot but let you know how much we are pleased therewith, judging that respect of yours towards our officers to be the true and natural fruit which demonstrates what fidelity and affection towards us is rooted in your hearts; and although your carriage doth of itself most justly deserve our praise and approbation, yet it seems to be set off with the more lustre by the contrary deportment of the colony of the Massachusetts, as if by their refractoriness they had designed to recommend and heighten the merit of your compliance with our directions, for the peaceable and good government of our subjects in those parts: you may therefore assure yourselves that we shall never be unmindful of this your loyal and dutiful behaviour, but shall, upon all occasions, take notice of it to your advantage, promising you our constant protection and royal favor, in all things that may concern your safety, peace and welfare; and so we bid you farewell. Given at our court, at Whitehall, the 10th day of April, 1666, in the eighteenth year of our reign. By his majesty's command,

WILLIAM MORRICE.

Superscribed to our trusty and well beloved,
 the governor and council of the colony of
 Connecticut, in New-England.

NUMBER XXIII.

An address to king William, June 13th, 1689.

To the king's most excellent majesty,
The humble address of your majesty's dutiful and loyal subjects, the governor and company of your majesty's colony of Connecticut, in New-England.
GREAT SOVEREIGN,

GREAT was that day, when the Lord, who sitteth upon the floods, and sitteth king forever, did divide his and your adversaries from one another, like the waters of Jordan forced to stand upon an heap, and did begin to magnify you like Joshua, in the sight of all Israel, by those great actions that were so much for the honor of God, and the deliverance of the English dominions from popery and slavery, and all this separated from those sorrows that usually attend the introducing of a peaceable settlement in any troubled state; all which doth affect us with the sense of our duty to return the highest praise unto the KING of KINGS, and LORD of HOSTS, and bless HIM, who hath delighted in you, to sit you on the throne of his Israel, and to say because the LORD loved ISRAEL forever, there-

APPENDIX.

fore hath he made you king to do justice and judgment, &c. also humble and hearty acknowledgment for that great zeal, that by your majesty hath been expressed in those hazards, you have put your royal person to, and in the expense of so great treasure in the defence of the protestant interest. In the consideration of all which, we, your majesty's dutiful and loyal subjects of your said colony, are encouraged humbly to intimate that we, with much favor, obtained a charter of king Charles the II. of happy memory, bearing date April 23d, 1662, in the 14th year of his reign, granted to the governor and company of his majesty's colony of Connecticut, the advantages and privileges whereof made us indeed a very happy people, and by the blessing of God upon our endeavours, we have made a considerable improvement of your dominions here; which, with the defence of ourselves from the force of both foreign and intestine enemies, has cost us much expense of treasure and blood; yet in the second year of the reign of his late majesty king James the II. we had a *quo-warranto* served upon us by Edward Randolph, requiring our appearance before his majesty's court, in England; and although the time of our appearance was elapsed before the serving the said *quo-warranto*, yet we humbly petitioned his majesty for his favor, and the continuance of our charter, with the privileges thereof; but we received no other favor but a second *quo-warranto*, and we well observing that the charter of London, and other considerable cities in England were condemned, and that the charter of the Massachusetts had undergone the like fate, plainly saw what we might expect, yet we not judging it good or lawful to be active in surrendering what had cost us so dear, nor to be altogether silent, we empowered an attorney to appear on our behalf, and to prefer our humble address to his majesty, to entreat his favor quickly upon it; but as Sir Edmond Andross informed us he was impowered by his majesty to regain the surrender of our charter, if we saw meet so to do, and to take ourselves under his government; also colonel Thomas Dungan, his majesty's governor of New-York, labored to gain us over to his government: we withstood all these motions, and in our reiterated addresses, we petitioned his majesty to continue us in the full and free enjoyment of our liberties and property, civil and sacred, according to our charter. We also petitioned, that if his majesty should not see meet to continue us as we were, but was resolved to annex us to some other government, we then desired, that (in as much as Boston had been our old correspondents, and people whose principles and manners we had been acquainted with) we might be annexed rather to Sir Edmund Andross his government, than to colonel Dungan's, which choice of ours was

APPENDIX.

taken for a resignation of our government, though that was never intended by us for such, nor had it the formalities in law to make it a resignation, as we humbly conceive, yet Sir Edmund Andross was commissioned, by his majesty, to take us under his government; pursuant to which about the end of October, 1687, he with a company of gentlemen and grenadiers, to the number of sixty or upwards came to Hartford (the chief seat of this government) caused his commission to be read and declared our government to be dissolved, and put into commission, both civil and military officers through our colony, as he pleased, where he passed through the principal parts thereof. The good people of the colony, though they were under a great sense of the injuries they sustained hereby, yet chose rather to be silent and patient than to oppose, being indeed surprised into an involuntary submission to an arbitary power, but when the government we were thus put under, seemed to us, to be determined, and we being in daily fear and hazard of those many inconveniences, that will arise from a people in want of government, being also in continual danger of our lives by reason of the natives being at war with us, with whom we had just fears of our neighbouring French to join, not receiving any order or direction what method to take for our security, we were necessitated to put ourselves into some form of government, and there being none so familiar to us as that of our charter, nor what we could make so effectual for the gaining the universal compliance of the people, and having never received any intimation of an enrolment of that, which was interpreted a resignation of our charter, we have presumed, by the consent of the major part of the freemen, assembled for that end, May 9th, 1689, to resume our government, according to the rules of our charter, and this to continue till further order, yet as we have thus presumed to dispose ourselves, not waiting orders from your majesty, we humbly submit ourselves herein, intreating your majesty's most gracious pardon, and that what our urgent necessity hath put upon us, may no ways interrupt your majesty's grace and favor towards us, your most humble and dutiful subjects, but that in your clemency you would be pleased to grant us such directions as to your princely wisdom may seem meet, with such ratifications and confirmations of our charter, in the full and free enjoyment of all our properties, privileges, and liberties both civil and sacred, as therein granted to us, by your royal predecessor, king Charles the II. which may yet further insure it an inheritance to us and our posterities after us, with what farther grace and favor your royal and enlarged heart may be moved to confer upon us; which, we trust, we shall not forget nor be unprofitable under; but as we have this day with the greatest expres sions of joy, proclaimed your majesty and royal consort king and queen of England, France, and Ireland, with the dominions thereto belonging, so we shall ever pray, that God would grant your majesties long to live, and prosperously to reign over all your dominions, and that great and happy work you have begun may be prospered here and graciously rewarded with a crown of glory hereafter.

ROBERT TREAT, Governor.
Per order of the general court of Connecticut, signed,
JOHN ALLEN, Secretary.

NUMBER XXIV.

Letter to governor Leisler, requiring the release of major-general Winthrop, &c. September 1st, 1690.

HARTFORD, Sept. 1st, 1690.

HONORABLE SIR,

BY an express from our captains, at Albany, of the 27th August last, we are certified, that major-general Winthrop is made a prisoner, and that on our officers' request to the commander of the fort for his liberty to officiate in the army, yourself being present at Albany, their answer was, that if they would speak with the general, they might go to York ; also that our commissary is under restraint ; these are very unexpected and surprising as well as grievous tidings to us, and put us upon signifying to you, that it was upon a certain knowledge of major Winthrop's fidelity, prudence, and valor, that we did solicit him to undertake this service, and used our interest in the Massachusetts gentlemen to prevail with him therein, who having the same confidence in his virtues did so, and we thereon recommended him to you, who gave us to understand as great a value of him, and therefore desired his acceptance, which his honor accepting, though he were worthy of a tenfold greater command, he waited on you and his country ; sir, these things are so radicated in all New-England, that your thus dealing cannot raise a jealousy in us of any thing unworthy so generous a soul, as is this gentleman, and though in honor to you, in your present capacity, we will suspend any censures which we might make on your unadvisedness in this action, yet we must in justice remember you of that article concluded by the commissioners at York, whereof you were one, namely, what was referred to the commander in chief and his council of war, which you in particular are not to overrule ; if the return from Wood Creek, done by a council of war, be the matter which offends you, as it is generally said to be, consider how far that article, and the reason it is grounded on, lead to it ; also, that the army being confederate, if you be concerned so are we, and the rest, and that you alone should judge upon the general's and council of war's actions, will infringe our liberty; but that which is worst in event is, that such actions will render our friendly correspondence too weak, to join in future attempts, which we may have but too much occasion for; for if our sending our best friends to join with you, prove a pitfall to them, it will necessitate our future forbearance, whatever the consequence be.

And sir, you necessitate us to tell you, that a prison is not a catholicon for all state maladies, though so much used by you, nor are you incapable of need of, nor aid from their majesty's subjects in New-England; nor could you in any one action have more disobliged all New-England, and if you shall proceed in this way, you will certainly put all that gentleman's friends on his vindication, be the matter controverted what it will, he is of such estate and repute, as could not shun a just trial, and if your adherence to Mr. Milborn (whose spirit we have sufficient testimony of,) and other emulators of the major's honor, be greater than to ourselves and the gentlemen of the bay, you may boast of the exchange, by what profit you find. Sir, you cannot expect but we shall be warm with these matters, unless you prevent us by a timely and honorable release of the major, which is the thing we advise unto, and desire to hear from you with all speed, what our expectations may be on this account. We are giving account of this matter to the governor and council of Massachusetts, it is justly expected that your declaration to us all of the grounds of this your action, should have been as forward as the thing itself. We also move you to set our commissary at liberty, since he is of such use to our soldiers as he cannot be spared.

NUMBER XXV.

The determination of the king, in council, relative to the militia of Connecticut, April 19th, 1694.

A PETITION having been presented to his majesty, by major-general Fitz John Winthrop, agent for the English colony of Connecticut, in New-England, in America, in behalf of the said colony, by the name of the governor and company of the English colony of Connecticut, in New-England, in America, setting forth, that the petitioners by letters patents, under the great seal of England, in the fourteenth year of the reign of the late king Charles the second, were incorporated by the name of the governor and company of the English colony of Connecticut, in America, with powers as well for the civil administra

APPENDIX.

tion of affairs, as the lieutenancy for the ordering, arraying, modelling, and conducting the militia, for the special defence of the colony; that from the date of the said grant, until the month of October last, they have enjoyed the said liberties and privileges, without forfeiture or molestation, except some interruption they received in the reign of king James the second; that colonel Fletcher, governor of New-York, in October last, by color of his majesty's commission, whereby for the uniting the forces of the said province and colony, he was created commander in chief of the militia of the said colony, did demand of the petitioners not only to submit to him, as lieutenant general and commander in chief over the full quota of the militia of that colony, in conjunction with those of New-York and the adjacent governments, but likewise the particular lieutenancy of the said colony and the power of assessing, modelling, and establishing the militia thereof, the petitioners therefore humbly praying the said commission may receive such explanation and restriction, as to his majesty in his royal justice and wisdom shall seem meet; and his majesty having been pleased to refer the said petition to the right honorable the lords of the committee of trade and plantations to consider the matter of the said petition, and to report what they conceive fit for his majesty to do therein; and the lords of the committee having received the report of their majesty's attorney general and solicitor general upon the matter of the said petition, together with the address of the colony of Rhode-Island, and touching the uniting the strength of those colonies against the French, which report is in the words following,

May it please your lordships,

In obedience to your lordship's commands signified to us by Mr. Blathwait, the 2d of January and the 3d of February last, by which we were to consider the several charters of Connecticut and Rhode-Island, and the grants of east and west New-Jersey, and to report our opinion upon the whole matter what may be done for the uniting the strength of those colonies and New-York under a chief commander, to be commissioned by their majesties, for the defence of their majesty's subjects in those parts against the French, and also to consider the annexed copy of the petition of the governor and company of Connecticut, and to report our opinion thereupon, we have considered the matter to us referred, and do find that king Charles the II. by his charter, dated the 23d of April, in the 14th year of his reign, did incorporate John Winthrop, and several other persons therein named and all others who then were or after should be admitted and made free of the company, to be a corporation by the name of the governor and company of the English colony of Connecticut in New-England in

APPENDIX.

America, with such powers, privileges and capacities, as are usually granted to corporations of like nature, and to have continuance and succession forever, and therein the bounds of the colony are described and a grant thereby made to the corporation of all land, soil, ground, havens, ports, jurisdictions, royalties, privileges, franchises and hereditaments, within the same or thereunto belonging, TO BE HOLDEN to the corporation and their successors in trust for the benefit of themselves and their associates, freemen of that colony, their heirs and assigns of the kings of England, as of the manor of East-Greenwich, by the 5th part of the ore of gold and silver there found, with power to the corporation to make laws, elect governors, deputy governors and assistants, erect judicatures and courts, and choose officers for the civil government, and thereby also power is granted to the chief commanders, governors and officers of the company and others inhabiting there, by their leave or direction for their special defence and safety, to assemble, martially array and put in warlike posture the inhabitants of the colony, and to commission such persons as they should think fit to lead and conduct the inhabitants, and to encounter, resist, kill and slay all that should attempt or interpose the invasion or annoyance of the inhabitants or plantations, and to exercise martial laws and take and surprise the invaders or attemptors of the plantation or hurt of the company and inhabitants, and, on just occasion, to invade and destroy the natives or other enemies of the colony.

We also find that king Charles the II. in the 15th year of his reign did incorporate divers persons by name, and such others as then were, or after should be admitted and free of the company by the name of the governor and company of the English colony of Rhode-Island and Providence plantation, in New-England in America, and granted them in effect the like powers and authorities both civil and military, as are before mentioned to be granted to Connecticut.

We find that the civil government, in those plantations or colonies, executed the military powers conferred by the charters; but that their majesties, in the third year of their reign, by their commission, constituted Sir William Phipps, lieutenant and commander in chief of the militia and of the forces by sea and land within the colonies of Connecticut, Rhode-Island and Providence plantation, king's province and province of New-Hampshire, and all forts and places of strength in the same with several powers and authorities, and that their majesties by their commission under the great seal, dated the 10th of June, 1693, revoked so much of Sir William Phipps his commission and powers, as related to the colony of Connecticut, and by the same commission constituted Benjamin Fletch-

APPENDIX.

er, Esq. their majesty's captain general and commander in chief of New-York, Pennsylvania, New-Castle, and the territories and tracts of land depending thereupon, to be the commander in chief of the militia and of all the forces by sea and land within the colony of Connecticut and of all forts and places of strength within the same, with power to levy, arm, muster, command, or employ the militia of the said colony, and upon any necessary and urgent occasion, during this war, to transfer to the province of New-York, and frontiers of the same, for resisting and withstanding enemies, pirates and rebels, both at land and sea, and defence of that province and colony, of which commission and the large powers therein contained as to Connecticut, the colony of Connecticut by their annexed petition do complain and pray redress against the exercise of it, in such manner over the whole militia, and therein shew their reasons against it. We have heard colonel Winthrop and his council, on the behalf of the colony of Connecticut, and Mr. Almey and his council, on the behalf of Rhode-Island and Providence plantation, and Dr. Cox appeared on the behalf of east and west New-Jersey, and produced some writings, shewing how the same were granted out from the crown to the duke of York, and by the duke of York to others, but the Dr. not claiming any title to himself it doth not appear to us in whom the estate in law of those places or of the government thereof, civil or military, doth now reside, nor how the same is exercised. But having read the annexed estimate from Mr. Blathwait, we communicated the same to the agents for Connecticut, Rhode-Island and Providence plantation, who declared their readiness during times of danger to provide their respective quotas therein contained, and in case of increase of danger, or other necessary occasions, during the continuance thereof, their respective quotas to be proportionably increased with other colonies; but as to the remaining militia beyond the quotas (which it seems in those countries consists of all males between sixteen and sixty years of age) they humbly desire that it may remain under the ordinary and usual government and command of the colonies according to their charters, and not to be commanded out, unless in times of actual invasion or imminent danger, for the necessary preservation of some of the colonies, and at such times only when such of the colonies whereout the forces shall be drawn, are not in danger, and that at all times a sufficient power of the militia may be always kept in each colony under the power of the government of it, for the safety and necessary preservation thereof.

We are humbly of opinion that the charters and grants of those colonies do give the ordinary power of the militia to the

APPENDIX.

respective governments thereof; but do also conceive that their majesties may constitute a chief commander, who may have authority, at all times, to command or order such proportion of the forces of such colony or plantation, as their majesties shall think fit; and farther, in times of invasion and approach of the enemy, with the advice and assistance of the governors of the colonies, to conduct and command the rest of the forces for the preservation and defence of such of those colonies as shall most stand in need thereof, not leaving the rest unprovided of a competent force for their defence and safety; but in time of peace, and when the danger is over, the militia within each of the said provinces ought, as we humbly conceive, to be under the government and dispositions of the respective governors of the said colonies, according to their charters.

All which, nevertheless, is most humbly submitted to your lordships' great wisdom.

EDWARD WARD,
THOMAS TREVES.

2d April, 1694.

And the lords of the committee having presented to his majesty's council the report of Mr. attorney and Mr. solicitor general upon the matters above mentioned, his majesty, in council, is pleased to approve the said report, and to signify his pleasure, that the quota, not exceeding one hundred and twenty men, be the measure of the assistance to be given by the colony of Connecticut, and all times during war to be commanded by the governor of New-York; and the right honorable Sir John Trenchard, his majesty's principal secretary of state, is to prepare letters for his majesty's royal signature, for the signification of his majesty's pleasure herein to the governor of New-York and Connecticut accordingly.

WILLIAM BRIDGEMAN.

NUMBER XXVI.

THE GREAT PATENT OF NEW-ENGLAND.

JAMES, by the grace of God, King of England, Scotland, France, and Ireland, Defender of the Faith, &c.

TO all to whom these presents shall come, greeting:— Whereas, upon the humble petition of divers of our well disposed subjects, that intended to make several plantations in the parts of America, between the degrees of thirty-four and forty-five, WE, according to our princely inclination, favouring much their worthy disposition, in hope thereby to advance the enlargement of the christian religion, to the glory of God Almighty, as also by that means to stretch out the bounds of our dominions, and to replenish those deserts with people, governed by laws and magistrates, for the more peaceable commerce of all that in time to come shall have occasion to traffic into those territories, granted unto Sir Thomas Gates, Sir George Summers, knights, Thomas Hamon, and Raleigh Gilbert, Esquires, and others their associates, for the more speedy accomplishment thereof, by our letters patents, bearing date the 10th day of April, in the fourth year of our reign of England, France, and Ireland, and of Scotland the fortieth, free liberty to divide themselves into two several colonies; the one called the first colony, to be undertaken and advanced by certain knights, gentlemen, and merchants, in and about our city of London; the other, called the second colony, to be undertaken and advanced by certain knights, gentlemen, merchants, and their associates, in or about our cities of Bristol, Exon, and our town of Plymouth, and other places, as in and by our said letters patents, amongst other things more at large, it doth and may appear.

And whereas, since that time, upon the humble petition of the said adventurers and planters of the said first colony, we have been graciously pleased to make them one distinct and entire body by themselves, giving unto them their distinct limits and bounds:

And have, upon their like humble request, granted unto them divers liberties, privileges, enlargements, and immuni-

APPENDIX.

...es, as in and by our several letters patents, it doth and may more at large appear.

Now forasmuch as we have been, in like manner, humbly petitioned unto by our trusty and well beloved servant, Sir Ferdinando Gorges, knight, captain of our fort and island, by Plymouth, and by certain the principal knights and gentlemen adventurers of the said second colony, and by divers other persons of quality, who now intend to be their associates, divers of which have been at great and extraordinary charges, and sustained many losses, in seeking and discovering a place fit and convenient to lay the foundation of a hopeful plantation, and have, divers years past, by God's assistance, and their own endeavours, taken actual possession of the continent hereafter mentioned, in our name, and to our use, as sovereign lord thereof, and have settled already some of our people in places agreeable to their desires in those parts, and in confidence of prosperous success therein, by the continuance of God's divine blessing, and our royal permission, have resolved, in a more plentiful and effectual manner, to prosecute the same; and to that purpose and intent, have desired of us, for their better encouragement and satisfaction therein, and that they may avoid all confusion, questions, or differences between themselves and those of the said first colony, that we would likewise be graciously pleased to make certain adventurers, intending to erect and establish fishery, trade, and plantation, within the territories, precincts, and limits of the said second colony, and their successors, one several distinct and entire body, and to grant unto them such estate, liberties, privileges, enlargements, and immunities there, as are in those, our letters patents, hereafter particularly expressed and declared.

And forasmuch as we have been certainly given to understand, by divers of our good subjects, that have, for these many years past, frequented those coasts and territories between the degrees of forty and forty-eight, that there is no other the subjects of any christian king or state, by any authority from their sovereign lords or princes, actually in possession of any the said lands or precincts, whereby any right, claim, interest, or title, may, might, or ought, by that means accrue, belong, or appertain unto them, or any of them.

And also, for that we have been further given certainly to know, that within these late years, there hath, by God's visitation, reigned a wonderful plague, together with many horrible slaughters and murders, committed amongst the savages and British people there heretofore inhabiting, in a manner to the utter destruction, devastation, and depopulation of that whole territory, so as there is not left, for many leagues together, in a manner, any that do claim or challenge any kind of interest

APPENDIX.

therein, nor any other superior lord or sovereign, to make claim thereunto, whereby we, in our judgment, are persuaded and satisfied, that the appointed time is come in which Almighty God, in his great goodness and bounty towards us, and our people, hath thought fit and determined, that those large and goodly territories, deserted as it were by their natural inhabitants, should be possessed and enjoyed by such of our subjects and people, as heretofore have, and hereafter shall, by his mercy and favour, and by his powerful arm, be directed and conducted thither; in the contemplation and serious consideration whereof, we have thought it fit, according to our kingly duty, so much as in us lieth, to second and follow God's sacred will, rendering reverend thanks to his Divine Majesty, for his gracious favour in laying open and revealing the same unto us, before any other christian prince or state; by which means, without offence, and, as we trust, to his glory, we may with boldness go on to the settling of so hopeful a work, which tendeth to the reducing and conversion of such savages as remain wandering in desolation and distress, to civil society and christian religion, to the enlargement of our own dominions, and the advancement of the fortunes of such of our good subjects as shall willingly interest themselves in the said employment, to whom we cannot but give singular commendations for their so worthy intention and enterprize.

We, therefore, of our special grace, mere motion, and certain knowledge, by the advice of the lords and others of our privy council, have, for us, our heirs, and successors, granted, ordained, and established, and, in and by these presents, do, for us, our heirs, and successors, grant, ordain, and establish, that all that circuit, continent, precincts, and limits, in America, lying and being in breadth from forty degrees of northerly latitude from the equinoctial line, to forty-eight degrees of the said northerly latitude, and in length by all the breadth aforesaid, throughout the main land, from sea to sea, with all the seas, rivers, islands, creeks, inlets, ports, and havens, within the degrees, precincts, and limits of the said latitude and longitude, shall be the limits, and bounds, and precincts of the said second colony.

And to the end that the said territories may for ever hereafter be more particularly and certainly known and distinguished, our will and pleasure is, that the same shall, from henceforth, be nominated, termed, and called by the name of New-England, in America, and by that name of New-England, in America, the said circuit, precinct, limit, continent, islands, and places in America aforesaid, we do, by these presents, for us, our heirs, and successors, name, call, erect, found, and establish, and by that name to have continuance for ever.

APPENDIX.

And for the better plantation, ruling, and governing of the aforesaid New-England, in America, we will, ordain, constitute, assign, limit, and appoint, and for us, our heirs, and successors, we, by the advice of the lords, and others of the said privy council, do, by these presents, ordain, constitute, limit, and appoint, that from henceforth there shall be for ever hereafter, in our town of Plymouth, in the county of Devon, one body politic and corporate, which shall have perpetual succession; which shall consist of the number of forty persons, and no more; which shall be, and shall be called and known by the name of the council established at Plymouth, in the county of Devon, for the planting, ruling, ordering, and governing of New-England, in America, and for that purpose, we have, at and by the nomination and request of the said petitioners, granted, ordained, established, and confirmed, and, by these presents, for us, our heirs, and successors, do grant, ordain, establish, and confirm our right trusty and right well beloved cousins and counsellors, Lodowick, duke of Lenox, lord steward of our household; George, lord Marquis Buckingham, our high admiral of England; James, marquis Hamiliton; William, earl of Pembroke, lord chamberlain of our household; Thomas, earl of Arundel; and our right trusty and right well beloved cousin, William, earl of Bath; and our right trusty and right well beloved cousin and counsellor, Henry, earl of Southampton; and our right trusty and right well beloved cousins, William, earl of Salisbury, and Robert, earl of Warwick; and our right trusty and right well beloved John, viscount Haddington; and our right trusty and well beloved counsellor, Edward, lord Zouch, lord warden of our cinque ports; and our trusty and well beloved Edmond, lord Sheffield, Edward, lord Gorges; and our well beloved Sir Edward Seymor, knight and baronet; Sir Robert Mansel; Sir Edward Zouch, our knight marshal; Sir Dudley Diggs, Sir Thomas Roe, Sir Ferdinando Gorges, Sir Francis Popham, Sir John Brooks, Sir Thomas Gates, Sir Richard Hawkins, Sir Richard Edgecomb, Sir Allen Apsley, Sir Warwick Heale, Sir Richard Catchmay, Sir John Bourgchier, Sir Nathaniel Rich, Sir Edward Giles, Sir Giles Mompesson, Sir Thomas Worth, knights; and our well beloved Matthew Sutcliff, dean of Exeter; Robert Heath, Esq. recorder of our city of London; Henry Bourgchier, John Drake, Raleigh Gilbert, George Chudley, Thomas Hamon, and John Argall, Esquires, to be, and in and by these presents, we do appoint them to be, the first modern and present council, established at Plymouth, in the county of Devon, for the planting, ruling, ordering, and governing of New-England, in America; and that they, and the survivors of them, and such as the survivors and survivor of them shall, from time to

APPENDIX.

time, elect and choose to make up the foresaid number of forty persons, when and as often as any of them, or any of their successors, shall happen to decease or to be removed from being of the said council, shall be, in and by these presents, incorporated, to have a perpetual succession for ever, in deed, fact, and name, and shall be one body corporate and politic; and that those, and such said persons, and their successors, and such as shall be elected and chosen to succeed them, as aforesaid, shall be, and, by these presents, are and be incorporated, named, and called by the name of the council established at Plymouth, in the county of Devon, for the planting, ruling, and governing of New-England, in America; and them, the said duke of Lenox, marquis Buckingham, marquis Hamilton, earl of Pembroke, earl of Arundel, earl of Bath, earl of Southampton, earl of Salisbury, earl of Warwick, viscount Haddington, lord Zouch, lord Sheffield, lord Gorges, Sir Edward Seymor, Sir Robert Mansel, Sir Edward Zouch, Sir Dudley Diggs, Sir Thomas Roe, Sir Ferdinando Gorges, Sir Francis Popham, Sir John Brooks, Sir Thomas Gates, Sir Richard Hawkins, Sir Richard Edgecomb, Sir Allen Apsley, Sir Warwick Heale, Sir Richard Catchmay, Sir John Bourgchier, Sir Nathaniel Rich, Sir Edward Giles, Sir Giles Mompesson, Sir Thomas Worth, knights; Matthew Sutcliff, Robert Heath, Henry Bourgchier, John Drake, Raleigh Gilbert, George Chudley, Thomas Hamon, and John Argall, Esquires, and their successors, one body corporate and politic, in deed and in name, by the name of the council established at Plymouth, in the county of Devon, for the planting, ruling, and governing of New-England, in America.

We do, by these presents, for us, our heirs, and successors, really and fully incorporate, erect, ordain, name, constitute, and establish, and that, by the same name of the said council, they, and their successors, for ever hereafter be incorporated, named, and called, and shall, by the same name, have perpetual succession.

And further, we do hereby, for us, our heirs, and successors, grant unto the said council established at Plymouth, that they, and their successors, by the same name, be, and shall be, and shall continue persons able and capable in the law, from time to time, and shall, by that name of council aforesaid, have full power and authority, and lawful capacity and ability, as well to purchase, take, hold, receive, enjoy, and to have to them and their successors, for ever, any manors, lands, tenements, rents, royalties, privileges, immunities, reversions, annuities, hereditaments, goods, and chattels whatsoever, of, or from us, our heirs, and successors, and of, or from any other person or persons whatsoever, as well in and within this our realm of

APPENDIX.

England, as in and within any other place or places whatsoever or wheresoever; and the same manors, lands, tenements, and hereditaments, goods, or chattels, or any of them, by the same name, to alien and sell, or to do, execute, or ordain and perform all other matters and things whatsoever, to the said incorporation and plantation concerning and belonging.

And further, our will and pleasure is, that the said council, for the time being, and their successors, shall have full power and lawful authority, by the name aforesaid, to sue and to be sued, implead and to be impleaded, answer and to be answered unto, in all manner of courts and places that now are, or hereafter shall be, within this our realm, and elsewhere, as well temporal as spiritual, in all manner of suits and matters whatsoever, and of what nature or kind soever such suits or actions be or shall be.

And our will and pleasure is, that the said forty persons, or the greater number of them, shall, and may, from time to time, and at any time hereafter, at their own will and pleasure, according to the laws, ordinances, and orders of, or by them, or by the greater part of them hereafter, in manner and form in these presents mentioned to be agreed upon, to elect and choose, amongst themselves, one of the said forty persons, for the time being, to be president of the said council, which president, so elected and chosen, we will shall continue and be president of the said council, for so long time as by the orders of the said council, from time to time to be made, as hereafter is mentioned, shall be thought fit, and no longer; unto which president, or, in his absence, to any such person as, by the orders of the said council, shall be thereunto appointed, we do give authority to give order for the warning of the said council, and summoning the company to their meetings.

And our will and pleasure is, that, from time to time, when, and so often as any of the said council shall happen to decease, or to be removed from being of the said council, that then, and so often, the survivors of them of the said council, and no other, or the greater number of them, who then shall be, from time to time, left and remaining, and who shall, or the greater number of which that shall be assembled at a public court, or meeting, to be held for the said company, shall elect and choose one or more other person or persons, to be of the said council, and which, from time to time, shall be of the said council, so that the number of forty persons of the said council may, from time to time, be supplied.

Provided always, that as well the persons herein named to be of the said council, as every other counsellor hereafter to be elected, shall be presented to the lord chancellor of England, or to the lord high treasurer of England, or to the lord

APPENDIX.

chamberlain of the household, of us, our heirs, and successors, for the time being, to take his and their oath and oaths, of a counsellor and counsellors, to us, our heirs, and successors, for the said company and colony in New-England.

And further, we will and grant, by these presents, for us, our heirs, and successors, unto the said council, and their successors, that they, and their successors, shall have and enjoy for ever, a common seal, to be engraven according to their discretions.

And that it shall be lawful for them to appoint what other seal, or seals, they shall think most meet and necessary, either for their use, as they are one united body, incorporate here, or for the public use of their government and ministers in New-England aforesaid, whereby the said incorporation may or shall seal any manner of instrument, touching the same corporation, and the manors, lands, tenements, rents, reversions, annuities, hereditaments, goods, chattels, affairs, and any other things, belonging unto, or in any wise appertaining, touching or concerning the said council, and their successors, or concerning the said corporation and plantation, in and by these our letters patents, as aforesaid, founded, erected, and established.

And we do further, by these presents, for us, our heirs, and successors, grant unto the said council, and their successors, that it shall and may be lawful to and for the said council, and their successors, for the time being, in their discretions, from time to time, to admit such and so many person and persons to be made free, and enabled to trade and traffic unto, within, and in New-England, aforesaid, and unto every part and parcel thereof, or to have, possess, and enjoy any lands or hereditaments in New-England aforesaid, as they shall think fit, according to the laws, orders, constitutions, and ordinances, by the said council and their successors, from time to time, to be made and established, by virtue of, and according to the true intent of these presents, and under such conditions, reservations, and agreements, as the said council shall set down, order, and direct, and not otherwise.

And further, of our especial grace, certain knowledge, and mere motion, for us, our heirs, and successors, we do, by these presents, give and grant full power and authority to the said council, and their successors, that the said council, for the time being, or the greater part of them, shall and may, from time to time, nominate, make, constitute, ordain, and confirm, by such name or names, style or styles, as to them shall seem good, and, likewise, to revoke and discharge, change and alter, as well all and singular, governors, officers, and ministers, which hereafter shall be by them thought fit and needful to be made

APPENDIX.

or used, as well to attend the business of the said company here, as for the government of the said colony and plantation.

And also, to make, ordain, and establish all manner of orders, laws, directions, instructions, forms, and ceremonies of government and magistracy, fit and necessary for and concerning the government of the said colony and plantation, so always as the same be not contrary to the laws and statutes of this our realm of England, and the same at all times hereafter, to abrogate, revoke, or change, not only within the precincts of the said colony, but also upon the seas, in going and coming to and from the said colony, as they, in their good discretion, shall think to be fittest for the good of the adventurers and inhabitants there.

And we do further, of our special grace, certain knowledge, and mere motion, grant, declare, and ordain, that such principal governor as, from time to time, shall be authorized and appointed, in manner and form in these presents heretofore expressed, shall have full power and authority to use and exercise martial laws, in cases of rebellion, insurrection, and mutiny, in as large and ample manner, as our lieutenants in our counties within our realm of England, have, or ought to have, by force of their commission of lieutenancy.

And forasmuch as it shall be necessary for all such our loving subjects as shall inhabit within the said precincts of New-England aforesaid, to determine to live together, in the fear and true worship of Almighty God, christian peace, and civil quietness, each with other, whereby every one may, with more safety, pleasure, and profit, enjoy that, whereunto they shall attain with great pain and peril.

We, for us, our heirs, and successors, are likewise pleased and contented, and, by these presents, do give and grant unto the said council, and their successors, and to such governors, officers, and ministers, as shall be, by the said council, constituted and appointed according to the natures and limits of their offices and places respectively, that they shall and may, from time to time, for ever hereafter, within the said precincts of New-England, or in the way by the seas thither and from thence, have full and absolute power and authority to correct, punish, pardon, govern, and rule all such the subjects of us, our heirs, and successors, as shall, from time to time, adventure themselves in any voyage thither, or that shall, at any time hereafter, inhabit in the precincts and territories of the said colony as aforesaid, according to such laws, orders, ordinances, directions, and instructions, as by the said council aforesaid, shall be established; and, in defect thereof, in cases of necessity, according to the good discretions of the said governors and officers respectively, as well in cases capital and

APPENDIX.

criminal as civil, both marine and others; so always as the said statutes, ordinances, and proceedings, as near as conveniently may be agreeable to the laws, statutes, government, and policy of this our realm of England.

And furthermore, if any person, or persons, adventurers, or planters, of the said colony, or any other, at any time or times hereafter, shall transport any monies, goods, or merchandizes, out of any our kingdoms, with a pretence and purpose to land, set, or otherwise to dispose the same, within the limits and bounds of the said colony, and yet, nevertheless, being at sea, or after he hath landed within any part of the said colony, shall carry the same into any other foreign country, with a purpose there to set and dispose thereof, that then all the goods and chattels of the said person, or persons, so offending, and transported, together with the ship or vessel wherein such transportation was made, shall be forfeited to us, our heirs, and successors.

And we do further, of our special grace, certain knowledge, and mere motion, for us, our heirs, and successors, for, and in respect of the considerations aforesaid, and for divers other good causes and considerations, us thereunto especially moving, and by the advice of the lords and others of our said privy council, have absolutely given, granted, and confirmed, and, by these presents, do absolutely give, grant, and confirm, unto the said council, called the council established at Plymouth, in the county of Devon, for the planting, ruling, and governing of New-England, in America, and unto their successors, for ever, all the aforesaid lands and grounds, continent, precincts, place, places, and territories, (viz.) the aforesaid part of America, lying and being in breadth from forty degrees of northerly latitude from the equinoctial line, to forty-eight degrees of the said northerly latitude inclusively, and in length of, and within all the breadth aforesaid, throughout the main land, from sea to sea, together also with all the firm land, soils, grounds, havens, ports, rivers, waters, fishings, mines, and minerals, as well royal mines of gold and silver, as other mines and minerals, precious stones, quarries, and all and singular other commodities, jurisdictions, royalties, privileges, franchises, and pre-eminences, both within the said tract of land, upon the main, and also within the said island and seas adjoining.

Provided always, that the said islands, or any the premises herein before mentioned, and, by these presents, intended and meant to be granted, be not actually possessed, or inhabited by any other christian prince or state, nor be within the bounds, limits, or territories of that southern colony, heretofore, by us, granted to be planted by divers of our loving subjects in the south parts.

APPENDIX.

To have and to hold, possess, and enjoy all and singular the aforesaid continent, lands, territories, islands, hereditaments, and precincts, sea waters, fishings, with all and all manner their commodities, royalties, liberties, pre-eminences, and profits, that shall arise from thence, with all and singular their appurtenances, and every part and parcel thereof, and of them to, and unto the said council, and their successors, and assigns, for ever, to the sole, only and proper use, benefit, and behoof of them, the said council, and their successors, and assigns, for ever, to be holden of us, our heirs, and successors, as of our manor of East-Greenwich, in our county of Kent, in fee and common socage, and not in capite, nor by knights' services.

Yielding and paying, therefore, to us, our heirs, and successors, the fifth part of the ores of gold and silver which, from time to time, and at all times hereafter, shall happen to be found, gotten and obtained in, at, or within any the said lands, limits, territories, and precincts, or in, or within any part, or parcels thereof, for, or in respect of all and all manner of duties, demands, and services whatsoever, to be done, made, or paid to us, our heirs, and successors.

And we do further, of our especial grace, certain knowledge, and mere motion, for us, our heirs, and successors, give and grant to the said council, and their successors, for ever, by these presents, that it shall be lawful and free for them, and their assigns, at all and every time and times hereafter, out of any our realms or dominions whatsoever, to take, lead, carry, and transport, in and into their voyages, and for and towards the said plantation in New-England, all such and so many of our loving subjects, or any other strangers that will become our loving subjects, and live under our allegiance, or shall willingly accompany them in the said voyages and plantation, with shipping, armour, weapons, ordnances, munition powder, shot, victuals, and all manner of clothing, implements, furniture, beasts, cattle, horses, mares, and all other things necessary for the said plantation, and for their use and defence, and for trade with the people there, and in passing and returning to and fro, without paying or yielding any custom or subsidy, either inwards or outwards, to us, our heirs, or successors, for the same, for the space of seven years from the day of the date of these presents.

Provided, that none of the said persons be such as shall be hereafter, by special name, restrained by us, our heirs, or successors.

And, for their further encouragement, of our special grace and favour, we do, by these presents, for us, our heirs, and successors, yield and grant to, and with the said council, and their successors, and every of them, their factors and assigns, that they, and every of them, shall be free and quiet from all subsidies and customs, in New-England, for the space of seven years, and from all taxes and impositions for the space of twenty and one years, upon all goods or merchandize, at any time or times hereafter, either upon importation thither, or exportation from thence, into our realm of England, or into any other our dominions, by the said council, and their successors, their deputies, factors, and assigns, or any of them, except only the five pounds per cent. due for custom upon all such goods and merchandizes as shall be brought or imported into our realm of England, or any other of our dominions, according to the ancient trade of merchants; which five pounds per centum only being paid, it shall be thenceforth lawful and free for the said adventurers, the same goods and merchandize, to export and carry out of our said dominions into foreign parts, without any custom, tax, or other duty, to be paid to us, our heirs, or successors, or to any other officers or ministers of us, our heirs, and successors. Provided, that the said goods and merchandizes be shipped out within thirteen months after their first landing, within any part of those dominions.

And further, our will and pleasure is, and we do, by these presents, charge, command, warrant, and authorize the said council, and their successors, or the major part of them, which shall be present and assembled for that purpose, shall, from time to time, under their common seal, distribute, convey, assign, and set over such particular portions of lands, tenements, and hereditaments, as are, by these presents, formerly granted unto each our loving subjects, naturally born, or denizens, or others, as well adventurers as planters, as, by the said company, upon a commission of survey and distribution, executed and returned for that purpose, shall be named, appointed, and allowed, wherein our will and pleasure is, that respect be had, as well to the proportion of the adventurers, as to the special service, hazard, exploit, or merit, of any person so to be recompensed, advanced, or rewarded.

And we do also, for us, our heirs, and successors, grant to the said council, and their successors, and to all and every such governors, or other officers, or ministers, as, by the said council, shall be appointed, to have power and authority of government and command, in or over the said colony and plantation, that they, and every of them, shall, and lawfully may, from time to time, and at all times hereafter, for ever, for their several defence and safety, encounter, expulse, repel, and resist, by force of arms, as well by sea as by land, and all ways and means whatsoever, all such person and persons as, without the special license of the said council, and their successors,

APPENDIX.

or the greater part of them, shall attempt to inhabit within the said several precincts and limits of the said colony and plantation.

And also, all and every such person and persons whatsoever, as shall enterprise or attempt, at any time hereafter, destruction, invasion, detriment, or annoyance to the said colony and plantation.

And that it shall be lawful for the said council, and their successors, and every of them, from time to time, and at all times hereafter, and they shall have full power and authority to take and surprise, by all ways and means whatsoever, all and every such person or persons whatsoever, with their ships, goods, and other furniture, trafficking in any harbour, creek, or place, within the limits and precincts of the said colony and plantation, and not being allowed by the said council to be adventurers or planters of the said colony.

And of our further royal favour, we have granted, and for us, our heirs, and successors, we do grant unto the said council, and their successors, that the said territories, lands, rivers, and places aforesaid, or any of them, shall not be visited, frequented, or traded unto by any other of our subjects, or the subjects of us, our heirs, or successors, either from any of the ports and havens, belonging, or appertaining, or which shall belong or appertain unto us, our heirs, or successors, or to any foreign prince, state, or potentate whatsoever.

And therefore, we do hereby, for us, our heirs, and successors, charge, command, prohibit, and forbid all the subjects of us, our heirs, and successors, of what degree or quality soever they be, that none of them, directly or indirectly presume to visit, frequent, trade, or adventure to traffic into, or from the said territories, lands, rivers, and places aforesaid, or any of them, other than the said council, and their successors, factors, deputies, and assigns, unless it be with the license and consent of the said council and company, first had and obtained in writing, under their common seal, upon pain of our indignation, and imprisonment of their bodies, during the pleasure of us, our heirs, or successors, and the forfeiture and loss, both of their ship and goods, wheresoever they shall be found, either within any of our kingdoms or dominions, or any the place or places out of our dominions, and for the better effecting of our said pleasure herein, we do hereby, for us, our heirs, and successors, give and grant full power and authority unto the said council, and their successors, for the time being, that they, by themselves, their factors, deputies, or assigns, shall and may, from time to time, and at all times hereafter, attach, arrest, take, and seize all and all manner of ship and ships, goods, wares, and merchandizes whatsoever, which shall be brought

APPENDIX.

from, or carried to the places before mentioned, or any of them, contrary to our will and pleasure, before in these presents expressed, the moiety, or one half of all which forfeitures, we do hereby, for us, our heirs, and successors, give and grant unto the said council, and their successors, to their own proper use, without accompt, and the other moiety, or half part thereof, we will shall be and remain to the use of us, our heirs, and successors.

And we, likewise, have condescended and granted, and, by these presents, for us, our heirs, and successors, do condescend, and grant to, and with the said council, and their successors, that we, our heirs, or successors, shall not, or will not, give and grant any liberty, license, or authority to any person or persons whatsover, to sail, trade, or traffic unto the aforesaid plantations of New-England, without the good will and liking of the said council, or the greater part of them, for the time being, at any their courts to be assembled.

And we do, for us, our heirs, and successors, give and grant unto the said council, and their successors, that whensoever, or so often as any custom or subsidy shall grow due or payable, unto us, our heirs, or successors, according to the limitation and appointment aforesaid, by reason of any goods, wares, or merchandize, to be shipped out, or any return to be made, of any goods, wares, or merchandize, unto, or from New-England, or any the lands or territories aforesaid, that then, so often, and in such case, the farmers, customers, and officers of our customs of England and Ireland, and every of them, for the time being, upon request made unto them by the said council, their successors, factors, or assigns, and upon convenient security to be given in that behalf, shall give and allow unto the said council, and their successors; and to all person and persons free of the said company as aforesaid, six months time, for the payment of the one half of all such customs and subsidy, as shall be due and payable unto us, our heirs, and successors, for the same; for which these, our letters patents, or the duplicate, or the enrolment thereof, shall be, unto our said officers, a sufficient warrant and discharge.

Nevertheless, our will and pleasure is, that, if any of the said goods, wares, and merchandizes, which be, or shall be, at any time hereafter, landed and exported out of any our realms aforesaid, and shall be shipped with a purpose not to be carried to New-England aforesaid, that then such payment, duty, custom, imposition, or forfeiture, shall be paid and belong to us, our heirs, and successors, for the said goods, wares, and merchandizes, so fraudulently sought to be transported, as if this our grant had not been made nor granted.

And we do, for us, our heirs, and successors, give and grant

APPENDIX.

unto the said council, and their successors, for ever, by these presents, that the said president of the said company, or his deputy, for the time being, or any two others of the said council, for the said colony in New-England, for the time being, shall and may, at all times hereafter, and from time to time, have full power and authority to minister, and give the oath and oaths of allegiance and supremacy, or either of them, to all and every person and persons, which shall, at any time and times hereafter, go and pass to the said colony in New-England.

And further, that it shall be, likewise, lawful for the said president, or his deputy, for the time being, or any two others of the said council, for the said colony in New-England, for the time being, from time to time, and at all times hereafter, to minister such a formal oath, as by their discretions shall be reasonably devised, as well unto any person or persons employed, or to be employed in, for, or touching the said plantation, for their honest, faithful, and just discharge of their service, in all such matters as shall be committed unto them, for the good and benefit of the said company, colony, and plantation, as also unto such other person or persons as the said president, or his deputy, with two others of the said council, shall think meet, for the examination or clearing of the truth, in any cause whatsoever concerning the said plantation, or any business from thence proceeding, or thereunto belonging.

And to the end that no lewd or ill disposed persons, sailors, soldiers, artificers, husbandmen, labourers, or others which shall receive wares, apparel, or other entertainment from the said council, or contract and agree with the said council, to go, and to serve, and to be employed in the said plantation, in the colony in New-England, do afterwards withdraw, hide, and conceal themselves, or refuse to go thither, after they have been so entertained and agreed withal, and that no persons which shall be sent and employed in the said plantation of the said colony in New-England, upon the charge of the said council, do misbehave themselves by mutinous, seditious, or other notorious misdemeanours, or which shall be employed, or sent abroad by the governor of New-England, or his deputy, with any ship or pinnace, for provision of the said colony, or for some discovery, or other business and affairs concerning the same, do, from thence, treacherously either come back again, or return into the realm of England, by stealth, or without license of the governor of the said colony in New-England, for the time being, or be sent hither as misdoers or offenders, and that none of those persons, after their return from thence, being questioned by the said council here for such their misbehaviours and offences, do, by insolent and contemptuous carriage, in the presence of the said council, shew little respect and reverence, either to the place or authority in which we have placed and appointed them, and others, for the clearing of their lewdness and misdemeanours, committed in New-England, divulge vile and slanderous reports of the country of New-England, or of the government or estate of the said plantation and colony, to bring the said voyages and plantation into disgrace and contempt, by means whereof, not only the adventurers and planters already engaged in the said plantation, may be exceedingly abused, and hindered, and a great number of our loving and well disposed subjects, otherwise well affected, and inclined to join and adventure in so noble a christian and worthy an action, may be discouraged from the same, but also the enterprise itself, may be overthrown, which cannot miscarry, without some dishonour to us and our kingdom.

We, therefore, for preventing of so great and enormous abuses and misdemeanours, do, by these presents, for us, our heirs, and successors, give and grant unto the said president, or his deputy, or such other person, or persons, as, by the orders of the said council, shall be appointed, by warrant, under his or their hand or hands, to send for, or cause to be apprehended, all and every such person and persons, who shall be noted, or accused, or found, at any time or times hereafter, to offend, or misbehave themselves, in any the affairs before mentioned and expressed; and, upon the examination of any such offender or offenders, and just proof, made by oath, taken before the said council, of any such notorious misdemeanours, by them to be committed, as aforesaid, and also, upon any insolent, contemptuous, or unreverent carriage, or misbehaviour, to, or against the said council, to be shewed or used, by any such person or persons, so called, convinced, and appearing before them, as aforesaid, that, in all such cases, our said council, or any two, or more of them, for the time being, shall, and may have full power and authority, either here to bind them over with good securities for their good behaviour, and further therein to proceed, to all intents and purposes, as it is used in other like cases within our realm of England, or else, at their discretions, to remand and send back the said offenders, or any of them, to the said colony of New-England, there to be proceeded against and punished, as the governors, deputy, or council there, for the time being, shall think meet, or otherwise, according to such laws and ordinances, as are, and shall be in use there, for the well ordering and good government of the said colony.

And our will and pleasure is, and we do hereby declare, to all christian kings, princes, and states, that, if any person or

APPENDIX.

persons, which shall hereafter be of the said colony or plantation, or any other, by license or appointment of the said council, or their successors, or otherwise, shall, at any time or times hereafter, rob, or spoil, by sea or by land, or do any hurt, violence, or unlawful hostility, to any of the subjects of us, our heirs, or successors, or any of the subjects of any king, prince, ruler, or governor, or state, being then in league and amity with us, our heirs, and successors; and that, upon such injury, or upon just complaint of such prince, ruler, governor, or state, or their subjects, we, our heirs, or successors, shall make open proclamation, within any of the parts of our realm of England commodious for that purpose, that the person or persons having committed any such robbery or spoil, shall, within the time limited by such a proclamation, make full restitution or satisfaction of all such injuries done, so as the said princes, or others so complaining, may hold themselves fully satisfied and contented; and if that the said person or persons, having committed such robbery or spoil, shall not make, or cause to be made, satisfaction accordingly, within such time so to be limited, that then it shall be lawful for us, our heirs, and successors, to put the said person or persons out of our allegiance and protection, and that it shall be lawful and free for all princes to prosecute with hostility the said offenders, and every of them, their and every of their procurers, aiders, abettors, and comforters in that behalf.

Also, we do, for us, our heirs, and successors, declare, by these presents, that all and every the persons being our subjects, which shall go and inhabit within the said colony and plantation, and every of their children and posterity, which shall happen to be born within the limits thereof, shall have and enjoy all liberties, and franchises, and immunities of free denizens and natural subjects, within any of our other dominions, to all intents and purposes, as if they had been abiding, and born within this our kingdom of England, or any other our dominions.

And lastly, because the principal effect which we can desire, or expect of this action, is the conversion of, and reduction of the people in those parts, unto the true worship of God and christian religion, in which respect we would be loath that any person should be permitted to pass, that we suspected to affect the superstition of the church of Rome, we do hereby declare, that it is our will and pleasure, that none be permitted to pass in any voyage, from time to time to be made into the said country, but such as shall first have taken the oath of supremacy; for which purpose, we do, by these presents, give full power and authority to the president of the said council, to

APPENDIX.

tender and exhibit the said oath to all such persons as shall, at any time, be sent and employed in the said voyage.

And we also, for us, our heirs, and successors, do covenant and grant to, and with the council, and their successors, by these presents, that if the council, for the time being, and their successors, or any of them, shall, at any time or times hereafter, upon any doubt which they shall conceive, concerning the strength or validity in law, of this our present grant, or be desirous to have the same renewed and confirmed by us, our heirs, and successors, with amendments of such imperfections and defects, as shall appear fit and necessary to the said council, or their successors, to be reformed and amended, on the behalf of us, our heirs, and successors, and for the furthering of the plantation and government, or the increase, continuing, and flourishing thereof, that then, upon the humble petition of the said council, for the time being, and their successors, to us, our heirs, and successors, we, our heirs, and successors, shall and will, forthwith, make and pass, under the great seal of England, to the said council, and their successors, such further and better assurance of all and singular the lands, grounds, royalties, privileges, and premises aforesaid, granted, or intended to be granted, according to our true intent and meaning, in these our letters patents, signified, declared, or mentioned, as by the learned council of us, our heirs, and successors, and of the said company, and their successors, shall, in that behalf, be reasonably devised or advised.

And further, our will and pleasure is, that, in all questions and doubts, that shall arise upon any difficulty of construction or interpretation of any thing contained in these our letters patents, the same shall be taken and interpreted, in most ample and beneficial manner, for the said council, and their successors, and every member thereof.

And we do further, for us, our heirs, and successors, charge and command all and singular admirals, vice admirals, generals, commanders, captains, justices of peace, mayors, sheriffs, bailiffs, constables, customers, comptrollers, waiters, searchers, and all the officers of us, our heirs, and successors whatsoever, to be, from time to time, and at all times hereafter, in all things aiding, helping, and assisting unto the said council, and their successors, and unto every of them, upon request and requests, by them to be made, in all matters and things, for the furtherance and accomplishment of all or any the matters and things by us, in, and by these our letters patents, given, granted, and provided, or by us meant or intended to be given, granted, and provided, as they, our said officer, and the officers of us, our heirs, and successors, do tender our pleasure, and will avoid the contrary, at their perils.

Made in the USA
San Bernardino, CA
07 February 2017